D1593572

Jesus and His Death

Jesus and His Death
Historiography, the Historical Jesus, and Atonement Theory

Scot McKnight

Baylor University Press
Waco, Texas

Scripture quotations are from the New Revised Standard Version Bible, copyright 1989, Division of Christian Education of the National Council of the Churches of Christ in the United States of America. Used by permission. All rights reserved.

Book Design by Helen Lasseter
Cover Design by David Alcorn
Cover Image: Death, copyright Anneke Kaai (2003). From *In a Word: See What You Believe.* Paraclete Press/Piquant Editions, 2003. Used with permission.

Library of Congress Cataloging-in-Publication Data

McKnight, Scot.
  Jesus and his death : historiography, the historical Jesus, and atonement
theory / Scot McKnight.
    p. cm.
  Includes bibliographical references and index.
  ISBN 1-932792-29-5 (hardcover : alk. paper)
  1. Jesus Christ--Historicity. 2. Jesus Christ--Person and offices.
3. Atonement.   I. Title.
BT303.2.M43 2005
232'.3--dc22

                                                                    2005021034

Printed in the United States of America on acid-free paper

For Jon, Mark, Matt, and Sam

Contents

Preface   ix

PART ONE: THE DEBATE

1   The Historical Jesus, the Death of Jesus,
Historiography, and Theology   3

2   Jesus' Death in Scholarship   47

3   Re-enter Jesus' Death   77

PART TWO: THE REALITY OF A PREMATURE DEATH

4   The Leading Foot in the Dance of Atonement   105

5   A Temporary Presence in God's Providence   121

6   Jesus and the Prophetic Fate   139

PART THREE: A RANSOM FOR MANY

7   The Authenticity of the Ransom Saying   159

    Excursus: The Son of man   171

8   Jesus and the Scripture Prophets   177

9   The Script for Jesus   189

Contents

10 Jesus and the Servant   207

11 The Passion Predictions   225

PART FOUR: JESUS AND THE LAST SUPPER

12 *Pesah* in Jewish History   243

13 *Pesah* and the Last Supper   259

14 This Bread and This Cup   275

15 Jesus and the Covenant   293

16 "Poured Out" and Eschatology   323

17 Conclusions   335

   Excursus: Chasing Down Paul's Theological Ship   372

Works Cited   375
Scripture Index   411
Author Index   439
Subject Index   449

Preface

This book began when N.T. Wright asked me, as a member of the steering committee for the Historical Jesus Section at the Society of Biblical Literature meeting in Nashville, to prepare a five minute introduction to the topic of that session: the death of Jesus. When the program appeared, I discovered that I was (a providential accident, so I believe) scheduled for a full paper, so I set out to survey recent scholarship on how Jesus understood his own death. Four years later I feel comfortable enough with the research to make it public.

I am grateful to my colleague Klyne Snodgrass for reading the entire manuscript and offering valuable comments. Klyne is a fair-minded, theologically adept, and loving teacher who gives his life for others. I am also grateful to my colleague and friend Greg Clark for our constant conversations about things hermeneutical. Greg's alert mind and compassion have been a source of joy for a decade, and I look forward to our every conversation. I wish also to mention that I received comments on presentations as well as on various sections and chapters from David Koeller, Dale Allison, John Koenig, and Paul Copan, as well as N.T. Wright.

This book is dedicated to my four dissertation students who have now gone on to be exceptional teachers and splendid friends. If you would like to know what Aristotle meant by friendship, I suggest you become friends with them as I have.

Part I

THE DEBATE

Chapter 1

The Historical Jesus, the Death of Jesus, Historiography, and Theology

IN HISTORY, AS ELSEWHERE, FOOLS RUSH IN, AND THE ANGELS MAY PERHAPS
BE FORGIVEN IF RATHER THAN TREAD IN THOSE TREACHEROUS PATHS THEY
TREAD UPON THE FOOLS INSTEAD.[1]

~G.R. ELTON

When academics stand before an audience and explain a view of the historical Jesus—in this case how Jesus understood his own death—and when the historical Jesus case is made in the context of a theological discipline and education, the scholar may think he or she is walking on water, but the voices of truth are calling out to the scholar to watch each step. The waters tend to swallow.

Shorn of metaphor, we might say these voices of truth ask three questions: What is history? What is a historical Jesus? What role is that historical Jesus to play in the theological curriculum? Each question needs to be answered, but particularly the third because very few historical Jesus scholars operate in a vacuum. Each makes meaning on the basis of the historical reconstruction. In the context of this monograph the questions are more focused: How did Jesus understand his own death? And, while not the specific focus of this monograph, What role is a reconstruction of how Jesus thought about his death to play in the theological curriculum and, in particular, in how one understands atonement?

Various answers might be proposed now in a preliminary and imaginative way.[2] One might say that Jesus did not think about his death in any profound sense and that, therefore, it was the early Christians who narrated a story that imputed meaning to that death. For some, such a chasm between Christian faith

I am grateful to Paul Copan for comments on an earlier draft of this chapter.
[1] G.R. Elton, *The Practice of History* (New York: Crowell, 1967), 89.
[2] See ch. 2, under "Some Highlights in the History of Scholarship."

3

and what Jesus actually thought would jar the foundations of faith; for others, the chasm might provide space for free thinking. One might, alternatively, argue that Jesus thought of his death in profoundly soteriological terms, even if undeveloped, and that the early Christians unfolded the theology Jesus gave to his impending death. And, however one answers these questions, many think that *whatever* answer one comes to ought to shape one's theology, and some are bold enough to think that the church, or at least the enlightened within the church, ought to revise its understanding of faith accordingly.

As I said, to come to terms with how Jesus understood his own death means we have to come to terms with three questions—about history, about the historical Jesus, and about the role of historical reconstruction in theological meaning-making. We begin with the first question: what is history?

MODERN HISTORIOGRAPHY: A BRIEF TAXONOMY[3]

Historical Jesus scholars appropriate a historiography, though very few of them spell their historiography out.[4] Those historiographies can be conveniently labeled postmodernist and modernist, with all sorts of shades within each label as well as a spectrum of how those historiographies have been used by historical Jesus scholars.[5] The most complete historiographies by historical Jesus scholars

---

[3] For a good survey of the history of historiography, see E. Breisach, *Historiography: Ancient, Medieval, and Modern* (2d ed.; Chicago: University of Chicago Press, 1994). It is not possible here to provide full bibliographies on matters historiographical. The standard journal is *History and Theory.*

The term *historiography,* which usually refers to the "history of historical studies" or (less often) to the "writing of history," is frequently used in scholarship as shorthand for "philosophy of history." When I speak of historical Jesus scholars operating with a historiography, I intend that to mean "a philosophically based, whether conscious or not, perception of what can be known about the past and how what can be known is discerned and represented." Peter Novick's well-known *That Noble Dream* (New York: Cambridge University Press, 1988), 8, n. 6 states: "the once respectable word 'historiology' has dropped out of just about everybody's vocabulary, and 'historiography' has had to do double duty for both 'historical science' [in which I would include the "philosophy of history"] and descriptive accounts of historical writing [i.e., "the history of history"]. Strictly speaking, 'the objectivity question' is an *historiological* [concerns the science of history] issue, but all historians speak of it as 'historiographical.' Go fight city hall." If Novick keeps the sword in the scabbard, I shall as well (and stand behind him).

[4] An informed study in this regard is the article by Halvor Moxnes, "The Historical Jesus," *BTB* 28 (1999): 135–49. He studies the historiography, with reference to "master narratives," of J.P. Meier, E.P. Sanders, R.A. Horsley, J.D. Crossan, and B.J. Malina. For my own survey of trends in Jesus studies, see "Jesus of Nazareth," in *The Face of New Testament Studies* (ed. S. McKnight and G.R. Osborne; Grand Rapids: Baker Academic, 2004), 149–76. See the recently published D.L. Denton Jr., *Historiography and Hermeneutics in Jesus Studies* (JSNTSSup 262; London: T&T Clark, 2004). This study was unfortunately not available to me during my research, but his emphasis on the role of holism and the place of narrative (or story) in historiography are most welcome and accord with the direction of my own understanding.

are those of N.T. Wright in the first two volumes of his multivolume series *Christian Origins and the Question of God*,[6] and the recent introduction by James D.G. Dunn in his *Jesus Remembered*.[7] While other studies are intensely informed at the level of philosophical discussion and technical method—one thinks of B.F. Meyer, J.P. Meier, J.D. Crossan, and Dale Allison,[8]—few are actually proposing a historiography as have Wright and Dunn. The reason I say this about Wright and Dunn (with reservations, of course), will become clear in our survey of postmodernist and modernist historiography, but in brief it is this: Wright proposes a plausible Jewish context and a plausible story for what Jesus was all about, while Dunn proposes a plausible method (oral traditioning) as the most likely process out of which the Jesus traditions grew and, thereby, Dunn is redefining what "authentic" means.[9] Both Wright and Dunn have put forth theories that are and will continue to reshape studies in the historical Jesus.

---

[5] A good textbook on how to do history is M. Howell and W. Prevenier, *From Reliable Sources* (Ithaca, N.Y.: Cornell University Press, 2001).

[6] See N.T. Wright, *The New Testament and the People of God* (vol. 1 of *Christian Origins and the Question of God*; Minneapolis: Fortress, 1992), 29–144. The historiography of Wright was then worked out in *Jesus and the Victory of God* (*Christian Origins and the Question of God* 2; Minneapolis: Fortress, 1996).

[7] James D.G. Dunn, *Jesus Remembered* (vol. 1 of *Christianity in the Making*; Grand Rapids: Eerdmans, 2003), 11–336. Dunn's book is a landmark when it comes to the exploitation of "oral theory" for understanding the Jesus traditions, though there is debate on how he understands that oral tradition and just how memory works. For his most recent statement, see Dunn, *A New Perspective on Jesus* (Acadia Studies in Bible and Theology; Grand Rapids: Baker, 2005). On oral tradition, see J. Vansina, *Oral Tradition as History* (Madison: University of Wisconsin Press, 1985); T.C. Mournet, *Oral Tradition and Literary Dependency* (WUNT 2; Tübingen: Mohr Siebeck, Jan./Feb. 2005). See the recent responses to Dunn in B. Holmberg, "Questions of Method in James Dunn's *Jesus Remembered*," *JSNT* 26 (2004): 445–57; S. Byrskog, "A New Perspective on the Jesus Tradition: Reflections on James D.G. Dunn's *Jesus Remembered*," *JSNT* 26 (2004): 459–71; and Dunn's response: "On History, Memory and Eyewitnesses," *JSNT* 26 (2004): 473–87.

[8] B.F. Meyer, *The Aims of Jesus* (London: SCM, 1979), 76–110, who famously adapted Bernard Lonergan's studies for historical Jesus scholarship; see also B.F. Meyer, *Critical Realism and the New Testament* (Princeton Theological Monograph Series 17; Allison Park, Pa.: Pickwick, 1989); *Reality and Illusion in New Testament Scholarship* (Collegeville, Minn.: Liturgical [Glazier], 1994); J.P. Meier, *A Marginal Jew: Rethinking the Historical Jesus* (3 vols.; ABRL; New York: Doubleday, 1991–2001), 1.1–201; J.D. Crossan, *The Historical Jesus* (San Francisco: HarperSanFrancisco, 1991); on Crossan's method, one must see the critical evaluation of D.C. Allison, Jr., *Jesus of Nazareth* (Minneapolis: Fortress, 1998), 10–33.

[9] One might say that there are three strands of historiography among historical Jesus scholars whose works will be cited when appropriate: (1) those of a modernist bent include scholars as diverse as N. Perrin, J.P. Meier, E.P. Sanders, B.D. Chilton, and M. Borg, even though their theologies differ wildly; (2) those of a postmodernist bent include E. Schüssler Fiorenza and perhaps James D.G. Dunn; and (3) those of a mediating line include N.T. Wright and more likely Dunn (his historiographical epistemology is chastened modernism rather than consistently postmodern). The critical separation occurs over the relation of Subject (historian) and Object (Jesus/Gospels/ancient evidence). The closer one gets to the Subject dominating the discourse, the closer one gets to the

POSTMODERNIST HISTORIOGRAPHY

Whatever postmodernism has going for it or against it, it has the confidence that when it comes to the matter of historiography it alone has the goose by the neck. Take, for example, Keith Jenkins, the United Kingdom's most confident post-modernist historiographer and (as is sometimes said of the radicals) "boa-deconstructor." Jenkins defines postmodernism as the "era of the aporia"; that postmodernism is a stance taken by *le tout intelligentsia*.[10] That is,

> By aporia I mean that this is an era when all the decisions we take—political, eth-ical, moral, interpretive, representational, etc., are ultimately undecidable (aporetic). That our chosen ways of seeing things lack foundations and that, as far as a discourse like history is concerned, it is essentially to be thought of as an aes-thetic—a shaping, figuring discourse— and not as an objective, true, or founda-tional epistemology.[11]

And:

> There are not—and nor have there ever been—any "real" foundations of the kind alleged to underpin the experiment of the modern; that we now just have to understand that we live amidst social formations which have no legitimising onto-logical or epistemological or ethical grounds for our beliefs or actions beyond the status of an ultimately self-referencing (rhetorical) conversation.[12]

Jenkins at times fawns over the earlier Hayden White, even though White isn't so antifoundationalist.[13] White, America's leading postmodernist (or, more

---

postmodernist enterprise. The closer one gets to seeing the Object as capable of speaking for itself, simply by uncovering the earliest original material, as is clearly the case with J.P. Meier, the closer one is to the modernist enterprise.

[10] A potent critique of Keith Jenkins and other postmodernists can be found in Richard J. Evans, *In Defence of History* (rev. ed.; London: Granta, 2000). See also G. Himmelfarb, *The New History and the Old* (rev. ed.; Cambridge, Mass.: Belknap, 2004); K. Windschuttle, *The Killing of History* (San Francisco: Encounter, 2000), whose rhetoric rivals Jenkins. There is no embracing definition of postmodernism, and what I mean by postmodernist historiography essentially can be narrowed down to Jenkins himself. There is not space here to develop the spectrum of postmodernist histo-riographies. On this, see K. Jenkins, *The Postmodern History Reader* (London: Routledge, 1997).

[11] Jenkins, *Refiguring History* (London: Routledge, 2003), 71 (Introduction, n. 1).

[12] Jenkins, *On "What is History?"* (London: Routledge, 1995), 7.

[13] Jenkins also utilizes Richard Rorty at a deep level. See Jenkins' *On "What is History?"* 97–133. While I'm only loosely conversant with Rorty, I am aware that Jenkins relies on the "linguistic turn" of Rorty but fails in his most recent book (*Refiguring History*) substantially to engage Rorty's later "pragmatist turn" and, even more recently, his "romantic polytheism turn," both of which put strain on Rorty's earlier linguistic turn and, therefore, on the cogency of Jenkins' appeal to Rorty. See R. Rorty, *Achieving Our Country* (Cambridge, Mass.: Harvard University Press, 1997). A sum-mary can be found in J. Boffetti, "How Richard Rorty Found Religion," *First Things* 143 (2004): 24–30. See also R. Rorty, "Religion in the Public Square," *JRE* 31 (2003): 141–49. According to the English philosopher Bernard Williams, Rorty's philosophical pragmatism was running on

accurately, structuralist) historiographer,[14] essentially claims that all history writing is a narrative created in the head of the historian out of discrete facts from the past.[15] His fundamental work *Metahistory* provided a taxonomy of the sorts of narrative games historians play. As a result, scholars today often speak of the linguistic turn in historiography, a radical reshaping of the discipline developed by postmodernists under the influence of the logocentrism of Jacques Derrida and Richard Rorty.

Everything a historian writes, it is claimed (rather objectively) by those like White and Jenkins, is emplotted in a narrative—and it is the narrative that matters in that it shapes the content. There is in that narrative, as White expresses it, "an inexpungeable relativity in every representation of historical phenomena."[16] The narrative one historian tells differs from the narrative another historian tells because they are telling different stories—as opposed to one story being less accurate as it corresponds to, or better yet coheres with, the "facts." Therefore, history is all rhetoric, all discourse, all language, and in effect all autobiography.[17] History is, after all, nothing but historiography, the history of histories and the history of historians.

The impact of this theory is at times quixotic. History, the postmodernist says, is the study of ancient texts, not the ancient past; it is, in other terms, *phenomenalism* (rather than *critical realism*, about which we will have more to say below). In effect, Dan Brown's *The Da Vinci Code* and Jaroslav Pelikan's *Christianity and Classical Culture* (to pick an egregious example) are simply different readings of phenomena, but neither is right, neither is wrong. Any search for the "best explanation" is removed from the map.[18]

Of a less extreme nature and whose work will not be explored in detail here, F.R. Ankersmit's recent study *Historical Representation* marks a singular advance on Hayden White in underscoring and developing what it means to provide a *narrative* about the past. Recognizing the inevitability of the historian's need to turn discoveries into narrative, Ankersmit finds *representation* to be the most

---

empty and led to changes: see Williams, *Truth and Truthfulness* (Princeton: Princeton University Press, 2002), 59.

[14] See Hayden White, *Metahistory* (Baltimore: The Johns Hopkins University Press, 1973); *Tropics of Discourse* (Baltimore: The Johns Hopkins University Press, 1978); *The Content of the Form: Narrative Discourse and Historical Representation* (Baltimore: The Johns Hopkins University Press, 1987); and, with some clear modification, *Figural Realism* (Baltimore: The Johns Hopkins University Press, 1999).

[15] See Jenkins, *Re-thinking History*; *On "What is History?"*; *Why History?* (London: Routledge, 1999).

[16] Hayden White, "Historical Emplotment and the Problem of Truth in Historical Representation," in his *Figural Realism* (Baltimore: The Johns Hopkins University Press, 1999), 27.

[17] For another recent study along this line, see F.R. Ankersmit, *Historical Representation* (*Cultural Memory in the Present*; Stanford: Stanford University Press, 2002).

[18] On this, see P. Lipton, *Inference to the Best Explanation* (2d ed.; International Library of Philosophy; London: Routledge, 2002).

plausible term for what is done, and he explores the significance of that term as the key factor involved in historical undertakings. Representations are linguistic "things" and they do not "refer to" so much as they are "about" the past.[19] A representation offers to the reading public a metaphor.[20] The discipline of history writing, of providing a re-presentation, is about subjectivity and aesthetics.[21] Whatever representation a historian puts forward is a proposal, and little more than that. It is not that historians build upon one another to construct an edifice of certain knowledge.

> Hence, history as a cathedral to which each historian contributes a few bricks for the greater glory of common effort has given way to history as a metropolis in which everybody goes their own way and minds their own business without caring much about what others do.[22]

Inevitably, postmodernist historians like Jenkins and Ankersmit have their share of critics.

A leading historiography all dressed up in the attire of a previous generation and who calls out from the starboard side of this debate, Sir Geoffrey Elton, calls the postmodernist approach to history the "ultimate heresy" and "frivolous nihilism."[23] A modernist historiographer[24] like Elton, Jenkins says in his accusing manner, thinks he is getting at the "facts" and "finding the truth," but in effect that sort of history can be turned on its head, as deconstructionists gleefully do, to see little but the historian's own narrative tale. As Richard Evans, who stands near on the starboard side Elton, sums it up:

> The implication is that the historian does not in fact capture the past in faithful fashion but rather, like the novelist, only gives the appearance of doing so.[25]

Jenkins throws down the gauntlet more than once: when speaking of (upper case) History, he says, "I mean, nobody really believes in that particular fantasy

---

[19] Ankersmit, *Historical Representation*, 13.

[20] Another helpful study of history as the exploration of mental metaphors is that of J.L. Gaddis, *The Landscape of History* (New York: Oxford University Press, 2002).

[21] Ankersmit, *Historical Representation*, 75–103.

[22] Ibid., 152.

[23] G.R. Elton, *Return to Essentials* (Cambridge: Cambridge University Press, 1991), 43, 49.

[24] Jenkins defines modernism as follows: "It is a general failure . . . of the attempt, from around the eighteenth century in Europe, to bring about through the application of reason, science and technology, a level of personal and social wellbeing within social formations which, legislating for an increasingly generous emancipation of their citizens/subjects, we might characterise by saying that they were trying, at best, to become 'human rights communities'" (*On "What is History?"* 6).

[25] R.J. Evans, *In Defence of History*, 98. Another staunch response to the postmodernist trend in historiography can be found in Himmelfarb, *The New History and the Old*, who is more concerned with the predominance of social history over political history. But, for her take on postmodernist historiography, see pp. 15–30.

any more" and when he speaks of (lower case) history, he says that view "is now unsustainable."[26] St. Paul had his thorn in the flesh and we, I'm prone to say, have the postmodernists. They keep us on our knees. Or, on our heels.

Roughly speaking, "History" pertains to macroscopic visions of history—like the Bible, like Augustine, Hegel, and Marx (an odd box of chocolates, to be sure), while "history" pertains to the microscopic attempts to shed light on smaller corners of real people in the real past. Except that there are some who believe the former, including many historical Jesus scholars—who have the confidence (and this is no strike against him), like Marcus Borg, to think that what they find in the past about Jesus has historic significance for understanding both history and life.[27] In fact, nearly every historical Jesus scholar operates at least with a lower-case history, and many with an upper-case sense of History.

We must be careful at this point because postmodernism is often inaccurately caricatured. It is not that there is no past and no attempt at description of that past. For postmodernist historiographers like Jenkins, there is indeed a past, a present, and a future. That past can be characterized as containing "facts," that is existential facts or better yet discrete facts. And, in contrast to what some Gospel Jesus scholars now claim, the historian can at times determine those facts or find them in spite of their present location within narratives (like the Gospels). However, those facts are discrete, according to the postmodernist, in that they are unrelated, uninterpreted, and meaningless in and of themselves. The facts are a proliferated, disparate lot.

> Which means that whenever such a proliferation and dispersal is disciplined into
> some specific unity, into some specific sort of significance [that is a historical

---

[26] Jenkins, On "What is History?" 8, 9.

[27] See the trajectory shaped in Marc Borg's writings by his *Jesus, A New Vision* (San Francisco: Harper & Row, 1987) to his most recent *The Heart of Christianity* (San Francisco: HarperSanFrancisco, 2003).

Martin Kähler laid down the maxim that Christian faith could not be based on the results of historians. Historians themselves mock his claim. Nearly every historical Jesus scholar I know believes in the portrait of Jesus he or she has painted on the canvas after historical research. Nor, so I think, can Kähler sustain the claim that "historical" knowledge and "theological" or "systematic" knowledge are epistemologically that different. Faith is inevitably shaped by what one knows and is not as certain as Kähler would like, and what one knows is shaped by one's historiography and epistemology. In other words, both faith and historical knowledge are shaped by a probabilistic epistemology at some level. On this, see Kähler, *The So-Called Historical Jesus and the Historic Biblical Christ* (ed. and trans. C.E. Braaten, 1896; rpr. Philadelphia: Fortress, 1964).

While it is wise to contend that the church's faith is not to shift every time a new historical Jesus study is offered, it is unwise to think that this is simply an epistemological issue. Put slightly differently, the church's faith is rooted in the New Testament and in the historic creeds, not in the shifting results of scholars; but that knowledge of the NT and the creeds contains a historiography and a "narrative" in the mind of every individual believer. The reason L.T. Johnson's *The Real Jesus* struck a nerve with Christian historical Jesus scholars is because he contended for a creedal faith, even if he mistakenly appealed to a Kähler-like foundation for such a contention. See *The Real Jesus* (San Francisco: HarperSanFrancisco, 1996).

> narrative] . . . then that unity is not, and cannot be, one which has arisen from
> the dispersed facts themselves; is not one which has arisen from the sources, but
> is a unity which is and can only be logically derived from outside these things—
> from theory; only theory can give history any unity of significance . . . theory ulti-
> mately reasserts itself as the inescapable determinant of meaning.[28]

Historians can make statements about these dispersed (or discrete, or existential, or proliferated) facts, and they can also connect them chronologically to form a chronicle, but that is not what history really is. History is the spinning of a narrative out of discrete facts in order to ascertain meaning. Importantly for the postmodernist historian, to discover facts is not to discover meaning. Meaning is created by the historian, who tells a narrative as a piece of aesthetics. Hayden White, who can be called back to the deck on this very question, sees history as a form of literature and not a form of science.[29]

Thus, Jenkins claims,

> we [all of us, so it seems] recognise that there never has been, and there never will
> be, any such thing as a past which is expressive of some sort of essence, whilst the
> idea that the proper study of history is actually "own-sakism" is recognised as just
> the mystifying way in which a bourgeoisie conveniently articulates its own inter-
> ests as if they belonged to the past itself. . . . Consequently the whole "modernist"
> History/history ensemble now appears as a self-referential, problematic expression
> of "interests," an ideological-interpretive discourse without any "real" access to the
> past as such; unable to engage in any dialogue with "reality." In fact, "history" now
> appears to be just one more "expression" in a world of postmodern expressions:
> which of course is what it is.
>
> ... modernist renditions are now naïve: their historical moment has passed.
>
> Saying true things about the past at the level of the statement is easy—anybody
> can do that—but saying the right things, getting the picture straight, that is not
> only another story but an impossible one: you can always get another picture, you
> can always get another context.
>
> ... then precisely insofar as the narrative endows real events with the kind of
> meaning found otherwise only in myth and literature, we are justified in regard-
> ing such a construct as an allegory.[30]

In other words, history as a discourse is not an epistemology.

Bingo! There you have it: a postmodernist understanding (with neo-Marxism as its tarragon) of what historical Jesus scholars are actually—unbe-

---

[28] Jenkins, On "What is History?" 82–83.

[29] See White, Metahistory.

[30] Jenkins, On "What is History?" 9, 10, 21, 24. "Own-sakism" is a critique of Sir G.R. Elton, who will be examined below.

knownst to them—doing: they are simply asserting their power and ideology through an aesthetic presentation about Jesus. Since postmodernism is the only game in town, it is the game historical Jesus scholars are playing. It would not be unfair, though it would be edgy, to describe postmodernist historiography as *semiotic fascism*. Words, and only words, rule—totally. Their own game of words is itself, ironically, a metanarrative.

Which view shows us that just about anything is possible in the world of scholarship.

Historical Jesus scholarship becomes, in Jenkins' categories, bourgeoisie— and it is the proletariat (read: postmodernist historiographers) that now runs the game. The classical studies of Joachim Jeremias, Geza Vermes, Ben Meyer, E.P. Sanders, M. Borg, J.P. Meier, J.D. Crossan, N.T. Wright, B.D. Chilton, and James D.G. Dunn turn out, in this neo-Marxist and linguistic turn, to be nothing but ideologies, nothing but personal expressions of power. They simply emplot the events or existential facts about Jesus in a narrative, and it is the narrative that determines which facts are to be emplotted. Each narrative is a game of power, played by the author and his intended audience. And, what makes one presentation of Jesus "true" and another "not true" or "less than true" is that the true one is connected to persons in power while the not true or less than true ones are not. Truth, then, is little more than the voice of privilege.[31] It might be easy for one historical Jesus scholar to make this accusation against another, but it is harder to admit that one's accusation itself is only the same game of power.

As Jenkins puts it in a way that "goes all the way down" to the bottom of the soul,

> Postmodern historians think that human beings can live ironic, reflexive, histori-cised lives, without the magic, incantations, mythologisations and mystifications spun by certaintist historians from across the board in both upper and lower cases. Postmodern historians see their own histories as being made not for "the past itself" but for themselves and for people whom they like (for when, they ask, was that ever not the case?).[32]

This is a bitter pill to swallow for most of us, and it is not the sort of thing often heard in historical Jesus scholarship, though some theologians have banged this drum for a few decades. Are they not, as the philosopher Bernard Williams suggests, "pecking into dust the only tree that will support them" when they abandon any goal of objectivity, any sense of truth having some sense of correspondence or coherence, and of texts having the intention of communicat-ing?[33] In the coherency theory of truth, one could say that one's "re-presenta-

---

[31] Jenkins, *On "What is History?"* 38–39.

[32] Ibid., 38.

[33] See Williams, *Truth and Truthfulness*, 19. See below, under "Historical Jesus Studies and the Theological Discipline."

tion" *characterizes* truth even if it does not *constitute* that truth.[34] But, as Jenkins counsels us, because we can't get to the truth, sometimes we just have to take our medicine, or swallow the dust, and hope to get better—which would mean we would need to stop thinking that what we are doing is what we are really doing, and start recognizing that we are nothing but ideologues.

This postmodern critique of historical scholarship, it needs to be recognized, is not the old, standard pointing of fingers within historical Jesus scholarship. This is not E.P. Sanders criticizing Joachim Jeremias for having a Lutheran gospel grid through which he forces Jesus; nor is this Marc Borg arguing that previous scholars have not sufficiently recognized the religious genius of Jesus; nor is this N.T. Wright claiming that previous scholars have not sufficiently recognized the profound grasp Jesus had on Israel's story; nor is this Jimmy Dunn contending that previous scholars have not recognized the significance of oral traditions.

No, what Jenkins is accusing us of is far more profound, and it closes the books on nearly every historical Jesus study ever done. He is saying that we are not finding the "real" Jesus behind the texts, the rediscovery of whom sheds light both on the real Jesus and a more genuine and authentic and historical faith. He is arguing that we are simply fooling ourselves: what we think we are doing is not what we are doing. We are not finding Jesus back there, hidden for all these years by the church and others. What we are "finding" is nothing; we are "imposing" pleasing narratives about our own ideologies in order to assert our own power. We impose our power in the form of rhetoric about Jesus. Historical Jesus scholars don't have a goose by the neck, after all; instead, they have a mirror by the top and they are looking at themselves. History, he is saying, is not the past. History is a narrative using discrete facts about the past. This sort of history is more imagined than it is found. The past remains there, discoverable in its historiographical representations (like the Gospels), but meaningless until it is spun into a narrative. History makes discoverable and discrete and existential facts meaningful; but the meaning one finds is not what happened, not the past itself, but a narrative spun in the mind of the historian.

Sometimes, of course, we recognize that historical Jesus scholars have such a heavy agenda that any notion of objectivity (which Jenkins excoriates) is tossed into the winds, but I've not yet met many who think they ought to abandon objectivity and instead simply tell a narrative of their own choosing, gathering bits and bobs of discrete facts and spinning them into a metanarrative of meaning. At least not at the conscious, intentional level. It ought also to be noted that the claim that there is no objectivity is ultimately a claim for an alternative objectivity rather than an alternative to objectivity.

Not all go "all the way down" with Jenkins. For instance, a standard textbook in the United States for history classes is that of Joyce Appleby, Lynn Hunt,

---

[34] I owe this observation to Paul Copan.

and Margaret Jacob, *Telling the Truth about History*.[35] While they appreciate and learn from the postmodernist perspective that history is created in the mind rather than a simple discovery of the past and that history writing shapes culture, their concern is to present a chastened postmodernist or, as I interpret them, an enlightened modernist perspective.[36] However we classify them, the authors mediate the voices—they are neither radical postmodernists nor classical modernists. In fact, they offer a stunning critique of classical modernism in their study of the "heroic model of science."[37] They can provide in this chapter a bridge to the modernist agenda in historiography.

For instance, Appleby, Hunt, and Jacob (AHJ) think the historian can find truth. Thus, in commenting on the discovery that science itself was historically conditioned and can be called to account as a historicist undertaking, AHJ observe: "Science can be historically and socially framed *and still be true*."[38] Furthermore, appealing to the value of realism, AHJ observe that "realism permits historians to aim language *at things outside themselves*."[39] The age-old quest for objectivity, disinterestedness, and distance in an effort to let the ancient world speak has led to renewed appreciations of what objectivity really is, and AHJ build on the work of E.H. Carr and approach critical realism (see below the following section on modernist historiography) when they say that:

> We have redefined historical objectivity as an interactive relationship between an inquiring subject and an external object. Validation in this definition comes from persuasion more than proof, *but without proof there is not historical writing of any worth*.[40]

And, this "persuasion" is defined as the result (progress?) of scholarly discussion:

> Objectivity is not a stance arrived at by sheer willpower, nor is it the way most people, most of the time, make their daily inquiries. Instead it is the result of the clash of social interests, ideologies, and social conventions within the framework of object-oriented and disciplined knowledge seeking.[41]

---

[35] J. Appleby, L. Hunt, and M. Jacob, *Telling the Truth about History* (New York: Norton, 1994) [= AHJ]. The three are historians (at the time of printing) at UCLA. Both Moxnes and Dunn use the study of these three historians in their attempts to come to terms with a more responsible historiography.

[36] At times this study recalls E.H. Carr, *What is History?* (The George Macaulay Trevelyan Lectures [January–March 1961]; New York: Knopf, 1962; 2d ed. 1987), especially in how the authors articulate what "objectivity" is (see pp. 241–70). For example, this comment dissociates the authors from Jenkins: "Every time people go down the relativist road, the path darkens and the light recedes from the tunnel" (192). In fact, they say, "In the final analysis, then, there can be no postmodern history" (237).

[37] AHJ, *Telling the Truth about History*, 15–125.

[38] Ibid., 171 (italics added).

[39] Ibid., 251 (italics added).

[40] Ibid., 261 (italics added).

[41] Ibid., 195.

As if to counter the work of Jenkins before his time, AHJ say,

> What this book insists upon is the human capacity to discriminate between false
> and faithful representations of past reality and, beyond that, to articulate stan-
> dards which help both practitioners and readers to make such discriminations.[42]

It is unfair to AHJ to cut them off at this point, but space forbids a lengthy analysis of their important place in the discipline. Yet, one of their comments transcends our space concerns, a comment that best expresses what history is all
about: "The human intellect demands accuracy while the soul craves meaning."[43]

(MORE OR LESS) MODERNIST HISTORIOGRAPHY

Keith Jenkins remonstrates with two historians whose books have shaped the modern discussion of historiography: the works of E.H. Carr[44] and G.R. Elton.[45] If
Carr, in his soft Marxist *modus operandi*, contends that a fact becomes history only
when it is absorbed into a meaningful history by a historian, Elton represents pure
modernism: history is the attempt to find out what happened and why *for its own
sake*, in its own context, in its own terms, and its own meaning.[46] Carr thinks what
matters is how we can use the past to predict and shape the future, while Elton
thinks what matters is not how something can be used but what it was really
like—to use the famous Rankean expression, *blos zeigen, wie es eigentlich gewesen
ist*, ("simply to show, how it really [or, essentially] happened").[47] While both Carr
and Elton are Rankean to one degree or another, Elton is the post-Rankean Ranke.
And Carr and Elton did not get along, famously.[48]

---

[42] Ibid., 261.

[43] Ibid., 262.

[44] Carr, *What is History?* See also J. Haslam, *The Vices of Integrity* (New York: Verso, 1999); M. Cox,
ed., *E.H. Carr* (New York: Palgrave, 2000).

[45] Elton, *Practice of History; Return to Essentials.* Teachers know that one of the most proven ways
to get students to learn is to present polar opposites so that students can find their own way. This,
I suppose, is why Carr and Elton have proven so popular (though more modern-day historians cur-
rently are Marxist, and more inclined toward Carr than toward Elton). I suspect Jenkins and Evans
can replace Carr and Elton as dialectical opposites.

[46] Thus, Howell and Prevenier, *From Reliable Sources*, 19: "Thus, historians are never in a position—and should never imagine themselves as being in a position—to read a source without attention to both the historical and historiographical contexts that gave it meaning."

[47] L. von Ranke, *Geschichten der romanischen und germanischen Völker von 1494 bis 1514*
(Sämmtliche Werke 33/34; 2d ed.; Leipzig: Duncker & Humbolt, 1874), preface to 1st edition, vii
(*apud* G. Theissen and D. Winter, *The Quest for the Plausible Jesus* [trans. M.E. Boring; Louisville:
Westminster John Knox, 2002], 43). For years I have said *wie es eigentlich gewesen ist*, while many
omit the *ist*. I am happy to see in Theissen and Winter a correct citation.

[48] See, e.g., Elton, *Practice of History*, 12–22. Carr, who was a Marxist, gets this insult from Elton:
"Marxism . . . [is] a truly remarkable achievement of scientific insight and ill-controlled specula-
tion" (37).

To play with the image we have already used, if Jenkins claims that both Carr and (especially) Elton are not holding the goose by the neck but a mirror instead, Elton has a counter. The modernist will claim that Jenkins, by admitting that his own ideology shapes his history, is the one with a mirror in his hands and that the goose can be had—if one has strong enough hands. In addition, the modernist historiographer is ashamed that Jenkins is proud of his own stance. Elton and his ilk will lay claim to the fact that it is they who have the goose by the neck, even if at times they are humble enough to admit their grip is tenuous, and at times the goose escapes. But at least, Elton would say, the modernist historian is interested in the goose of what remains from the past and not the mirror of a present ideology.

Jenkins thinks Elton's methodology is as passé as drinking tea from one's saucer, while Elton thinks Jenkins is cracked—cup and saucer. Jenkins may claim that postmodernism is no longer an option for historians but is instead the fate and condition of all who are at work at all time, but Elton (were he still alive) would simply say . . . perhaps I should use Elton's own words that get at this with his own savage wit:

> No one reads or writes history in a fit of total absentmindedness, though a fair amount of history has been written by people whose minds seem in part to have been on other things.[49]

In other words, Elton would think Jenkins has his mind on other things (and his eyes on a mirror), while Elton thinks he's got his own hand around the goose's neck and Jenkins' neck (the mirror was left at home as he trotted off to the library).

Whether the goose image is useful or not, the majority of historical Jesus scholarship can be categorized as Rankean, post-Rankean, *and* modernist. That is, they are concerned with finding facts, discovering what those facts meant at their time and in their original context, and then setting out an interpretation of those facts in a way that best corresponds to the originals. Perhaps the most representative modernist historians in early Christian studies (with footnote referencing omitted) would be scholars like Martin Hengel, E.P. Sanders, J.P. Meier, Richard Bauckham, and David Aune.

They aim to be scientific—hence preoccupied with method and neutrality and objectivity, and they breathe the air of the hopeful—hence convinced that proper methods, intelligence, and the suppression of one's own views can lead to an ever enlarging knowledge base about the past and its value for the present and future. This is a modernist historiography at work, though I'm not so sure most historical Jesus scholars are as conscious of this as perhaps they ought to be. What modernist historians assume is that language is not simply self-referential but is also other-referential.

---

[49] Elton, *Practice of History*, 39.

It would be unfair, however, to historical Jesus scholarship to suggest that historical Jesus scholars are simply working out the historiography of either Carr or Elton. In fact, the historiography of historical Jesus scholars is eclectic and often unconscious or uninformed of a specific historiography. Because historical Jesus scholarship is eclectic, we need to mention four other historiographers whose views come into play when one discusses the historiography of historical Jesus scholarship: Marc Bloch,[50] Jacques Le Goff,[51] Richard J. Evans,[52] and John Lewis Gaddis.[53] But, because historical Jesus scholarship seems largely unconscious of its historiography, or at least unwilling to trot out its essential features, it is important for us to bring to the surface some of these features.

If we care about the place of the historical Jesus in the theological curriculum, it becomes fundamentally important for us to become aware of what we are doing when we pursue the historical Jesus. Because, so it seems to me, most historical Jesus scholars are fundamentally Eltonian, I will focus on Elton's work.[54]

Sir Geoffrey Elton is best understood if we begin with these two claims:

> Historical method is no more than a recognized and tested way of extracting from what the past has left the true facts and events of that past, and so far as possible their true meaning and interrelation, the whole governed by the first principle of historical understanding, namely that the past must be studied in its own right, for its own sake, and on its own terms. . . . Its fundamental principles are only two, and they may be expressed as questions, thus: exactly what evidence is there, and exactly what does it mean? Knowledge of all the sources, and competent criticism of them—these are the basic requirements of a reliable historiography.

---

[50] M. Bloch, *The Historian's Craft* (trans. P. Putnam; New York: Vintage, 1953). This book is a draft of a volume that was never completed; Bloch was assassinated by the Third Reich on 16 June 1944, along with twenty-six others. The book has enjoyed enormous popularity.

[51] A member of the French *Annales* school with its social-scientific and objective approach, and following the lead of Marc Bloch, Jacques Le Goff is a major medievalist, and I am grateful to my colleage, Dr. Susan Rabe, for introducing me to Le Goff. See his *History and Memory* (trans. S. Rendall and E. Claman; European Perspectives; New York: Columbia University Press, 1992). This study is a collection of major articles originally translated into Italian for R. Romano, ed., *Enciclopedia* (Turin: Einaudi, 1977–1982).

[52] Closer to Elton than to Carr, but a mediating voice between them nonetheless, is Richard J. Evans' *In Defence of History*. His study is an elegantly written masterpiece of chastened modernist historiography. The decision to respond to his many, mostly postmodernist critics wounds the elegance of the book by this modern German history scholar.

[53] Standing on the shoulders of E.H. Carr, John Lewis Gaddis, an American historian of the Cold War period, gave a series of lectures at the University of Oxford as the George Eastman Visiting Professor at Balliol. They follow the lines set out by Carr and, like Carr, Gaddis writes masterfully. See his *Landscape of History*.

[54] For Jenkins' relentless critique of Elton, see Jenkins, *On "What is History?"* 64–96.

The historian must not go against the first conditions of his calling: his knowledge of the past is governed by the evidence of that past, and that evidence must be criticized and interpreted by the canons of historical scholarship.[55]

Never mind that Elton's sharp pen has what amounts to two "firsts": What does he mean by "evidence"?

Evidence is the surviving deposit of an historical event; in order to rediscover the event, the historian must read not only with the analytical eye of the investigator but also with the comprehensive eye of the story-teller.[56]

The historian, so claims the modernist historian G.R. Elton, can be objective:

In the process of learning, he already constructs, and in so far as the first is governed by the integrity imposed by the evidence the second flows from that evidence rather than from the historian's mind. However, it is he who uses the evidence: he chooses, arranges, interprets. As a researcher, he has his defences; we must see whether as a writer he can escape *the relativism of his personality.*[57]

In another context, Elton puts it with his usual flair for the dramatic:

Historians' personalities and private views are a fact of life, like the weather; and like the weather they are not really worth worrying about as much as in practice they are worried over. They cannot be eliminated, nor should they be. The historian who thinks that he has removed himself from his work is almost certainly mistaken; what in fact he is likely to have proved is the possession of a colourless personality which renders his work not sovereignly impartial but merely dull.[58]

He can't stop with this, so he continues:

But though dullness is no virtue, neither is self-conscious flamboyance. The historian need not try either to eliminate or to intrude himself; let him stick to the writing of history and forget the importance of his psyche. It will be there all right and will no doubt be served by his labours, but really it matters less to the result than critics lament or friends acclaim, and it matters a great deal less than does his intellect.

Which is not to say that the historian does not hop the rails of objectivity and reveal that he would rather continue alone and chase a different path. For Elton, awareness of this bias is critical in keeping the historian on the rails.

---

[55] Elton, *Practice of History*, 65, 35.

[56] Ibid., 84.

[57] Ibid., 91. Italics are mine. On "objectivity," see Evans, *In Defence of History*, 224–53; Novick, *That Noble Dream*; Gaddis, *Landscape of History*, 111–28; Le Goff, *History and Memory*, 111–15.

[58] Elton, *Practice of History*, 105.

The point is rather that whatever piece of the past the historian reconstructs must, to be present to the mind, achieve a shape of beginning and end, of cause and effect, of meaning and intent. If, as he ought to be, the historian is in addition an artist, a man wishing to create (in words) a thing of interest and beauty, the constructive element in the process can become overpowering; and if political motives supervene it becomes really dangerous.[59]

A nasty war has taken place between the historian and the social scientist over whether or not we focus on individuals shaping history or on history shaping, because it determines, individuals. A leading light in this discussion was Isaiah Berlin, both in his *Historical Inevitability*, wherein he fought against determinism of all kinds in the name of a humane, free-will-oriented and even moralistic historiography, and in his inimitable essay on Leo Tolstoy's historiography, "The Hedgehog and the Fox."[60] But Elton, building on that scholarship, cut through the brush (because he, too, was a hedgehog) with this:

> History does not exist without people, and whatever is described happens through and to people. Therefore let us talk about people, by all means imposing categories on them and abstracting generalizations from them, but not about large miasmic clouds like forces or busy little gnomes like trends.[61]

Elton has been attacked, especially of late by the postmodernists, and Elton's work responds with an only slightly chastened claim:

> Reality has to be rediscovered and described on the basis of knowledge which is invariably incomplete, often highly ambiguous, and cannot be enlarged once all the relevant survivals have been studied, all of which demands constant decisions based on choice among the possibilities . . . [but] the present must be kept out of the past. . . . That partial and uneven evidence must be read in the context of the day that produced it . . . [because] we must study the past for its own sake and guided by its own thoughts and practices.[62]

And, as he ends chapter 1 of his classic textbook: *Omnia veritas.*[63]

[59] Ibid., 97.

[60] I. Berlin, *Historical Inevitability* (Auguste Comte Memorial Trust Lecture 1 [12 May 1953]; London: Oxford University Press,1954); "The Hedgehog and the Fox," in *The Proper Study of Mankind* (ed. H. Hardy and R. Hausheer; New York: Farrar, Straus & Giroux, 1998), 436–98. For an informative and at times humorous setting of Berlin's historiography in context, see M. Ignatieff, *Isaiah Berlin: A Life* (New York: Metropolitan Books, 1998), 203–7.

[61] Elton, *Practice of History*, 102.

[62] Elton, *Return to Essentials*, 65.

[63] Elton, *Practice of History*, 50. On p. 51 he states that we are to recognize "that inability to know all the truth is not the same thing as total inability to know the truth."

WHAT IS HISTORY?

There is one fundamental issue in all philosophical discussions of historiography today: the relation of the Subject to the Object,[64] of the historian to what that historian wants to study—in our case, Jesus of Nazareth and the historical relics that survive about him, his world, and how he understood his own death. If the postmodernist, someone like Jenkins, wants to usurp the Object with the Subject by contending that history is narrative, history is rhetoric, and history is ideology, the modernist wants to blanket the Subject and find the Object, pure and simple and untouched, and build on that disinterested knowledge for a better world.

Let this be said before we go further: what the modernist wants to do cannot be achieved in its pure form. The postmodernists have made this clear. Unfortunately, too often they make this point with rhetoric and logic and not specific examples gleaned from historical spadework—the sort of examples that compel agreement by historians.[65] In our field, it is maddeningly clear that what one group sees as progress (e.g., the Crossan approach) is unacceptable to another group (e.g., the Allison approach). *Progress*, then, is a tricky term when it comes to historical research laden with meaning—as is historical Jesus study.

Back to the issue of the relationship of the Subject and the Object. Even before the postmodernists, E.H. Carr tossed blocks of ice on the heat of claimed neutrality and objectivity of the modernist, empiricist history, saying that such a day is now over.

> This [era of empiricist historiography] was the age of innocence, and historians walked in the Garden of Eden, without a scrap of philosophy to cover them, naked and unashamed before the god of history. Since then, we have known Sin and experienced a Fall; and those historians who today pretend to dispense with a philosophy of history are merely trying, vainly and self-consciously, like members of a nudist colony, to recreate the Garden of Eden in their garden suburb.
>
> Study the historian before you begin to study the facts. . . . When you read a work of history, always listen out for the buzzing. If you detect none, either you are tone deaf or your historian is a dull dog.
>
> Two books cannot be written by the same historian.[66]

---

[64] Few have discussed, so far as I know, the claim of Elton that the subject matter of history is more objective than that of the natural sciences because the material is independent and has what he calls a "dead reality" (p. 53). See Elton, *Practice of History*, 51–58.

[65] A weakness in the approach of Keith Jenkins is his lack of examples from historical work. This, in part, is what Sir Geoffrey Elton despised: Elton listened only to those who were doing actual historical work (e.g., Elton, *Return to Essentials*, 3–26, 34). At the level of style and example, the studies of Richard J. Evans and John Lewis Gaddis carry the day.

[66] Carr, *What is History?* 21, 26, 52.

But let this also be said before we go further: neither is the bold claim of Jenkins tenable. We cannot completely swallow the Object in our subjectivity. We remain differentiated ego masses—and can do nothing about it. This is why the "critical realism" of Ben F. Meyer, a historical Jesus scholar, has become so important to historical Jesus scholarship.[67] Or, in the words of AHJ, a "practical realism."[68] Or, as stated by Dunn,

> To conceive the hermeneutical process as an infinitely regressive intertextuality is a counsel of despair which quickly reduces all meaningful communication to impossibility and all communication to a game of "trivial pursuit."[69]

So what then is history? And, for our purposes, what kind of history is the historical Jesus scholar doing? First, history begins with "facts" that survive from the past as evidence (facts constituent of the Object).[70] This evidence confronts the Subject (observer),[71] which facts, even if one follows the dynamic flow of the French phenomenologist Michel Henry on life, time and truth,[72] can be captured as existential facts—a point permitted even by the postmodernist Keith Jenkins. The Subject does not completely swallow up the Object, and when it is claimed that it does, we are seeing what Richard Evans calls the "narcissism of much postmodernist writing" and "inflated self-importance, solipsism and pretentiousness."[73] The Object can be distinguished from the Subject, and while the Object is always at the level of perception or representation (what isn't?),[74] such Objects genuinely exist, even if they need to be sorted out through a critical procedure. The realism of the Object requires a critical, not naïve, approach, one in which the Subject and the Object interact.[75] To be sure, apart from perhaps archaeological remains, all existential facts have been through what Elton

---

[67] See Meyer, *Critical Realism*.

[68] AHJ, *Telling the Truth about History*, 247–51.

[69] Dunn, *Jesus Remembered*, 121.

[70] My own teacher J.D.G. Dunn distinguishes between the originating "event," as compared to the "data" and "facts," with the latter being the interpretive descriptions of the hard evidence of the former (a Nietzschean view). Facts are always interpretive. See Dunn, *Jesus Remembered*, 102–4.

[71] A nuanced historiography makes this distinction: we study not so much the past but what survives from the past. But, few historians question that they can look "through" what survives to say something about the past itself. "Facts" exist independently of the mind, whether they are discovered or not; that is, things were said and things occurred. "Evidence" is what survives of those "existential facts." The judgment that facts are "discrete" is a claim that facts have no meaning in and of themselves and that context and emplotment are not constitutive of those facts. I agree with R.J. Evans when he says: "The historian formulates a thesis, goes looking for evidence and discovers facts" (*In Defence of History*, 78).

[72] Henry, *I Am the Truth* (trans. S. Emanuel; *Cultural Memory in the Present*; Stanford: Stanford University Press, 2003).

[73] Evans, *In Defence of History*, 200.

[74] On this, see Gaddis, *Landscape of History*, 129–51.

[75] A good summary of this can be found in Wright, *New Testament and the People of God*, 31–46.

calls "some cooking process," noting that no existential facts are "raw."[76] As AHJ write, "Practical realists are stuck in a contingent world."[77] Nonetheless, the relic of that past remains and it can be studied—and some things can be known. As Jacques Le Goff puts it,

> In sum, I think history is indeed a science of the past, if it is acknowledged that this past becomes an object of history through a reconstitution that is constantly questioned.[78]

John Lewis Gaddis is not alone in countering postmodernity's fetishistic worry about the Subject when he states that "historians are relatively minor actors, therefore, in the coercive process."[79] But the necessary recognition that Subject and Object interact to form a knowledge rooted in critical realism means that all conclusions must be recognized as approximate, probabilistic, and contingent— and, not to be missed, shaped by the interaction of Object and the Subject's story.

An example of an existential fact, from the Gospels—which are not them- selves without narrative context[80]—would be Jesus' entering into the Jordan

---

[76] See Elton, *Practice of History*, 58. With his customary wit, Elton goes on: "one could at best then hope to find an historian [from the ancient past] learned, wise and sensitive enough to have cooked his materials in such a way that their natural flavour appears in the dish" (59).

[77] AHJ, *Telling the Truth about History*, 250.

[78] Le Goff, *History and Memory*, 108.

[79] Gaddis, *Landscape of History*, 146.

[80] A point made time and again in Dunn, *Jesus Remembered*, esp. 125–36. I cannot, however, agree with Dunn at all when he says that "narratives about Jesus never began with Jesus" (131). I, for one, cannot imagine a Jesus who did not have a narrative about himself that he communicated in vari- ous ways to those who heard him and who saw him. One might plausibly ask if statements by Jesus, now rendered with a positive verdict in matters pertaining to authenticity, do not contain within them some sort of hints about his own narrative about himself? If Jesus used "Son of man," if Jesus used some Mosaic allusion, if Jesus said something about "the one who is to come"—if Jesus said such things then we are face-to-face (however mediated through the sayings of Jesus as remembered by his followers) with a narrative that began with Jesus. Dunn's preoccupation with the *nature* of the evidence (the result of memory) too often obscures what the historian is to do and can do with that same evidence.

My criticism, however, is less a disagreement with what he does say about the evidence than with what that evidence can provide for us—which, in my judgment, finds more of an articulation in the body of Dunn's work than one might expect from his methodological discussions. Maybe all we have is the remembered Jesus, but Dunn's own study frequently speaks of a typical historical Jesus who is not quite the Jesus of Mark, Matthew, Luke, or John, but who is one just "behind" them—the one who is held in common by the oral tradition. And that Jesus is a historical Jesus distinguishable from the Evangelists' presentation. I give one quotation that seems, to me, to reveal that Dunn after all is talking in some senses of modernist study of the historical Jesus. "The crite- rion is this: any feature which is *characteristic within the Jesus tradition and relatively distinctive of the Jesus tradition* is most likely to go back to Jesus, that is, to reflect the original impact made by Jesus' teaching and actions on several at least of his first disciples" (333). What I am saying is this: this Jesus, this remembered Jesus of Dunn, is not the Jesus of the Gospels *tout simplé* but a Jesus distinguishable from those orally expressed Gospels, and also one who is in some sense behind

River near John the Baptist. If we are the Subject, and Jesus (as represented in
the Gospels and Josephus) is the Object, and one of the existential facts is that
he entered into the Jordan River, then Subject and Object can be distinguished—even if the Object can only be known through the mind of the
Subject.

Second, while there is something to be said for treating heuristically the
"existential facts" as genuinely discrete, the postmodernist wedge has been
driven in too deep: even existential facts emerge from the waters of context and
contingency and intention.[81] The existential facts we work with, say Jesus' entering the Jordan River, are embedded and emplotted in their own context because
humans intend and humans interpret as part of what makes them human.[82] It
wasn't just any river he entered; and it wasn't during the night; and the entry
wasn't disconnected from a John who was known for baptizing people; and
water, especially the Jordan, wasn't any water; and confessions aren't normal in
the Jordan; and others joining isn't typical. The social context, in other words,
shapes how the data or facts can be represented and should be represented.

It might be useful to think more clearly about *discrete facts* and *emplotted* or
contextualized facts. It can be just as easily claimed that no fact is genuinely discrete
because all facts occur in contexts, as a result of intentions, and therefore have
some sort of narrative or meaning constituent to their very existence.[83] If I were to
be seen walking around my car to open the door, one might interpret that action
discretely as an existential fact of walking around the car to open a door into which
I did not enter. Odd behavior, to be sure, but still discrete. But, if one widens the
context to see both contingency and intention in my action, one would see that I
opened the door for a female, who is from other contexts determined to be
my wife Kris, and that such behavior is characteristic of males such as I who
were reared to open doors as an act of courtesy. In such a context, any kind of
meaning-making would see my action as an act of love and kindness and chivalry.
(Of course, there are other truthful explanations of the action on other occasions:
maybe the door is jammed and she needs my help in prying the door loose, or
maybe her hands are full and mine are not.) In general, in context, my action
would be discernible and susceptible to accurate meaning-making. In such a context, treating my action as discrete would tell us less than we could and should

---

them. Yes, indeed, he is a Jesus of faith even at that level, but he is distinguishable. The fundamental question for me about Dunn's methodology is why we need a remembered Jesus more than
the Jesus of the Evangelists.

[81] On these matters, see Gaddis, *Landscape of History*, 71–109. On intention, see G.E.M.
Anscombe, *Intention* (Library of Philosophy and Logic; Oxford: Blackwell, 1979). With the rise of
Marxism especially, the issue of historical inevitability was pushed to the front by historiographers.
A definitive argument in favor of free will and contingency and against determinism is the engag-
ing essay, in his customary style of the winding road, of Berlin, *Historical Inevitability*, esp. 69–79.
The rest of the essay is a polemic against determinism as a legitimate hermeneutic of reality.

[82] Again, see Henry, *I Am the Truth*, 33-52.

[83] See the helpful comments in Evans, *In Defence of History*, 75–102.

know. This is important because, without defense, Jenkins and other postmodernist historiographers assume the fundamental importance of treating existential facts as discrete.[84] But, if as I have argued, existential facts and events were originally emplotted because of human intention and because humans "read" others' intentions through actions, etc., then there was an original meaning, however inchoate, and it is the aim of the historian to get as close to that original meaning as much as possible by working at the sources to find the original emplotment.

Third, it is at this level, at the level of contextualizing the existential facts, that meaning-making begins to take place. That is, if I understand Jesus' entry into the Jordan River to be connected, because of a discernible context, to John the Baptist, to John's message and mission (which were determined through other existential facts), and to Israel's historic associations with this very location at the Jordan, then the historian can discern some kind of meaning of what Jesus was doing and what his baptism meant. This meaning is brought to the surface through narration, through what Paul Ricoeur labeled the "fictive."[85]

In other words, history involves three *steps*—though we hasten to insert that *step* gives the wrong impression if one thinks that the historian proceeds from one step to the other. Actual historical study reveals that the three steps are taken at the same time because, as Marc Bloch put it so well, "In the beginning, there must be the guiding spirit."[86] In fact, meaning-making occurs from the beginning of the process. This was the insight of several earlier historiographers, including Benedetto Croce and R.G. Collingwood.[87] Back now to these three interrelated steps: They are (1) the *discovery* of existential facts—in our case the discovery of the gospel evidence by exegesis, or of archaeological data, or of political contexts. Then, (2) there is *criticism* of the existential facts. It is here that historical Jesus scholars have made big beds with billowy pillows and thick covers.[88] An existential fact often becomes nonexistential at the hand of a

---

[84] It may be observed here that this is precisely the strategy of the early form critics, who isolated events and sayings of Jesus, rendered their current contextual location in the Gospels as secondary, and then imagined more original and secondary contexts out of which those events or sayings emerged. Redaction critics followed soon after and sought to discover the theology inherent in the "fictive" or "imaginary narrative" imposed on the "discrete events" by the redactor. It is perhaps the social scientists, however, who have undercut this simplistic model of the early form critics by arguing that all persons/events/sayings are socially, culturally, and ideologically embedded and emplotted—in and of themselves. For recent studies bringing these issues to light, see Michael Moxter, "Erzählung und Ereignis: Über den Spielraum historischer Repräsentation," in *Der historische Jesus* (ed. Schröter and Brucker), 67–88; J. Schröter, *Jesus und die Anfänge der Christologie* (BTS 47; Neukirchen-Vluyn: Neukirchener Verlag, 2001); Theissen and Winter, *Quest for the Plausible Jesus*.

[85] The literature by Paul Ricoeur, not to mention about him and as an extension of him, is immense. I cite his three-volume set of essays: *Time and Narrative* (trans. K. McLaughlin and D. Pellauer; 3 vols.; Chicago: University of Chicago Press, 1984–1988).

[86] Bloch, *Historian's Craft*, 65.

[87] B. Croce, *History* (trans. D. Ainslie; New York: Russell & Russell, 1960); R.G. Collingwood, *The Idea of History* (Oxford: Clarendon, 1946).

[88] See below, under "The Issue of Historical Judgment."

skeptical historical Jesus scholar. Some scholars, many perhaps, think Jesus was baptized but know not where—not because there is not evidence that Jesus was baptized near where the children of Israel reportedly crossed the Jordan (e.g., John 1:22-23, 26) but because that evidence is judged, through criticism, to be unreliable.[89]

Now we get to the significance of the postmodernist enterprise. Next, (3) the historian begins to make meaning by interpreting what he or she judges to be critically reliable fact in its context and for the author's own intention.[90] It is

---

[89] So, when James D.G. Dunn disagrees with me because "the tradition contains no indication in that regard," he must mean that the evidence in John is not to be regarded as an "existential fact." See Dunn, *Jesus Remembered*, 378 n.182. That is, that John 3:26 is not part of the reliable tradition.

[90] There was a long-standing debate between E.H. Carr and G.R. Elton over whether something becomes historical only when it is swallowed up into a historical narrative, or whether events in and of themselves are historical. Carr, for himself, thought history was about taking facts and placing them into a narrative in order to shape the present and the future, and thought that objectivity was all about what from the past fit into the course of the future. See Carr, *What is History?* 36–69. Elton, on the other hand, had a different design: all facts were historical; some were more significant than others. But, whether or not they had functional use for the future had nothing to do with their being historical or objective. See Elton, *Practice of History*, 51–87. Carr has been followed in this regard by Gaddis, *Landscape of History*, 1–16.

It is my view that no historian ever studies anything purely for its own sake (though I have undertaken some studies because I had to for an assignment). All historians have a reason for what they are studying, even if that reason is curiosity—but nearly all of them render judgment about their Object in the process. As an example, some modern historical Jesus scholars trumpet rather boldly that they are not, at the personal level, Christians in any ordinary sense and that this makes them more objective or neutral in their judgments. But, what becomes clear upon examination of their narratives about Jesus is that their Jesus tends, more often than not (and I know of almost no exceptions), to lean in the direction of their own belief systems. Jesus, thus, can become an enthusiastic apocalyptic and not worthy of utter devotion, and (what I am suggesting) their own non-faith in such a Jesus can be confirmed. What would be rare is someone who came to the conclusion that Jesus was utterly divine but who did not think him worthy of devotion. In other words, all historical Jesus scholars have an aim in what they are writing about Jesus. Thus, knowledge and power are related, though I maintain they are not mutually determinative. See the excellent study of this topic in Evans, *In Defence of History*, 191–223.

A good example of this can be seen in J.H. Charlesworth, "The Historical Jesus and Exegetical Theology," *PSB* 22 (2001): 45–63, who begins his study (45) with this claim: "All scholars who are distinguished in Jesus Research acknowledge that the historical-critical method needs to be employed." A postmodernist of a deconstructionist spirit could be justified in seeing this as nothing more than the assertion of power—those who don't do historical Jesus studies by "my" or "our" method will not be acknowledged, and, because we acknowledge one another, "our" studies are the best. However, inasmuch as I think Charlesworth does state the facts straight in this regard—that the best scholarship is genuinely critical—I tend to think he is not playing the game of power, but objectively stating a historiographical truth. This, however, is not to say that genuine insights cannot be gleaned from those who operate with the historical-critical method. Inasmuch as Charlesworth is a modernist historian, his statement intentionally includes the postmodernist approach to Jesus. He speaks of "true historians," (48), of "virtually *bruta facta*" (49), and includes here "healing miracles"—which is not a "brute fact" but instead explanations of something else. He also speaks of the "purely historical and scientific methods" that must be "disinterested" (62). In

at this point that narration begins to shape the choice of facts, the order those facts are to find, and what meaning will occur as a result of that narration. That is, the historian makes meaning through narration, as a result of imagination,[91] through sorting through the evidence with a narrative that ties everything together, whether or not one prefers Ricoeur's "fictive" label. History is not just discovery and judgment, as if judgment will somehow work a magic that turns those discovered facts into meaningful story. No, the "task of the historian is to explain not only what happened, but why it happened and why it happened in the way it did."[92]

This occurs whether the historian is doing something large and formidable, as Peter Brown does in his *Rise of Western Christendom* or Martin Hengel does with his *Hellenism and Judaism* or E.P. Sanders does with his *Paul and Palestinian Judaism* or James D.G. Dunn with his *The Parting of the Ways*. Or, it occurs when some historian narrows his or her scope to a singular event, theme or saying, as can be seen in Kathleen Corley's *Women and the Historical Jesus* or in Tom Holmén's *Jesus and Jewish Covenant Thinking*. In each of these studies, whether big or small, it is the historian, not the existential fact, who makes meaning through what some classic historiographers call interconnectedness. It is the business of a historian to make meaning of existential facts by bringing them into a coherent narrative—and the better written the more likely it is that the narrative will catch on. Bloodless historians create bloodless meanings—with the proviso that the sanguine do not necessarily write better histories.

This raises the question of truth. Are some narratives or meanings more truthful than others? Is there, at times, meaning inherent to an existential fact. That is, does the very act of Jesus' baptism in the Jordan River at the hand of John the Baptist need anything more than exegesis (a "bringing out of what is there")? At this point a wedge can be pushed into the discussion. If, as some postmodernists suppose, all events are indeed discrete in the sense that they are not connected and there is no meaning inherent in the event itself, then one must conclude that no historical narrative is true in the sense of final. Why? Because there is no standard against which one can measure the narrative to claim that it is true (assuming here some sort of correspondence or coherency theory for truth). It is here that the postmodernist enjoys the role of using the dagger. Because of his or her position of irony, the postmodernist delights in the claim that all is rhetoric, or narrative, or language. But, as Richard J. Evans points out rather often, no postmodernist historiography permits the role to be reversed—that is, no postmodernist permits his or her narrative to be seen as nothing more than ideology and language, and nearly all such postmodernists

---

addition, Charlesworth proceeds to say that while the Christian faith is rooted in history, it transcends that history (62). This is an excellent article on the topic of this chapter.

[91] On imagination, which is discussed by most historiographers, see Gaddis, *Landscape of History*, 35–52.

[92] Dunn, *Jesus Remembered*, 101.

trumpet their claim to have a postmodernist method that tells that the (even if they don't use that term) story about method and about what can be known.[93] Oddly enough, the postmodernist claims his or her irony as the truth.

Call it common sense realism or critical realism,[94] or whatever else you'd like, no human lives in a total denial of some sense of truthfulness.[95] An example may help. We live in Chicago. We are fans of the American game of baseball, and that means we cheer for the Chicago Cubs. The Chicago Cubs have not won a pennant in decades, and last year, on the verge of clinching a decisive game and putting themselves in position to go to the World Series, an event occurred (so far as I can tell) in the sixth game of the National League Playoff Series. That event involved a Cubs fan named Steve Bartman (may he nonetheless live to a ripe old age). The fan reached up to snatch a baseball that had been hit by a batter into foul territory, and Chicago Cubs player Moises Alou reached out to catch the ball. The fan "interfered" by touching the ball. The result was that the player did not, and could not, catch the ball. Had Alou caught the ball, perhaps, just perhaps, the Cubs would have won the game and been able to go to the World Series—and who knows, perhaps they would have prevailed there as well. (A recent television game between the Chicago Cubs and their dreaded rivals, the St. Louis Cardinals, showed that some fans had a high opinion of Steve Bartman. A Cardinals fan projected a sign that said, "Bartman for President.")

Now, here's my point: according to a strict postmodernist interpretation, if we had not been in the stadium, all we would have known about the game is what newspaper writers told us, what radio announcers relayed to us, and what television analysts showed us. They communicated to us what they wanted to for their own reasons, according to their own ideologies, and for the assertion of their own power. What we don't know is the "reality" of the event, because there is no such thing as a singular reality. We could, by analyzing the residue of historical evidence—newspaper reports, eyewitnesses (one of whom was my son), and TV camera shots (which distort depth perceptions), come to our conclusion and tell our own story. But, no story would be true. All we would have would be rhetoric and all we would have would be ideology.

It might be added, as my colleague David Koeller—an avid baseball fan and a professional historiographer—pointed out to me, that the *social context* of a baseball game informs how we narrate the incident. That is, a social context involving how the game is played, how fans behave at games, how fans respond to fellow fans when they touch baseballs on the margins of the field of play, how contingencies at one moment in a game impact later events in the game. The

---

[93] Evans, *In Defence of History*, throughout.

[94] On "critical realism," see esp. Meyer, *Critical Realism*.

[95] A recent important examination of this can be seen in Williams, *Truth and Truthfulness*, where he explains what he calls a "State of Nature" in which Accuracy and Sincerity are required for humans to exist with one another.

debate that ensued in Chicagoland, which involved Steve Bartman finding himself at times a Wanted Man, was a debate between various individuals within the same social context—some thinking his act was trivial and others thinking he was to blame for the Cubs' loss.

A consistent postmodernist, however, would argue there are only narrations of this event, none of which has any claim either to truth or to accuracy when it comes to the significance of the event. I think this construction of reality is as difficult to live with as the denial of the law of contradiction.[96] More importantly, I think no postmodernist lives this way—most of them who heard about the game would think they knew what happened and most of them could make meaning out of it—and a meaning that they would think truthful at some level. (And this would be so even for those who only heard reports by friends and fans.) Most postmodernist historiographers, also, would have an opinion on contingency, what would have happened had the man not reached out and touched the ball. Many, and I am among that group, think Alou would have caught the ball and the Cubs would have most likely won the game. None, I think, would say that the fan touching the ball was simply a discrete event that had no connection to the baseball player or even to the outcome of the game.[97]

We live in a world where we have to make meaning to live, and some meanings are more realistic and truthful than others. The person who looks at a baseball coming at him or her and has a world in which meaning-making does not observe the rules of gravity may get whacked in the face—and what I am saying is that people don't live like this. Not even postmodernists, who seem to have plenty of starch in their drawers. One who has a meaning-making narrative in which the laws of gravity are at work has a more truthful narrative than the one who does not.

Returning from our digression into the pit of nether gloom that is Cubs baseball, we can look once again at what truth means when it comes to history and meaning-making. In contrast to the postmodernist agenda, *if* facts are not simply discrete, *if* events have context, *if* the contingency of existential facts is not simply chaos, *if* humans have intentions in their actions and sayings—that is, in the existential facts for which there is a historical residue—*then* some narratives and meanings are more truthful than others. Those that are most truthful are those that can be demonstrated to cohere more or less with the existential facts in their historical contexts. As Richard Evans puts it, in what can only be called a chastened post-postmodernist modernism,

> I will look humbly at the past and say despite them all: it really happened, and we really can, if we are very scrupulous and careful and self-critical, find out how it

[96] This is pointed out often by historiographers and philosophers. A notable example is Himmelfarb, *New History and the Old*.

[97] So meaningful was that event to some Cubs fans that the ball was enshrined for some time in a bar near Wrigley Field and this winter was blown up, in front of cheering fans, and at considerable expense. So ended, it is believed, the curse against the Cubs.

happened and reach some tenable though always less than final conclusions about what it all meant.[98]

Postmodernists teach us that our own narratives are not equivalent with that reality in the past, and they remind us that our narratives need to be held lightly with the obvious potential of being revised and even jettisoned, but they cannot steal from us this: that our narratives either more or less cohere with what we can know about existential facts and their contexts in such a way that we can derive a narrative that approximates truth. The best histories are those that narrate the most significant events in such a manner that meaning and events are close.

THE HISTORICAL JESUS: BRIEF REMARKS

We can begin with this: Christianity believes in history. Historiographers are fond of commenting that history as we now know it was washed into the tide of generations by Israel and the early Christians who believed, as is now clear, in "events" and "sayings" as put together into a "narrative."[99] As Dunn, joining a long line of English (and Scottish—may the land, "sae far awa'," retain its honor) theologians, states it,

> For those within the Christian tradition of faith, the issue is even more important. Christian belief in the incarnation, in the events of long ago in Palestine of the late 20s and early 30s AD as the decisive fulcrum point in human history, leaves them no choice but to be interested in the events and words of those days. . . . A faith which regards all critical scrutiny of its historical roots as inimical to faith can never hold up its head or lift up its voice in any public forum.[100]

Two brief points draw to the surface the issue about the fundamental significance, for faith itself, of the original Jesus and our historical representations of him—which representations can never be escaped, from the least informed to the most articulate believer. First, the Apostle Paul contends that the entirety of the Christian faith is founded on the fact of Jesus being raised from the dead.[101] He states this is the Christian tradition (i.e., narrative representation) from the very beginning (1 Cor 15:3-7). Perhaps his most pointed lines are these:

[98] Evans, *In Defence of History*, 253.

[99] E.g., Elton, *Practice of History*, 2; Bloch, *The Historian's Craft*, 31.

[100] The line is from Robert Burns, "My Native Land Sae Far Awa'," in *The Poems and Songs of Robert Burns (1759–1796)* (Collins: Glasgow, n.d.), 462. Dunn, *Jesus Remembered*, 100–101.

[101] On how Paul understood the resurrection, see now the exhaustive tome of N.T. Wright, *The Resurrection of the Son of God* (vol. 3 of *Christian Origins and the Question of God*; Minneapolis: Fortress, 2003), 207–398. See also M.J. Harris, *Raised Immortal* (Grand Rapids: Eerdmans, 1983); *From Grave to Glory* (Grand Rapids: Zondervan, 1990). For the broader discussion of how Paul expresses faith in past events, the brief section of Meyer, *The Aims of Jesus*, retains potency; see pp. 60–75.

If there is no resurrection of the dead, *then* not even Christ has been raised. And, *if* Christ has not been raised, *then* our preaching is useless and so is your faith (1 Cor 15:13-14).

That is, the Christian gospel is absolutely dependent on the understanding that Jesus Christ was dead, was buried, and came back to life—in the words of N.T. Wright in *The Resurrection of the Son of God*, acquired "life *after* life-after-death." This, in other words, is the claim that faith is rooted in the facticity of an event, a particular event, namely, the resurrection of Jesus from the grave. This is one reason why historiographers often claim Christianity is a religion of history.

A second example is from the Apostles' Creed, in which, whenever one dates it, the faith of Christianity is expressed not so much as a belief in the Bible as a belief in the events to which the Bible witnesses—namely those brought about by the Father, Son, and Spirit.[102] Events—as put into a holistic Christian narrative—are at the foundation of this unifying creed of Christians: God creating and the Son dying, descending, rising, and ascending.[103] To be sure, there is a narrative understanding of these existential events or, to use Ricoeur's language, a *fictive representation*, but if those events are simple fictions or myths, then some serious damage is done to the content of what it is that Christians affirm.

What is also affirmed today is that the historical Jesus matters.[104] What do historical Jesus scholars mean when they speak of the historical Jesus? In light of the brief survey of historiography above, it can only mean this: the historical Jesus is a narrative representation of the existential facts about Jesus that survive critical scrutiny. The reason N.T. Wright makes a strong case for the study of Jesus as an instance of history is because he renders history into a story, a narrative representation on the basis of a conscious method. That is, his study is not simply a study of existential facts that survive scrutiny, but it is a complete narrative representation of those existential facts. It puts all things together into a robust, engaging story. This is what, according to historiographers, genuine history does. I do not mean by this that N.T. Wright's study of Jesus is the best, though I am partial to much of what he says,[105] but what I do mean is that N.T. Wright's study of Jesus is exemplary when it comes to the matter of historiography. There are some historiographical rivals, namely the historical Jesus studies of B.F. Meyer, E.P. Sanders, R.A. Horsley, James D.G. Dunn, the imaginative J.D. Crossan and the even more imaginative B.D. Chilton, but none of these provides as rich or as complete a narrative representation.

---

[102] On creeds, see now J. Pelikan, *Credo* (vol. 1 of *Creeds and Confessions of Faith in the Christian Tradition*; ed. Jaroslav Pelikan and V. R. Hotchkiss; New Haven: Yale University Press, 2003); L.T. Johnson, *The Creed* (New York: Doubleday, 2003).

[103] See the comments of Charlesworth, "Historical Jesus and Exegetical Theology," 62–63.

[104] See, e.g., R. Bauckham, "The Future of Jesus Christ," in *The Cambridge Companion to Jesus* (ed. M. Bockmuehl), 265–80.

[105] As can be seen in my *A New Vision for Israel* (Grand Rapids: Eerdmans, 1999).

Scholars will no doubt dispute some, or much, of the evidence that has survived Wright's critical scrutiny—which they have a right to do if they are doing
history. In disputing the existential facts Wright uses, less evidence will survive
and a new narrative representation will have to be offered. The point here is not
which evidence survives, but what one does with the evidence that does survive.
For it to be good history it must be an engaging narrative. To be sure, some studies are only partial (*histoire en miettes*) because, as monographs or articles, they
examine only some of the evidence or are narrowly focused. But for something
to pass muster with the historiographers, a narrative is needed to give existential
facts their appropriate meaning.

Others, of course, tell a different narrative. B.F. Meyer and E.P. Sanders,
who have had their share of tussles, tell the narrative of the restoration of Israel;
J.D. Crossan tells the narrative of a countercultural Jesus; while Richard Horsley
tells the narrative of a socially engaged Jesus; and Bruce Chilton tells the narrative of a *mamzer* ("illegitimate child") who was also a mystic . . . and the narratives go on and on. And what needs to be seen as "on and on" is that each new
re-presentation of Jesus is, in effect, a new gospel to be believed by the historical
Jesus scholar and by any who care to agree with that scholar. I know of no other
way of putting this. Historical Jesus studies tend to construe existential facts into
a new narrative, and a new narrative adds up to a new Gospel.

It is this "on and on" that causes the problem we are facing: what role are
these narrative representations of Jesus to play in the theological discipline? The
issue here is found in one of the words italicized above: the historical Jesus is the
narrative *re-presentation* of the existential facts about Jesus that survive critical
scrutiny. Every historical Jesus placed on the table is a re-presentation of Jesus
and it is a re-presentation of the Jesus in the canonical four Gospels—sometimes
by eschewing the overall narrative of those four gospels for a non-canonical representation in favor of the historical Jesus scholar's own rendition of what Jesus
was "really like." It is this "on and on" of re-presentations that raises a critical
question for the theological discipline.

There are two deep traditions of a narrative about Jesus—the four canonical Gospels and the various creeds of the church—that have shaped the entire
history of the church and the role Jesus himself plays in that church. Are the new
narrative representations of Jesus to oust those two deep traditions? Are they to
supplement them? Or, are they to correct them?

It can be said without exaggeration that the church's own presentation of
Jesus in the four Gospels, or in the creeds, is the governing story of Jesus.[106] It
is this story, or history, that won the day and that has shaped the self-identity of
the church for two millennia.[107] This presentation is the church's "memory" and

---

[106] See F. Watson, "The Quest for the Real Jesus," in *The Cambridge Companion to Jesus* (ed.
Bockmuehl), 156–69; C. Stephen Evans, *The Historical Christ and the Jesus of Faith* (New York:
Oxford, 1996).

[107] Deconstructionists, of course, may suggest that the church's story is precisely the problem: it

it is *both* memorization of past and generation of identity and future.[108] The church makes the claim that neither the modernist nor the postmodernist has either the goose by the neck or the mirror by the top. Instead, the church claims it has the *gospel*, which can be found by reading the four canonical Gospels or by studying the church's creeds. By and large, the church doesn't eat goose and it does not care to look at itself in a mirror. It believes instead in the gospel, the narrative about Jesus that mediates Jesus to those who read it.[109]

The problem, therefore, with other re-presentations of Jesus is *scriptural*— what role is the Scripture to play in the church's understanding of Jesus? The problem is also *christological*—what role are the traditional affirmations of Jesus to play in the church's understanding of other re-presentations of Jesus? The problem is *epistemological*—how do the re-presentations of Jesus cohere with the already existing canonical presentations of Jesus? And, finally, it is *ecclesiological*— what role is the church's own self-identity to play in judging new re-presentations of Jesus? Is it not the case, whether we come at this from the angle of postmodernism, tradition history, or just common sense, that a new narrative of Jesus will re-shape the church's own self-identity? As Robert Morgan put it in his ruminative essay,

> The objection to this procedure [of re-presenting Jesus], and what some would call its theological *impossibility*, is that it substitutes a religiously indeterminate historical presentation of Jesus for the Gospels and most Christians' theological evaluation of him.... In proposing a substitute for Jesus as the subject of Christological predication, Strauss [who is the subject of Morgan's essay at this point] was abandoning Christian faith. . . . Those who place a historical reconstruction of Jesus at the head of their presentations [of NT theology] are wittingly or unwittingly placing a question mark against all traditional Christian ways of understanding Jesus. . . . [For] purely historical reconstructions are inevitably at odds with traditional Christianity. . . . [And, to] replace it [the Christian faith about Jesus Christ] with a historical statement about Jesus, however true in its own terms, is no mere modification but a radical break with historical

---

was an ideology that had sufficient power to control the story (as did Dante in his *Divine Comedy*). Constantine has been overestimated here, but having said that, we must recognize that (1) that story was not invented by Constantine; it had deep, original roots in the Christian tradition. And, (2) it is that story that has shaped the identity of the church ever since. To interfere with that story is to interfere with the identity of the church —which is what some want to do today (e.g., Elaine Pagels, *Beyond Belief* [New York: Random, 2003]; Bart Ehrman, *Lost Christianities* [New York: Oxford University Press, 2003]).

[108] On which, see esp. Le Goff, *History and Memory*, 51–99. See also Dunn, *Jesus Remembered*, 125–36; and Dunn's colleague, Stephen Barton, "Many Gospels, One Jesus?" in *The Cambridge Companion to Jesus* (ed. Bockmuehl), 170–83, esp. 178–83.

[109] The issue of the four-fold testimony cannot be explored here. One can say that the church forms its identity on the basis of a four-fold narrative and on the basis of a synthesis of those four narratives.

Christianity. . . . It is one thing to be interested in the historical reality of Jesus, and to see there the criterion of the kerygma (Ebeling), but quite another matter to substitute a purely historical for a kerygmatic presentation of Jesus in this context.[110]

Here is what I think is a stunning line:

But to make these hypothetically reconstructed early experiments [he is speaking here of hypothetical sources like Q, M, and L, but it applies *mutatis mutandis*] normative for Christian faith and life today would be an extraordinary novelty.[111]

An even more complicating factor, and one into which we cannot delve here, is that the church, in opting for the four canonical Gospels (and the creeds to which those very four Gospels contributed) also eschewed other narrative presentations of Jesus. That is, the church judged that the *Gospel of Thomas* and the *Gospel of Peter* were not consistent enough with the *canonical narrative* to be accepted as authoritative for shaping Christian theology and self-identity.[112]

This corners all other narrative re-presentations of Jesus and leads us to this question: did the church, by accepting only these four Gospels, render a judgment once and for all about all other attempted re-presentations of Jesus? We could answer this with a yes and a no—a yes for any grand narrative claiming final authority but no for any narrative claiming some sort of insight into the canonical Gospels or some kind of support or supplement to them. So, we ask again, how do the various historical Jesus re-presentations fit into the theological discipline?

HISTORICAL JESUS STUDIES AND THE THEOLOGICAL DISCIPLINE

What lurks behind much of the discussion of both modernist and postmodernist historiography is the simple observation that a Christian faith embraces,

---

[110] Robert Morgan, "The Historical Jesus and the Theology of the New Testament," in *The Glory of Christ in the New Testament* (ed. L.D. Hurst and N.T. Wright; Oxford: Clarendon, 1987), 187–206, here 191–95.

[111] Morgan, "Historical Jesus," 203. See also Dunn, *Jesus Remembered*, 125–27, though I think Dunn presses too far the representation of the historical Jesus and the church's Jesus as a contrary relationship. There is no necessary distinction between a historical Jesus and the church's Jesus. As an example, my friend Darrell Bock's book on Jesus is as close to the church's Jesus as one can get for a historical Jesus representation; see his *Jesus according to Scripture* (Grand Rapids: Baker Academic, 2002) and his methodological discussion in *Studying the Historical Jesus* (Grand Rapids: Baker Academic, 2002). I am not agreeing with Bock so much as pointing out that the motivation of historical Jesus studies is not simply to offer a representation of Jesus in competition with the church, and indeed the results of such presentations support my assertion.

[112] I do not wish to enter here into a debate about the role these other gospels are to play in the articulation of other representations of Jesus. Of course, they do have a role and will continue to do so. Consider, for example, Pagels, *Beyond Belief*, whose own story shows that personal faith and historical representation are not isolable (30–73).

at some level, an upper case History, a macro-scheme of where things started and where they are ultimately going.[113] In other words, because Christian faith by nature confesses both *aitios* and *telos*, it cannot be simply postmodernist—for postmodernity rejects such explanations in its disprivileging of any reading. Furthermore, to the degree that modernity eschews the "question of God" it also eschews a Christian, teleological understanding of history.[114]

This Christian tradition, seen in such formative thinkers as Augustine, Sextus Julius Africanus, Eusebius, Isidore of Seville and the Venerable Bede, grounds history for the Christian in a *genesis*, a *telos*, and an *eschatos*. So, while technical historiography moves along modernist or postmodernist lines, in the public forum where faith assumptions may need to be bracketed for the sake of conversation, a truly Christian historiography, not to say a Christian historio-graphical approach to Jesus and how he understood his death, will need to carve its own path. To use the inimitable terms of Isaiah Berlin, Christian historiog-raphers are more or less hedgehogs.[115] Perhaps they will wonder if they are gen-uine hedgehogs at times, but for a historian to qualify as a Christian, there will be a noticeable hedgehog quality about their work.

What is also noticeable is this: postmodernist historiography and Christian historiography do, on some stretches of the crossing of the waters, join hands in fellowship. At other times the postmodernist abandons the starboard side to the modernist or, one might say, the traditionalist. In light of our prior discussions about both postmodernist and modernist historiography and the historical Jesus, what can we say about the role of the historical Jesus in the theological discipline?

The prefatory word that was brought closer to the starboard side of the debate when Bultmann spoke of *Vorverständnis*, and now stands like an elephant on the poop deck, is this: everyone has an agenda, a motivation, and a purpose whenever studying the historical Jesus.[116] It is not enough to admit the role pre-suppositions play in interpretation, though this is where we ought to begin. What is needed is not so much frank admission and then a jolly carrying on as usual, as if admission is justification, but instead the willingness to let our pre-suppositions (Subject) be challenged by the evidence (Object). I cannot agree with the tone of F.R. Ankersmit's claim in his chapter, "In Praise of Subjectivity," when he says,

---

[113] I am grateful to my colleague, Bradley Nassif, for his response to this section of this chapter.

[114] On which, see N. Berdyaev, *The Meaning of History* (trans. G. Reavey; London: Geoffrey Bles/Centenary, 1945); *The Destiny of Man* (trans. N. Duddington; London: Geoffrey Bles/Centenary, 1945); C. Dawson, *Religion and the Rise of Western Culture* (New York: Sheed & Ward, 1950); S.J. Case, *The Christian Philosophy of History* (Chicago: University of Chicago Press, 1943).

[115] See Berlin, "Hedgehog and the Fox."

[116] An older, but still eminently valuable study of the role of presuppositions can be found in G.N. Stanton, "Presuppositions in New Testament Criticism," in *New Testament Interpretation* (ed. I.H. Marshall; Grand Rapids: Eerdmans, 1977), 60–71.

> Historical writing is, so to speak, the *experimental garden where we may try out different political and moral values* and where the overarching aesthetic criteria of representational success will allow us to assess their respective merits and shortcomings.[117]

Postmodernism teaches us that we will never thoroughly jettison our presuppositions (though this is hardly something new to postmodernity), but it tends to permit an admission to become a justification (Jenkins and less so with Ankersmit)—and a legitimate, proud one at that—while what is needed is the critical realism of B.F. Meyer or the practical realism of AHJ, a critical interaction with the evidence and scholarship so that a measure of objectivity is achieved. But this, as I say, is but the prefatory word of what we can learn from modern historiography. What it tells us is this: *if* we all have motivation, we can nonetheless ask if a given historical Jesus study qualifies to be a *Christian* motivation about Jesus. Maybe we can never write history objectively, but what we do write can be useful, and Christians can learn to write about Jesus in genuinely Christian ways. If we do so, as the historiographers Martha Howell and Walter Prevenier so eloquently state,

> We can thus implicate our audiences in the histories we write, making them see *how we see* as well as what we see. If we do so, we can produce useful knowledge about the past, or at least about our access to that past.[118]

From these considerations of what Christian history is and what role presuppositions do play in all historiographical undertakings, we can now turn to how today's scholars appropriate historical Jesus studies in theology. There are at least four uses of the Jesus traditions and the historical Jesus for constructing theology, and they apply *mutatis mutandis* to what Jesus thought about his death. First, for some the historical Jesus' perceptions of his death are but relics of history and, while questions about him are interesting and raise issues about religion, spirituality, and faith, ultimately neither he nor his perceptions matter to personal religion or to social vision.

Second, for some the historical Jesus, as reconstructed and re-presented, is the *norma normans* of the gospel itself. If, it would be argued, Jesus never thought of his death or never gave to it any significance, then the early developments about atonement theology and all the later accretions would be well-intended expressions of myth and ideology, but ultimately unimportant for faith and life. True, not everything can be traced back to Jesus, but it would make a great deal of difference to know that the central tenet of Christian faith—namely, that Jesus died for sins—was (or was not) at least traceable to Jesus himself.[119]

---

[117] Ankersmit, *Historical Representation*, 99 (italics added).

[118] Howell and Prevenier, *From Reliable Sources*, 148.

[119] There has been a constant appeal for biblical scholars to recognize the historical orientation of earliest Christianity. Thus, cf. E. Hoskyns and N. Davey, *The Riddle of the New Testament* (London:

Third, for some Jesus is known only *through* the Christian Scriptures in a narrative depiction: that is all we know, we can't really get behind it; and if we did, it wouldn't really matter for faith. Historical study is well and good, and plays some positively useful roles, but its role in theology is limited to what it can contribute to the Christian tradition. Fourth, for some what really matters is religious, historical, social, cultural, political, and intellectual development. Today we are enlightened moderns, and it does no good to pretend that we can get back to the "original truth" in order to critique our perceptions of religious faith by that pristine, reconstructed image. Religious faith is not dependent on historical study, and modern consciousness transcends antiquity. In fact, for many of these enlightened moderns, to absolve Christianity of concepts like atonement, expiation, and crucifixion would be a deed well done. In closing down the curtains on this section, I wish now to turn to three considerations of what we can learn from historiographical discussions about the historical Jesus' role in theological construction.

First, we can return to the postmodernist claim about what history is and offer this challenge: if our understanding of history and the historical Jesus is near the mark and we are concerned about how the historical Jesus fits into the theological discipline, historical Jesus scholars can only offer narrative representations of Jesus that fit with the relics about Jesus in the surviving evidence. That is, they cannot make of him what they will without being accused of the charge of historical misrepresentation. At this point the historical Jesus scholar (nearly all so far as I can see) parts company with the postmodernist radical who thinks we can make of history whatever we want because, after all, it is only rhetoric, language, and ideology; or, as Ankersmit states in the quotation above, an "experimental garden where we may try out different political and moral values." If history is merely a branch of aesthetics and literature, then the task of the historian is to offer as good a narrative as he or she can. I would counter with the words of Marc Bloch: "Explorers of the past are never quite free. The past is their tyrant."[120]

The limitation of every historical representation of Jesus to the evidence inevitably means that the canonical Gospels themselves are often held accountable to the evidence as well. At some level, at least for most historical Jesus scholars, the Gospels themselves become "authoritative" to the degree that the Gospels cohere with evidence that can be discovered about Jesus and judged "authentic" (on which see below).[121]

Faber & Faber, 1931); Jürgen Roloff, *Das Kerygma und der irdische Jesus* (Göttingen: Vandenhoeck & Ruprecht, 1970); G.N. Stanton, *Jesus of Nazareth in New Testament Preaching* (SNTSMS 27; Cambridge: Cambridge University Press, 1972); E.E. Lemcio, *The Past of Jesus in the Gospels* (SNTSMS 68; Cambridge: Cambridge University Press, 1992); R.A. Burridge, *What Are the Gospels?* (SNTSMS 70; Cambridge: Cambridge University Press, 1992).

[120] Bloch, *Historian's Craft*, 59.

[121] See the orthodox presentation in William Lane Craig, *Reasonable Faith* (rev. ed.; Wheaton: Crossway, 1994), esp. his chapter "The Problem of Historical Knowledge" (pp. 157–91). It is also

The evidence determines the parameters of what a historical Jesus scholar should say about Jesus. "In some cases," as Richard Evans states it, "the narrative is there in the sources."[122] The old cry of Sir Geoffrey Elton, "to the sources" (*ad fontes*), is at the foundation of nearly every historical Jesus study I know of. We have wildly different portraits of Jesus in the studies of B.F. Meyer, E.P. Sanders, R.A. Horsley, J.D. Crossan, J.P. Meier, N.T. Wright, and B.D. Chilton, but each of them claims—overtly—that their representation of Jesus is grounded in the evidence and that it comes from that evidence. They are each, to use our historiographical taxonomy, modernists through and through. They believe that we can discover the evidence, judge it through a critical process, find (rather than impose) its meaning in its context with clarity; and that they can, sometimes with more potency than other times, represent it all in a compelling narrative. But, as modernist historiographers, each believes in the evidence—and each is not all that unlike Sir Geoffrey Elton in orientation.

Since I have placed Carr and Elton in the same category of modernist historiographer, I must add that many if not most historical Jesus scholars tend to make a presentation of Jesus that fits with what they think the future of Christianity holds, as E.H. Carr so clearly argued. While each may make the claim that they are simply after the facts and simply trying to figure out what Jesus was really like—and while most don't quite say this, most do think this is what they are doing— nearly every one of them presents what they would like the church, or others with faith, to think about Jesus. Clear examples of this can be found in the studies of Marcus Borg, N.T. Wright, E.P. Sanders, and B.D. Chilton—in fact, we would not be far short of the mark if we claimed that this pertains to each scholar—always and forever.[123] And each claims that his or her presentation of Jesus is rooted in the evidence, and only in the evidence.

If that evidence is likened to a marble block, then the historical Jesus scholar may have to chisel away chunk after chunk, but the historical Jesus scholar is not permitted to add marble to the already determined block. E.P. Sanders, J.D. Crossan, Kathleen Corley, N.T. Wright, and James D.G. Dunn, for instance, each chisel away different parts of the marble block, but each confessedly is working on the same block and trying to find what the block was intended to be—as a good sculptor will always admit.

Second, a word about hermeneutics, a topic which (again) cannot be given here the attention it deserves. I build here on the profound work of A.C. Thiselton in his *New Horizons in Hermeneutics* and F. Watson in his *Text and*

---

found, in a completely unorthodox way, in the work of Maurice Casey. See his *From Jewish Prophet to Gentile God* (Edward Cadbury Lectures at the University of Birmingham, 1985–1986; Louisville: Westminster/John Knox, 1991). Both believe what should be believed is what we discover to be historically accurate.

[122] Evans, *In Defence of History*, 147.

[123] This is precisely why Martin Kähler's famous claim that faith is not based on historical study is disproven by history. Scholars and those who follow them—in the church or not in the church—believe in their own narratives.

Truth.[124] Thiselton demonstrates that postmodernity operates with a "hermeneutic of suspicion," and, as Keith Jenkins's works on historiography reveal, it is a hermeneutic that sees texts as ideological graspings for power written for a cadre who utilize that text as an assertion of power. Watson, for his part, demonstrates satisfactorily an older notion: a text is an attempt at communication. As Kevin Vanhoozer argues, texts are at some level persons and, as Alan Jacobs contends, texts must be treated as our "neighbors."[125] Perhaps another way of saying the same thing, only in terms of faith instead of love, is found in Robert Morgan:

> The conflict is thus no longer between faith and reason but between a reasonable faith and a faithless reason.[126]

I contend that a hermeneutic of suspicion is fundamentally at odds with the Christian gospel, which is what a theological discipline is most concerned with. In other words, what a Christian needs is not a hermeneutic of suspicion but, as Alan Jacobs brilliantly presents, a "hermeneutic of love"[127] or a "hermeneutic of trust."[128] Jacobs, building on the profound but often neglected study *On Christian Doctrine* by Augustine, notes that a charitable interpretation not only fully embraces the distinction between Subject and Object, but also knows that genuine hearing can only take place when the reader subordinates himself to the Other (or, Object) in order to hear and to understand and to love. This is not some soft-kneed nonsense that Jacobs offers us, but a hermeneutic that is finding echoes in other fields as well, as the study of Princeton philosopher Harry Frankfurt shows.[129] As Jacobs states it,

---

[124] A.C. Thiselton, *New Horizons in Hermeneutics* (New York: HarperCollins, 1992); *Interpreting God and the Postmodern Self* (Grand Rapids: Eerdmans, 1995); F. Watson, *Text and Truth* (Grand Rapids: Eerdmans, 1997).

[125] Kevin Vanhoozer, *Is There a Meaning in This Text?* (Grand Rapids: Zondervan, 1998), 455–68; Alan Jacobs, *A Theology of Reading: The Hermeneutics of Love* (Boulder: Westview, 2001), 9–35. The recent impact on hermeneutics by theology, as can for example be seen in Vanhoozer, ought to be felt by those historical Jesus scholars who believe (1) in God and (2) that God has revealed himself in Jesus Christ. A self-revealing God is the sort of God who makes interpersonal textual communication and historical knowledge possible.

[126] Morgan, "Historical Jesus," 199.

[127] I recently noticed that N.T. Wright spoke of this in his 1992 study; see *New Testament and the People of God*, 64, who himself points to Thiselton, *New Horizons*, 604–11.

[128] See Jacobs, *Theology of Reading*. On a larger scale, see also D.K. Clark, *Empirical Realism* (Lanham, Md.: Rowman & Littlefield, 2003); J. Rist, *Real Ethics* (Cambridge: Cambridge University Press, 2002); C. Smith, *Moral, Believing Animals* (Oxford: Oxford University Press, 2003).

[129] It is clearly anticipated in P. Stuhlmacher, *Historical Criticism and Theological Interpretation of Scripture* (trans. R.A. Harrisville; Philadelphia: Fortress, 1977); Meyer, *Critical Realism*, 3–96; see also Meyer's later study, *Reality and Illusion*. See H.G. Frankfurt, *The Reasons of Love* (Princeton: Princeton University Press, 2004).

Discernment is required to know what kind of gift one is being presented with, and in what spirit to accept it (if at all), but a universal suspicion of gifts and givers, like an indiscriminate acceptance of all gifts, constitutes an abdication of discernment in favor of a simplistic *a priorism* that smothers the spirit.[130]

Because the hermeneutic of love knows that genuine love is righteous and holy, the hermeneutic speaks the truth about what it reads, judges some things good and some things bad, but it nonetheless operates on the basis of trust and love rather than suspicion. While it may conclude that some texts are genuinely ideological graspings of power to be rendered worthless—who would not judge the Marquis de Sade's *In Praise of Folly* as a monstrosity?—a proper reading cannot begin with suspicion. Instead Christian and non-Christian readers need to recognize that texts are intended to be "communication events" between two humans made in the image of God and that a genuinely humane reader is one who trusts the words of the others.[131] This approach is as humane as it is Christian.

When it comes to the historical Jesus, I am not claiming that a Christian, because he or she adopts a chastened but genuine hermeneutics of love and trust, thinks everything in the Gospels is historical simply by inclusion.[132] This would miss the general strength of our point about hermeneutics. What it means is that the historical Jesus scholar would not assume the texts are unhistorical or so ideologically driven that they must be desconstructed and reshaped by one's own ideology. This sort of treatment of the Gospels is, in my view, the destruction of communication because it refuses to listen to the Other (Object, the Gospels) and it intends the Subject (reader) to swallow up the Object in his or her own ideological agenda. Communication, which is what happens in any genuine love, is broken when suspicion gains the upper hand. Again, this does not mean that the Gospels contain only red letters—to use the coding of the Jesus Seminar—but it does delay the judgment until after genuine encounter and reading of the text occur.

Third, history as defined by historiographers, especially of a structuralist and postmodernist sort, involves the narration of existential facts. When it comes to the theological discipline, therefore, there are some narrations that are "good" and there are some that are "bad," with both good and bad defined by what the theological discipline itself defines as its own narrative. Which means this: since history inevitably is a "narrative," there is either one defining narrative or there are an infinite number of narratives. Since the theological disciplines involve Scriptures and creeds, there is a single normative narrative, or what we could also call a four-fold normative narrative about Jesus.

---

[130] Jacobs, *Theology of Reading*, 24 (italics added.)

[131] See here Watson, *Text and Truth.*

[132] See the useful postscript on Old Testament theology and history in John Goldingay, *Israel's Gospel* (vol. 1 of *Old Testament Theology*; Downers Grove: InterVarsity, 2003), 859–83.

That is, if history is a narrative, and if we are concerned with the role of modern historical narratives in the overall theological discipline, we have no options other than surrendering either to the absence of normative narrative or to the church's normative narrative. To use the words of my professor's own book on the historical Jesus, all we have at the normative level is the "remembered Jesus." It is this remembered Jesus that was the normative narrative. If we recognize, as we have no choice but to do, the *ecclesial* context of nearly every representation of Jesus, we are bound to confess that narrations about Jesus are expressions of an ongoing, and living tradition. As Dunn has so well observed,

> This solution, applied to the Gospels, does not, of course, restore the old objectivity of the Gospels' meaning. But it does indicate a stronger possibility of recognizing a firmness to their perceived significance; it does prevent a falling apart into complete subjectivity and relativity; and from a Christian perspective in particular, it does attune with the more traditional thought of a trust-sustaining consensus (*sensus communis* = *sensus fidelium*) within which matters of faith and conduct can be discussed and determined.[133]

If we relate this comment to the structuralist and postmodernist rendering of what history is, and recall that Hayden White speaks of an "inexpungeable relativity in every representation," then we might say that there is one relativity that counts as Christian, a relativity found in the four-fold Gospel witness to Jesus Christ.[134] In fact, in this essay of White wherein he speaks of an inexpungeable relativity, White contends that there are some past events (and his concern here is the Shoah) that themselves set the parameters of the sort of narrative, or representation, that can be told if one is to retain any sense of integrity with respect to the original events. That is, White comes close to stating that some accounts are truer than others, and the that truer ones are those that bring to expression what is found at the deep level of the events. What I would be arguing here is that the events in the life of Jesus can only be represented in a historical Jesus discussion faithfully if they express the deep level of what they were all about. One cannot turn the life of Jesus into a comedy because the data (or facts) do not lend themselves to a comedy; the data, in other words, determine what is truthful in history.

While this observation cannot be developed here, it can be reasonably argued that there is an *inevitability to creedal orthodoxy* in Christian theological formulation because of the formative power of the foundational four-fold narrative about Jesus in the gospels. The genesis of Mark and John, which is no pun, finds its inevitable *telos* in the orthodox creeds of the church. One might plausibly counter that other creeds could have developed alongside those creeds, which is precisely why Protestantism has for five hundred years contended for

---

[133] Dunn, *Jesus Remembered*, 96.
[134] White, "Historical Emplotment," 27.

sola scriptura. But what is plausible to some finds its guiding parameters in the primal narratives of the four-fold witness to Jesus Christ in the New Testament.[135]

I offer now a fourth, but final, observation. If we are dealing with the theological discipline, we are probably dealing with both faith-based seminaries or colleges as well as state-based or university-based schooling. What is expected in one is not expected or even allowed, in the other. We can perhaps, as hedgehogs, cut through the brush with a rather simple observation: to the degree that the school that shapes the curriculum is itself shaped by the two deep traditions about Jesus (the canonical Gospels, the creeds),[136] to the same degree its openness or closedness to other representations of the historical Jesus is determined.

In a university setting where freedom of thought is championed as the one and only creedal statement,[137] there will be almost no restrictions on what a historical Jesus scholar may say and teach about Jesus (except of a conservative nature). In a more ecclesiastically shaped institution, there may well be restrictions, at different levels, on what can be said and taught about Jesus. Institutions of this sort vary on what is permitted and what is not permitted.

My contention is now clear: if a theological curriculum is based on a traditional confession in the narrative depiction of Jesus in the Gospels, or the historic creeds, then the historical Jesus has a distinct but limited role. The historical Jesus scholar's narrative representation of Jesus is of value only insofar as it supplements or supports the grand narrative of Jesus that is found in the Gospels or the creeds. A proposal or representation of Jesus by an individual historical Jesus scholar may have lesser values: showing how we got from the "original Jesus" to the present "canonical Jesus"; offering an apologetic for what the church believes by filtering through non-canonical evidence or other sorts of evidence and arguments; or simply writing out a history of early Christianity in order to explain to students and Christians how things became what they are. Historical Jesus scholarship certainly helps at the level of statement and description—or, in the words of Jimmy Dunn, with "data" and "facts"—and it may help with chronicle, clarification and context, but historical Jesus scholarship helps only to a limited, some would say a very limited, degree with the story or narrative that forms the foundation of Christian theology. What is clear is that

---

[135] There is plenty to say at this point about Scripture and how Christians are to understand it, but such issues cannot be explored here. I mention three important writers: K. Trembath, *Evangelical Theories of Biblical Inspiration* (New York: Oxford University Press, 1987); J. Goldingay, *Models for Scripture* (Grand Rapids: Eerdmans, 1994); *Models for Interpretation of Scripture* (Grand Rapids: Eerdmans, 1995); T. Work, *Living and Active* (Sacra doctrina; Grand Rapids: Eerdmans, 2002).

[136] I do not mean to suggest here the Tridentine theory of Scripture *and* tradition as authority. I see the classical creeds as the living, ongoing, even Spirit-led voice of the church coming to terms with what it believes. I see the Scripture as Protestants always have: as the final authority.

[137] This is a leitmotif in the historiography of many, including Jenkins, *Reforming History*, and AJH, *Telling the Truth about History*.

for the person who is committed to the canonical Gospels, or creeds as the church's definitive narrative about Jesus, another narrative about Jesus will not play a faith-determining role. It will not because it cannot. Why? Because, as Robert Morgan says,

> The task of this theological discipline is to interpret the canonical witnesses theologically, and so inform the life and thought of the Christian Church.[138]

Perhaps the clearest example of this can be seen in recent New Testament theologies. Georg Strecker begins his NT theology with the theology of Paul, proceeds only then to the early Christian traditions about Jesus in the Gospels, the Synoptic Gospels, and the Johannine School, and then to the literature he judges as part of the early church's movement into the early Catholic church and the Catholic letters.[139] P. Stuhlmacher, on the other hand, begins his two-volume NT theology with *die Verkündigung Jesu* and, as did Joachim Jeremias after tracing out the parameters set by Jesus, orients the theologies of Paul, the synoptic Evangelists, and John and his school within those parameters.[140] While I tend to agree with Stuhlmacher on matters historiographical pertaining to the historical Jesus, both Stuhlmacher and Strecker are struggling with what role historical reconstruction is to play as one sorts out what can only be called a "New Testament theology"—as opposed to "early Christian thought." Again, if both sort out historical questions in wildly different ways, each knows that the ultimate foundation for a normative shaping of theology is conditioned by the story and narrative found in the Gospels. Both are appropriating what can only be called a "Christian" historiography.

The reason for this is clear: theological curricula are shaped by larger bodies, by administrative and church-based boards, and they are shaped to foster students into the faith those bodies confess. The faith of such bodies, in most cases, is the result of two millennia of study of the Bible and the creeds, the result of two millennia of intense theological debate and discussion. It is unlikely, first, that a single historical Jesus scholar will completely change the theological conclusions of either the church or even of a smaller church body. Second, the swirl of ideas that emerges from a wide variety of historical Jesus scholarship makes clear that it is impossible for each of these to be adapted or adopted for use in the life of the church or in the theological curriculum.

In his recent, brilliant magnum opus, Larry Hurtado traces with exacting nuance how the early churches expressed devotion to Christ.[141] The church itself

---

[138] Morgan, "Historical Jesus," 203.

[139] G. Strecker, *Theology of the New Testament* (ed. and completed by F.W. Horn; trans. M.E. Boring; Louisville: Westminster John Knox, 2000).

[140] P. Stuhlmacher, *Biblische Theologie des Neuen Testaments* (2 vols.; Göttingen: Vandenhoeck & Ruprecht, 1992, 1997). Dan Bailey is completing his translation of Stuhlmacher, and it will be published by Eerdmans.

[141] Larry Hurtado, *Lord Jesus Christ* (Grand Rapids: Eerdmans, 2003).

came from the trajectory Hurtado sorts out. And many historical Jesus studies today would fit within the parameters sketched by Hurtado. Many, also, would not fit. Those narrative representations of Jesus that do not fit into that grid would also not fit into a theological curriculum intent on teaching a traditional understanding of Jesus.

Most theological curricula permit enough freedom of thought for the individual scholar to offer suggestions here and there, and to offer, under the watchful eye of both scholarship and theological context, a new narrative representation of Jesus. It does not surprise that both N.T. Wright and B.D. Chilton serve in the same church body: the church of England and its American family member, the Episcopalian church. Other church bodies would not be so supple, and they have a right to determine their own parameters. Such parameter-making, after all, is an expression of freedom of thought as free as in any scientific discipline that requires its professors and students to learn to explore the world within a set of categories well established by others.

The Issue of Historical Judgment

There are two major moments in the last century of historical Jesus scholarship that deal with the issue of critical judgment.[142] Perhaps I am biased by my own context and readings, but to me the major moments are two scholars: Norman Perrin and E.P. Sanders.[143] The former argued for historical Jesus studies operating as the disciplines of science while the latter argued that historical Jesus studies ought to operate as the disciplines of the humanities. Neither, to my knowledge, put it in these terms, so let me explain.[144]

Perrin argued that method precedes all else, that there are three criteria (*dissimilarity*, *multiple attestation*, and *coherence*) that can be applied to the evidence, and that when the evidence passes through the sieve of these criteria, certain sayings and events survive. It is from these sayings and events that one can discern

---

[142] The most complete study of the history of this scholarship is Theissen and Winter, *Quest for the Plausible Jesus*. But, see also the survey of S.E. Porter, *The Criteria for Authenticity in Historical-Jesus Research* (JSNTSup 191; Sheffield: Sheffield Academic, 2000) 28–123.

[143] No one disputes the significance of Ernst Käsemann's running the gauntlet in 1953 when he called the students of Bultmann back to the possibility of ascertaining the historical Jesus and, what was most significant, the positive significance of the historical Jesus for theology. One might replace Norman Perrin's name with Käsemann's, but it is the criteriological priority that gives Perrin an edge for how the discussion has evolved. See E. Käsemann, "The Problem of the Historical Jesus," in his *Essays on New Testament Themes* (trans. W.J. Montague; SBT 41; London: SCM, 1971), 15–47.

[144] Ultimately, of course, this sort of historical judgment owes more to Ernst Troeltsch's penetrating and pioneering essays on the relationship of faith and history, but especially on his famous three criteria: *probability*, *analogy*, and *correlation*. See his "Historical and Dogmatic Method in Theology," in *Religion in History* (trans. J.L. Adams and W.F. Bense; intro. J.L. Adams; 1898; repr. Minneapolis: Fortress, 1991), 11–32. On Troeltsch himself, see Hans-Georg Drescher, *Ernst Troeltsch* (trans. J. Bowden; Minneapolis: Fortress, 1993).

a methodologically sound and historiographically defensible understanding of Jesus. Sanders, on the other hand, while not eschewing the criteriological approach to the Gospels as much as he initially contends, argued that what is needed is not so much a microscopic analysis of individual sayings, collated and then narrated, but a big picture understanding of Jesus as discerned from what he did—through which we gain a view of what Jesus was all about, regardless of the debates about individual sayings and events and details.

Perrin has the most descendants: one thinks of Jeremias (his teacher) who supported him, and then of B.F. Meyer, J.P. Meier, J.D. Crossan, J. Becker, and the Jesus Seminar as led by R.W. Funk. Sanders has fewer descendants, and even those that descend from him, since they operate with a big picture approach, tend to disown their parentage in his methodological discussion. I think here of R.A. Horsley, M. Borg, B.D. Chilton, N.T. Wright, Dale Allison, and (if I may be so bold) my own study on the larger message of Jesus, *A New Vision for Israel*. The most recent spark in this discussion has been generated by Gerd Theissen and his student, Dagmar Winter. Inasmuch as they focus on the criterion of distinguishing Jesus from the early church, they belong in the line of Perrin; but inasmuch as they also focus on the larger picture of Jesus that fits plausibly within Judaism, they belong also in the line of Sanders.[145] As Theissen puts it,

> Jesus' singularity consists in a singular combination of Jewish traditions as well as in the fact that his words and deeds represent a unique stage in the development that leads from Judaism to Christianity.[146]

---

[145] More specifically, Theissen and Winter propose two criteria: *First*, a given factor is authentic if one finds (1) contextual plausibility as well as (2) plausibility of effects in the early church. *Second*, each of these has two subcategories. Beginning with plausibility of effects, they find an indicator of authenticity in any element of the tradition that shows opposition to traditional bias, which is similar to the older method of dissimilarity to, or tension with early-church tendencies. Authenticity is found in coherence of sources, which is similar to the older multiple attestation criterion. Moving back to contextual plausibility, they find an element authentic that is contextually appropriate, which is directly contrary to the older dissimilarity to Judaism criterion—and authenticity is found in a corresponding *contextual distinctiveness*: Jesus must cut his own figure within Judaism. And, to stretching the frequency of how often one can use the term *plausibility*, they propose an overarching *comprehensive historical plausibility*—which is the combination of elements in the life of Jesus that give us a distinctive form of Judaism that then gives rise to the effects we find in the early churches. Thus, contextual plausibility is (1) contextually appropriate and (2) contextually distinctive. Plausibility of effects entails (1) opposition to traditional bias and (2) coherence of sources.

I have two responses to Theissen and Winter: (1) they have corrected the criterion of double dissimilarity but in so doing have taken the second half back too much—they find tension with the early church to be too valuable, and hence they are seeking a Jesus who is too distinctive from the early churches; and (2) they are too unaware of the fundamental insights of postmodernist historiography's emphasis on the significance of the historian's narrative in shaping what we understand about the past. Their tendency is to think if we find something plausible then we have meaning, while the entire construction of the larger metanarrative that makes a contextually plausible Jesus needs to be recognized for what it is: a heuristic model derived at the level of critical realism.

[146] Theissen and Winter, *Quest for the Plausible Jesus*, 244.

As I assess the issue, deciding what is authentic cannot be reduced to a science, contra the approach of Perrin and his descendants. Nor is the criterion of dissimilarity all it is purported to be in this scientific tradition. The recent monograph of Gerd Theissen and Dagmar Winter has laid to rest, permanently, any idea that the criterion is either distinterested, objective historiography or that it can achieve anything like a consensus.[147] In fact, at some levels (not all, thankfully), the criterion of double dissimilarity is a criterion of double prejudice. On the one hand, it is designed to find a Jesus who is contra early Christian orthodoxy (thus, anti-church faith) and, on the other, it is designed to find a Jesus who is contra Judaism (thus, anti-Judaism or anti-Semitism). This is a bald statement of mine that needs nuance, not the least of which is the idea that genuine tensions between Jesus and Judaism or between Jesus and the early church—though it ought to be observed that these are often arguments from silence—can be genuine indicators of authenticity, but the overall thrust of finding a Jesus who is neither very Jewish nor very Christian is a chimera who never existed and who can only be the quest of scholars who have abandoned any notion of disinterestedness in order to find a Jesus of their own making.

Therefore, the criteria proposed by Theissen and Winter—that of a Jesus who is plausibly placed within Judaism and, at the same time, plausibly generative of the later Christian effects—is far closer to a genuine historical approach for studying Jesus than the old-fashioned approach that found its flashpoints in Paul Schmiedel and Rudolf Bultmann, and then in the later disciples of Bultmann (notably Ernst Käsemann). As a sidebar, I add that I am not sure Theissen and Winter's model is actually a criterion at all. Instead, it is an orientation—for as a method it hardly helps us to see if a given datum is genuine. Did Jesus say the first beatitude? Surely, it is plausible for Jesus the Jew to have said something like this, and it shows sufficient connection with early Christian ethics to be considered authentic. But few would find this argument sufficiently rigorous. However, as a counter to the criterion of double dissimilarity, the proposal of Theissen and Winter is a powerful and direction-turning alternative.

So, again, any method designed to help us "find Jesus" has to be more than some scientific criterion. I think this because human intention, which is what historical Jesus studies are really all about, cannot be reduced to a science. The fundamental problem with the criteriological approach to the sayings and events of Jesus is that they make *formal reason* and even *mechanistic* what is *material reason* or, to use other terms, they turn the *substance* into its *form*. Words cannot be turned into *things*, while it is *things* that can be turned into *form* and into *scientific reason*. Words, and humans who use these words, cannot be reduced to form. One might say that catching a baseball, to invoke my former illustration, is the *form*, but the *substance* can only be discerned by its socio-intentional contexts. To go back to the world of philosophy, the criteriological approach seeks

---

[147] See ibid., esp. the tracing of its development by Winter, 27–171.

to turn Kant's sense of *judgment* into his senses of either *pure* or *practical reason*.[148]

Having said that, however, I do believe there are occasionally patterns to be discovered in historical judgment. Perrin did not decide, without reason, that multiple attestation, dissimilarity, and coherence are the criteria, and then proceed to the evidence. In fact, as all recognize, Perrin's criteriological approach was indebted heavily to Rudolf Bultmann's *History of the Synoptic Tradition* and to Joachim Jeremias's studies on the Aramaic background to the sayings of Jesus. In essence, Perrin's own method is the synthesis of those of Bultmann and Jeremias, and thus his method is the distillation of how other historians were operating with concrete evidence. And I think Perrin's criteria are right. They just aren't right enough. One cannot sort the evidence sufficiently through these three criteria.

Careful study of the evidence, combined as it will be in historical Jesus study with historical judgment, will produce a vast array of logical judgments that cannot be reduced simply to these three. While they may sometimes find an earlier indicator in those three criteria, others will emerge. I take but one example. Stanley Porter has recently argued for a rather minimal new criterion.[149] His argument works like this: if we can assume that Jesus sometimes may have spoken in Greek, then there just may be occasions, when Jesus is dealing with a more Gentile audience, that we find authentic words in Greek. Whatever one thinks of Porter's point, his historical judgment is sound; if, at times, it is the case that Jesus spoke in Greek (and not all scholars agree), then a new criterion has been found. Porter's criterion can be used in Perrin-like fashion or, as I prefer, it can be recognized when historical judgments are being made.

My overall point is this: historical judgment is diverse, revealing itself more often in subtle judgment and overall picture than in a criteriological approach to the sayings and deeds of Jesus. That is, I doubt very much that any historical Jesus scholar actually begins with a *tabula rasa*, puts the criteria on the table, and then asks the evidence to come to judgment; if there is one exception to my doubt, it is the work of J.P. Meier. Instead, most have an overall representation of Jesus in mind and go about looking at evidence and making judgments about what is genuine from what is not genuine and, at times, revising the overall representation. This, so it seems to me, is what critical realism is calling us to do. It is what I see in the works of many historical Jesus scholars, even when they are ultimately contending for a method more in tune with Perrin.

In the end, it is a representation, or a narrative or story about Jesus that compels agreement and disagreement. Rarely, so it seems to me, is it the method that strikes the critic first. Instead, as we read the representation of Jesus—say in Crossan's or Chilton's studies—we either assent or dissent. We do so on the

---

[148] My inferences here are sparked by Ankersmit, *Historical Representation*, 11–17.

[149] See Porter, *Criteria for Authenticity*.

basis of whether or not the Jesus represented is like the Jesus we represent him to be in our mind. Postmodernity compels us to think of our work this way. It compels us to do so because this is, after all, how we do work.

In what follows I study how Jesus understood his own death according to such a method. Because the debates about how Jesus understood his death are so numerous and yet the topic so rarely examined "for its own sake" (a tip of my cap to Sir Geoffrey Elton), we need to examine the history of scholarship before we connect the evidence, bit by bit, making historical judgments in order to build a meaning-making narrative of what Jesus was all about and who he was.

Chapter 2

Jesus' Death in Scholarship

CAN CHRISTIANS TRUST A SOTERIOLOGY
ABOUT WHICH JESUS IS UNAWARE?

If Homer scholars never find Achilles' immortal shield and see firsthand the dance floor depicted by Hephaistos, the lame craftsman among Zeus's gods, it would not affect Homer's depiction of the cosmic dimensions of life, or his insight into the tragic flaws of human character, or his impact on the image of the heroic. If Achilles never fought Hector, life would remain the same. If Roman scholars were never to find any evidence of Aeneas, of his trip to northern Africa or his eventual triumph in Rome, most of us would still value Vergil's broad perceptions of the push of history toward a settled blessing over Rome, and his artistic capacity to turn life into a cosmic story. If Aeneas never sailed, the winds of Vergil would still blow. If medieval scholars never find a socially active Robin Hood from Nottingham (i.e., Edwinstowe), the yearning for social justice would still fill our hearts. If we agree with J.C. Holt's theory that the original Robin Hood was a certain Robert Hode who stole some chickens, the power of the Robin Hood story would not be affected.[1] We don't need a historical Achilles, Hector, Aeneas, or Robin Hood in order to have the story and message they became.

But, if Jesus scholars settle into a studied consensus that Jesus never thought about his death in saving terms,[2] if those scholars conclude that the early

---

A shortened version of this chapter was given to the SBL Historical Jesus Section in Nashville, Tennessee (19 November 2000) and is now an updated expansion of my article, "Jesus and His Death," *CurBS* 9 (2001): 185–228. I am grateful to those who offered suggestions and queries but especially to D.C. Allison, K. Snodgrass, and N.T. Wright.

[1] J.C. Holt, *Robin Hood* (London: Thames & Hudson, 1982).

[2] On those terms, see S.B. Marrow's fine study, "Principles for Interpreting the New Testament

Christian atonement theology was fictive and symbolic rather than grounded in something Jesus said or thought, then it would shake the faith of many today who see the essence of Christianity in the death of Jesus as an atoning death, even if Jesus "suffered the extreme penalty" (Tacitus, *Ann.* 15.44). Looking for Jesus' view of his death is to ask if the Christian interpretation of his death is grounded in some historical fact, if those various early Christian construals of his death were intended by the one who set the agenda for his followers. To be sure, as Umberto Eco has said so well, "the cultivated person's first duty is to be always prepared to rewrite the encyclopedia,"[3] but should we here? Should we prefer the view of the Apostle Paul and *Auctor Hebraeos* or that of Tacitus and the Talmud (*b. Sanh.* 43b [cf. Deut 13:1-11])? Or do we need to start all over again, as if for the first time?

The questions before us in this monograph are these: Did Jesus think he would die prematurely? If so, at what point in his life did that occur to him? from the outset? following the death of John the Baptist? after he was opposed by the leaders? or, only after he entered Jerusalem that last week? Furthermore, did Jesus think about his death in saving terms? Did he think it was of more than martyrological value or not? And, if not, what are we to make of the continued witness of the church to the atoning value of his death?

The chief export of the Christian faith is Jesus Christ and the cross[4]—articulated in jewelry, in architecture, and in theology. But, is this witness of the church little more than attributing to Jesus' death what it wishes to find in the relationship to God through Jesus Christ—whether he thought of his death in such terms or not? Is it, to use postmodernist language, simply meaning found in discrete events, a meaning valuable for some but not for others, meaning that is not inherent to the event itself, meaning used to justify and legitimate power structures? Is the church's witness to the death of Jesus as saving event simply an illustration that, in the words of the Peruvian savant Mario Vargas Llosa, "soci-

---

Soteriological Terms," *NTS* 36 (1990): 268–80; for a brief, if outdated, survey, see I.H. Marshall, "The Death of Jesus in Recent New Testament Study," *WW* 3 (1983): 12–21.

[3] Umberto Eco, *Serendipities* (trans. W. Weaver; San Diego: Harcourt Brace, 1998), 21.

[4] On crucifixion, besides the rather revealing account of Josephus (B.J. 5.11.1), see esp. M. Hengel, *Crucifixion in the Ancient World and the Folly of the Message of the Cross* (trans. J. Bowden; Philadelphia: Fortress, 1977); also J.H. Charlesworth, "Jesus and Jehohanan," *ExpTim* 84 (1972–1973): 147–50; H.-W. Kuhn, "Die Kreuzesstrafe während der frühen Kaiserzeit," *ANRW* 2.25.1 (1982): 648–793; J. Zias and E. Sekeles, "The Crucified Man from Giv'at ha-Mivtar," *IEJ* 35 (1985): 22–27; F. Zugibe, "Two Questions about Crucifixion," *BRev* 5 (1989): 35–43; J.H. Charlesworth and J. Zias, "Crucifixion," in *Jesus and the Dead Sea Scrolls* (ed. J.H. Charlesworth; ABRL; New York: Doubleday, 1992), 273–89. On how crucifixion was practiced and perceived in Judea, see David W. Chapman, *Perceptions of Crucifixion Among Jews and Christians in the Ancient World*, (Ph.D. diss., Cambridge, 1999), who provides a taxonomy of how Jews perceived crucifixion and in nearly every case shows that it was countercultural to find something good in a crucifixion (crucified brigand, crucified rebel, crucified martyr, innocent sufferer, biblical exemplars, cursing of the crucified). In addition, see also the positivist approach toward the evidence of J.S. McLaren, "Exploring the Execution of a Provincial," *ABR* 49 (2001): 5–18.

eties have the religions they require"?[5] No one has put this better than David
Brondos, who says,

> Ultimately, Jesus dies [according to theologians], not because his words and
> actions were viewed as offensive or dangerous to the Jewish and Roman authori-
> ties, but because his death is regarded as necessary for some theological reason:
> only through the cross could forgiveness be won and sin, death and evil overcome
> in us and our world. Instead of looking to history to determine the causes of his
> death, we look outside or above history to some type of "metastory": the stories of
> salvation which we tell have to do, not so much with a first-century Galilean Jew
> in conflict with the religious authorities of his day, but with God's holy nature and
> the satisfaction of its just demands, the enslavement of all humankind to Satan,
> sin, death and evil and our subsequent liberation, or the creation of a "new
> humanity" embracing all who follow Christ's teachings and example or participate
> in his death and resurrection.[6]

That is, does Jesus' death have ontological or narratological but not historical value? Did his death set into motion a sort of reflection on his death, a
reflection that had little to do with the intention of the one who died? Apart
from faith—Christian faith at that—one cannot state that Jesus' death outside
of Jerusalem in (say) 30 CE was an act of God in history. But, apart from faith,
one *can* try to determine if Jesus thought his death was atoning. And, if one were
to conclude that Jesus did not think in such categories, well, then I believe the
history of Christianity ought to be given a reappraisal. If the religion of
Christianity has given to Jesus' death both a central significance and an importance never given it by Jesus, then the religion itself becomes completely separated from Jesus himself.[7]

Let us return to the analogy of Homer. Since the days when young men
drew swords to settle scores, Christian scholars have invoked the gods, taken up
arms, and fought the battle for the honor of having the best theory of the atoning death of Jesus.[8] And, like the focused Achilles and the vacillating

---

[5] See M.V. Llosa, "Trench Town Rock," *American Scholar* 71.4 (2002): 56.

[6] David Brondos, "Why Was Jesus Crucified?" *SJT* 54 (2001): 484–503, here p. 485. Brondos proposes an alternative story to that offered by N.T. Wright, a story that focuses on the longing for
shalom in Israel.

[7] See the fine essay of N.T. Wright, "Jesus' Self-Understanding," in *The Incarnation* (ed. S.T. Davis,
D. Kendall, and G. O'Collins; Oxford: Oxford University Press, 2001), 47–61.

[8] Scholarship here is engaged and not soon to let go. I list only a few representative, recent studies:
C.E. Gunton, *The Actuality of the Atonement* (Grand Rapids: Eerdmans, 1989); G. Sloyan, *The
Crucifixion of Jesus* (Minneapolis: Fortress, 1995); T. Gorringe, *God's Just Vengeance* (Cambridge:
Cambridge University Press, 1996); S. Sykes, *The Story of Atonement* (Trinity and Truth; London:
Darton, Longman, & Todd, 1997); R. Schwager, *Jesus in the Drama of Salvation* (trans. J.G.
Williams and P. Haddon; New York: Crossroad, 1999); J.B. Green and M.D. Baker, *Rediscovering
the Scandal of the Cross: Atonement in New Testament & Contemporary Contexts* (Downers Grove:
InterVarsity, 2000); J. Denny Weaver, *The Nonviolent Atonement* (Grand Rapids: Eerdmans, 2001);

Agamemnon, they and their followers have sat in their boats and nursed their private war wounds. While Anselm, who completed the task of Augustine as Achilles did that of Patroclus, and Abelard have shouldered leadership in the primary battles, Gustav Aulén, a modern Ajax, forayed into battle and offered yet another historic interpretation of the atoning significance of Jesus. But the Hector of consensus has not yet been conquered, even if some are emboldened to think it is on the lam and shortly to be captured. Is it possible, perhaps, to make peace in the Christian war about the best theory of the atonement by probing the evidence of the Gospels to find what Jesus thought about his death?

It would be a tall order from Zeus to sail from the homeland to fight in both of these wars, the war over whether or not Jesus saw his death as atoning and the war over how atonement is to be understood. Instead, I have asked for a smaller mission—to ask how Jesus understood this death—but with a view to ventilating a suggestion or two about the theory of atonement.

RECENT SCHOLARSHIP: GENERAL REMARKS

Recent gospel scholarship has turned en masse to questions about the historical Jesus, and this not only because of the Jesus Seminar's publicity. Twenty years ago scholars were confronted with a methodological watershed: either narrative criticism or the historical Jesus. The fruits of choosing the latter are that nearly every year reveals a new, comprehensive, and provocative study of Jesus with one enduring blind spot: since the magisterial study of B.F. Meyer in 1979,[9] only one significant Jesus book has devoted more than passing interest to what Jesus thought about his death. The only scholar who has broached this question in a manner that integrates the message and mission of Jesus into his own understanding of his death is N.T. Wright.[10] Not to overstate the case, several studies have approached this question fairly, and judiciously, but they have not clarified their study of the death of Jesus by integrating that view into a larger study of Jesus' mission. In this and the next chapter, I will survey recent scholarship on how Jesus understood his own death. Because the issues are complex, we need to offer an overview in this chapter and then look more particularly at critical issues in the next chapter.

I will not, however, examine in any detail the "who was responsible for what" issue, that is, "who killed Jesus?" or, as Ellis Rivkin asked, "what crucified

---

and one should see, at the bottom of some of these discussions, R. Girard, *Things Hidden Since the Foundation of the World* (trans. S. Bann and M. Metteer; Stanford: Stanford University Press, 1987).

[9] B.F. Meyer, *The Aims of Jesus* (London: SCM, 1979).

[10] N.T. Wright, *Jesus and the Victory of God* (vol. 2 of *Christian Origins and the Question of God*; Minneapolis: Fortress, 1996). A traditional, if at times eccentric, answer can be found in J.C. O'Neill, "Did Jesus Teach That His Death Would be Vicarious as well as Typical?" in *Suffering and Martyrdom in the New Testament* (ed. W. Horbury, B. McNeil; Cambridge: Cambridge University Press, 1981), 9–27.

Jesus?"[11] And, even in the topic of how Jesus saw his own death, I do not claim to cover everything, especially in reference to a survey of historical and exegetical studies on the critical texts. These kinds of studies aid most of us in research, but few are interested in writing out their results of the history and contours of scholarship.

We can profitably begin by reminding ourselves of the fundamental importance that the death of Jesus took on in the earliest churches, most notably those connected to Paul and the writer of Hebrews. For Paul,[12] the death of Jesus became an *atonement* with Jesus as the "mercy seat" (Rom 3:21-25)[13] and for the author of Hebrews, especially at 9:15-22, Jesus' death put an end to the temple's sacrificial system. Morna Hooker's Didsbury Lectures were devoted to the variegated dimensions of the theme of the death of Jesus in the New Testament, and she presents the problem as contained in the word *for* in "he died for our sins."[14] The discussion, she states, started immediately. In fact, C.H. Dodd, who must have been born with a graceful pen in hand, once claimed the following: "It is often assumed that there was a time when the church could think of the cross only as a disaster retrieved by the resurrection, and that only subsequent reflection found a positive meaning in it. *It is impossible to deny that this may have been so; but if there was such a period, it is a period to which we have no access.*"[15]

As if to confirm Dodd's point, G. Feeley-Harnik has argued in her study *The Lord's Table* that each of the Synoptists may well have used sacrificial language connected to *Pesah*, or Passover, to retell the story of Jesus' last supper and death as a midrash on, and a counter to, the non-Christian, Jewish understanding of *Pesah*.[16] Methodologically, however, Feeley-Harnik is less concerned with the historical Jesus (though her language does not always contain itself) than with redaction and early Christian midrash. An important conclusion she draws then is that earliest Christianity, in nearly all of its expressions, interpreted the death of Jesus as a salvific event and did so in terms of *Pesah*. This last observation will not be without significance as this book unfolds.

---

[11] E. Rivkin, *What Crucified Jesus?* (Nashville: Abingdon, 1984); see also McLaren, "Exploring the Execution of a Provincial."

[12] See H.N. Ridderbos, "The Earliest Confession of the Atonement in Paul," in *Reconciliation and Hope* (ed. R. Banks; Grand Rapids: Eerdmans, 1974), 76–89; J.D.G. Dunn, *The Theology of Paul the Apostle* (Grand Rapids: Eerdmans, 1998), 207–33.

[13] D.P. Bailey, "Jesus as the Mercy Seat," *TynBul* 51 (2000): 155–58 (a summary of his dissertation).

[14] M. Hooker, *Not Ashamed of the Gospel* (Didsbury Lectures, 1988; Carlisle, UK: Paternoster, 1994).

[15] C.H. Dodd, *According to the Scriptures* (London: Nisbet, 1952), 123 (italics added).

[16] G. Feeley-Harnik, *The Lord's Table* (Symbol and Culture Series; Philadelphia: University of Pennsylvania Press, 1981; repr., Washington, D.C.: Smithsonian Institution, 1994). This is an anthropological study of *Pesah* as the generative nucleus of Christian midrash, and she explores such in the context of food as metaphor for life and salvation.

So here we ask a question behind these interpretations: what did Jesus think of his death? We know what several early Christians thought—to make the matter simple and distinguishable, that it was exemplary (1 Peter), that it was paradigmatic for discipleship (Mark), that it was atoning (Romans), and that it was covenant-forming (Hebrews)—but what did Jesus think of it? Did he think of his death as significant at all? Was he at the bottom of this soteriological attribution? The most recent question is even more fundamental: Does it matter what Jesus thought?[17] Few have written as pointedly about this as has J.A.T. Robinson in his signal essay on the self-consciousness of Jesus.[18] He asks. in what might be taken as the foundation for the quest for the historical Jesus,

> But what if he did not understand himself as anything like what the church pro-
> claimed him to be? Is it possible to be content with—let alone to believe—a
> Christ *malgré lui*? "Do you think you're what they say you are?" asks the chorus
> in *Jesus Christ Superstar*, representing, as choruses are supposed to, the ordinary
> man. And if he did not, then it is difficult to persuade the ordinary man or "sim-
> ple believer" that it is a matter of complete indifference. . . . I am not persuaded
> that it is possible to remain indifferent to the findings of the historian on how
> Jesus understood himself, nor that an ultimate scepticism is either tolerable or
> necessary. . . . In this sense the *self-knowledge* of Jesus is the indispensable heart of
> the mystery: to regard it as a matter of indifference or as a "no go" area is to leave
> a blank at the centre of Christian theology.[19]

Regardless of the many attempts to appreciate the *canonical witness*—whether through the lenses of aesthetic criticism or New Testament theology or Orthodox theology or kerygmatic theology or the "witness of the church"—and there is something important to each approach, one has difficulty in believing the atoning death of Jesus and then being told that we are not sure that Jesus

---

[17] Ultimately, this is one of the questions Luke Timothy Johnson asks. That is, he is the most recent revival of the theory of M. Kähler and Rudolf Bultmann's kerygmatic theology: see M. Kahler, *The So-Called Historical Jesus and the Historic Biblical Christ* (ed. and trans. C.E. Braaten, 1896; foreword by P. Tillich; Philadelphia: Fortress, 1964); R. Bultmann, *Jesus Christ and Mythology* (New York: Scribner, 1958); *The Presence of Eternity* (The Gifford Lectures, 1955; New York: Harper, 1957); L.T. Johnson, *The Real Jesus* (San Francisco: HarperSanFrancisco, 1996). Nonspecialists are entering the fray quite often and one notable example is P. Jenkins, *Hidden Gospels* (New York: Oxford University Press, 2001). I don't dispute the need to meet, at the methodological level, The Jesus Seminar. I am not persuaded that Luke Timothy Johnson's theory is as simple as it looks. See S. McKnight, "The Hermeneutics of Confessing Jesus as Lord," *ExAud* 14 (1998): 1–17, as modified below, under "Historical Jesus Studies and the Theological Discipline." In particular, while I agree with Johnson that the canonical and creedal perceptions of Jesus are what constitute a Christian perception of Jesus, I am not persuaded that faith and knowledge (*fiducia* and *scientia*) are as distinguishable as he tends to make them.

[18] A.T. Robinson, "The Last Tabu?" in his *Twelve More New Testament Studies* (London: SCM, 1984), 155–70.

[19] Ibid., 158–59, 161.

thought of his death in this way. A self-respecting thinker will move to a different table and eat a different meal or, as we are suggesting, request a different waiter.

Put more directly, we are saying this: in light of the previous chapter, we are claiming that a Christian understanding of Jesus sees his death as atoning, but in addition we are asking if the Christian understanding corresponds to what Jesus thought about his own death.[20] We are asking the Truth question, as long as we recognize that when it comes to historical truth we are not dealing with empirical and scientific certainty, or at least as modernists have so framed what truth can achieve. Yes, we are saying that the early Christians did think Jesus' death was atoning. Did they get it right? we are asking.

GENERAL REMARKS: HISTORICAL CONTEXT

At the level of basic history, we observe that it is highly probable that Jesus was crucified, close to *Pesah*, as a political and religious rebel.[21] Essentially, Jesus was put to death because he was accused of being a false prophet and magician who was in danger of leading the people astray.[22] Furthermore, it is only slightly less probable that Jesus' death was the inevitable result of a legal process that emerged from legal texts like Deuteronomy 13; 17:1-7; 18:20. One might toss into the brewing pot that Jesus was probably accused of being the rebellious son of Deuteronomy 21:18-21 (cf. Q 11:34).[23] From a Christian perspective, as David Brondos concludes, Jesus died because he was faithful to his mission to bring *shalom* to his people.[24] Jesus' stubborn commitment to what he knew to be God's will, however we sort out the data, must be considered as part of the mix when we consider the reason why Jesus was put to death.

Additionally, at the basic level of history and the *Sitz im Leben Jesu*, attributing *meaning* or *story* or *narrative power* to one's own death is completely appropriate within Jewish culture. As any reading of the scholarship of the last half-century indicates, one would think that representing Jesus as someone who

---

[20] See ch. 1, under "Historical Jesus Studies and Theological Discipline."

[21] See esp. R.A. Horsley, "The Death of Jesus," in *Studying the Historical Jesus* (ed. B. Chilton and C.A. Evans; NTTS 19; Leiden: E.J. Brill, 1994), 395–422; esp. pp. 396–99, 405–16; see also J.D.G. Dunn, *Jesus Remembered* (vol. 1 of *Christianity in the Making*; Grand Rapids: Eerdmans, 2003), 765–824.

[22] The details have been worked out by A. Strobel, *Die Stunde der Wahrheit* (Tübingen: Mohr Siebeck, 1980); G.N. Stanton, "Jesus of Nazareth: A Magician and a False Prophet Who Deceived God's People?" in *Jesus of Nazareth: Lord and Christ* (ed. J.B. Green and M. Turner; Grand Rapids: Eerdmans, 1994), 164–80; D. Neale, "Was Jesus a Mesith?" *TynBul* 44 (1993): 89–101.

[23] I use "Q 11:34" for the Q textual references in accordance with standard scholarly practice. Q 11:34 is found at Luke 11:34, but with possible variants from the Matthean parallel. For Q, the standard text is: J.M. Robinson, et al., *The Critical Edition of Q* (Hermeneia; Minneapolis: Fortress, 2000). On the rebellious son charge, cf. S. McKnight, "Calling Jesus *Mamzer*," *JSHJ* 1 (2003): 73–103.

[24] Brondos, "Why Was Jesus Crucified?" 495–96.

thought his death was atoning would be outside the norm of what scholars could do. In fact, for many scholars—most especially those who were influenced by the *Religionsgeschichteschule* as fed into early Christian scholarship through Bultmann—atonement is necessarily late and Hellenistic. It needs to be emphasized that this methodology and this conclusion about atonement are no longer tenable in light of what we know both about the relationship of Judaism and Hellenism as well as what we know would be conceivable for a first-century Jew like Jesus. There is simply too much evidence within classical strands of Judaism, leaving someone like Philo aside for the moment, that indicates atonement was an active issue to think Jesus could not have entertained atoning notions about his own death.[25]

Perhaps the most significant study in this regard was done nearly three decades ago by Marie-Louise Gubler, whose study, though it is devoted to early Christian interpretation, has been nearly completely ignored in scholarship on the death of Jesus—in spite of its clear presentation of Jewish views of how a death may be perceived as significant, including evidence that it could be seen as atoning.[26] Gubler traces four themes, each of which has deep roots in the traditions of Israel used by early Christians to provide narrative power to the death of Jesus. Those themes are:

(1)   the violent fate of the prophets,[27]
(2)   the suffering and exaltation of the innocent/righteous [e.g. Pss 22; 69; Dan 3:28; 6:25-27; 11:29-35; 12:1-2],[28]
(3)   soteriological or atonement interpretations [including Isa 53],[29] and
(4)   the *Aqedah* of Isaac [cf. 4Q225; 4Q266].[30]

[25] See, for example, A. Yarbro Collins, "Finding Meaning in the Death of Jesus," *JR* 78 (1998): 175–96.

[26] M-L. Gubler, *Die frühesten Deutungen des Todes Jesu* (OBO 15; Freiburg: Universitätsverlag, 1977).

[27] The standard study is that of Odil Hans Steck, *Israel und das gewaltsame Geschick der Propheten.* (WMANT 23; Neukirchen-Vluyn: Neukirchener Verlag, 1967).

[28] L. Ruppert, *Der leidende Gerechte* (FB 5; Würzburg: Echter, 1972); *Jesus als der leidende Gerechte?* (SBS 59; Stuttgart: Katholisches Bibelwerk, 1972); *Der leidende Gerechte und seine Feinde* (FB 6; Würzburg: Echter, 1973); K. Th. Kleinknecht, *Der leidende Gerechtfertigte* (WUNT 2/13; Tübingen: Mohr Siebeck, 1984).

[29] The literature here is enormous; see ch. 2, under "The Death of Isaiah's Servant (and the Messiah)."

[30] On this, see G. Vermès, *Scripture and Tradition in Judaism* (StPB 4; Leiden: E.J. Brill, 1961), 193–227; "New Light on the Aqedah from 4Q225," *JJS* 47 (1996): 140–46; B.D. Chilton, "Isaac and the Second Night" and "Recent Discussion on the Aqedah," in his *Targumic Approaches to the Gospels* (Studies in Judaism; Lanham: University Press of America, 1986), 25-37, 39-49 with bibliography; see also J.D. Levenson, *The Death and Resurrection of the Beloved Son* (New Haven: Yale University Press, 1993); A. Segal, "The Akedah: Some Reconsiderations," in *Judentum* (ed. Peter Schäfer; vol. 1 of *Geschichte–Tradition–Reflexion*, Cancik, Lichtenberger, and Schäfer, 1996, 99–116; B.N. Fisk, "Offering Isaac Again and Again," *CBQ* 62 (2000): 481–507; E. Noort and E. Tigchelaar, *The Sacrifice of Isaac* (vol. 4 of *Themes in Biblical Narrative*; Leiden: E.J. Brill, 2002).

Whatever one concludes about how Jesus understood his own death (and Gubler's task was not designed to explore historical Jesus questions), the idea that theological or soteriological meanings rose to the surface would hardly surprise a first-century Jew. On top of this one can easily add in the Maccabean martyrs (e.g., 4 Macc 6:28-29; 17:21-22), with clear connections to a death that atones; and one has plenty of plausible Jewish contexts for either Jesus himself or early Christians understanding death as an atonement.[31]

We can pause here to consider briefly the *Aqedah* tradition as an example. Clearly, in early Christian exegesis Abraham's binding of Isaac is interpreted in light of Christ or better yet, Christ was understood in light of the *Aqedah* (Rom 8:32). Even if for Paul the accent is on Abraham as analogous to the Father's love for his people rather than on Isaac as a figure of Christ, the tradition in Judaism provided narrative power for Paul. *Auctor Hebreos* understands a similar pattern at work in God's plan to redeem through Christ (11:17-19), even thinking that Abraham may have offered Isaac while knowing that God could indeed raise him from the dead. And, to complicate matters, *Jubilees* connects *Pesah* with the *Aqedah* (17:15–18:19) while the later rabbinic sources decide to present Isaac's death as atoning. Furthermore, they think he was raised from the dead (e.g., *Mek. de R. Ishm.*, tractate *Pisha* 7.78-82; 1.57/58 [on Exod 12:11-14]).

We have here then both Jewish and Christian witness to the *Aqedah* being understood as somehow connected to the atoning work of God. But, the decisive factor is not the suitability or even the use of the tradition to understand the death of Jesus, though the existence of a Jewish milieu and interpretive tradition provides plenty of evidence for thinking such could have been undertaken by early Christians and perhaps Jesus. Instead, the decisive factor is that, regardless of the potential explanatory power of this tradition, there is no evidence that Jesus understood his own death in terms of the *Aqedah*. As a part of general culture, of course, one can argue that such figures lurked on the surface, ready to be taken up into a story or narrative at any given moment. The *Aqedah* was one such figure. But each instance of using such figures (especially when it comes to the Christian story—is not the Son of man a clear example?) will result from a combination of the life of Jesus and an assortment of (often unused) texts from the Tanakh that are embroiled in a pot of polemics within and without.

If such meanings lurked at the surface of culture, it should hardly surprise if Jesus were to appeal to such paradigms to understand his own death. But we are getting ahead of ourselves. The question is not whether or not it was *possible* for Jesus to have attributed significance to his death, but instead whether or not it is *probable* or even almost *certain* and, if so, in what sense he did attribute meaning to his death? Furthermore, in what ways did what he had to say about his death correspond to early Christian interpretations of that death?

---

[31] See M. de Jonge, "Jesus' Death for Others and the Death of the Maccabean Martyrs," in *Text and Testimony* (ed. T. Baarda, et al.; Kampen: Kok, 1988), 142–51; *Christology in Context* (foreword by W.A. Meeks; Philadelphia: Westminster, 1988), 173–88.

So, to return to our concern in this chapter: according to Jesus scholarship, did Jesus anticipate a premature death? and, if so, did he attribute to that death any significance? Did he think his death would be a tragedy? the act of a prophet-martyr for the kingdom's cause?[32] a heroic example? a covenant-establishing death? an atoning sacrifice?[33] Would he be a prophet who must die for his message to his nation? a prophet who threw himself into God's hands as part of the last great tribulation? a righteous sufferer? a messianic servant? and, though few entertain this question, was his death, if construed as significant, for his chosen followers? for his people Israel? for the world?

SOME HIGHLIGHTS IN THE HISTORY OF SCHOLARSHIP

I begin with a brief overview of how scholars have comprehended Jesus' own perception of his death. There is simply not enough space for me to work through the nuances of each interpretation, or to provide a comprehensive listing of scholarship for each category. I shall detail some of the highlights; I hope most of the more important ones are sketched.[34] I shall group scholarship in six broad categories, but I confess that these are types and that the individual scholars espousing them always have nuances that swell beyond the type and even overlap with other types. One further caveat: in detailing this scholarship, I have attempted to keep each scholar in only one category. What we lose in sketching the nuances of an individual author we gain in space and simplicity. Again, much more can be said about definition (say, of what a scholar means when he or she speaks of Jesus seeing his death in terms of the Son of man), but our concern here is more with getting various views on the table than with defining the nuances.

AN ESCHATOLOGICAL DEATH: SCHWEITZER'S WHEEL OF HISTORY ROLLS ON

Modern scholarship on the death of Jesus begins with Albert Schweitzer; according to him, Jesus saw the final tribulation as the necessary precursor to the kingdom of God and, in the latter stages of his ministry, came to the conclusion that he must enter into that tribulation himself in his death—and so he entered Jerusalem to set the wheel of history in motion.[35] He died, in other words, voli-

---

[32] See P.E. Davies, "Did Jesus Die as a Martyr-Prophet?" *BR* 2 (1957): 19–30.

[33] The use of the term "sacrifice" has been problematized by B.H. McLean, "The Absence of an Atoning Sacrifice in Paul's Soteriology," *NTS* 38 (1992): 531–53. In what follows no attempt will be made to resolve this issue, though I tend to think the term and category of sacrifice has been, and will continue to be, used in discussions of early Christian soteriology, whether or not that usage reflects an adequate grasp of ancient Israelite sacrificial practices.

[34] See also J.B. Green, "The Death of Jesus and the Ways of God," *Int* 52 (1998): 24–37.

[35] Albert Schweitzer, whose views were based on the first edition of Johannes Weiss's book, *Die Predigt Jesu vom Reiche Gottes* (1892; repr. ed. F. Hahn; 3d ed.; Göttingen: Vandenhoeck & Ruprecht, 1964), published several books on Jesus early in his career: *The Mystery of the Kingdom of God* (trans. W. Lowrie; New York: Dodd, Mead, 1914); trans. of *Das Messianitäts—und*

tionally and intentionally—to force the hand of God. Schweitzer's notion of the final woes as Jesus' perception of his own death has been followed up in various ways but the most notable study since his time is that of D.C. Allison, Jr. In his published (and now unfortunately overlooked) dissertation,[36] Allison develops further the important solution of Schweitzer: Jesus saw his own death as the inception of the final, great tribulation, but through that tribulation he expected vindication as resurrection.[37] Allison, to borrow the rabbinic expression of R. Nahman, but this time with its positive sense, is "a bag full of books" (*b. Meg.* 28b). And most recently, Ulrich Luz builds on Schweitzer's thesis, but only by calling into question the eschatological motives of Jesus.[38] Recently, however, Brant Pitre has offered an entire reevaluation of the import of Schweitzer and

---

Leidensgeheimnis (Tübingen: Mohr Siebeck, 1901); *The Psychiatric Study of Jesus* (trans. C.R. Joy; Boston: Beacon, 1948) [the dissertation for his degree in medicine]; trans. of *Die psychiatrische Beurteilung Jesu* (Tübingen: Mohr Siebeck, 1913); and the most influential book ever written in historical Jesus studies, *Geschichte der Leben-Jesu-Forschung* (9th ed.; UTB 1302; Tübingen: Mohr Siebeck, 1984); the first title, published by Mohr 1906, was *Von Reimarus zu Wrede*; a second edition by Mohr, with the present title, was published in 1913; in 1966 J.M. Robinson wrote an informative preface to a new edition. There are now two English editions: *The Quest of the Historical Jesus* (trans. W. Montgomery; Baltimore: The Johns Hopkins University Press, 1998) and *The Quest of the Historical Jesus* (J. Bowden; trans. W. Montgomery, J.R. Coates, S. Cupitt, and J. Bowden; Minneapolis: Fortress, 2001). This latter new translation corrects W. Montgomery's occasional effusions of style and adds the translation of the fuller German second edition.

Several comments about the Bowden edition are in order: first, it is a pity that a completely new translation was not prepared. To the degree that this book is as important as Bowden claims (and I have no reason to doubt his claims) it deserves the extra time required to retranslate. Second, in spite of inserting Dennis Nineham's foreword from the 1970s, only patchily updated in 1999, the editors managed to omit the important foreword to the German edition by J.M. Robinson. Third, the same editors managed also to omit the important prefaces and various sorts of introduction by F.C. Burkitt and D.R. Hillers. Fourth, I found many typographical errors in the book, and the book contains no scriptural index, and this is sad for a book advertised as the first complete edition. Finally, I found numerous translational errors in my occasional checking, especially of the new material. However, we must remain grateful to Bowden for his persistence in publishing a translation of the "complete" Schweitzer; perhaps further editions will improve this important contribution. The Josiah touch of his Editor's Note (xi) gives the book a revivalist slant.

On Schweitzer, see J. Brabazon, *Albert Schweitzer: A Biography* (New York: Putnam, 1975); S.J. Gathercole, "The Critical and Dogmatic Agenda of Albert Schweitzer's *The Quest of the Historical Jesus*," *TynBul* 51 (2000): 261–83. I am unable to determine which translation of Weiss he is using; however, he seems not to have paid sufficient attention to the alterations in Weiss in Weiss's own second edition (1900). Nor does it appear that he has used the 6th edition of Schweitzer's self-aggrandizing history of Jesus studies.

[36] D.C. Allison, Jr., *The End of the Ages Has Come: An Early Interpretation of the Passion and Resurrection of Jesus* (Philadelphia: Fortress, 1985).

[37] D.C. Allison, Jr., *Jesus of Nazareth* (Minneapolis: Fortress, 1998); *The Intertextual Jesus* (Harrisburg: Trinity Press International, 2000). Allison, in *Jesus of Nazareth*, sees Jesus also in terms of servant (p. 54), illustrating our earlier point that many of the scholars I will mention could also be placed in other parts of this chapter.

[38] See Ulrich Luz, "Warum zog Jesus nach Jerusalem?" in *Der historische Jesus* (ed. J. Schröter and R. Brucker; BZNW 114; Berlin: Walter de Gruyter, 2002), 409–27.

Allison's theory, and has in effect built upon them a significant structure of understanding the death of Jesus as atoning as that death is understood to be part of the great tribulation.[39]

Other scholars have pointed to the eschatological tribulation as critical for Jesus' perception of his own death, but few have taken hold of this theme as so central to his perception of his death as have Schweitzer and Allison and Pitre.[40] More importantly, among those scholars who have explored the eschatology of Jesus, few have considered Jesus' death as part of that eschatology, and this omission needs to be corrected.

AN UNINTENDED DEATH: THE LEGACY OF BULTMANN

Rudolf Bultmann largely ignored the topic of Jesus and Jesus' own death. He did say that "we cannot know how Jesus understood his end, his death" and that this "death can scarcely be understood as an inherent and necessary consequence of his activity; rather it took place because his activity was misconstrued as a political activity."[41] Bultmann, however, attributed the death of Jesus as a saving event to the Hellenistic church's kerygma. The foundation of Bultmann's conclusion about Jesus' view of his own death was laid out in his *History of the Synoptic Tradition* and in his own understanding of the evolution of the earliest churches.[42] For him, the sayings that are used to claim that Jesus saw his death with an atoning significance are unreliable guides to Jesus; they reflect *Gemeindetheologie*. For many, this view of Bultmann nips the flower off the creed's rose, and a rose bush with no flowers draws few admirers.

One who does admire Bultmann's deflowered bush, at least in his courage, is J.D. Crossan. His books on Jesus adhere to this line of thinking on Jesus' perception of his death, though he uses (as he often does) more clever language: "prophecy historicized" is preferred to "history remembered."[43] For him, the

---

[39] See B.J. Pitre, "The Historical Jesus, the Great Tribulation and the End of the Exile," Ph.D. diss. (Notre Dame, 2004). This thesis, directed by David Aune, came to my attention after my own research was completed.

[40] But see Wright, *Jesus and the Victory of God*, 576–92.

[41] R. Bultmann, "The Primitive Christian Kerygma and the Historical Jesus," in *Historical Jesus and the Kerygmatic Christ* (ed. C.E. Braaten and R.A. Harrisville; New York: Abingdon, 1964) 15–42, here pp. 22, 23.

[42] R. Bultmann, *The History of the Synoptic Tradition* (1921; repr. trans. J. Marsh; rev. ed.; New York: Harper & Row, 1963).

[43] J.D. Crossan, *The Historical Jesus* (San Francisco: HarperSanFrancisco, 1991); *Jesus* (San Francisco: HarperSanFrancisco, 1994); *Who Killed Jesus?* (San Francisco: HarperSanFrancisco, 1995). The quoted words are discussed in the last book cited here, pp. 1–13. Apart from attributing the moment of creation to different sources (Bultmann to the early Christian prophets; Crossan more to the Evangelists), there is great similarity when it comes general conclusions on the historical reliability of the Jesus traditions, and so it becomes an oddity in Jesus scholarship to see no mention of Bultmann in Crossan's pioneering work, *The Historical Jesus*. In Crossan's earlier (and in some ways the book that set in motion his later work) *In Fragments* (San Francisco: Harper &

practice of open commensality was reinterpreted in light of the death of Jesus and became something else (eventually the Eucharist). Crossan is skeptical about the gospel records and thinks the traditional viewpoint of Jesus seeing his death as atoning is held together by genuflections, pins, and Hail Marys, to reuse the language of his fellow Irishman.[44]

Paula Fredriksen's book belongs in this "unexpected event" category, inasmuch as she thinks Jesus was surprised by what happened in the last week and because she thinks Jesus did not attribute significance to his death.[45] The discussion about what Jesus thought about his death, in other words, is for her, if not bankrupt, already filed. On another note, Fredriksen's research involved another, and I think very important, question: why was Jesus crucified but his disciples were not? She contends that it was the messianic announcement of the crowds that riled up the leaders and led to the death of Jesus.[46] It is for our purposes unfortunate that she does not tackle our question directly. I suspect she avoids the question because she doesn't think that Jesus thought about his death theologically, and certainly not soteriologically.[47] The best parts of the book summarize Judaism and the temple, setting the stage for a thesis that says the crowds extended themselves too far. Too much evidence, too many issues, and too much scholarship pertaining to Jesus' death are avoided to give her final resolution adequate form and tone. What I like about the book is, in other words, that the stage she sets prepares for a different drama than the one she depicts— or to use postmodernist terms, than the one she "storyfies."

What can we say then about this viewpoint of Jesus—that his death took him unaware and that he did not attribute to it any atoning significance? In all due respect to the erudition behind this view, it appears to me that this view blatantly dismisses Jesus' ability to perceive his environment. It is hard for me to imagine Jesus—and the following study will set out the arguments—being shocked by his arrest, trial, and execution at the hands of Rome. Why didn't he run when he had the chance? And, if he chose not to run, was he not choosing death? And, if that is so, why did he choose death? Even people with dimmer lights would have seen the authorities coming. This point was firmly established two decades ago by Lorenz Oberlinner, when he argued that though there is not

---

Row, 1983), there is a heavy indebtedness to Bultmann. For a potent response to J.D. Crossan's method, cf. Allison, *Jesus of Nazareth*, 10–33.

[44] So Frank O'Connor, *An Only Child* (New York: Knopf, 1961), 37.

[45] P. Fredriksen, *Jesus of Nazareth, King of the Jews* (New York: Knopf, 1999).

[46] See ibid., 235–59.

[47] A significant weakness in the argument is as follows: there is, in some sense, tension between the non-martyrdom of the disciples and Jesus' explicit words (e.g., Mark 8:34; Q 12:4-9; 17:33). Namely, we have Jesus predicting martyrdom of others alongside a text that shows that they escaped the entire matter. It is more likely that Jesus predicted such than that he did not. And, if he predicted their deaths, then he certainly predicted his own, which makes his trip to Jerusalem more than a sudden and unexpected turn of events.

sufficient evidence to think Jesus was certain of his own death, or that his death was inevitable, there is sufficient evidence to know that he knew he could die prematurely.[48]

THE DEATH OF ISAIAH'S SERVANT (AND THE MESSIAH): DEBATING ACROSS THE ENGLISH CHANNEL

Scholarship after Schweitzer and Bultmann has also taken a more traditional route. Since at least the 1930s, some historical Jesus scholarship in the United Kingdom has seen the death of Jesus in terms of figures in the Tanakh, especially Isaiah's Servant, but the challenge of German form criticism was formidable. Someone who accepted neither Bultmann's premises nor his consequences was C.H. Dodd, who held as a constant in his writings that Jesus expected his death and that it was the inevitable end of the path he had chosen, or was chosen for him by God.[49] Jesus chose that path intentionally as the ideal representative of Israel and as a sacrifice.[50] And he understood his entire life in the light of predictions and patterns in the Tanakh.[51]

Two years after Dodd's influential study of the parables of Jesus, we reach a landmark in how Jesus viewed his death. In 1937, Vincent Taylor published his justly famous *Jesus and His Sacrifice* and argued, wearing a method that we would say today is "well dressed in the style-before-last," for Jesus intending his death as an atonement as he embraced Isaiah's Servant.[52] It is indeed unfortunate that, since Taylor's book, no complete study of how Jesus envisioned his own death has been undertaken. A little remembered detail about one of Taylor's studies fits into this study: in 1954 Taylor succeeded Bultmann as the president of *Studiorum Novi Testamenti Societas* (SNTS). On the topic under consideration here, the difference could not be more dramatic. But the issue is not just one of radicals versus conservatives, for Taylor pleaded in his presidential address of SNTS to see the debate about Jesus' death in scholarly terms:

> The view that the [passion] sayings are *vaticinia ex eventu* is widely held, but
> no less so the belief that they are original utterances of Jesus. It would, I think, be

---

[48] See L. Oberlinner, *Todeserwartung und Todesgewissheit Jesus* (SBB 10; Stuttgart: Katholisches Bibelwerk, 1980).

[49] C.H. Dodd, *The Parables of the Kingdom* (London: Nisbet, 1935), 57–60.

[50] C.H. Dodd, *The Founder of Christianity* (London: Collins, 1971), 103–10. See also C.F.D. Moule, *The Origin of Christology* (Cambridge: Cambridge University Press, 1977), 151–53.

[51] Dodd, *According to the Scriptures*. Dodd's study generated a wealth of studies on how Jesus understood the Tanakh. See R.T. France, *Jesus and the Old Testament* (London: Tyndale, 1971). See further at ch. 3, under "Kingdom as Context for Jesus' Life" and "Jesus' Death and the Last Week."

[52] V. Taylor, *Jesus and His Sacrifice* (1937; repr. London: Macmillan, 1955), 270–71. It ought to be noted here that very similar notes were being sounded in Germany at the time by Rudolf Otto, *The Kingdom of God and the Son of Man* (trans. F.V. Filson and B.L. Woolf; Lutterworth Library 9; London: Lutterworth, 1938), 249–61, 265–329.

a tragedy if differences of opinion upon this question were regarded as signs of intellectual standing, as marking the distinction between learned and enlightened conclusions and the obscurantism of more conservative views.[53]

Four years after Taylor's original work, *Jesus and His Sacrifice*, C.J. Cadoux came to similar conclusions, though with a significantly different approach and context, to such convictions on the part of Jesus.[54] In particular, Cadoux argued that Jesus' assumption of the servant's role was to incite repentance. In 1943, two years after Cadoux, W. Manson, in self-confessed deep agreement with Vincent Taylor, argued for Jesus understanding his life and death in terms of the Servant of Isaiah.[55]

Another landmark is the elegant book, *The Servant-Messiah*, by another British scholar, T.W. Manson. A decade after his namesake, he contended that Jesus saw in his death the very climax to his mission as the Servant of Isaiah; it was, as he said, "the logical issue of his service."[56] In some senses T.W. Manson continues the ongoing scholarly notion of the representativeness of Jesus, a theme that emerges fairly consistently in UK scholarship and which finds its purest form in the works of H. Wheeler Robinson and, to a lesser degree, in H.H. Rowley and C.R. North.[57] This scholarship—from Taylor to Cadoux to W. Manson and to T.W. Manson—might be justifiably regarded as the UK's highpoint of affirming Jesus' perception of his death in terms of the Servant of Isaiah, but it would take one more scholar to offer the final blow to Bultmann as England fought Germany's reigning form-critical method.

In 1954, R.H. Fuller wrote one of the most important studies ever on how Jesus envisioned his own death: *The Mission and Achievement of Jesus* argues against Bultmann that Jesus saw his death as the means by which God would bring in the fullness of the kingdom, which in Fuller's view was already in operation in the ministry of Jesus.[58] Fuller argued that the kingdom was inaugurated through the death of Jesus and that Jesus saw his mission to die and so bring in the kingdom. He thought the Markan order (following here, in some senses, the

[53] V. Taylor, *New Testament Essays* (Grand Rapids: Eerdmans, 1972). I refer here to his "The Origin of the Markan Passion-Sayings," *NTS* 1 (1955): 159–67; reprinted in Taylor on pp. 60–71. Here p. 60.

[54] C.J. Cadoux, *The Historic Mission of Jesus* (London: Lutterworth, 1941), 37–38, 249–65.

[55] T.W. Manson, *Jesus the Messiah* (London: Hodder & Stoughton, 1943).

[56] T.W. Manson, *The Servant-Messiah* (Cambridge: Cambridge University Press, 1953), here p. 80.

[57] H. Wheeler Robinson, *Corporate Personality in Ancient Israel* (rev. ed.; Philadelphia: Fortress, 1980); *The Cross in the Old Testament* (Philadelphia: Westminster, 1955), 55–114; H.H. Rowley, *The Servant of the Lord and Other Essays on the Old Testament* (London: Lutterworth, 1952), 1–88; C.R. North, *The Suffering Servant in Deutero-Isaiah* (2d ed.; Oxford: Oxford University Press, 1956). A current example is found in the erudite studies of H.G.M. Williamson, *The Book Called Isaiah* (Oxford: Clarendon, 1994); *Variations on a Theme* (Didsbury Lectures, 1997; Carlisle, UK: Paternoster, 1998).

[58] R.H. Fuller, *The Mission and Achievement of Jesus* (SBT 12; London: SCM, 1954).

study of T.W. Manson) was important: the core of the passion predictions rang true to the facts. Also, he thought the words of institution by Jesus brought together Isaiah 52–53 with Isaiah 42 into a soteriological synthesis which he believed Jesus thought he was fulfilling. I quote: "Jesus was not only the prophet of the imminent advent of the eschatological Reign of God, but he also conceived it to be his mission to provide by his death the decisive occasion through and in which God would inaugurate that event whose imminence was the burden of his proclamation."[59] (Fuller, after he settled in the United States, assumed the thinking of the New Quest, altered these important conclusions to see the passion predictions as unhistorical, and left his former conclusions behind.)[60]

Across the English Channel, in Germany, it was time for Bultmann to receive home-grown criticism. It was to the idea of servant also that Joachim Jeremias, building squarely on the work of Gustaf Dalman,[61] appealed in order to explain Jesus' view of his death. The use of *servant* to explain Jesus' mission is a gloss on the already existing tendency of German scholarship to focus on the title *Messiah*, from W. Wrede onwards, as the critical issue for understanding Jesus' mission.[62] Further, either because so many attached themselves to Jeremias,[63] as tugboats do to incoming ships, or because of the kind of criticism that leads one to avoid mentioning Jeremias in fear of getting bopped on the head, the genius has been beaten out of Jeremias's various studies. It is a tragedy of modern Jesus scholarship that he has been chopped down and used for timber, or (to change imagery) described as an alchemist by an age of chemists.[64]

It is only fair to Jeremias to recall his contributions, even if in so doing we may not be able to resuscitate his once strong reputation. Nor will we always agree either with his overuse of Strack-Billerbeck, or all of his conclusions, or his lack of dating discretion in the use of Jewish sources, or his occasional altering of realities in order to fit ideas. In spite of these criticisms, many have been directed to the Jewish sources by Jeremias, and he did more, in his generation, for the return to Jewish sources in New Testament scholarship than perhaps anyone else—excepting perhaps W.D. Davies. It must be remembered that Jeremias

---

[59] Ibid., 79.

[60] R.H. Fuller, *The Foundations of New Testament Christology* (New York: Scribner, 1965), esp. 115–19; also his book with P. Perkins, *Who is This Christ?* (Philadelphia: Fortress, 1983). I am grateful to Dale Allison for pointing out Fuller's change of mind. For this reason, Fuller's earlier study takes a back seat in our discussion.

[61] E.g., G. Dalman, *The Words of Jesus* (1898; repr. trans. D.M. Kay; Edinburgh: T&T Clark, 1902); *Jesus-Jeshua* (trans. P.P. Levertoff; New York: Macmillan, 1929).

[62] M. Hengel, *Studies in Early Christology* (Edinburgh: T&T Clark, 1995). W. Wrede tossed down his *drei eckigen Hut* in *The Messianic Secret* (trans. J.C.G. Greig; 1901; repr. Cambridge: James Clarke, 1971).

[63] E.g., I.H. Marshall, *Last Supper and Lord's Supper* (Grand Rapids: Eerdmans, 1980).

[64] See the heated exchange of B.F. Meyer and E.P. Sanders in Meyer, "A Caricature of Joachim Jeremias and His Scholarly Work," *JBL* 110 (1991): 451–62; Sanders emptied his tail guns in "Defending the Indefensible," *JBL* 110 (1991): 463–77.

almost single-handedly resisted the drive of the German *Neutestamentlers* to set earliest Christianity in an exclusively Hellenistic context. Modern scholarship's preoccupation with the Jewishness of Jesus (and Paul)—leading Dom Crossan at times to the witty criticism that modern Jesus books are in a quest for who can say "my Jesus is more Jewish than your Jesus"—was set by Dalman, Strack-Billerbeck, and Jeremias.[65] The work of modern scholarship, so much more nuanced, critical, and informed, of Hengel, Davies, Black, France, Moo, Sanders, Wright, Charlesworth, Chilton, Allison—to name but a few—would not be what it is apart from the role Jeremias played.[66] Now, back to our task of noting the contribution Jeremias made in how Jesus understood his death.

Two directions of Jeremias's studies are noteworthy here: his study of the last supper and a gaggle of articles touching upon these themes, all brought together in his *New Testament Theology*.[67] First, Jeremias acknowledges that the passion predictions have been heavily influenced by later events;[68] second, Jesus must have anticipated a violent death because of the opposition he experienced as well as his *salvation-historical* view of the martyrdom of prophets;[69] third, there is a residue of historically valuable information in the passion predictions which themselves are variants of the passion prediction of Jesus, found most primitively in Mark 9:31a: "God will soon deliver up the man to men"; fourth, there is plenty of evidence for Jesus' perception of his own death, with various factors, including contextual embeddedness, unfulfilled dimensions, and the so-called "three days logia" (Mark 14:58; 15:29; Luke 13:32, 33; John 16:16, 17, 19) pointing toward early material. Jeremias concludes this section as follows: "there can be no doubt that Jesus expected and announced his suffering and death."[70]

But did Jesus attribute to his death atoning significance? Jeremias argues that the Jewish world of Jesus knew of four means of atonement (repentance,

---

[65] This is not to deny the importance of either G.F. Moore or of the profound scholarship undertaken in Jewish scholarship on Jesus and early Christianity. For the latter, cf. D.A. Hagner, *The Jewish Reclamation of Jesus* (Grand Rapids: Zondervan, 1984); "Paul in Modern Jewish Thought," in *Pauline Studies* (ed. D.A. Hagner and M.J. Harris; Grand Rapids: Eerdmans, 1980), 143–65.

[66] An excellent example of this is the most significant work on women in the Jewish world by Tal Ilan, whose first book is mostly a mining and explication of the references pointed out by Jeremias's chapter on women in his *Jerusalem in the Time of Jesus* (trans. F.H. and C.H. Cave; 1962; repr. Philadelphia: Fortress, 1969). See her *Jewish Women in Greco-Roman Palestine* (Peabody, Mass.: Hendrickson, 1996); followed by *Integrating Women into Second Temple History* (Peabody, Mass.: Hendrickson, 2001).

[67] J. Jeremias, *New Testament Theology* (trans. J. Bowden; New York: Scribner, 1971); thus, *The Eucharistic Words of Jesus* (trans. N. Perrin; 1966; repr. Philadelphia: Fortress, 1977); *Abba: Studien zur neutestamentlichen Theologie und Zeitgeschichte* (Göttingen: Vandenhoeck & Ruprecht, 1966); a recent collection of some of his smaller studies can be seen in *Jesus and the Message of the New Testament* (ed. K.C. Hanson; 1965; repr. Minneapolis: Fortress, 2002).

[68] Jeremias, *New Testament Theology*, 277–78.

[69] Ibid.,178–80; Jeremias, *Jesus and the Message of the New Testament*, 80-85.

[70] Jeremias, *New Testament Theology*, 286.

Yom Kippur, suffering, and death) and from this argues that it was not impossible Jesus thought of his suffering and death in terms of atonement. He then summarizes his studies of the eucharistic words, the ransom saying, the sword saying, the saying about Elijah, the phrase "delivered up," the striking of the shepherd, and intercession for the guilty—and concludes that always "we find the explanation of this suffering to be the representation of the many (Mark 10.45; 14.24) by Jesus."[71] He regularly appeals to a background in the Servant Songs of Isaiah, esp. 52:13–53:12.[72]

French scholarship, not frequently entering into this discussion apart from a focus on the last supper,[73] largely confirmed the substantive results of the work of Jeremias, though the work of A. George appealed to the theme of sacrifice more than to Servant of Isaiah.[74] For George, Jesus both anticipated his own death and did so with an understanding of it as the sacrificial dimension of his mission to redeem.

In response especially to the work of Jeremias and Heinz Schürmann (see below), a group of Roman Catholic German scholars convened in March of 1975 to discuss how Jesus understood his own death.[75] Complicating the focal issue of the conference was the emerging confusion of the debate about criteria for assessing the Jesus traditions. Anton Vögtle's extensive article in that volume focused on the complexities of asking what and how Jesus thought about his death. He then concluded that Jesus did not provide grounds for understanding this death as a *stellvertretende Sühne* ("representative atonement") until the last supper, but that such a revelation at that supper best explains the Jesus traditions as well as the emerging thoughts of the earliest churches.[76]

The probing and somewhat skeptical essays at that conference by Joachim Gnilka and (the previously mentioned) Vögtle were not satisfactory to Rudolf Pesch for, in spite of a fine essay in that same volume, he repeated and further explicated his ideas two years later in a monograph.[77] Among his conclusions a few need to be mentioned, though here I am entering into the complex field of the last supper of Jesus: (1) that both Matthew's and Luke's texts are a redaction of Mark's text; (2) that Luke 22:19-20 is a Lukan redactional *Mischtext* ("conflated text") based upon Mark 14:22-25 and 1 Corinthians 11:23-25; (3) that

[71] Ibid., 299.

[72] In this, Jeremias was followed consistently by L. Goppelt, *Theology of the New Testament* (ed. J. Roloff; trans. J.E. Alsup; 2 vols.; 1975; repr. Grand Rapids: Eerdmans, 1981), 1:193–99.

[73] X. Léon-Dufour, *Sharing the Eucharistic Bread* (trans. M.J. O'Connell; New York: Paulist, 1986).

[74] A. George, "Comment Jésus a-t-il perçu sa propre mort?" *LumVie* 101 (1971): 34–59.

[75] K. Kertelge, ed., *Der Tod Jesu* (QD 74; Freiburg: Herder, 1976).

[76] A. Vögtle, "Todesankündigungen und Todesverständnis Jesu," in *Der Tod Jesu* (ed. Kertelge), 51–113.

[77] J. Gnilka, "Wie urteilte Jesus über seinen Tod?" in *Der Tod Jesu* (ed. Kertelge), 13–50; R. Pesch, "Das Abendmahl und Jesu Todesverständnis," in *Der Tod Jesu* (ed. Kertelge), 137–87; *Das Abendmahl und Jesu Todesverständnis* (QD 80; Freiburg: Herder, 1978).

Paul's text is completely secondary and is a "cult aetiology"; (4) that the *Deuteworte* ("words of interpretation") of the last supper are authentic and reveal Jesus as Messiah, as servant, as establishing a new covenant, and as offering himself as an atoning, sacrificial death for Israel.

A year later, in Canada, B.F. Meyer followed Jeremias, arguing that Jesus intended to "charge with meaning his being repudiated and killed."[78] Meyer sees both the "expiation" and the "covenant" motifs in Jesus' mission as historical.[79] Meyer then developed his argument in interaction with recent scholarship in a later study that focuses more directly on the words of institution; here Jesus is Messiah, Servant of Isaiah, and the fulfiller of Israel's hopes.[80] Along the same path walked the Scottish scholar I. H. Marshall in his *Last Supper and Lord's Supper*. On the basis of his own reconstruction of the original last supper, opting for a Byzantine-type text of the last supper, Marshall argued that Jesus offered himself to his followers as the Servant of Isaiah who would forgive sins through a substitutionary sacrifice. The influence of Jeremias's German scholarship is evident on every page of the works of these two scholars.

More importantly, in 1980 both Martin Hengel and Peter Stuhlmacher published articles which sought to push the balance back in the direction of a more nuanced understanding of the servant but, in effect, both gave Jeremias the warm and Bultmann the cold shoulder.[81] This debate about Bultmann continues to concern these Tübingen scholars: one can say that Jeremias begot Hengel and Hengel begot Stuhlmacher. Hengel rooted the earliest Christian atonement theology in his all-important Hellenists of Jerusalem, who had learned from Jesus' own words at the last supper that his death was a "representative atonement" (*stellvertretende Sühne*).[82] And Stuhlmacher proposed that the ransom saying was authentic. He concludes, with the same oracular clarity found in Bultmann, as follows: "Accordingly, New Testament scholarship doesn't need to be at a loss to answer the important question of how Jesus understood his mission and his death. It can answer that Jesus ministered, suffered, and endured an expiatory death as the messianic reconciler."[83] In his most recent

---

[78] Meyer, *Aims of Jesus*, 218.

[79] Ibid., 219.

[80] B.F. Meyer, "The Expiation Motif in the Eucharistic Words: A Key to the History of Jesus?" in *One Loaf, One Cup* (ed. B.F. Meyer; New Gospel Studies 6; Macon: Mercer, 1993), 11–33.

[81] M. Hengel, "Der stellvertrentende Sühnetod Jesu. Ein Beitrag zur Entstehung des urchristlichen Kerygmas," *IKZ* 9 (1980): 1–25, 135–47; *The Atonement* (trans. J. Bowden; Philadelphia: Fortress, 1981); P. Stuhlmacher, "Vicariously Giving His Life for Many, Mark 10:45 (Matt. 20:28)," in his *Reconciliation, Law, and Righteousness* (trans. E. Kalin; Philadelphia: Fortress, 1986), 16–29.

[82] See also H. Merklein, "Der Tod Jesu als stellvertretender Sühnetod: Entwicklung und Gehalt einer zentralen neutestamentlichen Aussage," in *Studien zu Jesus und Paulus* (ed. H. Merklein; WUNT 43; Tübingen: Mohr Siebeck), 181–91.

[83] Stuhlmacher, "Vicariously Giving His Life for Many," 25–26; *Grundlegung Von Jesus zu Paulus* (vol. 1 of *Biblische Theologie des Neuen Testaments*; 2d ed.; Göttingen: Vandenhoeck & Ruprecht, 1997) 125–43. This theme of messianic reconciler has recently been picked up by the American

NT theology, Stuhlmacher states that "the crucifixion of Jesus was the historical, unavoidable consequence of the provocation of his ministry as the messianic
Son of Man" and "Jesus understood his death as a representative atoning death
for 'the many' (i.e., Israel and the nations)."[84] Furthermore, after arguing that
Mark 9:31 (Luke 9:44); Mark 10:45; and Luke 22:35-38 are essentially authentic, Stuhlmacher states: "In that Jesus representatively takes upon himself the
responsibility of guilt for the 'many' and erases it with the sacrifice of his life, he
effects for them the righteousness that was needed to live before God."[85] But, he
is quick to add that this representative death is neither about averting God's
wrath nor about satisfying the wounded honor of God (contra Anselm). This
death expresses the love and compassion of God, and the teaching of Jesus is
therefore the foundation for early Christian thinking about justification.

In proposing a servant consciousness on the part of Jesus in various publications,[86] Stuhlmacher is not without critics, of course. W. Zager has responded
forcefully in his *ZNW* article, now summarized briefly in his *Jesus und die
frühchristliche Verkündigung*.[87] Zager has revived the older line that Jesus didn't
see his death as atoning since that notion entered Christian belief through the
martyrdom theology of Hellenistic Judaism. Other Europeans have, in general,
supported the line of thinking that Jesus thought of his own death in atoning
categories, and one thinks here of the wide-ranging study of Raymund
Schwager, *Jesus in the Drama of Salvation*.

This *Tübingenschule* approach to the Servant of Isaiah, found in Hengel and
Stuhlmacher,[88] as the definitive background for Jesus' self-perception and mission (and surely there is some collegial back-slapping here) is perhaps best represented in English in the fine collection of essays edited by W.H. Bellinger, Jr.,
and W.R. Farmer.[89] Not persuaded by the German reaction to Stuhlmacher,
Otto Betz contends in the Bellinger and Farmer volume that Jesus offered his
very self in the last supper and so "enacted Isaiah 53:12."[90] He contends rightly

---

scholar John Koenig, *The Feast of the World's Redemption* (Harrisburg: Trinity Press International,
2000).

[84] Stuhlmacher, *Grundlegung Von Jesus zu Paulus*, 1:126, 142 (my translation).

[85] Ibid., 130 (my translation).

[86] P. Stuhlmacher, "Der messianische Gottesknecht," *JBTh* 8 (1993): 131–54; "Jes 53 in den
Evangelien und in der Apostelgeschichte," in *Der leidende Gottesknecht* (ed. Janowski and
Stuhlmacher), 93–105.

[87] W. Zager, "Wie kam es im Urchristentum zur Deutung des Todes Jesu als Sühnegeschehen?"
ZNW 87 (1996): 165–86; *Jesus und die frühchristliche Verkündigung* (Neukirchen-Vluyn:
Neukirchener Verlag, 1999), 35–61.

[88] D. Bailey, "The Suffering Servant: Recent Tübingen Scholarship on Isaiah 53," in *Jesus and the
Suffering Servant* (ed. Bellinger and Farmer), 251–59 (summarizes Janowski; on which see below).

[89] W. Bellinger and W.R. Farmer, *Jesus and the Suffering Servant* (Harrisburg: Trinity Press
International, 1998).

[90] O. Betz, "Jesus and Isaiah 53," in *Jesus and the Suffering Servant* (ed. Bellinger and Farmer),
70–87, here p. 86.

that Morna Hooker's criteria (see below) for recognizing the presence of the influence of servant themes are too restrictive, and he explores especially the resonances of "gospel."[91] Not to be as silent as the servant, Hooker announces no peace and wields her holy pen, but who has believed her report?[92] Not Farmer! In the same collection of essays, he provides a *traditionsgeschichtliche Studie* in which he contends that Jesus did think of himself in terms of the servant, especially expressed in the dominical tradition now found at Matthew 26:26-30.[93]

Finally, since the work of Fuller and Schürmann, the most complete study is that of N.T. Wright, and his work forms a transition to other suggestions as well as a summary of what precedes.[94] But before we get to Wright, we must pause momentarily to note the work of G.B. Caird, upon whom Wright built his case.[95] Caird presents a summary case for accepting the Servant of Isaiah as part of Jesus' entire framework of self-perception and, therefore, for seeing Jesus as thinking of himself as a sacrifice. Thus, "what sinful people could not do for themselves Jesus believed he was doing by giving his life 'a ransom for many.'"[96] For Jesus, the Servant of Isaiah 53 was a "'situation vacant' title, an unfulfilled 'job description,' which Jesus himself—and perhaps any who might be willing to join with him—was determined to fill."[97] A paragraph that will be foundational in N.T. Wright's *Jesus and the Victory of God* completes Caird's study of the death of Jesus, and in this paragraph he suggests that it might just have been Jesus who made the long leap from his own death as sacrificial to that death being a "vicarious sacrifice for the sins of the whole world."[98]

In N.T. Wright we find an extensive discussion of evidence, some of which has never been brought into the discussion (like the logia of the Great Commandment, the Green Tree and the Dry, as well as the Hen and Chickens), that leads to the conclusion that Jesus went to Jerusalem to die. Jesus did this as an intentional embodiment of Israel's history in order to effect a new exodus and end the exile,[99]—to wit, to inaugurate the kingdom. Wright's emphasis on Jesus

---

[91] Betz, "Jesus and Isaiah 53," 72, 74–82.

[92] M. Hooker, "Did the Use of Isaiah 53 to Interpret His Mission Begin with Jesus?," in *Jesus and the Suffering Servant* (ed. Bellinger and Farmer), 88–103.

[93] W.R. Farmer, "Reflections on Isaiah 53 and Christian Origins," in *Jesus and the Suffering Servant* (ed. Bellinger and Farmer), 260–80.

[94] Wright, *Jesus and the Victory of God*; "The Servant and Jesus: The Relevance of the Colloquy for the Current Quest for Jesus," in *Jesus and the Suffering Servant* (ed. Bellinger and Farmer), 281–97.

[95] See esp. G.B. Caird, *New Testament Theology* (completed and ed. by L.D. Hurst; Oxford: Clarendon, 1994), esp. 310–16, 369–84, 404–8. One should also read the weighty words of pp. 145–78, where Caird addresses directly the questions surrounding a theory of atonement.

[96] Caird, *New Testament Theology*, 407.

[97] Ibid.

[98] Ibid., 408. Caird concludes by citing Luke 24:25-27 and then transforms his pen into a flashing rapier: "To those who believe Luke's testimony, no further explanation is necessary. To those who do not, no further explanation is possible."

[99] N.T. Wright has been knocked about for his view of "end of exile"; though he may appeal to the

as the one who recapitulates and fulfills Israel's history is another example in UK scholarship of the emphasis on Jesus as representative of Israel. Wright states:

> Of course, if we are looking for a bit of detached teaching with an Old Testament background in which Jesus will say "[L]ook, I am the Servant of Isaiah 53," we will look in vain. . . . But in the middle of the picture [of Jesus] is a hypothesis that can be stated as follows: Jesus made Isaiah 52:7-12 thematic for his Kingdom announcement. . . . But if we ask how the message of Isaiah 52:7-12 is put into effect, the prophecy as Jesus read it had a clear answer. The arm of Yahweh, which will be unveiled to redeem Israel from exile and to put evil to flight, is revealed, according to Isaiah 53:1, *in and through the work of the Servant of Yahweh.*[100]

Understanding Jesus' view of his own death by appealing to the Servant Songs of Deutero-Isaiah has a long history with many fashionable ins and outs but, to steal the words of S.J. Perelman, the servant is "still standing there, slightly chipped but otherwise in very good condition."[101] It boggles to think so many Jesus books have been published in the last thirty years that have simply ignored the scholarship on Jesus and the servant.

Wright, of course, stands on the shoulders of Dodd,[102] T.W. Manson, and three others who will be described shortly: Barrett, Hooker, and Caird, the last who sadly carried to his resting place a book bag in which was to be found his extensive knowledge of our subject. From these shoulders, Wright leaps forward into a new synthesis of kingdom seen as Israel's "eschatological redemption."[103] Wright's brush is broad and sweeps across the entire spectrum, and his understanding of how Jesus saw his own death is not without the nuance of Son of man, to which I now turn.

THE SUFFERING SON OF MAN: THE UNAVOIDABLE CHARYBDIS

As a general point, it needs to be observed that *suffering* and the *expectation of suffering* do not necessarily evoke the Suffering Servant of Isaiah and neither is the "Servant of YHWH" necessarily a personal figure. It is to the credit of the

---

category too often, I side mostly with Wright. Compare the insightful volume of J.M. Scott, *Exile: Old Testament, Jewish, and Christian Conceptions* (JSJSup 56; Leiden: E.J. Brill, 1997). See esp., C.A. Evans, "Aspects of Exile and Restoration in the Proclamation of Jesus and the Gospels," 299–328; slightly different in "Jesus and the Continuing Exile of Israel," in *Jesus and the Restoration of Israel* (ed. C.C. Newman; Downers Grove: InterVarsity, 1999), 77–100.

[100] Wright, "The Servant and Jesus," in *Jesus and the Suffering Servant* (ed. Bellinger and Farmer), 291 (emphasis mine).

[101] S.J. Perelman, "Frou-Four, or, The Future of Vertigo," in *Most of the Most of S.J. Perelman* (ed. S. Martin; New York: The Modern Library, 2000), 58.

[102] One of the outstanding features of Wright's *Jesus and the Victory of God* is that it takes the OT texts of Dodd (and others) and explores their significance for understanding of Jesus, thus completing the task set out by Dodd.

[103] Wright, *Jesus and the Victory of God*, 576–92.

Schweitzer-Allison-Wright line of thinking that suffering can be linked to a *time*, rather than a *person* or *figure*, in history or prophecy. But, the attraction of the term suffering to the Servant of Isaiah is not easily resisted. Those who appeal to the Son of man[104] as the generative figure behind Jesus' perception of his suffering tend to dispute the servant imagery, as is especially the case with Morna Hooker and most recently with Jimmy Dunn.

In the Shaffer Lectures at Yale in 1965, C.K. Barrett undertook this same burden and did resist the reigning hypothesis in the UK: he argued that scholarship's discovery of the servant behind Jesus was a *trompe l'oeil* and, in clearer sight, Jesus understood his death within the categories of the Son of man.[105] To use another image, Barrett (and after him Hooker) pointed a "Servant" Geiger counter at the evidence and heard no clicking. That is, Daniel 7 as well as 11:35 and 12:2-3 give sufficient indication that the death of martyrs can atone. Furthermore, the Son of man figure, the representative of eschatological suffering and atonement and vindication, can be tied into such texts. Thus, as is a well-known theme for Barrett,[106] one need not appeal, as did T.W. Manson, to the Servant of Isaiah to understand Jesus' perception of his own death. Barrett directed the research of Morna Hooker, whose published dissertation, *Jesus and the Servant*, also influenced Barrett and argued this thesis more completely.[107] It ought to be noted here that for neither Barrett nor Hooker is this a debate about what is authentic; the texts are taken as reliable reports of Jesus' views and then subjected to rigorous examination. The texts, they argue, do not show an influence of the Servant Song of Isaiah 52–53.

This Barrett-Hooker line has had its critics, among whom should be mentioned at least four. In his published dissertation R.T. France, on the basis of the same evidence, argued forcefully for a servant background to the mission of Jesus.[108] In another carefully argued dissertation, Douglas J. Moo contended against the methodological restrictions of Barrett and Hooker, and concluded that several *ipsissima verba* evoked the servant.[109] Wright tipped his cap to both Barrett and Hooker but still found servant resonances in Jesus' perception of his death because that perception emerges from "Jesus' whole kingdom-announcement."[110] Rikki Watts presented, on the basis of a more rigorous and self-conscious method, a case that Mark 10:45 reflects the Servant of Isaiah.[111]

---

[104] On Son of man, cf. below, ch. 7 excursus.

[105] C.K. Barrett, *Jesus and the Gospel Tradition* (London: SPCK, 1967), 35–67.

[106] C.K. Barrett, "The Background of Mark 10:45," in *New Testament Essays* (ed. A.J.B. Higgins; Manchester: Manchester University Press, 1959), 1–18.

[107] M. Hooker, *Jesus and the Servant* (London: SPCK, 1959).

[108] France, *Jesus and the Old Testament*, 110–35.

[109] D.J. Moo, *The Old Testament in the Gospel Passion Narratives* (Sheffield: Almond, 1983), 165–72.

[110] Wright, *Jesus and the Victory of God*, 601–4, here p. 603.

[111] R. Watts, "Jesus' Death, Isaiah 53, and Mark 10:45: A Crux Revisited," in *Jesus and the Suffering Servant* (ed. Bellinger and Farmer), 125–51.

While many would not walk hand in hand with either Barrett or Hooker, scholarship today seems less confident of the servant imagery for understanding either Jesus or the early church.[112] As if he has heard a different oracle at Delphi, de Jonge can conclude just the opposite of Stuhlmacher: "All in all, we must conclude that the influence of Isa. 52:13–53:12 on the earliest Christian kerygma can hardly be demonstrated. A fortiori, there is no proof that Jesus himself was profoundly or uniquely influenced by this scriptural passage."[113] While he does not argue the case with such rhetoric, Jimmy Dunn has recently concluded that Jesus (as he was "remembered") understood his death in terms of the suffering of the Son of man and that, at the last supper, he seems to have seen his death as a covenant sacrifice.[114]

THE DEATH OF THE PROEXISTENT ONE: ATONEMENT WITHOUT A THEORY

Of German studies since Jeremias, the most notable research is that of Heinz Schürmann.[115] His many writings—revised, republished, and rarely translated—are more difficult to unravel than Kloppenborg's Q, and neither is his German style user-friendly. In his careful research, Schürmann avoids forcing the evidence into one biblical category (servant, Son of man) and also slides by the need to use a term that reveals an atonement theory. From the beginning of his research, a 1973 essay called "Wie hat Jesus seinen Tod bestanden und verstanden?" (How did Jesus endure and understand his death?) to the final redaction of this and other essays in his book *Jesus: Gestalt und Geheimnis* (*Jesus: Form and Secret*) twenty years later, Schürmann has had a single line of thought: Jesus' entire life was a life of *Proexistenz* (a complicated but useful category expressing an active, intercessory, and representative role in speaking grace to sinners). Jesus knew he was to die *and* he interpreted his own death salvifically.

Schürmann's study argues for *Proexistenz* more from the actions and gestures of Jesus at the last supper (the *ipsissima facta*) than from specific logia. He calls the final three actions of Jesus (entry, temple event, and last supper) *Erfüllungszeichen* ("fulfillment signs") and the last supper action is the climax of such actions. In particular, in his last study he emphasized the "gestures" of Jesus at the last supper as revealing a soteriological intention of his imminent death.[116] A notable detail of his study is that Jesus urged his followers to drink from *his* cup rather than from individual cups. Such an action was contrary to *Pesah* customs, and leads Schürman to think of that action as salvific—Jesus' followers participate in his death. Schürmann is less confident than many that Jesus

---

[112] Thus, M. de Jonge, *God's Final Envoy* (Grand Rapids: Eerdmans, 1998), 30–33.

[113] Ibid., 33.

[114] See Dunn, *Jesus Remembered*, 805–18.

[115] H. Schürmann, *Jesu ureigener Tod* (Freiburg: Herder, 1975); *Gottes Reich—Jesu Geschick* (Freiburg: Herder, 1983); *Jesus—Gestalt und Geheimnis* (ed. K. Scholtissek; Paderborn: Bonifatius, 1994).

[116] See also J. Schlosser, *Jésus de Nazareth* (2d ed.; Paris: Agnès Viénot, 2002), 281–301.

thought in terms either of servant or martyr. His concept of *Proexistenz*, before it arrives at its destination, walks the long plank between the two without jumping in either direction.[117] Put differently, Schürmann constructed a new path for comprehending how Jesus understood his death, but it was Pesch, Stuhlmacher, and Wright who walked that path to the end. It is a pity that very few scholars have either interacted with Schürmann or have seen the path he was charting and followed it.[118]

One of the few who did was Joachim Gnilka, who wrote an extensive article summarizing what can be known from a solid methodological basis about Jesus' view of his own death.[119] His study records how Ernst Käsemann, Joachim Jeremias, and Ferdinand Hahn were reassessing the historical Jesus in the aftermath of Käsemann's famous essay on the historical Jesus. Back to Gnilka. He argues that a Jesus who forces the issue in Jerusalem is unlikely (contra Schweitzer). Furthermore, he thinks that there was a widespread early Christian interpretation of Jesus' death as the violent death of a prophet. Gnilka thinks Jesus provided clues to interpret his death: he expected the renewal of table fellowship after his death, and the atoning language about his death emerges from the last supper traditions. Stepping back, Gnilka contends that a "dying for" (*Sterben für*) is the oldest meaning attributed to Jesus' death and builds a bridge to the shape of Jesus' very life and work: in other words, his *Proexistenz*.[120] Though not interacting with the work of these German scholars, P.M. Casey's study of the development of Christology, sometimes radical and sometimes conservative, outlines the bare details of a Jesus who thought of his own death as atoning but who also foresaw an imminent vindication.[121]

THE DEATH OF A MARTYR OR A PROPHET OR THE RIGHTEOUS ONE OR AS EXAMPLE: DEATH WITHOUT ATONEMENT

Many scholars, perhaps a majority today, think Jesus was innocent, that he was righteous, that his death was splendidly exemplary, and/or that he died as a result of his self-claim and his mission, but that his death was not undertaken (consciously and deliberately) as an atonement. As innocent and righteous, the paradigm for Jesus' death is to be found deep in Israel's traditions, most notably in Psalms 22 and 69. The largely German view owes its boost to Eduard Schweizer and was then completely presented by Lothar Ruppert, though one

---

[117] Schürmann, *Jesus—Gestalt und Geheimnis*, 286–345.

[118] See Vögtle, "Todesankündigungen und Todesverständnis Jesu," in *Der Tod Jesu* (ed. Kertelge), 90–92.

[119] Gnilka, "Wie urteilte Jesus über seinen Tod?" in *Der Tod Jesu* (ed. Kertelge), 13–50.

[120] A similar, but not always clear, study is by C.J. den Heyer, *Jesus and the Doctrine of the Atonement* (trans. J. Bowden; Harrisburg: Trinity Press International, 1998). The author concludes that Jesus died "for others" (p. 17), but his work varies little from that of Schürmann or Gnilka.

[121] M. Casey, *From Jewish Prophet to Gentile God* (Edward Cadbury Lectures, 1985–1986; Louisville: Westminster/John Knox, 1991), 64–67.

rarely finds this view on the table today.[122] Its lack of fashion appears to me to be related to the theology it inevitably invokes: the sinlessness of Jesus.

In its simplest form, this rubric contends that Jesus was a prophet who died as a martyr for his mission and his cause.[123] Death as a martyr was a heroic option in Judaism.[124] In using the term *martyr*, however, I do not mean to attribute to these scholars the atoning work of a martyr that some have argued for.

Perhaps no one has expressed this view more articulately than C.F.D. Moule[125] who says,

> Jesus . . . did not seek death; he did not go up to Jerusalem in order to die; but he did pursue, with inflexible devotion, a way of truth that inevitably led him to death, and he did not seek to escape. It seems that he went up to Jerusalem on that last, fatal journey, partly to keep the Passover, like any good Palestinian [sic] Jew; and partly, like the passionate prophet that he was, to present his nation with one last challenge—to make a final bid to save them from their disastrous course of religious and political blindness. But he knew he was, in fact, bound to die, and he made no attempt either to escape or to defend himself. In that sense, he was the victim of his own loyalty to his vocation. . . . But not for a moment does Jesus treat it [his inevitable death] merely as something to be endured. Always, he exercises a sovereign mastery over it. . . . All this [texts, like Mark 8:35, just cited] is in no spirit of mere resignation. It bespeaks a most positive and affirmative attitude. Thus, the external necessity is, in the inward life of the will, turned into an act of sovereign, creative power, as is the case whenever the surrender of life rises to the heights of martyrdom.

Another early study from this angle was that of P.E. Davies, who argued that Jesus was a prophet, a martyr, and an Ezekelian Son of man. The outcome of his life was the martyrdom of a prophet.[126]

---

[122] On this, see E. Schweizer, *Lordship and Discipleship* (London: SCM, 1960), 22–41. An excellent survey of the viewpoint can be found in Gubler, *Die frühesten Deutungen des Todes Jesu*, 95–205; the most complete study is that of Ruppert, *Der leidende Gerechte*.

[123] A good, but older, collection of data can be found in E. Stauffer, *New Testament Theology* (trans. J. Marsh; London: SCM, 1955), 331–34. An important essay developing the early Christian idea that martyrdom was the occasion for Spirit-inspired witness and behavior has been developed by G.W.H. Lampe, "Martyrdom and Inspiration," in *Suffering and Martyrdom in the New Testament* (ed. Horbury and McNeil; Cambridge: Cambridge University Press, 1981), 118–35. See also J. Pobee, "The Cry of the Centurion—A Cry of Defeat," in *The Trial of Jesus* (ed. E. Bammel; SBT 2.13; London: SCM, 1970), 91–102.

[124] See D. Daube, "Death as Release in the Bible," *NovT* 5 (1962): 82–104; D.W. Palmer, "To Die is Gain," *NovT* 17 (1975): 203–18; J.J. Collins, "The Root of Immortality: Death in the Context of Jewish Wisdom," *HTR* 71 (1978): 17–92; A.J. Droge and J.D. Tabor, *A Noble Death* (San Francisco: HarperSanFrancisco, 1992); D. Boyarin, *Dying for God* (Stanford: Stanford University Press, 1999); Alan Segal, *Life After Death* (New York: Doubleday, 2004), 248–81.

[125] Moule, *The Origin of Christology*, 109, 110.

[126] Davies, "Did Jesus Die as a Martyr-Prophet?" 37–47.

Sanders's book on Jesus[127] marks a watershed: few have been able to get to the heart of the issues, none has had the impact at the methodological level,[128] and few have reshaped questions as he has. Sanders thinks the Jesus of many Christian interpretations is "weird"[129] but that a more rigorous historical method yields very little confirmation of tradition: Jesus did not go to Jerusalem to die, he did not attribute salvific significance to his death (though he may well have anticipated his death), but he did think his death would not thwart the coming of the kingdom.[130] Further, Jesus may have thought he would be vindicated.[131] For our purposes, we should observe that Sanders thinks it is possible that he "died for his self-claim."[132] Little more can be known.

Jürgen Becker's book on Jesus argues, quite similarly if independently, that the knowledge of his own death did not weaken Jesus' resolve to continue working and praying for the kingdom of God.[133] And de Jonge's monograph on the origins of NT Christology concludes that is very likely Jesus saw his death in terms of the fate of the prophet and perhaps the righteous sufferer, but de Jonge has no confidence that atoning and salvific significance can be traced back to Jesus.[134] The study of David Brondos fits in this category.[135] For Brondos, whose view is a development of the classical Abelardian theory, Jesus had a ministry of *shalom* for others and, because Jesus was so faithful to that calling, he was put to death. Thus, "it is not Jesus' death *per se* that is salvific, but his *faithfulness unto death*" and therefore "the New Testament affirmations regarding the saving significance of the cross take on a different meaning."[136] The faithfulness of Jesus becomes efficacious as a result of the resurrection. Thus, "God did not send his Son in order for him to *die*, . . . but to serve as his instrument for establishing

---

[127] E.P. Sanders, *Jesus and Judaism* (Philadelphia: Fortress, 1985).

[128] Excepting perhaps R. Bultmann, especially as mediated through the criteria set out by Norman Perrin. See Perrin, *Rediscovering the Teaching of Jesus* (New York: Harper & Row, 1967), 15–53. Though his method is finely nuanced and more consistent, the work of J.P. Meier continues that line of thinking: see his *A Marginal Jew: Rethinking the Historical Jesus* (3 vols.; ABRL; New York: Doubleday, 1991), 1:167–95. Sanders, on the other hand, propounds a theory of historiography less parochial to Jesus scholarship, operating as he does on the basis of actions, intentions, historico-contextual fit, and rock-solid commonsense; cf. his *Jesus and Judaism*, 1–58. If, at times, Sanders barely extends the New Quest criteria approach, his fundamental proposal has transformed Jesus studies. See ch.1, "The Issue of Historical Judgment."

[129] Sanders, *Jesus and Judaism*, 333; see also Cadoux, *Historic Mission of Jesus*, 250–51. Cadoux thought, in Abelardian fashion, Jesus gave his life to shame others (Israel) into repentance; cf. pp. 262–65.

[130] Sanders, *Jesus and Judaism*, 324.

[131] Ibid., 332.

[132] Ibid., 333.

[133] J. Becker, *Jesus of Nazareth* (trans. J.E. Couch; New York: Walter de Gruyter, 1998), 327–42.

[134] De Jonge, *God's Final Envoy*, 12–33; see also Luz, "Warum zog Jesus nach Jerusalem?" in *Der historische Jesus* (ed. Schröter and Brucker; Berlin: Walter de Gruyter, 2002), 409–27.

[135] Brondos, "Why Was Jesus Crucified?"

[136] Ibid., 496.

the promised reign of *shalom* and justice; his commitment to this task led to his death . . . but it was the fulfillment of that task rather than the death resulting from it which constituted his objective."[137]

For each of these scholars, all we have is a martyr for one's beliefs—someone who died for what he believed, whether intentionally or not. But, that death was not given by Jesus an atoning sense.[138]

GENERAL OBSERVATION: GEOGRAPHICAL BLINDERS

First, my reading of scholarship reveals a disappointing parochialism. North American scholarship, especially in its more recent skeptical orientation, has almost completely avoided the discussion of Jesus' understanding of his death. I have mentioned some exceptions, the most recent of which is Koenig. UK scholarship has tended to focus on Jesus as a representative of a figure in Israel's scriptures, or even of Israel itself, in both his ministry and his death (and here I think of Dodd, both Mansons, Caird, and Wright). German scholarship, in part because of the heavy influence of Jeremias, who was himself responding to Bultmann, has led the fleet across the broad-backed sea in considering the atoning significance of Messiah and Servant.[139] No one has devoted as much attention to this subject of Jesus' death as has Schürmann, but one should not forget the contributions of Gnilka, Pesch, Goppelt, Hengel, and Stuhlmacher. Further, the tradition-critical conservative conclusions of Gnilka on the last supper, in which he affirms an atonement theology on the part of Jesus, should not be ignored in this setting. It ought to be noted, however, that Bultmann and friends unanimously concluded that Jesus did not attribute special meaning to his death, though they are just as clear that he was killed for his message of calling Judaism to authenticity by decision.[140]

Perhaps American scholarship's tendency to search for its own identity since the days of European dialectical theology has led its academy to fashion its own approach to questions about Jesus. At any rate, Jesus' perception of his death is worthy of renewed consideration, and it would be nice to see more North Americans read the most recent form of the *Tübingenschule*. (I add that it is no longer true to say that graduates of and professors at American universities are reading and interacting with even the seminal studies of German scholars. This

---

[137] Ibid., 499.

[138] One could place B.D. Chilton here as well: cf. his *Rabbi Jesus: An Intimate Biography* (New York: Doubleday, 2000). An older view, though focusing on but one logion (Mark 10:38-39) with considerable finesse, is that of V. Howard, "Did Jesus Speak about His Own Death?" *CBQ* 39 (1977): 515–27.

[139] Cf. R. Bieringer, "Traditionsgeschichtlicher Ursprung und theologische Bedeutung der UPER-Aussagen im Neuen Testament," in *The Four Gospels 1992* (ed. F. Van Segbroeck, et al.; BETL 100; Leuven: University Press, 1992), 1:219–48.

[140] See here Horsley, "Death of Jesus," in *Studying the Historical Jesus* (ed. Chilton and Evans), 399–401.

blindness to international discussion works, as it does, both ways, but not to the benefit of scholarship.) It is not possible, of course, to read everything, but the parochialism seen in scholarship on Jesus surely makes one ask why we are not reading one another more. (I confess my own parochialism, but I have tried to read the better studies so far as possible.)

A second general comment: the five most important studies of this topic are by the earlier work of Fuller, the various contributions of Jeremias, the many essays of Schürmann, the study by Pesch, and the recent treatment by Wright. Fuller, Schürmann, and Pesch are almost totally neglected in current scholarship. Neither Sanders nor Wright cite Fuller's book (perhaps because he changed his mind?). Sanders quotes only one page of the earliest of Schürmann's books but does not interact at all with Schürmann's theses about Jesus' death;[141] he ignores Gnilka's and Pesch's essays as well as the two important 1980 studies of Stuhlmacher and Hengel. Wright does not quote Schürmann, Gnilka, or Pesch. Sanders would have made his book better by interacting with this line of scholarship more completely since he denies much of what they argue; Wright, in some ways, reveals an awareness of their ideas since he follows up the lines of all three of these German scholars. Let me add that I am not saying that these scholars did not read these studies (I don't know that); what I am saying is that their discussions could have been sharpened by interacting with them. Since each of these scholars took the time to address the issue of Jesus' perception of his death, it confounds why they have not interacted with those who have studied the issues the most.

The fundamental reason for not citing Schürmann seems clear: either it is his intense tradition criticism or the *Garstigkeit* of his German diction and neologisms. It ought to be recorded here that neither Hengel nor Stuhlmacher interact with Schürmann either. In fact, when Stuhlmacher lists scholars on his side, he fails to mention Schürmann. However, I can think of no good reason for not interacting with Gnilka or Pesch. In other words, some scholars seem to pass through these important studies on how Jesus looked at his death like the children in the fiery furnace, untouched. Not everything new is good; not everything old (two decades at that) is bad.

---

[141] Sanders, *Jesus and Judaism*, 336.

Chapter 3

Re-enter Jesus' Death

It is not yet my intention to adjudicate between these scholars, resolve all the issues, or expound a consensus on how Jesus viewed his death. The evidence and contexts for the evidence are so complex that a consensus may never be reached. However, several foundational issues need to be brought to the surface and examined more completely than was possible in chapter 2, where we surveyed the history of scholarship. In this chapter we will circle back around scholarship but attempt to show the major issues involved in coming to terms with what Jesus thought about his death.

Perhaps the most notable issue is this: traditional Christian faith, in its several manifestations, structures the gospel itself around the saving death of Jesus. Yet, almost none of the major books about Jesus since the reawakening of historical Jesus scholarship conceptualizes the mission and vision of Jesus as having anything to do with his death. Besides observing the obvious chasm between traditional faith and critical scholarship, one should ask two questions: Why have the major studies of Jesus so completely neglected the history of scholarship sketched in the previous chapter, a scholarship clearly diverse but also just as clearly concerned with how Jesus understood his own death? The more important question, lurking behind all that we shall argue, is this: Could the church have been wrong from the beginning in attributing historic, saving significance to the death of Jesus? The embedded question is this: Is it possible that the church endowed the death of Jesus with a saving significance beyond anything Jesus ever considered?

At the core also is another question: Is it possible that critical scholarship has simply lolled away from a fundamental dimension of Jesus that, long ago, was missed and somehow has not re-entered the conversation? To quote Umberto Eco once again, "The real problem of a critique of our own cultural models [that is, how Jesus saw his death] is to ask, when we see a unicorn, if by any chance it is not a rhinoceros."[1] Scholarship tends to think its own scholarship is on some dynamic and ineluctable path of progress, like a Hegelian synthesis, but such a belief assumes a map that corresponds to no known reality, though it might apply to friends who neglect most others. Two examples without footnotes: one might argue that the most likely explanation of Jesus' view of his death could be traced from the time of Bultmann's denial of Jesus' thinking in terms of atonement into the more recent scholarship of E.P. Sanders, J.D. Crossan, and P. Fredriksen, who have denied once again the historicity of such a belief on the part of Jesus. Or, as an alternative history of scholarship, one might pursue the question of Jesus' use of the Old Testament, especially as it pertains to his reuse of the Servant of Isaiah as a blueprint for his own life. Thus, one might argue that C.H. Dodd set out the positive case, which was then taken up by C.K. Barrett and M.D. Hooker. Strangely, the figure survived due to the efforts of R.T. France, D.J. Moo, M. Hengel, P. Stuhlmacher, C.A. Evans, and N.T. Wright. But, scholarship works on texts, on ideas, and on methods. The notion that it marches courageously forward, while onlookers applaud, lacks foundation in the hard world of shifting paradigms. The *only* progress of scholarship along this marching path is if one examines a specific *school* of thought. The eclectic scholar, however, will soon realize that what some take to be a unicorn of development is actually a rhinoceros of a different order, and rhinos are not so tame.

What we need to consider now are eight main lines of research, even at times reaching a near consensus—occasionally even unicorns are spotted—discovered in the last half century of discussion of how Jesus understood his death. By way of preface, I register an agreement with Barrett in his discussion of the passion predictions: "We have achieved nothing of note if we have merely abstracted from the predictions the conclusion that Jesus may have had some inkling of his fate before it overtook him."[2] Barrett added wryly the following imaginary reflection of Jesus: "It is clear that, if I [Jesus] pursue my present course, my adversaries will attempt to put me out of the way. Indeed, I fear they will succeed in doing this, and so my proclamation of the kingdom will come to an end, and we shall all be back where we were when I began my ministry."[3] Thus, on the same page he concludes: "if Jesus predicted his death (and there is no reason why he should not have done so), he also interpreted it." If we can establish *that* Jesus expected a premature death, we can justifiably ask (and expect some sort of answer to) *how* he thought of his premature death.

---

[1] Umberto Eco, *Serendipities: Language and Lunacy* (trans. W. Weaver; San Diego: Harcourt Brace 1998), 75.

[2] C.K. Barrett, *Jesus and the Gospel Tradition* (London: SPCK, 1967), 37.

[3] Ibid., 38.

THE EVIDENCE: BROADER THAN THE SCHOLARSHIP SUGGESTS

The potential evidence in the Jesus traditions about Jesus thinking of his own death is broader and deeper than one suspects by reading the literature, and so we intend here to place a good amount of it on the table to make the issue clear. At this point the evidence is merely *potential*; historical judgment must be used to determine what is *actual*. The (1) evidence needs to be set into (2) a commonsensical tradition as well as into (3) the interpretive tradition of early Christian apologetics.

One can't settle into thinking that we need only look at Mark 10:45 and then the last supper traditions, touch perhaps on the Lukan tradition in 13:31-35, discern which words—if any—are authentic, interpret and move on.[4] In fact, Jesus' anticipation of his death and, at times, interpretation of that death, is a thread woven throughout the Jesus traditions. Whether one agrees with N.T. Wright's interpretations of these bits of evidence or not, the point must be made that he can present a great number of texts, from a variety of sources and in a menagerie of forms, that speak either directly or indirectly about Jesus' perception of his own death. In what follows, the evidence is set out in the order of the classic Oxford Hypothesis, which I intend neither to prove nor to debate but instead to assume throughout.[5] I list here the traditions that must at least be considered (others could be listed), though in the following chapters not all will be examined:

THE MARKAN TRADITION

2:20:	the bridegroom being taken
8:31; 9:31:	passion predictions
10:32-34:	passion predictions
9:12:	the Son of man's suffering and rejection in the context of Elijah's restoration
9:13:	John the Baptist's death
10:38:	the cup and baptism
10:45:	the ransom saying
12:1-12:	parable of the vineyard workers
14:1-9:	anointing at Bethany

---

[4] See J. Gnilka, "Wie urteilte Jesus über seinen Tod?" in *Der Tod Jesu: Deutungen im Neuen Testament* (ed. K. Kertelge; QD 74; Freiburg: Herder, 1976), 13–50; P. Stuhlmacher, *Biblische Theologie des Neuen Testaments* (2 vols.; 2d ed.; Göttingen: Vandenhoeck & Ruprecht, 1997), 1:125–43.

[5] For bibliography and brief annotations, cf. S. McKnight, M.C. Williams, *The Synoptic Gospels* (IBR Bibliographies; Grand Rapids: Baker, 2000), 37–50. On Q, see now D.C. Allison, Jr., *The Jesus Tradition in Q* (Harrisburg: Trinity Press International, 1997); J.S. Kloppenborg Verbin, *Excavating Q* (Minneapolis: Fortress, 2000). But, no attempt will be made in this study to "layer" Q, not the least of which reasons would be that I think it too speculative.

14:21:	warning of the traitor
14:22-25:	last supper tradition
14:27-28:	smitten shepherd
14:36:	the Gethsemane cup
14:49:	the arrest is connected to a scriptural necessity
14:50:	the flight of the disciples
14:60-61, 65:	the silence of Jesus
15:3-4:	the silence of Jesus[6]
15:34:	cry of dereliction

THE Q TRADITION

11:4:	prayer to be preserved from temptation
9:58:	no place to lay one's head
11:30:	Jonah's obscure prophecy

THE LUKAN TRADITION

12:49-50:	Jesus' fire and baptism
13:31-33:	a prophet needing to die in Jerusalem
17:25:	the Son of man must first be rejected
22:35-38:	the need for a sword
23:27-31:	nursing women and the green and dry trees

THE MATTHEAN TRADITION

23:29-32:	the death of prophets
23:34-36:	sending out prophets who will be put to death
23:37-39:	the riddle about the hen and chicks
26:2:	the Son of man will be betrayed to crucifixion.

THE JOHANNINE TRADITION[7]

1:29:	Lamb of God
2:19:	destroy temple
3:14:	Son of man lifted up
8:28:	Son of man lifted up
10:15, 17-18:	laying down one's life

---

[6] E. Schnabel, "The Silence of Jesus," in *Authenticating the Words of Jesus* (ed. B. Chilton and C.A. Evans; NTTS 28.1; Leiden: E.J. Brill, 1999), 203–57, who suggests that Jesus' silence is indicative of his intention to die.

[7] See R.E. Brown, *The Death of the Messiah* (2 vols.; ABRL; New York: Doubleday, 1994), 1484–86. One thinks also of 6:51; 7:33; 12:23-24; 13:1, 36; 14:28; 16:5, 7, 10, 16-17, 28.

12:3, 7:   anointing at Lazarus' house
12:33-34:   Son of man lifted up

There is a widespread *source* and *form* attestation for Jesus having thought of his death as premature. S.H.T. Page has concluded on the basis of this kind of evidence: "the extensiveness of the sayings which refer to Christ's death, their allusive character, and the variety of forms utilized demonstrate convincingly that Jesus was aware that He would meet with a violent end."[8]

If we follow the lead of Dodd,[9] we will also consider the following logical factors that would have influenced Jesus:

(1)   Jewish traditions spoke fairly widely about the great tribulation;
(2)   Prophets suffered frequently;
(3)   Jesus' predecessor John was put to death;
(4)   Jesus warned his followers about persecution and death.

Because the evidence is so variable, any study of how Jesus thought of his death (assuming, for the argument, that he did) will be a constant balancing act of exegesis, historical judgment, and overall fit into the emerging picture one has of Jesus. Reducing the discussion to the ransom saying and the last supper is unworthy of historical integrity; and simply adding a study of some of the Son of man sayings doesn't give the full picture. Several approaches to the discussion call our attention to the need for Jesus scholarship to turn once again to the question of Jesus' view of his own death to see if it might shed light on how he understood his mission. To recall our previous discussion,[10] any study that attempts to present a singular feature about Jesus that does not absorb that feature into the overall narrative representation of Jesus fails at a basic level of historiography. Conversely, any study that fails to integrate salient singular features into the narrative (following historical judgment), as many have perhaps done with respect to Jesus' understanding of his death, also fails at the basic level of historiography.

J.B. Green is not alone in thinking that a crucified Messiah would be unthinkable, or at least "weird," in Judaism at that time.[11] If so, it would not have been 15 minutes into Easter faith before someone would have countered Christian claims with the question: "Then why crucified?"[12] Morna Hooker has participated in the discussion of Jesus and his death for more than five decades,

---

[8] S.H.T. Page, "The Authenticity of the Ransom Logion (Mark 10:45b)," in *Studies of History and Tradition in the Four Gospels* (ed. R.T. France and D. Wenham; Gospel Perspectives 1; Sheffield: JSOT, 1980), 137–61, here p. 144.

[9] C.H. Dodd, *The Parables of the Kingdom* (London: Nisbet, 1935), 57.

[10] In chapter 1, under "What is History" and "The Historical Jesus: Brief Remarks."

[11] J.B. Green, *The Death of Jesus* (WUNT 2/33; Tübingen: Mohr Siebeck, 1988), 164–69, where he replies to critics of his view.

[12] See also D.J. Juel, *Messianic Exegesis* (Philadelphia: Fortress, 1988), 89–133.

and in the fourth decade she stated: "The first task of the early Christian preachers . . . was to deal with the problem of Christ's death."[13]

The ubiquity of the evidence above, then, suggests that at least the early Christians needed an apologetic from the very beginning for Jesus' death. Following on the heels of C.H. Dodd, one of the burdens of Barnabas Lindars was to explain the New Testament's use of the OT in an apologetical framework, with cross apologetics a featured dimension.[14] In fact, Lindars finds several criticisms at work: that the Messiah dies, that the Messiah is crucified, that the Messiah was humiliated, that the Messiah was betrayed by a follower, that his disciples fled him in his gravest hour, that the Messiah's death could be redemptive, and that Messiah's memorial meal had scriptural foundation.[15] It is, therefore, plausible to think that the charge of dying on a spike as a curse from God was a Jewish response to the early Jesus movement's claims (Deut 21:23). Such a charge was then given a new spin after Christian exegesis took place: it was God's means of salvation (Gal 3:13). Did Jesus set the agenda for the texts the early Christians appealed to in their apologetic? So thought C.H. Dodd.[16]

Widespread evidence, common sense, and an early Christian apologetic each suggests that we should at least look to the evidence to see if Jesus anticipated and interpreted his own death. The evidence is complex, the arguments need to be clear and forthright, and the starting point is important, but there is sufficient evidence for scholars to consider the death of Jesus when constructing a comprehensive account of Jesus' mission.

KINGDOM AS CONTEXT FOR JESUS' DEATH

No theory of Jesus' perception of his death can endure the test of scholarship if it does not anchor death into the vast sea of kingdom and larger themes of Jesus' mission, including his warning of judgment if Israel does not repent.[17] I have sketched this view of Jesus' ministry in another context and will allow that statement to sustain this point, but the issue is important. Jesus died in the context of a mission to establish the kingdom of God, to restore Israel.[18] For instance,

---

[13] M. Hooker, *Not Ashamed of the Gospel* (Carlisle, UK: Paternoster), 12 (italics mine). W. Manson, *Jesus the Messiah* (London: Hodder & Stoughton, 1943): "From saying that Jesus was the Messiah despite the event of the cross they came to say that he was the Messiah in virtue of that event" (169).

[14] B. Lindars, *New Testament Apologetic* (London: SCM, 1961).

[15] Ibid., 75–137.

[16] C.H. Dodd, *According to the Scriptures* (London: Nisbet, 1952), 109–10.

[17] So J. Schlosser, *Jésus de Nazareth* (2d ed.; Paris: Agnès Viénot, 2002), 299–301; M. Reiser, *Jesus and Judgment* (trans. L.M. Maloney; Minneapolis: Fortress, 1997), 313; C. Riniker, "Jesus als Gerichtsprediger?," *ZNT* 5 (2002): 2–14.

[18] S. McKnight, *A New Vision for Israel* (Grand Rapids: Eerdmans, 1999), with bibliography. Of the immense bibliography on kingdom, I mention only the following three items: H. Schürmann, "Das Zeugnis der Redenquelle für die Basileia-Verkündigung Jesu," in *Logia* (BETL 59; Leuven:

scholars are aware that death and kingdom rarely converge in the Jesus tradition, but two traditions should come to mind and gain a fair hearing: Mark 14:25, which has at least three variants in its tradition (Mark 14:25, 1 Cor 11:25 ["as often as you eat, you proclaim the Lord's death until he comes"], and Didache 10:6 ["Maranatha! Our Lord come!"]); and the enigmatic isolated logion at Luke 22:28-30, which states "You are those who have continued with me in my trials; as my Father appointed a kingdom for me, so do I appoint for you that you may eat. . . ." While there may be some problems for these traditions when it comes to matters of authenticity, many have found them worthy of the bedrock tradition about Jesus. If so, their interpretation is not quickly attached to early Christian atonement theology, but instead plays a slightly different language game. And one should consider Matthew 11:12-13 in this context, for opposition and kingdom are interrelated.

In the words of Jürgen Becker: "Since all of Jesus' activity was dedicated to the Kingdom of God, it would make sense that he saw his anticipated death as having some relation to that kingdom."[19] This, of course, was an important foundation of Schweitzer's own perception of how Jesus saw his death, and it is best accessed in his earliest work, *The Mystery of the Kingdom of God: The Secret of Jesus' Messiahship and Passion*. Recently, Craig Evans has successfully made the same connection to kingdom.[20] So, too, has Raymund Schwager who argues, correctly I think, that if Jesus' entire mission is about the kingdom, then his actions as well as words are kingdom actions.[21]

But once again, the study that relates kingdom to Jesus' view of his own death most directly is that of Schürmann, whose most recent recensions of his studies reveal two separate essays on Jesus' death and the kingdom. In the first, he addresses issues like the "lack of success" (*Erfolgslosigkeit*), the danger of Jesus' life, and martyrdom. In the second, he devotes an entire essay to integrating the two themes of kingdom and death.[22] Not to be forgotten here are the works of W. Manson, R. Otto, and the earlier R.H. Fuller, who each argued that Jesus thought he would inaugurate the kingdom precisely through his death.[23]

Leuven University Press, 1982), 121–200; E.P. Sanders, "Jesus and the Kingdom," in *Jesus, the Gospels and the Church* (ed. E.P. Sanders; Macon, Ga.: Mercer University Press, 1987), 225–39; J.D.G. Dunn, *Jesus Remembered* (vol. 1 of *Christianity in the Making*; Grand Rapids: Eerdmans, 2003), 383–487.

[19] J. Becker, *Jesus of Nazareth* (trans. J.E. Couch; New York: Walter de Gruyter, 1998), 341; see also H. Merklein, "Der Tod Jesu als stellvertretender Sühnetod," in *Studien zu Jesus und Paulus* (WUNT 43; Tübingen: Mohr Siebeck, 1987), 181–91, here pp. 184–85.

[20] C. Evans, "From Public Ministry to the Passion," in his *Jesus and His Contemporaries* (AGJU 25; Leiden: E.J. Brill, 1995), 301–80.

[21] See R. Schwager, *Jesus in the Drama of Salvation* (trans. J.G. Williams and P. Haddon; New York: Herder & Herder, 1999), 82-118.

[22] H. Schürmann, *Jesus—Gestalt und Geheimnis* (ed. K. Scholtissek; Paderborn: Bonifatius, 1994), 157–67, 168–85.

[23] See W. Manson, *Christ's View of the Kingdom of God* (intro. H.R. Mackintosh; Bruce Lectures; London: James Clarke, 1918), 140–44; R. Otto, *The Kingdom of God and the Son of Man* (trans.

Unfortunately, neither Hengel nor Stuhlmacher integrate the two themes, though Stuhlmacher does hint at such in his essay on why Jesus died.[24]

Also on a more positive side, I think here of how Allison, Meyer, and Wright, and Schweitzer before them, have integrated the theme of the final tribulation in the teachings of Jesus as that which shapes his expectation of death, though Allison mutes this theme slightly in his Jesus book as a hermeneutical grid through which to read Jesus' mission and intention.[25] To be sure, the interpretations of these scholars differ, but their approaches are fundamental to a basic solution: integration of major themes from both Judaism and Jesus into how a death might be construed. It should be remembered that Schweitzer thought Jesus had the passion in mind in his entire ministry, a passion understood as suffering preceding glory.[26]

The consequence of these three recent studies, in each case, is a perception of Jesus' death somewhat at variance with the earliest Christian presentation of Jesus' death as vicarious atonement, expiating sacrifice, or propitiation. If Jesus' death is understood as martyrdom, or as assumption of the tribulation prior to vindication, or as new exodus, while we may have some dimensions for a continuity to the early Christian kerygma, more substantially we have less continuity between the death of Jesus as he construed it and as it was later construed by Christian interpretation. In fact, we have factors that meet the criterion of dissimilarity head-to-head. This issue will be explored later.

Before moving on to a third dimension of recent scholarship, we should record the insight of Vögtle's seminal essay.[27] Vögtle argued that at whatever time or date a scholar believes that Jesus thought his death was certain, and an integral part of his kingdom mission, then from that time on that death has to be seen as fundamental to that mission. Jesus' death then needs to be related not only to the larger themes of his mission, but also to the broad sweep of his life—so far as we can reconstruct it. Vögtle thus puts full weight on the *Todesankündigungen* of Jesus.

JESUS' DEATH AND THE LAST WEEK

Others place significant weight on the connection between Jesus' death and the events of the last week, from his temple demonstration to the last supper, as one

---

F.V. Filson and B.L. Woolf; London: Lutterworth, 1938); R.H. Fuller, *The Mission and Achievement of Jesus* (SBT 12; London: SCM, 1954).

[24] P. Stuhlmacher, "Why Did Jesus Have to Die?" in *Jesus of Nazareth—Christ of Faith* (trans. S.S. Schatzmann; Peabody, Mass.: Hendrickson, 1993), 39–57; here pp. 47–49.

[25] D.C. Allison, Jr., *Jesus of Nazareth* (Minneapolis: Fortress, 1998).

[26] A. Schweitzer, *The Mystery of the Kingdom of God* (trans. W. Lowrie; 1901; repr. New York: Schocken, 1964), 223.

[27] A. Vögtle, "Todesankündigungen und Todesverständnis Jesu," in *Der Tod Jesu* (ed. Kertelge), 51–113, here pp. 56–57.

continuous action—a series of dots intentionally connected by Jesus. That the temple incident and the death of Jesus are connected unites scholarship from Jeremias to Sanders.[28] Leander Keck makes this connection poetically: the Galilean Jesus who was "God's finger" becomes in Jerusalem "God's fist."[29] A study important here is the recent biography of Jesus by Chilton, the fecundity of whose pen is no less surprising than its variety.[30] The temple demonstration is understood by Chilton, distinct among a chorus of singers of other parts, as an occupation—or, better yet, as a temporary occupation. More importantly, Chilton connects the temple to the last supper tradition,[31] where Jesus explains that his meal is a substitute for the inadequate sacrifices being offered in the temple by the corrupt leaders now reigning. In his words: "In the absence of a Temple that permitted his view of purity to be practiced, Jesus proclaimed wine his blood and bread his flesh of sacrifice."[32] That this line of thought is developed in Hebrews is well known; that it had its origins in Jesus is a new part in the song led by Chilton.[33]

If Sanders and Fredriksen minimize the connection of temple incident and last supper, both Chilton, who may be following up a suggestion of Jacob Neusner[34] and N.T. Wright[35] maximize it: temple action and last supper belong together. A uniform line of thought directs the actions of both, and one needs to connect the two dots to see what is going on. Israel's temple is in need of reform, but the last meal of Jesus is to replace or substitute for that temple's activities. To be sure, each understands the meal in different categories (Chilton more generally as a replacement of sacrifice; Wright as a new exodus with soteriological overtones), but each connects the events and in so doing sheds light on how Jesus (ostensively) saw his own death. Peter Stuhlmacher thinks Jesus "himself triggers the final mortal conflict in Jerusalem via the act of the temple cleansing."[36] Confirming a connection to temple, Martin Hengel thinks the

---

[28] J. Jeremias, *New Testament Theology* (trans. J. Bowden; New York: Scribner, 1971), 279; E.P. Sanders, *Jesus and Judaism* (Philadelphia: Fortress, 1985).

[29] L. Keck, *Who is Jesus?* (Columbia: University of South Carolina Press, 2000), 121.

[30] B.D. Chilton, *Rabbi Jesus* (New York: Doubleday, 2000); see also his *The Temple of Jesus* (University Park: The Pennsylvania State University Press, 1992), 137–54.

[31] Chilton has a complex, and speculative, theory on the origins of the last supper, but he also sees its origins beginning prior to the last week of Jesus: on this, cf. his *A Feast of Meanings* (NovTSup 72; Leiden: E.J. Brill, 1994); *Rabbi Jesus*, 248–59.

[32] Chilton, *Rabbi Jesus*, 255; Chilton contends that Jesus believed in the Zecharian vision of a pure temple (Zech 14) that would be eschatologically realized when the offerings of *Sukkoth* were presented by both Jews and non-Jews in the temple.

[33] The study of Baruch Bokser on the Seder in later Jewish tradition proposes an analogous point: the *Pesah* meal becomes the *Pesah* offering, and the community at the meal becomes the temple. See his *The Origins of the Seder* (Berkeley: University of California Press, 1984).

[34] J. Neusner, "Money-Changers in the Temple," *NTS* 35 (1989): 287–90.

[35] N.T. Wright, *Jesus and the Victory of God* (Christian Origins and the Question of God 2; Minneapolis: Fortress, 1996), 557–58.

[36] Stuhlmacher, "Why Did Jesus Have to Die?" 53.

early Hellenists' displeasure with the temple and sacrifice reveals that at the foundation of the Christian movement's memorial of Jesus' last supper must be something about sacrifice.[37] Daniel J. Antwi insightfully explores the temple incident, not in light of what followed, but in light of what preceded it: Jesus' attitude toward the temple as well as his claims to forgive.[38] It must be added, at this point, that some scholars today contest the historicity of the temple incident and so dissolve the "connect the dots" game some scholars are playing.[39]

The connection many Jesus scholars are making today between the temple incident and the last supper, or at least between the temple incident and Jesus' death, forces the question of Jesus' intention: did he storm the temple to make a statement about his mission? And, if so, what likelihood is there that Jesus thought he would survive the incident? And, if he divined a probable death, is it not at least a possibility worth considering that Jesus saw his death as part of his mission? Why, if he didn't see value in a mission that could lead to death, would he have acted as he did in the temple? Or, as Craig Evans has recently concluded, perhaps it is only after the temple incident—that is after Mark 11–12—that Jesus began to speak of his death.[40] This set of questions is being asked in modern scholarship, though very little of its answer shows up, in books related to Jesus, in the discussion of the overall purpose of Jesus' mission.

EXPLORING SCRIPTURAL PRECEDENTS: JESUS AS "SCRIPTURE PROPHET"

Discovering the scrolls at the Dead Sea confronted biblical scholars with a live, imaginative, and socially determinative exegesis of the Tanakh, and led many scholars to a fresh appraisal not only of how the various exegetes of that community used the Scriptures, but also to how the same Scriptures were used within the Tanakh and New Testament.[41] Scholars today are scrambling over one another to see who can find the most plausible figure or motif that best sets Jesus' perception of his death in context.

The issue of Jesus' uses of Scripture to explain his own death is more complex than traditional scholarship permits. We should face this central question head-on: How was it even possible for a Jew who believed in God's sovereign

---

[37] M. Hengel, *The Atonement* (trans. J. Bowden; Philadelphia: Fortress, 1981), 55–75.

[38] D.J. Antwi, "Did Jesus Consider His Death to be an Atoning Sacrifice?," *Int* 45 (1991): 17–28, here p. 27.

[39] D. Seeley, for instance, concludes that the temple incident is a Markan creation; cf. his "Jesus' Temple Act," *CBQ* 55 (1993): 263–83. One who thinks the event is historical is C.A. Evans, "Jesus' Action in the Temple and Corruption in the First-Century Temple" and "Jesus and the 'Cave of Robbers'," in *Jesus and His Contemporaries* (AGJU 25; Leiden: E.J. Brill, 1995), 319–44, 345–65.

[40] C.A. Evans, "Did Jesus Predict his Death and His Resurrection?" in *Resurrection* (ed. S.E. Porter, M.A. Hayes, and D. Tombs; JSNTSup 186; Roehampton Institute London Papers 5; Sheffield: Sheffield Academic, 1999), 86–91.

[41] See below, chs. 8–10.

and providential care, who surely believed that God had accomplished forgiveness through the sacrificial system of the temple—especially on Yom Kippur, and who preached the arrival of the long-expected kingdom that was interrelated to these themes about God and forgiveness—how was it even possible, we must ask, for such a person suddenly to think his death was the sacrifice of all sacrifices, the end of the temple system, and a sure atonement for all people? While some have answered this question in the negative, others have found clues to Jesus' perception of his death in the Tanakh. And that scholarship has taken several tacks into this oceanic question. But a warning, in neon, of Dodd should be kept before us at all times when examining Old Testament background for Jesus. We need to discern "where associations of ideas in the critic's own mind have been treated as evidence for original connections."[42]

The bewildering variety of those connections, with their fecund interpretive possibilities for understanding what Jesus was all about, ought to lead us to greater clarity and care at the methodological level, and the most recent insight at this level is from the pen of Dale Allison, in his short, but definitive discussion of the principles that need to be consulted when detecting allusions.[43] He finds five indices indicating the use of an intertext by the text under study:

first, one should begin by consulting the history of interpretation;
second, the text and its intertext should share vocabulary, word order, themes, imagery, structure, and/or circumstances;
third, the commonalities between text and intertext ought not to be commonplaces;
fourth, the intertext or its themes ought to be prominent in the specific author;
fifth, the intertext's allusion ought to enhance meaning congruent with the text's themes.

Now to the variety of scriptural contexts to which Jesus may have appealed in order to understand this death. From Schweitzer to Allison and Wright, scholars have appealed to the great tribulation as a penetrating insight into how Jesus understood his impending death.[44] The older scholars, like Dodd and T.W. Manson, wanted to anchor Jesus' mission and perception of his death in the Servant Songs of Isaiah, and their statements remain persuasive to many.[45] Following this traditional argument with added nuance, Stuhlmacher contends that both Isaiah 43:3-4 and 52:13–53:12, in combination with Daniel 7:9-14,

---

[42] Dodd, *According to the Scriptures*, 28.

[43] D.C. Allison, Jr., *The Intertextual Jesus: Scripture in Q* (Harrisburg: Trinity Press International, 2000), 9–13.

[44] A. Schweitzer, *The Mystery of the Kingdom of God*, 315–54; D.C. Allison, Jr., *The End of the Ages Has Come* (Philadelphia: Fortress, 1985), 115–41; Wright, *Jesus and the Victory of God*, 576–92.

[45] Dodd, *According to the Scriptures,* 92–96, 107–10; T.W. Manson, *The Servant-Messiah* (Cambridge: Cambridge University Press, 1953).

are behind the mission of Jesus.[46] Standing on these shoulders but looking in a
slightly different direction is Martin Hengel, who traces atonement theology
more to Graeco-Roman sources which made their impact through a more hell-
enized Judaism after Alexander the Great.[47] Chilton turns to a completely different set of texts, and finds Zechariah 14's vision of purity shaping the mission
and vision of Jesus, especially his temple occupation.[48]

N.T. Wright, speaking for many, contends for a multiphasic scriptural background to Jesus' perception of his death, and, as he is prone to do, discusses his
options at length: Daniel, the Psalter, Zechariah, Ezekiel, and especially Isaiah.[49]
Allison, also along with others, thinks the death of Jesus needs to be connected
with the Son of man.[50] A most recent and innovative suggestion by John Koenig
is that Jesus' last supper intentionally draws together the threads of vine and
kingdom from Genesis 49:8-12.[51] An influential study of H. Gese explores the
Jewish *Todah* meal ("thank offering") as the initial context for understanding
Jesus' death and resurrection.[52] Adding to this variety of suggestions, we include
the death of prophets, the image of the righteous sufferer, as well as the Jewish
martyrs as manifested in the Maccabean traditions (1 Macc 2:50; 2 Macc 7:37-
38; 4 Macc 1:11; 6:27-29; 9:23-24; 17:21-22; 18:4).[53] Some refer to specific
texts in Jewish literature (e.g., Sir 29:15; *T. Benj* 3:8), but especially to the targum to Isaiah.[54]

But, of late, attention has shifted programmatically to the Dead Sea Scrolls.
I shall mention here the important study of Michael O. Wise, a book that has

---

[46] Stuhlmacher, "Vicariously Giving His Life for Many, Mark 10:45 (Matt. 20:28)," in his
Reconciliation, Law, and Righteousness (Philadelphia: Fortress, 1986), 16–29.

[47] Hengel, *The Atonement*, 33–75, with nn. On a more particular note, Martin Hengel has recently
argued that we find potential evidence for a pre-Christian interpretation of suffering as atoning in
such texts as Daniel 11–12, the Aramaic *T. Levi*, and also in 4Q540/541 [=4QahA]. See his "Zur
Wirkungsgeschichte von Jes 53 in vorchristlicher Zeit," in *Der leidende Gottesknecht* (ed. B.
Janowski and P. Stuhlmacher; FAT 14; Tübingen: Mohr Siebeck, 1996), 49–91.

[48] B.D. Chilton, *Temple of Jesus* (University Park: The Pennsylvania State University Press, 1992),
113–59.

[49] Wright, *Jesus and the Victory of God*, 540–611.

[50] Allison, *The End of the Ages Has Come*, 128–37.

[51] J. Koenig, *The Feast of the World's Redemption* (Harrisburg: Trinity Press International, 2000),
26–28.

[52] H. Gese, *Essays on Biblical Theology* (trans. K. Crim; Minneapolis: Augsburg, 1981), 117–40.

[53] On this, cf. esp. C.A. Evans, "From Anointed Prophet to Anointed King," in his *Jesus and His
Contemporaries* (AGJU 25; Leiden: E.J. Brill, 1995), 437–56.

[54] It should perhaps be noted here that German scholarship sharply divides on whether atonement
theology first emerges from Palestinian Judaism, and later from Palestinian Jewish Christianity, or
from Hellenistic Judaism, and later from the Hellenistic churches. The first was argued by
Lohmeyer, and the second by Wengst. Wengst has been followed in the important monograph of
Hengel, and the important essay of Merklein. See E. Lohmeyer, *Märtyrer und Gottesknecht*
(FRLANT 64; Göttingen: Vandenhoeck & Ruprecht, 1964); K. Wengst, *Christologische Formeln
und Lieder des Urchristentums* (SNT 7; Gütersloh: Gerd Mohn, 1972); Hengel, *The Atonement*; H.
Merklein, "Der Tod Jesu als stellvertretender Sühnetod."

the rare combination of readability and technical expertise, the latter mostly wrapped snuggly into the endnotes.[55] Wise sees the messianic figure in the DSS to be a prototype for Jesus, as the community itself is "proto-Christianity."[56]

Wise names the messianic figure at Qumran "Judah"; he was the first to see himself as a hidden Messiah, and Wise thinks he can recover significant bits of Judah's biography, especially through the *Thanksgiving Hymns*. Wise thinks he can see Judah anticipating suffering, and that violent men (1QH X), in particular Hyrcanus II, were seeking his life because of his beliefs about the temple and its Pharisaic leadership (esp. Shimeon ben Shetah). These complaints of his were written up as they were in a protest form now found in 4QMMT. Judah was put on trial as a false prophet and exiled; shortly thereafter he died a violent death, "smitten by the sword" (in 72 BCE). But this Judah also believed that he was to fulfill the role of Isaiah's Suffering Servant (1QH VIII–IX) and that it was he, not the Pharisees, who was faithful to God's covenant. God rewards him, so his followers believe, with glory at the right hand of God (XXVI, 2–10). Wise sees no place where the death of Judah was understood as an atonement, but Judah did anticipate his own vindication (1QH XV). In a private letter, Wise told me that he thinks it is only a possibility that Judah, since he considered himself the servant, could have thought in terms of "redemptive suffering." It is unclear what Judah thought of atonement since he did not exegete such Scriptures of himself. In fact, Judah's perception of death, or at least that of his followers, was much along the lines of Mark 14:25: death would not thwart the divine plan.

Wise's book, of course, is an experiment and, because it is the first such full-scale, critical experiment, it will be examined, twisted, and squeezed. Whether Qumran scholars agree with his portrait of the figure behind the *Thanksgiving Hymns* or not, his proposal that Jesus fits into a Jewish model of a scripture prophet confirms the flow of so much scholarship as the context of Jesus' vision: at the heart of Jesus was reflection on Scripture, and he directed his followers to certain portions of Scripture.

SELF-IDENTITY SHAPES DEATH

A point of near consensus is that Jesus' death emerges from his self-identity or, in the words of E.P. Sanders, his "self-claim."[57] For most scholars Jesus' death was not an accident, and he was not stunned by the actions of the establishment in the final week. This is what disappoints so much in Paula Fredriksen's study

[55] M.O. Wise, *The First Messiah* (San Francisco: HarperSanFrancisco, 1999).

[56] Wise, *First Messiah*, 256. Though Israel Knohl has also recently published a book with a similar purpose and an identical title, I find his theory too speculative to be discussed in this brief survey; see his *The Messiah Before Jesus* (trans. D. Maisel; Berkeley: University of California Press, 2000). One wonders if the piano is not playing the pianist in Knohl.

[57] Sanders, *Jesus and Judaism*, 333. Sanders thinks the assertion that Jesus died for his self-claim is "true in part."

of why Jesus died; she does not consider the pervasiveness of scholarship's conviction that Jesus' death and his self-claim were somehow connected.[58] Some think Jesus brought this all on himself intentionally[59] and went to Jerusalem with the *specific intention to die*—Dodd once said Jesus "was putting his head into the lion's mouth."[60] While few historical Jesus scholars agree with J.C. O'Neill in his attempt to prove that Jesus "went to his death as the eternal Son of God offering himself as a sacrifice for the sins of the world,"[61] more think it is likely that he went to Jerusalem to worship and to celebrate Passover as a good Jew but that his past mission and actions forced the issue of his status to the fore.[62] He was prepared for such trouble but did not go to Jerusalem to provoke it so he could die.

Not a few think that Jesus had tossed his hat over the wall and knew that he was now obligated to climb that wall to follow the path. In fact, many do think Jesus went to Jerusalem to provoke a national response. For instance, Martin Dibelius once made this claim:

> All this [his demand to be heard in Jerusalem] may be concluded from the fact that Jesus took his followers with him to Jerusalem. It is the one and only indication known to us of a development in the history of Jesus. The movement that Jesus set going in Galilee was transferred by this change of scene to the religious center of the country. Thereby, so it appears, it was brought to the bar of decision.[63]

Several studies, some of a general nature and others with a specific label, deserve to be mentioned. Perhaps one of the earliest studies to argue for a chain of links from the early Christian atonement theology back to Jesus was Joachim Gnilka's essay which, though exceedingly cautious in historical conclusion, finds the very shape of Jesus' life to lead to an interpretation of his death as saving.[64] This notion was developed with a bolder link four years later in a way only Germans (plying their neologisms) can do: L. Oberlinner[65] developed a line of thought found in Vögtle[66] that Jesus had a *Todeserwartung* but perhaps not a

[58] P. Fredriksen, *Jesus of Nazareth, King of the Jews* (New York: Knopf, 1999).

[59] A. Schweitzer, *The Quest of the Historical Jesus* (ed. John Bowden; trans. W. Montgomery, et al.; foreword by D. Nineham; Minneapolis: Fortress, 2001), 349.

[60] C.H. Dood, *The Founder of Christianity* (London: Collins, 1971), 94.

[61] J.C. O'Neill, *Who Did Jesus Think He Was?* (BibInt 11; Leiden: E.J. Brill, 1995), 135.

[62] E.g., C.F.D. Moule, *The Origin of Christology* (Cambridge: Cambridge University Press, 1977), 109–11.

[63] M. Dibelius, *Jesus* (trans. C.B. Hedrick and F.C. Grant; Philadelphia: Westminster, 1949), 63. See also G. Bornkamm, *Jesus von Nazareth* (12th German ed.; Stuttgart: W. Kohlhammer, 1980), 137–39.

[64] Gnilka, "Wie urteilte Jesus über seinen Tod?"

[65] L. Oberlinner, *Todeserwartung und Todesgewissheit Jesu* (SBB 10; Stuttgart: KBW, 1980).

[66] Vögtle, "Todesankündigungen und Todesverständnis Jesu," 53–58, where he distinguishes between *Todesbereitschaft* and *Todesgewissheit* ["readiness for death," "certainty of death"]); Jesus had a *Todeserwartung* ["expectation of death"] but perhaps not a *Todesgewissheit*.

Todesgewissheit.[67] Either way, Jesus' view would have emerged from conviction about who he was and why he was sent.[68] Some have sought to trace the death of Jesus back to his message.[69]

An important study along this line that avoids some of this "to die or not to die" pluckiness is by Kim Huat Tan, *The Zion Traditions and the Aims of Jesus.*[70] To refocus the question about Jesus' intention, Kim contends that the Zion traditions provide a scheme that explains Jesus' intention and actions in the last week. Zion traditions can be found in Jesus' entry, the temple incident, and his last supper. Earlier in his study, Kim had argued that Luke 13:31-33 and 34-35 reveal that Jesus saw Jerusalem as the locus of his mission's goal and his death. In seeing Jerusalem as the focus of his mission, Jesus simultaneously expresses his sentiments about Jewish leadership and expects that God will assert his kingship in Jerusalem. This puts a new color in an old garment: yes, Jesus did go to Jerusalem for the express purpose of carrying out his mission in and for Jerusalem's restoration. In this sense, Kim diverges from Schweitzer (Jesus went to die) and converges with Chilton (Jesus went to accomplish something major for the nation). The death of Jesus becomes what happens to Jesus for pursuing his mission. Apart from specifics, this is as close to a consensus as we have in Jesus studies on Jesus' view of his death.

Put differently, Jesus' idea of self: he thought he was a prophet from God, or the Messiah, or the final agent of God—depending on one's view of Jesus' self-claim—and who he thought he was led to what he did. And what he did got him in trouble in Jerusalem. So it can be said that his *identity* and his *death* are connected. But the consensus ends right there: Sanders wants no more than a minimal statement (Jesus' death is related to his self-claim) while others want a more developed sense. In general terms, then, I think most would have to agree with Borg's viewpoint, if not his words: "He [Jesus] was killed because he sought, in the name and power of the Spirit, the transformation of his own culture."[71] Others find a more specific identity of Jesus that is connected to his death.

Recently, German scholars, especially those at Tübingen, have shoved the *messianic identity* and self-consciousness of Jesus onto front stage for all to see, and then have asked if the death of Jesus and his messianic identity are to be welded. The most important collection of essays in this regard can be found in the 1993 edition of *Jahrbuch für Biblische Theologie*, in which there are notable essays by K. Koch on the Son of man and Messiah in apocalyptic literature; O.

---

[67] That is, an expectation but not certainty of his death.

[68] On which, cf. the observations of Brown, *The Death of the Messiah*, 1488–1489.

[69] For example, Evans details in an essay the link between message and death that "kingdom of God" can sustain ("From Public Ministry," 301–18).

[70] Kim Huat Tan, *The Zion Traditions and the Aims of Jesus* (SNTSMS 91; Cambridge: Cambridge University Press, 1997).

[71] M. Borg, *Jesus, A New Vision* (San Francisco: Harper & Row, 1988), 183.

Hofius on how Jesus does and does not correspond to the Messiah as the eschatological king of Israel and how an entirely new concept of Messiah is fashioned by Jesus; P. Stuhlmacher on Jesus embracing self-consciously the mission to be the messianic servant; and D. Zeller on Paul's use of the title Messiah.[72] It is noticeable that Stuhlmacher's essay is entitled "Der messianische Gottesknecht" ("the messianic servant of God"), not the "Der gottesknechtliche Messias" ("the servant-of-God Messiah"). The messianic identity of Jesus is subsumed under his role as servant; as servant he offers himself as an atonement. Again, self-claim/identity and death coalesce to understand who Jesus was and what his mission was all about.[73]

However, messianism is not the only angle scholars have taken as they approach the identity and self-claim of Jesus. The classic appeal to Jesus as servant remains a viable option for many. But, the majority of scholars are more content to speak of some general orientation of Jesus' life that led to his death. Thus, Heinz Schürmann saw this all under the rubric of Jesus' *Proexistenz*.[74] N.T. Wright expresses the same theme as Jesus enacting his own *kingdom story* and argues that Jesus had to bring his "act" to Zion.[75] B.F. Meyer notes, rather abstractly: "The national restoration that Jesus proposed he first of all incarnated in himself. His was a selfhood independent of routine," and we should consider "his mission in terms of *realized personal authenticity*."[76] In fact, J.P. Galvin, in his lucid survey of both German exegetes and systematicians, concludes that the very life and death of Jesus betray a kind of soteriology: a freely accepted consequence of the kind of life he lived.[77] Most recently, Leander Keck, who evidently has some ambrosia in his pen, argues: "He went [up to Jerusalem] to do what

---

[72] Titles in *Jahrbuch für Biblische Theologie* 8 (ed. Ingo Baldermann, et al., 1993) are: K. Koch, "Der Messias und Menschensohn" (73–102); O. Hofius, "Ist Jesus der Messias?" (103–29); D. Zeller, "Zur Transformation des Χριστός bei Paulus " (155–67); P. Stuhlmacher, "Der messianische Gottesknecht" (131–54).

[73] An American conference in 1987 led by James H. Charlesworth devoted itself to the same set of questions about Jewish messianism. See his *The Messiah* (Princeton Symposium on Judaism and Christian Origins; Minneapolis: Fortress, 1992). Separate essays are found on messianic ideas in the Hebrew Scriptures, in early Judaism and rabbinics, in social contexts and Philo; and then nine essays address the evidence regarding Jesus and the beliefs of the early Christians. Of particular importance for our question here is the essay by James D.G. Dunn on the historical Jesus. This study by Dunn, when compared to those by Stuhlmacher and Hofius, dovetails into a sharply focused angle: Jesus was as much a shaper of, as one shaped by, Jewish messianism. Dunn states it most memorably when he says that Jesus was "in no sense a tailor's dummy draped convincingly or otherwise in the robes of Jewish messianic hope" ("Messianic Ideas and Their Influence on the Jesus of History," in *The Messiah* [ed. Charlesworth, et al.], 381).

[74] Schürmann, *Jesus—Gestalt und Geheimnis*, 219; see also J. Roloff, "Anfänge der soteriologischen Deutung des Todes Jesu (MK. X. 45 und LK. XXII. 27)," *NTS* 19 (1972–1973): 62–64.

[75] Wright, *Jesus and the Victory of God*, 564–65.

[76] B.F. Meyer, *Christus Faber* (Allison Park: Pickwick, 1992), 123, 122.

[77] J.P. Galvin, "Jesus' Approach to Death," *TS* 41 (1980): 713–44, here p. 743.

he had always done: embody what he knew was coming. In the temple he took the risk of symbolizing it."[78]

If the debate continues, at least it will follow the path set by establishing Jesus' identity. The fundamental question becomes: would someone with Jesus' self-claim, vision, and mission attribute significance to his death, if he realized ahead of time that death was inevitable or probable? And, more pointedly, what was Jesus' self-claim?

THE CAUSE OF JESUS' DEATH AS *ENTRE*

Most seem to think we can learn about Jesus' understanding of his own death if we can determine the cause, or causes, of his death. It is well known that some scholars connected Jesus' death pointedly to his regular praxis of table fellowship with sinners,[79] but Sanders has called such a conclusion into serious question.[80] Bruce Chilton connects Jesus' death to his temple occupation,[81] while Paula Fredriksen contends that it was a boisterous but not very large crowd that led to Jesus' death.[82]

The consensus is probably represented in Jürgen Becker's multiphasic understanding of why Jesus died: because of his deeds and his teachings, and because ultimately he was (perceived by those with power as) leading the nation astray.[83] If there is a new trend, it is to connect the death of Jesus with his temple action; thus, Géza Vermès: "Doing the wrong in the wrong place and in the wrong season resulted in the tragic death of Jesus on the Roman cross."[84]

It is the Roman cross that deserves some consideration at this point. There is an early and stubborn point of view on Jesus' death that spans the first to fifth centuries CE and which finds itself tucked into the clothing of Jews, pagans, and Christians: Jesus was put away by the Jewish (and Roman) authorities because he had led people astray. We find evidence for this view in Acts 5:40, Acts 10:39, and Galatians 3:13 (each rooted in its own way in Deut 21:22); we find the same in Tacitus, *Annales* 15.44; and we find the same among the talmudic scholars (*b. Sanh.* 43b). In other words, Jesus was put away because of views that gave rise to both actions and symbols that threw into question the views, actions, and symbols of Israel's leaders.

---

[78] Keck, *Who is Jesus?* 124.

[79] N. Perrin, *Rediscovering the Teaching of Jesus* (New York: Harper & Row, 1967).

[80] Sanders, *Jesus and Judaism*, 202.

[81] Chilton, *Rabbi Jesus*, 211–27.

[82] Fredriksen, *Jesus of Nazareth*.

[83] Becker, *Jesus of Nazareth*, 327–36.

[84] Géza Vermès, *The Changing Faces of Jesus* (London: Penguin, 2000), 262; cf. also U. Luz, "Warum zog Jesus nach Jerusalem?" in *Der historische Jesus* (ed. J. Schröter and R. Brucker; BZNW 114; Berlin: Walter de Gruyter, 2002), 419–21.

That Jesus was opposed during his life should not be questioned; that he
was accused (both technically and generally) is also obvious. We should consider
of what he was accused. First, Jesus was accused, for a variety of reasons, of being
a *lawbreaker*, where law should include both the Tanakh or its interpretive tradition. Thus, Jesus ran into opposition over issues pertaining to Sabbath (e.g.,
Mark 2:24; Luke 13:14; 14:1-6) and food law customs (Mark 7:1-4), especially
as they were embodied as a vision for Israel in table fellowship (Mark 2:13-17).
Even if some might argue that Jesus did not, technically speaking, break Tanakh
in these instances, others would argue that, technically or not, he did. In light
of the sociological significance of labeling someone successfully, whether or not
Jesus actually broke a law is of less significance in this context than if he were
successfully labeled as such. As Bruce Malina and Jerome Neyrey have stated:

> To label a person or group negatively is a social act of retaliation for some alleged
> deviance. . . . In the hands of influential persons or powerful groups, they can
> inflict genuine injury, since they serve to define a person as out of social place,
> hence as permanently deviant . . . in a society built on grades of status, degrad-
> ing terms that stick almost necessarily lead to collective avoidance, ostracism and
> isolation.[85]

Second, Jesus was accused, because he exorcized demons, of allegiance with
Satan.[86] The well-known Beelzeboul/-bub logion emerged most likely from an
accusatory situation in the life of Jesus (Mark 3:22). The same accusation can be
found in other early traditions (Matt 9:34; 10:25), which ought not to surprise
since exorcism can be firmly anchored in Jesus' understanding of his own mission to Israel (Q 11:20).

Third, in the often misunderstood logion of Matthew 11:19—where Jesus
is reported to be a glutton and drunkard—it is most likely that Jesus was
accused, during his lifetime, of being a rebellious son. The language of Matthew
11:19 clearly derives from Deuteronomy 21:18-21: If a father has a "rebellious
son" (*sorer vu-moreh*) who does not respond properly to discipline, the son is to
be arraigned before the community's elders and charged with being a "glutton
and drunkard" (*zolel ve-sobe*), and he is to be stoned on the spot. Tough guys,
these ancients! The charge of glutton and drunkard, functioning as it does as a
label for a rebellious son, has probably less to do with *what* the son is doing
(carousing) and more with an appropriate *label* that can be pinned on his tunic
for dishonoring his parents (Exod 20:12). The accusation of Matthew 11:19,
then, probably refers to the sorts of inferences that can be plausibly leveled
against Jesus for disruption and disrespect of family (Q 14:26 [cf. *Gos. Thom.*
55; 101.1-2]; Mark 3:31-35; cf. also Mark 10:29-30; 12:18-27; 13:12; Luke
9:59-60; Q 12:51-53; Matt 19:10-12).[87] One might say that the accusation of

[85] B.J. Malina and J.H. Neyrey, *Calling Jesus Names* (Sonoma, Calif.: Polebridge, 1988), 37.

[86] For a full study of this label, though at the level of the evangelist, cf. Malina and Neyrey, *Calling Jesus Names*, 1–32.

glutton and drunkard is the *legal* category for the actual crime behind the expression *friend of tax collectors and sinners*. At least one is entitled to ask if the asceticism of John was not followed by the Jesus who had no home (Q 9:57-58), who prayed for daily provisions (Q 11:3; Q 12:2-31), and who reportedly sent out his followers with nothing, counting on hospitality (Mark 6:6-13, 30 pars.).[88] And if Jesus did follow the practices of John in substantial ways, then the accusation of Matthew 11:19 becomes all the more ironical and legal, rather than descriptive.

Fourth, it is likely that Jesus was accused of *blasphemy* at some level. Scholarship is not as clear as it once was on the meaning of blasphemy, and in the lull before the matter is defined, scholars are beginning to fill in the gaps with such evidence as (a) the accusation of blasphemy in the words of Jesus about forgiveness (Mark 2:7); (b) the indignation of the leaders at the entry (Matt 11:11-18; Luke 19:39); and (c) the high priest's words in Mark 14:64. The recent monograph of Darrell Bock argues that the accusation of blasphemy, while it does not necessarily fit the legal definition of m. Sanhedrin 7:4-5, probably derives from the generic claim of an exalted nature or from some kind of an insult to the divine majesty, while others see here the diversity of views within Judaism.[89] The language Jesus used, the claims he was making, were outside the bounds of the leaders' acceptable definitions of Jewish behavior; therefore, he was a blasphemer.

Fifth, it is also likely that Jesus was accused of being a *false prophet*. If most leaders have their naysayers, we can rely on Jesus having experienced the same about his claims to be speaking as a prophet—that is, for standing in the breach and declaring to Israel what he thought God wanted the nation to hear.[90] If we

---

[87] See McKnight, *New Vision for Israel*, 179–87. That the logia dealing with Jesus and family disruption have a firm anchor in the mission of Jesus was shown long ago in the seminal article of J.A.T. Robinson, "Elijah, John and Jesus," in his *Twelve More New Testament Studies* (London: SCM, 1984), 28–52. It is probable that Jesus and John discussed who were the main figures in the Malachi program of restoration. See below, ch. 10, under "Mark 9:9-13."

[88] In general, cf. Allison, *Jesus of Nazareth*, 172–216, where the evidence and bibliography are summoned to the bar.

[89] D. Bock, *Blasphemy and Exaltation in Judaism* (WUNT 2/106; Tübingen: Mohr Siebeck, 1998), whose view is not dissimilar to the view of C.H. Dodd: "Jesus was charged with blasphemy because he spoke and acted in ways which implied that he stood in a special relation with God, so that his words carried divine authority and his actions were instinct [sic] with divine power" and he was "a profanation of sanctities" ("The Historical Problem of the Death of Jesus," in his *More New Testament Studies* [Grand Rapids: Eerdmans, 1968], 84–101, here p. 99). See also A.Y. Collins, "The Charge of Blasphemy in Mark 14.64," *JSNT* 26 (2004): 379–401.

[90] On Jesus as prophet in this sense, see still the always suggestive A.J. Heschel, *The Prophets* (2 vols.; New York: Harper & Row, 1962); E.P. Sanders, *Jesus and Judaism*; R.A. Horsley, *Jesus and the Spiral of Violence* (San Francisco: Harper & Row, 1987); also his *Jesus and Empire* (Minneapolis: Fortress, 2003); Wright, *Jesus and the Victory of God*; McKnight, *A New Vision for Israel*; S. Bryan, *Jesus and Israel's Traditions of Judgement and Restoration* (SNTSMS 117; Cambridge: Cambridge University Press, 2002).

combine *false prophet* with *deceiver*, and set such accusations in the context of such evidence as Acts 5:30; Galatians 3:13; Josephus, *A.J.* 18.63; Tacitus, *Ann.* 15.44; Justin, *Dial.* 69:7 and *b. Sanh.* 43a,[91] we are standing on firm ground when we see in the following evidence a credible accusation against Jesus during his lifetime: (a) Luke 7:39—where a Pharisee thinks Jesus is acting unlike a prophet; (b) Mark 8:11-13—where the Pharisees again query Jesus about a sign; (c) Mark 14:65—where at the trial Jesus is expected to put on a street-theater performance of his prophetic abilities; (d) Luke 23:2, 5, 14—where Jesus is accused of stirring up trouble, refusing to pay taxes to Caesar, and so subverting the nation (cf. again *b. Sanh.* 43b); and (e) Matthew 27:62-64—where Jesus is called an "impostor" *(ho planos)* who leads a "deception" *(he eschate plane)*. Again, this kind of language emerges from the Jewish lawbook against law-breakers and deceivers and impostors: Deuteronomy 13:2-6 and 18:15-22. In each case, the offender is to be put to death, like the rebellious son, and proba-bly by stoning. It will not go unnoticed that the intended results—death by stoning—are found in a variety of contexts and sources, and make it all the more likely that during Jesus' lifetime the opponents of Jesus wanted him put to death. It would not be far from the truth that penalities could be found, in the Tanakh itself, that could lead the opponents to their accusations.

Sixth, the *titulus* of the crucifixion narrative reflects what is most likely a historical accusation against Jesus (cf. Mark 15:2, 9, 12, 16-20, 26, 32), at least during the last week of his life, and no doubt in rumbles and murmurs after hearing Jesus speak so consistently of the imminent arrival of the kingdom of heaven (Mark 1:15). Some Jews thought Jesus presumptuously claimed to be "King of the Jews."

Seventh, a recent, gently rolling wave of scholarship has argued that Jesus was accused of being a *mamzer* ("bastard," "illegitimate son") by his contempo-raries and that far-reaching conclusions about Jesus' mission can be derived from the status that would result from such an accusation. In fact, the recent use of this category for understanding Jesus' social status must be assigned to a list of breakthroughs, and it is to the credit of Bruce Chilton that the category is to be given a front-row seat in recent discussion.[92] I am unaware that any scholar, prior to Chilton, has given the category the attention it might deserve.[93] One can infer that early Christians didn't invent such a social status for Jesus, and we can see their straining already in Matthew's own geneaology. Here we find a series of names, punctuated by women with a reputation (Matt 1:1-17: Tamar in v. 3, Rahab and Ruth in v. 5, the wife of Uriah in v. 6) who are then used to

---

[91] On this, cf. the recent excellent study of G.N. Stanton, "Jesus of Nazareth," in *Jesus of Nazareth, Lord and Christ* (ed. J.B. Green and M. Turner; Grand Rapids: Eerdmans, 1994), 164–80; D. Neale, "Was Jesus a Mesith?" *TynBul* 44 (1993): 89–101; see also the older study of C.H. Dodd, "The Historical Problem."

[92] Chilton, *Rabbi Jesus*; "Jésus, le mamzer (Mt 1.18)," *NTS* 46 (2001): 222–27.

[93] See my recent evaluation, some of which appears (in slightly edited form) here again: "Calling Jesus *Mamzer*," *JSHJ* 1 (2003): 73–103.

set the stage for Mary. Evidently, we are to understand Mary also had the same sort of reputation, though she is guiltless since the conception in her case was virginal (1:16, commented on in 1:18-25). Some scholars remain convinced that the language of Mark 6:3 ("the son of Mary")[94] reflects accusations and labels at the time of Jesus, which Matthew felt uncomfortable with and so changed to "the son of the carpenter" (13:55): the normal *Yeshua ben Yosep* is abandoned in favor of the scurrilous *Yeshua ben Miriam*.[95] Since scholars today are rethinking John's Gospel as a legitimate source for information about the historical Jesus,[96] we are possibly justified to find historical confirmation of our issue in John 8:41, where the Jews (John's problematic term for Jesus' opponents) protested to Jesus: "We are not illegitimate children; we have one father,

---

[94] For the text-critical issues, cf. R.E. Brown, *The Birth of the Messiah* (2d ed.; ABRL; New York: Doubleday, 1993), 537–39.

[95] E. Stauffer, "Jeschu ben Mirjam (Mk 6:3)," in *Neotestamentica et Semitica* (ed. E.E. Ellis and M. Wilcox; Edinburgh: T&T Clark, 1969), 119–28: "Ale mysteria Christi sind paradoxe Tatbestände, die eine dialektische Deutung hervorrufen, positv oder negativ, doxologisch oder polemisch. Das gilt von der Geburt Jesu genau so wie vom Faktum des Leeren Grabes, von seiner Wundertätigkeit genau so wie von seinem Selbstzeugnis. Darum entfaltet sich die christliche Jesusbotschaft a principio in der Kontroverse" (128). For others who see a slur here, cf. M.D. Hooker, *The Message of Mark* (London: Epworth, 1983), 153; J. Marcus, *Mark* (2 vols.; New York: Doubleday, 2000), 374–75. See also H.K. McArthur, "Son of Mary," *NovT* 15 (1973): 38–58; R.E. Brown, et al., *Mary in the New Testament* (Philadelphia: Fortress, 1978), 59–67; Brown, *Birth of the Messiah*, 537–41; J.P. Meier, *A Marginal Jew* (3 vols.; ABRL; New York: Doubleday, 1991–2001), 1:225–27; T. Ilan, "'Man Born of Woman . . .' (Job 14:1)," *NovT* 34 (1992): 23–45. In spite of this trend to find in "son of Mary" little more than an ordinary remark, (1) the oddity of the expression—since sons were named by their father unless the mother's lineage was superior; (2) the context of conflict; (3) later evangelical modification of the language; and (4) the presence of a woman who at least later is to be accused of illicit sexual union, beg for explanation, and one solid such explanation is that it hints at illegitimacy. Furthermore, Meier offers the suggestion that the statement is "glib" without a shred of evidence. Also, that the "brothers and sisters" are mentioned in Mark 6:1-6 does not necessarily include them in the same accusation. Finally, it should not be argued that "son of Mary" was, as a form, indicative of illegitimacy; there could be other motives for labeling a son by his mother. I am of the suspicion that too much of this scholarly trend seeks to find the Jewish accusation later than the Christian affirmation, rather than the reverse. From a completely different angle, and with far less care at the historical level, cf. J. Schaberg, *The Illegitimacy of Jesus* (San Francisco: Harper & Row, 1987), 160–64. For her response to some caustic reactions to her study, see J. Schaberg, "A Feminist Experience of Historical-Jesus Scholarship," in *Whose Historical Jesus?* (ed. W.E. Arnal and M. Desjardins; vol. 7 of *Studies in Christianity and Judaism* 7; Waterloo: Wilfrid Laurier University Press, 1997), 146–60.

[96] See J.A.T. Robinson, *The Priority of John* (ed. J.F. Coakley; Oak Park, Ill.: Meyer-Stone, 1985); M. Hengel, *The Johannine Question* (Philadelphia: Trinity Press International, 1989); D. Moody Smith, "Historical Issues and the Problem of John and the Synoptics," in *From Jesus to John* (ed. M.C. de Boer; Sheffield: JSOT, 1993), 252–67; J. Ashton, *Understanding the Fourth Gospel* (Oxford: Clarendon, 1991) and *Studying John* (Oxford: Clarendon, 1994); D. Tovey, *Narrative Art and Act in the Fourth Gospel* (Sheffield: Sheffield Academic, 1997); S. Byrskog, *Story as History— History as Story* (Tübingen: Mohr Siebeck, 2000); R.T. Fortna and T. Thatcher, eds., *Jesus in Johannine Tradition* (Louisville: Westminster John Knox, 2001); C.L. Blomberg, *The Historical Reliability of John's Gospel* (Downers Grove: InterVarsity, 2002).

God himself." That is, their claim probably labels Jesus one more time with his suspected illegitimacy.[97] The Hebrew equivalent here would probably be "offspring of fornication" (זנונים ילדי, *yaldey zenunim*). This suspicion is covered rather gently by John in 6:42 with the following: "Is not this Jesus, the son of Joseph?" No need, so reasons John, to poke at a deep wound. That the audience accuses Jesus of being a "Samaritan" and "demon-possessed" in John 8:42 probably speaks to the same suspected status of Jesus, and it may just as well lurk behind John 9:16 ("a sinner").

That Mary was pregnant before cohabiting with Joseph is indisputable; no Christian would have invented such a problem for Jesus in order to dismiss it. How the pregnancy was discovered (prior to cohabitation or a birth too early not to be noticed), or *why* or *how* Mary was impregnated was explained differently. As for the followers of Jesus, there was a virginal conception (hence, Matt 1:18-25; Luke 1:26-38;[98] *Prot. Jas.* 7:1–16:2; *Ps.-Mt.* 6–12).[99] For others in the Diaspora, from the mid-second century CE onwards, Mary had been caught *en flagrant*—Mary and someone other than Joseph had intercourse, and she was discovered when signs of pregnancy were visible (cf. Origen, *Cels.* 1.28 [Mary is cast out by Joseph for adultery with a certain Panthera], 32–33, 69; 2:5, 8–9, 31; Tertullian, *Spect.* 30.6; *Gos. Thom.* 105; Acts *Pil.* 2:3; *m. Yebam.* 4:13; *t. Ḥul.* 2:24; *b. Sanh.* 67a; *y. 'Abod. Zar.* 40d; *y. Sabb.* 14d).[100] (On the issue of Galilean customs differing from Judean customs, the evidence is unclear for the first century and should not be factored into the discussion.[101])

The social stigma attached to Mary, that is, the label that gave to her a *master status* of some sort, would have been telling (cf. Wis 4:3-6). The Christian tradition claims Mary was saved by a benevolent act of Joseph.[101] He avoided the public-shaming event described or alluded to in *m. Soṭah* and broke Jewish custom by marrying her, cohabiting with her, and raising Jesus (and the other children). Whatever explanation one prefers today is not the issue; clearly, Jesus' origins were *irregular* and that irregular origin gave rise to an accusation. Jesus was labeled by his contemporaries as a *mamzer*. And such a label would have carried with it socio-religious implications with a powerful significance for Jesus.

---

[97] So Schaberg, *Illegitimacy of Jesus*, 157–58 (with n. 39); *pace* Meier, *Marginal Jew*, 1:227–29; Brown, *Birth of the Messiah*, 541–42.

[98] For a fair-minded discussion of the value of the infancy narratives, cf. Meier, *Marginal Jew*, 1:208–14.

[99] For study, cf. Brown, *Birth of the Messiah*, 517–33, 697–712; J. Schaberg, *Illegitimacy of Jesus*, 178–92; Meier, *Marginal Jew*, 1:220–22.

[100] Cf. Brown, *Birth of the Messiah*, 534–42; J. Schaberg, *Illegitimacy of Jesus*, 169–74.

[101] That Jews in Galilee were more strict on premarital customs than Jews in Judea can be seen in *t. Ketub.* 1:4; *b. Ket.* 9b, 12a; but cf. the earlier text at m. Ketub. 1:5 where the distinction is not raised. Scholarship is not decided on the feasibility of this distinction for first-century Judaism, and neither have many paid sufficient attention to the context of these statements; cf. B. Chilton, "Jésus, le mamzer."

As Malina and Neyrey have argued, though they failed to note that *mamzer* may have been one of the labels pinned to Jesus:

> Negative labelling bears the force of stigma. When carried out publicly or at times secretly, such labelling can carry with it an institutional sanctioning of overwhelming proportions: positively by granting symbolic reward potential, negatively by granting symbolic devastation potential, both of deep and enduring quality. . . . Labelling is intended to create a master status. . . .[103]

What this long digression on the accusations against Jesus reveals is that from the very beginning Jesus was held under suspicion by his contemporaries. It is no longer necessary to isolate one ground for his accusation. Jesus was a marked man well before he entered Jerusalem that last day. Enough groups were against him to get him put away. To study what he thought about his death, accordingly, involves computing what role these various accusations played in his life and how he was able to carry them along with him when he carried about his mission. Therefore, to suggest that his death caught him by surprise flies in the face of too much evidence.

ALL ABOUT METHOD

It comes as no surprise to say that method determines the outcome. If one has a general skepticism about the historical reliability of the logia in the Jesus traditions, then significant information is eliminated from view in sorting out the evidence about the question. This sort of agnosticism, of course, is confident and has its advantages. Our discipline inherited this through the critical studies emerging from the Enlightenment when applied to texts dealing with faith claims. It has been said best, perhaps, by Xavier Léon-Dufour, one of France's eminent scholars: "As a general rule, what is historically certain is somewhat vague, and what is sharply defined is usually not historically certain."[104]

A different kind of methodological agnosticism is that of Sanders, who helpfully chose to focus his attention on Jesus' actions, in particular the temple incident, rather than sayings, because he knew all too well what a quagmire one fell into when one entered that kind of rope-pulling context.[105] It is entirely possible that Sanders, had he pursued an approach that took into consideration the logia tradition as well, might have known more about how Jesus saw his death. Others, in fact most, approach the issue mostly through the logia tradition and, once they land upon what they think is authentic, come to a more precise

---

[102] The deliberations behind Matthew 1:18-25 concern Deuteronomy 22:13-21, 23-27, 28-29, and pertain to Mary's motives and options, as well as to Joseph's options.

[103] Malina and Neyrey, *Calling Jesus Names*, 38, 39.

[104] E.P. Sanders, *Sharing the Eucharistic Bread* (trans. M.J. O'Connell; New York: Paulist, 1986), 160.

[105] Sanders, *Jesus and Judaism*.

perception. In fact, some still argue for the view that the Jesus traditions are preserved with sufficient integrity to force the historian to see items as authentic
unless there are compelling reasons to the contrary.[106]

In what follows we will focus on the logia tradition, but knowing that a full
narrative can only be put together in light of Jesus' overall mission to bring the
kingdom, and in light of the sorts of things he did.

A TAXONOMY OF JESUS' DEATH

To sum up: there is a gradation in specifics that scholars will assign to Jesus' perception of his death. I offer this final typology as a means of summarizing where
scholarship is today; names will not be attached. At one end, Jesus is surprised
and shocked by the turn of events; here he must have thought his death a waste
of talent and his trip to Jerusalem an unintended mistake. At the other, Jesus
dies as an atonement for sins, for the entire human race. We think here, for one
example, of Paul's *hyper* statements, as we see in 2 Corinthians 5:14-15 or 5:21.
I would chart the scale of what various scholars think to be something like what
I will explain in the following paragraphs, though a reading of scholarship will
reveal that some sing on different levels of the scale at the same time.

First, Jesus died an *unintended and shocking death*. Second, Jesus' death was
either *heroic* or *exemplary*, but such is what others have made of it. Third, there
are *three martyr types*. This category maximizes the term *martyr* and forces three
other terms (*prophet, righteous sufferer,* and *atoning sacrifice*) to play the role of
glossator or epexegesis. My intent is this: for these three types, Jesus' death is
understood not in the terms of classical Christianity, but in the terms of figures
in Jewish history who gave themselves to God for Israel as a result of their calling. For each of these options, Jesus' death is part of his human and self-claimed
destiny. Three subtypes may be noted: martyr—as prophet; martyr—as the righteous sufferer; and martyr—as the atoning sacrifice for the people.

The next three types begin to assume, in increasing degree, heavier theological and soteriological freight, and fill Jesus' intention with sacrificial and
atoning significance. From each of the three following types one can trace neater
and more direct lines to the various theories of Christian atonement theology.
Fourth, Jesus self-consciously assumed the eschatological woes, sometimes as
"the first" and other times in a "vicarious role" and often in conjunction with
the representative role of the Suffering Servant of Isaiah or the Son of man of
Daniel, or both and more! Fifth, some see in Jesus' own intention a self-claim
that involves his death as having atoning significance. Two subtypes may be
noted: *atoning sacrifice for his people* (construed as disciples or nation), usually as
the Suffering Servant but sometimes as the Son of man; and *atoning sacrifice for
the world*.

---

[106] So, e.g., Stuhlmacher, "Why Did Jesus Have to Die?" 41.

CONCLUSION

Joan Didion, one of America's great essayists, once said: "It is easy to see the beginnings of things, and harder to see the ends."[107] Not so with historical Jesus studies and especially not so with how Jesus thought of his death. We know the end; it is the beginning that baffles us. For some scholars, Jesus' view of his death is more than just an interesting question. For some the issue of the *discontinuity* between a credible understanding of what Jesus thought of his death, on the one hand, and the Pauline and the Epistle of Hebrews' portraits, on the other hand (embodied as they are in the architecture of churches), is no small problem. Indeed, according to Dahl, discontinuity between the proclamation of the early Christians and the historical Jesus is fatal for faith.[108] Consequently, the discussion on this table is of massive significance to some. For instance, it was C.J. Cadoux, who said,

> Such an inquiry [into Jesus' understanding of his own death] does not mean a discussion of the whole problem of the Atonement; but it does mean the first part of such a discussion. The meaning Jesus himself, so far as we can discover it, must in the nature of things furnish the basis for any satisfactory doctrine of the Atonement; and no doctrine will be entitled to acceptance which either contradicts, or even gives no essential place to, the thoughts of Jesus on the topics concerned.[109]

Some may prefer to keep answers to historical questions of this sort in the subjunctive mood, but the constant contingency one is thereby forced to live in will not permit the settling that many require.

When Christians confess the creeds, affirmations are made of the significance of historical events. For many, this necessitates that the tools of historiography are trotted out and used with care, with caution, but with critical determination. It matters, then, to many creedal Christians that Jesus' death occurred and for some it matters what Jesus thought of his death. It matters for some, too, that what early Christians thought about the death of Jesus is in some sense consonant both with what happened and with what Jesus thought about his death. Was atonement theology arbitrarily imposed on the Jesus traditions or was it an organic evolution from the Master himself? What are we to make of these traditions, and what role does historiography play in the construction of theological knowledge? For those who approach the Jesus traditions as Christians, what role is to be given to historical Jesus scholarship?

To the texts we now must turn.

---

[107] J. Didion, *Slouching Towards Bethlehem* (New York: Farrar, Straus & Giroux, 1968), 225.

[108] N.A. Dahl, *Jesus the Christ* (ed. D.H. Joel; Minneapolis: Fortress, 1991).

[109] C.J. Cadoux, *The Historic Mission of Jesus* (London: Lutterworth, 1941), 258. For a brief survey of Cadoux's contribution, cf. W.P. Weaver, *The Historical Jesus in the Twentieth Century, 1900–1950* (Harrisburg: Trinity Press International, 1999), 193–99.

Part II

THE REALITY OF A PREMATURE DEATH

Chapter 4

The Leading Foot
in the Dance of Atonement

Historical Jesus scholarship of the second half of the twentieth century has avoided a question to which C.H. Dodd thought there was a firm answer. In Dodd's influential book, *The Parables of the Kingdom*, he discussed the predictions of Jesus that do not mention the kingdom of God,[1] but in so doing he also offered a poignant response to the charge that all passion predictions were *vaticinium ex eventu*:

> We may observe (1) that the whole prophetic and apocalyptic tradition, which Jesus certainly recognized, anticipated tribulation for the people of God before the final triumph of the good cause; (2) that the history of many centuries had deeply implanted the idea that the prophet is called to suffering as a part of his mission; (3) that the death of John the Baptist had shown that this fate was still part of the prophetic calling; and (4) that it needed, not supernatural prescience, but the ordinary insight of an intelligent person, to see whither things were tending, at least during the later stages of the ministry.[2]

As Jesus scholarship takes its first steps into the twenty-first century it has to wonder if there is solid enough footing to dance with C.H. Dodd. Can we any longer agree with R.S. Barbour, who said, "If it is important to be able to say anything about the historical Jesus, it is important to attempt to say something about his attitude to his death"?[3] Or, to put the matter quite directly, has the floor so weakened that the "dance of atonement with Jesus" is over? If Jesus does not take the lead step in the dance, is there a dance at all?

---

[1] C.H. Dodd, *The Parables of the Kingdom* (2d ed.; London: Nisbet, 1942), 56–80, esp. 56–67.
[2] Ibid., 57.
[3] R.S. Barbour, "Gethsemane in the Tradition of the Passion," *NTS* 16 (1969–1970): 231–51, here p. 251.

BOOKENDS FOR AN ORIENTATION

It does little good to discuss *how* Jesus thought of his death if we do not first establish *that* Jesus believed he would die prematurely. No one questions that Jesus suffered at the hands of his contemporaries, whether we see that suffering at the level of innuendo or of overt persecution.[4] If he did suffer at the hands of others, is there reason to think he considered that he might die prematurely?

In this section of our book we will begin with the question of *if* Jesus thought he would die prematurely before we begin sorting out the question of *how* he thought of that death. Because of the massive details and parallels involved, and because of the intensity of discussions in the bibliography on various passages, it is simply not possible at each venture to display all the pertinent evidence. The study would swell beyond what it already is. Instead, we will often refer the reader to more careful displays of data and to analyses elsewhere, and appeal to results and logical arguments.

One of the more neglected traditions about Jesus that may shed light into the thinking room is the Our Father and especially the sixth request ("do not lead us into temptation"). Here we find a tradition where Jesus evidently wanted to *avoid* situations where God would put him and his followers through a life-probing test. A similar reflection by Jesus comes on the final free night of Jesus: in Gethsemane Jesus asks his Father to remove this "cup" from him, and he asks this in the context of a "test/temptation" (Mark 14:36-38). Here are bookends for an orientation to sorting out some traditions that suggest Jesus knew of his death—but these bookends frame the entire issue as the door through which Jesus did not want to enter.[5] Here, I suggest, is a good place to begin this section that is concerned with if Jesus came to the conviction that he was to die prematurely.

Q 11:4 (MATTHEW 6:13 PAR. LUKE 11:4)

We need concern ourselves here only with two issues: (1) the authenticity of the request and, if authentic, (2) the meaning of *temptation*.[6] It was a bit of a sen-

---

[4] Ch. 3, under "The Cause of Jesus' death as *Entre*"; S. McKnight, "Calling Jesus *Mamzer*," *JSHJ* 1 (2003): 73–103; A.J. Hultgren, *Jesus and His Adversaries* (foreword by R.H. Fuller; Minneapolis: Augsburg, 1979); J. Schlosser, *Jésus de Nazareth* (2d ed.; Paris: Agnès Viénot, 2002), 177–214.

[5] Luke 22:28, in its tradition-historical proximity to Mark 14:36, 38, and evidently non-Lukan origin, makes for an even tighter fit for the last days of Jesus being experienced as the climactic text to a life of being tested. On the Lukan (de)emphasis, cf. S. Brown, *Apostasy and Perseverance in the Theology of Luke* (AnBib 36; Rome: Pontifical Biblical Institute, 1969), 8–9, 12–19.

[6] Bibliography on the Lord's Prayer is immense, worthy of seven histories of interpretation. Bibliography on prayer is also growing: see here M. Kiley, et al., *Prayer from Alexander to Constantine* (New York: Routledge, 1997), with a notable essay on the Lord's Prayer by R. Conrad Douglas, "A Jesus Tradition Prayer (Q 11:2b-4; Matt 6:9b-13; Luke 11:2b-4; Didache 8.2)," 211–15. For a recent study of the Lord's Prayer in historical, ecclesial, and spiritual contexts, cf. D.L. Migliore, ed., *The Lord's Prayer* (Grand Rapids: Eerdmans, 1993). Alongside the important

sation in the United States when the Jesus Seminar's conclusions on the Lord's Prayer were made public, for it was reported in the news that only *Abba* was authentic. However, their views are not as radical as appeared at first blush, if one considers the "pink" words as probably authentic at some level.[7] Their conclusions:

> "Our Father" (authentic: red);
> "your name be revered. Impose your imperial rule" . . . "Provide us with the bread we need for the day. Forgive us our debts to the extent that we have forgiven those in debt to us" (probable: pink);
> "And please don't subject us to test after test" (unlikely: gray);
> "in the heavens" . . . "enact your will on earth as you have in heaven" . . . "but rescue us from the evil one" (inauthentic: black).

It is not my purpose here to engage in direct discussion with the Jesus Seminar in its philosophy, its methodology, its general conclusions, or its sort of Jesus—others have done this and done it well[8]—instead, I wish simply to include them in the debate, but without letting them take over the conversation.[9] The traditional argument for the general authenticity of the Lord's Prayer might best be summarized by the following four claims, which can be broken down into thirteen separate considerations.

---

newer commentaries on Matthew (W.D. Davies and D.C. Allison, U. Luz, D.A. Hagner, H.D. Betz, and C.S. Keener) and Luke (J.A. Fitzmyer, D. Bock, J. Nolland, and J.B. Green), a very considered study can be found in the ageless O. Cullmann, *Prayer in the New Testament* (OBT; Minneapolis: Fortress, 1995), 37–69; here cf. pp. 58–66 especially. Cullmann's insistence on God's omnipotence sheds considerable light on the supposed dark corner of God's *tempting* or God's *testing*. He translates: "spare us temptation as such" (p. 62). See also G.R. Beasley-Murray, *Jesus and the Kingdom of God* (Grand Rapids: Eerdmans, 1986), 147–57. An older study of the term remains valuable: M. Andrews, "Peirasmos—A Study in Form Criticism," *AThR* 24 (1942): 229–44.

[7] R.W. Funk, R. Hoover, and the Jesus Seminar, *The Five Gospels* (Polebridge; New York: Macmillan, 1993), 148–50.

[8] See, e.g., the celebrated (but largely Bultmannian) response of L.T. Johnson, *The Real Jesus* (San Francisco: HarperSanFrancisco, 1996). (See my review in *CBQ* 59 [1997]: 159–61.) See also N.T. Wright, *Jesus and the Victory of God* (Christian Origins and the Question of God 2; Minneapolis: Fortress, 1996), 28–82; James D.G. Dunn, *Jesus Remembered* (Grand Rapids: Eerdmans, 2003).

The issues are so serious, scholars from other fields have pulled their chairs up to the table; cf. P. Barnett, *Jesus and the Logic of History* (Grand Rapids: Eerdmans, 1997); C. Stephen Evans, *The Historical Christ and the Jesus of Faith* (New York: Oxford University Press, 1996); R. Martin, *The Elusive Messiah* (Boulder: Westview, 1999); P. Jenkins, *Hidden Gospels* (New York: Oxford, 2001).

[9] See H. Taussig, *Jesus Before God* (Santa Rosa, Calif.: Polebridge, 1999), 65–67, where he appeals to his reconstructed Q community; see also his "The Lord's Prayer," *Forum* 4 (1988): 25–41, esp. 36–37. Taussig prefers a Q setting for the origin of the temptation clause, though his parallel to Q 12 does not use the term, and neither does he consider the eschatology of the "test" adequately. In some senses sympathetic with the Jesus Seminar, D.E. Oakman orders the Lord's Prayer into two tables (Petitions 1–3 and Petitions 4–7), and thinks *Abba* and Petitions 4–7 (including the temptation clause) authentic; see "The Lord's Prayer in Social Perspective," in *Authenticating the Words of Jesus* (ed. B. Chilton and C.A. Evans; NTTS 28.1; Leiden: E.J. Brill, 1999), 137–86.

First, the *liturgical shape* of the Lord's Prayer indicates antiquity:

(1)   liturgical texts tend to be treated conservatively, as can be seen in that the *Didache* (8:2) largely repeats the Matthean tradition; the tradition is at least early Christian praxis.[10]

Second, *source-critical observations* indicate an early tradition:

(2)   the Lord's Prayer is found embedded in the Q tradition,[11] a tradition considered by many to be the earliest "surviving" Christian tradition;

(3)   the Lord's Prayer evoked commentary and extrapolation, indicating that the Lord's Prayer that drew such commentary existed independently and in an earlier form;[12]

(4)   the signature additions (if they are that)[13] in the Matthean text appear to be pre-Matthean or (less possibly) Matthean redaction, leaving some clear lines of demarcation between tradition and extrapolation.[14]

Third, *theological observations* indicate historical reliability:

(5)   there is little development of a Christian theological nature in the Lord's Prayer;

(6)   there are no parallels in earliest Christianity for the command to remember and recite a set prayer;[15]

(7)   the theology of the Lord's Prayer, with its emphasis on kingdom, remarkably coheres with the overall tenor and focus of Jesus' own mission; the temptation clause itself is a theme found in other contexts

---

[10] On liturgical developments of the Lord's Prayer, see the older study of T.W. Manson, "The Lord's Prayer," *BJRL* 38 (1955–1956): 99–113, 436–48.

[11] Most judge the Lord's Prayer to be from Q; the evidence supports the judgment, as long as one permits a liturgical text to have its own life apart from the written tradition. I do not understand the Jesus Seminar's omission of the sixth petition from the original Q text (cf. Funk, et al., *The Five Gospels*, 149; on p. 327 it is included). All standard editions and scholars include Q 11:4.

[12] So A. Finkel, ""The Prayer of Jesus in Matthew," in *Standing Before God* (ed. A. Finkel and L. Frizzoli; New York: Ktav, 1981), 131–69, here p. 132 with n. 11.

[13] On Matthew's text, see B. Gerhardsson, "The Matthaean Version of the Lord's Prayer (Matt 6:9b-13)," in *The New Testament Age* (2 vols.; ed. W.C. Weinrich; Macon, Ga.: Mercer University Press, 1984), 1:207–20, here pp. 207–9, where it is shown that the Lord's Prayer in Matthew is not only an interpolation but remains intact as a tradition. On the sixth petition in Matthean theology, cf. now M. Kiley, "The Lord's Prayer as Matthean Theology," in *The Lord's Prayer and Other Prayer Texts from the Graeco-Roman Era* (ed. J. Charlesworth, et al.; Valley Forge: Trinity Press International, 1994), 19–21.

[14] It is not uncommon to read that an author would not revise his community's set prayer. This claim is a stranger to reality, e.g., cf. Finkel, "Prayer of Jesus," 131.

[15] So R. Riesner, *Jesus als Lehrer* (WUNT 2/7; Tübingen: J.C.B. Mohr [Paul Siebeck], 1981), 445–47.

and forms (e.g., Mark 14:36, 38); the liturgically reshaped *Shema* of Judaism (cf. Mark 12:29-31), with its amendment in the "love others" clause, provides a plausible historical platform for Jesus to revise the Qaddish by adding prayer concerns for the same "others";[16]

(8)   the prayer, and our clause itself, can be interpreted potently from the standpoint of eschatological imminency, a viewpoint characteristic of Jesus.[17]

Fourth, the *Jewish flavor* of the prayer indicates historical plausibility:

(9)   the prayer fits into a Jewish prayer context and stands at a distance at the same time (e.g., Sir 23:1, 4; 51:10; cf. Ps 139:23);[18]

(10) the Lukan *Sitz im Leben* for the Lord's Prayer is believable and provides the sociological reason for the prayer—group formation (Luke 11:1);[19]

---

[16] I have worked out this suggestion about the Shema in a popular format and am working on a piece for a more academic setting. See for now *The Jesus Creed* (Brewster, Mass.: Paraclete, 2004), 14–23 (ch. 2).

[17] On which one still finds the best exposition in R.E. Brown, "The Pater Noster as an Eschatological Prayer," in his *New Testament Essays* (Garden City, N.Y.: Doubleday, 1968), 275–320, esp. p. 276: ". . . The petitions of the PN [=Pater Noster] do not refer to daily circumstances but to the final times." While Brown is not concerned with the historical Jesus, to the extent that he addresses questions of eschatology to a close degree he is speaking also of Jesus. But, cf. A. Vögtle, "Der 'eschatologische' Bezug der Wir-Bitten des Vaterunsers," in *Jesus und Paulus* (ed. E.E. Ellis and E. Gräßer; Göttingen: Vandenhoeck & Ruprecht, 1975), 344–62, who finds eschatology prominent in the "you" but not the "we" petitions. So also Gerhardsson, "Matthaean Version," 214–15. Other discussions at R. Schnackenburg, *All Things Are Possible to Believers* (trans. J.S. Currie; Louisville: Westminster John Knox, 1995), 81–90; H. Schürmann, *Praying with Christ* (trans. W.M. Ducey; New York: Herder & Herder, 1964), 83–92. I have expounded Jesus' eschatology in my *A New Vision for Israel* (Grand Rapids: Eerdmans, 1999), 12–55.

[18] So J. Wellhausen, *Das Evangelium Matthaei* (Berlin: Reimer, 1904), 26; J. Heinemann, "The Background of Jesus' Prayer in the Jewish Liturgical Tradition," in *The Lord's Prayer and Jewish Liturgy* (ed. J.J. Petuchowski and M. Brocke; New York: Seabury, 1978), 81–89; Finkel, "Prayer of Jesus." In particular, the brevity of Jesus' prayer may not only build on the *Qaddish* but form a resistance to the *Shemoneh 'Esreh*.

[19] Thus, the Lord's Prayer is tied into Jesus' baptism by John, as well as into the calling of the Twelve; cf. S. McKnight, "Jesus' New Vision within Judaism," in *Who Was Jesus?* (ed. P. Copan and C.A. Evans; Louisville: Westminster John Knox, 2001), 73–96, esp. 78–81; see also "Jesus and the Twelve," *BBR* 11 (2001): 203–31.

For a good survey of the historical context of the Lord's Prayer, cf. J. H. Charlesworth, "Jewish Prayers in the Time of Jesus," in *The Lord's Prayer* (ed. Migliore), 36–55, who provides evidence for six themes in Jewish prayers: (1) need for God, (2) need for acceptance, forgiveness, and justification; (3) need to converse with God spontaneously; and he shows that Jewish prayers were (4) public and collective, (5) able to solidify Israel, and (6) cosmic and calendrical. See also Heinemann, "Background of Jesus' Prayer"; Finkel, "Prayer of Jesus"; Kiley, et al., *Prayer from Alexander to Constantine*, 9–120.

(11) there are plausible Semitic constructs that could have given rise to the current Greek texts;[20]

(12) at the level of surface grammar, our clause stands alone in the world of Judaism where no one would presume to escape temptation—escape succumbing, yes, but temptation itself, never;[21]

(13) ending any prayer with no formal closure is without Jewish parallel.[22]

Some of these arguments are tepid, while others, depending on one's starting point, have probative force of various strengths. A person who sets out after morning breakfast to deny the substantial veracity of the Lord's Prayer will be found, before supper, curled up in a corner chair, exhausted, and with little hope of success. Consequently, most scholars today judge the Lord's Prayer in general to be authentic, especially in its Lukan form, but do so with various sorts of modifications.[23] Gerd Lüdemann, not one to think highly of the historicity of the Gospels, states, "With the exception of v. 10b, in all probability the Our Father goes back to Jesus."[24]

Those who don't think the Lord's Prayer is authentic tend to be those who also argue against the eschatological understanding of Jesus. R.W. Funk's direction of the Jesus Seminar does not force all to agree with him, but one ought to note, for the general interest of this study of mine, the correlation between his proposal for a Christianity absent of atonement and the consistent judgment of inauthenticity to those sayings of Jesus that betray value in his death.[25] Back to the Lord's Prayer and the Jesus Seminar: while the printed form in the Seminar's publication gives the impression that the various original Q petitions were inauthentic (gray), the comments themselves make one think that they are in essence authentic.[26] Hence, "They [the fellows] think it more likely, given the conditions under which oral discourse is transmitted, that he [Jesus] employed the

---

[20] For Aramaic, cf. J.C. de Moor, "The Reconstruction of the Aramaic Original of the Lord's Prayer," in *The Structural Analysis of Biblical and Canaanite Poetry* (ed. P. Van der Meer and J.C. De Moor; JSOTSup 74; Sheffield: JSOT, 1988), 397–422; for Hebrew, cf. J. Carmignac, "Hebrew Translations of the Lord's Prayer: An Historical Survey," in *Biblical and Near Eastern Studies* (ed. G. Tuttle; Grand Rapids: Eerdmans, 1978), 18–79.

[21] E.g., E. Lohmeyer, *The Lord's Prayer* (trans. J. Bowden; London: Collins, 1965), 194.

[22] So W. Popkes, "Die letzte Bitte des Vater-Unser," *ZNW* 81 (1990): 1–20.

[23] See B.F. Meyer, *The Aims of Jesus* (London: SCM, 1979), 208; R.A. Horsley, *Jesus and the Spiral of Violence* (San Francisco: Harper & Row, 1987), 174–75; J.P. Meier, *A Marginal Jew* (3 vols.; ABRL; New York: Doubleday, 1991–2001), 2:291–94; J. Becker, *Jesus of Nazareth* (trans. J.E. Crouch; New York: Walter de Gruyter, 1998), 265–71; Wright, *Jesus and the Victory of God*, 292–94; D.C. Allison, Jr., *Jesus of Nazareth* (Minneapolis: Fortress, 1998), 71; G. Theissen and A. Merz, *The Historical Jesus* (Minneapolis: Fortress, 1998), 240–80; B. Chilton, *Rabbi Jesus* (New York: Doubleday, 2000), 59, n. 4, and his *Jesus' Prayer and Jesus' Eucharist* (Valley Forge, Pa.: Trinity Press International, 1997), 24–51.

[24] G. Lüdemann, *Jesus after Two Thousand Years* (Amherst, N.Y.: Prometheus, 2001), 147.

[25] Thus, R.W. Funk's *Honest to Jesus* (San Francisco: HarperSanFrancisco [Poleridge], 1996), 312.

[26] Funk, et al. *The Five Gospels*, 325–27 (pp. 148–50 contain mostly assertion).

four petitions [traditional categories of kingdom, bread, forgiveness, and temptation] from time to time but as individual prayers."[27] In light of their muted voice—muted in part because their renderings of the various petitions are non-eschatological—of protest against the authenticity of the various petitions, it seems fair to conclude that the sixth petition of the Lord's Prayer is authentic.

Another muted voice is the one who attempts to declare a clear meaning for the term *temptation/test* (Greek: *peirasmos*) because, in and of itself, the petition creates a dilemma.[28] The sixth petition is authentic; what it means, however, needs clarity in order to determine how Jesus may have understood the future as expressed in that sixth petition. As P.S. Cameron put it, "Either *peirasmos* is a bad thing—temptation to sin—which doesn't come from God, and therefore it doesn't make sense to ask him to refrain from leading us into it; or it is a good thing—testing—which does come from God, and it doesn't make sense to ask him to change his mind."[29] In the same journal, S.E. Porter said, "In any case the text seems on the surface to implore God not to bring the petitioner into a situation of temptation or testing, with the inference that God could or in fact *does* tempt men."[30] What can this request mean?

After reconstructing the Aramaic original to the Lord's Prayer, Joachim Jeremias, seeing the corporateness of the "us" and basing his interpretation on *wᵉla ta 'elinnan lᵉnisyon*,[31] argued famously that the term *temptation/test*

> does not mean the little temptations or testings of everyday life, but the final great Testing which stands at the door and will extend over the whole earth—the disclosure of the mystery of evil, the revelation of the Antichrist, the abomination of desolation (when Satan stands in God's place), the final persecution and testing of God's saints by pseudo-prophets and false saviours. What is in danger, is not moral integrity, but faith itself. The final trial at the end is—apostasy! Who can escape?[32]

[27] Ibid., 327.

[28] See H. Seesemann, "πεῖρα," in *Theologische Wörtenbuch zum Neuen Testament* (10 vols.; ed. G. Kittel and G. Friedrich; Stuttgart: W. Kolhhammer, 1932–1979) 6:23–37; Lohmeyer, *Lord's Prayer*, 191–208; see also J. Gibson, *The Temptations of Jesus in Early Christianity* (JSNTSup 112; Sheffield: Sheffield Academic, 1995), 245–47, esp. n. 33; Oakman, "Lord's Prayer in Social Perspective," in *Authenticating the Words of Jesus* (ed. Chilton and Evans), 175–76, understands the sixth petition as a plea to be delivered from "trials in rigged courts before evil judges" (176).

[29] P.S. Cameron, "Lead Us Not into Temptation," *ExpTim* 101 (1989–1990): 299–301, here p. 299.

[30] S.E. Porter, "Mt 6:13 and Lk 11:4: 'Lead Us Not into Temptation,'" *ExpTim* 101 (1989–1990): 359–62, here p. 359.

[31] B.D. Chilton modifies to *'al ta 'elenyi lenisyona*; cf. *Jesus' Prayer and Jesus' Eucharist* (Valley Forge: Trinity Press International, 1997), 46; J.C. de Moor, "Reconstruction of the Aramaic Original of the Lord's Prayer," 411–13, suggests *wela 'aytena lenisyon*. The DSS equivalent, in Hebrew, occurs only once (1QHa IV, 22). A more common term, *bahan*, can be seen at 1QM XVI, 11; 1QHᵃ X, 13; f 2 I, 8; 4Q177 II, 10; 4Q443 2.4.

[32] Joachim Jeremiah, "The Lord's Prayer in the Light of Recent Research," in his *The Prayers of Jesus* (London: SCM, 1967), 105–6; similarly Brown, "Pater Noster as an Eschatological Prayer,"

Or, in the words of Ernst Lohmeyer, "The focal point here is no longer the individual or even a particular community, but the final encounter between God and (the) evil (one) which ushers in God's kingdom."[33]

This eschatological apprehension of the term temptation/test as the Final Ordeal, like a hermit crab, has climbed into the shells of many kinds of scholars. Jesus' vision of the future for Israel (embedded now in the apocalyptic texts like Luke 22 and Mark 13) would suggest he had an above average understanding of its bleakness and therefore, also, the suitability of this sort of request. Thus, for this view the sixth petition is less about timidity and more about a profound perception of history, of the severity of what is shortly to come to pass in the land.

The following arguments deserve consideration in any interpretation of the meaning of the sixth petition.[34] First, it is highly unlikely that a first-century Jewish teacher would think humans can arrive at a state of moral perfection where they will no longer be tempted, in the sense of enticement, to do sinful things. The request, in that context, almost certainly cannot mean that Jesus prayed that his followers would no longer be tempted to sin in this life for, as C.F.D. Moule once tartly observed, "Would it [asking not to be tempted] not be about as logical as saying 'We know we are at war; but let there be no fighting!'?"[35]

Second, while the text is not as clear in its meaning as we might like,[36] the Jewish context of this petition emerges from the view that God, who himself can be "tested" (cf. Exod 17:7; Deut 6:16; 9:22; Ps 95:9), does not himself tempt

---

314–20; B.F. Meyer, *Aims of Jesus*, 206–8; the best survey of the evidence is D.C. Allison, Jr., *The End of the Ages Has Come* (Philadelphia: Fortress, 1985), 5–25; cf. also pp. 83–179, where the connections and implications are exposed. For the opposing view, namely, that "temptation" means not succumbing to daily temptations, which was the prevalent view of the early church, cf. K. Froelich, "The Lord's Prayer in Patristic Literature," in *The Lord's Prayer* (ed. Migliore), 86. See the strong response in Cullmann, *Prayer in the New Testament*, 58–66.

[33] Lohmeyer, *The Lord's Prayer*, 206 (cf. pp. 204–6); see also B.F. Meyer, *Aims of Jesus*, 208.

[34] It remains easiest to refer to the enumerated petitions in the Matthean version:

	Matthew	Luke	*Didache*
1.	Name	Name	Name
2.	kingdom	kingdom	kingdom
3.	Will		Will
4.	Bread	Bread	Bread
5.	Debts	Sins	Debts
6.	Temptation	Temptation	Temptation

[35] C.F.D. Moule, "An Unsolved Problem in the Temptation Clause in the Lord's Prayer," in his *Forgiveness and Reconciliation and Other New Testament Themes* (London: SPCK, 1998), 190–204, here p. 197.

[36] In fact, H.D. Betz thinks Matthew 6:13a reaffirms the old wisdom Jewish tradition in which God was the *source* of temptation, and the prayer is for God to complete his work of redemption so evil can be wiped away. See Betz, *Sermon on the Mount* (ed. Adela Yarbro Collins; Minneapolis: Fortress, 1995), 411–13.

humans to sin (*tentatio*).[37] Instead, he tests humans (*probatio*), especially the righteous, in order to reveal their covenant loyalty (cf. preeminently Adam and Eve [Gen 3], Abraham [22:1], Job, and David [Ps 26:2]; cf. also Exod 15:25; 16:4; 20:20; Deut 8:2, 16; 13:4; 33:8; Judg 2:22; 2 Chr 32:31; Prov 3:12; esp. Sir 2:1;15:11-20; 33:1; 44:19-20; 1 Macc 2:52; Wis 11:10; *Mart Isa* 5:4-16; Jdt 8:12-14, 22-23, 25-27). Along with this view in the Jewish tradition is the conviction that humans are seduced into sin by their own sinful nature as prodded by the world and the Evil One (cf. Gen 3; Acts 14:22; Jas 1:13-15; 1 John 2:15-17).[38] Temptations are contained within God's circumscribed omnipotence and God's knowing of the human possibilities (1 Cor 10:13; Jas 1:2, 12). Adjoined to God's protection of humans is the view that, left alone, humans could not handle what God could put them through (e.g., Ps 143:2),[39] which makes a connection to the exodus-wilderness experience a possible background.[40]

Third, the prayer of *b. Berakot* 60b provides a plausible, noneschatological, moral setting for the sixth petition—should one be so inclined to think Jesus was also noneschatological in orientation: "Bring me not into the power of sin, and not into the power of guilt, and not into the power of temptation, and not into the power of anything shameful." The same general request is found at *b. Sanhedrin* 107a, where David becomes the negative example in comparison to Abraham, Isaac, and Jacob. Earliest Christianity absorbed this framework (2 Pet 2:9; Polycarp, *Phil.* 7:1-3 [where theological apostasy threatens]) and set out some of its boundaries (1 Cor 10:13).[41] In effect, the petition would then be a litotes, with the positive expressed in the next petition.

Fourth, there are plenty of texts[42] that speak of the final days as the "messianic woes" and do so with the assumption that they will be a faith-challenging

[37] On this, cf. Porter, "Lead Us Not into Temptation," 359–62, who explores God's part in temptation.

[38] See Tertullian, *De oratione* 8; Cyril of Jerusalem, *Catecheses*, 23.17–18.

[39] See M.H. Sykes, "'And Do Not Bring Us to the Test,'" *ExpTim* 73 (1962): 189–90; like the professor who ends up purchasing two copies of the same book, Cameron put forth the same view in the same magazine some three decades later; cf. his "Lead Us Not into Temptation," 299–301.

[40] On which, cf. J.J. Lewis, "The Wilderness Controversy and *Peirasmos*," *Colloquium* 7 (1974): 42–44, where the possibility is raised that this is a prayer about not provoking God.

[41] The issue here is a narrowing of "do not lead us" into "do not allow us to succumb to," or "to escape from within." Cf. Moule, "Unsolved Problem in the Temptation Clause," 190–204; on the textual history of this view, cf. Manson, "The Lord's Prayer," 443–45; G.G. Willis, "Lead Us Not into Temptation," *DRev* 93 (1975): 281–88. See also the lengthy discussion in Davies and Allison, *Matthew*, 1:612–15; D.C. Allison, Jr., *The Sermon on the Mount* (New York: Crossroad, 1999), 129–31; J.M. Lachmann, *The Lord's Prayer* (trans. G.W. Bromiley; Grand Rapids: Eerdmans, 1998), 125–46, esp. 142–46; Betz, *Sermon on the Mount*, 408–10, who draws swords with Moule; Beasley-Murray, *Jesus and the Kingdom of God*, 156. On the Latin textual history of this permissive sense, see A.J.B. Higgins, "Lead Us Not into Temptation," *JTS* 46 (1945): 179–83; "'Lead Us Not into Temptation,'" *ExpTim* 58 (1946–47): 250. Important responses include O. Cullmann, *Prayer in the New Testament*, 62–65; Moule, "Unsolved Problem in the Temptation Clause."

[42] See Keener, *Matthew*, 224, esp. n. 183; Meyer, *Aims of Jesus*, 206–8; Allison, *End of the Ages Has Come*.

test.[43] From earliest Christianity we choose Revelation 3:10: "Because you have kept my word of patient endurance, I will keep you from *the hour of trial* that is coming on the whole world to test the inhabitants of the earth." The terms attributed to Jesus in the apocalyptic tradition are of the same cloth: "This is but the beginning of the birthpangs" (Mark 13:8; cf. Matt 24:8; diff. Luke 21:11). The theme of preservation during the final tribulation is a topos in apocalyptic expectations:

> You, however, if you prepare your minds to sow into them the fruits of the law, he shall protect you in the time in which the Mighty One shall shake the entire creation (*2 Bar.* 32:1; cf. 32:1-7; 40:1-4; *4 Ezra* 9:1-13; *Mek. de R. Ishm.*, Vayassa 5 [on Exod 16:25]).

> But You have appointed me as a banner for the chosen of righteousness, and an informed mediator of wonderful mysteries, so as to test [the men] of truth and to try the lovers of correction (1QH X, 13-14; cf. also 1QS III, 22-25; IV, 16-19; 4Q176 frag 15:3; 4Q177 II, 10).

Evidence of this sort led Raymond Brown to interpret the sixth petition as a prayer of escape from the "titanic struggle between God and Satan which must introduce the last days."[44] The evidence for the eschatological interpretation is indeed impressive, especially if one adds the early Christian gloss to the sixth petition, "Deliver us from the Evil One" (Matt 6:13), and understands that petition in a similar eschatological context. One thinks here of Luke 10:18, where Jesus sees Satan's expulsion from heaven and usurpation of earth. What is needed, he states, is mighty power as Satan's diminishing power heads for its fatal blow (Luke 22:53).[45] The Apocalypse illustrates this graphically. The more eschatological one's view of Jesus, the more likely it is that the Lord's Prayer and the sixth petition are to be given an eschatological interpretation.[46]

Consequently, the muted voice of the eschatological view has gained enough attention to be considered the lead voice:[47] the sixth petition most likely

---

[43] Davies and Allison, *Matthew*, 1:613, sufficiently respond to the view that the anarthrous εἰς πειρασμόν indicates a more general temptation rather than the specific eschatological ordeal. I am not persuaded by their logic, namely that (a) all affliction is embedded in the sixth petition; (b) therefore the final affliction is implicit; (c) the early Christians understood the present as the messianic woes; (d) therefore every test belongs to the eschatological drama. The language of early Christianity, instanced in Mark 13:8, clearly demarcates an *intensification* of the test, even if they understood the last days as realized. The issue thus becomes whether or not the test is a "last days test" (which has begun) or the "final ordeal test" (which is emerging from the horizon). See also Allison's discussion in *End of the Ages Has Come*, 140–41.

[44] Brown "Pater Noster as an Eschatological Prayer," 314.

[45] See Schürmann, *Praying with Christ*, 85–86.

[46] See Meyer, *Aims of Jesus*, 207.

[47] There has been, since C.H. Dodd and G.B. Caird, another test: whether or not the language of Jesus will be permitted its literal sense of time or transferred (at times) into a *timelessness*. It strikes

meant, in Jesus' context, "Lord, do not let us succumb[48] in the final ordeal that will utterly test us." I take it as an assumption that the prayer Jesus *taught* is the same prayer that he *prayed for himself.* While it would take us into deep waters too quickly here to explore this theme, it should be observed that Brant Pitre, in his dissertation, has made a strong case for seeing the Lord's Prayer as ripe with allusions to a new exodus and that the temptation clause is just as much related to the Passover traditions of Exodus 12 (cf. Deut 4:27-34; 7:19 [LXX]; 29:3 [LXX]) as it is to later tribulation traditions. This is suggestive of what will be argued throughout this monograph.[49]

The significance of this statement for our study cannot be missed: Jesus, in his heart of hearts (which is how I understand the Lord's Prayer), did not want to go through that final ordeal alone or with his followers. Either he hoped for a national repentance that would avert that ordeal or he hoped for a premature deliverance.[50] On balance, I think the second option is as likely as the first. But, what matters in this context is this: Jesus seems to have recognized the *possibility* (even if at this stage remote) of a premature death, and his earnest prayer was for the Father to shape history so it would take a different course.

MARK 14:36, 38

That eschatological ordeal becomes personal in Gethsemane,[51] and shows that Jesus, from start to finish, did not relish what seemed just over the horizon.[52] Until these two texts are given clear explanations and set as they must be in the larger context of his mission, one must refrain from stating that Jesus' mission was simply to die for the sins of the world. I am loath to deny the centrality of his death for comprehending his accomplishment, but I am also deeply aware that the traditional Christians' framing of his mission in terms of a "life to die"

---

me that N.T. Wright, in his *Jesus and the Victory of God*, while helpfully clarifying the metaphorical language of, say, Mark 13:24-27, fails to render what the analog to the metaphor might be: and my view is that time, in the sense of imminency and the end of the world, cannot be erased from those metaphors. In other words, while I agree with Wright on the metaphorical nature of the language of Mark 13:24-27, I believe he fails to ask the question of when and the significance of that when.

[48] The permissive sense of "do not lead" has been recognized often; cf. Joachim Jeremias, *The Prayers of Jesus* (London: SCM, 1967), 104–5; Davies and Allison, *Matthew*, 1:613.

[49] See B.J. Pitre, "The Historical Jesus, the Great Tribulation and the End of the Exile," Ph.D. diss. (Notre Dame, 2004), 145–81.

[50] So A. Schweitzer, *The Kingdom of God and Primitive Christianity* (ed. and intro. by U. Neuenschwander; trans. L.A. Garrard; New York: Seabury, 1968), 118–19.

[51] On the Gethsemane event, cf. R.S. Barbour, "Gethsemane in the Tradition of the Passion," 231–51; Gibson, *Temptations of Jesus in Early Christianity*, 238–55; see also the masterful sweep of discussion in C.A. Evans, *Mark*, 2:404–7.

[52] For an exploration of the connection between Gethsemane and the Lord's Prayer, cf. Popkes, "Die letzte Bitte des Vater-Unser," 8–17.

needs a much more nuanced statement. As D.E.H. Whiteley, who was no stranger to the Christian faith, once stated, "the accounts of the Agony in the Garden of Gethsemane are not easy to reconcile with the theory that Christ at all times regarded His death as inevitable."[53] No one has captured the implication of the prayer of Jesus here any more vividly than Jeff Gibson, whose informed study is concerned with Markan theology, but whose words would apply to Jesus himself if the words are considered history. Here are his observations:

> It is clear that the aim of this petition is *nothing less than the elimination of the cross from the messiahship. Jesus prays that as Messiah he will not have to suffer and die* . . . the anguish and bewilderment, the hesitation and uncertainty to which Jesus is subject in Gethsemane arises [sic] out of a conflict between Jesus' desire to be faithful to his calling and to accomplish the Messianic task and the apparent irrationality of submitting in obedience to a divinely decreed plan of action when it seemed that to obey was to jeopardize God's worthwhile purposes. . . . It also shows that the petition of Jesus entails the desire to be allowed to implement a plan of action to accomplish the Messianic task which is the very opposite of God's will in this regard, one, namely, that uses violence and domination, instead of suffering and service, to achieve this end and envisages the punishment and destruction, not the inclusion within the mercies of God, of those "not of Israel."[54]

Some of that evidence we are in search of finds itself in the classic text, Mark 14:35-36 and 38:

> And going a little farther, he threw himself on the ground and prayed that, if it were possible, the hour might pass from him. He said, "Abba, Father, for you all things are possible; remove this cup from me; yet, not what I want, but what you want." . . . "Keep awake and pray that you may not come into the time of trial [or, into temptation]."

The Christology of this text, to the degree that we know it, swims upstream against the flow of early Christian christological reflection, as can be seen both in the Gospel traditions themselves (cf. John 18:11) and noncanonical evidence (cf. Justin, *Dial.* 99; Celsus in Origen, *Cels.* 2:24). It presents a Jesus who either (1) did not want to die and wanted God to change his will[55] or expected, at Passover, for the end to occur (cf. *Mek. de R. Ishm.* on Exod 12:42 [pp. 115–16][56]) or almost impossibly, was (2) afraid of death (some appeal to Mark

---

[53] D.E.M. Whiteley, "Christ's Foreknowledge of His Crucifixion," *SE* I (= TU 73 [1959]): 100–14; here pp. 100–101.

[54] Gibson, *Temptations of Jesus in Early Christianity*, 248, 251, 253 (italics mine).

[55] Contingency in God's will is pervasive in ancient Israel and Judaism; cf. Gen 18; 22; Exod 32:10-14; 2 Kgs 20:1-6; 2 Sam 15:25-26; Judg 2:1-3; Jer 18:5-11. Cf. P.D. Miller, *They Cried to the Lord* (Minneapolis: Fortress, 1994), 55–134; Cullmann, *Prayer in the New Testament*, 132–42.

[56] Which reads: "In that night were they redeemed and in that night will be redeemed in the future—these are the words of R. Joshua, as it is said: 'This same night is a night of watching unto

14:33). Both Matthew and Luke toned down the emotions of Jesus found in Mark 14:32-42.[57]

Also, it is hard, despite some voices to the contrary, to set this text in the context of the Maccabean martyr theology tradition. In fact, there is no Jewish martyr story that sheds light on the potential martyr's anxiety about death, as the classic text of 2 Maccabees 7 shows. The stories were about those with the courage of Daniel and the Maccabee boys, or for those with classical ancestors; about Thermopylae and King Leonidas, King of Sparta, not about fear and prayer for release. Hence, we might legitimately appeal to the so-called criterion of dissimilarity for defense. And, the Christology reveals a human being[58] who is suddenly attacked by intense anguish and pain, and who therefore "contemplates a route around suffering."[59]

The essence of this logion's concern to avoid suffering makes cameo appearances in John 12:27 (a troubled soul); 18:11 (drinking the cup as metaphor for death); and Hebrews 5:7 ("loud cries and tears"). If the logion is judged to be too explicit, or at least hard to accept because it required eavesdropping on Jesus' prayer (while stating the followers were at a distance and evidently failing Jesus by sleeping;[60] cf. Mark 14:32-42), the narrative report of Mark 14:35 (he prayed in anguish of what he was to face) provides all that is necessary for our purposes for understanding how Jesus saw his death.[61] In fact, one can mute the evidence of Mark 14:36 because 14:35 gives the fundamental datum: Jesus was in anguish about death. That is, the variations on the Markan logion in Matthew (26:42, where Matthew in his parallel to Mark 14:39 duplicates the earlier wording from 14:36, emphasizing the desire to avoid the pain) and Luke (22:42) can be used to support the view that Mark 14:36 is a Markan (or pre-Markan) explication of Mark 14:35 that both Matthew and Luke expand. Even so, and the arguments are far from convincing, the general thrust of Mark 14:36 remains

---

the Lord.'" There follows a disagreement by R. Eliezer, who speculates the final redemption to be in Tishri, and cites Ps 81:4-5 in defense.

[57] Cf. Barbour, "Gethsemane in the Tradition of the Passion," 236–42.

[58] So Fitzmyer, *Luke*, 2:1442.

[59] Davies and Allison, *Matthew*, 3:502.

[60] The sleep of the disciples, however, might be construed as a piece of the theological portrait of Mark in the so-called messianic secret. There is still no better text for this than C. Tuckett, ed., *The Messianic Secret* (IRT 1; Philadelphia: Fortress, 1983). C.K. Barrett: "In these circumstances men may run away, but they do not normally fall asleep" (*Jesus and the Gospel Tradition* [Philadelphia: Fortress, 1968], 47). On sleep, cf. D. Daube, *The New Testament and Rabbinic Judaism* (1956; repr. Peabody, Mass.: Hendrickson, n.d.), 332–35, who points us to *m. Pesah.* 10:8 and *b. Pesah.* 120b where dozing is distinguished from deep sleep; if the deep sleep occurs at *Pesah*, the meal is reckoned over. See also Whiteley, "Christ's Foreknowledge of His Crucifixion," 111–12.

[61] Mark Kiley suggests that Mark 14:36 was *Gemeindetheologie* under the influence of the *Hallel* hymn now found at Psalm 116:4. Cf. his " 'Lord, Save My Life' (Ps 116:4) as Generative Text for Jesus' Gethsemane Prayer (Mark 14:36a)," *CBQ* 48 (1986): 655–59. The links he forges, however, are too imprecise to persuade.

stubbornly historical because it merely makes explicit what is in Mark 14:35, and almost no one questions the anguish of Jesus in the garden of Gethsemane.

What makes the logion's thrust even more historically solid is the use of "test" in Mark 14:38 (par. Matt 26:41; Luke 22:40b, 46), leading one back to the "cup" sayings (Mark 10:38)[62] and to the sixth petition as a leitmotif of Jesus' life and mission: Jesus foresaw the Final Ordeal on the horizon and yearned for God to deliver him (and his people) from that hour. The use of *Abba*,[63] the affirmation of God's sovereignty, and the distinctively dissimilar resignation to God's will[64] each feature in Jesus' teachings and mission, and in fact are anchored in the Lord's Prayer. Even if there is a thin layer of early Christian dust under our feet,[65] we are standing on solid ground when claiming that Mark 14:35-36 reflects an event in the life of Jesus.[66] As James Dunn said, "For myself I find it difficult to attribute the origin of this record to any other source than the all too vivid scene brutally etched on the memory of even the dullard disciples."[67]

If we understand the meaning of this event in Jesus' life along the lines of the sixth petition, which itself is echoed in the same scene (Mark 14:38), we are on firm ground to argue that Jesus yearned to escape the final ordeal and once again prayed, *sans arrière pensées*, to the Father for this cup to pass him by.[68] In other words, he asked God to preserve him from that hour or he asked for that hour to be suspended, or he asked, in essence, for the bell to ring before the clock's final tick.[69] However we take it, we have before us an insight into Jesus' expectation and understanding of his death: since opposition to God's final call to Israel would bring on the Final Ordeal, his death must be understood as part of that ordeal. These two requests are bookends to the life of the public Jesus, and they demonstrate a unity of vision. Neither at the beginning nor at the end

---

[62] See below, ch. 5, under "Mark 10:38."

[63] The Markan ἀββα ὁ πατήρ is clearly redundant and partakes of early Christian language (cf. Gal 4:6; Rom 8:15); see also Finkel, "Prayer of Jesus in Matthew," 152–58.

[64] See here Heinemann, "Background of Jesus' Prayer," 86, who points to the novelty of Jesus' surrender: "It is clear beyond all doubt that these words of Jesus are directed against the prayer of the synagogue, and against fixed, statutory public prayer in general. In its place, he prefers a simple prayer conforming to the tradition of popular private prayer" (89). See also R.T. France, *Mark*, 585.

[65] R.S. Barbour sees in the Gethsemane tradition "almost the only point at which the Passion narrative has not altogether yielded to the overriding sense of predestination and fulfilment of the Scriptures . . ."; cf. "Gethsemane in the Tradition of the Passion," 247.

[66] Most scholars: cf. e.g., J. Nolland, *Luke*, 3:1082, who wonders if the logion is not so strongly contrary to what is otherwise known of Jesus to suggest inauthenticity.

[67] James Dunn, *Jesus and the Spirit* (Philadelphia: Westminster, 1975), 19. Dunn offers the best defense of the essential authenticity of the prayer in Gethsemane; pp. 17–20.

[68] One cannot fail to quote the laconic stance of Fitzmyer in contrast to the many psychological interpretations: after listing several such, he comments: "His [Jesus'] foresight of all this would have caused the distress and the agony" (*Luke*, 2: 1440).

[69] See Barrett, *Jesus and the Gospel Tradition*, 46–49.

was his desire for God to bring about the cup of judgment against his people. His desire was to realize the kingdom of God.

If many discover here some fragility on Jesus' part, I confess (in the Christian tradition) that I think that—in light of Jesus' mission, his steadfast teachings on the need to face persecution, and his resolute determination that night not to flee—a deeper meaning not often mentioned can be seen in this text. In essence, the temptation logia can be understood as *petitions*: Jesus' desire not to endure them is an *appeal* to the Father to redeem his people, preserve the honor due his name, and to do so speedily and soon and, if God so acts, Jesus himself will be relieved of this pain.

The eschatological nature of the request is confirmed in the term *cup*, which (as will be shown below), is a metaphor for YHWH's judgmental word, the day of YHWH, about Israel's covenantal disobedience.[70] From the days of John the Baptist until now, the axe has been laid against the tree; Jesus prayed that neither he nor his followers would be near the tree when God picked up the axe and slammed it into the tree in judgment. This leads to the observation that Jesus must have understood his death as an aspect of his eschatology:[71] that is, since what was about to occur to him was part of the Final Ordeal, his death must be understood as eschatological, as part of that eschatological scenario about to unfold on the stage of Jerusalem's history. And his desire is that God would postpone the lifting of the axe. Even more profoundly, however, he relinquishes his petition to the will of God (cf. Mark 14:36, 38b, 41).

From beginning to end, then, we can affirm that Jesus wanted God to usher in the kingdom. He knew, however, that history does not often follow one's hopes. If history chose another path, he was ready to change directions himself and follow the will of God. Consequently, he prayed for his people and for himself that God would find some way to intervene to alter history. This conclusion can surround the other texts that deserve consideration in our study, one set of which concerns Jesus' seeming view that his life would not run to the end of the three score and ten, his view that he would be present with his followers only temporarily.

---

[70] Cf. A.T. Hanson, *The Wrath of the Lamb* (London: SPCK, 1957), 27–36; Keener, *Matthew*, 638 n. 87.

[71] So also R.E. Brown, *The Death of the Messiah* (2 vols.; ABRL; New York: Doubleday, 1994), 1:154, 159–60, et passim.

Chapter 5

A Temporary Presence in God's Providence

If Jesus saw his death as a *possibility* and could see his death in connection to the arrival of the Final Ordeal, the great tribulation, the next step in our study is to determine if his thoughts moved beyond possibility to *probability*. Did Jesus, in other words, not only comprehend that the eschatological coursing of time *could* put his life in jeopardy, but also that it *would* almost inevitably make his death a likelihood? Was this coursing of history part of God's plan for his life? Was his death a way for him to absorb the blows of that Final Ordeal?

A scattering of Jesus traditions raises these issues in one form or another, and evidently from both earlier and later parts of his life. While these texts never broach the issue of a theory of atonement, they each do suggest that Jesus thought his death would be premature. We examine then those texts that, if authentic, speak to Jesus' death as a part of God's plan for Israel's history.

A TEMPORARY PRESENCE

MARK 2:19-20

In a tradition found in all three Synoptic Gospels, Jesus defends his and his followers' practice of not fasting and, in doing so, suggests that he might not be around for a normal life span (Mark 2:18-22; par. Matt 9:14-17; Luke 5:33-39):

> [18]Now John's disciples and the Pharisees were fasting; and people came and said to him, "Why do John's disciples and the disciples of the Pharisees fast, but your disciples do not fast?" [19]Jesus said to them, "The wedding guests cannot fast while the bridegroom is with them, can they? As long as they have the bridegroom with them, they cannot fast. [20]The days will come when the bridegroom is taken away from them, and then they will fast on that day.

[21]"No one sews a piece of unshrunk cloth on an old cloak; otherwise, the patch pulls away from it, the new from the old, and a worse tear is made. [18]And no one puts new wine into old wineskins; otherwise, the wine will burst the skins, and the wine is lost, and so are the skins; but one puts new wine into fresh wineskins."

All scholars are agreed that Mark 2:18-22 is an expanded tradition, but most also argue that there is very little evidence of Markan redaction;[1] instead, the tradition has grown into the present unit prior to Mark. Many would argue that Mark 2:18-19a and 2:21-22 were the original unit, with 2:19b-20 added later, but prior to Mark.[2]

What matters for our study is whether or not the traditions are plausibly authentic. Norman Perrin pounded in the stake in front of the little pond of this pericope and pinned to it the sign "No Fishing" (read: inauthentic), but soon thereafter a big group of scholars (the Jesus Seminar) ignored his sign, came upon the pond, tossed in some lines, and found fish (read: authentic).[3] The ground for concluding that 2:19a and 2:19b are authentic is that Jesus' disciples did not fast, while the disciples of other Jewish leaders at the time did fast. The logion simply expresses this social fact.

It is reasonable to argue that, if Jesus and his disciples did not follow customary fasting practices,[4] he offered some sort of defense.[5] Thus, that defense can be seen in 2:19a-b: Jesus is with them, it is time to celebrate (cf. Q 7:31-35); the kingdom is here, but the days are coming when it won't be appropriate to fast. According to this same branch of scholarship, Mark 2:20 makes explicit in a parenthetical aside that fasting would resume when Jesus died (cf. also Acts 13:2-3; 14:23; Matt 6:16-18). But, that verse according to most is a later piece

---

[1] J. Gnilka finds Markan redaction only in Mark 2:18a and "the new from the old" phrase of 2:21 (*Markus*, 1:111–13), while E.J. Pryke finds Markan redaction only in "and the Pharisees were fasting" as well as in the "and the disciples of the Pharisees" phrase in 2:18 (*Redactional Style in the Marcan Gospel* [SNTSMS 33; London: Cambridge University Press, 1978], 154).

[2] On this, cf. the studies of R. Pesch, *Markusevangelium*, 1:171, 174–75; M.D. Hooker, *Mark*, 97–101; J. Marcus, *Mark 1–8*, 237; R.A. Guelich, *Mark 1–8:26*, 107–8; J. Roloff, *Das Kerygma und der irdische Jesus: Historische Motive in den Jesus-Erzählung der Evangelien* (Göttingen: Vandenhoeck & Ruprecht, 1970), 223–37. The older studies of V. Taylor, *Mark*, 211–12, and C.E.B. Cranfield, *Mark*, 110–11, defend the authenticity of Mark 2:19-20.

[3] R.W. Funk and R.W. Hoover, *The Five Gospels* (New York: Macmillan [Polerbride], 1993), 47; R.W. Funk and the Jesus Seminar, ed. and trans. *The Acts of Jesus* (San Francisco: HarperSanFrancisco, 1998), 67; contra N. Perrin, *Rediscovering the Teaching of Jesus* (New York: Harper & Row, 1967), 79.

[4] We are to suppose here that Jesus does not follow the Monday–Thursday fast, not that he does not fast at all (cf. Matt 4; Mark 14:25; and the fast on Yom Kippur as stipulated in Lev 16).

[5] Roloff, among others, has argued that this text does not provide a defense of early Christian practices; cf. *Das Kerygma und der irdische Jesus*, 223–29. For some important early Christian evidence, consider Matthew 6:16-18; Acts 13:2-3; *Did.* 1:3; 8:1.

of Christian theologizing[6] from a christologically developed angle (see also Luke 17:22).

Mark 2:19 can be defended also on eschatological grounds: the basis of Jesus' defense of the suspension of fasting is that a new day has dawned and its light is shed on fasting practices. Those practices are not for the celebrants of the arrival of God's kingdom. That Jesus' departure from the customary fasting is tied into the characteristic practice of table fellowship[7] confirms a coherent picture: those who formerly fasted for the completion of God's promises are now celebrating the completion of those promises in the kingdom mission of Jesus. In addition, the choice of nuptial imagery for expressing eschatological arrival is historically plausible for a Jewish prophet (cf. Hos 2:14-15; Isa 61:10; 62:4-5; Matt 22:1-14; 25:1-13; John 3:29; Rev 19:7). Also, Jesus' sense of eschatological imminency seems present, and the saying can be understood as a "veiled messianic claim,"[8] the sort of veiling so typical of Jesus. The practice of Jesus and his followers, the defense by Jesus, and the imagery chosen fit his mission in general.[9]

A dating wedge can be placed in the discussion if one can determine from the attitude expressed toward John the Baptist and his disciples whether or not Jesus' mentor has departed the scene. We can infer from the Q tradition (Q 7:18-35; 16:16) that Jesus and John debated their roles and spent time considering what parts of scripture they were to act out.[10] That they differed on some matters, perhaps even crucial matters, can be inferred from the parting of their ministries. It is probable that, since the tradition in front of us does not begin with "*John and* his disciples" (Mark 2:18a) approaching Jesus, John is no longer with them. In such a case, the people who are concerned are contrasting the two movements.[11] This leaves us with several logical steps, none of which can be adequately demonstrated here, but which are highly probable.

First, John is gone, and I take it as certain that Jesus would have thought of his own death as a possibility in the wake of John's. If so, *second*, we can suggest

---

[6] We find here a shift in topic, tone, and genre: from the suspension of fasting and the eschaton to a new day of fasting; from defense of the suspension of fasting to warning; and from straightforward statement to prophecy; on this, cf. esp. Guelich, *Mark 1–8:26*, 111–14; contra France, *Mark*, 139–40.

[7] So Roloff, *Das Kerygma und der irdische Jesus*, 227.

[8] See France, *Mark*, 139.

[9] *Pace* J.E. Taylor, *The Immerser* (Grand Rapids: Eerdmans, 1997), 206–7.

[10] On this, cf. my conclusions below, ch. 8, under "John the Baptist." And, cf. J.A.T. Robinson, "Elijah, John and Jesus," in his *Twelve New Testament Studies* (London: SCM, 1984), 28–52. On this view of "Scripture prophets," cf. again, ch. 8, under "John the Baptist."

[11] So also Roloff, *Das Kerygma und der irdische Jesus*, 228. One can consider John 3:29 in this light: here John and Jesus are contrasted over joy, though in John it is the Baptist who attributes joy to the Jesus movement, and it is seen to be a concern of various followers. It is not far from joy to the suspension of fasting. It might even be more credible to suggest that it was the suspension of fasting that led to the joy! See C.H. Dodd, *Historical Tradition in the Fourth Gospel* (London: Cambridge University Press, 1976), 282–85.

that Mark 2:19 is late rather than early in the public ministry of Jesus. It would postdate John's own abstemious "last supper" of edible bits found in the desert. And, if John is gone and Jesus has considered the possibility of his own death in light of John's violent death, then, *third*, we might suggest that 2:19a-b affirms not only the suspension of fasting but also, *while* and *as long as* the temporary presence of Jesus occurs. We have already concluded in the previous section that an early Christian redactor added 2:20 to make precisely this point,[12] probably under the influence of reports about Jesus' death and a new reading of Amos 8:9-14. (I am open, however, to the suggestion that Mark 2:20 could be rendered authentic in light of the life connections Jesus had with John.) But this conclusion that Jesus anticipated a premature death, however tantalizing, is not firm enough here to shape our understanding of Jesus' view of his own death, and so requires supporting evidence from the life of Jesus to tip the conclusion from the possible to the probable.

MARK 10:38

One such piece of evidence can be found in a text enormously significant for understanding several features about Jesus, not the least of which is his understanding of the fate of his own life. Thus, Mark 10:38 reads:

> But Jesus said to them, "You do not know what you are asking. Are you able to drink the cup that I drink, or be baptized with the baptism that I am baptized with?"

A general consensus considers this logion as apparently "untouched" by Mark,[13] though some still maintain that there are some traces of it in the sayings of early Christianity.[14] The first group also tends to argue that the logion is substantially authentic.[15]

---

[12] So Pesch, who states that the logion shifts from the "*Wann* der Nicht-Fastenzeit in Richtung der Frage nach dem *Wie lange* ihrer Dauer verschoben wird: aus 'während' wird 'solange'!" (*Markusevangelium*, 1:174).

[13] My study tabulates the conclusions in the commentaries and redactional studies of R. Pesch, J. Gnilka, E.J. Pryke, and C.A. Evans.

[14] Matthew has omitted the baptism half of the logion at Matthew 20:22. For possible motives, cf. Davies and Allison, *Matthew*, 3:89. See also G. Braumann, "Leidenskelch und Todestaufe (Mc 10 38f.)," *ZNW* 56 (1965): 178–83, who invents an early Christian *Sitz im Leben* in which there is a debate about the propriety of drinking wine prior to the eschatological banquet, and the possibility of not undergoing baptism.

[15] A defense of Mark 10:38 can be seen in A. Feuillet, "La coupe et le baptême de la passion (Mc, x, 35-40; cf. Mt. xx, 20-23; Lc., xxii, 50)," *RB* 74 (1967): 356–91, here pp. 358–70; V. Howard, "Did Jesus Speak About His Own Death?" *CBQ* 39 (1977): 515–27, who argues, with a nuanced use of the so-called "criteria," that a saying like this provides the substantial link between Jesus' life and the call by Jesus for his followers to endure martyrdom; M. Casey, *Aramaic Sources of Mark's Gospel* (SNTSMS 102; Cambridge: Cambridge University Press, 1998), 206; see also E.P. Sanders, *Jesus and Judaism* (Philadelphia: Fortress, 1985), 147.

But, the discussion is not about tallying votes by recognized authorities, so we need to consider the following evidential and historical arguments. Counting in favor of the *inauthenticity* of the logion is that the "cup" dimension of the saying may recall rather than forecast Gethsemane (Mark 14:36) or perhaps even the last supper (Mark 14:22-25). Scholarship tends to value Jesus' creative use of metaphor,[16] but it is the choice of metaphors here that leads toward skepticism. "Baptism," as an indicator of one's death, suggests a possible connection to Paul (Rom 6:3-4) and, therefore, early church exegesis rather than historical Jesus.

On the other hand, while the strengths of these observations are obvious, it is first of all the Christology of the pericope that leads to the suggestion of the possibility of a judgment of *authenticity*: here we have a Jesus who is limited in power, in eschatological power, because he is not given the authority to assign places in the eschatological banquet (Mark 10:40). Where else but in the earliest dimensions of the Jesus tradition do we find such a Christology? But there are other supporting arguments that lead to a decisive conclusion for the authenticity of the logion.

Second, the double attestation of the baptism metaphor (cf. Mark 10:38; Luke 12:49-50) reveals that this is a logion used in different traditions (*multiple attestation*).[17] And yet, anchored as this logion is in terms and ideas found in sayings by John the Baptist, it stands out as a variant of what John meant with the similar terms and ideas (cf. Q 3:16). Our logion is clearly not a repetition of John but a performance of John's saying in a new and refreshing way, this time by Jesus. A third argument on behalf of Mark 10:38: John, the son of Zebedee, was not in fact martyred so far as we know and the logion hints at such a fate for John. Therefore, at least part of the logion is not a *vaticinium ex eventu* (cf. Irenaeus, *Haer.* 2.22.5; 3.3.4; Eusebius, *Hist. eccl.* 3.23).

Fourth, the baptism of Christ in Romans, and Jesus' "baptism" here are not as similar as some have stated, even if the language shows similarities. In particular, Romans 6:3-4 refers to a unique death of Christ into which the early Christians are also plunged. This, at a deep level, needs to be distinguished from the coequality of a baptismal death described in Mark 10:38-39. If the early Christian tradition has invented the logion on the basis of Romans 6:3-4, then that creator has dechristologized the Pauline sentiment and turned the saying on its head: baptism in Christ (incorporative) has become baptism of Jesus himself (alone). This, too, would fight the tendency of early Christian Christology. Fifth, the "baptism" of Q 3:16 about which John spoke needs to be seen for

---

[16] For two good studies of the metaphor here, see Feuillet, "La coupe et le baptême de la passion"; G. Delling, "βαπτισμα βαπτισθηναι," *NovT* 2 (1957–58): 92–115.

[17] On which, cf. below, ch. 6, under "Luke 12:49-50." See also James D. G. Dunn, "The Birth of a Metaphor—Baptized in Spirit," in his *Pneumatology* (vol. 2 of *The Christ and the Spirit*; Grand Rapids: Eerdmans, 1998), 103–17; *Jesus Remembered* (vol. 1 of *Christianity in the Making*; Grand Rapids: Eerdmans, 2003), 802–4.

what it was: a metaphor of judgment rather than a liturgical action.[18] The logion
of Mark 10:38 can be credibly assigned to Jesus.

It appears then that Jesus and John share a common metaphor vis-à-vis the
early church—even if Jesus reshapes the Baptist's metaphor slightly. Such a conclusion satisfies the *criterion of dissimilarity* because the meaning of the saying is
technically not that of the early church.

An important observation once again needs to be recalled: Jesus' connection
to John undoubtedly—at least following his death—led Jesus to think of his
potential death at the hands of Roman leadership. That connection alone establishes an even firmer link to John's image of baptismal judgment as a spring-
board for Jesus' own rendition of that image. As John thought of the coming
trouble, so also did Jesus—and Jesus did so in the mentor's terms. This makes
the logion historically plausible because both sayings emerge from a similar context (Final Ordeal) and they are not quite the same as the early Christian use of
those images.

There is more support for the authenticity of the logion. The ecclesial setting assumed in the *ex eventu* interpretation fits no known realities: where John
is martyred, where John and James are elevated in importance, and where no
mention is given to Peter.[19] Furthermore, Maurice Casey has proposed a plausible Aramaic rendering of the logion.[20] In addition, *cup* has a plausible prophetic,
targumic or Jewish setting (e.g., Isa 51:17, 22; *Tg. Neof.* on Deut 32:1; *Tg. Neof.*
on Gen 40:23; *Mart. Ascen. Isa.* 5:13; *T. Ab.* 16:11) and should be carefully distinguished from cup in the last supper (Mark 14:22-25). Finally, some argue
that the logion is so like Markan denigration of the apostles/disciples that it
must stem from his own creative hand. However, in spite of statements that
Mark's Gospel is harsh on the disciples, and therefore the harshness may be a
Markan motif rather than historical memory, the evidence for wholesale invention of the obtuseness of the disciples is not compelling. It is not historical reasoning to contend that since Mark has a motif, every instance of that motif
indicates creation by Mark. Matthew, who has been accused of idealizing the
Twelve, retains plenty of incidents reflecting a less than flattering light on the
figure of the disciples. Thus, we must reckon fairly with the observation that it
is as possible for the disciples to have been this blind as it is for Mark to have
invented the motif out of whole cloth. The foundation for Markan creativity
here is not significant enough to be used.

But what might this logion have meant in the life of Jesus? We have
assumed a death-related interpretation: "Can you disciples drink the cup (of
death) I drink? Can you be baptized with the baptism (of death) I am baptized
with?" But is that the most accurate way to render *cup* and *baptism*? A close reading of cup allusions in the Hebrew Bible suggests, instead, that our above-

---

[18] So Dunn, "Birth of a Metaphor," in his *Pneumatology*, 104–7.

[19] So Sanders, *Jesus and Judaism*, 147.

[20] Casey, *Aramaic Sources of Mark's Gospel*, 193–218, esp. 201–5.

mentioned bookends—Matthew 6:13 and Mark 14:36—bracket the discussion and enclose our cup and baptism logion within the category of the Final Ordeal, the great tribulation, rather than simply the category of a premature death.[21] One thinks, for instance, of the following passage:

> Rouse yourself, rouse yourself!
>> Stand up, O Jerusalem,
> you who have drunk at the hand of the LORD
>> the cup of his wrath,
> who have drunk to the dregs
>> the bowl of staggering. (Isa 51:17; cf. 43:1-2)

> Thus says your Sovereign, the LORD,
>> your God who pleads the cause of his people:
> See, I have taken from your hand the cup of staggering;
> you shall drink no more
>> from the bowl of my wrath. (Isa 51:22)

> For thus the LORD, the God of Israel, said to me:
> Take from my hand this cup of the wine of wrath, and make all the
> nations to whom I send you drink it. (Jer 25:15; cf. 25:17, 28; 49:12; 51:7)

> You have gone the way of your sister; therefore I will give her cup into
>> your hand.
> Thus says the Lord GOD:
> You shall drink your sister's cup,
>> deep and wide;
> you shall be scorned and derided,
>> it holds so much.
> You shall be filled with drunkenness and sorrow.
> A cup of horror and desolation
>> is the cup of your sister Samaria. (Ezek 23:31-33)

> You will be sated with contempt instead of glory.
>> Drink, you yourself, and stagger!
> The cup in the LORD's right hand
>> will come around to you,
> and shame will come upon your glory! (Hab 2:16)

> On the wicked he will rain coals of fire and sulfur;
>> a scorching wind shall be the portion of their cup. (Ps 11:6; cf. 75:8)

---

[21] See the various suggestions in J.D.M. Derrett, "Christ's Second Baptism (Lk 12:50; Mk 10:38-40)," *ExpTim* 100 (1988–1989): 294–95. The most complete survey of the ancient evidence is D.C. Allison, Jr., *The End of the Ages Has Come* (Philadelphia: Fortress, 1985), 5–25.

With this evidence in the Tanakh, we can stand on firm ground to state that when he said *cup* his audience would have understood the purification of the Final Ordeal, the tribulation that was about to come as God poured out his judgment on unfaithfulness and (and this is an emphasis in the biblical theme of wrath) prepared his people for redemption.[22] The metaphor of baptism is but a case of hendiadys or parallelism with *cup*: the cup of judgment/suffering and the baptism he is to endure are each images of the impending case of YHWH against Israel's covenantal unfaithfulness and the judgment he will mete out as he displays faithfulness to his promises (Gen 6–8; Pss 9:15-17; 88:6-7; Q 17:26-27).[23] There is substantial confirmation of this Final Ordeal understanding of Mark 10:38: Luke 12:49-50, a variant of Mark 10:38, connects baptism to "fire," showing that in that context a tribulation as purification is in view. Again, John, whose mentor role for Jesus should not be neglected in this regard,[24] apparently made the same connection (Q 3:16): the baptism about which both John and Jesus spoke was an image of what will happen to those who experience the day of YHWH when he comes to purify his land and his people for his perfect rule.

Here we have found our way back to what Jesus had in mind in Mark 10:38. We find not a passion prediction but the prediction of a passion, that is, a prediction of suffering in the Final Ordeal. In the concern of this study, what we have here is a clear statement that Jesus sees suffering on the horizon, and it just may be that he thinks this suffering will lead to death. We would be safe to infer from suffering the possibility of death, but that is not yet established. Nor is it wise at this point to think that Jesus' drinking of the cup or immersing himself in the baptismal waters are in any way a vicarious act for the others, though clearly in Mark 10:38 there is a hint that the disciples, after all, may very well experience the same (but after Jesus, who may be paving the way for them).[25] If there is anything here, it would be that Jesus, like the Son of man in Daniel 7, sees himself at the head of a people who will undergo a terrible ordeal of suffering. But, again, such an inference is pushing the evidence before us far beyond its intent at this point.

Because the issue of the Final Ordeal and Jesus' perception of his own death are so intertwined, it is important to pause to set out a brief survey of the data and issues. It is not possible to sort out all the data in this context but, because Dale Allison and Brant Pitre have done so, our task can be abbreviated and their evidence reused.[26] In spite of the seminal work of Albert Schweitzer (*The Quest*

---

[22] For *cup* in the DSS, cf. 1QpHab XI, 10, 14; 4Q169 3-4 IV, 6; 4Q176 6 VII, 2; 4Q386 1 III, 1.

[23] G. Delling severed "baptism" from the water rite in his "βαπτισμα βαπτισθηναι," 95–102.

[24] On this, cf. esp. J.P. Meier, *A Marginal Jew* (3 vols.; ABRL; New York: Doubleday, 1991–2001), 2:19–233.

[25] So also France, *Mark*, 416.

[26] See Allison, *The End of the Ages Has Come*, 5–25; B.J. Pitre, "The Historical Jesus, the Great Tribulation and the End of the Exile," Ph.D. diss. (Notre Dame, 2004), esp. 41–142. In addition, others have made use of Allison's ground-breaking study, including N.T. Wright, *Jesus and the Victory of God* (Christian Origins and the Question of God 2; Minneapolis: Fortress, 1996);

of the Historical Jesus) and the more recent study of Allison, it is noteworthy that Pitre must spell out how infrequently the tribulation is substantive in historical Jesus scholarship.

Jewish literature, especially the apocalypses, vary on the order of events that will unfold before the Age to Come—but this one thing is sure: there will be a tribulation period before the Age to Come is established. That tribulation involves religious apostasy, political upheaval, physical suffering, and cosmic disturbances.[27] While some thought that tribulation was present (e.g., *T. Moses; 4 Ezra*), others thought it was yet to come (*1 Enoch* 91–105; *2 Bar.* 25–29). Jesus clearly belonged to the latter group but he sees it as in the very process of realization from the time of John the Baptist on (Q 16:16), and it becomes fundamental to understanding what he thought of his death to relate the two ideas: did he see his death as part of, or the onset of, the tribulation? It should be noted that some expectations were that only the wicked would suffer (*2 Bar.* 71:1), but it was more common to think that the tribulation would become a severe test for the people of God (Dan 7:21-22; 12:1; *As. Mos.* 9:1–7). Again, Jesus belonged to the latter group, for he clearly connects his own suffering and that of his followers with the tribulation (cf. e.g. Q 16:16; 12:51-53; Luke 13:31-35; Mark 10:38-39; 13). Because Allison mapped the Evangelists' use of this motif for understanding the death of Jesus so well, it is now a commonplace to interpret the death of Jesus as informed by tribulation imagery.[28] The issue for us in this study is whether or not Jesus did the same. In what follows I will not need to trot out the evidence for Jesus harboring thoughts that a tribulation was either being realized or imminent, and instead, I will use this construct to understand how Jesus thought about his own death.[29]

McKnight, *A New Vision for Israel* (Grand Rapids: Eerdmans, 1999); see also J. Lunde, "The Salvation-Historical Implications of Matthew 24–25 in Light of Jewish Apocalyptic Literature," Ph.D. diss. (Trinity Evangelical Divinity School, 1996), 28–129, who provides a helpful taxonomy of various understandings of salvation-history schemes in Jewish apocalypses, including various views within 1 Enoch itself.

[27] See esp. now Pitre, "Historical Jesus, the Great Tribulation," 5–10. It is to Pitre's credit that he interacts with N.T. Wright's theory of the "end of the Exile," and contends that Wright's definition of *exile* is in need of modification. *Israel*, so Pitre contends, refers not to *all of Israel* but to the northern, lost ten tribes, and he contends that Wright mixes the Assyrian and Babylonian exiles as one and the same. Pitre helpfully distinguishes between Israel (the lost ten tribes) and Jews (those who have returned from Babylon), and that Jesus' vision was for a restoration of pan-Israel. That Jesus comes from Galilee is of no small moment to his vision for all of Israel. "Wright," he says, "has the *right insight* but the *wrong exile*" (37). Further research needs to be undertaken to confirm the distinction of Israel as northern ten tribes and Judah/Jews as southern tribes.

[28] See Allison, *End of the Ages Has Come*, 26–61. Allison, it should be noted, did anchor this theme in the historical Jesus as well (115–41). This study informs my own study from beginning to end.

[29] Pitre, "The Historical Jesus, the Great Tribulation," has clearly demonstrated that Jesus thought of his death in terms of the tribulation and that the suffering of the tribulation could be described as atoning (see esp. pp. 483–653); my concern is the broader question of the *atoning significance* of what Jesus thought about his death. Tribulation is one nest into which such a theme needs to be placed.

MARK 14:3-9

In a narrative laced with aesthetic ironies[30]—a woman[31] destined to be famous but who has no name, who anoints Jesus prior to his burial,[32] in which a poor itinerant is anointed with costly nard, and in which is heard a bumbling reproach for spilling this nard over Jesus when it could be given to the poor— we find (evidently) Jesus anticipating his own death just prior to his betrayal, arrest, trial, and crucifixion.[33] Like most Jesus traditions, this one has its own history.[34] E.J. Pryke, to take but one specific example, concludes that Mark 14:8-9 is Markan redaction,[35] and this would cast a doubtful glance on any claim that the text preserves an indication Jesus anticipated his own death.[36]

That the story appears in three separable forms (Mark 14:3-9; Luke 7:36-50;[37] John 12:1-8)[38] suggests that some kind of anointing of Jesus by a woman has a secure historical foundation, even if Jesus' reflections on such an anointing

[30] For a nice study of this text in its Markan context, cf. E.K. Broadhead, "Mark 14:1-9," *Paradigms* 1 (1985): 32–41.

See J. Jeremias, "Die Salbungsgeschichte Mk. 14,3-9," 107–15 and "Markus 14,9," 115–20 in his *Abba* (Göttingen: Vandenhoeck & Ruprecht, 1966); R. Pesch, "Die Salbung Jesu in Bethanien (Mk 14,3-9)," in *Orientierung an Jesus* (ed. P. Hoffmann, N. Brox, and W. Pesch; Freiburg: Herder, 1973), 267–85; Mary Rose D'Angelo, "Mark 14:3-9," in *Women in Scripture* (ed. C. Meyers, T. Craven, and R.S. Kraemer; Grand Rapids: Eerdmans, 2000), 434–36; M.A. Beavis, "Women as Models of Faith in Mark," *BTB* 18 (1988): 3–9; J. Blank, "Frauen in den Jesusüberlieferungen," in *Die Frau im Urchristentum* (ed. G. Dautzenberg, et al.; QD 95; Freiburg: Herder, 1983), 22–28, 42–48. A definitive study on how women have been studied in Jesus scholarship, and where one finds a deconstruction of Jesus as the feminist Christian liberator, can be seen in A.-J. Levine, "Lilies of the Field and Wandering Jews," in *Transformative Encounters* (ed. Ingrid Rosa Kitzberger; BIS 43; Leiden: E.J. Brill, 2000), 329–52.

[31] Mark/Matthew: a woman; Luke: a sinful woman; John: Mary.

[32] M. Black has not convinced all with his suggestion that the woman used pistachio nut oil (ἀλάβαστρον μύρου νάρδου πιστικῆς, with the latter term being a transfer of *pistaqa*); cf. his *An Aramaic Approach to the Gospels and Acts* (3d ed.; Oxford: Clarendon, 1967), 223–25.

[33] There is no evidence that the sort of anointing commonly associated with sexual pleasure is to be found here; contra K. Corley, *Private Women, Public Meals* (Peabody, Mass.: Hendrickson, 1993), 102–6; a similar approach intending more to scandalize than to reconstruct events on the basis of evidence and probability is found in B.L. Mack, "The Anointing of Jesus," in *Patterns of Persuasion in the Gospels* (ed. B.L. Mack and V.K. Robbins; Sonoma, Calif.: Polebridge, 1989), 85–106.

[34] For example, see Mack, "Anointing of Jesus," 85–106, who argues for a no longer recoverable core that was elaborated by Mark, Luke, and John.

[35] Pryke, *Redactional Style in the Marcan Gospel*, 171; contra Pesch, *Markusevangelium*, 2:328–29, who sees 14:3-9 as an unredacted tradition.

[36] So also R. Bultmann, *The History of the Synoptic Tradition* (trans. J. Marsh; rev. ed.; New York: Harper & Row, 1976), 36–37, 60; C.-P. März, "Zur Traditionsgeschichte von Mk 14, 3-9 und Parallelen," *SNTSU* A 6/7 (1981–1982): 89–112.

[37] On Luke's text, cf. S. Demel, "Jesu Umgang mit Frauen nach den Lukasevangelium," *BN* 57 (1991): 41–95, esp. 60–67.

[38] For a careful comparison, cf. Fitzmyer, *Luke*, 1:684–86.

are irrecoverable.[39] Furthermore, there are elements in this narrative that suggest a historical core. First, the harsh word on the poor sounds like Deuteronomy 15:11 and yet is contrary to the early Christian pictures of Jesus as one who cared for the poor (Mark14:7).[40] Second, the elevation of a woman's ministry, described here as quasi-prophetic or as an actual prophetic symbolic action[41] or just a performative action (Mark 14:3; cf. 1 Sam 10:1; 16:13; 1 Kgs 1:34-40; 2 Kgs 9:6),[42] suggests an earlier rather than later tradition. Third, Jesus' presence in the house of a (former?) leper (Mark 14:3; cf. John 12:1-2; 11Q19[Temple] XIVI, 16-18) conforms to his habit of doing the unusual. Fourth, Jesus' defense of the marginalized, even a prostitute, with "she has done me a courtesy" (Scholar's Version) or "a beautiful thing"[43] (14:6), is just like Jesus. Fifth, if the woman was a prostitute (so Luke), Jesus' accepting her offering as a renunciation becomes an *Ersatz* for the Temple priesthood (cf. Deut 23:18-19; Josephus, *A.J.* 4.206; *b. Tem.* 29a-b), and would confirm other suggestive traces of Jesus' criticism of the Temple authorities.

I would also suggest that the harsh word about the poor in Mark 14:7a is unusual for Jesus (but, then again, he is not easy to predict). If he said something like 14:7a, the balancing line of 14:7c (leaving 14:7b as editorial[44]) is required. A possible clue to Jesus' harshness is latent in Mark 14:4; perhaps the question was asked by Judas (cf. John 12:4-8). Is it possible Jesus is expressing his disturbance with Judas?

It is normal for historical Jesus scholars to argue that Mark 14:9 is *Gemeindetheologie*, reflecting the already active Gentile mission of the early church,[45] but 14:8 sounds like the sort of deconstruction Jesus liked to do: a woman anoints Jesus in a royal manner (a legitimate perspective on Jesus for some), but Jesus sabotages her action by reinterpretation:[46] "What you have

[39] So Funk, et al., *Acts of Jesus,* 135–36; Blank, "Frauen in den Jesusüberlieferungen," 22–23.

[40] It is not impossible that Jesus saw himself as a poor man and, therefore, the expense was an act of charity; cf. the discussion of charity in G.F. Moore, *Judaism in the First Centuries of the Christian Era* (3 vols.; New York: Schocken, 1971), 2:162–79.

[41] Mary Rose D'Angelo's comment is worthy of permanent record: "the woman who was to be remembered is also the prophet who has been forgotten" ("Mark 14:3-9," 436).

[42] J.F. Coakley's arguments against an anointing of the head reverse to be potent arguments for authenticity on the grounds of near dissimilarity and shocking innovation; cf. "The Anointing at Bethany and the Priority of John," *JBL* 107 (1988): 241–56, here pp. 248–49.

[43] On the term *kalon,* cf. D. Daube, "The Anointing at Bethany and Jesus' Burial," in his *The New Testament and Rabbinic Judaism* (Peabody, Mass.: Hendrickson, n.d.), 312–24, here esp. 315–16; Jeremias, "Die Salbungsgeschichte Mk. 14, 3-9," 107–15, where he poses a credible historical context in the discussion of relative values of alms and deeds of mercy. See also E. Schüssler Fiorenza, *In Memory of Her* (New York: Crossroads, 1985), 126–30. The author chose Mark 14:9 as the biblical text upon which she constructs the title of the book (cf. pp. xiii–xiv).

[44] So Gnilka, *Markus,* 2:222.

[45] See März, "Zur Traditionsgeschichte von Mk 14, 3-9," 98–99.

[46] The reversal of estimation pulled here by Jesus fits the social context described by D. Daube in n. 39 above: if "good work" refers to something like almsgiving, and not burial, then Jesus' words

[actually] done," he says to her, "is not what you [think you] have done!" Jesus'
commentary builds on Mark 14:7c but adds nothing substantially new: "You've
anointed me as a king, but I am about to die!"[47] Thus, if a woman anointed
Jesus late in his mission to Israel it is likely that Jesus made some kind of comment, and it is not at all surprising he made this sort of comment.

On the other hand, that Mark 14:3-9 intrudes into the narrative of Mark
14:1-2, 10-11, suggests that Mark has brought the tradition into this scene. Its
original location is not easy to discern, but perhaps John 12:1-8 preserves that
part of the tradition best.[48] If John preserves the original setting, an event like
this late in Jesus' life would permit a scene in which Jesus may well have
expressed the sentiment that he was about to die. We have seen glimpses of this
already (and will see more later), but we should at least admit these two facts: it
is almost certain Jesus perceives that he will die prematurely and it is more than
likely that he thinks through what a premature death might mean for his kingdom mission. Probably then, just prior to his last week, a woman suddenly
intrudes upon a dinner at the home of (perhaps) Lazarus, anoints Jesus' feet[49]
(or, as I think, head), and Jesus accepts her action. But, Jesus gives her action
feet when he turns it on its head: instead of a prophetic act of anointing royalty,
her action is actually a preemptive anointing of his body for an imminent death,
in effect, a performative utterance.

Thus, though with different degrees of opacity, when historical judgment is
rendered on Mark 2:19-20, 10:38, and 14:3-9, we can come to the conclusion
that there is significant evidence suggesting that Jesus anticipated a premature
death and that he was to have a temporary presence among his followers.
Fundamentally, Jesus' perception of his own life and death appears to be
anchored in the experience of his mentor, John the Baptist. One other tradition
confirms this conclusion.

LUKE 13:32-33

Just how early the thought came upon Jesus that he might die is hard to know.
But we are certain that the death of his mentor was undoubtedly scorched into
his memory. When, we might ask, did Jesus first express his conviction that he
would die? Luke 13:32-33 can help us in answering such a question. The tradi-

---

shock his audience into a new perception of this good work—now a burial rite. Daube contends
that Jesus received no post-death burial anointing; thus, the event in Mark's Gospel was then used
as a pre-event anointing. Put differently, if the anointing was originally more of a royal anointing,
and was later used as an indication of a burial anointing, then it is likely that the anointing is historical because it becomes a stubborn historical fact that had to be used for a new purpose.

[47] Cf. also Gnilka, *Markus*, 2:222; contra März, "Die Tradition von Mk 14, 3-9," 101–2.

[48] For a slightly overcooked defense of the independence and historical priority of John 12:1-8, cf.
J.F. Coakley, "Anointing at Bethany."

[49] For a display of the evidence, cf. Coakley, "Anointing at Bethany and the Priority of John,"
246–52.

tion is classically located in L, and it was Joachim Jeremias who began the serious discussion of this tradition. I have provided the NRSV with Jeremias' redactional words printed in italics:[50]

> [32]He said to them, "Go and tell that fox for me, 'Listen, I am casting out demons and performing cures today and tomorrow, and on the third day I finish my work. [33]Yet today, tomorrow, *and the next day* I must be on my way, because it is impossible for a prophet to be killed outside of *Jerusalem*.'"

Some recent developments of the discussion disagree. These have concluded that Luke 13:33—because of characteristic Lukan language in "yet," "I must," "be on my way," and "Jerusalem"—is probably entirely a piece of Lukan redaction. Verse 33, it is argued, was designed to adapt 13:32 to the Lukan journey to Jerusalem, or at least to make explicit what is implicit (if that) in 13:32.[51]

The most complete recent study of Kim Huat Tan, *Zion Traditions and the Aims of Jesus*, however, has argued quite conclusively that Luke 13:33 contains both Lukan tradition and redaction.[52] Luke 13:32-33 has much to commend it as historical, and Tan has argued that "the pronouncement is substantially from Jesus, although there is a likelihood that Luke may have substituted or used certain of his favourite words."[53] If one permits the vocabulary to have been touched by Luke, then other considerations are to be used in determining authenticity.

The theme of suffering, as D.C. Allison has observed, is pervasive in the Jesus traditions.[54] That a premature death would have crossed the threshold of Jesus' mind was nearly a certainty once John was beheaded. That Jesus died in Jerusalem leads to a simple question: is it likely that such a horrendous ending could have occurred completely unexpectedly? In other words, would it have been mentally possible for Jesus to have gone to Jerusalem that last time either confident that nothing would happen to him or completely unaware that the situation was not in his favor? Thus, the presence of Jerusalem in Luke 13:33 is not at all impossible in an authentic *mot* of Jesus.[55] One item deserves

---

[50] See J. Jeremias, *Die Sprache des Lukasevangeliums* (K-EKNT Sonderband; Göttingen: Vandenhoeck & Ruprecht, 1980), 233–34.

[51] See M. Rese, "Einige Überlegungen zu Lukas XIII, 31-33," in *Jésus aux origines de la christologie* (ed. J. Dupont; BETL 40; Gembloux/Leuven: Duculot/Leuven University Press, 1975), 201–25; A. Denaux, "L'hypocrisie des Pharisees et le dessein de Dieu," in *L'Evangile de Luc* (ed. F. Neirynck; rev. ed.; BETL 32; Leuven: Leuven University Press, 1989), 245–85; Nolland, *Luke*, 2:739; Fitzmyer, *Luke*, 2:1028: "One could, however, further debate whether v. 33 was really part of 'L' or stems from Lucan composition, as a sort of commentary on v. 32, which it parallels (in part at least)."

[52] See K.H. Tan, *Zion Traditions and the Aims of Jesus* (SNTSMS 91; Cambridge: Cambridge University Press, 1997), 57–69, esp. 65–67.

[53] Ibid., 67.

[54] D.C. Allison, Jr., *Jesus of Nazareth* (Minneapolis: Fortress, 1998), 46.

[55] See P. Stuhlmacher, *Biblische Theologie des Neuen Testaments* (2 vols.; 2d ed.; Göttingen: Vandenhoeck & Ruprecht, 1997), 1:127–28.

consideration here: Jerusalem as the place of death for prophets was a *topos* by the time of Jesus (cf. Jer 26:20-23; 38:4-6; Amos 7:10-17; 2 Chr 24:20-22; Josephus, *A.J.* 10.38; *Mart. Isa.* 5:1-14; Justin, *Dial.* 120:14-15; cf. also *Liv. Pro.* 1–3).[56] Put differently, here is how the logic works: John died; I might, too. John and I are both prophets. Prophets often die in Jerusalem; I may die there, too.

But the critical feature in Luke 13:32-33 for our purposes is the (probably) Aramaic time limitations:[57] "today and tomorrow, and on the third day [perhaps *yoma den weyomachra*] I finish[58] my work," along with the not altogether harmonious "Yet today, tomorrow, and the next day." Not only are the two parts hard to harmonize, but neither has an unambiguous interpretation—leading even more clearly to the stage of early Christian prior to *ex eventu* composition. Again, it is not unlike Jesus to offer a little ambiguity to a hostile audience. These two expressions are intended to cover an indefinite time period followed by a certain, imminent event.

The authenticity of the "three days" motif of the Markan passion predictions (8:31; 9:31; 10:33-34)[59] has found plenty of detractors, but the Lukan logion in our context lacks the kind of specificity that betrays later perspective. Furthermore, the "third day" motif of Luke 13:32-33 does not refer to resurrection, but to death. The logia of Luke 13:32-33, then, don't evince early Christian theology but instead the kind of things Jesus appreciated: ambiguity, questioning, and mystery.

We can return once again to Jesus' mentor, John: the use of "fox" for Herod Antipas strikes one as coherent with Jesus' relation to John and a response to what Herod did to John.[60] The attitude expressed through this term did not endear the early Christians to the ruling authorities of their day, but it is quite consistent with Jesus' attitude toward other authorities—one thinks here of the

---

[56] When scholars make the claim that Jerusalem was not a place of persecution for prophets, they fail to take two considerations into sufficient account: (1) the tomb-building projects done for prophets and (2) the sort of evidence cited in this paragraph. E.g., R.J. Miller, "The Rejection of the Prophets in Q," *JRL* 107 (1988): 225–40, here pp. 234–35. On tomb building, see J. Jeremias, *Heiligengräber in Jesu Umwelt* (Mt. 23, 29; Lk. 11, 47). *Eine Untersuchung zur Volksreligion der Zeit Jesu* (Göttingen: Vandenhoeck & Ruprecht, 1958).

[57] For a staunch defense, cf. Black, *Aramaic Approach to the Gospels and Acts*, 205–7, where a connection is drawn back to the "daily" in the Lord's Prayer. He sees four lines: (1) Behold I cast out demons, and I do cures *day by day.* (2) But *one day* soon I am perfected. (3) But *day by day* I must needs work. (4) Then *one day* soon pass on [die]. The point is a short indefinite period followed by another indefinite but imminent event.

[58] On the puns latent in the text and especially in "finish" (τελειοῦμαι), see J.D.M. Derrett, "The Lucan Christ and Jerusalem," *ZNW* 75 (1984): 36–43. His suggestion on pp. 40–41 that Jesus was urging the Jewish people to be sanctified, in stages, against the Day of YHWH's coming, however, is built on one questionable piece of evidence (Exod 19:10-11; his other texts are irrelevant).

[59] See below, ch. 11, under "After three days."

[60] See R.A. Batey, *Jesus and the Forgotten City* (Grand Rapids: Baker, 1991), 105–18.

undeniable criticisms Jesus made of Pharisees.[61] The same criticisms may be found in rabbinic documents (e.g., *b. Ber.* 28a; *b. Yebam.* 109b; *t. Shab.* 1:4). It is the *attitude*, I am suggesting, that betrays the authenticity of the tradition. The context, the style, and the meaning each speak more of the context of Jesus than a later rewriting of the Jesus tradition.

We can put our findings together here by summarizing the results of Tan's study on the meaning of these expressions:[62] the Pharisees suggest that Jesus must be on his way or suffer at the hands of Herod Antipas. As they asked him to "go," Jesus takes up that word *go* and, as is often his practice, plays with it: "You *go*. And, I will *go* when my work is done. I may die, but it will not be at his hands but instead in Jerusalem." The irony of it all is that Jesus *does* go and *still dies*.

And this takes us to the edge of our concern: there is sufficient evidence to think that Jesus was aware that he was not to live his three score and ten. Everyone's life is temporary in some sense. However, some are aware that their life is even more temporary, and Jesus was one of those. Furthermore, the evidence studied above suggests over and over that Jesus saw in his own end a connection to John the Baptist, whose death precipitated Jesus' reflection.

The Lord's Prayer and the Gethsemane incident intimate that such a death was not his desire, but he was committed to carrying out the will of his Father. These logia and events in Jesus' life suggest that Jesus attached his premature death to the eschatological tribulation or better yet, that Jesus envisioned his participation in that tribulation and that meant premature death. And, the evidence also leads us to think that Jesus came to this conviction sometime after John died and when he himself was experiencing a similar kind of opposition at the hands of authorities. That Jesus connected his death to the Final Ordeal leads us across the threshold from the "that-ness" of a death to the "why-ness" of that death. Are there clues in the Jesus traditions that imply Jesus processed the certainty of death through the sieve of significance? We conclude this chapter with one general reflection by Jesus that suggests he saw his premature death as part of God's plan.

IN GOD'S PROVIDENCE

It is clear that John's death precipitated reflection by Jesus on the likelihood of his own death, a death probably at the hands of the same authorities. We are led to ask if it is possible for someone like Jesus, who showed himself to be intelligent, reflective, and theological, to have offered insights into the significance of his death.[63]

[61] Pre-Markan evidence can be found in Mark 2:16a; 7:5, 6, 9, 15; 10:2; 12:13, 15; Q 11:37-41; cf. also Rom 2:1-11, 17-29; Phil 3:2.

[62] Zan, *Zion Traditions and the Aims of Jesus,* 69–74.

[63] See J. Jeremias, *Jesus and the Message of the New Testament* (ed. K.C. Hanson; 1925; repr. Minneapolis: Fortress, 2002), 82.

MARK 14:36 AND LUKE 13:32-33

A place to begin is at the end: we are reasonably sure that Mark 14:36 reflects an authentic saying of the historical Jesus. This saying reveals an important insight by Jesus into the significance of his imminent death: that it might be the *will of God.* C.E.B. Cranfield expressed this poignantly: "Thereby in full awareness of the cost he embraces the will of God and sets his lips to the cup."[64] Most scholars are persuaded of two things about the Lord's Prayer: (1) the petition for God's will to be done is a Matthean comment (cf. Matt 6:10b), and (2) that it nonetheless unfolds the kingdom petition and reflects the mission of Jesus.[65]

When Jesus responds to the suggestion that he ought to leave the area of danger and head for a safer region outside the grasp of Antipas, his wording, however difficult to articulate with precision, nonetheless embraces the same ideal of surrender to God's will (Luke 13:31-33). In effect, he says, "Tell Herod that I have a task to perform and God will protect me until that task is complete. My prophetic ministry will end, as have the ministries of others, in Jerusalem, but not at the hands of Antipas." In other words, as Kim Huat Tan has stated, "Jesus believed his death fell under the ambit of divine necessity."[66] One cannot, I suppose, find anything more Jewish (cf. the *Qaddish* and the *Amidah*) than a piety that finds in God's will the supreme center point for human direction. The following from *m. 'Abot* illustrates the point, as translated by Jacob Neusner:

> Rabbi says:
> E. "And keep your eye on three things, so you will not come into the clutches of transgression:
> F. "Know what is above you:
> G. "(1) An eye which sees, and (2) an ear which hears, and (3) all your actions are written down in a book" (2:1).
>
> Rabban Gamaliel, son of R. Judah the Patriarch, says:
> A. He would say, "Make his wishes into your own wishes, so that he will make your wishes into his wishes.
> B. "Put aside your wishes on account of his wishes, so that he will put aside the wishes of other people in favor of your wishes" (2:4).

But this individualistic and ethical sense needs to be set into Jesus' larger eschatological context: God's will is the final, full realization of his plan on earth. That final plan includes the individual and ethical decisions made on earth by humans. The stance of Jesus in these three passages (Q 11:4; Mark 14:36; Luke

---

[64] Cranfield, *Mark*, 434.

[65] See, e.g., Davies and Allison, *Matthew*, 1:605–7; G. Lüdemann, *Jesus after Two Thousand Years* (Amherst, NY: Prometheus, 2001), 147, finds only this clause as unhistorical in the Lord's Prayer.

[66] Tan, *Zion Traditions and the Aims of Jesus*, 75.

13:32-33), then, is not just micro-ethical decisions, but a disposition in life characterized by yearning for God's glory to return to the temple, for God's people Israel to become splendid through Mount Zion, and for God's Torah to govern the affairs of humans. It is this eschatological, and therefore ethical, will to which Jesus regularly resigned himself. If the disposition is not equivalent to walking in the Torah (*halakhah*), it finds its perfect expression in the Torah. Unfolded even further, we find that Jesus knows that God's will, previously revealed in the Torah, is now being fully realized on earth and that God has clarified Jesus' part in that realization. If that will means death, then so be it.

JOHN 10:15-18

The christologization that occurs under the monochromatic ink of the Fourth Gospel expresses the providential plan of God to which Jesus submits:

> [14]"I am the good shepherd. I know my own and my own know me, [15]just as the Father knows me and I know the Father. And I lay down my life for the sheep. [16]I have other sheep that do not belong to this fold. I must bring them also, and they will listen to my voice. So there will be one flock, one shepherd. [17]For this reason the Father loves me, because I lay down my life in order to take it up again. [18]No one takes it from me, but I lay it down of my own accord. I have power to lay it down, and I have power to take it up again. I have received this command from my Father."

This Johannine logion exceeds the Synoptic tradition in at least two respects: first, it transforms Jesus' death from the exclusive will of God into a mutual decision by the Father and the Son who has power over his own life but now willingly lays down that life (John 10:14, 17, 18); and, second, the Father's will has become an explicit *command*: "I have received this command from my Father" (10:18). It is not far, if one wants to conscript the criterion of coherence, from the will of God to the command of the Father. And neither is resignation to God's will far from power to decide one's fate (cf. John 13:37 [Peter]; 15:13 [Jesus for his friends]; 1 John 3:16 [ethical principle]; cf. Mark 10:45 below). After all, Jesus could have run back to Galilee had he wanted; he could have avoided Antipas and his comrades in knife. Both of these considerations are worthy of debate. And C.H. Dodd has argued that even though John 10:15 reflects Johannine theology, it is a reflection upon genuine traditions of Jesus,[67] even earlier than Matthew 11:27,[68] and that the language of John 10 here reflects a prophetic mission.[69] Raymond E. Brown's mulling over this text led to

---

[67] Dodd, *Historical Tradition in the Fourth Gospel,* 76–80.

[68] Ibid., 359–61.

[69] C.H. Dodd, *The Interpretation of the Fourth Gospel* (Cambridge: Cambridge University Press, 1953), 151–63.

a great likelihood that the shepherd tradition of John 10 is rooted in genuine material (cf. Luke 15; Mark 14:27).[70] Granted these arguments, we still would have to be cautious if we were to suggest these verses as authentic in the normal sense of the word. But, it is precisely here that we stand before John, both recognizing what he has accomplished and knowing that behind him stand fecund sayings of Jesus that could give rise the sorts of sayings John attributed to Jesus. No one has said this better than John Robinson:

> Yet when we come to the teaching of Jesus we see him [John] using a different technique to the same end, though the difference is one of degree rather than of kind, for the works and words of Jesus are not sharply distinguished. John is still concerned with what Jesus is really saying and meaning, and the words, like his actions, can be understood at very different levels. Yet he does not simply set them down straight, and then comment upon them—allowing the sayings and their interpretation to stand side by side, with the raw material presented in its untreated state. Rather, it is worked up; the interpretation is thoroughly assimilated and integrated.[71]

However, our point is to require less of this text: we are not asking that it contain authentic logia of Jesus in the normal sense of the term. Instead, we are asking what material John has worked up and what was there behind him, and it seems credible that behind this material is the genuine reflection by Jesus that (1) God had somehow and for some reason willed his death, and (2) that Jesus had resigned himself to that will. In these two senses we can see in John 10:15-18 a genuine reflection of the historical Jesus.[72]

CONCLUSION

We can pause now to summarize the argument: first, it is all but certain that Jesus would have had to think that he *could* and *might* die prematurely, especially from the time of John's death; second, it is just as certain that Jesus did not desire to die; third, it is very probable that Jesus came to the conclusion, sometime after John died, that he would die, and he expressed this in language of a temporary presence among his disciples; and, fourth, it is very probable that Jesus came to the view that this death was willed by God as a dimension of the Final Ordeal. Thus, in our quest for understanding Jesus' own understanding of his death, we can be confident that Jesus thought he would die prematurely and that this death was willed by God as part of his eschatological plan to purge Israel at the end of times.

[70] R.E. Brown, *John*, 1:398–99.

[71] J.A.T. Robinson, *The Priority of John* (ed. J.F. Coakley; Oak Park, Ill.: Meyer Stone, 1987), 298.

[72] For a potent examination of John's understanding of Jesus' death, and how John has worked up the tradition about Jesus' understanding of his own death, cf. J. Ashton, *Understanding the Fourth Gospel* (Oxford: Clarendon, 1991), 485–501.

Chapter 6

Jesus and the Prophetic Fate

Approximately three miles northeast of Nazareth, off the left shoulder of the path toward Tiberias as the hawk flies, lay a village traditionally connected to Jonah, son of Amittai. The village was called Gath-Hepher (2 Kgs 14:25; later called Gobebatha and under Sepphoris' direction; now called el-Meshhed). Jerome informs us that there was a sacred tomb in Jonah's memory in Gath-Hepher, as did also Rabbi Levi (*Gen. Rab.* 98:11).[1] As a Galilean and speaking for Galileans,[2] Jesus identified himself with that prophet but not because of Jonah's prophecy of the expansion of the land under Jeroboam II (2 Kgs 14:23-27). Instead, it was Jonah's embodied warning (in the whale?[3] in his preaching? in his Galilean anti-Jerusalem stance?) that Jesus reused for himself:[4] as Jonah was a sign to the Ninevites, so Jesus was to be a sign to "this generation" (Q 11:29-30; cf. *Liv. Pro.* 10).[5] A shocking set of comparisons, to be sure: to make Ninevites and "this generation" parallel is subversive in the extreme.

---

[1] Details can be found in J. Jeremias, *Heiligengräber in Jesu Umwelt* (Mt. 23, 29; Lk. 11, 47). *Eine Untersuchung zur Volksreligion der Zeit Jesu* (Göttingen: Vandenhoeck & Ruprecht, 1958), 24–28; J.L. Reed, *Archaeology and the Galilean Jesus* (Harrisburg: Trinity Press International, 2000), 204–11.

[2] John 7:52 probably refers to "the" messianic prophet, for surely the opponents knew of Jonah (and perhaps Nahum).

[3] So G.R. Beasley-Murray, *Jesus and the Kingdom of God* (Grand Rapids: Eerdmans, 1986), 256–57.

[4] Perhaps the request for a sign is connected to Deuteronomy 13:1-2 (cf. *Sipre Deut.* 92a [on Deut 13:2]). On the tradition-history, see Reed, *Archaeology and the Galilean Jesus*, 200–203; for interpretive issues, see Beasley-Murray, *Jesus and the Kingdom of God*, 252–57.

[5] Matthew clarifies "sign" as the correlation of a three-day entombment: Jonah in the fish, and Jesus in the grave (Matt 12:40). See D. Schmidt, "The LXX Gattung 'Prophetic Correlative,'" *JBL* 96 (1977): 517–22, for the "just as . . . so" expression (cf. also Q 17:24, 26, 28, 30). For our purposes, it is sufficient if Q 11:29 can be anchored in the life of Jesus; Q 11:30 shows signs of a later stage in Q's development. See Beasley-Murray, *Jesus and the Kingdom of God*, 252–58.

The imagery is perhaps more rooted in popular Galilean perceptions of Jonah than in the Hebrew Scriptures. In his reluctant openness to Gentiles, Jonah is depicted as a loyalist to Israel in the Hebrew Scriptures, but Jewish tradition turns him against Jerusalem (Tob 14:4; Josephus, *A.J.* 9:208–14; *Liv. Pro.* 10:11; *b. Sanh.* 89b).[6] Jesus, too, was a finger-pointer at Jerusalem's leadership and was open (slightly more than Jonah) to Gentiles (cf. Q 7:1-10; 10:11-13; 13:28-29). The Galilean image of a local prophet has shifted: Jonah the Dove had become Jonah the Hawk, and as a hawk Jonah has become a paradigm for Jesus.[7]

As Jonah's historian eulogized him for his wonderful words of promise, his contemporaries castigated Jesus for his awful words of warning. They had given outward respect to John; but John was put to death by Herod Antipas, and his death had made the public pause to ascribe praise to Jesus. Now Jesus was face to face with a similar end: as a prophet announcing the coming judgment of God against the unfaithfulness of Israel,[8] Jesus was likely to consider the rejection of his words and the opposition by the leaders as something that could possibly lead to death. Such, so Jesus would have thought, is the fate of the prophet—a martyr's fate, as history demonstrates in all its various forms (e.g., from Neh 9:26 to Q 6:22-23 and Acts 7:52).[9] If Jesus divined his own death, we are led to ask if he interpreted that death. A glimpse of interpretation is found in Jesus' seeing his death as part of God's eschatological plan to purify Israel through the Final Ordeal, as we saw in the previous chapter. This chapter will examine if he interpreted his death as the fate of the prophet.[10]

[6] Cf. S. Bryan, *Jesus and Israel's Traditions of Judgement and Restoration* (SNTSMS 117; Cambridge: Cambridge University Press, 2002), 41–44.

[7] Most scholars recognize that Matthew 12:40 is a Matthean clarification of the Q logion in which the "sign" is taken to be death and vindication: as Jonah was delivered, so also will Jesus be. So Davies and Allison, *Matthew*, 2:352. While there is ample ground for building a case for Matthew's redaction being an unfolding of the obvious (after all, one thinks of Jonah in terms of the fish and his deliverance), the logion prior to Matthean redaction might have had a more local color (as presented above). One can hardly be certain.

[8] See R.A. Horsley, *Jesus and Empire* (Minneapolis: Fortress, 2003), 79–104.

[9] See P.W. Barnett, "The Jewish Sign Prophets—A.D. 40–70—Their Intentions and Origins," *NTS* 27 (1981): 679–97. At a broader level, see the informative study of H. Lenowitz, *The Jewish Messiahs* (New York: Oxford, 1998).

[10] See E. Stauffer, *New Testament Theology* (trans. J. Marsh; London: SCM, 1955), 331–34; Odil Hans Steck, *Israel und das gewaltsame Geschick der Propheten* (WMANT 23; Neukirchen: Neukirchener Verlag, 1967); M.-L. Gubler, *Die frühesten Deutungen des Todes Jesu* (OBO 15; Freiburg: Universitätsverlag, 1977), 10–94; D.E. Aune, *Prophecy in Early Christianity and the Ancient Mediterranean World* (Grand Rapids: Eerdmans, 1983), 156–59; U. Luz, "Warum zog Jesus nach Jerusalem," in *Der historische Jesus* (eds. Schröter and Brucker), 412–19.

JESUS AND THE PROPHETIC FATE

LUKE 23:27-31

The paradoxical deconstruction of the woman's act of anointing Jesus, examined in the last chapter, might be connected at the level of style and method with Jesus' last (and dark) beatitude for the women. With a touch of the macabre,[11] some women begin weeping for Jesus as he walks the storied road for the last time:

> [27]A great number of the people followed him, and among them were women who were beating their breasts and wailing for him. [28]But Jesus turned to them and said, "Daughters of Jerusalem, do not weep for me, but weep for yourselves and for your children. [29]For the days are surely coming when they will say, 'Blessed are the barren, and the wombs that never bore, and the breasts that never nursed.' [30]Then they will begin to say to the mountains, 'Fall on us'; and to the hills, 'Cover us.' [31]For if they do this when the wood is green, what will happen when it is dry?" (Luke 23:27-31)

The Jesus Seminar, contrary to some recent trends in Jesus scholarship, finds the women's actions as only a possibility (gray), but the logion of Jesus impossible.[12] Others, however, render a positive judgment for the statements of Jesus.[13] To begin with, as J.A. Fitzmyer and John Nolland have recently argued, the pericope shows little, if any, trace of Luke's redactional stamp,[14] though there are reasons to think that Luke may have glued together various bits of tradition.[15] Luke 23:31 certainly did not circulate as an independent and adaptable logion. Thus, a possible history might be, as Nolland argues, that (1) Luke 23:27-28 was an original unit; (2) 23:29 was perhaps a separate, but authentic, word of Jesus (cf. *Gos. Thom.* 79); and (3) 23:30-31 was later added to expound 23:27-28 or 23:27-29. It is hard to imagine a context for the "days are surely coming" logion (23:29) much more likely than Luke 23:27-28.

---

[11] So Caird, *Luke*, 249.

[12] R.W. Funk and R.W. Hoover, *The Five Gospels* (New York: Macmillan, 1993), 395–96; R.W. Funk and the Jesus Seminar, *The Acts of Jesus* (San Francisco: HarperSanFrancisco, 1998), 360, where they rebound off R.E. Brown's cautious words. In fact, their words are less cautious than Brown's (*The Death of the Messiah* [2 vols.; ABRL; New York: Doubleday, 1994]), 2:930. Brown finds Luke 23:29 as authentic and 23:30 as prophetic and 23:31 as proverbial accompaniments, perhaps traditional. So also M.L. Soards, "Tradition, Composition, and Theology in Jesus' Speech to the 'Daughters of Jerusalem' (Luke 23, 26-32)," *Bib* 68 (1987): 221–44, who finds Lukan use of early Christian traditions in 23:29 and 23:31a-b.

[13] E.g., see K.G. Kuhn, "ξύλον," in *Theologische Wörtenbuch zum Neuen Testament* (ed. Kittel and Friedrich) 5.37, n.7.

[14] Fitzmyer, *Luke*, 2:1494; Nolland, *Luke*, 3:1135.

[15] See J.H. Neyrey, "Jesus' Address to the Women of Jerusalem (LK. 23.27-31)—A Prophetic Judgment Oracle," *NTS* 29 (1983): 74–86; S. Demel, "Jesu Umgang mit Frauen nach den Lukasevangelium," *BN* 57 (1991): 41–95, here pp. 78–82.

Besides the thoroughly Jewish and plausible historical context of the peri-cope (cf. *b. Moʻed Qaṭ.* 25b; *b. Sanh.* 93a),[16] one should observe the surprising lead given to women in their recognition of the moment and their willingness to be associated with a criminal—and this in contrast to the cowardice of the disciples. In turn, another surprising feature is the jarring word from Jesus. Vasiliki Limberis describes the statements of Jesus as "potent, terrifying words."[17] There is no serious parallel (Isa 54:1 has the opposite meaning) in either Judaism or early Christian faith to Jesus' dark beatitude (Luke 23:29). But, the centrality of a concern with Jerusalem's doom, in a minatory saying, is consistent with the prophetic warning of both John (Q 3:7-9, 16b-17) and Jesus (cf. Mark 12:9; Q 13:34-35; Luke 19:41-44).[18] And, as can be seen quite easily, there is nothing overly christological or developed theologically. In particular, the running statement implies the death of Jesus and connects that death with Jerusalem's fate, but offers absolutely no thought of the benefit of that death. The absence of an atonement theology speaks on behalf of the logion.

On average, it is dubious to argue from *ambiguity* to *historicity*, but in this case the argument deserves some consideration: the ambiguity of Luke 23:31 ("green" and "dry") argues slightly against an early church creation. Care should be exercised, for it could just as easily be asked why Jesus would have used an ambiguous image. Perhaps the logion is not as ambiguous as some have stated. R.E. Brown speaks for the majority and suggests that this logion has Jesus' oppo-nents as the subject of the protasis ("they . . . when green"; cf. 1QHᵃ XVIII, 25) but God as the subject of the apodosis (what will God do to Jerusalem when its time has come?).[19] Thus, the green wood and the dry wood are two times of his-tory: now (Jesus) and the time of Jerusalem's woes—the Final Ordeal (cf. Isa 10:16-19; Ezek 21:3 [MT; cf. 20:47]).[20] The imagery has contemporary Jewish parallels, and ought to be compared to the *Hodayot* use of the term *dry* for the condition of a tree *after* the fire (1QHᵃ XVI, 18, with XVI, 20; cf. also XI, 29). If such a specific rendering of green and dry is to be found in the logion of Jesus, then Jesus was contrasting the *hope of fecundity* in the present with the *doom of*

[16] Cited in Str-B 2:263–64, with some later midrashic quotations as well.

[17] Vasiliki Limberis, "Women Lamenting Jesus," in *Women in Scripture* (ed. Meyers, Craven, and Kraemer; Grand Rapids: Eerdmans, 2000), 452.

[18] On the tradition history of the central text, Mark 13 and other similar texts, cf. esp. D.W. Wenham, *The Rediscovery of Jesus' Eschatological Discourse* (vol. 4 of *Gospel Perspectives*; Sheffield: JSOT, 1984); for the substantial historical veracity of this theme for Jesus, cf. D.C. Allison, Jr., *Jesus of Nazareth* (Minneapolis: Fortress, 1998), 34, 120–21. This theme divides the camp today: the noneschatologists and the eschatologists; the Jesus Seminar, M. Borg, and D. Crossan from A. Schweitzer, E.P. Sanders, and D.C. Allison. C.H. Dodd and N.T. Wright, who accept the warnings about Jerusalem as historical, diminish the sense of time by interpreting the language as metaphor for more ultimate realities.

[19] Brown, *Death of the Messiah*, 2:926–27.

[20] See also N.T. Wright, *Jesus and the Victory of God* (vol. 2 of *Christian Origins and the Question of God*; Minneapolis: Fortress, 1996), 567–70.

sterility after the Day of YHWH. Poetry draws its magic from its imagery, and the imagery here is not as ambiguous as a first encounter suggests.

What we can infer from this discussion for Jesus' understanding of his death is this: unlike the early Christians who saw in his death an atonement for sins previously committed, Jesus sees in his death a foretaste of the imminent judgment of God on the city of Jerusalem for its recalcitrance. Thus, he sees his death and Jerusalem's fate as tied together, perhaps so closely that one speaks of the other. The eschatology inherent in such an understanding of Jesus, and his desire for the city to turn from its ways confirm the interpretation offered. Jesus evidently, at this time in his life, sees no hope for the city to turn; the judgment is inevitable, and he will go down as part of that city's defeat. Such a rendering of this pericope coheres with the findings of chapters 4 and 5 where we saw that Jesus may have viewed his death in terms of the Final Ordeal.

Q 9:58 (Luke 9:58 par. Matt 8:20)

This connection of Jesus' death to the fate of Jerusalem needs to be connected also with the pervasive theme of the rejection of the prophets at the hands of their own people. We have already put on the table solid evidence for Jesus sensing that he would be rejected as the particular form of his premature death (e.g., Mark 10:38; Mark 14:3-9; Luke 13:31-33 and Matt 23:29-32), but other evidence, as well as another inspection of this previously discussed evidence, leads to a deeper perception of what Jesus understood about his own death.

The skeptical boilerplate of the Jesus Seminar is transcended when its attention turns to Q 9:58, and many scholars today consider the following logion authentic: "Foxes have holes, and birds of the air have nests; but the Son of Man has nowhere to lay his head." The issue for us becomes the reason for the Son of man's (=humans?) treatment with inhospitality. Or, is it simply the unsure existence of an itinerant? or, more broadly, the unsure existence of humans?

In a later chapter, I will present a more complete case, but the following outline of that evidence leads us to think Jesus, by using "Son of man," is here referring to himself as representative, humiliated human being.[21] First, "Son of man" is a reuse of the creation narrative (cf. Gen 1:26-28; Pss 8:4-8; 144:3-4; Sir 17:4; *Tg. Psalm* 8; *Gen. Rab.* 79:6) in the sense of humiliation (cf. Job 7:16-20; Ps 144:3; 1QS XI, 20–21). Second, the "foxes" and "birds" of this Q logion evoke the opponents of Jesus (cf., e.g., Deut 28:6; 1 Sam 17:44, 46; 1 Kgs 14:11; 16:4; 21:24; Jer 7:33; 15:3; 16:4; 19:7; 34:20; Ezek 29:5; 32:4; 39:4), and Luke 13:32 suggests we are pointed in the right direction in suggesting a polemical setting for the logion. The language, then, should not be seen as Arcadia. Instead, this language speaks of the harsh, experienced realities of rejection at the hands of the ruling authorities (cf. 1QHª XII, 9; 4Q177 I, 8, 9).

[21] See below, ch. 7.

This rejection is to be charged to the account of the political leaders, and the one at whom Jesus was most likely pointing was Herod Antipas. John the Baptist was snuffed out by Antipas. Jesus' response to John's death, as we have surmised, was to ponder his own fate. This language of Q 9:58 and Luke 13:32 suggests that Jesus looked at Antipas as the one who might also bring his own life to a premature end. The political rats, so Jesus says, have plenty of places to lay their head, just as they have plenty to wear at their Petronian feats (cf. Q 7:24-28). Jesus' life is threatened because of his connection to John, because his message and vision threaten the rule of the leaders, and because he is calling for a national repentance (cf. Q 10:13-15; 11:31-32; 13:28-29, 34-35; also Luke 14:16-24).

We cannot infer from this logion that Jesus thought the rejection he was experiencing was because he was a prophet. The language does not permit that conclusion, but the substance of the logion leads us just short of such a view, and it should not be ruled out. If we pause to consider again the sayings we have already studied (cf. Mark 10:38; Luke 13:32-33; 23:27-31), we should observe that in these there is an interlacing of imminent eschatological woes and the *inevitability* of this tribulation. There appears to be a time limit on Jesus' life (Luke 13:32-33); the time limit is so overwhelming that Jesus sees it as a baptism (Mark 10:38); and that time will lead to a horrible fate for Jerusalem (Luke 23:27-31). If these three pericopes reflect a later time in Jesus' life, which they probably do, we are nonetheless excused if we find in Q 9:58 a preliminary taste of that perspective. There is an inevitable judgment on covenantal unfaithfulness, and Jesus, as the representative Son of man, is called to declare the judgment. If we baptize Q 9:58 in the wider context of Jesus' own mission, then, we are justified in thinking that it is his (prophetic) mission that leads to inhospitality. It is as the mission of the representative Son of man, the one who stares prophetically at the luxuriance of the royal dandies with the glare of God, that leads to the Son of man's rejection.

LUKE 12:49-50

Jesus' sense of *mission* is seen in the carefully crafted parallelism of Luke 12:49-50:

> [49]I came to bring fire to the earth, and how I wish it were already kindled! [50]I have a baptism with which to be baptized, and what stress I am under until it is completed![22]

The baptism logion of Mark 10:38 has been mulled over, and we find in that (eschatological) baptism not only an inevitability—an external constraint—but

---

[22] See the discussion in Nolland, *Luke*, 2:706–10; S.J. Patterson, "Fire and Dissension: Ipsissima Vox Jesu in Q 12:49, 51-53?" *Forum* 5 (1989): 121–39, who provides a consensus report on the logia here; Luz, "Warum zog Jesus nach Jerusalem?" 422–25; D.C. Allison, Jr., *The End of the Ages Has Come* (Philadelphia: Fortress, 1985), 124–28; Beasley-Murray, *Jesus and the Kingdom of God*, 247–52.

instead the very mission of Jesus—an internal misson. While much of scholarship doubts the "I have come" sayings of Jesus,[23] others have blown fire and smoke in the eyes of a simplistic denial on the basis of form. Anyone, it is argued, of Jesus' status would have a sense of mission, and a sense of mission could be expressed (or later reexpressed in a new form) in such a manner. Our concern is not with the precise "I have come" words. But, form is not the only problem for those who want this logion to be placed in the databank of secure information about Jesus.

What is more difficult is the seemingly aggressive tone Jesus expresses with respect to initiating that time of fire in Luke 12:49b.[24] Such a posture of desiring such a baptism conflicts at some level with the bookend statements of Jesus about the eschatological travail as an ordeal he did *not* want to enter (cf. Matt 6:13 and Mark 14:36). It is the second line of 12:50, however, that suggests we should be cautious about attributing to Jesus too much aggression, and instead understand here a logion about the *inevitability* of a confrontation and destiny.[25] The constraint of 12:50 suggests that the Final Ordeal is to occur at someone else's initiative: in other words, it is not so much pursued as inevitable. If so, Luke 12:49 and 12:50 are a case of synonymous parallelism of the two logia and lead to an interpretation of 12:49b and 12:50b that is quite similar to the meanings concluded for Q 11:4 and Mark 14:36. Here is a yearning not for the Final Ordeal to bring it on, but a firm resignation on the part of Jesus to endure the will of God, whatever that might entail.[26]

It is only a possibility that Luke 12:49 is from Q,[27] but it is the two or three variants elsewhere of the terms of this logion that lend credibility to Jesus having said something like what is now found in Luke 12:49. Matthew contains a substantially similar logion at 10:34, where the image of a "sword" is used instead of the image of a "fire" (the Final Ordeal), and the *Gospel of Thomas* has sayings that reveal an independent strain of the same logion.[28] Thus:

> Jesus said: I have cast fire upon the world, and see, I guard it until it [the world] is afire. (10)

---

[23] On which see E. Arens, The ΗΛΘΟΝ-Sayings in the Synoptic Tradition (OBO 10; Göttingen: Vandenhoeck & Ruprecht, 1976). See ch. 7 below.

[24] The problems here were unsuccessfully exploited by A. Vögtle, "Todesankündigungen und Todesverständnis Jesu," in *Der Tod Jesu* (ed. Kertelge), 51–113.

[25] See Beasley-Murray, *Jesus and the Kingdom of God*, 248, who defends their being an original connection between the two lines.

[26] See the fresh rendering of the logion in J.D.G. Dunn, "The Birth of a Metaphor—Baptized in Spirit," in his *Pneumatology*, 103–17, here p. 110.

[27] J.M Robinson, et al., *The Critical Edition of Q* (Hermeneia; Minneapolis: Fortress, 2000), give it a "C" rating and enclose Q 12:49 in double brackets (376–77).

[28] See A. Guillaumont, et al., *The Gospel according to Thomas* (San Francisco: Harper & Row, 1984); cf. Patterson, "Fire and Dissession," 126–30, 134–37.

> Jesus said: Men possibly think that I have come to throw peace upon the world
> and they do not know that I have come to throw divisions upon the earth, fire,
> sword, war. (16)

The logion, even if we can only condense the logia to a more general idea, conflicts with the early Christian depiction of Jesus as the one who came to save (J.P. Meier's criterion of embarrassment).[29] Also counting in its favor is that the harsh image of fire (cf. Isa. 30:27-28) coheres reasonably with the overstating tack Jesus often takes in response to others. Furthermore, we can once again draw a line back to John the Baptist, who also spoke of fire as part of the eschatological work of God (cf. Q 3:16b-17).

It is likely, then, that Jesus saw in his own mission the beginning of the judging/refining fire of the Final Ordeal (cf. 2 Kgs 1:10; Isa 66:14-16; Ezek 38:22; 39:6; Amos 1:4, 7, 10, 14; Mal 3:19).[30] This is only slightly confirmed by noting that fire is occasionally on the lips of Jesus in the Jesus traditions (cf. Mark 9:43, 48, 49; Matt 5:22; 7:19; 13:40, 50; 25:41; Luke 9:54; *Gos. Thom.* 82).[31] The remarkable distinction of this text is that it is Jesus' *own calling* that will engulf him.[32] He is the *first* to enter into this fire and water, this new era of history. As with Q 9:58, discussed immediately above, Jesus seems to see himself as the representative who will undergo the Final Ordeal, either at the lead of his followers or on their behalf.

His adaptation of the imagery of the purging/judging fire could be further confirmed by the important, and usually neglected, study of the meaning of *fishers of men*. The metaphor is more than a cute pun designed for ministers so they can build bridges to various vocations. Instead, the imagery reflects the dual task of announcing the presence of salvation and the warning of judgment (Hab 1:14-17; Jer 16:16; Ezek 29:4-5; Amos 4:2; Prov 6:26b; Eccl 9:12; 1QH II, 29; III, 26; V, 8; 1QHᵃ XIII, 8; CD IV, 15-16; *T. Dan* 2:4).[33] The other use of fishing imagery by Jesus is found in Matthew 13:47-50, where (whether authentic or not) the image is one of both preserving and destroying. If this fishing imagery reasonably coheres with what Jesus had to say about his mission, we would have further confirmation that Luke 12:49, then, reports secure information about Jesus: he saw his mission resulting in purgation and judgment.

[29] See Meier, *A Marginal Jew* (3 vols.; ABRL; New York: Doubleday, 1991–2001), 1:168–71.

[30] See Dunn, "Birth of a Metaphor," in his *Pneumatology*, 106; G. Delling, "βαπτισμα βαπτισθηναι," *NovT* 2 (1957–58): 92–115, here pp. 104–8; Beasley-Murray, *Jesus and the Kingdom of God*, 249; Allison, *End of the Ages Has Come*, 125–27.

[31] A similar usage can be found at Qumran: e.g., 1QM XI, 10; XIV, 1, 17; 1QHᵃ IV, 13; XIV, 18; XVI, 20; 4Q174 IV, 1; 4Q177 III, 7; 4Q189 1-2 I, 9; 4Q434 1 I, 6, 13.

[32] Delling, "βαπτισμα βαπτισθηναι," 109–11.

[33] W. Wuellner, *The Meaning of "Fishers of Men"* (Philadelphia: Westminster, 1967); C.W.F. Smith, "Fishers of Men," *HTR* 52 (1959): 187–203; so also Davies and Allison, *Matthew*, 1:398–99.

Yet another line can be drawn back to John in the "baptism" of Luke 12:50,[34] which is similar to Mark 10:38, for here we discover "baptism" and "fire." Each is used by Jesus, in different contexts, to define his mission. John said Jesus would baptize with the Holy Spirit and fire. In Luke 12:49-50 Jesus announces that his mission involves fire and baptism. However, there is a subtle, if also significant, shift in meaning in Jesus' adaptation of the metaphors. Both the fire and the baptism of Luke 12:49-50 appear to be headed at Jesus rather than coming from Jesus. Evidently, we can conclude that Jesus now knows that John's words are coming about in a personally realized sense: Jesus is the one who must endure that Final Ordeal and it causes him pain and anguish to think of what is about to occur. As Jesus stepped forward as a representative Israelite to be baptized by John, so he steps forward as one who is rejected (Q 9:58) and as one who must undergo the fire and the baptism (Luke 12:49-50). In each, Jesus is to be seen as heading into the eschatological ordeal[35] as the representative of his followers. To think such might not involve death is to play a game of abstraction with closed eyes.[36]

Jesus thought that he would die prematurely at the hands of someone like Antipas. Jesus understood this death to come about as the result of a divinely destined mission that involved the onset of the Final Ordeal that, in larger categories, is somehow (we don't know how) connected to the kingdom of God. It should be emphasized here that when we connect *mission* with *death*, we need to do so under the severest of conditions: the bookends of Q 11:4 and Mark 14:36 drain any exuberant enthusiasm of thinking Jesus thought from front to back in terms of dying as the way to define his mission. In fact, this can be turned on its head: if Jesus saw his mission in terms of the kingdom of God, and if he saw the kingdom as necessarily connected to the Final Ordeal (which would be very Jewish of him), and if he comprehended his participation in that Final Ordeal as being plunged into it as the representative Israelite who would die, then there is reason to connect his mission and his death. But, this is getting ahead of ourselves. Before we connect death and mission under the umbrella of kingdom, we need to define what kind of mission Jesus had in mind, and it is to this that we now must turn.

MATTHEW 23:29-36 (= FROM Q; CF. LUKE 11:47-51)

> [29]"Woe to you, scribes and Pharisees, hypocrites! For you build the tombs of the prophets and decorate the graves of the righteous, [30]and you say, 'If we had lived in the days of our ancestors, we would not have taken part with them in shedding the blood of the prophets.' [31]Thus you testify against yourselves that you are

---

[34] We have already argued that Jesus used the image of baptism; see above, pp. 125–30.

[35] The evidence is wide-ranging, but see Gen 6–8; Pss 9:15-17; 88:6-7; Isa 30:27-28; Ezek 38:22; *L.A.E.* 49:3; *Sib. Or.* 3:689–90; 1QHIII, 29-30; Q 17:26-27; 2 Pet 3:6-7.

[36] So also Beasley-Murray, *Jesus and the Kingdom of God*, 251.

descendants of those who murdered the prophets. [32]Fill up, then, the measure of your ancestors. [33]You snakes, you brood of vipers! How can you escape being sentenced to hell? [34]Therefore I send you prophets, sages, and scribes, some of whom you will kill and crucify, and some you will flog in your synagogues and pursue from town to town, [35]so that upon you may come all the righteous blood shed on earth, from the blood of righteous Abel to the blood of Zechariah son of Barachiah, whom you murdered between the sanctuary and the altar. [36]Truly I tell you, all this will come upon this generation.

This set of logia coheres substantially with Luke 13:31-33, discussed above, and even if it extends beyond the life of Jesus in its strong invective against the temple and/or the Pharisees,[37] there are indications that the unit's substance derives from Jesus.[38] The graphic images, even aesthetics, of the unit are consistent with the concrete style of Jesus' teachings.[39] There are few images as rhetorically potent as these: "you build the tombs of the prophets and decorate the graves of the righteous" (Matt 23:29). The evident turning of their action on its head is typical of Jesus' style, as we have seen already several times (cf. Mark 14:3-9; Luke 13:31-33; 23:27-31).

Also part of his style was the direct controversy, if not overt diatribe, he engaged. C.H. Dodd spoke of the "irreconcilable breach" that occurred between Jesus and his contemporaries. It is clear from a critical reading of the Jesus traditions that such a breach led to an "increasing bitterness," and it encouraged his followers to give his sayings a "sharper edge." But, Jesus "did deliberately criticize them, and sometimes in trenchant terms."[40] If Jesus could call Antipas a fox, and if he could expose in graphic terms the hypocrisy among leaders, and if he was centrally concerned with the exploitation of the poor by the rich, it would not be surprising to find him expressing himself in strong terms and drawing some deep lines in the sand. In general, then, we must permit sayings like this to have a chance at poking their heads above the genuine line. But gen-

---

[37] So Funk, et al., *Five Gospels*, 244. However, this rhetoric should not be assigned to some mean-spirited Christian groups upset about losing control in the synagogues; such rhetoric found its origins in the prophets and became a feature of Jewish infighting. See here L.T. Johnson, "The New Testament's Anti-Jewish Slander and Conventions of Ancient Rhetoric," *JBL* 108 (1989): 419–41; see also R.A. Horsley and J.A. Draper, *Whoever Hears You Hears Me* (Harrisburg: Trinity Press International, 1999), 285–91; Kyu Sam Han, *Jerusalem and the Early Jesus Movement* (JSNTSup 207; Sheffield: Sheffield Academic, 2002), 169–83; also S. Légasse, "L'oracle contre 'cette génération' (Mt 23,34-36 par. Lc 11,49-51) et la polémique judéo-chrétienne dans la source des Logia," in *Logia: Les Paroles de Jésus* (ed. J. Delobel; BETL 59; Leuven: Leuven University Press, 1982), 237–56.

[38] Contra R.J. Miller, "The Rejection of the Prophets in Q," *JBL* 107 (1988): 225–40; E.P. Meadors, *Jesus, the Messianic Herald of Salvation* (Peabody, Mass.: Hendrickson, 1995), 46–49.

[39] See J.D.M. Derrett, "'You Build the Tombs of the Prophets' (Lk. 11, 47-51, Mt. 23, 29-31)," *TUGAL* 102 (1968): 187–93. Derrett, never at a loss for suggesting that moderns have failed to discern the hidden context of a given saying of Jesus, makes the suggestion that expenditure for monuments was complicity with those who had not paid the blood-guilt money to the victims.

[40] C.H. Dodd, *Founder of Christianity* (London: Collins, 1971), 69.

eral arguments do not prove these logia as genuine. The general argument that the logia fit admirably into Jesus' concern with inner vs. outer morality has been claimed throughout the history of Protestant liberalism to carry the weight of Jesus' ethic, but general arguments add only bitty weights to the scale.

We can move to more specific considerations to determine the pedigree of our pericope. The opening woe of Matthew 23:29 finds a substantial parallel in Luke 11:47, and most assign it to Q.[41] As Dale Allison has pointed out, Matthew 23:30-32 has no Lukan parallels but may derive from Q,[42] and the fact that 1 Thessalonians 2:16 contains a parallel to Matthew 23:32 (and assumes awareness of the entire complex) suggests it should be attributed to tradition (Q?).[43] Furthermore, the truncation of these verses suggests that we have to do with tradition, rather than with redactional clarification: Matthew 23:31 attempts to clarify 23:30, but the attempt is not as successful as some would prefer.[44] Both Matthew and Luke clarify Q 11:47 (Matt 23:29) differently, revealing a common underlying core dealing with fathers amd sons.[45]

The critical logical factor in determining the pedigree of this unit is the theme: (1) does Jesus speak elsewhere, or was it likely for him to have spoken at all, of the rejection of the prophets, largely in terms of Jeremiah 7:25 and 29:18-20, and (2) did Jesus personalize the tradition to lead us to think he saw his fate like other prophets?[46] The answer to these two questions hovers between *maybe* and *probably*. Importantly and once again we must think of John: he was a prophet and he was decapitated for it. An intelligible universe requires that one plus one is two. Jesus mulled over his own fate after John's death, and we must

---

[41] Robinson, et al., *Critical Edition of Q,* 282–83; Q 11:47-51 was probably an existing unit; on this, cf. Miller, "Rejection of the Prophets in Q," 227–29; S. Légasse, "L'oracle contre 'cette génération'" 237–56, for a careful tradition-critical analysis.

[42] See Davies and Allison, *Matthew,* 3:305. A connection, not altogether plausible, with Psalm 5:10 has been explored in J.D.M. Derrett, "Receptacles and Tombs (Mt 23:24-30)," *ZNW* 77 (1986): 255–66.

[43] See also D.C. Allison, Jr., *The Jesus Tradition in Q* (Harrisburg: Trinity Press International, 1997), 58–60, who uses the connection of our passage to 1 Thessalonians to show that Q (all three stages) had its origins in the 40s of the first century CE.

[44] Luke's wording sharpens the blade and drives it into the belly of the lawyers: "but your fathers killed them" (Luke 11:47). The logic, however, is clear enough: (1) you decorate the tombs of the prophets; (2) you are related to the prophet-killers as a son is to his father; (3) relation to the prophet-killers is a taking of the wrong side; (4) therefore, your decorating is a sham. What is not proven, but assumed, is point (2): the gravity of the logion is in the assumption that the Jewish leaders otherwise show the signs of rejecting the prophets and join with those who killed the former prophets. The behavior triggering the accusation is found in both versions: decorating the tomb of a prophet connects the person to the murderer of the prophet. Thus, "tomb-building serves only to ratify these past treacheries" (Miller, "Rejection of the Prophets in Q," 230).

[45] For an argument that Matthew's text is closer to the Q source, see Légasse, "L'oracle contre 'cette génération'" 237–39. I am invoking the criterion of G. Theissen and D. Winter, *The Quest for the Plausible Jesus* (trans. M.E. Boring; Louisville: Westminster John Knox, 2002).

[46] I have presented a case for Jesus as prophet (and more) in *A New Vision for Israel* (Grand Rapids: Eerdmans, 1999).

think that anyone who knew Israel's Tanakh as well as Jesus must have thought of other prophets who were rejected by their generation (cf. 1 Kgs 18:4, 13; 19:10, 14; 2 Chr 24:20-21; 36:15-21; Neh 9:26; Jer 2:30; 7:25; 26:20-24; 29:18-20; 11Q19[Temple] LIV; LXI). Prophets were firmly connected to martyrdom in non-biblical Judaism (cf. *Jub.* 1:12; Josephus, A.J. 10:38).[47] And there are various settings in which this very theme surfaces in the Jesus tradition: one thinks of Q 6:23 and of Mark 12:1-12, which we will examine shortly, and our text. However much the unit may have been touched by Matthew (or Luke) to sharpen the language and tone, there is nothing overtly Christian or nothing unconnectable to Jesus about the main substance—the rejection of prophets by Jewish leaders.

As has been made clear by Joachim Jeremias, there is abundant evidence (cf., esp. *Liv. Pro.*; Josephus, *C. Ap.* 2.205) for an increase of tomb (i.e., monument) building at the time of Jesus, and this provides a plausible Jewish context for the logion.[48] Jeremias examined the case for forty-nine figures whose graves were considered sacred in early Judaism and Christianity. In particular, in addition to Jonah, whom I mentioned at the outset of this chapter, he contends that no fewer than ten are of note for setting this pericope into a realistic first century context:

(1)   Joseph [Josh 4:5; Acts 7:15-16];
(2)   the Maccabeans at Modein;
(3)   the royal Necropolis in Jerusalem [Acts 2:29];
(4)   the prophetess Hulda [2 Kgs 22:14; 2 Chr 34:22; *t. B. Bat.* 1:11];
(5)   Isaiah (Heb 11:37);
(6)   Zechariah ben Jehoida [Heb 11:37];
(7)/(8) Rachel and Bilhah, Zilpah and Dinah (Matt 2:18; *Jub.* 34:15-16];
(9)   Davidids;
(10)   Patriarchs in Hebron [Acts 7:16].

Tombs were a favorite for pilgrims not only because of who was buried there but also because the sites were connected to wonders and successful intercession with the divine.[49]

To draw these threads together—the style, the substance (if not some of the particulars), the historical context, Jesus' relationship to John the Baptist, multiple attestation, and the rough-edged relationship Jesus had with the authorities of Jerusalem—each leads to the same conclusion: the unit's substance can be attributed to Jesus. But, before we draw conclusions from the substance of this text for determining how Jesus understood his death, we need to examine Mark 12:1-12.

[47] On this, cf. esp. Steck, *Israel und das gewaltsame Geschick der Propheten.*

[48] Jeremias, *Heiligengräber in Jesu Umwelt.* T.Y. *Shek.* 2:5 states that monuments are not to adorn the burial places of the righteous; instead, their works are their memorial. Jesus evidently agreed with this sentiment and would have also argued that the obedience of that prophet was what mattered.

[49] Jeremias, *Heiligengräber in Jesu Umwelt,* 126–43.

MARK 12:1-12 (PAR. MATT 21:33-46; LUKE 20:9-19); GOSPEL OF THOMAS 65

R.W. Funk concludes: "The Fellows of the Seminar were of the opinion that a version of this parable, without allegorical overtones, could be traced to Jesus."[50] They prefer the version found in the *Gospel of Thomas* 65, which deserves here to be quoted in full:

> He said: A good man had a vineyard. He gave it to husbandmen so that they would work it and that he would receive its fruit from them. He sent his servant so that the husbandmen would give him the fruit of the vineyard. They seized his servant, they beat him; a little longer and they would have killed him. The servant came, he told it to his master. His master said: "Perhaps he did not know them." He sent another servant; the husbandmen beat him as well. Then the owner sent his son. He said: "Perhaps they will respect my son." Since those husbandmen knew that he was the heir of the vineyard, they seized him, they killed him. Whoever has ears let him hear.

According to the Jesus Seminar report, the original parable ends with a crime, like the parable of the unjust steward (Luke 16:1-7), and evokes the themes of realism and loss.[51] But even shorn of allegorical details the parable of the *Gospel of Thomas* speaks of the rejection of a servant, the owner pondering the acceptance of his son, the sending of his son nonetheless, and the son's death. One is led to the inevitable question: what would Jesus have meant in contrasting "servant" with "son"?[52] Added to this question it is natural also to ask: Who were the servants? And is it also hard for us to think that Jesus would not have had Israel, or the temple (which is more likely), in mind with the "vineyard" (cf. the juridical parable at Isa 5:1-7)?

In other words, Morna Hooker is almost certainly accurate when she claims that the parable has irremovable allegorical details;[53] and many scholars have argued that the parable, shorn here and there of specific Christian details,[54] goes

---

[50] Funk, et al., *Five Gospels*, 101.

[51] *Ibid.*

[52] M. Lowe, "From the Parable of the Vineyard to a Pre-Synoptic Source," *NTS* 28 (1982): 25–63, makes the suggestion that the original parable was about John the Baptist. So also C.S. Mann, *Mark*, 462; D. Stern, "Jesus' Parables from the Perspective of Rabbinic Literature: The Example of the Wicked Husbandmen," in *Parable and Story in Judaism and Christianity* (ed. C. Thoma and M. Wyschogrod; New York: Paulist, 1989), 42–80, here pp. 64–68. The attraction of "son" to John the Baptist is offset, perhaps fatally, by who it was who put John to death—and Antipas makes no appearance in the parable. See B.H. Young, *Jesus and His Jewish Parables* (New York: Paulist, 1989), 305–6, n.1. R.D. Aus, *The Wicked Tenants and Gethsemane* (USFISFCJ 4; Atlanta: Scholars, 1996), 1–64, here esp. pp. 56–57, suggests the "son" was Isaiah.

[53] *Mark*, 273–74.

[54] C.H. Dodd, for instance, found the original parable in Mark 12:1b-3, 5a, 6-9a; cf. his *The Parables of the Kingdom* (London: Nisbet, 1935), 124–32.

right back to Jesus himself.[55] The allegorical details are minor: "only" (Gen 22:2; *Tg. Neof.*; Gen 22:2), "son" need not mean "Son of God," "vineyard" is Israel/temple but not the church (Hos 10:1-2; Isa 27:2-6; Jer 2:21-22; 12:9-13; Ezek 19:10-14; Ps 80:9-19 [MT]).[56] The bizarre action of the owner is consistent with the shocking style of Jesus.[57]

Four considerations separate the parable from the early church: (1) the absence of the son's resurrection in the parable speaks against its origin among post-Easter Christians,[58] (2) the Christology is undeveloped (prophetic), (3) the polemic is with "leaders" (e.g., perhaps the priests as usurpers of the vineyard; *Tg. Isa.* 22:12-25; 28:1-29; T. Levi 14:2-15:1; 2 Chr 36:14-16) and not Israel as a whole, and (4) the owner's prediction in Mark 12:9 is hard to harmonize with earliest Christianity. In addition, making it historically plausible, the details are consistent with first-century Jewish socio-economic conditions,[59] and the parable squares neatly with the demonstrably current targumic renderings of Isaiah 5:1-7 as an indictment of the temple.[60] What is more, the death of the son acquires no atoning significance whatsoever and is instead the description of the death of a prophet (Mark 12:8; cf. Jer 26:20-23; 1 Kgs 18:4, 13; 19:10, 14; 2 Chr 24:21; Neh 9:25-26).

We are left then with a parable by Jesus that spoke of servants being sent to a vineyard, with those servants being rejected and/or killed, and with a rather incomprehensible owner who, in spite of the violent treatment of his servants, sends his son into the fray and thinks somehow he will be treated more kindly. That is, the parable fits with other shocking statements by Jesus about how God deals with humans (cf. Luke 15:1-32). There are similar rabbinic parables that are unlikely to have been borrowed by early Christians (cf. *Sipre Deut.* 312).[61] What gives this parable its singularity is that Jesus envisions (contra Isa 5) new

[55] So Taylor, *Mark*, 472–73; Pesch, *Markusevangelium*, 2:222; K.R. Snodgrass, *The Parable of the Wicked Tenants* (WUNT 27; Tübingen: Mohr, 1983), 108–9, who provides a sizable list of scholars who think the parable genuine; C.A. Evans, *Mark*, 2:224; A. Hultgren, *The Parables of Jesus* (Grand Rapids: Eerdmans, 2000), 360–67.

[56] Cf. Stern, "Jesus' Parables from the Perspective of Rabbinic Literature," 64–68.

[57] See Hooker, *Mark*, 274; Hultgren, *Parables of Jesus*, 362. But see also J.D.M. Derrett, *Law in the New Testament* (London: Darton, Longman & Todd, 1970), 286–312.

[58] On the debate about Psalm 118:22-23, cf. C.A. Evans, *Mark*, 2:228-30.

[59] W. Schottroff, "Das Gleichnis von den bösen Weingärtnern (Mk. 12:1-9 par.): Ein Beitrag zur Geschichte der Bodenpacht in Palästina," *ZDPV* 112 (1996): 18–48.

[60] So J.C. De Moor, "The Targumic Background of Mark 12:1-12: The Parable of the Wicked Tenants," *JSJ* 29 (1998): 63–80; W.J.C. Weren, "The Use of Isaiah 5, 1-7 in the Parable of the Tenants (Mark 12, 1-12; Matthew 21, 33-46)," *Bib* 79 (1998): 1-26; Young, *Jesus and His Jewish Parables*, 282–316; Aus, *Wicked Tenants and Gethsemane*; G.J. Brooke, "4Q500 1 and the Use of Scripture in the Parable of the Vineyard," *DSD* 2 (1995): 268–94. In particular, Aus draws attention to the singing of Exodus 15 at Passover in the temple (cf. *b. Meg.* 31a), and connects our passage to *Mek. de R Ishm. Shir.* 7 (on Exod 15:9), 9 (on Exod 15:15), *Besh.* 1 (on Exod 13:21).

[61] H.K. McArthur and R.M. Johnston, *They Also Taught in Parables* (Grand Rapids: Zondervan, 1990); cf. in particular *Mek. Shir.* 2:130-33; *Sipre Num.* 131; *Sipre Deut.* 40; 305.

leaders and a new beginning, both themes being inherent to Jesus' kingdom mission.

We are prepared now to combine Matthew 23:29-32 with Mark 12:1-12 (or *Gos. Thom.* 65) to suggest that Jesus not only saw a connection between John and the fate of Israel's prophets, but placed himself in the same line of rejection. This means that Jesus must have thought of his own death as a martyr like the martyrs of other (recent and ancient) prophets in Israel. But this perception by Jesus is more than "mere clairvoyance. They [the predictions of Jesus about his death] are a dramatization in terms of history of the moral realities of the situation."[62] Which is to say: Jesus sees his death, not in terms of an isolated individual who is granted insight by God into the next few days, but as one who sees his life on the stage of a history that will soon turn to Act II, and he will not be a part of it. He is escorted off the stage because his part in Act I is not accepted by the temple actors who are writing the lines for Act II. His martyrdom is not the fate of an individual; it is the inevitable impact of his calling in his time. To mimic the words of E.P. Sanders, the "smoke" of Jesus' death is the result of the "fire" he knew himself called to live and declare.[63]

As a summary statement of this section on the prophetic fate of Jesus, we agree with the following judgment of Ulrich Luz: "Jesus also, who belongs to the prophetic tradition of Israel, must have been conscious of the connection between his prophetic vocation, the city of Jerusalem [as a place of rejection of prophets], and a possible martyrdom."[64]

RUNNING THE GAUNTLET

We need to pause momentarily to see where we've been. The bookends of Q 11:4 and Mark 14:36 reveal an attitude of Jesus toward death: from the beginning of his public ministry to the end he was not *intent* on dying as a form of entrance into the Final Ordeal. But there is significant evidence (Mark 2:19-20; 10:38; 14:3-9; Luke 13:31-33) to show that Jesus thought he would not be granted a normal span of life. And this premature death appears to have been understood by Jesus as part of God's providential will for him and was thus part of his mission. Jesus' first clear interpretation of his death is that, like other prophets, the fate of his mission would be a martyrdom. That is, there is clear evidence that Jesus understands his death in terms of tragedy.

MARK 8:34

One point of tension with the bookends found at Q 11:4 and Mark 14:36, is the apparent *courage* we find in Jesus to face that premature death. Theological

---

[62] Dodd, *Parables of the Kingdom*, 131.

[63] E.P. Sanders, *Jesus and Judaism* (Philadelphia: Fortress, 1985), 3–22.

[64] Luz, "Warum zog Jesus nach Jerusalem?" 415 (author's translation).

convictions are not easily translated into courageous behavior; knowing that one's death is willed by God, and even accepting death as the fate of a prophet, might not lead to courageous forward movement. But Jesus had courage, and it is perhaps best seen at Mark 8:34 (par. Matt 16:24; Luke 9:23): "If any want to become my followers, let them deny themselves and take up their cross and follow me." Many scholars would see the use of the cross as an image for death as a later Christian intrusion, and they could be justified in their doubt.[65] But the surrounding logia, which have been brought together in the course of transmission, support one central and revealing thought: life is not as valuable as faithfulness, and death should not threaten integrity (cf. Mark 8:34, 35, 36-37, 38).[66] Furthermore, there are clear doublets, leading one to suspect that there is something deeply dominical behind the traditions: Mark 8:35 has a doublet at Q 14:27 (cf. Matt 10:38-39; Luke 17:33) and Mark 10:38 has a doublet at Q 12:9 (cf. Matt 10:33). As if the logion became a source for comments, there are variants of the logion in the early church (cf. John 12:25; Phil 2:6; Rom 6:8; 2 Cor 5:15-16).[67]

What surprises is that a cross logion is found in a variety of sources. One should not be hasty in pronouncing these logia as early Christian *Gemeindetheologie* simply because the image of the cross is used; for, after all, crucifixion was a part of the Roman penal system.[68] If we are careful to peel away any notion of an atoning cross and leave the image as simply metaphorical, and then combine that with the images of "saving one's life" (cf. Mark 8:35; Luke 17:33; John 12:5), we have adequate evidence to think Jesus encouraged his followers to assume the same courage he had: to face death if that is the blow dealt by history.[69] John was an example to Jesus in this regard; the prophets who were before him were also examples. And who could forget the potent stories surrounding the Maccabees? Death for one's faith was such a common occurrence that we would be surprised if Jesus *didn't* embrace the same stance and call his followers to resist violence and oppression with martyrdom. The theme is

---

[65] Funk, et al., *Five Gospels*, 78–79.

[66] This notion has a widespread presence in the Gospels and early church; it reflects a fundamental item of continuity between Jesus and the early church, as well as between (certain groups within) Judaism and Jesus. Cf. W. Rebell, "'Sein Leben Verlieren' (Mark 8.35 par.) als Strukturmoment vor- und nachösterlichen Glaubens," *NTS* 35 (1989): 202–18. For a good study of the courage of the Zealots, cf. M. Hengel, *The Zealots* (trans. D. Smith; Edinburgh: T&T Clark, 1989); on the Maccabees, cf. E. Bickermann, *The God of the Maccabees* (trans. H.R. Moehring; SJLA 32; Leiden: E.J. Brill, 1979). One thinks of the Daniel 7–12, 1–2 Maccabees, and the sectarians at Qumran, not to mention the holdouts at Masada.

[67] See H.J. de Jonge, "The Sayings on Confessing and Denying Jesus in Q 12:8-9 and Mark 8:38," *NovT* 89 (1997): 105–21, for a careful and judicious tradition-critical analysis, concluding that Mark 8:38/Q 12:8-9 is possibly from Jesus; see also J. Lambrecht, "Q-Influence on Mark 8,34–9,1," in *Logia* (ed. J. Delobel), 277–304, who argues that Mark used Q to his own ends.

[68] On which cf. still M. Hengel, *Crucifixion* (trans. J. Bowden; Philadelphia: Fortress, 1977).

[69] See V. Howard, "Did Jesus Speak about His Own Death?" *CBQ* 39 (1977): 515–27; Luz, "Warum zog Jesus nach Jerusalem?" 417–19.

prevalent in Judaism and in early Christianity and, *therefore*, more than likely to have been a conviction of Jesus.

The logic is simple and unavoidable: if Jesus called his disciples to a willing martyrdom, for which there is plenty of evidence (Q 12:4-9; 14:27; 17:33), we can infer with the utmost of probability that he, too, saw his own death approaching. He therefore faced his death with open eyes.

CONCLUSIONS

Modern Jesus scholarship has rarely examined the question of what Jesus thought of his death, if he even knew of that death. This stands so contrary to the Christian perception of Jesus as having suffered a sin-forgiving and atoning death, that it simply boggles how the question can be avoided for so long. It is the contention of this book that this question needs to be asked again, and this first section of bits and bobs in the Jesus tradition suggests the beginnings of an answer: yes, Jesus did think he was to die, and it can be reasonably connected to a final feature of his mission. And the evidence so far studied also suggests that he thought of his death in terms of a divinely destined martyr for his prophetic calling. But we have not yet studied the most critical expressions on the lips of Jesus regarding a potential atoning significance to his death, namely, Mark 10:45 and the last supper tradition.

Several other ideas have surfaced and need to be dealt with in passing at this point. The first is this: there are some slight indicators that Jesus saw himself, in his mission and his role in that mission to Israel, as the *representative Israelite*. Anyone who thinks of himself as Jesus did, as one who was called by YHWH to call Israel to repentance and to the arrival of God's kingdom, surely saw himself as a representative Israelite in a profound sense. But Mark 10:38, and its companion at Luke 12:49-50, suggests that Jesus' baptism is the first in a line of others. His enduring of the Final Ordeal is as one who represents what God has called others to accomplish; his suffering initiates the eschatological tribulation. One needs to be careful in what to draw from this, and we are certainly not capable of arguing from these two logia that Jesus' end was somehow vicarious or substitutionary, as later Christians were to infer. But, we are driven by the evidence to the conclusion that Jesus thought his death was somehow representative of what happens when God's call involves the sort of thing Jesus was sent to declare and do.

Second, the notion of Jesus' baptism triggers, in the Markan context, the Son of man saying in Mark 10:45. We will examine this logion soon enough, but for now it must be said that the connection is obvious: if Jesus must suffer in the Final Ordeal, then (as a Scripture prophet himself) he would have pondered over Scriptures that might shed light on his destiny—and at least one place he might look to see his life inscripturated would be Daniel 7. In spite of some scholarship's denial, that text speaks of the Son of man's suffering, and there the Son of man is clearly a representative figure for Israel, the saints of the Most High.

Third, the theme of *vindication* has lurked in the background in a few of these logia, and surely has one of its anchors in Psalm 118:22.[70] To return to Mark 12:1-12, though many scholars have argued that Mark 12:10-12 parallels have been added to the original parable of Jesus, one would be hard-pressed to think of any Jewish prophet who thought his martrydom would not be vindicated ultimately by God. So, even if Mark 12:10-12 reflects (as it does) early Christian coloring, they were on to something that would have been at some level implicit. When Jesus opines over the tombs as indicators that the Jewish leaders were participants in putting to death the prophets (Matt 23:23-36), that unit is followed (in Matthew, but not Luke) by Jesus' lament over Jerusalem, where vindication is clearly present (Q 13:34-35).[71] The Final Ordeal, suffering as martyrdom, and final vindication are part and parcel of the Jewish context of Jesus; it is historically plausible to connect them.

But the major theme that fails to appear is an atoning significance to his death. The above three themes—representation, Son of man, and vindication—seem likely, but there is no indication in these various logia that Jesus saw his death as atoning. And the scattering of the evidence across source-critical and form-critical lines, along with simple historical logic, suggests that the theme is limited to two other pieces of evidence that will be the subject of lengthier analysis in what follows. It is only in John that something like purgation of sin, or atonement, appears: John 1:29, where John claims that Jesus is the Lamb of God who takes away the sin of the world. The question that concerns this study is whether the John of John 1:29 stood on the other side of the cross. We won't be able to decide that until we have sorted through the enormously significant passages of Mark 10:45 and the last supper narrative.

Jesus' anticipation of his own premature death needs to be changed from a criterion indicating inauthenticity to a criterion of authenticity. As Bultmann used the "eschatological" criterion, so scholarship should be able to use the "premature death" criterion. From the time of John the Baptist's death onwards, it is highly unlikely that Jesus anticipated a premature death. That he contemplated its place in God's plan is inevitable. That he contemplated it being atoning, however, needs further examination—and it is to that examination that we now turn as we examine the two critical texts about Jesus having contemplated an atoning significance to his death: Mark 10:45 and 14:24.

---

[70] See further at ch. 11, "Tradition History and Authenticity."

[71] This is not to deny that the Q logion hasn't been edited and updated; cf. Miller, "Rejection of the Prophets in Q," 235-40, where the "how often" is given considered attention.

Part III

A Ransom for Many

Chapter 7

The Authenticity of the Ransom Sayings

Apart from the words reported of Jesus in the last supper, no statement attributed by the Evangelists to Jesus is more significant for the debate over how Jesus understood his death than the following words: "For the Son of man came not to be served but to serve, *and to give his life a ransom for many*" (Mark 10:45). And neither is there a logion of more disputed authenticity than this "Son of man" ransom saying.[1] But, as Barnabas Lindars observed in his contribution to *Expository Times*' well-received pieces on texts about salvation, "Few people are likely to be satisfied with relegating this idea to the creative reflection of the church . . . [as it] lies close to the heart of the gospel. There is bound to be a strong desire to retain it as genuinely the word of Jesus."[2] Desires, however, don't always make for good history.

We immediately confront a serious methodological factor. Two contradictory claims have been made. First, the claim has been made that the saying is inauthentic because it has the flavor of the Hellenistic churches. Second, as if mining a different quarry, some scholars have argued vehemently for the authenticity of this logion because it has a Jewish background. As a *point-d' appui*, we note that Bernd Janowski and Peter Stuhlmacher find a plausible Jewish background for the ransom saying in various texts.[3] Thus,

> Psalm 49:7 (Heb 49:8): Truly, no ransom avails for one's life, there is no price one can give to God for it.

---

[1] On Son of man, see the excursus at the end of this chapter. That bibliography is assumed from this point on.

[2] B. Lindars, "Salvation Proclaimed," *ExpTim* 93 (1981–1982): 292–95, here p. 292.

[3] See P. Stuhlmacher, *Biblische Theologie des Neuen Testaments* (vol. 1 of *Grundlegung von Jesus zu Paulus*; Göttingen: Vandenhoeck & Ruprecht, 1997), 128–29, referring to the work of Janowski.

Isaiah 43:3-4: For I am the LORD your God, the Holy One of Israel, your Savior. I give Egypt as your ransom, Ethiopia and Seba in exchange for you. Because you are precious in my sight, and honored, and I love you, I give people in return for you, nations in exchange for your life (cf. also Isa 45:14-17; *Sipre Deut.* 333 on 32:43 [Neusner, 382]).

4Q508, 3.I, 5-6: Of the wicked you shall make our ransom, while for the upright [you will bring about] the destruction of all our enemies.

This evidence permits them a connection also to Isaiah 52:13–53:12. But there is a methodological issue involved, even if we for now suspend judgment on the issue of whether this view can be justified at the level of historiography. Here is the tendency in their procedure: the evidence is completely sorted on the table; the logion is compared to Jewish and Greek sources; when it is discovered that the "ransom for many" element of the saying is Jewish, rather than Greek, the conclusion occurs: it is from Jesus. The leap is made. It remains, however, a leap and not a simple short step.[4] This methodological tendency to equate what is Jewish with what is Jesus is frequently observed in the conservative reaction to Bultmann, who argued that atonement sayings like this are not Jewish but emerged instead from the Hellenistic churches. To be sure, for a saying to be assigned to Jesus there needs to be evidence that the saying is plausible in a *Jewish context*, as Gerd Theissen and Dagmar Winter have argued.[5] But establishing something as Jewish is not the same as establishing it as from Jesus.

The argument is messier than it looks. Thanks to the pioneering reminders of Martin Hengel,[6] few today accept the simple bifurcation of Jewish and Hellenistic Christianity. Rendering judgment on Jewish vs. Hellenistic simply is no longer an option. Many, however, retain Bultmann's negative judgment on the authenticity of Mark 10:45 that emerged from his bifurcation of Hellenistic and Jewish Christianity. Bultmann's opponents, like the spies of the clan of Joseph (Judg 1:22-26), scouted Judaism to find sacrificial and atoning and vicarious perceptions of death—and then, once those texts were discovered, the case about a text like Mark 10:45 was considered closed. The mistake can be stated simply: just because something is Jewish doesn't mean it is from Jesus. To assign this logion to Jesus another approach must be taken. To be sure, assigning the logion to Jesus is more persuasive if there is a Jewish context and if it meets general criteria for assessing historicity. But not all are agreed that those criteria can be met.

[4] Cf. B.D. Chilton, *A Galilean Rabbi and His Bible* (GNS 8; Wilmington, Del.: Michael Glazier, 1984), 90.
[5] G. Theissen and D. Winter, *The Quest for the Plausible Jesus* (trans. M.E. Boring; Louisville: Westminster John Knox, 2002).
[6] M. Hengel, *Hellenism and Judaism* (trans. J. Bowden; Minneapolis: Fortress, 1974); *Jews, Greeks and Barbarians* (trans. J. Bowden; Philadelphia: Fortress, 1980); M. Hengel and C. Markschies, *The 'Hellenization' of Judaea in the First Century after Christ* (trans. J. Bowden; Philadelphia: Trinity Press International, 1989).

In the rest of this chapter we will begin our exploration of the historical pedigree of Mark 10:45 and, more importantly, the pedigree of "a ransom for many."

THE AUTHENTICITY DISCUSSION

The context and ethical focus of Mark 10:35-45 (par. Matt 20:20-28; Luke 22:24-30)[7] seems to be breached by the addition of the ransom saying in Mark 10:45b. A brief review of the Markan context puts the tension of the logion in sharper focus.[8] James and John, like the centurion (Q 7:1-10), believe Jesus can do whatever he wants, so they ask if they might be given seat numbers two and three in the final kingdom of God (Mark 10:35-37), which request bears resemblance to Daniel 7:9-10, 14, 26-27. Jesus asks them if they are to share his fate by using the images of baptism and cup (10:38-39), which is a set of terms judged authentic in the previous chapter. These images anticipate his death. When they shockingly respond that they are up to the challenge of ingesting his cup and enduring his baptism, Jesus shifts to a different argument: God is in charge of seating in the kingdom banquet (10:40).

Naturally, the other disciples, who are just as influenced by an honor and shame culture, find the request of James and John presumptuous. Into this discussion about who gets to sit where in the kingdom Jesus inserts his timeless, upside-down wisdom about service as the fundamental virtue of a leader. A Gentile-like lust for power and authority is all too common and, instead, his followers are to be noted by serving one another in love (10:41-44). Then he appeals to his own life's course as an example: he, too, will serve them. But, then he adds what seems incongruous to the ethical concern: he will serve them to the point of offering his life as a *ransom*[9] for the *many*.[10]

It is the italicized words that are considered inappropriate for the life of Jesus, and more appropriate for early Christian faith in Jesus' death as atoning. This is partly confirmed by both John's and Peter's emphases on Jesus' life as the paradigm of loving service.[11] John's Gospel constructs the entire last supper as a

---

[7] Luke's parallel does not begin until Mark 10:41 (Luke 22:24-27) and is anchored into a different setting (the last supper). Many have attempted to connect Mark 10:45b to the last supper by riding through the room on Luke 22:26-27. Thus, the redemptive sense of Mark 10:45b is articulated in the context of the Pesah or quasi-Pesah meal. A sketch of the development of redemption in the NT was hammered out, on the basis of connecting Mark 10:45 and 14:24, by I.H. Marshall, "The Development of the Concept of Redemption in the New Testament," in *Reconciliation and Hope*, 15–69.

[8] See France, *Mark*, 414–21; Green, *Luke*, 765–70.

[9] Recently, to no avail, J.C. O'Neill tried to resurrect the likelihood of MS W's original reading (*loutron* instead of *lutron*). See his "Did Jesus Teach that His Death Would be Vicarious as Well as Typical?" in *Suffering and Martyrdom in the New Testament* (ed. Horbury and McNeil), 9–27.

[10] The Lukan context for the *logion* (Mark 10:45 par. Luke 22:27) is the last supper, at which time the disciples break into an argument about greatness in the kingdom.

[11] Both also clearly move into atonement or into the purifying value of Jesus' life: cf. John 13:7-10 and 1 Peter 2:18-25.

meal during which Jesus enacted this very lesson: his followers are to be noted by serving, so he washes their feet (John 13). 1 Peter has a similar pattern: the Christian slaves are encouraged to endure their sufferings because Jesus' very life was a life of suffering followed by vindication (1 Pet 2:18-25). The logion, even at the level of moral example, could be *Gemeindetheologie*. But, if the early churches thought of Jesus' life as the paradigm of service, the notion of serving leadership could also be from Jesus himself. Had the words of Jesus not moved into the realm of a ransom for many, few would have doubted these words as genuine.[12]

The lust for power, the social context behind this logion, is as common as blood. The challenge to serve instead of enacting that power is not common, and can be seen as turning the social context on its head. Deconstructing power is typical of Jesus, but the notion is hardly innovative. The notion of loving one's friends, of serving within one's community—even to the point of dying—is a commonplace in the ancient world (Aristotle, *Eth. nic.* 9.8; Strabo, Geogr. 16.4.26; Philo, *Contempl.* 70–72; *b. Hor.* 10a; *b. Ta'an.* 10b). There is nothing here uncharacteristic of the ancient world, distinctive to Christianity, or out of place for Jesus: it is historically plausible.[13] And the entire conversation found now in Mark is believable: from the lust for power to the challenge of loving service to the example Jesus offers of his own life of service. Until we get to the ransom for many—and that is what matters for us. We are led then to think that the context is credible and the drift of the conversation is as well. Apart from the ransom for many are there any other obstacles?

The "I came" saying (Greek: *elthen*, aorist) sums up the life of Jesus—his mission and vision—from the angle of early Christian theology, and can strain our perception of the kinds of things that would have been said by Jesus. In fact, there are a number of "I came" or "I was sent" sayings that, more or less, express early Christian theology. A list includes the following:

> Mark 1:38: Let us go on to the neighboring towns, so that I may proclaim the message there also; for that is what I came out to do.

> Mark 2:17: I have come to call not the righteous but sinners.

> Matthew 5:17: Do not think that I have come to abolish the law or the prophets; I have come not to abolish but to fulfill.

---

[12] Thus, cf. S. Kim, *The "Son of Man" as the Son of God* (WUNT 30; Tübingen; J.C.B. Mohr, 1983), 38–41; P. Stuhlmacher, "Why Did Jesus Have to Die?" in *Jesus of Nazareth—Christ of Faith* (trans. S.S. Schatzmann; Peabody, Mass.: Hendrickson, 1993), 39–57; S.H.T. Page, "The Authenticity of the Ransom *Logion* (Mark 10:45b)," in *Studies of History and Tradition in the Four Gospels* (vol. 1 of *Gospel Perspectives*; ed. R.T. France and D. Wenham; Sheffield: JSOT, 1980), 137–61. Contra, e.g., Pesch, *Markusevangelium*, 2:162–66; J.D. Crossan, *In Fragments* (San Francisco: Harper & Row, 1983), 285–94. B.J. Pitre, "The Historical Jesus, the Great Tribulation and the End of the Exile," Ph.D. diss. (Notre Dame, 2004), has an extensive defense of the historicity of Mark 10:45 (pp. 534–83).

[13] P.M. Casey, "General, Generic and Indefinite," *JSNT* 29 (1987): 21–56, here pp. 42–43.

Matthew 10:34-36: Do not think that I have come to bring peace to the earth; I have not come to bring peace, but a sword. For I have come to set a man against his father, and a daughter against her mother, and a daughter-in-law against her mother-in-law; and one's foes will be members of one's own household.

Matthew 11:19: the Son of man came eating and drinking.

Luke 12:49: I came to bring fire to the earth, and how I wish it were already kindled! (cf. Matt 10:34-36)

Luke 19:10: For the Son of man came to seek out and to save the lost.

John 9:39: I came into this world for judgment so that those who do not see may see, and those who do see may become blind.

John 10:10: I came that they may have life, and have it abundantly

John 12:47: For I came not to judge the world, but to save the world.

Also, the "sent" pattern needs to be seen in this light:

Mark 9:37: Whoever welcomes one such child in my name welcomes me, and whoever welcomes me welcomes not me but the one who sent me.

Matthew 10:40: Whoever welcomes you welcomes me, and whoever welcomes me welcomes the one who sent me.

Matthew 15:24: I was sent only to the lost sheep of the house of Israel (cf. 10:5-6).

If we take seriously the criterion of multiple attestation, in forms as well as sources, we are led inescapably to the conclusion that Jesus probably reflected on and spoke about his call from the Father in the "I have come" form. It should not be argued that each and every one of these statements is *ipsissima verba Jesu*; but the breadth of the evidence as well as the inherent truncation of the various missions suggest that an "I have come" statement should not be ruled out because of its form. We need to distinguish between form and substance.

It is indisputable that Jesus thought he had been called by God as a prophet to announce a message to his people. In that sense, Jesus knew he was sent and that means he could have thought in terms, as did other prophets, of an "I have come to" type language. If that is bedrock tradition, then an "I have come" saying, *in substance*, has every right to be heard as potentially an authentic word from Jesus.[14] We have a credible first century moral context; the form of the logion is not at all inconsistent with the sort of thing Jesus may have said. If the form has been reshaped by an early Christian who liked the "I have come" sayings, the substance of what Jesus intended remains unaltered. These are not the problems, however.

[14] Stated carefully in Kim, *The "Son of Man" as the Son of God*, 40–43.

It is the absence of the ransom saying in the Lukan parallel that presents the most formidable challenge to the authenticity of Mark 10:45b.

Mark 10:45	Luke 22:27
For the Son of man came not to be served	For who is greater, the one who is at the table or the one who serves?
	Is it not the one at the table?
but to serve	But I am among you as one who serves.
and to give his life a ransom for many.	

A first read through these two texts might lead one to think that they are not parallel, but there are several factors that suggest otherwise. (1) The general flow of the context is identical:

in both Mark and Luke the context is a dispute about greatness (Mark 10:35-41; Luke 22:24);

Jesus responds by pointing out the arrogant lust for power among Gentile (read: Roman; read: Antipas-like) leaders (Mark 10:42; Luke 22:25);

Jesus informs them that service is the fundamental moral category for his followers (Mark 10:43-44; Luke 22:26); and

Jesus points to his own example as the moral norm (Mark 10:45; Luke 22:27).

(2) There are significant verbal parallels that are not, by themselves, a commonplace in the teachings of Jesus: *gentiles, lording it over others, those in authority,* and *servant.* (3) Since Luke's parallel is found in the last supper traditions of Luke 22 and Mark's elsewhere, it matters that Luke has no doublet.[15] (Luke may have knowingly relocated the pericope, and so chosen to omit the section when he was using Mark 10.) It is unlikely that Luke is describing a separate event or a second occurrence of this logion, and it is also likely that Luke has inserted this tradition in his last supper tradition.[16]

But the two traditions are nonetheless somewhat independent. While the right words are present in both accounts, the scarcity of substantial lengthy parallels suggests that either Luke has completely rewritten Mark, or to use the terms of J.D.G. Dunn, he has "re-performed" the oral tradition "performed" also in Mark.[17] Or, that he has used a different source for the same material (in which case someone else has rewritten the tradition). The second argument is

---

[15] Ibid., 43–52.

[16] A case has been made for two different events by Page, "The Authenticity of the Ransom *Logion* (Mark 10:45b)," 137–61; I.H. Marshall, *Luke: Historian and Theologian* (Grand Rapids: Zondervan, 1989), 813–14, sees omissions by both Mark and Luke.

[17] See J.D.G. Dunn, *Jesus Remembered* (vol. 1 of *Christianity in the Making*; Grand Rapids: Eerdmans, 2003).

persuasive since the language of Luke 22:24-27 is not heavily Lukan, even if it does reflect some Hellenistic influence (e.g., "greater," "benefactor," "youngest," and "leader"). The two, then, are most likely variants of the one saying of Jesus. Accordingly, we are now left with a saying of Jesus in a credible context, an acceptable form, but found in two variants—which is the more original? Allowing for different oral performances of the saying does not prevent us from asking which is closer to what Jesus said (*pace* Dunn).

One factor may suggest that Luke *omitted* the soteriology inherent in the expression *ransom for many*. There are only two exceptions to Luke's general tendency to avoid, downplay or erase atonement theology: Luke 22:20 and Acts 20:28. In a later chapter we will see that Luke 22:20 is probably secondary (the shorter reading is preferred). Thus, the only place Luke has atonement theology[18] explicitly is at Acts 20:28. If this indicates the general direction and interest of Lukan theology, it could be argued that Luke has omitted the ransom expression. This is a weighty consideration but not finally determinative. The exception at Acts 20:28 hardly supports the case: if Luke can have it there he would not be opposed to having it elsewhere. More importantly, we cannot be sure the notion of ransom was in Luke's source since dependence on Mark in this instance is far from clear. (Furthermore, we could argue that Luke *does* have some atonement theology, but that it is clearly not central to his designs and, *on that basis*, argue he has omitted it.)

We are left to judge the possibility of Jesus having said *ransom* and *for many* as something appropriate to his life and his mission. As for the two expressions, the latter is likely to have emerged from a Jewish milieu, since it is a translation of the Hebrew/Aramaic *rabbim* or (as Casey has it) the Aramaic *chlp sgyʾyn* ("in the place of many"), and is almost surely from Semitic-speaking sectors of the church or from Jesus.[19]

Could Jesus have said "ransom"?[20] There can be little doubt that at some level what is said here is precisely what did happen: Jesus was arrested and his

---

[18] I add here the observation that what I mean here by "atonement theology" pertains to stating explicitly how the death of Jesus atones. In other words, we are speaking of mechanics (see below, under "Conclusions"). If we define *atonement* broader, as I will in the Conclusion to this book, then it would be inaccurate to say, as I have, that "the only place Luke has atonement theology is at Acts 20:28." But more of that later.

[19] On this, see H. Kosmala, *Hebräer—Essener—Christen* (StPB; Leiden: E.J. Brill, 1959), 174–91.

[20] The Greek term *lutron* refers to purchase money used to manumit slaves; in a more general sense it refers to liberating a person from some sort of confinement, e.g., Josephus, *A.J.* 14.107, 371; *B.J.* 2.273. There is massive debate about the Aramaic/Hebrew behind the Greek term. Casey prefers *prq/pwrqn* ("redeem"), while older scholars preferred the Hebrew *asam* ("sin offering"). See M. Casey, *Aramaic Sources of Mark's Gospel* (SNTSMS 102; Cambridge: Cambridge University Press, 1998), 211. See also B. Janowski, "Auslösung des verwirkten Lebens," *ZTK* 79 (1982): 25–59; C. Spicq, "*lutron,*" *TLNT* 2:423–29. Cf. Luke 1:68; 2:38; 21:28; 24:21. Thus: Jesus gives himself so they can be set free (cf. John 18:8-9, 14); and they were set free because he was taken captive. See also M. Wilcox, "On the Ransom-Saying in Mark 10:45c, Mat 20:28c," in *Frühes Christentum* (ed. H. Lichtenberger; vol. 3 of *Geschichte–Tradition–Reflexion*; ed. H. Cancki, H. Lichtenberger, and P. Schafer; Tübingen: Mohr Siebeck, 1996), 173–86, here pp. 177–79.

followers were not; he was put to death on a cross and his disciples were set free. Many fail to see the liberation focus of the term *lutron*, or focus that which they are set free from onto the one particular of sin. *Lutron* here needs to be understood as an emancipation from whatever it is that Jesus sees as resolved in his kingdom message. In other words, *lutron* is kingdom language—if it is to be connected to Jesus. A glance at the Tanakh shows this (e.g., Exod 6:6-8; 2 Sam 7:23; Ps 78:42; Isa 43:1; 52:3; Jer 31:11; Mic 4:10; Zech 10:8).[21] He was the ransom price, and they were the ones set free. In context, then, the political overtones are unmistakable: if the problem is the Gentile/Roman authorities' use of power, Jesus (as Son of man) has come to liberate his "many" from their rule. Jesus gives his life in order to save the lives of his followers, a fact consistent with the substance of Mark 10:35-45. And the old tradition about the discussion of one person being taken so the community can be saved, found in John 11:51-52; 18:8-14, may well reflect what can be seen as the very bottom of a discussion of the significance of the death of Jesus. Jesus is put to death to save the rest of the community.[22] Was there more to it than this? Perhaps. To explore this we will need to venture into other areas before we return to this altogether believable and historically credible understanding of the ransom saying of Mark 10:45.

And to explore the other options means we have arrived at another vista: do we see evidence for Jesus thinking of himself or his mission in terms of Isaiah's Servant, which is one of the most widely accepted understandings of the background of the ransom *logion*? Bultmann, and the many who followed him, said no.[23] It is not just that the language of Mark 10:45 (but see above) is so atypically Jewish in Bultmann's view. Rather, Jesus does not elsewhere (apart perhaps from Mark 14:24) describe his death with such a soteriological category, and neither is *Servant* as firm in the Jesus traditions as some have thought.[24] That Jesus

[21] See the fine study of Alberto de Mingo Kaminouchi, *"But it is Not So Among You"* (JSNTSup 249; New York: T & T Clark International, 2003), 139–56, who broadens the sense of ransom and in so doing creates connections (which he does not explore) with Jesus' broader kingdom mission. His denial of sin as that from which the followers of Jesus are liberated is mitigated when one recognizes that sin and forgiveness both have a social-theological scope. See McKnight, *A New Vision for Israel* (Grand Rapids: Eerdmans, 1999), 224–27. For a confirmation of Kaminouchi's thesis and how *lutron* may have been understood by Christians under the influence of Hellenistic cultic traditions, see A. Yarbro Collins, "The Signification of Mark 10:45 among Gentile Christians," *HTR* 90 (1997): 371–82. Pitre, "The Historical Jesus, the Great Tribulation and the End of the Exile," contends that *lutron* sets free Israel and sets off the restoration of the twelve tribes of Israel (pp. 497–34).

[22] So Wilcox, "On the Ransom-Saying in Mark 10:45c, Mat 20:28c," in *Frühes Christentum* (ed. Lichtenberger), 179–83.

[23] R. Bultmann, *History of the Synoptic Tradition* (trans. J. Marsh; rev. ed.; New York: Harper & Row, 1976), 144.

[24] One who respects the evidence but still finds in Servant the heart of the christological problem of the New Testament is O. Cullmann, *The Christology of the New Testament* (trans. S.C. Guthrie and C.A.M. Hall; rev. ed.; Philadelphia: Westminster, 1963), 79–82.

rarely (if ever) describes his death as soteriologically effective is undeniable. On the other hand, whether or not this kind of language is credible within Judaism (and we should instance examples of understanding a person's death as having soteriological value—and not just look for parallels to the Greek term *lutron* and probable Hebrew/Aramaic equivalents) is a fort guarded of late mostly by European, especially German, scholars. It is mistake, however, to look exclusively to Isaiah 52–53. Death as a saving event is found in other places as well.

Recent scholarship dealing with Jewish leaders and movements has demonstrated that Jesus *could have* said something like this—but I hasten to add that arguing for a plausible Jewish context does not prove that Jesus used the ransom expression of Mark 10:45, or that one must then automatically appeal to the Servant of Isaiah as the only plausible Jewish context out of which this saying could emerge.[25] Scholarship seems to need to be constantly reminded that Mark 10:45 speaks, not of the Servant, but of the Son of man, and that figure is most likely derived from Daniel 7 and 9.

A case can be made for Mark 10:45 as a reflection by Jesus on his own mission in light of the fourth Servant Song. The argument begins with terms like *ransom* and *many* and ends with whether Jesus as a Jewish prophet could have thought of himself or his followers in terms of the Servant of Isaiah. The following deserve consideration: first, διακονέω is never a translation of עבד in the LXX, pushing Mark 10:45 away from the Servant Song. However, the Markan context uses the term δοῦλος as a synonym (Mark 10:44), and that term clearly can evoke עבד (e.g., Isa 49:3, 5). Second, the expression δοῦναι τὴν ψυχὴν αὐτοῦ can evoke Isaiah 53:10 ("if he made himself an *offering for guilt*"; e.g., אשם) or 53:12 ("For he exposed himself to death" and/or "whereas he bore the guilt of many"), even if the language is hardly a direct translation.[26] Regardless of personal bias and in spite of exaggerated claims by some (e.g., Jeremias, France), one must admit both that the language of Mark 10:45 is uncommon and thematically similar to Isaiah 53. Third, the term λύτρον could be seen as a free translation of אשם (Isa 53:10) but without any supporting evidence in the LXX. M.D. Hooker is known for her case that this Hebrew term is never translated by that Greek term in the LXX; instead, the Greek term translates גאל, כפר, or פדה.[27] Fourth, the securest link to the fourth Servant Song

---

[25] An alternative is that of B. Lindars, who concludes that a man (i.e., the man to whom such a call is given) may risk his life for the sake of the many. See his "Salvation Proclaimed," 294.

[26] So W. Zimmerli and J. Jeremias, *The Servant of God* (trans. H. Knight, et al.; SBT 20; Naperville, Ill: Alec R. Allenson, 1957), 95–96, who give other traces of allusion to Isaiah 53. C.K. Barrett truncates the evidence here: cf. his "The Background of Mark 10:45," in *New Testament Essays* (ed. A.J.B. Higgins; Manchester: Manchester University Press, 1959), 4–5. See W.J. Moulder, "The Old Testament Background and Interpretation of Mark x.45," *NTS* 24 (1977): 120–27.

[27] M.D. Hooker, *Jesus and the Servant* (London: SPCK, 1959), 76–77; see also Barrett, "The Background of Mark 10:45," 5–7; "Mark 10:45: A Ransom for Many," in his *New Testament Essays* (London: SPCK, 1972), 20–26; Wilcox, "On the Ransom-Saying in Mark 10:45c, Mat 20:28c," 3:179. For the further discussion, see also D. Hill, *Greek Words and Hebrew Meanings* (SNTSMS

is found in the expression ἀντὶ; πολλῶν an expression that can be seen as a direct translation from the fourth song (e.g., 52:14, 15; 53:11, 12 bis), especially when an atonement act is connected to the "many" in 53:12. Finally, it is the choice of "Son of man" in Mark 10:45 that leads some to Daniel 7 and others, by way of tradition-criticism, from Daniel 7 to the Servant Song of Isaiah 53. To use D.C. Allison's categories for detecting allusions: Mark 10:45 shares vocabulary, themes, and imagery; the language is uncommon; as well, the history of interpretation is in favor of an allusion to Isaiah 53.[28]

As a preliminary conclusion, we must state that "ransom for many" may owe its inspiration to Isaiah 52:13–53:12. We are thus led to two other sorts of questions: first, is each of these terms authentic? And, is there corroborative evidence that Jesus thought of himself in terms of the servant?[29] Could Jesus have seen his personal death as an atonement for others? Could he have thought he would die as a substitution for others, a sin offering for others? Is it credible for a first-century Jew to have thought in such terms and, pulling from the other side, would other Jews have understood such a claim? We are led to ask the second set of questions first: is there sufficient evidence from Judaism to think Jesus could have made himself understandable in claiming that his death was atoning? The first place one naturally makes the connection is to the Maccabeans, but one should not limit the evidence to them.[30]

Thus, one finds atoning features about the Maccabean martyrs and other figures in Jewish history.

2 Maccabees 7:37-38: I [the youngest of the seven sons martyred one by one in front of their mother], like my brothers, give up body and life for the laws of our ancestors, appealing to God to show mercy soon to our nation and by trials and plagues to make you confess that he alone is God, and through me and my brothers to bring to an end the wrath of the Almighty that has justly fallen on our whole nation.

4 Maccabees 6:27-29: [Eleazar prays] "You know, O God, that though I might have saved myself, I am dying in burning torments for the sake of the law. Be merciful to your people, and let our punishment suffice for them. Make my blood

---

5; Cambridge: Cambridge University Press, 1967), 58–80. But see also the evocation of אשם at Leviticus 5:17-19.

[28] D.C. Allison Jr., *The Intertextual Jesus: Scripture in Q* (Harrisburg: Trinity Press International, 2000), 9–13.

[29] Without attempting a complete listing, I mention here that the positive answer has been given by V. Taylor, *Jesus and His Sacrifice* (1937; repr. London: Macmillan, 1955); R.T. France, *Jesus and the Old Testament* (London: Tyndale, 1971), 110–35; D.J. Moo, *The Old Testament in the Gospel Passion Narratives* (Sheffield: Almond, 1983), 122–27. The negative has been offered in the studies of Hooker, *Jesus and the Servant*, and Barrett, "The Background of Mark 10:45," 1–18.

[30] M. de Jonge, "Jesus' Death for Others and the Death of the Maccabean Martyrs," in *Text and Testimony* (ed. T. Baarda, et al.; Kampen: Kok, 1988), 142–51.

their purification, and take my life in exchange for theirs (*katharision auton poieson to emon haima kai antipsychon auton labe ten emen psychen*)."

4 Maccabees 17:22: And through the blood of those devout ones and their death as an atoning sacrifice (*tou hilasteriou*), divine Providence preserved Israel that previously had been mistreated.

4 Maccabees 18:4: Because of them [those who gave their bodies in suffering for the sake of religion; 18:3] the nation gained peace.

1QS V, 6: They are to atone (*kpr*) for all those in Aaron who volunteer for holiness, and for those in Israel who belong to truth, and for those who join them in community (cf. also III, 6; VIII, 6).

1QS IX, 4-5: They shall atone (*kpr*) for the guilt of transgression and the rebellion of sin, becoming an acceptable sacrifice for the land through the flesh of burnt offerings, the fat of sacrificial portions and prayer, becoming—as it were—justice itself, a sweet savor of righteousness and blameless behavior, a pleasing freewill offering (cf. 4Q257 III, 9; 4Q259 II, 15; 4Q265 7 II, 9).

4Q541 9 I, 2-3: And he [the future priest] shall make atonement (*kpr*) for all those of his generation, and he shall be sent to all the children of his people (cf. also 1QM II, 5; 4Q159 1 II, 2).

1Q34bis 3 I, 5: And You have appointed the wicked as our ransom (*kwpr*) and by the upright (cf. 4Q508 I, 1; 4Q513 2 II, 4).

11Q10 (TgJob) XXXVIII, 2 (=Job 42:9-12): and God heard Job's voice and forgave (*shbq*) them [his friends] their sins on his account.

Pseudo-Philo, *Bib. Ant.* 18:5: And he [Abraham] brought him [Isaac] to be placed on the altar, but I [God] gave him back to his father and, because he did not refuse, his offering was acceptable before me, and on account of his blood I chose them.

Sipre Deuteronomy Pisqa 333.5 (on Exod 32:43): How do we know that the murder of Israelites by the nations of the world serves as atonement for the [Israelites] in the world to come? [the author answers by appealing to Ps 79:1-3 and then asks], And how on the basis of Scripture do we know that the descent of the wicked into Gehenna serves as atonement for the [Israelites too]? [the author answers by appealing to Isa 43:3-4]

The notion of a *person* dying for the sake of others, for the benefit of others, or for the benefit of the nation (to purge the land for a holy dwelling) can be plausibly set in a Jewish context. The notion of "dying for" that forges an exchange between God and the person or group that benefits from that death—that is, an atonement of some sort—is Jewish. It is not typical of Judaism to think of its leaders dying with such effects, but an atoning death doesn't have to be imported from Graeco-Roman religious beliefs.[31] Personal death as atonement may have (and may not have) entered Judaism through Hellenistic sources,[32] but it is nonetheless plausibly Jewish. The entire sacrificial system, at least on Yom Kippur, memorializes atonement through the death of an innocent victim as a "ransom" or "vicarious sacrifice" (Lev 16; Num 29:7-11; cf. *Sir.* 50:14-21; 1Q34 I-II, 6; perhaps 4Q504 1-2 VI, 5; 4Q508 2; 11Q19 [Temple] XXV, 10-16; *m. Yoma*).

However Jewish personal atonement might be, a connection of atonement to the Servant of Isaiah is not found when the above-cited texts describe Jewish heroes in death. The notion of personal death as an atonement is credible within Judaism, even if exceptional. In that context, it must be emphasized, it was not readily connected to Isaiah 52:13–53:12. It would be entirely inaccurate to think Jews would have immediately made a connection between someone's death being atoning and the fourth Servant Song of Isaiah.

The question we ask now is, Can a saying like this be from Jesus? Is it credible for Jesus to have thought his death could be a ransom for the many? Some have argued so. As Vincent Taylor claimed: "As a 'community-product,' the saying is much too discreet; as an utterance of Jesus, it has just that air of mystery, and the note of provocativeness, constantly found in His words."[33] However, the logion can only be authenticated if it can be demonstrated that Jesus thought of his own death in these terms, or at least terms not unlike them. Appeals to provocativeness and an air of mystery deserve their day in court, but they rarely are given the final word. We need firmer ground on which to stand if we are to take the first step toward an understanding of Jesus' death as atoning. To do this we must explore first how Jesus understood his own mission, how Jesus expressed that mission in the context of the Tanakh. We can do this most accurately by examining how other Jewish leaders thought of themselves and, in particular, we need to examine which figures of their rich scriptural tradition they relied on or evoked to understand their own circumstances and mission. Only then can we broach the question of how Jesus would have understood his own

---

[31] According to *Jub.* 17:15, the binding of Isaac (*Jub.* 18) takes place at Pesah; and the narrative places the binding on Mount Sinai (18:13). Both targums to Genesis 22:14 see the acts of both Abraham and Isaac as beneficial for later generations, but probably as a token of obedience (cf. *Tg. Ps.-J.* 22:14; *Tg. Onq.* 22:14). See also *Mek. de R. Ishm.*, on Exodus 12:23, where the blood of Isaac will protect as did the blood at the Passover. But, the earlier evidence found at Qumran suggests a non-atoning interpretation. 4Q225 2 cols. I, II understands the binding of Isaac in terms of Job: as Satan sought to destroy Job, so the Prince of Animosity seeks to destroy Abraham.

[32] See esp. M. Hengel, *The Atonement* (trans. J. Bowden; Philadelphia: Fortress, 1981). Hengel's appeal to LXX Daniel 3:35 (OT Apocrypha Pr Azar 12) misses the mark; this prayer is about the inviolable promise given to Abraham and his descendants that the seed would remain permanent (Pr Azar 13; LXX Dan 3:36). Atonement, perhaps even personal, is found at LXX Dan 3:40 (NRSV differs here; cf. Pr Azar 17).

[33] Taylor, *Jesus and His Sacrifice*, 105.

mission, and whether or not that understanding had recourse to the Servant of Isaiah.

But before we do this we must notice a stubborn and oft-neglected element of the Jesus traditions: whatever swirled in the dust of first-century Galilean and Judean Judaism, the notion that the coming Messiah would die was at best a speck in that dust swirl. In fact, the Jesus traditions consistently evince an astonishment on the part of Jesus' followers when the subject of death emerges (e.g., Mark 8:32b; 9:32). W. Wrede may have resorted to dogmatic ideas to explain such a feature of the Jesus traditions, but in so doing, he nipped the rose off Christian theology. We think it more likely that death was so implausibly a part of the Jewish expectation of the coming redeemer that this witness to astonishment evinces historical verisimilitude. And furthermore, its presence shows that death was neither central to Jesus' teachings nor comprehensible within the normal parameters of Jewish expectation.

Again, we are driven to a crucible of time: somewhere between the day Jesus learned of John the Baptist's death and the early church's explanation of Jesus' death, the critical category of Jesus' death as atoning emerged. We now must examine whether this most critical text, Mark 10:45, witnesses to one side or the other of the Easter faith in Jesus' atoning death. Does it reveal the historical Jesus thinking of himself as servant or does it show later *Gemeindetheologie*? Or, not to be forgotten, is the ransom for many to be explained by appeal to something Jewish other than the Servant of Isaiah?

EXCURSUS ON SON OF MAN

The debate about the Son of man and the authenticity of Jesus' referring to himself with that expression shows no signs of abating. Older scholarship teetered on a present/suffering Son of man vs. a future/judging Son of man, with the latter pole seeing a direct reference to Daniel 7. Most of scholarship sees the expression as having been used by Jesus, though there is heated debate regarding which meaning he assumed in his use. I set out some conclusions assumed in this chapter. For the history of discussion, see D. Burkett, *The Son of Man Debate: A History and Evaluation* (SNTSMS 107; Cambridge: Cambridge University Press, 1999).

(1) German scholarship, spearheaded by Bultmann, found authentic those references to the Son of man in which Jesus was referring to a heavenly figure other than himself, but later *Gemeindetheologie* found that same Son of man to be Jesus. It revised the traditions in light of this conviction.

Cf. his *Theology of the New Testament* (trans. K. Grobel; 2 vols.; New York: Scribner, 1951, 1955), 1:26–32; also H.E. Tödt, *The Son of Man in the Synoptic Tradition* (trans. D.M. Barton; London: SCM, 1965); P. Vielhauer went further in this tradition to see all Son of man sayings as *Gemeindetheologie*; cf. his "Gottesreich und Menschensohn in der Verkündigung Jesu," in *Festschrift für Günther Dehn* (ed. W. Schneemelcher; Neukirchen: Erziehungsverein, 1957),

51–79; "Jesus und der Menschensohn: Zur Diskussion mit Heinz Eduard Tödt und Eduard Schweizer," *ZTK* 60 (1963): 133–77; A. Vögtle, "Bezeugt die Logienquelle die authentische Redeweise Jesu vom 'Menschensohn'?" in *Logia: Les Paroles de Jésus–The Sayings of Jesus. Mémorial Joseph Coppens* (ed. J. Delobel; BETL 59; Leuven: Leuven University Press, 1982), 77–99. The Bultmannian line was challenged by M. Black, "The 'Son of Man' Passion Sayings in the Gospel Tradition," *ZNW* 60 (1969): 1–8; L. Goppelt, *Theology of the New Testament* (ed. J. Roloff; trans. J.E. Alsup; 2 vols.; Grand Rapids: Eerdmans, 1981), 1:178–93. An opposite view to Bultmann was maintained in the magisterial Beginnings of Christianity project; cf. *The Acts of the Apostles* (ed. F.J. Foakes Jackson and K. Lake; part 1 of *Beginnings of Christianity*; 5 vols.; Grand Rapids: Baker, 1979), 1:368–84.

(2) The traditional, especially British, view was that Jesus combined Son of man with servant categories.

Cf. the earlier study of R.H. Fuller, *The Mission and Achievement of Jesus* [SBT 12; London: SCM, 1954]); O. Cullmann, *The Christology of the New Testament* (trans. S.C. Guthrie and C.A.M. Hall; rev. ed.; Philadelphia: Westminster, 1963), 137–92.

(3) An independent line was taken by E. Schweizer who argued in fact that the most authentic Son of man sayings pertain to Jesus in his humility and suffering; however, the future Son of man is Jesus as chief witness at the judgment after vindication and exaltation.

Cf. the summary statement in his *Jesus* (trans. D.E. Green; London: SCM, 1971), 18–22; *Lordship and Discipleship* (SBT 28; Naperville, Ill.: Alec R. Allenson, 1960), 39–41.

(4) A fresh breakthrough occurred when Morna Hooker contended that the expression Son of man cannot be atomized but instead must be treated as a coherent expression of Jesus' authority proclaimed, denied, and vindicated.

Cf. her *The Son of Man in Mark: A Study of the Background of the Term "Son of Man" and Its Use in St. Mark's Gospel* (London: SPCK, 1967); "Is the Son of Man Problem Really Insoluble?" in *Text and Interpretation: Studies in the New Testament presented to Matthew Black* (ed. E. Best and R. McL. Wilson; Cambridge: Cambridge University Press, 1979), 155–68; see also O. Michel, "Son of Man," in *New International Dictionary of New Testament Theology* (ed. Colin Brown; 3 vols.; Grand Rapids: Zondervan, 1978), 3:613–34.

(5) The most recent trend is to see in the expression an Aramaic idiom with more or less a self-reference or reference to humans (e.g., a circumlocution for "I"; the human; the speaker in particular; an equivalent of "one"; a group to whom the speaker belongs; a modesty idiom).

On this see esp. M. Black, *An Aramaic Approach to the Gospels and Acts* (3d ed.; Oxford: Clarendon, 1967), 310–30 (app. by Vermès); G. Vermès, *Jesus the Jew* (London: Fontana/Collins, 1973), 160–91; M. Casey, *Son of Man: The Interpretation and Influence of Daniel 7* (London: SPCK, 1979); B. Lindars, *Jesus Son of Man: A Fresh Examination of the Son of Man Sayings in the Gospels in Light of Recent Research* (Grand Rapids: Eerdmans, 1983); R. Bauckham, "The Son of Man: 'A Man in My Position' or 'Someone'?" *JSNT* 23 (1985): 23–33; D.R.A. Hare, *The Son of Man Tradition* (Minneapolis: Fortress, 1990); M. Casey, "Idiom and Translation: Some Aspects of the Son of Man Problem," *NTS* 41 (1995): 164–82. This scholarship has been given a thorough treatment in D. Burkett, "The Nontitular Son of Man: A History and Critique," *NTS* 40 (1994): 504–21; P. Owen and D. Shepherd, "Speaking Up for Qumran, Dalman and the Son of Man: Was Bar Enasha a Common Term for 'Man' in the Time of Jesus?" *JSNT* 81 (2001): 81–122. Casey answers back: "Aramaic Idiom and the Son of Man Problem: A Response to Owen and Shepherd," *JSNT* 25 (2002): 3–32. The title has been taken in a completely innovative direction in W. Wink, *The Human Being: Jesus and the Enigma of the Son of Man* (Minneapolis: Fortress, 2002).

(6) For a recent defense of the Son of man as an individual, heavenly being, cf. T.B. Slater, "One Like a Son of Man in First Century CE Judaism," *NTS* 41 (1995): 183–98.

It is impossible here to adjudicate the issues involved in this debate, but the following positions will be assumed:

(1) Methodologically, Hooker's point about coherence and unity has yet to be gainsaid: authority is involved in each of the three strands of Son of man sayings.

(2) The collective interpretation—Son of man refers to the suffering and vindication of the saints in the last days; thus, Jesus *and* his disciples fulfill what was expected of Daniel's Son of man—remains the most likely view since it permits connections of various themes (on this, cf. the informed note of D.C. Allison, Jr., *Jesus of Nazareth: Millenarian Prophet* [Minneapolis: Fortress, 1998], 65–66, n. 242).

(3) The decision on whether one opts for an eschatological orientation, based of course on Daniel 7, emerges from other conclusions. Thus, the study of Tödt is a tradition-historical examination of the expression with the non-self-referencing Son of man forming the earliest stratum; the suffering and rising Son of man is *Gemeindetheologie*.

(4) Intense researches by M. Casey, some of which will be cited in what follows, have demonstrated positively that the study of Vermès led to an important climax on what the Aramaic expression intends, though I disagree (along with many others) that Daniel 7 can be eliminated from the Son of man tradition of Jesus. Casey, in particular, tends to prefer, as authentic, sayings that have an idiomatic Aramaic counterpart.

Cf. his *From Jewish Prophet to Gentile God* (Edward Cadbury Lectures 1985–1986; Louisville: Westminster/John Knox, 1991).

(5) The theory of an idiomatic self/non-self reference (e.g., Vermès, Casey, Lindars) has recently been seriously challenged by D. Burkett as well as by P.

Owen and D. Shepherd. These authors contend that this scholarship operates too often with an uncritical understanding of Eastern versus Western as well as middle versus late Aramaic, leading to a biased use of texts. Further, they point to the widespread but mistaken theory that Aramaic at the time of Jesus no longer distinguished between the emphatic (*bar enasha*) and absolute (*bar enash*) state. The idiomatic sense is pressed into service only occasionally with compelling success (e.g., Mark 2:10, 28).

See Burkett, "Nontitular"; *Son of Man Debate*; P. Owen and D. Shepherd, "Speaking Up for Qumran, Dalman and the Son of Man: Was Bar Enasha a Common Term for 'Man' in the Time of Jesus?" *JSNT* 81 (2001): 81–122.

(6) It remains an astonishing fact of the tradition that Son of man is almost exclusively found on the lips of Jesus (82 times in the gospels [cf. also John 12:34]; 4 times elsewhere [Heb 2:6; Rev 1:13; 14:14; Acts 7:56], with only the latter being used apart from a quotation of Scripture). Son of man, apart from the theology of an Evangelist or his predecessors, plays no role in early Christian worship. Short of arguing that this usage was created by early Christians who left no impact elsewhere, one is driven to the conclusion that Son of man, in general, is from Jesus. If there is a case for double dissimilarity, it is here. However, an observation frequently unnoticed: to the degree that Son of man is developed by early Christians in the gospel tradition, is that the above-mentioned lines are somewhat blurred. There are examples of early church insertion into the Jesus traditions, and those do reflect early church usage of the expression. As such, they weaken the argument from dissimilarity to the early church. However, the general argument remains sturdy.

On this, cf. D.C. Allison, Jr., *The End of the Ages Has Come: An Early Interpretation of the Passion and Resurrection of Jesus* (Philadelphia: Fortress, 1985), 129–33.

(7) The doubly articular ὁ υἱὸς τοῦ ἀνθρώπου most likely reflects the emphasis Jesus gave to the expression; this suggests that Jesus is thinking of a specific figure, undoubtedly the one in Daniel 7, and it therefore carries (as Hooker has pointed out) a sense of authority—always.

See C.F.D. Moule, "Neglected Features in the Problem of the 'Son of Man,'" in *Neues Testament und Kirche: Für Rudolf Schnackenburg* (ed. J. Gnilka; Freiburg: Herder, 1974), 413–28; *The Origin of Christology* (Cambridge: Cambridge University Press, 1977), 11–22; "'The Son of Man': Some of the Facts," *NTS* 41 (1995): 277–79; see also S. Kim, *The "Son of Man" as the Son of God* (WUNT 30; Tübingen: J.C.B. Mohr, 1983), 32–37.

(8) It is likely that Jesus backed away from the title *Messiah* during his lifetime; but, the term "Son of man" may well have carried a similar eschatological meaning.

See Burkett, *The Son of Man Debate*.

(9) Some evidence used by scholars probably postdates Jesus and should be avoided in this discussion; cf. e.g., *1 Enoch* 37–71; *4 Ezra* 13.

(10) Finally, there is an unfortunate drive toward consistency in the scholarship on Son of man: that is, the expression has *either* the connotations of Daniel 7 *or* the idiomatic use *or* the connotations of a text like Psalm 8. Oddly, it is not considered that the author of Daniel 7 knew of other uses, and his successors should likewise not be deprived of the same flexibility. This is an extension of the view of Hooker.

See here I.H. Marshall, "The Synoptic 'Son of Man' Sayings in the Light of Linguistic Study," in *To Tell the Mystery: Essays on New Testament Eschatology in Honor of Robert H. Gundry* (ed. T.E. Schmidt and M. Silva; JSNTSup 100; Sheffield: Sheffield Academic, 1994), 72–94.

In general I agree with M.D. Hooker and G.B. Caird, completed by L.D. Hurst, *New Testament Theology* (Oxford: Clarendon, 1994), 369–84, in which there is clearly a connection to Daniel 7 and the corporate sense of Son of man. As Hooker, "Is the Son of Man?" 167, states it: "the phrase is better understood as a reference to a role than a title." In this view an important notice is drawn to the pioneering work of T.W. Manson, *The Teaching of Jesus: Studies of Its Form and Content* (Cambridge: Cambridge University Press, 1939), 211–36; also his "The Son of Man in Daniel, Enoch and the Gospels," in *Studies in the Gospels and Epistles* (ed. M. Black; Philadelphia: Westminster, 1962), 123–45. See also J.D.G. Dunn, *Christology in the Making: A New Testament Inquiry into the Origins of the Doctrine of the Incarnation* (2d ed.; London: SCM Press, 1989), 65–97; Allison, *End of the Ages Has Come*, 136–37; Moule, *Origin of Christology*, 11–22; and for a nice summary of collective or corporate thinking and Christology, see C.F.D. Moule, *The Phenomenon of the New Testament* (London: SCM Press, 1967), 21–42; Schweizer, *Lordship and Discipleship*, 42–48.

Chapter 8

Jesus and the Scripture Prophets

We have established that Jesus thought he would die prematurely, in the providence of God, and would probably die at the hands of those who rejected his mission as a potential source of rebellion. It only makes sense that one who thought he would die, who on other grounds considered himself a prophet, also tried to make sense of that death. We can assume that Jesus did not think of his death as a sad tragedy or as a total accident of history. After all, Jesus could have escaped Jerusalem during the night; he could have avoided all public confrontation; and he could have worked harder to maintain his innocence.

The entire record of history suggests otherwise: Jesus thought he was to die and apparently knew it was his fate. He connected his mission and his death, and he did so in terms of the Final Ordeal. Can we go further? We have seen that Mark 10:45 would throw a morning light over the mission of Jesus if the ransom elements of that logion came from Jesus. Any Jew of Jesus' status in the first century would have sought to solve the riddle of a premature or violent death by searching the Scriptures to find God's mind. The question before us now concerns whether or not the ransom saying can be placed into the life of Jesus on the basis of his reflecting on Scripture to see his life inscripturated. There are significant examples of Jews who faced death as a result of their calling to declare God's will to the nation. Some of these are what we might call Scripture prophets, prophets who searched the Scriptures to discover their own life and destiny in the pages of the Tanakh. These Scripture prophets provide a plausible context for understanding Jesus' mission, and they will enable us to come closer in determining the pedigree of the ransom saying.[1] Put in a differ-

---

[1] In general, see P.W. Barnett, "The Jewish Sign Prophets—A.D. 40–70—Their Intentions and Origin," *NTS* 27 (1981): 679–97; for an excellent discussion of "messianic scripts," see C.A. Evans, "Messianic Claimants of the First and Second Centuries," in his *Noncanonical Writings and New Testament Interpretation* (Peabody, Mass.: Hendrickson, 1992), 239–52.

ent question: Is there a background in the Tanakh to move from a prophet's suffering to the prophet's suffering being atoning? We begin by looking at how rough contemporaries of Jesus appealed to the Tanakh to understand the fate of their own lives.

MATTATHIAS AND HIS SONS

A family that did search the Scriptures in a crisis and weaved itself into the fabric of the Jewish story is the Maccabees. Because of a compromise with Gentile customs, certain Jews (most notably Jason; cf. 2 Macc 4:7) formed an unholy covenant with Antiochus Epiphanes, and from this alliance the Maccabean movement was sparked (1 Macc 1:1-15). One of the first actions of Antiochus was to strip the temple of its sacred possessions (1:20-28; cf. Dan 9:24-27), leading to even deeper compromise of Israel's principles (1 Macc 1:41-43, 52). Israel was put to the test by Antiochus' double demand to renounce its temple system and to prohibit circumcision (1:44-61). Some resisted the reforms of Antiochus (1:62-63), but little came of their protest. A priest named Mattathias and his five sons grieved over Jerusalem, its temple, and the people's sins (2:6-14). When Antiochus' officers requested Mattathias and his sons to renounce the faith so they could become "friends of the king" (2:18), he resisted in words (2:19-22). But when a fellow Jew capitulated to the Gentile king's demand, Mattathias erupted into murdering the apostate Jew (2:23-26) and called for all those so committed to the covenant of Moses with Israel to flee to the hills and caves as a place of divine deliverance, and there prepare to fight (2:27-28).[2] Some, refusing to fight on the Sabbath, were senselessly murdered (2:29-38), but Mattathias and his associates decided to honor God by fighting on the Sabbath (2:39-41). Along with the "Hasideans," great victories were won by the Maccabeans, pagan altars were destroyed, circumcision was reinstituted, and a new commitment to the Torah was covenanted (2:42-48).

What concerns us is how Mattathias, and hence all his party, legitimated their actions: the words of 1 Maccabees provide the entire framework:

> Remember the deeds of the ancestors, which they did in their generations; and you will receive great honor and an everlasting name. Was not *Abraham* found faithful when tested, and it was reckoned to him as righteousness? *Joseph* in the time of his distress kept the commandment, and became lord of Egypt. *Phinehas* our ancestor, because he was deeply zealous, received the covenant of everlasting priesthood. *Joshua*, because he fulfilled the command, became a judge in Israel. *Caleb*, because he testified in the assembly, received an inheritance in the land. *David*, because he was merciful, inherited the throne of the kingdom forever. Elijah, because of great zeal for the law, was taken up into heaven. *Hananiah,*

[2] It is indeed likely that the decision to flee to the caves is an act of eschatological fulfillment of Isaiah 32, esp. 32:9-14; 55–56.

Azariah, and *Mishael* believed and were saved from the flame. *Daniel*, because of his innocence, was delivered from the mouth of the lions. (2:51-60)

For our purposes we should note that Mattathias (or at least his chronicler) plugged his life into this roll call of exemplary heroes of holy zeal, and so he moved forward in faith and courage to fight for YHWH. He and his family will act in the same obedience, with the same zeal, and so shall be inscribed in the same roll of the zealous (2:64).

The individual figures of Israel's history become *types* for Mattathias and the Maccabean movement. Accordingly, these types shaped the consciousness, the identity, the hopes, and therefore the behavior of the Maccabeans. Their theory: zealous obedience is rewarded by God; therefore, we will act in zealous obedience and God will vindicate us. The examples are selected with reason: Abraham was asked to sacrifice his son (Gen 22; 1 Macc 2:15-22); Phinehas was the descendant of Mattathias's priestly line (2:1; 2 Macc 4:23-25; 3:4); and Elijah was himself zealous for the Torah (1 Kgs 19:10, 14). Mattathias, then, reenacts the zealous obedience of his forbears. A type became his life-script. Their success confirmed the legitimacy of the type (cf. Josephus, *A.J.* 12.246–357). If God delivered his people at the Red Sea, he can do so again (1 Macc 4:8-9; 2 Macc 15:6-11). Furthermore, if the decision to flee into the desert (1 Macc 2:28-38) was a deliberate act to fulfill Isaiah 32:55–56, as well as Deuteronomy 32, then we should observe that YHWH promises revenge for the "blood of his children" (Deut 32:43). Death, then, is an event that God uses as a lever in judgment (cf. *T. Mos.* 9).

It is a short step to the atoning value of these martyrdoms, an atonement understood by the authors of these texts mostly as exhausting God's wrath against disobedience (2 Macc 7:37-38; 4 Macc 6:27-29; 17:22; 18:4) and enabling victory against the enemies (2 Macc 8:3-5, 27-33). It is another short step to connect Jesus to such ideas, even though the decisive element of Jesus' death as an eschatological event altering history is clearly not present in the Maccabean martyrs.[3]

JUDAH MESSIAH: THE TEACHER OF RIGHTEOUSNESS[4]

When the crisis between the Sadducees and Pharisees reached a zenith at the appointment of Alexandra's son, Hyrcanus II, a leader from an opposition party

---

[3] See M. de Jonge, "Jesus' Death for Others and the Death of the Maccabean Martyrs," in *Text and Testimony* (ed. T.J. Baarda, et al.; Kampen: Kok, 1988), 142–51.

[4] On this see esp. M.O. Wise, *The First Messiah* (San Francisco: Harper Collins, 1999), whose daring presentation illustrates the point I am making. I do not intend, by presenting Wise's theory here, to suggest that I agree in every detail. Rather, his thesis regarding "Judah Messiah" expresses what would otherwise be known of the Teacher of Righteousness under critical scrutiny of the scrolls. Wise performs a technical redaction-critical operation on 1QH, as well as on other texts, and reads from their bottom layer the biography of Judah Messiah. Thus, there are "teacher" hymns

arose. Michael O. Wise calls him "Judah Messiah," but he is known from the Dead Sea Scrolls as the Teacher of Righteousness. Statements in the Tanakh about temple service were the cutting edge of the dispute (cf. 4Q39–99 [MMT]; 1QH X, 33), and hence it is best to describe Judah as a Scripture prophet.[5] A Scripture prophet is someone who, as a result of contemplating scriptures as an active, combustible presence, is bound by those traditions; and those traditions shape the person's identity, behavior, and mission. The Scripture prophet connects the dots of various passages, and that leads to "a consistent drama of past, present, and future, and yet so comprehensively explanatory, that its discovery strikes their followers as beyond human capacity."[6] The most significant perception of the Scripture prophet is that he (or she) sees himself (or herself) *in the various figures of Tanakh*. A few examples of Judah Messiah establish the point.[7] If the reader examines the hymns carefully it will be observed that Judah's prayers are laced together with scriptural language—a mosaic of hermeneutical reflection.

Judah perceives his situation to be that of Malachi's prophecy: "You have ordered my steps within the wicked realm" (from Mal 10:6-22 [10:8]). When he explains his situation as "within the wicked realm," he is in Jerusalem, in the context of priestly law debates, and sees the words of Malachi 1:4 reactualized: "They may build, but I will tear down, until they are called *the wicked country*, the people with whom the LORD is angry forever." Judah thinks his situation is the fulfillment of Malachi's words and so the Pharisees he faces in the temple courts are the enemies of God; he alone, as the representative of his followers, is true to the prophet's words. In fact, Malachi's situation is perceived later to be a threat of death for Judah. A later follower of Judah commented on Psalm 37:32-33 in the following words: "'The wicked man [*Hyrcanus* II] observes the righteous man [*Judah*] and seeks [to kill him. But the Lo]rd [will not leave him in his power and will not co]ndemn him when he comes to trial.' (Ps 37:32-33) This refers to the wicked [pri]est who ob[serv]es the [teach]er of righteous[ness and seeks] to kill him [. . .] and the Law that he sent to him, but God will not le[ave him in his power] and will not [condemn him when] he comes to trial" (4Q171 1 IV, 7-8; italics are interpretations).

But not only Malachi's and the Psalmist's words apply to Judah: Zechariah's also apply. Judah states that he has been called by God "to open the fount of

---

and "community" hymns. See also M. Douglas, "Power and Praise in the Hodayot," Ph.D. diss.; University of Chicago, 1998. An alternative, more speculative, but substantially similar (in general orientation) view can be seen in I. Knohl, *The Messiah Before Jesus* (trans. D. Maisel; Berkeley: University of California Press, 2000).

5 For the important clarification of this category, cf. Wise, *First Messiah*, 263–69. Scripture prophets are distinguished from "free" prophets, with the latter operating on the basis of revelations.

6 Wise, *First Messiah*, 264.

7 In what follows I give, first, the traditional column and lines; the numbers in brackets are to the forthcoming edition of Wise and Douglas. The translations are from Wise.

knowledge for all the initiated" (from 1QH X, 6-22 [X, 18]). Now Zechariah 13:1 reads: "On that day a *fountain* shall be *opened* for the house of David and the inhabitants of Jerusalem, to cleanse them from sin and impurity." That only here, in the entire Hebrew Bible, *fountain* and *open* occur together clinches the case: "Zechariah had spoken of him."[8] Judah, called by God to reveal the truth, is rejected by the establishment led (according to Michael Wise) by Shimeon ben Shetah[9] and is in danger of death. Even though these interpreters rewrite the Psalms from a later angle, we can be sure that Judah knew his life was up for grabs.

How did he explain his death? There is indisputable evidence that Judah Messiah thought of himself, his mission, his situation, and his death in terms of the Servant Songs of Isaiah.[10] When Judah refers to his followers as "trees of life," "pools of water" in a "dry land," "cypress," "the elm, and the pine together"—here he is referring to Isaiah 41:18-19: "I will open rivers on the bare heights, and fountains in the midst of the valleys; I will make the wilderness a pool of water, and the dry land springs of water. I will put in the wilderness the cedar, the acacia, the myrtle, and the olive; I will set in the desert the cypress, the plane and the pine together" (from 1QH 9 [XVI, 4-10a]).

And, in the first line of Wise's hymn 9 we have Judah claiming to be a source of streams in a dry land, an allusion to Isaiah 53:2. In an allusion to 53:3-4, we read "[As for me], I sojourn with sickness and [my] heart is st[rick]en with afflictions. I am like a man forsaken in his anguish" (from 1QH 9 [XVI, 26-27]). This forsaken and stricken man, Judah Messiah, believes that God will vindicate him (1QH 8 [XV, 22-25]). His followers saw in his death a fulfillment of Zechariah's famous passage about the stricken shepherd (Zech 13:7; CD 19:5-10).

Particulars about the Teacher of Righteousness will be debated by scholars for generations. But this remains firm: the writer of the *Thanksgiving Hymns* was a singular individual who saw his life in terms of Scriptures. That is, he was a Scripture prophet who saw in the shadowy images of the ancient prophecies a glimpse and prophecy of his own calling, his rejection, his suffering, and his vindication.

TAXO AND HIS SONS

An alternative but roughly parallel hope for triggering God's victory can be found in the Testament of Moses, a pseudepigraph deriving from the Maccabean

---

[8] Wise, *First Messiah*, 60.

[9] See ibid., 68–73.

[10] See the chart in Wise, *First Messiah*, 290, where he cites parallels in 1QH XV, 8-27 and XVI, 4–XVII, 36 to Isaiah 41:11, 12; 42:1, 6; 49:1, 8; 50:4; 53:2, 3, 4. This evidence, Wise avers, also suggests the Servant Songs were connected. See his translations of these (his hymns 8 and 9) at pp. 192–96.

era but revised in the first decades of the first century CE (cf. 6:1-9). Here—in the prophetic testamentary words of Moses, the mediator of the covenant (1:14)—the figure Taxo, whether historical or literary, contends that God's deliverance of Israel will come by absorbing punishment rather than by meting out violence. In an apparent rehearsal of the story of 2 Maccabees 7, Taxo, father of seven sons, steps forward to speak to his sons. His burden is obedience to the Torah and covenant as well as faithfulness to the Tribe of Levi (9:4-5). His strategy is to reenact or, more accurately, to *fulfill* the guidelines of Deuteronomy 32 and Isaiah 32:55–56, where hiding in caves correlates with God's vengeance. His words: "We shall fast for a three-day period and on the fourth day we shall go into a cave, which is in the open country. There let us die rather than transgress the commandments of the Lord of Lords, the God of our fathers" (9:6). Here, evidently, Taxo responds to Mattathias's strategy of breaking Sabbath in order to exhibit zeal for the Torah. Taxo continues: "For if we do this, and do die, *our blood will be avenged before the Lord*" (9:7). This last line clearly connects with Deuteronomy 32:43 and shows that Taxo thinks their death will trigger God's vengeance. What is more, Taxo thinks that vengeance will usher in the kingdom of God (10:1-10). The following thematic connections to Jesus might be observed: (1) "Then his kingdom will appear" [10:1]; (2) "then the devil will have an end" [10:1]; (3) "And the earth will tremble. . . . And the high mountains will be made low" [10:4]; (4) "The sun will not give light" [10:5]. When faced with the threat of death, instead of violent zeal Taxo proposes peaceful, non-violent obedience to the Torah, an act that he is assured will trigger the favor of the avenging God.

THEUDAS

A less noble example of reenacting Jewish history or the biography of another can be seen in Theudas, who considered himself to be a prophet. Josephus, offering observations like a curmudgeon sitting in a public park, considered Theudas to be like the magicians in Pharaoh's court (*A.J.* 2.286, 302, 332, 336), namely a fraud (Greek: *goes*; *A.J.* 20.97-99; see also 20.167, 188; cf. also Eusebius, *Hist. eccl.* 2.11:1-3). This Joshua[11] imitator exhorted his 400 followers[12] to pack up their possessions (cf. Josh 3–4) and follow him to the Jordan where they would see the hand of God part the river as at the crossing of the Jordan of old. We

[11] Two other figures remain options: Moses (Exod 12–13) and Elijah and Elisha (2 Kgs 2:8, 13-14). Since the river is the Jordan and since they were not liberated before crossing the waters, Moses typology is unlikely. The presence of possessions makes one think of Joshua rather than the prophets. Our decision to think of Joshua does not change the structure of the typological thinking of Theudas. For a defense, cf. J.A. Trumbower, "The Role of Malachi in the Career of John the Baptist," in *The Gospels and the Scriptures of Israel* (ed. C.A. Evans and W.R. Stegner; JSNTSup 104/SSEJC 3; Sheffield: Sheffield Academic, 1994), 28–41, here pp. 29–32.

[12] From Acts 5:36, which probably refers to the same Theudas. Josephus says he persuaded the "majority of the masses," a typical Josephan exaggeration (*A.J.* 20.97).

must assume that Theudas intended the people to cross the river (going east-ward) and then come back (westward) to reenact the capture of the land.

Theudas's action was the desperate action of a charismatic leader in a time of crisis. Cuspius Fadus, whom Claudius Caesar appointed procurator of Judea in 44 CE instead of Agrippa II but who had no sensitivity to Jewish laws (cf. Josephus, *A.J.* 20.6), realized the political implications of Theudas's actions and sent a squadron to kill and capture the misguided followers. Theudas himself suffered the ignominy of decapitation and a public flaunting in Jerusalem. Theudas evidently thought of himself as a second Joshua who, through convincing the people by a Jordan miracle, could deliver Israel from Roman bondage and reenact the conquest of the land of Israel. We don't know how his followers explained his violent death. We do have a good grip on what he thought of himself and what his source for that identity was: the Tanakh.

Jesus ben Ananias

In the years immediately prior to the destruction of Jerusalem, at the Feast of Tabernacles, a certain Jesus ben Ananias declared woe on Jerusalem and the temple (autumn of 62 CE). Other contemporaries saw it as a time of peace.[13] A certain Jesus, whom Josephus dubs a "foolish peasant" (ἰδιωτῶν ἄροικος), stood at the temple and said, "A voice from the east, a voice from the west, a voice from the four winds; a voice against Jerusalem and the sanctuary, a voice against the bridegroom and the bride, a voice against all the people" (*B.J.* 6.301). These words are clearly a reenactment of Jeremiah (7:34; 16:9; 25:10; 33:11), and it is probable that Jesus ben Ananias sees his calling in terms of Jeremiah: he is to announce doom and gloom to the nation. Like Jeremiah, he was beaten (Josephus, *B.J.* 6.302), and again like Jeremiah, such persecution did not dissuade him from persisting in his message of destruction. Josephus's last words are as follows: "So for seven years and five months he continued his wail, his voice never flagging nor his strength exhausted, until in the siege, having seen his presage verified, he found his rest. For, while going round and shouting his piercing tones from the wall, 'Woe once more to the city and to the people and to the temple,' as he added a last word, 'and woe to me also,' a stone hurled from the *ballista* struck and killed him on the spot" (*A.J.* 6.308–9).

From the second century BCE to the end of the first century CE we find various figures who reenacted the lives of famous figures, or who found in the examples of the figures of biblical pages a prototype that could be followed in order to shape the direction of their calling and mission. The lives of these famous figures (Phinehas, Joshua, the Servant-figure of Isaiah, Jeremiah) become *scripts* the later antitypes can follow with courage and the knowledge that God will reenact both that history and that vindication on their behalf.

[13] τὰ μάλιστα τῆς πόλεως εἰρηνευομένης καὶ εὐθηνούσης ("when the city was enjoying profound peace and prosperity") are the words of Josephus (*B.J.* 6.300).

These figures provide a plausible context for understanding Jesus' words now found in Mark 10:45. But before we turn to Jesus once again, we need to examine another prophet, so close to Jesus in time and relationship that his example makes Jesus' absorption in Israel's figures almost a certainty.

JOHN THE BAPTIST

A case can be made for John thinking of himself as Elijah, in particular the eschatological Elijah as prophesied by Malachi (3:1-3, 19-24 [4:5-6]). This is not, however, the only nor necessarily the fundamental category to understand John. Rather, *Elijah* is one category John applied to his mission to Israel.[14] It should be observed that the final editor of Malachi probably identified the messenger who was to prepare the way for YHWH's return to the temple with Elijah (cf. Mal 3:1-5 and 4:5-6). The hope for an Elijah-*redivivus* was thereby set in motion (cf. Mark 9:11-13).[15] John may have thought he was that Elijah.[16] Some of the evidence, while not always equally sturdy, supports such a conclusion.[17]

It is a given that early Christianity understood John as Elijah and Jesus as the Christ, and early Christians also thought the Messiah was the "coming one" spoken of in Malachi (cf. Mark 9:11-13). Did John think of himself as Elijah? One sturdy leg for supporting this view can be found in the following coherent complex about John: Q 3:7-9; Mark 1:4-5, 7-8; Q 3:16b-17; 7:18-19, 22-23.[18] The following expressions, with their parallel in Malachi, make a connection between John and Elijah secure: (1) "the coming one" expression which evinces a view that is pre-Christian [cf. Q 7:19 with Mal 3:1-2]; (2) the image of purifying fire [cf. Q 3:16b with Mal 3:2b-3, 19-20a (4:1)]; (3) the tree image [Q 3:9 with Mal 3:19 (4:1)]; (4) Elijah's role of announcing repentance before the Day of YHWH [Q 3:7-9; cf. Matt 21:28-32; Luke 3:10-14; Mark 1:4-5 with Mal 3:23-24 (4:5-6); Josephus, *A.J.* 18:116–19].[19]

---

[14] See also J.D.G. Dunn, "John the Baptist's Use of Scripture," in *The Gospels and the Scriptures of Israel* (ed. Evans and Stegner), 42–54, who, by limiting his analysis to Q III, 7-9, focuses more on an Isaianic context.

[15] See J.E. Taylor, *The Immerser* (Grand Rapids: Eerdmans, 1997), 281–94.

[16] It need not be argued that belief in the return of Elijah was prevalent for John to have conceptualized his own mission as that of Elijah. For the debate, cf. M.M. Faierstein, "Why Do the Scribes Say That Elijah Must Come First?" *JBL* 100 (1981): 75–86; D.C. Allison, Jr., "'Elijah Must Come First'" *JBL* 103 (1984): 256–58; J.A. Fitzmyer, "More about Elijah Coming First," *JBL* 104 (1985): 292–94.

[17] On this, cf. R.L. Webb, *John the Baptizer and Prophet* (JSNTSup 62; Sheffield: JSOT, 1991), 250–54; Trumbower, "Role of Malachi in the Career of John the Baptist," 33–40.

[18] On which, see J.M. Robinson, et al., *The Critical Edition of Q* (Hermeneia; Minneapolis: Fortress, 2000), 8–17, 118–27.

[19] I cannot agree with Trumbower's connection of Mal 3:24 with Sir. 48:10 and *Sib. Or.* 4:165 to show that baptism was the means by which John thought the wrath of God would be averted. John's baptism is an innovation. Cf. S. McKnight, *A Light Among the Gentiles* (Minneapolis: Fortress, 1991), 82–85.

A second leg may be found in John's modus operandi: his appearance seems to be that of Elijah (Mark 1:6; Q 7:24-28; 2 Kgs 1:8; 1 Kgs 19:13, 19; 2 Kgs 2:8, 13-14; *Tg. Ps.-J.* on 2Kgs 2:8; cf. also Zech 13:4).[20] A third leg is that John's location for ministry was that of the ancient Elijah: both operated on the eastern side of the Jordan (John 1:28; 10:40; 2 Kgs 2:8), and this connection by John contrasts with his overt statement in John 1:21. A table may stand on a tripod, but a fourth leg makes the table even sturdier: John's vehement criticism of Herod Antipas's marriage to Herodias probably owes its impetus to Malachi 2:13-16, even if his words also echo Leviticus 18:16; 20:21. Malachi's stinging words are a singular criticism of divorce in the Hebrew Bible, and a book that makes the connection to Elijah. These four legs then support a table on which John placed his life: the table of Elijah. Thus, some agree that John saw himself as Elijah and structured his life in his image.[21]

However, the case is not quite as clear as the previous discussion might indicate. A closer examination suggests the clarity of Mark 9:11-13 comes from hindsight.[22] First, the most important connection of John to Elijah is in the term *the coming one*, found behind the words of both Mark 1:11 and Q 7:19. These are words John speaks of Jesus, not himself. Now, if as seems the case, the coming one of Malachi 3:1; 4:5-6 is Elijah, then John thought Elijah was Jesus, not himself. Second, John's words are that the one coming after him would baptize with "the Holy Spirit and fire" (Q 3:16). The words of Malachi are that the messenger's (read: Elijah's) words will be like fire, a fire that would purge the temple's systemic flaws—and once again, it appears John thought Jesus was that messenger, and that messenger was Elijah (Mal 3:2b-4; cf. 1 Kgs 18:20-40; 2 Kgs 2:9-11). And Sirach 48:1-3 identifies Elijah as a man of fire. Further, John sees in the coming one, that is Jesus, the burning of felled trees (Q 3:9) and the purging of the threshold flood (Q 3:17), and that lines up once again with the Elijah of Malachi 3:2b-4; 4:1.

Third, John denies that he is Elijah according to John 1:19-28. Fourth, an interesting variant at Luke 9:54 occurs: when the disciples wonder if Jesus wants to bring down fire, some good MSS add "as did also Elijah" (ACDW f1.13 Maj). If this text is correct, and we must say that its witnesses are credible, then these disciples may have thought of Jesus as *Elijah*. Fifth, we remember that when Jesus acts in the temple (cf. Mark 11:15-17 pars.; John 2:14-16), he is immediately questioned about his authority and he appeals to John the Baptist—perhaps because it was John who publicly made the connection of the "coming one"

---

[20] M. Hengel, *The Charismatic Leader and His Followers* (trans. J.C.G. Greig; Edinburgh: T&T Clark, 1981), 36, n. 71.

[21] The priestly criticism of Malachi 3:3 can be connected to John's antipriestly stance. Cf. on this C.H. Kraeling, *John the Baptist* (New York: Scribner, 1951), 1–32.

[22] See esp. J.A.T. Robinson, "Elijah, John and Jesus: An Essay in Detection," in *Twelve New Testament Studies* (London: SCM Press, 1962), 28–52.

with the temple's purification (Mark 11:27-33 pars.).[23] Finally, when John queries Jesus from prison about his identity, he appeals once again to Malachi 3–4. He wants to know who Jesus is. He asks if Jesus is the "coming one." Jesus replies that, no, he takes his cue from texts other than Malachi. John is perhaps shocked that Jesus has shifted from being the Elijah figure to being the agent of the kingdom realizations of Isaiah 29:8-9; 35:5-6; and 61:1. And Jesus, evidently, had to take some time to explain who John was (cf. Q 11:7-19). It may have been at that time that John first made the connection between the messenger of Malachi 3–4 and himself. But it was too late for him to do anything about it. Whatever he had done was all he could do now. Soon a soldier would sever his head from his body, and, at the prompting of Jesus, Christians would forever assign the Elijah script to him.

These two cases are a stalemate with, however, a notable conclusion. John may have seen himself as Elijah, and John may have seen Jesus as Elijah; it is also likely that Jesus saw John as Elijah. The conclusion is this: both were in search of a script for explaining their role in the nation's dilemma, and they sought for their answers in the pages of the Tanakh. John and Jesus asked, "Who am I?" and "Who is he?" and "Who are we?" The answers they had do not seem clear. That there is confusion over who is Elijah only lends support to our suspicion that they were reenacting the lives of pivotal figures in Israel's history. They were debating the issue. Clearly, the technique of identifying yourself by setting your life into the history of Israel was part of their missions.

CONCLUSION

The argument here presented is not dependent on each detail being accepted. Instead, a general impression has been presented in which Jewish leaders understood their mission as a reenactment of ancient figures from Israel. The degree of correspondence between life and script may vary from case to case, but the impression is secure: there were leaders at and around the time of Jesus who found a script for life in ancient biblical and historical figures. In so conducting their lives, they used a typological interpretation of the Tanakh. It appears that Jesus, at one time, may have been understood as the man of fire from Malachi, the eschatological Elijah. But it also appears that Jesus shifted (or John shifted) from this self-identity and moved back in his Bible to the prophecies of Isaiah.

Now a critical question with potential implications for interpreting Mark 10:45 can be asked. Did Jesus also appeal to any of the various scripts in the Tanakh and Jewish history to understand himself and his mission? In particular,

---

[23] It should be observed here that J.A.T. Robinson has a case for the temple action occurring earlier in the life of Jesus, just after his baptism, and therefore in the spot John records it rather than where the Synoptics locate it. If, as they say, John had been out of the way for some time prior to the last week of Jesus, appeal to John's baptism would be a weak argument. Cf. his "Elijah, John and Jesus," 40.

it will be asked, did Jesus understand himself as the servant in those prophecies? If there is evidence Jesus thought of himself as the Servant of Isaiah, we can drive a wedge into the issue of when history began to interpret Jesus' death as atoning—and that wedge would cut in such a way that it began with Jesus. However, if there is no supporting evidence that Jesus thought of himself in terms of the Servant of Isaiah, we would have to argue that the ransom dimensions of the logion are probably inauthentic or from some other Jewish tradition. Once again, did Jesus find a script for his life in the Tanakh? Was one of Jesus' typically Jewish scripts for his life and mission the Servant of Isaiah? In the next chapter evidence for Jesus' appeal to various scripts will be presented and then in the following chapter we will turn to the issue of Jesus and the Servant of Isaiah.

Chapter 9

The Script for Jesus

We enter here into a "mindfield." Buried under the mental surface of our concern is the following set of issues: Jesus' intentions, Jesus' vision for a restored Israel, and Jesus' use of the Old Testament as a source for finding a script for his life. That Jesus searched the Tanakh to understand his mission is a commonplace;[1] that in so doing he went directly to, or even later found himself drawn to, the servant passages of Isaiah is not beyond doubt. We should remind ourselves that it was C.H. Dodd who dramatically impressed upon New Testament scholarship that it was not a book of isolated testimonies but instead a set of passages to which Christians first appealed as they sought to understand Jesus, explain their identity, and then construct the basis of early Christian theology.[2] Dodd saw behind this reflection a set of primary passages: Genesis 12:3; 22:18;

---

[1] On Jesus' use of Scripture, the literature is vast and increasingly complex. The following represent the spectrum: L. Goppelt, *Typos* (trans. D.H. Madvig; 1939; repr. Grand Rapids: Eerdmans, 1982); C.H. Dodd, *According to the Scriptures* (London: James Nisbet, 1952); J.A.T. Robinson, "Did Jesus Have a Distinctive Use of Scripture?" in his *Twelve More New Testament Studies* (London: SCM, 1984), 35–43; R.T. France, *Jesus and the Old Testament* (London: Tyndale, 1971); R. Longenecker, *Biblical Exegesis in the Apostolic Period* (Grand Rapids: Eerdmans, 1975), 51–78; C.F.D. Moule, *The Origin of Christology* (Cambridge: Cambridge University Press, 1977), 127–34; D.J. Moo, *The Old Testament in the Gospel Passion Narratives* (Sheffield: Almond, 1983); B.D. Chilton, *A Galilean Rabbi and His Bible* (GNS 8; Wilmington: Michael Glazier, 1984); E.E. Ellis, *The Old Testament in Early Christianity* (Grand Rapids: Baker, 1992), 125–38 (on scholarship, cf. pp. 53–74); B.D. Chilton and C.A. Evans, "Jesus and Israel's Scriptures," in *Studying the Historical Jesus* (ed. B. Chilton and C.A. Evans; Leiden: E.J. Brill, 1994), 281–335; D.C. Allison, Jr., *The Intertextual Jesus:* (Harrisburg: Trinity Press International, 2000). An independent study, but still useful, is E. Schweizer, *Lordship and Discipleship* (SBT 28; Naperville, Ill.: Alec R. Allenson, 1960), 42–55.

I make no assumptions about Jesus', or Jewish, literacy; on this cf. W.V. Harris, *Ancient Literacy* (Cambridge, Mass.: Harvard University Press, 1989); A. Millard, *Reading and Writing in the Time of Jesus* (The Biblical Seminar 69; Sheffield: Sheffield Academic, 2000).

[2] Dodd, *According to the Scriptures*.

Deuteronomy 18:15, 19; Psalms 2; 8; 22; 31; 34; 38; 41; 42–43; 69; 80; 88; 110; 118; Isaiah 6:1–9:7; 11:1-10; 28:16; 40:1-11; 42:1–44:5; 49:1-13; 50:4-11; 52:13–53:12; 61; Jeremiah 31:10-34; Daniel 7; Hosea; Joel 2–3; Zechariah 9–14.[3] The more important conclusion for our purposes is that Dodd saw these as behind the entire Christian reflection. I quote:

> This [set of passages and the conclusions drawn from them] is a piece of genuinely creative thinking. Who was responsible for it? The early church, we are accustomed to say, and perhaps we can safely say no more. But creative thinking is rarely done by committees, useful as they may be for systematizing the fresh ideas of individual thinkers, and for stimulating them to further thought.[4] It is individual minds that originate. Whose was the originating mind here?
>
> Among Christian thinkers of the first age known to us there are three of genuinely creative power: Paul, the author to the Hebrews, and the Fourth Evangelist. . . . What forgotten geniuses may lurk in the shadows of those first twenty years of church history about which we are so scantily informed, it is impossible for us to say. But the New Testament itself avers that it was Jesus Christ Himself who first directed the minds of His followers to certain parts of the scriptures as those in which they might find illumination upon the meaning of his mission and destiny. . . . To account for the beginning of this most original and fruitful process of rethinking the Old Testament we found need to postulate a creative mind. The gospels offer us one. Are we compelled to reject the offer?[5]

These words of C.H. Dodd, some of the most memorable in biblical scholarship, set the tone for the important studies of (to stay with writing in English) B.D. Chilton, R.T. France, D.J. Moo, D. Juel, R. Hays, N.T. Wright,[6] C.A. Evans, W.H. Bellinger/W.R. Farmer, and D.C. Allison, and need to be kept before us.

Jesus never really appeals to any of the scrolls found near Qumran, but he does appeal quite often to the Tanakh. Indeed, the case has been made that Jesus' identity, his mission, and his vision for Israel are the result of his reflection on those very Scriptures. As we have seen, such an appeal is not unusual in Judaism, as a history of a text like Psalm 22 and the ambiguous "I" of that text clearly testifies.[7]

---

[3] In addition, Dodd saw some other subordinate and supplementary sources. See Dodd, *According to the Scriptures*, 107–8, for his chart.

[4] Dodd's and my experiences differ here.

[5] Dodd, *According to the Scriptures*, 109–10.

[6] In fact, N.T. Wright's entire book on Jesus can be seen as a fleshing out of Dodd's passages assigned to Jesus! See N.T. Wright, *Jesus and the Victory of God* (vol. 2 of *Christian Origins and the Question of God*; Minneapolis: Fortress, 1996).

[7] See on this Esther M. Menn, "No Ordinary Lament: Relecture and the Identity of the Distressed in Psalm 22," *HTR* 93 (2000): 301–41.

There is plenty of room for debate about which sayings of Jesus alluding to the Tanakh are authentic, which texts were his favorites, which textual tradition set his agenda, and how his interpretations are to be compared to other competing Jewish interpretations. But there is no longer any platform on which to stand if one wants to announce that Jesus set out on an independent course of teachings. His course was determined by the Tanakh, and Jesus was a Scripture prophet. Like the figures described in the previous chapter, Jesus also found in the Tanakh statements, figures, books, and visions that he thought applied directly to himself, to those around him, and to his world.[8]

Before proceeding to that task, however, a word about methodology. It is a mistake to begin, as so many have, with the Tanakh and Judaism, trace out a figure (say, Messiah), and then ask, Does Jesus fit this or that figure?—yes or no? The problem herein is that this gives the term or category a finality. The more historical question to ask is this: What was Jesus like? and, then, How does he correspond to various figures? and, Did Jesus make such a connection? If one asks the first question, one presumes upon a fixed category—Messiah is like this—and one must enter into a history of polemics: Jesus is or is not the Messiah of the Tanakh. The second question gives precedence to what we know about Jesus; the former to the term Messiah.[9] The second, in contrast to the first, permits a greater flexibility on the part of Jesus to shape his definition of a given category. But Jesus did appeal to scripts in the Tanakh.

Q 9:58: SON OF MAN

A good place to begin is with Q passages assigned by nearly everyone to Jesus to see how these passages use Scriptures to elucidate the meaning of his mission.

---

[8] A good example of this sort of detective work, which can easily be multiplied to volumes of evidence and examples, is Jesus' connection to Zechariah and to the images of that prophet. On this, cf. S. Kim, "Jesus—The Son of God, the Stone, the Son of Man, and the Servant," in *Tradition and Interpretation in the New Testament* (ed. G.F. Hawthorne and O. Betz; Grand Rapids: Eerdmans, 1987), 134–48; C.A. Evans, "Jesus and Zechariah's Messianic Hope," in *Authenticating the Activities of Jesus* (ed. B.D. Chilton and C.A. Evans; NTTS 28.2; Leiden: E.J. Brill, 1998), 373–88.

[9] Messiah has become a favorite discussion again: see J. Becker, *Messianic Expectation in the Old Testament* (trans. D.E. Green; Philadelphia: Fortress, 1980); J. Neusner, et al., eds., *Judaisms and Their Messiahs at the Turn of the Christian Era* (Cambridge: Cambridge University Press, 1987); J.H. Charlesworth, et al., eds., *The Messiah* (Princeton Symposium on Judaism and Christian Origins; Minneapolis: Fortress, 1992); *Jahrbuch für Biblische Theologie* 8 (1993); P.E. Satterthwaite, et al., eds., *The Lord's Anointed* (Tyndale House Studies; Grand Rapids: Baker, 1995); J.J. Collins, *The Scepter and the Star* (ABRL; New York: Doubleday, 1995); C.A. Evans and P.W. Flint, eds., *Eschatology, Messianism, and the Dead Sea Scrolls* (SDSSRL; Grand Rapids: Eerdmans, 1997); D. Cohn-Sherbok, *The Jewish Messiah* (Edinburgh: T&T Clark, 1997); W. Horbury, *Jewish Messianism and the Cult of Christ* (London: SCM, 1998). The fundamental issue here is how one defines *messianic* or *Messiah*; see esp. Horbury, *Jewish Messianism and the Cult of Christ*, 6–7; and the careful essay by J.G. McConville, "Messianic Interpretation of the Old Testament in Modern Context," in *The Lord's Anointed* (ed. P.E. Satterthwaite, et al.), 9–15.

This brief survey highlights the importance of various figures and statements in the Tanakh for how Jesus understood himself and his mission to Israel. No large theory will be built upon the specifics. Scholars might quibble with a point here and there; all should permit the general point.

I begin with Q 9:58 (cf. *Gos. Thom.* 86)[10] a poetic *mot* of irony almost surely from Jesus:[11] "Foxes have holes, and birds of the air have nests;[12] but the Son of man has nowhere to lay his head." One source in the Tanakh for this logion is Genesis 1:26-28, where God makes humankind in "our image" and gives the same "dominion . . . over the birds of the air." A claim picked up by the psalmist at 8:4-8,[13] as the psalmist, who alone combines son of man with birds of the air, surveys creation, he wonders, "what are human beings [e.g., the literal son of man] that you are mindful of them . . . you have given them dominion over the works of your hands . . . [over beasts and] the birds of the air" (cf. Ps 144:3-4; Sir 17:4; *Tg. Psalm* 8; *Gen. Rab.* 79:6). This dominion comes to a climax in that Son of man who appears before the Ancient One where he is given "dominion and glory and kingship" (Dan 7:13-14). Another tradition finds in the comparison of the Son of man with animals the assurance that God will surely provide, through whatever trade he is called to, for the Son of man (*m. Qidd.* 4:14; *b. Qidd.* 82b), unless—so reads the interpretation—that person sins.

But this privilege of the Son of man is subverted by another biblical, exegetical tradition.[14] Namely, Job 7:16-20 (cf. 25:6), Psalm 144:3 and 1QS XI, 20-21, where each writer finds in the Genesis 1:26-28//Psalm 8:4 (cf. Sir 18:1-14, esp. v. 8), instead of glory, an example of the humiliation of humans. Thus, Job: "I loathe my life; I would not live forever. . . . What are human beings that you make so much of them, that you set your mind on them. . .?" In a prayer for protection in war, we read of the psalmist, "O LORD, what are human beings that you regard them, or mortals that you think of them? They are like breath; their days are like a passing shadow" (Ps 144:3-4). At 1QS XI, 20-21, we find: "Who, indeed, is man among Your glorious works? As what can he, born of woman, be reckoned before You? Kneaded from dust, his body is but the bread of worms; he is so much spit."

---

[10] Thomas adds "and to rest." See on the Q logion, Allison, *Intertextual Jesus*, 160–63. See further, on the Son of man debate here, M. Casey, "The Jackals and the Son of Man (Matt. 8:20//Luke 9:58)," *JSNT* 23 (1985): 3–22; "General, Generic and Indefinite," *JSNT* 29 (1987): 21–56.

[11] See M.H. Smith, "No Place for a Son of Man," *Forum* 4 (1988): 83–107, here p. 92 (on authenticity).

[12] See Job 39:27-28.

[13] On the importance of Psalm 8, cf. Dodd, *According to the Scriptures*, 32–34, 104; F.J. Moloney, "The Re-interpretation of Psalm VIII and the Son of Man Debate," *NTS* 27 (1981): 656–72.

[14] Smith, "No Place for a Son of Man," 102–3, fails to note this second exegetical tradition and so sees Jesus himself subverting Psalm 8:4.

Two exegetical traditions emerge then from the creation narrative:[15] the Son of man is either the apex of God's good creation as God's climactic creative act, or, ironically, the son of man is the most humble being on earth. Jesus, as recorded at Q 9:58, opts for the latter interpretation as a result of his trying circumstances and homelessness, and sees in his[16] life the representative humiliated human being. Birds (cf. Ps 84:3) and foxes (cf. Lam 5:18) have more than does he. This logion fits with the collective understanding of "son of man."[17] Jesus does not thereby make himself unique on earth; but he classifies himself outside the majority—those who do have a place to rest nightly—and sees his life as an example of a humiliating turn of events.[18]

Jesus finds in the expression Son of man (cf. 1 Cor 15:27; Heb 2:6-8) an exegetical interpretation that applies specially to his own life. His view subverts one biblical tradition (that of glory) by appeal to another (the humiliation of humans on earth). The Q tradition (9:58) clearly makes Jesus someone special and not just an ordinary human being. The appeal of Jesus is to his status as a rejected prophet (e.g., Sir 36:27 LXX) rather than an ordinary human being.[19] I hold it as quite possible that Son of man in Q 9:58 is collective—Jesus and his followers are itinerants in need of sustenance and shelter.[20] In addition, to anticipate later discussion, it must remain a distinct possibility that Son of man here echoes Daniel 7: the suffering of the saints there are collectively vindicated under the more exalted figure of the Son of man. A collective element to the logion obtains whether or not one finds a possible echo of Daniel 7.[21]

More can perhaps be said to define the contours of Q 9:58. If this *mot* of Jesus emerges from the harsh realities of opposition, as Son of man sayings frequently do, then one is entitled to ask if the "birds" and "foxes" might not evoke

---

[15] Otherwise, see also similarities in Sir 36:31 (LXX 36:27); Plutarch, *Tiberius Gracchus* 9:5 (Tiberius: "The wild beasts that roam over Italy," he would say, "have every one of them a cave or lair to lurk in; but the men who fight and die for Italy enjoy the common air and light, indeed, but nothing else; houseless and homeless they wander about with their wives and children."). The parallels adduced from other traditions are unhelpful (e.g., Prov 1:20-33; Job 28:20-22; *1 En.* 42; 94:5; 2 Sam 15:19-22). So also Davies and Allison, *Matthew*, 2:43; Smith, "No Place for a Son of Man," 96–97; contra Gnilka, *Matthäusevangelium*, 1:311–12; Keener, *Matthew*, 274–75.

[16] An important clarification of Casey, "Jackals and the Son of Man," 9–12.

[17] On which, see the excursus at the end of chapter 6.

[18] Contra R. Bultmann, *History of the Synoptic Tradition* (trans. J. Marsh; rev. ed.; New York: Harper & Row, 1963), 28 with n. 3; H.E. Tödt, *The Son of Man in the Synoptic Tradition* (trans. D.M. Barton; London: SCM, 1965), 120–23, contends that the logion is about Jesus' authority but fails to see the significance of Q 9:58c.

[19] See Nolland, *Luke*, 2:541.

[20] See B. Lindars, *Jesus Son of Man* (London: SPCK, 1983), 29–31.

[21] On this, cf. Casey, "Jackals and the Son of Man," 10; Smith, "No Place for a Son of Man," 97–98, restricts an echo of Daniel 7 exclusively to Daniel 7:13-14, without respect for contextual features. See also M.D. Hooker, "Is the Son of Man Problem Really Insoluble?" in *Text and Interpretation* (ed. E. Best and R.M. Wilson; Cambridge: Cambridge University Press, 1979), 155–68, here esp. p. 167–68.

the opponents of Jesus, for which there is ample scriptural warrant. Thus, one should observe how various animals[22] evoke opponents at Deuteronomy 28:26 (1) (prophetic); 1 Samuel 17:44, 46 (1, 2) (Goliath and David's taunt); 1 Kings 14:11; 16:4; 21:24 (1, 3) (prophetic); Jeremiah 7:33 (1, 2); 15:3 (1, 3); 16:4 (1, 2); 19:7 (1, 2); 34:20 (1, 2) (prophetic); Ezekiel 29:5 (1, 4); 32:4 (1, 4); 39:4 (5, 4) (prophetic).[23] This topos speaks of those who devour the people of God and are uniformly foreigners. One thinks here of Jesus calling Herod Antipas "that fox" (Luke 13:32). The language, inasmuch as the one other time refers to Antipas, suggests the illegitimate Herodians who oppressed Israel, especially financially. This situation gives the logion its generic nature. Further, this theme of Jesus' opponents being in positions of both power and opulence is evident also in Q 7:25. Here Jesus contrasts once again the external circumstances of the prophet and the king. If one does not share the specific interpretation offered here, one cannot deny that such terms as are found in Q 9:58 were frequently used in the Tanakh for those who were destined to oppose the people and prophets of Israel. I suggest then that the "birds" and "foxes" of Q 9:58 may be more than Jesus' penchant for bucolic imagery. Jesus as the Son of man, along with his followers, knew the harsh realities of opposition by foreign authorities to God's inbreaking kingdom.[24]

Q 9:61-62: Elijah and Elisha

If Jesus saw the psalmist's Son of man as a script for his own and his followers' fate, Q 9:61-62 suggests Jesus sees in Elijah's calling of Elisha a script for his own calling of others.[25] There is a strong reason to doubt Q 9:61-62 was originally in Q: there is no Matthean parallel. However, not convinced that all of Q was swallowed whole by each Evangelist, many scholars find its coherence with Q 9:57-60 as well as its non-Lukan features to tip the balance in favor of Q.[26] As we will see shortly, this logion scripts the life of Elijah for Jesus. But, as we concluded above, Elijah was for the early church the forerunner of the Messiah, and there was some discussion between Jesus and John over Elijah (see ch. 8, "John

---

[22] In what follows, I use the following numbers and references: (1) for birds [עוֹף]; (2) for beasts; (3) for dog; (4) for living thing; (5) for bird [עַיִט].

[23] The term for fox (שׁוּעָלִים; e.g., Ezek 13:4; Lam 5:18; Ps 63:11), was sometimes confused with jackal (תַנִים)—and jackal is the dog of the prophetic taunts/threats.

[24] See M. de Jonge, "Jesus' Rôle in the Final Breakthrough of God's Kingdom," in *Frühes Christentum* (ed. Lichtenberger; vol 3 of H. Cancik, H. Lichtenberger, and P. Schäfer; Tübingen: Mohr Siebeck, 1996), 265–86.

[25] See now S. Bryan, *Jesus and Israel's Traditions of Judgement and Restoration* (SNTSMS 117; Cambridge: Cambridge University Press, 2002), 88–110.

[26] On this, see esp. J. Kloppenborg, *Q Parallels* (Sonoma, Calif.: Polebridge, 1988), 62–65. He lists the following as arguing the logion's presence in Q: Crossan, Edwards, Hahn, Hawkins, Hengel, Hunter, Kloppenborg, Knox, Marshall, Polag, Schürmann, Streeter, Vassiliadis, and Wernle. To which list can now be added Allison, *Intertextual Jesus*, 78–81. The Q Project excludes it: J.A.T. Robinson, et al., *The Critical Edition of Q* (Hermeneia; Minneapolis: Fortress, 2000), 156–57.

the Baptist"). So this saying must come from a very early period when John thought Jesus was Elijah[27] and John thought of himself as the messenger.[28] The logion's radical demand to abandon family (cf. Mark 1:16-20; 3:31-35; 10:15; Q 9:59-60; Q 14:26-27),[29] its graphic imagery, as well as its focus on the present kingdom of God speak on behalf of the authenticity of the logion,[30] even if some particulars are more literary than historical.[31] The evidence from 1 Kings suggests that Jesus patterned his calling of others on that of Elijah's calling of Elisha:

> So he set out from there, and found Elisha son of Shaphat, who was plowing. There were twelve yoke of oxen ahead of him, and he was with the twelfth. Elijah passed by him and threw his mantle over him. He left the oxen, ran after Elijah, and said, "Let me kiss my father and my mother, and then I will follow you." Then Elijah said to him, "Go back again; for what have I done to you?" He returned from following him, took the yoke of oxen, and slaughtered them; using the equipment from the oxen, he boiled their flesh, and gave it to the people, and they ate. Then he set out and followed Elijah, and became his servant. (19:19-21)

An allusion to this text/event is established by nearly all of Allison's criteria for detecting allusions.[32] Scholarship has seen an allusion to the Elijah-Elisha episode[33] and several important and distinctive themes and terms connect the two: *after* in "ran after" and "followed"; "plow/plowing"; the theme of saying farewell to the family; total abandonment of one's livelihood. The controversy between Jesus and John over who was Elijah sets this allusion into a credible tradition history with Jesus; and this Q logion, when contrasted to Jesus' actions, highlights Jesus' prophetic mission.[34]

---

[27] This early identification might explain Luke 9:52-56: the disciples of Jesus want to call down fire on the Samaritans; cf. 2 Kgs 1:9-16.

[28] Contra Allison, *Intertextual Jesus*, 144–45, who finds the tension as perhaps part of the evolution of Q.

[29] On this, cf. esp. R. Schnackenburg, *Die sittliche Botschaft des Neuen Testaments* (HTKNTSonderband 1–2; Freiburg: Herder, 1986–1988), 1:144–55; J. Becker, *Jesus of Nazareth* (trans. J.E. Crouch; New York: Walter de Gruyter, 1998), 308–23. For the broader context, see S. McKnight, *A New Vision for Israel* (Grand Rapids: Eerdmans, 1999), 170–71, 179–87.

[30] Bultmann, *History of the Synoptic Tradition*, 28, sees Q 9:62 as authentic but Q 9:61 as an "imaginary situation." M.G. Steinhauser thinks Q 9:62a and 9:62b are inauthentic, but his argument that "kingdom" is a place or a community is too sharply focused. See his "Putting One's Hand to the Plow: The Authenticity of Q 9:61-62," *Forum* 5 (1989): 151–58.

[31] So also Nolland, *Luke*, 2:540; Fitzmyer, *Luke*, 1:837.

[32] Allison, *Intertextual Jesus*, 9–13, 78–81, 142–45, though I find more allusion to Elijah than does Allison.

[33] Recent scholarship on intertextuality in Luke has found Luke 9:51-62 to be a gold mine for Lukan creativity, though rarely is the historical question faced squarely. For good studies, cf. T.L. Brodie, "The Departure for Jerusalem (Luke 9:51-56) as a Rhetorical *Imitatio* of Elijah's Departure for the Jordan (2 Kgs 1:1-2:6)," *Bib* 70 (1989): 96–109; "Luke 9:57-62," *SBLSP* (1989): 237–45.

[34] Allison, *Intertextual Jesus*, 78–81, draws a suggestive parallel to Lot's wife (Gen 19:17, 26) most

Like Elijah, Jesus (1) finds his followers in the midst of life and summons them out of their vocational world to follow him by trusting in the Father's care, (2) expects his followers to abandon all for the call to announce the kingdom, (3) sees his followers drawn into the task of a prophet (cf. Q 6:23), and (4) expects his followers to attend to him (cf. Luke 8:1-3). However, *unlike* Elijah, Jesus permits no delay, and neither does he literally toss his mantle over his followers. Elijah permits Elisha to return to his family and kiss them goodbye. Jesus permits no such diversion; the kingdom has drawn near and it is time to act, now and decisively. In fact, the statement of Jesus about putting one's hand to the plow and not looking back may also be directly connected to the act of Elisha. When Elisha went back, the text says, he boiled the oxen by using the equipment he had at hand—namely, he cooked the oxen by setting the plow on fire. If this is the case, it could be that Jesus is saying that his followers, like Elisha, are to burn the bridges to their former lives and not look back as they turn to follow him as Elisha followed Elijah.[35]

If Elijah's words reveal an ambiguous relationship, Jesus' call creates a life-altering change of dominion.[36] Family has been reconstructed for Jesus: the cherished establishment of family (Gen 1:27-28; 2:23-24; 3:16) has been reevaluated by Jesus and now, since the kingdom is at the point of arrival, will be reconstituted around him and his followers (Mark 3:31-35; Q 14:26-27).

This conclusion is strengthened by recalling the calls of the first four disciples (Mark 1:16-20) as well as Levi/Matthew (Mark 2:13-17; Matt 9:9-13). These calls are each patterned after the call of Elisha by Elijah in 1 Kings 19:19-21. We can draw two possible conclusions: either Jesus saw himself *as* Elijah with an eschatological twist, or he saw himself as *more than* Elijah. In either case, he saw himself as Elijah and found in that figure a script for his calling of others as they abandoned vocation and family to follow him. Jesus sees himself in the Tanakh, or he finds in that Tanakh examples to follow.

---

likely through *gezerah shewa*. M. Hengel exaggerates the contrast between Elijah and Jesus, with the former calling being more prompted by God; cf. his *The Charismatic Leader and His Followers* (trans. J. Greig; Edinburgh: T&T Clark, 1981), 16–17.

[35] See H.J. Blair, "Putting One's Hand to the Plough. Luke ix. 62 in the light of 1 Kings xix. 19-21," *ExpTim* 79 (1967–68): 342–43.

[36] Elijah's words in 1 Kings 19:20, "for what have I done to you?" surprise. Well, one might say, tossing the prophet's mantle over someone is not typical and is fundamentally a passing over of prophetic charisma. Perhaps the *ki* should be adversative: "Go back (*shuv*). But (think) what I have done to you" (so J. Gray, *I & II Kings* [OTL; 2d ed.; Philadelphia: Westminster, 1970], 413). The LXX is otherwise: ᾿Ανάστρεφε, ὅτι πεποίηκά σοι. Josephus follows the LXX: after adding that when the mantle was tossed over Elisha the latter began to prophesy, Elijah ordered him to say farewell to his parents (*A.J.* 8.354).

Q 11:20 AND PROPHETIC ACTIONS: MOSES

A third example of Jesus' evocation of a scriptural figure to shape his life and mission can be found in Q 11:20 as a virtually uncontested saying of Jesus: "But if it is by the finger [Matt: spirit] of God that I cast out the demons, then the kingdom of God has come to you."[37] Everything hinges in this example on whether Jesus said "finger" or "spirit." This is not to deny that, at some level, spirit, finger, God, and power could be functional equivalents (cf. Pss 8:3; 33:6; Ezek 3:14; 8:1, 3; 37:1; 1 Chron 28:11-19). But the *specific* evocation of each would give a different impression of what Jesus was doing and which script he was following. To name one: if *Spirit* is original, then Jesus is perhaps evoking the outpouring of the Spirit in the final days (e.g., Isa 32:15; 61:1-2; Ezek 37:14; Joel 2:28-29), though the closer the functional equivalent of spirit and finger, the closer we could be to a Mosaic image. It is not as important here to have certainty on which reading is the more primitive as it is to explore the possible implications of one reading (finger) for understanding how Jesus understood his role by finding a script for his life in the Scriptures. The general point, that Jesus did look to Scripture for a life-script, is more established by the accumulation of examples than by one specific example.

The majority of Q scholarship[38] leans to the view that it is more likely that Matthew would have altered finger to Spirit than that Luke, who is especially fond of pneumatic theology, would have changed Spirit to finger.[39] Matthew's

[37] See esp. G.H. Twelftree, *Jesus the Exorcist* (Peabody, Mass: Hendrickson, 1993), 98–113; Gnilka, *Matthäusevangelium*, 1:456; Allison, *Intertextual Jesus*, 53–57, 68–73. See also R. Hamerton-Kelly, "A Note on Matthew XII.28 par. Luke XI.20," *NTS* 11 (1965–65): 167–69, where it is shown that *hand/finger* and *Spirit* are closely associated; A. George, "'Par le doigt de Dieu' (Lc 11, 20)," in his *Études sur L'Oeuvre de Luc* (SB; Paris: Gabalda, 1978), 127–32 (Luke altered the original *Spirit* to *finger*.) So also J.-M. Van Cangh, "'Par l'esprit de Dieu—par le doigt de Dieu,'" in *Logia: Les Paroles de Jésus* (ed. J. Delobel), 337–42; H.K. Nielsen, *Heilung und Verkündigung* (ATDan 22; Leiden: E.J. Brill, 1987), 28–45; G.R. Beasley-Murray, *Jesus and the Kingdom of God* (Grand Rapids: Eerdmans, 1986), 75–80.

[38] E.g., Fitzmyer, *Luke*, 2:918; Allison, *Intertextual Jesus*, 53–57, 70–73.

[39] *Pace* J.D.G. Dunn, "Matthew 12:28/Luke 11:20–A Word of Jesus?" in *Eschatology and the New Testament* (ed. W.H. Gloer; Peabody, Mass: Hendrickson, 1988), 29–49; also his *Jesus and the Spirit* (London: SCM, 1975), 44–46. See also R.W. Wall, "The Finger of 'God'," *NTS* 33 (1987): 144–50; Nolland, *Luke*, 2:639–40; Davies and Allison, *Matthew*, 2:339–40. This discussion has been slightly skewed toward a discovery of which of the Evangelists, Luke or Matthew, got his fingerprints on an original saying of Jesus. Our question comes from a different angle: which is more likely to have been said by Jesus? There is a consensus that pneumatic language, while possible for Jesus, is hardly typical. On the other hand, there is a growing scholarship on Jesus and Moses. For the former, the standard studies are Dunn, *Jesus and the Spirit*, and C.K. Barrett, *The Holy Spirit and the Gospel Tradition* (2d ed.; London: SPCK, 1966). On Jesus and Moses, see esp. Allison, *Intertextual Jesus*, 25–100; his *The New Moses: A Matthean Typology* (Minneapolis: Fortress, 1993); S. McKnight, "Jesus and Prophetic Actions," *BBR* 10 (2000): 197–232; C. Chavasse, "Jesus: Christ and Moses," *Theology* 54 (1951): 244–50, 289–96.

redactional desire, apparently, was to connect back to his quotation of Isaiah 42:1-4 at 12:17-21 (cf. also 12:31) or, less likely since he was steeped in the sacred text, to avoid anthropomorphisms.[40] In the ultimate contest between Moses and Pharaoh, after striking the Nile to turn it into blood (Exod 7:20-25), blighting the land with frogs (8:1-15), and filling the land of Egypt with gnats (8:16-17), the battle came to a head. The first two plagues the Egyptian magicians were able to duplicate, but the third they could not. When they came to this conclusion, the magicians surrendered, saying, "This is the finger of God!" (8:19 [8:15]). Pharaoh's heart was nonetheless hardened (8:20). This is the allusion Jesus makes: "finger of God" occurs only three times in the Hebrew Bible (Exod 8:19; 31:18; Deut 9:10; but cf. Ps 8:3 [8:4]), and neither Exodus 31:18 nor Deuteronomy 9:10 show any connection to the logion of Jesus. Further, "sign" is found in both the Q and Exodus traditions (Q 11:16;[41] Exod 7:3, 9; 8:23; 10:1, 2; 11:9, 10). Surely a contest over exorcisms/miracles makes for a thematic connection between Jesus and Moses, with the opponents of Jesus lining up with Pharaoh's magicians. A reference to Spirit seems out of place in Jesus' contest. One final thought: the logion probably makes an eschatological claim. Jesus' exorcisms evince the fulfillment of end-time expectations of the defeat of Satan (e.g., Isa 24:21-22; *1 En.* 10:4-8; *Jub.* 23:29; 1QS IV, 18-19; *T. Mos.* 10:1; *T. Levi* 18:12; *T. Jud.* 25:3; Rev 20:2-3).[42]

The implication of this discussion is clearly that Jesus sees himself as (perhaps even the eschatological) Moses, at least in this particular: Jesus is like Moses in that his exorcistic ministries are challenged about origins. For Jesus, his exorcisms evince the power of God; for Aaron and Moses, the same attribution is made. In this contest between Jesus and his opponents, Jesus finds a script for his life in the response of the contemporaries to Moses. The significant difference is that whereas the ancient magicians confessed the gnat-miracle to be of divine origin (from the finger of God), it is Jesus who must announce the divine origin of his own exorcisms by claiming they demonstrate the presence of the kingdom of God. This self-claim ties the allusion to Moses even more specifically into Jesus' conception of his mission. Further, just as the prophet of Deuteronomy 18:15-18 becomes an eschatological expectation, so Jesus, by

[40] For a full discussion, cf. J.P. Meier, *A Marginal Jew: Rethinking the Historical Jesus* (3 vols.; ABRL; New York: Doubleday, 1991–2000), 2:410–11 (esp. n. 51); also cf. T.W. Manson, *The Teaching of Jesus: Studies of Its Form and Content* (Cambridge: Cambridge University Press, 1939), 81–82.

Tg. Onq. to Exod 8:15 has "It is a plague from before the Lord." *Tg. Neo.* on Exod 8:15: "This is the finger of might from before the Lord." *Tg. Ps.-J.* on Exod 8:15: "This is not from the power of the strength of Moses and Aaron, but it is a plague sent from before the Lord." These three renderings of Exodus 8:15 [8:19 in English] each seek to avoid anthromorphisms. *Finger* was eventually distinguised from *hand;* cf. *Mek. de R. Ishm.* on Exod 14:26-31, 7:109–16, where, because God uses his hand at the sea, there must be fifty plagues.

[41] See Robinson, et al., *Critical Edition of Q,* 246–47.

[42] See Twelftree, *Jesus the Exorcist,* 217–24; but cf. E.P. Sanders, *Jesus and Judaism* (Philadelphia: Fortress, 1985), 133–36.

claiming his actions are like those of Moses at the time of the exodus, can infer that the kingdom of God has been inaugurated. The logic is necessary for finger to evoke kingdom: something of a fulfillment must be present in Jesus' reenactment of Moses' signs. If the eschatological redemption is a new exodus (e.g., Isa 40:3-5; Hos 2:14-16, etc.), and there will be a prophet like Moses, then Jesus claims his actions are that fulfillment (cf. "strong man" in Q 11:20 and Isa 49:24). This perception of Jesus is historically plausible (4Q175 I, 1-8), even if early Christians found in Jesus a similar characteristic (Acts 3:12-26; 7:35-40).[43]

We cannot extend this discussion into an exploration of Mosaic themes in the life of Jesus, but I want to call attention to the persistent absence in modern reshapings of Christology in appealing to Moses as a prototype for Jesus. Perhaps because of the Reformation's call away from law to gospel/grace, or perhaps because of Protestant liberalism's fear of turning Jesus into a demanding lawgiver and prophet, or perhaps for other reasons—regardless, the connection has been largely ignored by Jesus scholars. A recent, incredibly detailed and massively documented study of Moses and Jesus in Matthew's theology has given rise to what I suspect to be a deeper perception by Dale Allison. Not only does Matthew present Jesus as a new Moses, but he thinks Jesus saw himself in such categories. To be sure, various nuances have to be spelled out when one asserts that Jesus saw himself in terms of Moses. However, the pattern is more than a peripheral dimension of the Jesus traditions.[44]

One other brief example may bring this to light.[45] It is not possible here to place on the table all the evidence, nor to adjudicate the historicity of the various bits of evidence that surface from a survey of Mosaic traces in the Jesus traditions, but most scholars permit today that Jesus did miracles, and many also permit that his actions were at times the sort that are often called "prophetic actions."[46] One thinks of the prophetic actions of the prophets in such passages as 1 Samuel 15:27-29; 1 Kings 11:29-40; 2 Kings 2:12-18; Hosea 3:1-5; Isaiah 20:1-6; Jeremiah 13:1-11; 18:1-12; 19:1-13; 27:1–28:17; 51:59-64; Ezekiel 2:8–3:3; 4:1-3, 7; 5:1-4; 37:15-28; Zechariah 6:9-15. One also thinks of the

---

[43] Allison, New Moses, 98–106.

[44] See Allison, New Moses; for Jesus, see various comments in Allison, Intertextual Jesus, esp. 25–73.

[45] See my "Jesus and Prophetic Actions," which is summarized in what follows.

[46] On this cf. C.H. Dodd, "Jesus as Teacher and Prophet," in Mysterium Christi (ed. G.K.A. Bell and A. Deissmann; London: Longmans, Green, 1930), 53–66; H. McKeating, "The Prophet Jesus," ExpTim 73 (1961–62): 4–7, 50–53; D.E. Aune, Prophecy in Early Christianity and the Ancient Mediterranean World (Grand Rapids: Eerdmans, 1983), 161–63; F. Schnider, Jesus der Prophet (OBO 2; Göttingen: Vandenhoeck & Ruprecht, 1973), 79-88 (who is too reliant upon the literary characteristics set up by G. Fohrer [see below]); J.W. Bowker, "Prophetic Action and Sacramental Form," in The New Testament Message (ed. F.L. Cross; part 2 of Studia Evangelica II–III; TUGAL 88; Berlin: Akadamie, 1964), 129–37; M.D. Hooker, The Signs of a Prophet (Harrisburg: Trinity Press International, 1997). For the prophetic actions in the Hebrew Bible, see W.D. Stacey, Prophetic Drama in the Old Testament (London: Epworth, 1990); K.G. Friebel, Jeremiah's and Ezekiel's Sign-Acts (JSOTSup 283; Sheffield: Sheffield Academic, 1999); G. Fohrer, Die symbolischen Handlungen der Propheten (2d ed.; Zürich: Zwingli, 1968).

Jewish sign prophets in Josephus, *A.J.* 18.85-87; 20.97-99; 20.167–68, 169–72, 188; *B.J.* 6.285–86. More importantly, we need to note the following actions of Moses: Exodus 5:1–12:51; 14:1–15:12; 15:23-26; 16:1-36; 17:1-7, 8-13; 19:9–20:26; 24:1-8; 32:15-24, 25-29; Numbers 11:16-30; 16:1-50; 17:1-13; 20:2-13, 22-29; 21:4-9; 27:12-23. These, then, are a brief sampling of the prophetic actions from which it is clear Jesus drew some energy.

Thus, a broad sampling of the evidence shows that Jesus exorcised demons (Q 11:20); healed (Q 7:18-23); gave, as did Hosea and Isaiah, special names (Mark 3:16; Matt 16:17-19); ate with the unlikely (Mark 2:13-17);[47] infringed on sabbatical practices (Mark 2:23-28) and handwashing principles (7:1-23); urged disciples to wipe the dust off their feet (6:11); entered into Jerusalem in an act of drama (11:1-10); cleansed the temple (11:11-19); cursed the barren fig tree (11:15-17, 20-25); held the last supper (14:22-25); fed the multitude (6:30-44); and was baptized in the Jordan (1:1-13). Many would not consider each piece of evidence historical; few would dispute that Jesus did some of the above and that the connections of the actions with the prophetic actions sketched above can be used heuristically to comprehend what Jesus thought he was all about.

Three observations are of note when one compares this widespread assortment of data from the Jesus traditions to the prophetic actions of others: (1) Jesus' actions are not modeled upon those of the ancient prophets of Israel and Judah; (2) Jesus' actions are occasionally similar to the actions of the Jewish sign prophets mentioned by Josephus; but (3) the actions of Jesus are most notably modeled upon the actions of Moses (and Joshua), and evoke the themes of restoration, redemption, and liberation. Once again, we come to the same conclusion we drew with respect to Q 11:20: Jesus, in some senses, modeled his own mission and identity on that of Moses—in particular, the expectation of the eschatological Moses.

THE TWELVE: A JOSHUA THEME

Nearly all Jesus scholars today contend that Jesus called the Twelve, even if the names are somewhat blurry on the edges, and this will be our fourth consideration.[48] What most have not asked is what the Twelve evoked. To be sure, nearly all those who contend the Twelve existed argue, with little thought about the issues, that twelve evokes the restoration of the twelve tribes of Israel.[49] This is

---

[47] On which see now J. Bolyki, *Jesus Tischgemeinschaften* (WUNT 2/96; Tübingen: Mohr Siebeck, 1998); E. Rau, *Jesus: Freund von Zöllnern und Sündern. Eine methodenkritische Untersuchung* (Stuttgart: W. Kohlhammer, 2000).

[48] On this, I summarize my article "Jesus and the Twelve," *BBR* 11 (2000): 203–31. For the question of historicity, cf. pp. 205–11; see also J.P. Meier, "The Circle of the Twelve: Did It Exist during Jesus' Public Ministry?" *JBL* 116 (1997): 635–72; J.D.G. Dunn, *Jesus Remembered* (vol. 1 of *Christianity in the Making*; Grand Rapids: Eerdmans, 2003), 507–11.

[49] E.g., J. Jeremias, *New Testament Theology: the Proclamation of Jesus* (trans. J. Bowden; New York:

probably accurate, but there is another theme evoked by the choice of twelve that suggests that Jesus had more in mind than just the renewal of the twelve-tribe nation. The evidence cannot be completely sorted out here, but the following evidence needs to be placed on the table: Genesis 17:20, 21; 35:22-26; Exodus 24:4; Numbers 1:5-16; Deuteronomy 1:22-23; Joshua 4:2, 3, 8-9, 20; 18:24; 19:15; 21:7, 40; Ezra 6:17. That is, the term is used throughout for the ecclesial body of Israel, especially in its covenant formation (e.g., Gen 12; 15; Exod 24:4; esp. Josh 4). When twelve are chosen they represent the nation: Numbers 1:44; 31:5; Deuteronomy 1:23; Joshua 3:12; 4:2. The same ecclesial shape of twelve is found in the Dead Sea Scrolls and the Pseudepigrapha. Thus: 1QS VIII, 1, 2, 3; 1Q28a 11-22; 4Q159 2-4:3-4; 1QM II, 1-3; 11Q19 XVII, 11-14 as well as *T. Abraham* 13:6; *T. Judah* 25:1-2; *T. Benjamin* 10:7. What is noticeable is that twelve is hardly used of Israel as an eschatological body; instead, when twelve is used, it denotes the ecclesial, covenant community to whom God grants redemption.[50]

A thorough study of Jesus and the Twelve (which can't be undertaken here)[51] uncovers the following: (1) the Twelve are somewhat like the twelve representatives of ancient Israel, when twelve functioned as the whole nation; (2) more importantly, Jesus' Twelve shows dramatic parallels with the formation of the nation by Joshua at the Jordan River: it is about covenant renewal and crossing the Jordan and overtaking the land—and one ought to hear resonances of the baptism of Jesus and his mission of the Twelve; (3) there is evidence to think that Jesus was thinking of the reunification of the tribes in the land of Israel; and (4) Jesus' choice of twelve is about the nation of Israel and its restoration. Thus, we are led to think that Jesus may have had Joshua and Joshua's covenant renewal in mind when he chose the Twelve, if we are also led to think that Jesus had the restoration of Israel in mind as well (e.g., Q 22:30).

Q 12:51-53: Micah

A final example comes from Q 12:51-53 (*Gos. Thom.* 10).[52] Again, the response Jesus experiences at the hands of his contemporaries, leading in the previous example to the experience of Moses, now leads—in contrast to Mark 6:10 and Q 10:5-9, and like Mark 6:14 and Q 10:3, 10-12—to the prophecy of Micah, through which we find a "rare glimpse into the inner mind of Jesus."[53] There are

---

Scribner, 1971), 234–35; B.F. Meyer, *The Aims of Jesus* (London: SCM, 1979), 153–54; E.P. Sanders, *Jesus and Judaism* (Philadelphia: Fortress, 1985), 104 *et permulti*.

[50] The term tribe has a similar connotation; cf. McKnight, "Jesus and the Twelve," 218–20.

[51] Ibid., 220–31.

[52] Q 12:52 appears to be a Lukan creation, the numbers explicating Q 12:53.

[53] So Caird, *Luke*, 167. On the history of interpretation, cf. Luz, *Matthew 8–20*, 109–10; see also P. Grelot, "Michée 7,6 dans les évangiles et dans la littérature rabbinique," *Bib* 67 (1986): 363–87.

two elements to this Q logion:[54] a claim by Jesus that his mission is not national peace but instead (certainly apocalyptic) national division/sword, and an appeal to Micah 7:6 as fulfilled in his mission.[55]

There are two plausible contexts for this logion. First, the realization by Jesus that his own family had spurned his mission and vision for Israel (see above on Q 9:61-62). We should not fail to notice the humility he experienced in that rejection (see above on Q 9:58). This logion fits with the earlier Q logia situationally, though the Evangelists do not so connect them. Jesus seems to be splitting families, a theme that does not fit the early Christian depiction of Jesus, lending support to its authenticity.

A second plausible context would be Jesus' reflections on John the Baptist: if the eschatological Elijah is to usher in family peace (Mal 4:6), then Jesus' previous statement to John (that Jesus was not Elijah) could lead Jesus to the conclusion that he has not been destined to bring in that eschatological, family peace. This, too, contrasts with a generalized Christian depiction of Jesus.[56]

These two contexts can be plausibly united: family discord (context one) is a focus of Elijah's mission (context two) in restoring Israel (Mal 4:5-6). Perhaps Jesus' own family's response to him correlates with and sets into context his own and John's debates about identity and mission, as well as correlates with John's decapitation (observe that a sword is involved). This eschatological peace and unity expected in the prophetic corpus, esp. Isaiah 40–55, have failed to materialize; instead, there is family discord of an apocalyptic nature (cf. Amos 5:16; Joel 1:15; 2:1-2, 11, 31; 4 Ezra 6:24; *Jub.* 23:16; 29:13).[57]

How to explain this? Jesus finds in Micah 7:1-7 an answer; the battery of parallels makes that abundantly clear. This doleful, skeptical lament of a depressed (perhaps later redactor of) Micah reflects the prophet's own experience and so is probably not a prophecy.[58] Jesus quotes:

> "[they will be divided:]
> father against son
>   and son against father,

---

[54] Robinson, et al., *Critical Edition of Q*, 376–87, includes 12:49 as probable, excludes 12:50 and 12:52, and includes 12:51, 53.

[55] For the most thorough discussion, see D.C. Allison, Jr., "Q 12:51-53 and Mk 9:11-13 and the Messianic Woes," in *Authenticating the Words of Jesus* (ed. B. Chilton and C.A. Evans; NTTS 28.1; Leiden: E.J. Brill, 1999), 289–310; see also his later summary in Allison, *Intertextual Jesus*, 132–34. See also M. Black, "'Not Peace but a Sword': Matt 10:34ff; Luke 12:51ff," in *Jesus and the Politics of His Day* (ed. E. Bammel and C.F.D. Moule; Cambridge: Cambridge University Press, 1984), 287–94 (apocalyptic, Zealot expectation); O. Betz, "Jesu heiliger Krieg," *NovT* 2 (1958): 116–37.

[56] For how Lukan theology can be synthesized here, cf. Green, *Luke*, 510–11. See also ch. 8, "John the Baptist."

[57] For a defense of the historicity on other grounds, cf. Allison, "Q 12:51-53," 300–306.

[58] See H.W. Wolff, *Micah: A Commentary* (trans. G. Stansell; Minneapolis: Fortress, 1990), 200–10.

> mother against daughter
>> and daughter against mother,
> mother-in-law against her daughter-in-law
>> and daughter-in-law against mother-in-law." (Q 12:52-53)

Jesus finds in rejection of his mission the end of all community, of all national peace, and of all hope for Israel. The system is rotten to the core, from the royal throne (cf. Mic 7:3-4) to the family hearth! Neighbors cannot be trusted (7:5a) and a husband cannot even trust his wife with what he has to say (7:5b). The prophet, however, not undone by chaos, asserts his trust in God (7:7; cf. Pss 31:14; 55:16-17). This text was understood eschatologically as the social condition of the time just before the messianic woes (cf. Mal 4:6; *Tg. Micah* adds "in that time" at 7:6; 4 Ezra 5:9 arm[?]; *Jub.* 23:19; *Sib. Or.* 8:84; 1Q14 17-18 on VI, 14-15;[59] *m. Soṭah* 9:15; *b. Sanh.* 97a), and Jesus apparently draws upon this interpretive tradition (Q 12:51-53; cf. the later Mark 13:12). From Micah 7:7 Jesus may have taken his encouragement to wait (cf. Mark 13:13).

A final thought of an eschatological nature: if Malachi 4:6 [3:24] (Elijah's restoration of families) echoes Micah 7:6—and I think it does—a clearer vision is attainable. First, Elijah's mission is to bring peace and reverse the family chaos of Micah; second, Jesus denies that he brings peace (cf. Jer 8:8-13; 28:9; Dan 12:1) and has, in fact, experienced the family discord (see above); third, this means that Jesus is not Elijah and, thus, the logion belongs to a period in his life after he has come to the conclusion that John was Elijah (and probably after the latter's death). Instead of being Elijah, Jesus is more like Micah.[60]

Micah's role for Jesus is difficult to define, but he is at least a mediator (Mic 7:2, 5, 7). H.W. Wolff thought the prophetic figure of Micah 7 was a forerunner of the righteous sufferer whose suffering atones.[61] Perhaps it is from reflecting on Micah's life that Jesus came to the conclusion that from the time of John forward there would be a time of tribulation (Q 16:16). His own commitment to his Father's will would lead him to face that Final Ordeal and would lead him to death.

If the eschatological fulfillment theme is thought too speculative, another line of thinking may be considered: Jesus may see Micah as a figure (a type, if you will) anticipating his own life. As Micah found chaotic family disintegration and mourned over the lack of the righteous, so Jesus may have seen in the rejection of his own family a reenactment of Micah's experience as a prophet of God. Once again, Micah's words are not a prophecy but an interpretation of current affairs. Jesus' words, apart from the future tense of the words in Q 12:52 (and

---

[59] This is slightly confirmed by 1Q14 [Micah Pesher] 17-18, line 5: "[Its interpretation] concerns the last generations . . ." in that this text, in close proximity of Micah 7, finds signs of the last days.
[60] Allison, "Q 12:51-53," brings in Elijah but does not see the connection of John with Elijah and therefore the foundation for Jesus' use of Micah 7:6.
[61] Wolff, *Micah*, 210.

the verse is difficult to assign to Q), are a statement of what is happening even now. Because Jesus sees the same situation occurring now, at his own expense, he sees the words of Micah reenacted.

CONCLUSION

Jesus finds in the Tanakh of Israel a script for his own life, for his identity, for his mission, for his perception of his own contemporaries and their responses to him, and for how to explain that opposition. There can be no question that Jesus sought answers to his own life in the Tanakh. This premise for him cannot go unobserved in historical Jesus scholarship: we can make the observation that whatever situation Jesus found himself in he would understood it in the light of sacred Scriptures. Jesus was a Scripture prophet, someone who found his own life in the pages of Holy Writ.

In particular, Jesus found in an exegetical tradition based on Psalm 8:4 a prototype of his own humiliation, opposition, and potential suffering: as the Son of man is humble, so he finds strength in his own humiliation. He found in Elijah's calling of Elisha (1 Kgs 19:19-21) a prototype of his own calling of his followers, with one notable exception: Jesus permits no delay, because of the urgency of the hour. He finds in the response of the magicians of Pharaoh to Moses a prototype of how his opponents have responded to him (Exod 8:19). Again, Jesus offers a significant shift: if it were the magicians who announced that Moses' and Aaron's actions were of divine origin, Jesus himself declares that his actions are of divine origin. Along the same line, the action of Joshua in forming a new covenant people becomes the prototype for Jesus to structure his own set of followers (Josh 3–4).

And, in the fundamental link we have observed time and again between Jesus and John, Jesus and John evidently debated about who was Elijah. Jesus had found in Micah himself a pattern to understand family opposition, and this is confirmed in a connection between John and Micah. However John came out on that issue, Jesus had come to the firm resolve that it was John (now dead) who was Elijah—though destined to bring peace, the Roman leaders had put him away (Mic 7:6 *and* Mal 4:6). Jesus has come to terms with his own mission and his own identity: he was not Elijah and his mission was not to restore peace to the land. He was more like Micah. Indeed, his mission was to trigger the Final Ordeal.

Jesus worked his way from his own experience and situation into the Tanakh and found providential designs for the structure and substance of his life, including how to understand opposition and the lurking reality of a premature death. If this dimension of the story of Jesus' life coheres with the clear evidence, then we can say that Jesus clearly found in the Tanakh the exegetical tools with which to make sense of his own life. If it is almost certain that Jesus would have comprehended from the fate of John a similar fate for himself, it is also almost certain that he would have gone to the Tanakh to understand that fate. The evidence cited above, and other evidence that could be summoned to support those claims, reveals that this is what he did.

In each of these four examples Jesus finds in the Scriptures a script for his own life. Jesus does not fully identify himself with any of these figures: he is both like and unlike each (Son of man, Elijah, Moses, Joshua, and Micah). But from each he finds a pattern sufficient to guide his own life. Notably, none of these is concerned explicitly with his death, though *tribulation* and *opposition* emerge in nearly every one of these figures in the Tanakh. Since death is the likely outcome of that opposition, and since John's own life led to a premature death, we must say that a premature death is likely a part of his own self-awareness. In fact, we can say that the combination of John's death, opposition to Jesus—beginning at home—conviction that he was headed for the Final Ordeal, and a clear conviction that he would die prematurely led Jesus to the Tanakh. In other words, we have credible evidence that Jesus went to the Tanakh to discover what role his death might play in his mission.

This broaches another question: Did Jesus search out Isaiah's marvelous poetry and vision, including the so-called Servant Songs, to get a grip on his premature death? Once again, we are searching for evidence that confirms or denies whether or not Jesus said "a ransom for many" in Mark 10:45. We have established that Jesus appealed to the Tanakh to find categories to understand his own life. We ask if his appeal landed upon any texts in the Tanakh that suggest that Jesus considered his death a ransom. The most commonly appealed to text is found in Isaiah 52–53, and it is to discover if Jesus appealed to that text that we now turn.

Chapter 10

Jesus and the Servant

It has been established that Jesus thought he would die prematurely, that it was part of God's providence, that he was like other prophets who met a similar fate, that this death was part of the Final Ordeal. And, we have also discovered that Jesus found his life and his patterns in various heroic figures of the Tanakh. We have argued also that from the time of John's death forward, Jesus knew he could meet a similar end and that he went to the Tanakh in search of a hermeneutical grid to understand his premature death.

This leaves an age-old question for Jesus scholarship: did Jesus see his life inscripturated in the Servant of Isaiah who emerges in at least four song-like passages?[1] The Qumran *Isaiah Scroll* of 52:13–53:12 reveals enough variation to

---

[1] I cannot enter here into a discussion of the original meaning of servant: Was it pre-Isaian, Isaian, or Deutero-Isaian? Was it inserted into the text by Deutero-Isaiah's students? Was it a referent with its own complicated evolution? Did Servant refer to a corporate body [Israel, the remnant] or to an individual? Did the Christian interpretation radically alter the coordinates of the fourth Servant Song? Four major views of the identity of the Servant have been espoused: (1) a historical individual, e.g., Cyrus; (2) an autobiographical reference to the author of Deutero-Isaiah or Trito-Isaiah; (3) a collective reference, either to the empirical Israel or to the Ideal Israel/Remnant; and (4) a prediction of the eschatological Messiah. Alongside this view, of course, is how the Servant Songs have been appropriated in the Christian history of exegesis.

For discussion, the following are noteworthy: C.R. North, *The Suffering Servant in Deutero-Isaiah* (2d ed.; London: Oxford University Press, 1956); H.W. Wolff, *Jesaja 53 im Urchristentum* (2d ed.; Berlin: Evangelische Verlagsanstalt 1950); H.W. Robinson, *The Cross in the Old Testament* (Philadelphia: Westminster, 1955), 55–114; W. Zimmerli and J. Jeremias, *The Servant of God* (trans. H. Knight, et al.; SBT 20; Naperville: Alec R. Allenson, 1957); H.H. Rowley, *The Servant of the Lord and Other Essays on the Old Testament* (London: Lutterworth, 1952), 1–88 [two essays: survey of scholarship and exploration of the relationship of servant to David Messiah]; H.G.M. Williamson, *Variations on a Theme* (The Didsbury Lectures 1997; Carlisle: Paternoster, 1998); G.P. Hugenberger, "The Servant of the Lord in the 'Servant Songs' of Isaiah," in *The Lord's Anointed* (ed. P.E. Satterthwaite, et al.; Grand Rapids: Baker, 1995), 105–39 [a Mosaic rendering of the

assert that an individual reading of at least one of those songs is now entirely plausible on historical grounds.[2] Did Jesus think of himself in terms of the Servant of Isaiah? Thinking of himself in terms of the Servant of Isaiah from one section of Isaiah, however, does not necessitate that he embraced the entire Servant picture of Isaiah as an image of himself, or that his appeals to that tradition meant he saw his death in terms of the Servant. Nor should we be unaware of the Christian tradition, which as Peter Stuhlmacher has shown, nearly stands the Servant image on its head and turns it into a cipher for Jesus Christ.[3] Each element requires clear evidence.

Servant]; W.H. Bellinger, Jr. and W.R. Farmer, eds., *Jesus and the Suffering Servant* (Harrisburg: Trinity Press International, 1998 [important essays on the Isaianic texts by a variety of scholars]; a recent analysis, a socio-rhetorical approach, is A.R. Ceresko, "The Rhetorical Strategy of the Fourth Servant Song (Isaiah 52:13-53:12)," *CBQ* 56 (1994): 42–55; B. Janowski, "Er trug unsere Sünden," in *Der leidende Gottesknecht* (ed. B. Janowski and P. Stuhlmacher; FAT 14; Tübingen: Mohr Siebeck, 1996), 27–48; and, in the same volume, the intense study of M. Hengel, "Zur Wirkungsgeschichte von Jes 53 in vorchristlicher Zeit," 49–91; C. Markschies, "Der Mensch Jesus Christus im Angesicht Gottes," 197–248; H.-J. Hermisson, "Gottesknecht und Gottes Knechte," in *Frühes Christentum* (ed. Lichtenberger; vol. 1 of *Geschichte–Tradition– Reflexion* [ed. Cancik, Lictenberger, and Schäfer; Tübingen: Mohr Siebeck, 1996]), 1:43–68.

In the history of New Testament scholarship, an early warning about an unreflective, casual appeal to Isaiah's Servant was issued by H.J. Cadbury, but it was not for some decades and in England that the warning was heard in the works of C.K. Barrett and M.D. Hooker. See the piece by the editors titled "Christology," in *The Acts of the Apostles* (ed. F.J. Foakes Jackson and K. Lake), 1:384–92; see H.J.Cadbury, "The Titles for Jesus in Acts," in *Acts of the Apostles* (ed. Foakes Jackson and Lake), 5:364–70.

The bibliography on Jesus and the servant is immense. I mention only the following: Wolff, *Jesaja 53 im Urchristentum*; M.D. Hooker, *Jesus and the Servant* (London: SPCK, 1959); R.T. France, *Jesus and the Old Testament* (London: Tyndale, 1971); Belllinger and Farmer, *Jesus and the Suffering Servant*; O. Betz, "Jesus und Jesaja 53," in *Frühes Christentum* (ed. Lichtenberger), 3:3–19; in the same volume, H.-J. Hermisson, "Gottesknechte und Gottes Knechte," 43–68. Betz follows his study up with an English, revised version in "Jesus and Isaiah 53," in *Jesus and the Suffering Servant* (ed. Bellinger and Farmer), 70–87; in the same volume he receives a response by Hooker, "Did the Use of Isaiah 53 to Interpret his Mission Begin with Jesus?" 88–103. The study of Rikki Watts, in itself quite valuable, is of less value for this study because its concern is with Mark's Gospel: see in the same volume "Jesus' Death, Isaiah 53, and Mark 10:45: A Crux Revisited," 125–51. See also J.D.G. Dunn, *Jesus Remembered* (vol. 1 of *Christianity in the Making*; Grand Rapids: Eerdmans, 2003), 809–18.

Recent commentaries also carry the discussion forward: see the speculative approach of J.D.W. Watts, *Isaiah 34–66* (WBC 25; Waco, Texas: Word, 1987), esp. 115–18, with relevant passages as well (Israel; Persian rulers, esp. Darius; and believing, obedient worshipers in YHWH's new city; the sufferer of the fourth song is Zerubbabel); also, see the canonical and theological approach in B.S. Childs, *Isaiah* (OTL; Louisville: Westminster John Knox, 2001), esp. 40–23.

[2] See the translation of M. Wise, M. Abegg Jr., and E. Cook, *The Dead Sea Scrolls* (San Francisco: HarperSanFrancisco, 1996), 358–60.

[3] See P. Stuhlmacher, "Jes 53 in den Evangelien und in der Apostelgeschichte," in *Der leidende Gottesknecht* (ed. Janowski and Stuhlmacher), 93–127, here p. 127: "Jesus Christus in seiner Person und in seinem Werk wird also nicht bloß und auch nicht primär durch Jes 53 ausgelegt, sonder *er selbst* legt Jes 53 aus." He suggests that Isaiah 53 becomes a new text at the hand of Christian interpretation.

Another methodological point is this: Jesus, on nearly every count, anchored the shape and the tone of his ministry in Isaiah 40–66. This argument has been made plausible by the German veteran Otto Betz, who concentrates especially on the term *gospel*, and in the complete study of Jesus by the British exegetical theologian N.T. Wright, as well as in the study of Rikki Watts. It is beyond our scope to detail the evidence here, but the point deserves to be made and needs to be given full consideration: to the degree that Jesus' teachings, ministry, and mission are rooted in the great Isaian traditions (40–55 or 40–66), to that same degree we can say that Servant imagery is thereby incorporated into that same teaching, ministry, and mission.[4] Jews of the first century didn't invade texts like these, excerpt a favorite portion, and then forget forever its larger contexts.

Similarly, a grey-bearded British tradition claims that Jesus was the first to combine a royal, Davidic vocation with the Servant of Isaiah.[5] In fact, there is the astonishing fact that Jesus, who thought of himself in royal terms and envisioned himself as head of an imminent kingdom—what else can kingdom language evoke?—did not shrink from death. This hermeneutical tradition explains the evocation of both images (David *and* Servant) by appealing to Jesus' need for scriptural warrant, and the most plausible set of Scriptures (it argues) must be those emerging from the servant texts of Deutero-Isaiah (without forgetting their cousin, Isa 61:1-9).[6] Can this connection of royal and servant imagery be demonstrated with sufficient force?

---

[4] See Betz, "Jesus and Jesaja 53," in *Frühes Christentum* (ed. Lichtenberg); N.T. Wright, *Jesus and the Victory of God* (vol. 2 of *Christian Origins and the Question of God*; Minneapolis: Fortress, 1996), 588–91; Watts, "Jesus' Death and Mark 10:45," in *Jesus and the Suffering Servant* (ed. Bellinger and Farmer). See also "H.-J. Hermisson, "Das vierte Gottesknechtslied im deuterojesajanischen Kontext," in *Der leidende Gottesknecht* (ed. Janowski and Stuhlmacher), 1–25.

[5] E.g., the combination was considered central by T.W. Manson, *The Servant-Messiah* (Cambridge: Cambridge University Press, 1953), 50–64; Robinson, *The Cross in the Old Testament*, 80; *Redemption and Revelation in the Actuality of History* (New York: Harper, 1942), 199; North, *Suffering Servant in Deutero-Isaiah*, 24–25; F.F. Bruce, *The New Testament Development of Old Testament Themes* (Grand Rapids: Eerdmans, 1969), 83–99; M. Black, "The 'Son of Man' Passion Sayings in the Gospel Tradition," *ZNW* 60 (1969): 1–8; G.B. Caird, *New Testament Theology* (ed. L.D. Hurst; Oxford: Clarendon, 1994), 310–16; Wright, *Jesus and the Victory of God*, chs. 11, 12.

An echo of this view may be found in Peter Stuhlmacher, and other German scholars, who think Jesus modified the Son of man expectation by combining it with the servant theme; cf. his "Vicariously Giving His Life for Many, Mark 10:45 (Matthew 20:28)," in his *Reconciliation, Law, & Righteousness* (trans. E. Kalin; Philadelphia: Fortress, 1986), 16–29, esp. 24–26; see the earlier studies of O. Cullmann, *The Christology of the New Testament* (trans. S.C. Guthrie and C.A.M. Hall; Philadelphia: Westminster, 1963), 65, 158; L. Goppelt, *Theology of the New Testament* (ed. J. Roloff; trans. J.E. Alsup; 2 vols.; 1975; repr. Grand Rapids: Eerdmans, 1981), 1:190–93.

[6] I list here only the names of the scholars. In favor: T.W. Manson, C.H. Dodd, G.B. Caird, R.T. France, D.J. Moo, P. Stuhlmacher, O. Cullmann, V. Taylor. Against: C.K. Barrett, M.D. Hooker, M. de Jonge, E. Schweizer.

There are five texts in the Jesus traditions that can be plausibly connected to the servant figure of Deutero-Isaiah, and to these we now turn.[7] We do so with less concern for historicity than for an Isaianic allusion, for if the latter is not proven the former is unimportant.

MARK 9:9-13[8]

Jesus has come to terms with the scriptural basis of his mission: he is not Elijah, but John is Elijah; Jesus is more like Micah. This discussion between Jesus and John over their scripturally based role in history is deeply embedded in the fabric of Jesus' life. The factor leading to clear delineations in roles, as we have seen, is the reality of John's death and the potentiality of his own suffering. To explain his own suffering, Jesus connects his experience to the Final Ordeal, the outbreak of evil and violence just prior to the arrival of the kingdom. The scribes, so say the followers of Jesus, think Elijah must first come.[9] Everyone is looking for Elijah, for he is a figure connected to the tribulation of the last days (e.g., Mal 4:5-6 [cf. LXX at 3:22-23]; 4 *Ezra* 6:26; Sir 48:10; *Sib. Or.* 2:187–88; 4Q521 1 III, 1; 4Q558 1 II, 4; Luke 1:17; John 1:21, 25; Rev 11:1-13; *m. Soṭah* 9:15). Jesus affirms such an eschatology: "To be sure Elijah must come first to restore all things." But, Jesus also asks, "If Elijah brings a restoration, how then is it written about the Son of man, that he is to go through many sufferings and be treated with contempt?" (Mark 9:12).[10] How, he asks, do we combine expectation of restoration (restoring the fortunes of Israel) and suffering?

---

[7] See Hooker, *Jesus and the Servant*, 62–102, for the most complete analysis of the evidence. Of her approximately forty possible allusions and citations, I consider only five that have stronger merit: Mark 1:11 pars.; 3:27 pars.; 9:9-13 pars.; 10:45 pars.; 14:24 pars; Luke 4:16-21 pars. with Q 7:22. I will examine Mark 10:45 later in this chapter and Mark 14:24 in the next chapter.

[8] For discussions, cf. J.A.T. Robinson, "Elijah, John and Jesus," in his *Twelve New Testament Studies*, 28–52; J. Taylor, "The Coming of Elijah, Mt 17, 10-13 and Mk 9, 11-13: The Development of the Texts," *RB* 98 (1991): 10–19; M. Casey, *Aramaic Sources of Mark's Gospel* (SNTSMS 102; Cambridge: Cambridge University Press, 1998), 111–37; S. Bryan, *Jesus and Israel's Traditions of Judgement and Restoration* (SNTSMS 117; Cambridge: Cambridge University Press, 2002), 88–110. See also the older view of V. Taylor, *Jesus and His Sacrifice* (1937; repr. London: Macmillan, 1955), 92–93; *Mark*, 393–95. For modern commentaries, see Pesch, *Markusevangelium*, 2:69–84; Davies and Allison, *Matthew*, 2:711–12; Gundry, *Mark*, 485. B.J. Pitre, "The Historical Jesus, the Great Tribulation and the End of the Exile," Ph.D. diss. (Notre Dame, 2004), 206–34, who draws out a connection of John's death to the tribulation.

[9] On the Elijah expectation, see the discussion of M.M. Faierstein, "Why Do the Scribes Say that Elijah Must Come First?" *JBL* 100 (1981): 75–86; J. Fitzmyer, "More about Elijah Coming First," *JBL* 104 (1985): 295–96; D.C. Allison, Jr., "'Elijah Must Come First,'" *JBL* 103 (1984): 256–58. On *first*, the implication is either to Elijah coming first, that is before either the "coming of the Day of YHWH" (Mal 3:22-23) or before the kingdom itself (Mark 9:1).

[10] I leave aside the debate about the authenticity of Mark 9:12b since our concern is whether or not Mark 9:12b reflects Servant Christology. A discussion of authenticity can be postponed until a positive case can be presented. I am not persuaded that Mark 9:12a and 12b identify Elijah and the Son of man. Rather, the two are mildly adversative: Elijah is to bring a restoration *but* the Son

This is no small concern of Jesus. The lines in this discussion are clearly drawn: it is about *how* the eschatological conditions arrive.[11] Jesus sees two notable features about the coming of the kingdom and queries his followers (presumably) about their view of the relationship of (1) the eschatological restoration—either as the coming of the Messiah or, what is more likely, the coming of YHWH,[12] and (2) the sufferings detailed in the prophet Daniel. In particular, so the focus of these words would seem to be, which comes first: Elijah's restoration (thus, Mal 3–4) or the suffering of the Son of man (thus, Daniel 7)?[13]

The Elijah debate between John and Jesus provides firm ground into which we can anchor these words in the life of Jesus. In fact, what was believed about John—that he was Elijah and that he would restore all things—did not come true. In fact, just the opposite: "they did to him whatever they pleased" (Mark 9:13). Thus, the logic of some that the Elijah material is an early Christian fiction creates its own problem:[14] the early church would have to have invented something (John was Elijah; a precursor to the Messiah) only to discover that the figure it chose didn't really fit the evidence (John doesn't fit what Malachi said). It is much more likely that the evidence about Jesus, John, and Elijah is to be explained as a discussion between the two historical figures than that the early church invented the material ex nihilo.[15]

Turning back to the narrative, Jesus now connects the notion about John and Elijah's restoration to the Son of man and sufferings. That is, according to Jesus and an old tradition,[16] the restoration of Israel is preceded by a time of suffering.[17] First, the Final Ordeal; then, the kingdom.

Materially, what Jesus says here coheres with what we argued above: Q 12:51–53 affirms that Jesus is not Elijah; Jesus is connected with the Final Ordeal in that context. Thus, he can expect to see suffering in his days, and suffering fills in what Jesus means when he says he did not come to bring peace but instead a sword.[18] For Jesus, suffering precedes the restoration of all things.

---

of man will suffer. How do these two predictions coalesce? That, at least, is how I understand Mark 9:12.

[11] On this, cf. Keener, *Matthew*, 439–40, n.122.

[12] See Bryan, *Jesus and Israel's Traditions*, 98–101.

[13] It is not true, as some have maintained, that for the Son of man to carry overtones of suffering it must have been glossed with the image of the Servant of Isaiah (so Taylor, *Jesus and His Sacrifice*, 94); the Son of man, when properly studied, can carry this theme as well (so Hooker, *Jesus and the Servant*). Casey's relentless polemically driven approach to Mark 9:11-13 in his *Aramaic Sources of Mark's Gospel*, 111–37, has been answered in the brief, but incisive, note of Bryan, *Jesus and Israel's Traditions*, 109, n.70.

[14] See R.W. Funk, et al., *The Five Gospels* (New York: Macmillan, 1993), 82–82[??].

[15] See ch. 8, under "John the Baptist."

[16] See D.C. Allison, Jr., *The End of the Ages Has Come* (Philadelphia: Fortress, 1985), 6–19, surveys the evidence, demonstrating the diversity of Jewish thinking on the tribulation.

[17] So Bryan, *Jesus and Israel's Traditions*, 101–11.

[18] On authenticity, see D.C. Allison, Jr., "Q 12:51-53 and Mark 9:11-13 and the Messianic Woes,"

Furthermore, the humble "Son of man" of Mark 9:12, whom most tend to think
is an appeal to the Son of man of Daniel 7, could perhaps be connected to the
bedrock Q tradition noted above: Q 9:58, where Jesus sees Psalm 8:4 as a script
for his life. In either case, the Son of man is a collective: Jesus the representative
and his followers are this Son of man. But it is the two expressions that follow
that concern us now: *many sufferings* and *treated with contempt*.

What is the source for these expressions? Are there any specific passages in
mind when Jesus says "many sufferings" (*polla pathe*) and "treated with contempt" (*exoudenthe*)? We begin with the four themes of Mark 9:9-13: (1) Son of
man; (2) resurrection; (3) Elijah; (4) suffering. We have here a tall order since
no text in the Tanakh connects each of these four themes. Son of man makes
one think of texts like Psalm 8 or Daniel 7. Resurrection probably recalls Daniel
12:1-2, though it could be connected to Isaiah 26:16-19 or even less likely to
Ezekiel 37. The figure Elijah most likely suggests Malachi 3–4 while suffering
many things, as well as treated with contempt, leads one to the fourth Servant
Song (Isa 52:13–53:12) or perhaps to one of the Psalms (22; 80; 118). Since
Elijah is peripheral to our saying, and Jesus in fact is contrasting his mission with
that of Elijah, we can limit the themes to the other three. Which text, if any, is
uppermost in Jesus' mind?

At the thematic level, the evidence is a toss-up. We can begin with Daniel.
Daniel is certainly a quarry for Jesus' use of "Son of man," but in Daniel 7 the
Son of man is not only an eschatological figure but one who receives authority
and glory after a time of suffering (7:21-22). In favor of Daniel is the coherence
of the theme of resurrection (12:1-2; cf. Mark 9:9-10) and it could be that Jesus
is thinking of that very Son of man as a prototype of his own life, but *only after*
he has suffered. Though often neglected and sometimes perhaps overvalued,
there is suffering in Daniel: (1) Daniel 7:21-22 shows that the saints were persecuted but then vindicated (cf. 7:25); (2) Daniel 11 records the battles of the
north and the south against one another, with the land of Israel suffering as a
buffer zone. Antiochus' second campaign to Egypt results in his defeat by Rome
(here "Kittim"; 11:30). Antiochus reacts in rage against Jerusalem, its inhabitants, its holy place, and its covenant (11:30-35); its leaders will "fall by sword
and flame, and suffer captivity and plunder" (11:33). But, the apocalyptist
writes, "Some of the wise shall fall, so that they may be refined, purified, and
cleansed, until the time of the end" (11:35). Those "wise" are said to be raised
as well (12:1-3). We have in Daniel, then, a plausible setting: we have Son of
man, resurrection, and suffering.

What of Isaiah? Unquestionably, the critical theme of suffering is detailed
in Isaiah 52:13–53:12 in a manner otherwise unparalleled in the Tanakh. One
cannot think of this servant without thinking of suffering many things—a
marred appearance (52:14), despised and rejected (53:3), considered struck

---

in *Authenticating the Words of Jesus* (ed. B. Chilton and C.A. Evans; NTTS 28.1; Leiden: E.J. Brill,
1999), 289–310, here pp. 306–10.

down by God (53:4), wounded and crushed (53:5), oppressed and afflicted (53:7), cut off through injustice (53:8), buried with the wicked (53:9), crushed by God (53:10)—but his death was overturned by God's will (53:10-12). There is obviously no Son of man reference here, but the theme of resurrection is possibly glimpsed in the servant's vindication: he will startle many nations (52:15); in spite of his death, he will see his offspring and prolong his days (53:10); he will see light (53:11), will find satisfaction (53:11b), will be assigned to the lot of the righteous (53:12), and will divide the spoil with the strong (53:12b). This may not be directly resurrection language, but it broaches the topic of final vindication. And, Isaiah 26:16-19 is a text in the same prophetic book that does broach resurrection (and is behind Daniel 12:1-2).

Possibly behind Mark 9:12 are the Psalms. At Psalm 22:6, a psalm considered behind Jesus' own perceptions at times, we find this same term: "despised by the people" (LXX 21:7: ἐχουδένημα λαοῦ; MT: עָם וּבְזוּי). This psalm shares only this one term, clearly no commonplace, with our logion. However, the general themes of suffering and resurrection are both present in this psalm. The psalmist prays for deliverance (22:19-21), and counts on God's deliverance (22:24) and vindication (22:25-31). At times the language here is not unlike Isaiah 53.[19]

Acts 4:11 has the same Greek verb, ὁ ἐχουθενηθείς, as a translation of Psalm 118:22, and that verb appears in Mark 9:12 (diff. Matt 17:12b). It is possible, therefore, that Psalm 118 lies behind the saying of Jesus—as it is apparently, at some level, behind the passion predictions (cf. ch. 11 below) and the parable of the wicked vinedressers (Mark 12:10-11 pars.). That Psalm focuses on vindication and deliverance at the hand of God, and it seems likely to me that Psalm 118 was a text in which Jesus saw his own fate inscripturated. But, Psalm 118 is more remote from Mark 9:12 than the other three, even if it does have connections to Jesus' life (cf. Ps 22:22, 26). Obviously, *Son of man* is absent as also is *suffer many things*; vindication can be broadly understood within the more specific category of resurrection, and of course, Elijah does not figure in this psalm. But, the general thrust of Psalm 118 is not unlike the general thrust of our passage—general thematics, however, are not concrete enough to tip the balance in favor of this passage.

An interesting collocation of terms and themes can also be seen in Psalm 89:38-39 where the "anointed one" is "rejected" (וְאַתָּה זָנַחְתָּ וַתִּמְאָס הִתְעַבַּרְתָּ שִׁיחֶךָ). This context fits the theme of suffering, though the themes of Elijah, Son of man and resurrection are not present. However, the orientation of this chapter would fit more the theme of God's rejection of his anointed rather than the people's rejection, and the psalm is a cry of a royal figure who seeks restoration (cf. Ps 89:38-51). If this psalm is behind Jesus' saying, he is emphasizing that his death is destined in God's plans.

---

[19] Acts 4:11 has the same Greek verb, ὁ ἐχουθενηθείς, as a translation of Psalm 118:22. It is possible, therefore, that Psalm 118 lies behind the saying of Jesus. That psalm focuses on vindication.

The sayings of Jesus behind Mark 9:9-13 share broad thematic relations with both Daniel 7 and 11–12, as well as with Isaiah 52:13–53:12; the connections to the various Psalms show some potential as well. Furthermore, at a broader level, two of these textual complexes played a more important role in the life of Jesus: both Daniel 7 and Isaiah 40–55. The specific terms *suffer many things* and *treat with contempt* are not found in either Daniel 7 or Isaiah's fourth Servant Song (though Malachi shows parallels to the latter term: 1:7, 12; 2:9).

However, some have argued that the Greek term of Mark 9:12, ἐξουδενηθῇ ("treat with contempt"), is the natural translation at Isaiah 53:3 of the Hebrew נִבְזֶה (*nibezeh*, niph. of *bzh*, "to despise").[20] We should look at this evidence more carefully since, if one can determine with confidence that the Greek term translates *bazah* and the Hebrew term occurs at Isaiah 49:7 and twice in 53:3, we would have an indicator that Jesus had the Servant in mind.

The Hebrew term *bazah* (and morphological variations) is behind several Greek terms that translate it:

(1) ἀτιμάζειν (e.g., Isa 53:3);
(2) ἐξατιμάζειν (e.g., 1 Kgs 17:42);
(3) ἐξουδενεῖν, ἐξουδενοῦν, ἐξουδένημα, κ.τ.λ., with variant spellings (e.g., Aquila at Isa 53:3; Symmachus twice at Isa 53:3; Theodotion at Isa 53:3; otherwise, e.g., Amos 6:1; Mal 2:9);
(4) καταφρονεῖν (e.g., Prov 19:16);
(5) μυκτηρίζειν (e.g., Prov 15:20);
(6) φαυλίζειν (e.g., Isa 49:7);
(7) ἀπαναίνεσθαι (e.g., Sir 6:23);
(8) ἀλισγεῖν (e.g., Mal 1:7).

At least twenty times the Hebrew *bzh* root is translated with ἐξουδεν–. Furthermore, since Aquila, Symmachus, and Theodotion each translate Isaiah 53:3 with the term now found in Mark 9:12, we are on even more solid ground. Because the themes of Mark 9:9-13 correlate with the themes of Isaiah 52:13–53:12, we should cautiously conclude that the term ἐξουδενθῇ at Mark 9:12 can plausibly be connected with the Servant passage. The oddity of this term as well as the need to find an OT text in which to anchor it each point us in the same direction. One can say, rather cautiously, that scholars have generally endorsed this conclusion.[21]

---

[20] So France, *Jesus and the Old Testament*, 123–24; on the term, cf. M. Görg, "*bazah*," *TDOT* 2:60–65.

[21] E.g., B. Lindars, *New Testament Apologetic* (London: SCM, 1961), 81; C.H. Dodd, *According to the Scriptures* (London: Nisbet, 1952), 92–93, n. 2; Taylor, *Jesus and His Sacrifice*, 91–97: "it is hypercriticism to doubt that this Scripture [Isa. 53] is in mind" (97). Pesch, *Markusevangelium*, 2:79, connects the term mostly with Psalms 89:39; and 22:6, 25; 69:33; 118:22, as well as with Isaiah 53—he sees the pre-Markan passion narrative mixing Son of man, the fate of the suffering righteous one, the Servant of God, as well as the eschatological prophet.

It is my judgment that Mark 9:12 contains a possible allusion to the Servant Song of Isaiah. The absence of Son of man is significant, and the presence of the term *contempt* at Psalm 22:6, the interesting parallels at Psalm 89, and the early Christian rendering of Psalm 118:22, in a context of not dissimilar themes, leaves one with the impression that Jesus may have been alluding to several texts or, more likely, he had derived from several Scriptures the notion that he would have to suffer, as many of God's chosen messengers had suffered.

Whether he was thinking of any one text is neither necessary nor sure. He could have in mind the righteous sufferer of Psalm 22, the anointed one of Psalm 89:38-51, the rejected stone at Psalm 118:22, the Suffering Servant of Isaiah 52:13–53:12, or an extended perception of the Son of man in Daniel 7 (cf. chs. 11; 12:1-3). If I had to choose one, I would opt for the fourth Servant Song because of the various Greek versions of Isaiah 53:3 in a context where all but the Son of man appear. It should be remembered, however, that Daniel is not an implausible context for all but the Elijah theme of Mark 9:9-13. Dogmatism is unwarranted here,[22] and other evidence will need to be examined to render a confident judgment on whether or not Jesus found in the Servant an image to whom he could relate.

LUKE 22:35-38

Mark 9:12 is a "Son of man" saying, not a "Servant" saying. And it is precisely the Son of man expression of Mark 9:12 that diverts the interpreter's attention away from Isaiah 52:13–53:12: if the Son of man is not present, we are led more immediately to the fourth Servant Song or to one of the psalms. Our next text, Luke 22:37, is less comprehensive in theme but more explicit in quotation.

The pericope of the two swords has no plausible context among early Christians,[23] conflicts with the general pacifistic stance Jesus seemed to have taken (e.g., Mark 8:34-38 pars.; 12:13-17 pars; Matt 5:9, 39, 43-48; 26:52; cf. Luke 3:14-15),[24] demonstrates an urgency as intense as one finds in the Jesus

---

[22] So also D.J. Moo, *The Old Testament in the Gospel Passion Narratives* (Sheffield: Almond, 1983), 89–91.

[23] There is an absence of Lukan vocabulary in the substance of our concern: cf. Fitzmyer, *Luke*, 2:1429.

[24] There is much good bibliography on this theme, but the foundational argument has been presented by J.H. Yoder, *The Politics of Jesus* (2d ed.; Grand Rapids: Eerdmans, 1994); recent Jesus books along this line are E. Bammel and C.F.D. Moule, eds., *Jesus and the Politics of His Day* (Cambridge: Cambridge University Press, 1984); M. Borg, *Jesus: A New Vision* (San Francisco: Harper & Row, 1988), 137–41; Wright, *Jesus and the Victory of God*; for an alternative view, see R.A. Horsley, *Jesus and the Spiral of Violence* (San Francisco: Harper & Row, 1987); the older views, which build to some degree on our text, are S.G.F. Brandon, *Jesus and the Zealots* (Manchester: Manchester University Press, 1967); G.W. Buchanan, *Jesus: The King and His Kingdom* (Macon, Ga.: Mercer University Press, 1984); these two studies were set in context by M. Hengel, *The Zealots* (trans. D. Smith; Edinburgh: T&T Clark, 1989).

traditions (22:36: "But now"), but was not fulfilled—if it expects the onset of
the Final Ordeal—and slides rather quietly into the sheath of the last evening
with his disciples (Mark 14:43-52 pars., with Matt 26:52).[25] The connection to
a secure event in the life of Jesus, the sending out of his followers to proclaim
the kingdom (cf. Luke 22:35-36 with Q 10:1-12[26] and Mark 6:9-13 pars.) without care for provisions, is now reversed: now his followers will need a purse, a
bag, and a sword—the latter so important his followers will have to sell the cloak
to buy one! In general, then, one must say the pericope is an oddity among the
Jesus traditions, which counts more *for* its authenticity than against it.

In this context, Jesus states that his imminent fate is a divine necessity (Luke
22:37) and quotes Isaiah 53:12: "and he was counted among the lawless." The
quotation from memory, seen in traces of connection to the Hebrew and LXX,[27]
can only be explained as integral to the context *if* the eschatological urgency of
Luke 22:36 ("but now") means that the days of peaceful proclamation are over:
"The authorities are on our case, and I am about to be arrested." The absence of
peace requires a sword. When the disciples claim to have two swords, Jesus says,
"It is enough."[28]

We need to pause to consider the role the Final Ordeal has played in the discussion so far: Jesus, from the days of John's death onwards, began to think of
his own fate. He connected his own fate with the Final Ordeal. And now, so the
text seems to imply, that moment has arrived. The imminency of the eschatology is unmistakable.

Two fundamentally different meanings can be derived from the use of Isaiah
53:12.[29] Either Jesus thinks he is the Servant of Isaiah's fourth song and is alluding to the entire line as a soteriology for his followers,[30] or Jesus simply perceives
that he is about to be arrested and, in being arrested, will be stigmatized[31] as a
thug (cf. Mark 15:28 in some MSS), or as one outside the bounds of Israel—
and that perception leads him to a Scripture like his experience, a script to go
by (Isa 53:12).[32] If the latter, his disciples are also in danger. It is entirely possible that this label for Jesus is not unlike his previous label as a "friend of tax col-

---

[25] See J. Jeremias, *New Testament Theology* (trans. J. Bowden; New York: Scribner, 1971), 294;
France, *Jesus and the Old Testament*, 114–15; Moo, *Old Testament in the Gospel Passion Narratives*,
138.

[26] Lukan vocabulary clearly appeals to Luke 10:4 (cf. 9:3), the mission of the seventy(-two). This
proves that Luke has either built this logion on Q or it was a pre-Lukan complex rooted in Q.

[27] For a full discussion of this mixed text, cf. Moo, *Old Testament in the Gospel Passion Narratives*,
133–34.

[28] It is unlikely that Luke intended to evoke a parallel here with Luke 23:33, for there he does not
use *anomoi* but *kakourgoi*.

[29] See G.W.H. Lampe, "The Two Swords (Luke 22:35-38)," in *Jesus and the Politics of His Day* (ed.
Bammel and Moule), 335–51.

[30] So France, *Jesus and the Old Testament*, 114–16.

[31] Isaiah 53:12 uses *nmnh* ("to number with," "to classify," "to label"; see *BDB, s.v.*).

[32] See ch. 3, under "The Cause of Jesus' Death as *Entré*."

lectors and sinners" (Q 7:34). In this case, nothing more is intended: his social value is shaped by a death with thugs, or sinners, as was the servant's, but no soteriology is implied. A fortiori: if he is so labeled, so too his disciples.

Along with T.W. Manson, many find in the words of Jesus a figure of the change of times, painted with an irony that leads to disappointment in his followers in Luke 22:38: "That will do!" (cf. Deut 3:26).[33] That the later sword incident in the garden suggests such a hush-hush interpretation is too easy (cf. Mark 14:51), and the language of Luke 22:35-36 has every appearance of being literal. This leads me to the conclusion that Jesus has in fact quoted Isaiah 53:12 and sees in that figure a fate like his own: the fate of dying with a bad label— with the wicked. The quotation then is not soteriologically designed (even if identification with sinners be added to the database), but biographical.[34]

Accordingly, my judgment is that Jesus does find in the Servant Song a script to go by in this sense: he is like the servant in that he identifies with those who have been misclassified.

MARK 1:11 PARS.; MARK 9:7 PARS.; LUKE 23:35

On these three occasions—the baptism, the transfiguration, and the cross— Jesus is labeled the elect one of God.[35] In the first two, the tradition has it that Jesus is called "the beloved one" (ὁ ἀγαπητός) while in the third he is called "the elect one" (ὁ ἐκλεκτός).[36] A plausible connection can be made to Isaiah

---

[33] T.W. Manson, *The Sayings of Jesus* (London: SCM, 1949), 341–42: "It is simply a vivid pictorial way of describing the complete change which has come about in the temper and attitude of the Jewish people since the days of the disciples' Mission. The disciples the saying literally and so missed the point; but that is no reason why we should follow their example" (341). So also Fitzmyer, *Luke*, 2:1432; Green, *Luke*, 774–75.

[34] See also Bock, *Luke*, 2:1748; Moo, *Old Testament in the Gospel Passion Narratives*, 137, too quickly slides from "does not explicitly include" to "easily include."

[35] In scholarship, the more critical term Son dominates the discussion, but those debates can be left to the side to focus on servant issues. J.P. Meier, *A Marginal Jew* (3 vols.; ABRL; New York: Doubleday, 1991–2001), 2:188–89, proposes *yahid* behind the logion. He presses the direction of the translation one way: while *yahid* can be *agapetos*, *agapetos* can be rendered otherwise. On this, cf. J.E. Taylor, *The Immerser* (Grand Rapids: Eerdmans, 1997), 270–72, who does not give enough attention either to the parallels at Mark 9:7 and Luke 23:35 or to *bahir*. Her take, appealing to texts like Daniel 9:23b and 10:11, is a prophetic one: "There seems to be a good case, then, for understanding the term 'beloved' in Jesus' baptismal vision in light of the notion that prophets are especially beloved, chosen, treasured, or desired by God" (p. 272). See also I.H. Marshall, "Son of God or Servant of Yahweh?," *NTS* 15 (1968–1969): 326–36.

[36] Hooker, *Mark*, 47, has a succinct discussion of "son" (Mark 1:11): here she shows it to have emerged from Psalm 2:7 and also from the king as representative of the nation. Furthermore, this corporate perspective dovetails into John's call as well as into a corporate sense of servant in the words of Mark 1:11. Further, the absence of direct LXX parallels to Isaiah 42:1 leads to a follow-up query: are these echoes of Semitic-language parallels? The answer appears to be yes. For an excellent discussion, cf. Marcus, *Mark*, 161–63 (where the expressions of Mark 1:11 are tied into Ps 2:7 and various other texts including Gen 22, and Isa 42:1).

42:1, the first of the Servant Songs.[37] The words are:

בְּחִירִי רָצְתָה נַפְשִׁי

ʼ Ἰσραὴλ ὁ ἐκλεκτός μου, προσεδέξατο αὐτὸν ἡ ψυχή μου[38]

My chosen/elect one, in whom I delight.

It is possible that "beloved one" and "elect one" are translational variants of the Hebrew *beḥiri* (Isa 42:1). Isaiah 42:1 possibly stands behind Mark 9:7 ("beloved one"), Luke 9:35 ("elect one"), and John 1:34 ("elect one"). Some have argued that "Servant" (*ebed, pais*) (cf. Isa 42:1) was altered in the early Christian tradition to "Son" (*huios*) as a legitimate translation variant of either *ebed* or *pais*, or the term *ebed* was filtered through the son-dimension of *pais* to become *huios*. This is only a possibility, and Matthew 12:18 uses *pais* when the writer quotes Isaiah 42:1. That Isaiah continues with "I have put My spirit upon him," suggests that Isaiah 42:1 could be behind the baptismal *bath qol*, if it is accurate to classify a direct statement by God as a *bath qol*.[39]

Thus, the influence of Isaiah 42:1 is entirely plausible for this text, as seen in a confluence of echoes: words that are not commonplace, the themes of election or belovedness and the Spirit coming on special persons; an early Christology—for, if this is servant Christology, it is not a soteriological but a prophetic representative who is in view, and, finally, *huios* remains a plausible translation of the Hebrew *ebed*.

Along with the troubled conscience early Christians must have lived with in redacting God's very own words (cf. Mark 1:11 pars.; 9:7 pars.), we must face the historical reality of how we can know that these words reflect Jesus' own mind.[40] These two observations notwithstanding, many today would argue that these words do indeed reflect Jesus' perception of his vocation (descent of Spirit, fall of Satan) as well as his view of himself and how God considered him, and that it was he who passed on the hidden revelation of who he was and what God thought of him that came to him in a vision when he was baptized.[41] That Jesus thought he was the elect one is slightly confirmed by the leaders at Luke 23:35, where they mock Jesus by labeling him the elect one.

---

[37] On this, cf. esp. Zimmerli and Jeremias, *The Servant of God*, 80–82; B.D. Chilton, *A Galilean Rabbi and His Bible* (vol. 8 of *Good News Studies*; Wilmington: Michael Glazier, 1984), 125–31 (who argues that Jesus did not identify himself with the figure of the servant [cf. pp. 199–200], but he did use the language of the servant to explain his own relationship to God).

[38] Matthew 12:18 quotes Isaiah 42:1 and uses ὁ ἀγαπητός as his translation of *bahir*.

[39] On this, cf. Hooker, *Mark*, 46–47; Guelich, *Mark*, 1:33; and esp. Keener, *Matthew*, 133–34.

[40] *That* Jesus was baptized is indisputable; e.g., J. Marcus, "Jesus' Baptismal Vision," *NTS* 41 (1995): 512–21, here p. 512; for a full defense, cf. Meier, *Marginal Jew*, 2:100–105 (with extensive notes); S. McKnight, "Jesus' New Vision within Judaism," in *Who Was Jesus?* (ed. Copan and Evans), 73–96, here pp. 78–81.

[41] Cf. Chilton, *Galilean Rabbi and His Bible*, 127; see the full defense in Marcus, "Jesus' Baptismal Vision," where he argues that Luke 10:18 originated in the same event (vision). See also Taylor, *The Immerser*, 264–77.

The terms associated with the divine words at Mark 1:11 and 9:7, then, can be plausibly connected to Isaiah 42:1 and to Jesus' own perception of his mission. Three critical terms can be connected to Isaiah 42:1: *beloved, pleased,* and *son.* The coincidence of these terms together at Isaiah 42:1, the presence of the middle term in the Targum to Isaiah (cf. 41:8-9; 43:10, 20; 44:1-2), and the similar collation of these terms at the baptism make the connection firmer.[42] A connection to the Servant passage, then, is possible. The previous sections in this chapter ("Mark 9:9-13" and "Luke 22:35-38") would make such a connection plausible and it seems possible that Jesus found some "scripts" for life in the servant imagery of Isaiah 40–55.

One must be careful, however, before concluding from such a view that Jesus therefore thought of himself *as the* servant and, if so, must have thought he was to die on behalf of the nation in order to announce salvation to the nations. What we have in the baptismal words is not an unambiguous affirmation that Jesus is the Servant of Isaiah, in some titular sense, but instead *a possibility* that he saw himself in similar terms.[43] And that possibility revolves around Jesus' intention, in his baptism, to be anointed by God's Spirit as God's elect one, an individual in whom God takes delight. If Jesus thought God's evaluation of him was that he was the elect one of Isaiah 42:1, we have firm grounds for linking Jesus to the Servant of Isaiah. To think that Jesus connected the dots from Isaiah 42:1 to all the Servant Songs, and then saw that figure as a prediction of his entire mission—including how to understand his progressive realization that his fate would not be unlike John's—requires more evidence than presently is available at our table.

I would suggest also the following: Christian scholars have long been troubled by the apparent confession of sins required by Jesus to join in John's baptism. After all, John's baptism was a "baptism of repentance for the forgiveness of sins" (Mark 1:4), and Jesus joined in such. Furthermore, we are aware that Matthew's rendition of the baptism of Jesus seeks to eliminate just this problem: here John states that he needs to be baptized by Jesus instead (Matt 3:14-15). I suggest that instead of seeing Jesus as vicariously atoning for sins through baptism (the older Lutheran view of Jesus' baptism), we should see Jesus' baptism as a representative national act of repentance. That is, Jesus underwent a baptism of repentance (as did others) to reenact a moral confession prior to his entry into the land of Israel on behalf of Israel. This was the first step toward the nation's restoration. His act of standing in for others would not be unlike the servant's own mission.

But, again, his baptism is a self-conscious act of solidarity with a new vision for Israel and as such was a collective, corporate act instead of an individualistic

---

[42] At a greater extension, Mark 1:10 echoes Isaiah 63:11–64:1.

[43] Cf. the nuanced statement of D. Juel, *Messianic Exegesis* (Philadelphia: Fortress, 1988), 119–33; France, *Mark,* 81.

confession of sins.[44] His action is Israel's action, at least what Israel ought to be doing now that John is declaring eschatological salvation and warning of an imminent doom. Taking this perspective of Jesus' baptism, we might be led to a corporate sense of servant in the baptism itself. The Son as servant, according to the *bath qol*, then, is not just Jesus but also all those who participate in this act along with Jesus to reconstitute and restore Israel.

LUKE 4:16-21; Q 7:22

The quotation of Isaiah 61:1-2a at Luke 4:18-19a and the allusion to Isaiah 61:1, and probably also to 16:18-19; 29:18-19; 35:5-6 and 42:18, at Q 7:22, though not an allusion to a Servant Song per se, has been drawn into the discussion of Jesus and the servant because Isaiah 61:1-3a reutilizes significant themes from the Servant Songs.[45] Thus, in each the messenger receives the Spirit (Isa 42:1; 61:1), and each seems to be cast in the prophetic role so central in Isaiah 40–55.[46]

The text (Isa 61:1-2) was used at Qumran to describe the jubilee of salvation effected through Melchizedek (11Q18[Melchizedek]).[47] That jubilee is the "Last Days," the "inheritance of Melchizedek," a "releasing th[em from the debt of a]ll their sins," the "year of Melchiz[edek]'s favor," a "righteous ki[n]gdom," a "vi[sitation]," and the "Day of [Salvation]." This figure will effect a judgment where he will "thoroughly prosecute the veng[ea]nce required by Go[d's] statu[te]s." In fact, the messenger of Isaiah 61:1-2 is the *[An]ointed of the spir[it]* in Daniel 9:26.

With this as a plausible Jewish context, we ask if Jesus' words here are authentic and, though Luke 4:18-19a is taken by many to be a Lukan creation on the basis of the LXX,[48] few have questioned the historicity of Q 7:22.[49] Their historical verisimilitude has recently been boosted by the publication of some fragments now known as 4Q521 (cf. Ps 146):

---

[44] On this, cf. my "Jesus' New Vision within Judaism." In the larger context of theologizing, see especially J. McLeod Campbell, *The Nature of the Atonement* (1856; repr. Grand Rapids: Eerdmans, 1996); R. Moberly, *Atonement and Personality* (London: John Murray, 1901). See my more popular, *The Jesus Creed* (Brewster, Mass.: Paraclete, 2004), ch. 25.

[45] Cf. D.C. Allison, Jr., *The Intertextual Jesus* (Harrisburg: Trinity Press International, 2000), 109–14.

[46] On this, cf. esp. Williamson, *Variations on a Theme*, 174–88.

[47] Its use at *Mek. de R. Ishm.* on Exodus 20:21 (*Bahodesh* 9:102–3), *Lauterbach* 2:273, 274, is more personal, illustrative of the presence of God upon the humble.

[48] So Fitzmyer, *Luke*, 1:526–27.

[49] A case can be made for Luke 4:18-19 deriving from Q 7:22 as scriptural warrant. If so, it still needs to be noted that Luke 4:18-19 is early Christology. Its location at the front of Luke's Gospel is Lukan even as it is precisely the kind of text Jesus must have seen as parallel to his mission. On this, cf. the important comments by Nolland, *Luke*, 1:193.

[For the hea]vens and the earth shall listen to His Messiah. . . . For the Lord seeks the pious and calls the righteous by name. . . . For He will honor the pious upon the th[ro]ne of His eternal kingdom, setting prisoners free, opening the eyes of the blind, raising up those who are bo[wed down]. . . . For He shall heal the critically wounded, He shall revive the dead, He shall send good news to the afflicted. He shall . . . and the hungry He shall enrich.

This text looks forward to a Messiah who will accomplish the salvation expected in the kingdom expectations of Deutero-Isaiah. And, so it appears, Jesus thought that a similar expectation was fulfilled in his very mission.[50] If Q 7:22 reflects the mission of Jesus, Luke 4:16-21, however redactional it might be, ably expresses what Jesus' mission was all about.

Here we are on firm ground: Jesus connects his mission with the vision of salvation in Isaiah and, as we have already noted, disconnects it from the figure of Elijah in Malachi 3–4, as did John the Baptist.[51] While these texts do not mention the servant and neither are there allusions to the Servant Songs, the themes of Jesus' mission are those of the servant's mission as they are explicated throughout Isaiah, especially in Deutero-Isaiah. Jesus saw his mission as the work of God as expected in Isaiah's predictions. He saw fulfillment in what he was bringing about. His connection to the servant here then is secondary and implicit, and only possibly does he depict himself as Isaiah's Servant.

MARK 3:27 PARS.

In the excitement of salvific blessings, Deutero-Isaiah announces:

Thus says the Lord GOD:
I will soon lift up my hand to the nations,
    and raise my signal to the peoples;
and they shall bring your sons in their bosom,
    and your daughters shall be carried on their shoulders.
Kings shall be your foster fathers,
    and their queens your nursing mothers.
With their faces to the ground they shall bow down to you,
    and lick the dust of your feet.
Then you will know that I am the LORD;
    those who wait for me shall not be put to shame. (49:22-23)

One role for the Servant of Deutero-Isaiah, according to his thinking (49:4), was to restore his people, but the servant realizes it is God who will restore the exiled

---

[50] The substantial parallel at 4Q521 also has a significant parallel at 11Q13[Melch] II, 2-7 (on Luke 4:19a), II, 13-20 (on Q 7:22). The pastiche at 11Q13 suggests the vision of Isaiah shaped the expectations of eschatological salvation—whether mediated by a prophetic or messianic figure (cf. *Tg. Isa.* 61:1; 1QH XVIII, 14).

[51] Q 7:23 may be an oblique statement to John.

community to the land (49:5) and so honor his servant. The Servant here is Israel (49:3). When the Servant is honored it will be through a universal announcement of God's salvation (49:6). Then Israel, his Servant, will return to the land, as YHWH "will have compassion on his suffering ones" (49:13). Abundant numbers of Israelites will return to the land (49:20). And then the author announces the words cited above: kings will fall and all the nations will elevate Israel.

The question of the exiles is close at hand: "How can we overcome our captors?" Deutero-Isaiah has the answer:

Can the prey be taken from the mighty,
    or the captives of a tyrant be rescued?
But thus says the LORD:
Even the captives of the mighty shall be taken,
    and the prey of the tyrant be rescued;
for I will contend with those who contend with you,
    and I will save your children.
I will make your oppressors eat their own flesh,
    and they shall be drunk with their own blood as with wine.
Then all flesh shall know
    that I am the LORD your Savior,
    and your Redeemer, the Mighty One of Jacob. (49:24-26)

In light of the firm conclusion that Jesus drew primary inspiration for his mission to Israel from Isaiah 40–55, we are led to ask if Mark 3:27 might not be seen as Jesus' actualization of Isaiah 49:24-26. An appeal to this text becomes more valuable if, as some have maintained, the baptismal vision included a vision of Satan's downfall (cf. Mark 1:11; Luke 10:18).

Mark 3:27 reads: "But no one can enter a strong man's house and plunder his property without first tying up the strong man; then indeed the house can be plundered." In spite of no verbal connections between Isaiah and Mark 3:27, Morna Hooker, who disputed vigorously Jesus' having used the Suffering Servant Songs as the background to his understanding of his death, nonetheless concludes: "there is little doubt that Jesus had this passage in mind when he spoke these words."[52] While we are in Deutero-Isaiah, we are also led to Isaiah 53:12: "and he shall divide the spoil with the strong." Hooker minimizes this potential allusion, even though the LXX and Mark use the same term for "strong" (*ischuron*). The Lukan parallel, considerably different and possibly a part of Q,[53] raises the same themes though with a less triumphal orientation (11:21-22). Nonetheless, Jesus, "the stronger man," conquers the enemy and plunders the house. That such ideas were connected with the kingdom is wit-

[52] Hooker, *Jesus and the Servant*, 73.
[53] See J.S. Kloppenborg, *Q Parallels* (FF; Sonoma, Calif.: Polebridge, 1988), 92.

nessed in *T. Levi* 18:12-13,[54] where one might find an echo of Isaiah 49 in the joy of the Lord over his children. A thematic trace may also be found in Isaiah 24:21-23 (binding) and its expectation of an eschatological binding of hostile powers (cf. Rev 20:2-3).

In Isaiah 49, the "strong man" is YHWH, and emphatically so. This expectation of God's decisive action in history is picked up, linguistically at least, in Psalms of Solomon 5:3 ("For no one takes plunder away from a strong man, so who is going to take [anything] from all that you have done, unless you give [it]?"). If Jesus sees Isaiah 49 fulfilled in his exorcisms, there is a significant act of intertextual intepretation: Jesus assigns the action of YHWH to his own exorcisms (the finger of God?). The work destined for God's own action, not that of his servant, Jesus assumes as his own job description in Mark 3:27: his exorcisms are God's work of liberation. The same primary actor is found in Isaiah 53:12: YHWH will "allot him [the servant] with the great" but "he [the servant] shall divide the spoil with the strong" (JPS: "He shall receive the multitude as his spoil"). Thus, though apparently deprived of due justice, the servant will regain power (52:13-15; 53:12).

A connection to a specific text in Isaiah 49 or 53 is hard to make. In each of these cases the author is concerned with political restoration of the nation to a position of power and that restoration *follows* suffering. What the Servant could not do, YHWH did. Mark 3:27 is concerned with exorcisms and the stripping away of Satan's power over individual Israelites (cf. Luke 10:18) as evidence that the kingdom of God is present (Q 11:20). An appeal by Jesus to this text appears to be only at the level of similar notions, and we would be wrong to pursue theological implications in the direction of Jesus' assumption of the servant's role. Jesus' language echoes Isaiah's, but he is not thereby assuming the role of the Servant of Isaiah. In fact, if he assumes any figure, it would be that of YHWH!

What is clear, though, is that there are sufficient indicators that Jesus did see Isaiah 40–55 to be paradigmatic for what God was doing in him. And, with a small bundle of passages that either do or possibly allude to the Servant of Isaiah, we are on firm ground to say that Jesus did seem to consult the Servant figure at various periods in his life. The figure is nowhere near as central as Son of man, but the servant does seem to be standing still.

CONCLUSION

These five complexes of sayings of Jesus have been mined by scholars in search of Jesus thinking of himself as the Servant of Isaiah. We can conclude that we have three possible texts (Mark 9:9-13; "the elect one" texts; Mark 3:27) and one clear text (Luke 22:35-38). Luke 22:35-38, where Jesus sees his imminent death as a reversal of his status—he will be killed with the thugs—clearly connects

---

[54] More references can be found in Gundry, *Mark*, 182.

Jesus, the Servant, and death. Not in a soteriological sense, but the connection is made. The most significant Servant text we have is Q 7:22 (possibly Luke 4:16-21), where Jesus clearly affirms that his mission to Israel was outlined previously in Isaiah's vision for the future. His mission is drawn from Isaiah, especially 40–55, to be sure. But, and this must be emphasized, the evidence is not unambiguously in favor of contending that Jesus saw his destiny as that of the Servant of Isaiah.

The Servant of Isaiah is not an upper case figure for Jesus; instead, the Servant of Isaiah is Israel, and that figure in Isaiah betrays that common interchange between the individual and the collective. There are dimensions to Jesus' life that form analogies to what took place to the Servant: in particular, as the Servant suffered and was exalted, so Jesus will suffer and be exalted; as the Servant was misclassified, so Jesus was too. But that Jesus saw in the Servant of Isaiah a figure of prophecy whose destiny he was to fulfill, particularly with respect to his death, is far from clear.

We can conclude, then, that among the images and figures which Jesus consulted in his life in order to make sense of what God's plan for him was, the Servant of Isaiah was one figure among others. It does not seem to stand above the others, and it certainly does not stand as tall as the Son of man. But, the Servant image does still stand as one of the candidates for how Jesus understood himself.

If we are to find in Mark 10:45's "ransom for many" an indication of what Jesus thought of his own death, then we will have to find other evidence on which to build if we want a solid foundation. What this chapter provides for us is possible evidence that Jesus did see some scripts for his life in the servant, and that ransom for many possibly looks to Isaiah 52–53. But if we want more secure footing, and I think we need more secure footing than we presently have, we will have to move to other evidence. The next place to which we can turn appears to be the passion predictions of Jesus.

Chapter 11

The Passion Predictions

Standing tall among the press of evidence for Jesus and how he understood his death, and whether or not that understanding moved into the realm of the Servant of Isaiah, are the passion predictions. In the passion predictions it is made clear that death for Jesus is not a tragedy but the *telos* of his mission. Perhaps it is here that the potential of the allusions to the Servant that convey an atoning sense of Jesus' death can be actualized, for the following reason: if the language of the passion predictions touches upon the language of the Servant, then we would have sufficient foundation to say that not only did Jesus at times appeal to the Servant but that he did so for comprehending the meaning of his death.

Assuming that Jesus "sensed the direction the wind was blowing and fore-saw his fate,"[1] we can now ask if the passion predictions enable us to see how Jesus divined his own death.[2] Again, did he connect these predictions with the Suffering Servant figure of Isaiah 52:13–53:12? Is the "influence of the Servant Songs of Isaiah on the conception and formulation of the Passion sayings . . . extensive and undeniable"?[3] Did he speak of his own death as atoning and redemptive? The problem we face here, once again, is the evidence itself. Just what did Jesus say and what has been added as explication? As Morna Hooker has said,

---

[1] So Davies and Allison, *Matthew*, 2:654–55; Fitzmyer, *Luke*, 1:779.

[2] R. Bultmann dismissed the idea; cf. his *The History of the Synoptic Tradition* (trans. J. Marsh; rev. ed.; 1963; repr. New York: Harper & Row, 1963), 152; *Theology of the New Testament* (trans. K. Grobel; 2 vols.; New York: Scribner, 1951, 1955), 1:29; see also Gundry, *Mark*, 428–31; Nolland, *Luke*, 2:459–64; Pesch, *Markusevangelium*, 1:47–56 (where it is argued that the passion predictions belong to the pre-Markan narrative).

[3] So D.J. Moo, *The Old Testament in the Gospel Passion Narratives* (Sheffield: Almond, 1983), 111.

Certainly it is difficult to believe that Jesus could have predicted his death and resurrection with the precision attributed to him, for though Mark tells us that Jesus
spoke plainly, the subsequent behaviour of the disciples is incomprehensible if the
predictions were as clear as Mark suggests.[4]

But has it all been created by later Christian theology? Again, Hooker, in a
muted echo of C.H. Dodd, clarifies:

The fact that the early Christian communities combed the scriptures for passages
which would explain the death of Jesus does not rule out the possibility that he,
too, looked in the scriptures for guidance.

And our task now is to find what Jesus found when he went to the Tanakh.
And the pointed words of D.E.H. Whiteley, in the generation before last, give
us direction when we ponder the Jesus traditions:

Granted that the early Christians were motivated by a desire to counter the difficulty raised by the fact that their Messiah had been crucified, it does not follow
that they had to counter this difficulty by telling a lie; why should they not, for
apologetic reasons, have told the truth?[5]

GENERAL OBSERVATIONS

The study of these predictions is dog-eared, and the evidence has been frequently discussed (cf. Mark 8:31 pars.; 9:31 pars.; 10:33-34 pars.).[6] A gaggle of
scholars argues these predictions demonstrate that Jesus thought of his death as
atoning and did so because the necessity of his death can be anchored to only
one bedrock tradition in the Tanakh, namely, the Servant of Isaiah's fourth song
(Isa 52:13–53:12). More, I suppose, think the predictions are *Gemeindetheologie*
written into the fabric of the life of Jesus by Christians who had embraced his
death as providential and atoning. "Can there be any doubt," Bultmann asks,
"that they are all *vaticinia ex eventu?*"[7] This was in the generation of theologians

---

[4] Hooker, *Mark*, 204. Hooker concludes that Jesus spoke of his rejection in general terms and, "If
we allow Jesus to have spoken in advance of his rejection, then he must also have expressed confidence in his subsequent vindication" (205). So also Taylor, *Mark*, 378.

[5] D.E.H. Whiteley, "Christ's Foreknowledge of His Crucifixion," in *SE* I (=TU 73 [1959]),
100–14, here p. 108.

[6] See Davies and Allison, *Matthew*, 2:657–61; C.A. Evans, "Did Jesus Predict His Death and
Resurrection?" in *Resurrection* (ed. S.E. Porter, M.A. Hayes, and D. Tombs), 82–97; H.F. Bayer,
Jesus' Predictions of Vindication and Resurrection (WUNT 2/20; Tübingen: Mohr Siebeck, 1986); P.
Hoffmann, "Mk 8,31," in *Orientierung an Jesus* (ed. P. Hoffmann, N. Brox, and W. Pesch;
Freiburg: Herder, 1973), 170–204; G.R. Beasley-Murray, *Jesus and the Kingdom* (Grand Rapids:
Eerdmans, 1986), 237–47; J.D.G. Dunn, *Jesus Remembered* (vol. 1 of *Christianity in the Making*;
Grand Rapids: Eerdmans, 2003), 798–802.

[7] Bultmann, *Theology*, 1:29.

before last. Since those days scholars have reevaluated Bultmann's powerful judgment, but has the tide shifted?

EVIDENCE DISPLAYED

MOTIFS		FIRST PREDICTION Mk 8 Mt 16 Lk 9			SECOND PREDICTION Mk 9 Mt 17 Lk 9			THIRD PREDICTION Mk 10 Mt 20 Lk 18		
1	*Necessity*	x	x	x						
1.1	Jerusalem		x					x	x	x
1.2	Fulfill prophets									x
2	*Son of man*	x		x	x	x	x	x	x	x
2.1	Jesus Messiah		x							
3	*Actions against Jesus*									
3.1	Suffer many things[8]	x	x	x						
3.2	Betrayed				x	x	x	x	x	
3.3	Rejected	x		x						
3.4	Condemned							x	x	
3.5	Delivered to Gentiles							x	x	x
3.6	Mocked							x	x	x
3.7	Spat on							x		x
3.8	Flogged							x	x	x
3.9	Insulted									x
3.10	Crucified								x	
3.11	Killed	x	x	x	x	x		x		x
4	*Actors against Jesus*									
4.1	Men[9]				x	x	x			
4.2	Elders	x	x	x						
4.3	High priests	x	x	x				x	x	
4.4	Scribes	x	x	x				x	x	
5	*Raised: Third Day*	x	x	x	x	x		x	x	x
6	*Responses*									
6.1	Ignorance				x		x			x
6.2	Fear				x	x	x			
6.3	Peter's rebuke	x	x							
7	*Boldness of Jesus*	x								

We need then to sort out this evidence. To keep it before our eyes the chart above might help remind us of what Jesus is purported to have said about his

[8] See M. Casey, "General, Generic, and Indefinite: The Use of the Term 'Son of Man' in Aramaic Sources and in the Teaching of Jesus," *JSNT* 29 (1987): 21–56, here p. 43, who sees behind this a "will die."

[9] Cf. here Gundry, *Mark*, 503.

imminent death in the passion predictions. I have classified the data in seven motifs with subthemes, and the evidence is plotted by textual references. For ease of reference, the first prediction is found at Mark 8:31-32; Matthew 16:21; Luke 9:22; the second prediction at Mark 9:31-2; Matthew 17:22-23; Luke 9:44-45; the third prediction at Mark 10:33-34; Matthew 20:18-19; Luke 18:31-33.[10]

We can begin with the following formal observations:[11]

(1)   the predictions of passion see the suffering of Jesus as a divine necessity, and this means that the rejection and vindication are almost certainly anchored in the Tanakh, either explicitly or implicitly;[12]

(2)   the predictions of suffering are described as the sufferings of the Son of man in all but one instance (Matt 16:21);[13]

(3)   the actors against Jesus are specific levels of Jewish leaders in the first and third prediction, while in the second prediction Jesus is handed over to "men" and in the third to the Gentiles;

(4)   Mark invariably has "after three days" for his prediction of resurrection while Matthew and Luke each correct this to "on the third day."

TRADITION HISTORY AND AUTHENTICITY

In addition to these formal observations, I offer the following tradition-critical observations:[14] (1) that a passion prediction can be spun from a hint of suffering is evident in Matthew 26:2 when one compares it to Mark 14:1:

---

[10] Other parallels are minor and do not contribute to the discussion substantively (e.g., Matt 17:13; 26:2). For the source-critical issues, one needs to read W.R. Farmer, "The Passion Prediction Passages and the Synoptic Problem: A Test Case," *NTS* 36 (1990): 558–70, who shows yet again that a simplistic approach to the Synoptic problem is untenable. But the formulaic nature of the passion predictions and the relative consistency of each Evangelist lends the suggestion that Matthew's and Luke's (so-called) agreements against Mark are not as potent as they first seem.

[11] For Aramaic reconstructions, cf. Casey, "General, Generic, and Indefinite," 40–49.

[12] Cf. here S.V. McCasland, "The Scripture Basis of 'On the Third Day,'" *JBL* 68 (1949): 124–37; B.M. Metzger, "A Suggestion Concerning the Meaning of I Cor. xv. 4b," *JTS* 8 (1957): 118–23.

[13] Casey, "General, Generic, and Indefinite," 43–46, fails to explore the intertextual rootedness of Mark 8:31 where a connection to Daniel 7 seems apparent.

[14] An early tradition history was mapped by J. Jeremias, *New Testament Theology* (trans. J. Bowden; New York: Scribner, 1971), 277–78, 281–86. First, "it is necessary" is Hellenistic; second, ἐγερθῆναι is later than ἀναστῆναι; third, the passion predictions of the passion narrative are overlayed with Christology; fourth, the παραδίδοται is the core of the tradition and was an original Aramaic participle (*mitmesar*). On this basis, Jeremias conjectures a punning *mashal*: "the son of man is delivered [by God] into the hands of men." He finds support at Luke 22:22; Mark 14:21; 9:12; Luke 24:7. This *mashal* is authentic and the core of the tradition; the rest is Christian explication. Dunn evidently agrees; see *Jesus Remembered*, 801.

Mark 14:1	Matthew 26:2
It was two days before the Passover and the festival of Unleavened Bread.	You know that after two days the Passover is coming, and the Son of man will be handed
The chief priests and the scribes were looking for a way to arrest Jesus by stealth and kill him.	over to be crucified.

The suggestion of Mark that *Pesah* was imminent was enough to send Matthew into the thought of a prediction of his death. We must be prepared for *mutatis mutandis* with respect to other hints about a premature death. A firm indicator within the passion predictions of clarifying details *post eventu* can be seen when Matthew converts Mark's "be killed" (10:34) into "to crucify" (Matt 20:19). Accordingly, few today doubt that details have been added like this.

(2) Undoubtedly, the least developed passion prediction is the second one: Mark 9:31.[15] The most developed is the third (Mark 10:33-34), where the actions taken against Jesus are filled in *post eventu*.[16] During the last week, confusion was smeared all over the faces of the disciples; this confusion, a realistic touch of genuine memory, reveals a Christian hand at work in some of the passion predictions. They are explicit enough that, if Jesus said them as they now are, the disciples should not have been as confused as they were. I say this as a teacher who knows what students do retain, but I do so with a conviction that the urgency and gravity of Jesus' words would have intensified memory. The threat of death tends to increase one's alertness.

(3) In spite of Jeremias' clever proposal of an underlying *mashal* at Mark 9:31, I find it highly unlikely that Jesus would have predicted his *death* and not his *vindication*. The two features of the passion predictions are so tightly interwoven that we are driven to accept, in however reduced form, that the root tradition spoke both of rejection and vindication. It is not possible, in my judgment, for someone like Jesus—prophet, potential martyr (all the signs pointed this way), charismatic figure, one who saw parts of his life inscripturated, and one who was reared in an atmosphere that connected resurrection and martyrdom and apocalyptic[17]—to have thought he would die prematurely

---

[15] In addition to the previous note, see the discussions of Casey, "General, Generic, and Indefinite," 46–47; Hooker, *Mark*, 226. P. Hoffmann's essay is concerned to critique the many Germans who contend Mark 9:31 is the most primitive form, and to replace that text with Mark 8:31 as the most primitive. See his "Mk 8,31."

[16] See Taylor, *Mark*, 436. However, as Gundry, *Mark*, 574–75, has shown, there is no clear pattern of borrowing, and he concludes that Mark 10:33-34 may be a genuine prediction. The order of events differs enough that one must conclude that the passion prediction was not based on anything but a general knowledge of the Passion Narrative. But the confusion of the disciples remains problematic for any attempt to defend the details of Mark 10:33-34.

[17] See on this now A. Segal, *Life After Death* (New York: Doubleday, 2004), 285–321, 351–98.

and not think his Father would vindicate him. I overstate: it may be possible, but it is extremely unlikely for someone like Jesus to have thought of martyrdom without vindication.

The examples and the ideas connected with Jewish martyrs have long memories (e.g., 2 Macc 7). Resurrection, while not an old tradition in Israel, was part and parcel of apocalyptic and sectarian groups (e.g., Isa 24–27; Ezek 37; Dan 12:1-2), and, if I might say so without discussion, therefore of groups not unlike the one so many scholars think behind Q.[18] If Jesus thought of premature death, Jesus also thought of ultimate vindication. So D.C. Allison:

> One may confidently hold that Jesus did not simply predict his own death and the dissolution of his movement. Surely he assumed that God would vindicate his cause notwithstanding the coming time of trouble. It would have been altogether natural for one who had faith in God's justice and power to look beyond present and expected troubles and hope for the Lord's favourable verdict. Such faith and hope in fact together mark the heart of Jewish eschatology, and we scarcely err supposing that Jesus shared them.[19]

And, because it is likely that Son of man is both authentic and drawn from Daniel 7, there is reason to think here of a collective vindication, and probably in terms of the general resurrection.[20] That is, the logion envisions not only the vindication of Jesus but of his followers.

(4) A notable feature, sometimes skipped, of the passion predictions is that they are devoid of soteriology and reflection on the significance of Jesus' death. It may be assumed that the *Tradents* and Evangelists knew what they believed about the significance of Jesus' death, but they eschewed every opportunity to insert anything of "for us" or "on our behalf." As a result, we have here three predictions of Jesus' death which do simply that: predict that he will be handed over and subsequently vindicated. There is no trace that his death will atone or accomplish salvation. In fact, it breathes the air of the martyrdom of a prophet or Jewish leader.

---

[18] On this, see N.T. Wright, "Resurrection in Q?" in *Christology, Controversy and Community* (ed. D.G. Horrell and C.M. Tuckett; NovTSup 99; Leiden: E.J. Brill, 2000), 85–97; and Segal from previous note.

[19] So Davies and Allison, *Matthew*, 2:660. Allison also contends that the notion of vindication would have involved that of resurrection. See D.C. Allison, Jr., *The End of the Ages Has Come* (Philadelphia: Fortress, 1985), 137–40; also cf. M. Black, "The 'Son of Man' Passion Sayings in the Gospel Tradition," *ZNW* 60 (1969): 1–8, here pp. 7–8; P.M. Casey, *From Jewish Prophet to Gentile God* (Edward Cadbury Lectures, 1985–1986; Louisville: Westminster/John Knox, 1991), 65–66; Dunn, *Jesus Remembered*, 818–24. For older studies, see G. Stählin, "'On the Third Day,'" *Int* 10 (1956): 282–99; E. Schweizer, *Lordship and Discipleship* (SBT 28; Naperville, Ill.: Alec R. Allenson, 1960), 22–41.

[20] See now Dunn, *Jesus Remembered*, 821–24. See also his study of the resurrection traditions at pp. 825–79.

(5) Perhaps the most noteworthy observation in favor of the view that Jesus uttered a passion prediction (in general) is the conclusions we've already come to: that from the time of John forward, Jesus must have recognized that he could also die; that there is significant evidence that Jesus thought he could die prematurely; that he connected his death and the Final Ordeal; that he identified himself with the ancient prophets, who often met a violent end, and with other figures in the tradition, some of whom met a premature death. In other words, it would be unusual if something like a prediction of his own death (and final vindication) were not to appear on the lips of Jesus and in the Jesus traditions. Such a comment by Jesus, in other words, is nearly inevitable in light of what we have so far argued.

In conclusion, it is my judgment that Jesus uttered something, whether one time or more than once doesn't matter at this point, about his being handed over to death and vindication and that such an action was part of the scriptural plan (that no text is specifically cited or even clearly discoverable makes the latter claim even more solid). In light of his regular comments about ruling authorities and his knowledge of the experience of John at the hands of authorities, it is likely also that he may have expressed who would be the primary actors. For the purposes of our investigation, however, specific details are not significant. What we need to know is not so much the *specific content* of those passion/vindication predictions as whether or not they could have expressed some kind of *understanding* of how he understood his death. Our concern is not so much if Jesus knew about his death, but how he understood his death. To do that, we will examine three expressions that are taken by many to be at the bedrock of the passion predictions: *after three days, betrayal/hand over,* and *divine necessity.*

It is easy, especially for Christian theologians, to appeal to figures or images or sacrifices in the Tanakh as the *historical background* to the passion predictions and then, because that evidence has been put into the cooking pot, to taste it everywhere. One sees this with the Servant and one sees it with other figures, and these figures also then heavily influence how Jesus understood his death. The question we need to ask is not if the passion predictions can be explained in light of such figures but what figures the specific expressions most likely refer to.

I give one example here. Even though Psalm 118:22 does not help us when it comes to issues of how Jesus understood his death, it does deserve to be put on the table at this point. Thus, it should be observed here that the Hallel Psalm 118:21-25, esp. v. 22, evidently played a significant role in Jesus' life and, it ought to be noted, was featured at *Pesah* and sometimes understood eschatologically. The psalm is probably behind Mark 8:31, it is quoted explicitly at Mark 12:10-11 in a manner consistent with a parable's *nimshal* and consistent with Jesus' regularly blaming Jewish leadership, and the stone imagery is also found in use by early Christians, as evidenced at Acts 4:11 and 1 Peter 2:4, 7. C.H. Dodd classified the stone citation with his "primary sources of testimonies," and recently Klyne Snodgrass's careful research has reinserted the stone testimony as a reliable word of Jesus and at the bedrock of how he faced his death.[21] It is of some interest, as well, that Zechariah 3:8-9 connects "stone" and "Branch/ Servant" and that the "stone" of Psalm 118 can be connected to the Son of man in Daniel 7 through the "stone" of Daniel 2.

What must be observed is that Psalm 118:22 has an *identical structure* with the passion predictions, a structure of rejection and vindication. At this point we can say that the structure of rejection-vindication on the part of a prophet is entirely plausible in a Jewish context; and inasmuch as Jesus does go to the Tanakh to explore for meaning, it is not impossible for him to have gone to a text like this one. But, for Psalm 118:22 to be considered the *specific* text to which Jesus appealed when he predicted his own death (assuming that he did) and for the verse to be used to understand how he interpreted his death, we need specific evidence that that text is in mind in the predictions. The same applies to other figures. Such contexts are plausible Jewish contexts, but that is all they can be at this point in our discussion. The point needs to be underlined: It is entirely Jewish for Jesus to have reflected on his death; the issue is *how* he did so (if he did).

And not to go unnoticed in any discussion about the authenticity of these logia, the predictions reveal a promise of resurrection and vindication (using ἀναστῆναι instead of the more confessional ἐγείρειν; cf. Rom 4:24-25; 1 Cor 15:4), but they clearly omit the very commonly believed early Christian view of the Parousia and of the coming of the Son of man in judgment. Jesus will be crucified and will be raised; that is all these logia state. His death is not interpreted, and his resurrection is left alone as well.

It is the general plausibility of such a saying within Judaism as well as the absence of soteriology and early Christian eschatology, in my judgment, that most support a passion prediction as an authentic reflection of something Jesus said. Mark 9:31, as a basic core to the kind of thing Jesus must have said, remains untouched by primitive Christian theologizing on the death of Jesus. Furthermore, a plausible Semitic/Aramaic *Vorlage*, whether as articulated by J. Jeremias (Mark 9:31) or M. Casey (Mark 8:31),[22] supports the notion that Jesus predicted his death. And the rebuke of Jesus by Peter has no plausible early Christian setting apart from some kind of statement by Jesus about impending rejection (Mark 8:32b-33).[23] If we accept the core of the passion prediction as authentic, what does it tell us about how Jesus thought of his death? Are there specific allusions to texts in the Tanakh? Does Jesus explore the Servant? or any other imagery? We need now to turn to specific expressions to explore their potential background.

---

[21] See C.H. Dodd, *According to the Scriptures* (London: Nisbet, 1952), 107–8; K.R. Snodgrass, *The Parable of the Wicked Tenants* (WUNT 27; Tübingen: Mohr Siebeck, 1983), esp. 95–106.

[22] See Jeremias, *New Testament Theology*, 277–78, 281–86; Casey, "General, Generic, and Indefinite."

[23] So also R.E. Brown, et al., eds., *Peter in the New Testament* (Minneapolis: Augsburg, 1973), 67–68, which cites in support F. Hahn, R.H. Fuller, and E. Dinkler.

AFTER THREE DAYS

Because "*after* three days" (Mark 9:31; others have "on": Matt 16:21 [but cf. 27:63]; Luke 9:22; 1 Cor 15:4; Acts 10:40; John 2:19)[24] cannot easily be assigned to early Christian theologizing (after all, Jesus was not raised after three days),[25] we can begin here.[26] If we cast aside later Christian understandings of what Jesus must have meant when he said "after three days" and ask instead what he might have meant and what his disciples would have understood, we are led to two primary texts: Hosea 6:1-2[27]and Daniel 7:25, the latter of which has to be connected to Daniel 12:1-2.[28]

Hosea 6:1-2 expresses the prophet's hope of religious revival and national restoration in the form of self-initiated renewal ("let us turn back"; 6:1 [*wenashubah*]) because the YHWH who has "torn" can "heal."[29] In fact, "after two days he will revive us; on the third day he will raise us up"—that is, YHWH can restore our nation to the land (cf. also Isa 26:19; Ezek 38:14; Dan 12:2; *Tg. Hos.* 6:1-2 makes resurrection explicit for what "after two days . . . on the third day" suggests). He will do this, so Hosea says, if his people will "press on to know YHWH" (6:3; JPS "pursue obedience" for *wenedeʿah*).

The expression *after two days* can be interpreted in two senses: it can mean either "soon,"[30] not unlike the overtones of Luke 18:7-8, or a "set time," leading

---

[24] Matthew and Luke consistently used "on the third day": Matt 16:21; 17:23; 20:19; Luke 9:22; 18:33.

[25] Cf. Acts 28:13 where "after one day" means "on the second day," and John 4:43 where "after two days" probably suggests something like "on the third day."

[26] See E.L. Bode, *The First Easter Morning* (AnBib 45; Rome: Biblical Institute Press, 1970), 105–26, who argues that the "three day" motif emerges from the *general* Old Testament idea that the third day was the day of salvation (cf. Gen 22:4; Exod 15:22; 19:10-11, 16; Josh 3:2; Judg 20:30; 1 Sam 9:20; 21:5; 2 Kgs 20:5, 8; Ezra 8:15, 32; Esth 5:1; Hos 6:2; Jonah 2:1; 2 Macc 13:12). He mixes ideas and texts in some of this listing but, more importantly, too often his logic is dependent upon the use of *Genesis Rabbah*. See also H.K. McArthur, "'On the Third Day,'" *NTS* 18 (1971–1972): 81–86; J.M. Perry, "The Three Days in the Synoptic Passion Predictions," *CBQ* 48 (1986): 637–54, who finds the core of the tradition in Luke 13:32-33, and that "*after* three days" is more primitive than the on the third day tradition. Norman Walker, "'After Three Days,'" *NovT* 4 (1960): 216–62, suggested that after three days referred to three days after the rejection, while "on the third day" was calculated from the death of Jesus. The problem for this is that Mark has *after* immediately after the death, not the rejection of Jesus in his passion prediction (8:31).

[27] On this view, cf. e.g., Dodd, *According to the Scriptures*, 77, 103; J. Wijngaards, "Death and Resurrection in Covenantal Context (Hos. vi. 2)," *VT* 17 (1967): 226–38; McArthur, "'On the Third Day,'" 81–86.

[28] There are interesting parallels at Genesis 42:17-18 and 2 Chronicles 10:5, 12.

[29] See now N.T. Wright, *The Resurrection of the Son of God* (vol. 3 of *Christian Origins and the Question of God*; Minneapolis: Fortress, 2003), 118–19.

[30] So J. Jeremias, "Die Drei-Tage-Worte der Evangelien," in *Tradition und Glaube* (G. Jeremias, et al., eds.; Göttingen: Vandenhoeck & Ruprecht, 1971), 221–29; so most recently, Evans, "Did Jesus Predict His Death and Resurrection?" 96.

the intertextual mind to Hosea 3:4-5.[31] *If* this is the background for Jesus' statement, he stated only that, as suffering has a set divine period, so also does vindication. If the other view is preferred, he implied that, though suffering is
imminent, vindication will come shortly.[32] The singular problem for this text as
the scriptural foundation for the three day motif is that Hosea 6:2 is not cited
anywhere in the NT and does not (evidently) figure in early Christian exegesis,
even though one might argue that it was possibly interpreted with reference to
the resurrection in Jewish (proto-rabbinic) interpretation.[33]

But a more general metaphorical sense of "after three days" finds support in
the Jesus traditions and needs to be kept in mind in assessing the meaning of the
passion predictions. Jesus is accused of saying he would destroy the temple but
rebuild it *in three days*, this time with a temple made without hands (Mark
14:58; 15:29). Unless we think Jesus inaccurate, three *literal* days simply cannot
have been his intention. And there are other similar texts: the sign of Jonah tradition (at Q 11:30) was probably originally without the three day motif, but
there is a Johannine tradition that Jesus spoke of being gone for "a little while"
(John 16:16-19), though the details are hard to recover. Further, Luke 13:32-33
offers a similar kind of reflection by Jesus:

> He said to them, "Go and tell that fox for me, 'Listen, I am casting out demons
> and performing cures today and tomorrow, and on the third day I finish my work.
> Yet today, tomorrow, and the next day I must be on my way, because it is impos-
> sible for a prophet to be killed outside of Jerusalem.'"

These traditions lead us back to consider another text, Daniel 7:25, as a
potential source of reflection for the passion predictions.[34] I continue to be
amazed by scholars who refuse to think Daniel 7 could be the context for a suffering Son of man. Daniel predicts suffering in the following words: "He shall
speak words against the Most High, shall wear out the holy ones of the Most
High, and shall attempt to change the sacred seasons and the law; and they shall
be given into his power for a *time, two times, and half a time.*" The Son of man
of Daniel 7 is vindicated *precisely because* the Son of man, a figure for the saints
of the Most High, has suffered. Vindication is what one promises to those who

---

[31] There Israel will be "many days without king" but "afterward, the Israelites shall return." But it
is a mistake to say, as have some, that there was no Hebrew equivalent for "a few"; cf. מעט. This
notwithstanding, "after three days" or "three days" are possibly capable of meaning "soon" even if
the references cited in Davies and Allison, *Matthew,* 2:661, n. 45, do not increase confidence. One
finds a possible meaning of "soon" at Hosea 6:1-2. But some see the two expressions *after* and *on*
as equivalent (Gnilka, *Markusevangelium,* 2:16). This would require both Matthew and Luke to
have independently altered the expression.

[32] See V. Taylor, *Jesus and His Sacrifice* (1937; repr. London: Macmillan, 1955), 89; Casey,
"General, Generic, and Indefinite," 44.

[33] So McArthur, "'On the Third Day,'" 85–86.

[34] So J. Schaberg, "Daniel 7,12 and the New Testament Passion-Resurrection Predictions," *NTS*
31 (1985): 208–22; contra Moo, *Old Testament in the Gospel Passion Narratives,* 102.

suffer; those who don't suffer expect not vindication but reward (see Deut 28). This prediction of Daniel means that Antiochus will enjoy power for a short time, for "three and half years" (Dan 9:27) or, perhaps more precisely, "for a limited period." (Daniel 8:14 and 12:11-12 further clarify this time period and 1 Maccabees 4:54 states that the period was exactly three years.)

At this point it would not be impertinent to observe that the two dead witnesses of Revelation lay on the street for "three and a half days" (Rev 11:1-13). If this exegetical tradition (Daniel; 1 Maccabees; Revelation), emerging probably from Hosea 6:1-2 is the context for Jesus' statement, the meaning shifts from the hope of an imminent vindication to a *shortened period of suffering*. Suffering is to come, but God is in control; he will ensure that the period is not lengthy, and he will also vindicate his chosen ones. While far from certain, the tradition found in Daniel and Revelation appears to be the most likely context for Jesus' statement. This being so, we are led once again, not to the Servant Songs of Isaiah, but to the Son of man passage in Daniel.

To be fair, however, to the classical view that the Servant of Isaiah is behind this notation of vindication, though without the critical expression of *after three days*, we should consider the following string of texts. Isaiah 53:11-12 speaks of exaltation in some sense of vindication. This very idea is picked up in Daniel 11:33–12:10, and then again at *T. Mos.* 10:9; Wis 2:12-20; 5:1-6 and perhaps at 4Q491. That is, the righteous servant of God suffers and is vindicated. If one is looking for the general theme of the righteous sufferer who is vindicated, one can surely take this avenue from the Servant of Isaiah into the first century, but (as I have mentioned) the critical *after three days* is not part of this tradition—and it is fundamental to the passion predictions. Nor is the three day motif a part of the Psalm 118:22 tradition.

BETRAYAL

The same Danielic background seems to apply to another passion prediction expression: "the Son of Man *is to be betrayed* into human hands" (Mark 9:31).[35] It, too, finds a parallel in the same vision of Daniel: "they [the suffering saints] *shall be given* into his power" (Dan 7:25). The LXX uses the same term (*paradidomi*) as does the Markan tradition (Mark 9:31; 10:33).[36] It is not accidental that we find two significant connections: *betray* and a generalized expression *after three days* in one text in Daniel 7:25, and occurring together once again in what appears to be a genuine word of Jesus.[37]

[35] See here N. Perrin, "The Use of (παρα)διδόναι in Connection with the Passion of Jesus in the New Testament," in *Der Ruf Jesu und die Antwort der Gemeinde* (ed. E. Lohse, C. Burchard, and B. Schaller; Göttingen: Vandenhoeck & Ruprecht, 1970), 204–12.

[36] On the authenticity question here, cf. Casey, "General, Generic, and Indefinite," 40–42.

[37] Perhaps the term is even more general, referring only to the fate of the prophets; on this see F. Hahn, *The Titles of Jesus in Christology* (trans. H. Knight and G. Ogg; New York: World, 1969), 38–39. See Matt 23:37; Rom 11:13; 1 Thess 2:15.

The clinching, weighty argument that the passion predictions are a reflection on Daniel 7 (with Dan 12:1-2 filtering Dan 7:25, and perhaps Daniel 7 filtering Ps 118:22 through Daniel 2) is that Jesus sees his suffering as the suffering of the Son of man. The bedrock of the passion predictions is that each is about the Son of man's suffering, not the servant figure from Isaiah. Indeed, Morna Hooker cuts a clear figure in the icy discussion here: "he would hardly have appealed to his hearers concerning the things which are written about the Son of Man if he were referring primarily to passages which they connected with a totally different concept [namely, the Servant of Isaiah]."[38] Thus, in the passion predictions we see Daniel 7:12 (the one like a Son of man) reactualized by Jesus for his own life and fate: as the Son of man represents the vindication of the suffering saints, so also the limitation of suffering for God's people is an encouragement to await God's vindication.[39]

THE DIVINE NECESSITY

This leads to the firm tradition throughout the early evidence that Jesus thought his life was scripted in the Bible and in the divine drama: it is necessary is rooted deep in the tradition.[40] If one thinks of passages in the Tanakh that might be taken to imply the necessity of suffering with the implication of vindication, one may be led to Genesis 22, to Psalm 22 or 118, or to Isaiah 52:13–53:12.[41] Each

---

[38] M.D. Hooker, *Jesus and the Servant* (London: SPCK, 1959), 96; so also Dunn, *Jesus Remembered*, 807.

[39] One can expand discussion of "suffer many things" (Mark 8:31) and see herein a synthetic profile of the "suffering righteous one," so much the darling of scholarship at one time. Thus, cf. Pss 34:7, 18, 20; 20:20; LXX 30:9; 68:17; 101:2; etc.; cf. also Isa 53:4, 11. On this, cf. Schweizer, *Lordship and Discipleship* , 22–41, who offers a brief of this view. That the early church thought of Jesus in such terms is possibly the implication of Acts 3:14; 7:52; 22:14; Matt 27:4 (B etc.); 23:28, 35.

[40] Luke 18:31 is probably Lukan, explicating in more graphic terms the sense of necessity. On Luke 22:37, cf. the comments of Moo, *Old Testament in the Gospel Passion Narratives*, 133 (and n. 4). That δεῖ can translate Aramaic/Hebrew expressions of necessity can be seen in Lev 5:17; 4 Kgdms 4:13-14; Isa 30:29; Dan 2:28, 45. On this, cf. Gundry, *Mark*, 446; see W.J. Bennett, Jr., "'The Son of Man Must . . .,'" *NovT* 17 (1975): 113–29.

[41] Specifically, the following may be noted: (1) ἐμπτύω is found three times in the LXX; one can compare Isa 50:6 and Job 7:19; 30:10. The term is also found at Mark 14:65 and 15:19 and is most likely *post eventu*; furthermore, it is not found in Isaiah 52:13–53:12 and neither is it a soteriological term. (2) μαστιγόω is found at Isaiah 50:6 and also at Mark 14:65; it is probably *post eventu*. But the vocabulary and themes are not commonplace; thus, it is possible the writer is thinking of the Servant figure of Isaiah. Hooker, *Jesus and the Servant*, soft-shoes her way through this term. (3) ἀποδοκιμάζω is probably an allusion to Ps. 118:22. (4) παραδίδωμι: Romans 4:25 is based on *Tg. Isa.* 53:5 (cf. Rom 8:32) and the term could be rooted in Isaiah 53:6, 12 bis. Significantly, the term has a different meaning in the passion predictions, but insignificantly, the difference of an active vs. a passive gets us nowhere for determining origins. On this, cf. Moo, *Old Testament in the Gospel Passion Narratives*, 95–97, who finds influence on the passion predictions from Isaiah 50:6; 53:12; and Psalm 118:22.

of these texts may play a role in Jesus' understanding of his mission, and methodologically there is no reason for us to limit the reservoir to one corner. But the persecution of the saints in Daniel 7, the obvious appeal Jesus found in the Son of man figure's vindication in that passage, the *explicit* use of Son of man in the passion predictions themselves, and the collective interpretation of Daniel 7 each lead, on different paths, to Jesus' creative constellation of capturing his own suffering in the Son of man figure of Daniel 7. We should observe that each passion prediction is followed by Jesus' warning of potential suffering for his followers—with yet another inkling of their vindication. The Son of man's suffering, then, contains allusions in the words of Jesus to a representative of a group. The passion predictions, of all the texts that can be considered, breathe the themes of Daniel 7.[42]

OTHER PASSION PREDICTIONS

Few today reckon the Johannine traditions at the same level as the Synoptic traditions when it comes to information for retrieving the historical Jesus.[43] However, one should not forget that John's (three) passion predictions also are tied into the themes of necessity, the Son of man, and vindication: John 3:13-14 (lifting up the Son of man); 8:28 (lifting up the Son of man); 12:31-34 (lifting up the Son of man).[44] It appears that Jesus, indeed, envisions that his suffering will lead to death, but he sees beyond his death to a vindication. As the Son of man, as representative of the saints of the Most High, suffered and was vindicated, so also will he be vindicated following suffering.

We can now expand our net more widely to consider the following as passion predictions that, in essence, confirm our previous study of the conventional passion predictions. *First*, from Q we should observe Q 11:47-48, 49-51, and 13:34-35.[45] Here we find the prophet of God who is persecuted for obedience and for declaring to a recalcitrant people what God has emboldened him to declare. *Second*, from Mark we note Mark 2:18-22 (bridegroom); 12:8 (Son); 14:21 (Son of man); 14:27 (shepherd); 14:36 (Son). Here we find the Son of God and Son of man and Shepherd who are each rejected and who suffer. And, *third*, from Luke we find 13:33; 12:49-50; and 22:35-38.

---

[42] On this, cf. the observations of Morna Hooker that the Son of man tradition in the Synoptics, in its earliest phase, was collective and inclusive. Cf. her "The Son of Man and the Synoptic Problem," in *The Four Gospels 1992* (3 vols.; BETL 100; Leuven: Leuven University Press, 1992), 1:189–201.

[43] The entire scholarship has recently been surveyed, from a conservative angle, by C.L. Blomberg, "John and Jesus," in *The Face of New Testament Studies* (ed. S. McKnight and G.R. Osborne; Grand Rapids: Baker, 2004), 209–26; see also Blomberg's most recent study, *The Historical Reliability of John's Gospel* (Downers Grove: InterVarsity, 2002).

[44] Note that ὑψόω/δοξάζω are found together at Isaiah 53:12, and that the texts share common vocabulary, themes, and terms that are not commonplace.

[45] Cf. here the (unfulfilled theme of) stoning of Luke 4:29; John 8:59; 10:31-36; 11:8.

The result of this quick glance at other passion predictions leads to similar conclusions: that Jesus saw his own death as that of a prophetic martyr; that he envisioned his suffering in terms of the Son of man's role in Daniel 7; that various images could be the vehicles of expressing his future death; that appeal to the Servant is present but not the front-ranking interpretation; but that in none of these instances does Jesus see his death in terms of atonement. Jesus sees his death as a representative death, as the death of one who embodies the fate of his followers. He, with his followers, is the Son of man who suffers and is vindicated.

CONCLUSION

The passion predictions offer no theology of the atonement, and neither is there a consistent, firm reflection on Jesus' death in light of the Servant of Isaiah. Instead, they are a genuine reflection of Jesus, not so much about his death as about his *vindication*,[46] and the scriptural text on which they are based appears most likely to be Daniel 7, though it would be unjustified to limit his reflection to that passage alone. Jesus, as Son of man, knows that the present suffering will escalate but suffering is not the final word. God, the Ancient of Days, will vindicate the Son of man after three days—that is, soon thereafter.

This places us in the position, after reflecting on Jesus' own scripting of his life, where we left off in our study of Jesus' anticipation of his premature death. Jesus, from the time of John's death, thought about his possible death. And what he seems to have thought about was that he would die prematurely, that it was part of God's plan, that he was like other martyrs and prophets and figures in the Tanakh, and, most especially, that his death would occur at the onset of the Final Ordeal. The connection Jesus makes in the passion predictions to the Son of man is similar: as the Son of man experienced (what can only be called) eschatological tribulation, so Jesus himself, as one like that Son of man, will also suffer the Final Ordeal. And, like that Son of man, Jesus will also be vindicated. This is the narrative, or emplotted story, that seems to cohere most with the evidence we can find about Jesus' own state of mind.

If one examines this evidence carefully, two features rise to the surface: *first*, that Jesus thought he would die in accordance with some scriptural warrant and, second, that this death is not seen as atoning so far as we can tell. We have evidence to suggest that Jesus did appeal to the Servant of Isaiah; we are not sure that "ransom for many" can be assigned to what Jesus said in the context of Mark 10:35-45, but we must admit that his own appeal to the Servant does make "ransom for many" a possible saying of Jesus. What we do see is clear: Jesus knew he would die, and he sought for answers in the Tanakh.

---

[46] Resurrection, and its precise meaning in Judaism, has become a serious discussion of late. See the interesting article of J.D. Crossan, "The Resurrection of Jesus in its Jewish Context," *Neot* 37 (2003): 29–57; N.T. Wright, "Jesus' Resurrection and Christian Origins," *Greg* 38 (2002): 615–35; *Resurrection of the Son of God*, 85–206 (where he contends for a "life after life-after-death"); Segal, *Life After Death*, chs. 3, 6–7, 9, 12, 14 (who in several ways is anticipated by Crossan).

The atoning interpretation of his death, however, does not appear in what most take to be a foundational statement of Jesus about his death: the passion prediction (or predictions). Clearly, Jesus thought he had to die, but the passion predictions simply offer no explanation of the effect or the saving value of a premature death. With so many possible hints about such themes in Isaiah 53, and with Jesus having at times appealed to servant imagery, we are amazed that Jesus did not appeal to this text to explain his death. We are confident of this: Jesus saw himself in terms of the suffering and vindicated Son of man of Daniel 7.[47]

Mark 10:45 Again

Our previous conclusion on Mark 10:45 was a stalemate: to authenticate the atonement language of Mark 10:45 one would have to demonstrate that Jesus thought of himself and his fate primarily in terms of the servant, in fact Servant, of Deutero-Isaiah. As a result, we demonstrated that it was in fact a part of the outlook of various Jewish charismatic leaders to think of themselves as fulfilling scripts found in the pages of the Tanakh. Further, we found that Jesus thought of himself in light of various figures, though it was only the Son of man that seems to predominate among those figures for Jesus. The closer we look, in fact, the more the Servant disappears and the more to the fore marches the enigmatic, collective figure of Daniel 7: the Son of man. Once again, we need to remind ourselves that Mark 10:45 is rooted deeply in Daniel 7 and its exegesis, and in that text the Son of man suffers with a view to atoning for sins (9:24).[48]

But, we are not done. The *Pesah* tradition offers us one more opportunity to find something about what Jesus thought of his death, and what it offers are some images that suggest that Jesus, or someone after him, thought hs death was atoning. To that we now turn, but we need to observe at this point that a study of that text will lead us one more time back to Mark 10:45 and the ransom saying.

[47] Beasley-Murray, *Jesus and the Kingdom of God.*
[48] See B.J. Pitre, "The Historical Jesus, the Great Tribulation and the End of the Exile," Ph.D diss. (Notre Dame, 2004), 508–34.

Part IV

JESUS AND THE LAST SUPPER

Chapter 12

Pesah in Jewish History

The Eucharist is one of the elements of church life which moderns may well like or dislike, but no intelligent person dare ignore it in seeking to understand Jesus. The elements served at Eucharist are the most stable dimension of Christendom. Questions abound, and the answers to those questions provide interpretations that shape the worshiper. But, on each Sunday, throughout Christendom, Christians sit, kneel, stand, and so partake of the "body of the Lord" and the "blood of the Lord." To many it brings relief, a sense of forgiveness, and a feeling of being at peace with God, self, and others. The Eucharist embodies the Christian's theology of atonement, forgiveness, reconciliation, and mission. It reveals a Christology as much as it also announces an eschatology. It forms an ecclesiology as much as it shapes the liturgy.

But are these theological themes and shapings from Jesus himself? Reshaping our question in more first-century terms: did Jesus see his last supper with his disciples as the foundation for the Christian practice of the Eucharist or, even more, as the embodiment of his own understanding of atonement? We should not relegate these questions either to the corners of history or to the ends of our consciences. In fact, Christianity has become a *cruciform religion*, a religion of the cross. Did the early Christian shapers of the emerging movement get this right? Was their conceptualizing of the Jesus traditions into a cruciform theology consistent with the very life of Jesus: his mission, his teachings, his actions? Or, somehow, was the simpler idea of Jesus derailed? Has the cross taken on a life of its own?

This is no small set of questions. Indeed, Christian identity today is rooted in this cruciform shape of the gospel. What would happen to Christian faith if it were suddenly discovered, by fresh discoveries, that Jesus did not intend to die to forgive sins? that he did not understand his death as atoning? Or that he didn't even anticipate his death? that, in fact, the last week was a blur of surprises

243

that only became clear when he faced an angry crowd from a cross? And then it was too late to do anything about it. To answer these questions, we need to answer other questions.

Was the last supper the Passover meal proper (*Pesah*)? If so, does *Pesah* provide clues about how Jesus divined his own death? And, even further, do such clues point us in the direction of an interpretation of a death that provides immediate and direct continuity to the early Christian interpretation that Jesus' death was in fact representative or substitutionary or vicarious or propitiatory or sacrificial and sin-absorbing? These questions are many, and they do not permit easy answers. But before we can inquire into the last supper as a *Pesah* meal we must first examine what *Pesah* was like in the first century.

Here, too, there have been serious historical blunders—of two sorts: (1) that the Exodus 12 tradition was practiced completely and continuously for centuries, and (2) that the Mishnah tractate *Pesahim*, often equated with the modern Passover *Haggadah*, reveals the details of practice in the first century. A survey of the history of the practice of *Pesah*, embedded as it is in the formalities of the Week of Unleavened Bread (*Massot*), reveals both of these historical lapses and sets our feet on firmer ground for analyzing the gospel traditions of the last supper.

PESAH IN HISTORY

Christian observance of the Eucharist as well as Jewish observance of *Pesah* blinker the practitioners into equating modern observance and rabbinic ritual with first-century practice.[1] Indeed, our liturgical practices shape our religious identity, and our identity then influences our understanding of the liturgy. The liturgies of *Pesah* and Eucharist tell the story of how Israelites and Christians understand themselves and their beliefs. These rites, in fact, embody their story. Can we find the original stories or, at least, a good approximation? Fleeting snapshots of the observance of *Pesah* in Jewish history—this is all we have—provide us with a sweep of the history of the festival as well as a contoured perception of what was most important to various Jewish communities. But, whether or not the last supper of Jesus was originally *Pesah* and, if not, at least a *Pesah* week meal, is very important. Accordingly, we begin with the development of *Pesah* in Jewish history. Once again, we enter a plethora of historical puzzles, exegetical debates, and theological ramifications—most of which will simply have to be ignored.

We should remember this one thought: when we enter into the world of various celebrations of *Pesah*, we are entering into a sacred world, a world in which the Israelite believed that God was speaking, in which time stood still as

---

[1] A good example of confusion with respect to historical time periods can be seen in D. Stern, *Jewish New Testament Commentary* (Clarksville, Md.: Jewish New Testament Publications, 1992), 77–82.

Israelites told their old story—a story in which meaning was determined by memory and recital of ancient events, and in which a people came together to express its identity in solidarity, worship, and memory. When Israelite celebrants began the *Pesah*, they joined hands with countless predecessors who had been to temple and table—even with familial, tribal, cultural, linguistic, theological, and political variations—for the same reason: to remember God's deliverance from Egypt. They were links in a living chain of memory. When the pilgrim left Jerusalem or entered into more ordinary time, he or she reentered the normal world refreshed and perhaps even revitalized to trust God to deliver his people yet once more—from Rome as well as others. This faith expressed itself often enough that written records survive, and to these we now turn.

There are roughly nine separate ancient witnesses to the *Pesah* and its celebration.[2] I provide here a listing:

(1) the foundational accounts in Exodus 12–13, which chapters are a combination of the putative sources P (12:1-20, 28, 40-50), E (12:21-27, 29-39; 13:1-19, 21-22) and J (13:21-22);[3]

---

[2] The most important study on this is J.B. Segal, *The Hebrew Passover From the Earliest Times to A.D. 70* (London Oriental Series 12; London: Oxford University Press, 1963). Among other things, he argues that the biblical order is also roughly the chronological order, and does so by pushing against the hallowed traditions of the Graf-Wellhausen documentary theory. See also A.B. Bloch, *The Biblical and Historical Background of the Jewish Holy Days* (New York: Ktav, 1978), 101–66, for a more traditional explanation; also see the following important essays: Joseph Tabory ("Towards a History of the Paschal Meal," 62–80) and I. J. Yuval ("Easter and Passover as Early Jewish Dialogue," 98–126) in *Passover and Easter* (ed. P.F. Bradshaw and L.A. Hoffman; vol. 5 of *Two Liturgical Traditions*; Notre Dame: University of Notre Dame Press, 1999): L.A. Hoffman, "The Passover Meal in Jewish Traditions," 8–28; Blake Leyerle, "Meal Customs in the Greco-Roman World," 29–61; B.S. Childs, *The Book of Exodus* (OTL; Louisville: Westminster John Knox, 1974), argues against Segal (pp. 184–86; see pp. 178–214. The *ne plus ultra* in Jesus studies is J. Jeremias, *The Eucharistic Words of Jesus* (trans. N. Perrin; Philadelphia: Fortress, 1977) who is himself quite dependent upon G. Dalman, *Jesus-Jeshua* (trans. P.P. Levertoff; New York: Macmillan, 1929) and H.L. Strack and P. Billerbeck, *Kommentar zum Neuen Testament aus Talmud und Midrasch* (6 vols.; München: C.H. Beck'sche, 1922–1961), 4:1, pp. 41–76; Strack and Billerbeck, in spite of their moil of examining ancient texts, operated with the tendency to typologize and so to cover every detail with the overlay of legend. See also A.J. Saldarini, *Jesus and Passover* (New York: Paulist, 1984); R. Pesch, *Das Abendmahl und Jesu Todesverständnis* (QD 80; Freiburg-Basel-Wien: Herder, 1978); X. Léon-Dufour, *Sharing the Eucharistic Bread* (trans. M.J. O'Connell; New York: Paulist, 1986).

[3] For the most recent attempt to break it down, see W.H.C. Propp, *Exodus 1–18* (AB 2; New York: Doubleday, 1999), 355–58, who sees Exodus 12:1–13:16 to be from P and most likely E. Source analysis of the pentateuchal traditions, including also the *Pesah* traditions, are in disarray today. Propp's study is complete enough to be a small monograph itself (cf. pp. 355–461). A popular, but eminently useful, source is R.E. Friedman, *The Bible with Sources Revealed* (San Francisco: HarperSanFrancisco, 2003); Friedman has a readable study of his more modern rendition of pentateuchal source analysis also in his *Who Wrote the Bible?* (New York: Summit, 1987). See also the various views in F. Crüsemann, *The Torah* (trans. A.W. Mahnke; Minneapolis: Fortress, 1996); I. Knohl, *The Sanctuary of Silence* (Minneapolis: Fortress, 1995). No attempt at critical evaluation will be given here, nor is anything substantial rooted in such positions. An informed, if traditional,

(2)   the disparate traditions found now in Exodus 23:14-17 (E); 34:18, 23 (J); Leviticus 23 (P); Numbers 9:1-14 (P); 28:16-24 (either P or the pentateuchal redactor);

(3)   the influential Deuteronomic rendition in Deuteronomy 16;

(4)   the historical traditions of Joshua 5:10-12; 2 Kings 23:21-23 par. 2 Chronicles 35; Ezra 6:19-22; Ezekiel 45:21-24;

(5)   *Jubilees* 49;

(6)   various texts in Josephus; 11QTemple XVII, 6-9 (of little significance);

(7)   Philo at *Spec.* 2.145–75, esp. 145–49;[4]

(8)   *Mishnah*, especially tractate *Pesahim*; various rabbinic texts;

(9)   the gospel traditions about the last supper (Mark 14:22-25 par. Matt 26:26-29; cf. Luke 22:19-20 and 1 Cor 11:13-26; John 13).

Other texts, such as John 6, provide for us only possible information about early Christian perceptions of *Pesah*/Eucharist traditions and will be used only in passing. The various *Pesah* practices of Jews are from roughly five periods, though dating is problematic: first, the foundational documents in Exodus 12–13; second, contributions from later Jewish traditions added into the Pentateuch and various historical books; third, the Deuteronomic tradition; fourth, the evidence from the first centuries BCE and CE; and fifth, the mishnaic evidence. There are at least seventeen separate elements of the *Pesah* tradition, and the evidence can be complex, so a chart of the discussion ends this section.

THE ELEMENTS OF PESAH: *A SURVEY*

All the fundamentals of *Pesah* are found in the traditions in Exodus 12–13. J.B. Segal,[5] author of the most important book on *Pesah*, thinks *Pesah* evolved out of an original New Year festival. Most scholars think *Massot* (Feast of Unleavened Bread) and *Pesah* were originally separate feasts, but were shaped into an organic unity by the realities of agricultural life.[6] From the foundational traditions the following elements of *Pesah* emerge:

---

approach to the broader issues of history in the Tanakh can be seen in V. Philips Long, et al., *Windows into Old Testament History* (Grand Rapids: Eerdmans, 2002).

[4] On Philo, see C.T.R. Hayward, *The Jewish Temple* (London: Routledge, 1996), 13–35. Philo calls *Pesah* the "crossing over" (διαβατήρια), and this refers to crossing over the Red Sea and the land of Israel (but not the crossing over of the avenging angel at the foundational *Pesah*). The note at the bottom of the Loeb edition of *Spec.* says that in "classical Greek *diabateria* are offerings made before crossing a boundary, and also (Plutarch, *Luc*, 24) before crossing a swollen river" and point to par. 147 in Philo's *Spec.* 2.

[5] See Segal, *Hebrew Passover*, 114–54; Saldarini, *Jesus and Passover*, 6–8.

[6] The ancient evidence is unclear on the earliest season for the New Year festival: it could have been either spring (*Pesah*) or fall (Rosh Hashanah and Yom Kippur).

- all Israel, with a focus on the circumcised, isolates and sacrifices an unblemished, male lamb (Nisan 10);
- all Israel kills the victim in the home on the evening of Nisan 14;[7]
- Israel is to smear blood on the lintel and doorposts with hyssop (marjoram);
- Israel is to roast the entire lamb and eat it with unleavened bread and bitter herbs;
- Israel is to eat the meal in haste;
- YHWH "passes over" the home if the blood is properly visible;
- the firstborn dies in the homes where the door has no such blood reminder, and the household discovers death the next morning;
- the feast is perpetual and celebrated along with *Massot* (a seven-day festival);
- the 1st and 7th day are "holy convocations";
- children are given an interpretive explanation of the meal and its festival habits;
- Israel inherits wealth from their neighbors, the "spoil of the Egyptians."

Along with a few other items (e.g., that the lamb was to remain in the house, that no bones were to be broken, and that the firstling sacrifice memorializes the *Pesah*), these are the essentials of the later *Pesah*: the march of time led to alterations, adaptations, and omissions, but the basics are all here. The meal served, whether specifically intended or not, as a meal that shaped identity and cohesiveness for all Israel—as it did then, so it does now.

A second and later phase of *Pesah*, however, is found when we examine other pentateuchal traditions that appear to reflect *Pesah* as celebrated in the land of Israel (Exod 23:14-17; 34:18, 23; Lev 23; Num 9:1-14; 28:16-25). In particular, *Pesah* appears to be fundamentally a *male feast* connected to the military census. Further, the victim is sacrificed, no longer in the home, but at a *sacred shrine*, and a sacrifice occurs *daily* during *Massot*. Accompanying such a celebration is a second-day sheaf offering of cereal and wine that permits harvest throughout the land and the eating of new crops; such an act anticipates Pentecost and integrates the two festivals. For those who "missed" *Pesah*, a *Second Pesah* is established. Finally, there is now a threat, perhaps because of the military census, of extirpation for those who do not participate. (One suspects that the days under Pharaoh needed no such warning.)

The so-called Deuteronomic revolution in Israel influenced *Pesah*, and this can be seen in the practices encoded in Deuteronomy 16.[8] The most unusual innovation—eventually frowned upon and perhaps even removed—is the

---

[7] For the rabbinic discussion of why there was a four-day wait from selection to sacrifice, see the interesting piece by J.M. Cohen, *Moments of Insight* (London: Vallentine, Mitchell 1989), 37–63, who suggests it had to do with the necessary three days following circumcision.

[8] For a critical study of the so-called Deuteronomic history, see A.F. Campbell and M.A. O'Brien, *Unfolding the Deuteronomistic History* (Minneapolis: Fortress, 2000).

permission to take the *Pesah* victim from the herd (16:2; *Tg. Onq.*; Deut 16:2, where it is also clarified that the herd sacrifice pertains to the festive offering of the week; assumed in *m. Pesah*; cf. also *m. Menah* 7:6). Again, showing the growing centralization of the festival, the victim is slain and eaten at the shrine/temple in Jerusalem. The celebrants return to their "tents" (16:7) in the morning after the celebratory meal. The bread of the *Pesah* meal is now known as the "bread of affliction" (16:3) and the victim may be "boiled" instead of roasted (16:7), another interesting but disputed innovation.

Later Jewish traditions, found now in the historical books as well as in texts like *Jubilees*, reveal more adaptations. Joshua 5:10-12 informs the reader that when the children of Israel ate unleavened bread, their manna ceased. Both 2 Kings 23:21-23 and 2 Chronicles 35 reveal the emerging priestly centrality in the feast: priests and Levites do the slaying and pouring of blood for the household groups gathered in the temple. The king and princes provide a victim for the people. As a clarification of the earlier Deuteronomic tradition, the offerings of the week could be boiled but not the *Pesah* victim. The Levites look after the details for the priestly celebration, while singers and gatekeepers assume new roles for the feast. Little new tradition is found in either Ezra 6:19-22 (where Levites and priests have central roles) or Ezekiel 45:21-24 (though here the prince gets more attention as a provider, and *Pesah* is merged [contra the previous traditions] with ideas of atonement).

Jubilees 49, based as it is on both Exodus 12 and Deuteronomy 16, reveals a few noteworthy features that take us to at least one person's perception of the practices at the cusp of the first century.[9] First, in contrast to the foundational traditions, joy characterizes the week and participants drink wine.[10] There are now praises and blessings as an apparent routine within the meal. Evening is "between the evenings from the third part of the day until the third part of the night" (e.g., roughly from 2:00 p.m.–2:00 a.m.). The victim cannot be boiled, nor is the slain animal to be eaten raw. This stipulation is confirmed by the copies of Deuteronomy from roughly the same period found at Qumran (Deut 16:7: "Then you shall cook and eat"). Participation in *Pesah*, showing the prophylactic dimension of ancient religious rites, will protect from plagues throughout the year. Apparently, the primary participants are males twenty years and older. Again, all is to take place in the temple, and the emphasis given to this demand (cf. 49:16-21) probably reveals a countervailing practice by some Jews outside Jerusalem.[11] *Pesah*, as can be seen, is a living stream of merging traditions, practices, and styles.

---

[9] Hayward, *Jewish Temple*, 103–7.

[10] Cf. Philo, *Congr.* 161: "And yet we all know that feasts and high days produce cheerfulness and gladness, not affliction [quoting Deut 16:3: "bread of affliction"]."

[11] See E.P. Sanders, *Judaism* (Philadelphia: Trinity Press International, 1992), 133–34, where Philo's evidence and the term sacrifice in Josephus, *B.J.* 14:260 (for the Sardinians) are also sifted.

By the first century, the Greek symposium and banquet (known to us especially through Plato's *Symposium*, Plutarch's *Table-Talk*, Petronius's shocking satire *Satyricon*, as well as Athenaeus's *Deipnosophistae*) began to make its presence felt in Judaism. Here we find an official meal with subsequent intellectual discussion (cf. Plato, *Symp.* 176E; Philo, *Contempl.* 75–78).[12] A clear example on Palestinian soil is the debauched dinner of the Roman rulers during which the bloodthirsty and no doubt drunken guests demand the head of John the Baptist (Mark 6:21-29). Possibly, even the much-earlier Amos refers to such banquets (Amos 6:4-7). The most significant impact of the symposium for Judaism (if any encouragement for such practices was needed) is the prominence that table fellowship has among Jewish sects. We think of Jesus eating with and teaching his disciples (e.g., Mark 2:13-17 pars.), the austere and orderly meals of the Essenes (1QS VI), and the solid connection the Mishnah makes between table fellowship and the Pharisees (e.g., *m. Toh.* 9:7; *m. Or.* 2:5; *m. Ed.* 1:7).[13] One suspects that much of Jesus' teaching found expression in such settings (e.g., Luke 15:1-2), and evidently rabbinic teaching finds its first expressions in such settings.

To return to the thread of our discussion: *Pesah* was probably influenced as well by the symposium. *Pesah* was an official meal followed by instruction consisting of reciting the exodus and some psalms as well as an explanation of the events of the exodus for the family. That *Pesah* concerned Israel's exodus does not mean it could not have been shaped by the symposium structure—though Jews were quick to dissociate *Pesah* from the ribaldry of the fashionable symposia.

The first century, our fourth snapshot into the history of the rite, clarifies some details. Our first witness to testify is Philo (*Spec.* 2.145–75). He begins:

> In this festival many myriads of victims from noon till eventide are offered by the whole people, old and young alike, raised for that particular day to the dignity of the priesthood . . . on this occasion the whole nation performs the sacred rites and acts as priest with pure hands and complete immunity (2.145).

Defended by Philo as having its etiology in the impatience of the people in waiting for a priest to be the one who offered the sacrifices, the *diabateria* becomes for him a festival of joy. His remark is that "these are the facts as discovered by the study of ancient history" (2.146). When these "literal facts" (2.147) convert to allegory, they describe the "purification of the soul" (2.147), the *diabateria*

---

[12] On this, cf. Leyerle, "Meal Customs in the Greco-Roman World" and Tabory, "Towards a History of the Paschal Meal," in *Passover and Easter* (ed. Bradshaw and Hoffmann). More widely, see W.J. Slater, ed., *Dining in a Classical Context* (Ann Arbor: University of Michigan Press, 1991); F. Lissaggargue, *The Aesthetics of the Greek Banquet* (trans. A. Szegedy-Maszak; Princeton: Princeton University Press, 1990); D.E. Smith, *From Symposium to Eucharist* (Minneapolis: Fortress, 2003), 133–72.

[13] On the latter, see esp. J. Neusner, *The Rabbinic Traditions about the Pharisees Before 70* (3 vols.; South Florida Studies in the History of Judaism 202–4; Atlanta: Scholars, 1999).

from body and passions. Philo suggests that the home is turned into a temple and the victim is slain on Nisan 14 (= two sevens; 2:148–49). I don't see how Philo can be read apart from thinking the victim was also slain in the home. We know from other Jewish sources that by the time he was writing it was customary for the victims to be slain by the laity, but they did so at the temple where the priest then properly took care of the blood (cf. 2 Chron 30:15-16).

A second witness is Josephus. (The NT will be examined in due course.) Most notably, Josephus tells us that purity for *Pesah* celebration involved a pre-liminary seven-day period. Israelites, evidently, now come to Jerusalem a week early to insure their purity. During this time they dwell in tents in and around Jerusalem. The sacrifice of the *Pesah* (from the flock; cf. *Tg. Onq.* on Deut 16:2) victim occurs between 2:00 p.m.–5:00 p.m. Reversing what we saw in earlier traditions, both women and children participate in the *Pesah* meal, and the number of celebrants at a *Pesah* was roughly between ten and twenty. In addition, as a reminder of the connection of the feast to the agricultural year, when the sheaf offering took place, the trade in Jerusalem was triggered. People could now consume grain cut from the new harvest.

Finally, our next piece of serious evidence is *m. Pesahim*, especially chapter 10, by the time of which the symposium structure was long-forgotten and reversed, and the celebration was shaped by a seder that has shaped the custom for centuries.[14] Two conditions shape this tractate: *Pesahim* attempts to make sense of the *Pesah* traditions in light of (1) a competing Christianity and (2) a destroyed temple. B. Bokser, one of our foremost scholars of this mishnaic evidence, has pointed out that the *Pesah* meal itself substitutes for the *Pesah* sacrifice.[15] We learn here that priests and Levites divided the crowds in thirds,[16] that authorities whitened the stones of the temple (cf. Q 11:44 as explicated in Matt 23:27-28), and that the laymen killed the victim but the blood was handled by the priests. Wine was not to be involved in the sacrifice, but it was prominent in the meal. The Israelites fasted from the time of the sacrifice until the meal. As an act of solidarity and equality, each person reclined at the meal,[17] including both the poor and slaves, and gifts were given to women and children. With the father at the lead, portions of the Bible were read aloud and explained, perhaps even the same passages now found in the Passover Haggadah (e.g., Deut 26:5-8; Pss 113–18), a text emerging in definitive form in the ninth and tenth

---

[14] So Hoffman, "The Passover Meal in Jewish Tradition," 14.

[15] B.M. Bokser, *The Origins of the Seder* (Berkeley: University of California Press, 1984); see also L.A. Hoffman, *Beyond the Text* (Bloomington: Indiana University Press, 1987), 86–102; Tabory, "Paschal Meal" and Yuval, "Easter and Passover as Early Jewish-Christian Dialogue," in *Passover and Easter* (ed. Bradwhaw and Hoffmann), 98–124.

[16] On the possibilities, see Sanders, *Judaism*, 136–37.

[17] See Leyerle, "Meal Customs in the Greco-Roman World," in *Passover and Easter* (ed. Bradshaw and Hoffmann), 30–31.

centuries CE.[18] There is in the Mishnah an emphasis on the theme of redemption.[19] While not always prominent in the evidence we have surveyed, this theme drives the feast itself.

Notably *absent* at this time were the following elements that were part of the *Pesah* of Egypt: selecting the victim on Nisan 10, smearing blood on the lintel and doorposts, and eating in haste. The important *additions* of the Mishnah include: Israelites removed all by-products of grain from the house (*m. Pesah* 3:1), and various grains were not mixed. Unleavened bread was made from grain of the previous year, and what was left over was burned. A victim had to be at least eight days old; its purity was given more attention. The victim could be basted or dipped, but it could not be boiled. The purity of the celebrants was humanized: if the majority of the family was clean, all were considered clean for participation. To be considered a participant, one needed to consume an olive's bulk of the victim and an olive's bulk of unleavened bread: in other words, some but not much. The meal was done by midnight; they burned the remains on the evening of Nisan 16. The second *Pesah* was more relaxed in atmosphere and celebration.

THE ELEMENTS OF PESAH: A CHART

The following charts the development of *Pesah* from the exodus *Pesah* to the Mishnah's regulations. The numbered items printed in italics are elements from the foundational traditions. All other items are elements added over the course of history.

---

[18] I have used N.N. Glatzer, *The Schocken Passover Haggadah* (New York: Schocken, 1981); see also N. Martola, "Passover Haggadah," *The Encyclopedia of Judaism* (ed. J. Neusner, A.J. Avery-Peck, and W.S. Green; 5 vols.; New York: Continuum, 1999–2004), 3:1052–1062.

[19] The entire tradition of the *aphikoman*, the piece of bread broken off, saved until the end of the meal (which itself had variations), and perhaps signifying the Messiah, is hard to date (cf. *m. Pesah* 10:8 where J. Neusner translates אֲפִיקוֹמָן as "dainties"). One debate concerned the propriety of sweets ending the taste of the *Pesah* victim or the *massa*. D. Daube, *He That Cometh* (St. Paul's Lecture 5; London: London Diocesan Council for Christian-Jewish Understanding, 1966), and "The Significance of the *Afikoman*," *Pointer* 3.3 (1968): 4–5, makes a valiant effort to anchor this into the life of Jesus and argues that Jesus could not have both introduced a rite as messianic and fulfilled it at the same time. See also D. Carmichael, "David Daube on the Eucharist and the Passover Seder," *JSNT* 42 (1991): 45–67; W.D. Stacey, "The Lord's Supper as Prophetic Drama," *Epworth Review* 21 (1994): 65–74. Daube's claims, and those of his followers, may be true; what is difficult, however, is to determine whether Jesus was suggesting that he was (only this broken) piece of bread. If so, Jesus would be discreetly disclosing to his small band of followers that he was the Messiah. General probabilities weigh against Daube: what we know of the *Pesah* liturgy at the time of Jesus is minimal, certainly not enough to anchor this suggestion firmly into the time of Jesus. Further, as I shall argue below, it is unlikely the last supper was Pesah, even if it shared with *Pesah* several of the themes of the *Pesah* week. For a critique of Daube, see Bokser, *Origins*, 65–66; Tabory, "Paschal Meal," 72–74, 79–80, n. 50. It is known, however, that *Pesah* was connected to messianic expectation, but what date we are unsure: cf. e.g., *Mek. de R. Ishm.* (on Exod 12:42); *Exod. Rab.* 18:12.

Elements of Exod 12–13	Exod/Lev/Num	Deut	Others	Jewish 1st c.[20]	Mishnah
a1. Preliminary purity for 7 days.	x				
a1.1 If majority are clean at offering, all clean.					x
a2. Stones of ramp and altar whitened.					x
1. Unblemished male; 1year old; household secured on Nisan 10.					
1a. Male feast; military census.	x				
1a.1 20 years and older.			x		
1a.2 Women and children.				x	
1b. Intentional absence means extirpation.	x				
1c. Victim from herd.		x			
1c.1 Lamb and kids.					x
1d. Victim from king/princes.		x			
1d.1 From 8th day old.					x
1e. Celebration protects against plagues.			x		
1f. Feast emphasizes redemption.			x (Ezek.)		x
1g. Purity of victim a great concern.					x
2. Killed in home on evening of Nisan 14.					
2a. Sacrifice at shrine daily.	x				
2b. Must be at shrine; temple.		x			x (Philo?)
2c. Priests slay and pour blood.			x		
2c.1 *Pesah* offering slain 2:00 p.m. to 5:00 p.m.				x	
2c.2 Laity kills; blood handled by priests.				x (Philo?)	x
2d. Priests sprinkle; Levites flay; roasted portions given back.			x		
2e. Evening defined: from 3d of day to 3d of night.			x		
3. Smear blood on door; stay until morning.					—
4. Eat entire roasted lamb that night; unleavened bread; bitter herbs; burn remainder in morning.					
4a. Called bread of affliction		x			
4b. Victim may be boiled.	x				
4b.1 Boil offerings, not victim.		x			
4b.2 Do not boil victim.			x		
4b.3 Basted or dipped, not boiled.					x
4c. Sacrifice must occur at shrine.	x				
4d. Morning return to tents.	x				
4e. Levites prepare meal for priests.		x			
4f. Wine introduced into meal.				x Philo: no wine.	
4g. Liturgical praise and blessings added.				x	
4h. Do not eat victim raw.			x		
4i. Fast from sacrifice to *Pesah.*					x
4j. All recline; including poor and slaves.					x
4k. Exodus haggadah and *Hallel* read aloud.				x(Philo?)	x
4l. Gifts for women and children.					x
4m. Celebrants must eat one olive's bulk of victim and bread.					x
4n. Meal done by midnight.					x
4o. Remains burned evening of Nisan 16.					x
5. Clothing: girded loins; sandals on; staff; haste.					—
6. YHWH passes over protected homes.					
7. Perpetual feast.					

[20] By which I mean a combination of Philo, the NT, and Josephus.

Elements of Exod 12–13	Exod/Lev/Num	Deut	Others Jewish	1st c.	Mishnah
8. Feast of unleavened bread: 7 days; Nisan 15-21; threat for eating leaven.					
8a. Sacrifice at shrine daily.	x				
8b. Sheaf offering of first fruits.	x				
Permits harvest/eating crops.					
Pentecost climaxes feast.					
8b.1 Triggers trade in Jerusalem.				x	
8c. When eaten, manna ceases.		x			
8d. Prince provides sheaf offering.		x			
8e. Joy characterizes week.			x	x	
8f. By-products of grain removed from house.					x
8g. Leaven destroyed by burning.					x
8h. Mixing of grains prohibited.					x
8i. Unleavened bread made from previous year's grains.					x
9. 1st and 7th days of Massot are holy convocation.					
10. Explain ritual to children.					
11. Firstborn slain redeems Israel;					
* Egyptians share wealth.*					
12. Circumcision required for participation.					
13. Lamb stays in house.					
14. No bones to be broken.					
15. Firstling sacrifice memorializes Pesah.					
16. Second Pesah *established*	x				
16a. Requirements and rituals relaxed.					x
17. Singers and Gatekeepers contribute to feast.		x			

JESUS AND THE *PESAH* MEAL

To discern what Jesus and his followers would have done at a *Pesah* celebration, I propose the following methodological procedures as indicative of historical probability: what is *core* to the tradition and what is *consistent* from the later Jewish traditions to the Mishnah.[21] Admittedly, this is a maximalist historiographical approach, but, for reasons that will emerge in chapter 13 below, this procedure is tolerable for the moment.

No one should question the victim being a lamb, and neither should we doubt what is found consistently in *Jubilees*, Josephus, and the Mishnah. Nor should one question that *Pesah* was fundamentally a national celebration of redemption, or that it followed a routine order (seder), even if we can't completely identify that order and even if it was flexible enough to permit local variation. That such a festival awakened Jewish hopes for national liberation should

---

[21] Jonathan Klawans, in a public paper for the SBL Historical Jesus Section in Nashville, stated that there is a growing consensus of "non-Neusnerian scholars" who think there are historical bits in the Mishnah but that, when it comes to pre-70 *Pesah* data, very little can be known. His paper has now been revised and published as "Was Jesus' Last Supper a Seder?" *BibRev* 17 (2001): 24–33, 47. He interacts with Hoffman, *Beyond the Text*, 89–93, who argues that the form of the seder known in rabbinic writings is post-70 CE. See also R. Routledge, "Passover and Last Supper," *TynBul* 53 (2002): 203–21.

not be doubted (Josephus, *A.J.* 17:149-167; 20:112; *Pesiqta de Rab Kahana* 7.11.3). Thus: "The celebration was designed to keep fresh the memory of the momentous struggle against slavery and the revelation of God through Moses. It was also to reassure the people that the Almighty would smite all future tyrants as he had done to Pharaoh."[22] We should keep in mind that *Pesah* was kept alive by oral memory rather than by fixed, written text. As such, the event would have been both firm and flexible—a father might have a style and a region (say, Galilee or Judea), or a set pattern for certain features, but the nation had a memory and a founding text: Exodus 12.[23]

To return to a method for digging out information for the first century CE celebration, some features that were likely part of the *Pesah* are not witnessed in the Mishnah, and so we will, at times, need to classify some elements as only likely or possible. In light of this procedure, we now provide a sketch of what the elements of the last supper of Jesus would have been if a *Pesah* meal.[24] I assume here that the Jesus traditions about the last supper are about a *Pesah* meal in order to give the event a local, realistic color. If the last supper was not *Pesah*, then all the details of the meal drop out and we are left with a simple *Pesah* week meal. But more of that in the next chapter.

It is likely that Jesus and his "fictive kin" and "family" arrive in Jerusalem seven days early to purify himself (and themselves) from corpse impurity,[25] and it is probable that he participates in daily worship and rituals at the temple. However, if Jesus does not arrive in Jerusalem seven days early to secure purity, a priest in Galilee would have performed purity rites over Jesus and other Galileans who that year were planning to attend *Pesah* (cf. Josephus, *B.J.* 6.290 [gathering in Jerusalem on Nisan 8]; Philo, *Spec.* 1.261).[26] It is certain that purity is a major concern for all celebrants. No one thinks of flouting purity laws when it comes to *Pesah*, or any of the high holidays.

When the time for sacrifice comes on Nisan 14 (between 2:00/3:00 p.m. and 5:00 p.m.),[27] Jesus takes an unblemished male lamb to the priest and Levites on behalf of a household that, typically, includes males and females, adults and children. To be sure, there is no evidence at the last supper that women were participants, but that may simply confirm the invisibility of women in Jewish records. I contend that it is possible that Mary was in attendance for three reasons: (1) it is highly likely Mary would have attended, as custom, *Pesah*, and she

---

[22] Bloch, *Biblical and Historical Background of the Jewish Holy Days*, 102; see also 117–18.

[23] This understanding of traditions has now been worked out in detail in J.D.G. Dunn, *Jesus Remembered* (vol. 1 of *Christianity in the Making*; Grand Rapids: Eerdmans, 2003). See ch.1, n. 7.

[24] The following summary may be compared with Sanders, *Judaism*, 132–38; also Saldarini, *Jesus and Passover*, 35–40, even though he does not operate critically enough with later rabbinic evidence.

[25] See here Sanders, *Judaism*, 113, 134.

[26] This element would not have featured in *m. Pesah* since attendance at the temple was no longer possible.

[27] If on a Sabbath, from 2:00 p.m. to 5:00 p.m.

would have naturally done so with her family; (2) the early Jesus traditions may suggest she was present during this last week of Jesus' life [cf. Mark 15:40, 47; 16:1]; (3) a later tradition implies her presence during the last week in Jerusalem [John 2:1-10; 19:25-27].[28]

Back to the sacrifice of the victim. Jesus, in this case the *paterfamilias* of this *Pesah* household, hands over a pure lamb to the priest, who probably slays the lamb in the presence of Jesus and any who accompany him. (In light of the mishnaic evidence, it is possible that Jesus would have slain the lamb.) Then the authorities impale the lamb on a stake and prop up the impaled victim on the shoulders of the Levites. They perhaps hook the lamb onto a wall to facilitate removing its parts (*m. Pesah* 5:9). The priest then flays the lamb with two separate procedures taking place: first, he returns the hide and meaty portions to Jesus for the family's *Pesah* meal; second, he catches the blood in a basin and tosses the blood against the base of the altar (probably through a series of passing bowls of blood from one Levite to another), while the fatty portions are removed in order to be burnt on the altar (immediately above the celebrants).

Along with his followers, Jesus finds a place to celebrate the *Pesah*. The gospel evidence implies a prearranged dining room, perhaps with padded couches placed in a U-shape so each could see and talk with everyone (Mark 14:12-16 pars.).[29] There they are to eat the roasted (not boiled) *Pesah* lamb. They (or someone for them) prepare the room and the tables. It is unclear if the leaven and other grains were at this time removed from the dining room—probably the owner had guaranteed that. Perhaps the disciples had already done so since the house had to be cleansed of leaven on Nisan 13. It is possible that they all fast during these few hours; maybe some do, maybe none. The *Pesah* victim is possibly basted or dipped in seasonings. Unleavened bread, possibly made from last year's grain, is made available, and bitter herbs are prepared. A fruit sauce also is prepared, and wine featured as the primary drink for the evening. I assume it is virtually certain that all of those with Jesus recline at table. Since we are unsure if children are present with Jesus and his followers, we cannot be sure that the *Pesah* memorial is explained to children. I take it for granted that, had children been present, such an explanation would have been forthcoming.

It is possible that a rough and ready seder was already in existence to guide the *Pesah* celebration. What would have been in it? It is a certainty that the *Pesah*

---

[28] See esp. D.A. Lee, "Presence or Absence?" *Pacifica* 6 (1993): 1–20. So also Jeremias, *Eucharistic Words of Jesus*, 46. For women at Western meals, cf. Leyerle, "Meal Customs in the Greco-Roman World," in *Passover and Easter* (ed. Bradshaw and Hoffmann), 4–45. For the time of Jesus, see esp. K.E. Corley, *Private Women, Public Meals* (Peabody, Mass: Hendrickson, 1993); T. Ilan, *Jewish Women in Greco-Roman Palestine* (Peabody, Mass: Hendrickson, 1996), 176–204, who among other deficiencies, fails to examine women in festal settings.

[29] See Leyerle, "Meal Customs in the Greco-Roman World," in *Passover and Easter* (ed. Bradshaw and Hoffmann), 33–34; he points to another possiblity: the *stibadium*, a semicircular couch with a large D-shaped table. The number at the last supper would require more than one *stibadium*, and that is not impossible.

text of Exodus 12 was part of that seder, if not read aloud at the *Pesah*—why else have the feast? I take it as likely, however, that the levites had already begun to use the *Hallel* psalms (113–118) in their singing at the temple (*t. Sukkah* 3:2); it is also likely, though less so, that such a set text was mentioned, recited, or sung at the *Pesah* meal as well. The use of Psalm 118:22-23 (Mark 12:10-11) and 118:25-26 (Mark 11:9-10), during Jesus' last week, speaks highly of an existing use of the *Hallel* psalms at the time of Jesus. The evidence that the followers of Jesus sang a hymn would confirm the existence of a seder, but only if we knew those psalms were already being sung at the meal—and we don't know this confidently (cf. Mark 14:26). However, there is evidence from the later Jewish period, as well as the Mishnah, that praises and blessings were offered. To balance the evidence, we observe that it was customary to sing at the end of a symposium as well (Athenaeus, *Deipn.* 15.702A–B). Only late at night (after midnight?) do they leave Jerusalem (Mark 14:26, 32) and take care, if they need to, of what remains of the lamb.[30]

To tie this together under the condition that the last supper tradition is a *Pesah* meal *and* (and this is a big condition) the Passover *Haggadah* reflects an early liturgical practice, the following elements are suggestive but impossible to determine with certainty.

1. Preliminary Meal.
    1.1 Word of dedication over first cup.   Luke 22:16?
            Blessing of feast day and cup.   Luke 22:17-8?
    1.2 Preliminary dish: herbs and fruit sauce.
    1.3 Meal proper served: 2d cup is mixed (but not drunk).
2. Liturgy.
    2.1 Passover *Haggadah* by father in Aramaic.
    2.2 Passover *Hallel*: first part (in Hebrew).
    2.3 Second cup.   Luke 22:16?
                                    Luke 22:17-18?
                                    Mark 14:23-25?
3. Main Meal.
    3.1 Grace by father over unleavened bread.   Mark 14:22
    3.2 Meal: *Pesah* lamb, unl. bread, bitter herbs,
            fruit sauce, wine.
    3.3 Grace over third cup.   Mark 14:23-25?
                                      Luke 22:17-18?
4. Conclusion.
    4.1 Second part of *Hallel* (in Hebrew).
    4.2 Praise over fourth cup (*Hallel* cup).   Mark 14:23-25?

As I have indicated above, there are grave doubts that the Passover *Haggadah* was a first century liturgical custom. And there are doubts about the very text of Luke and where the various elements line up with the Passover seder. Accordingly, the elements for a meal in the last supper traditions can be applied

---

[30] Questions arise here: was Olivet considered part of Jerusalem proper (cf. Mark 11:1)? If not, did they depart from custom and leave the city early? Could such take place on *Pesah*?

to nearly any Jewish meal but certainly to most festal meals celebrated in Jerusalem during a major feast.

What of the remaining portions of the lamb? The evidence is mixed, and three possibilities present themselves. First, Jesus' party consumed the entirety of the roasted lamb that evening. Second, they did not consume it all but took the remaining portions and burned them somewhere (presumably in Bethany) the next morning. Third, they did not consume it all but burned the remainder on Nisan 16, in the evening, according to the later custom. If the Synoptic traditions are a *Pesah* meal, then there is no evidence for any of the views. The first is more likely since they would have left the home at night—before morning and with no evidence for carrying around smelly roasted lamb portions. That Jesus and his followers might have left at night implies that the original demand of Exodus 12 to remain in the home until morning had been suspended; it also implies that the demand to return to tents in the morning was also suspended. In light of the followers of Jesus leaving at night, it is possible that the mishnaic stipulation to finish *Pesah* by midnight was already in effect.

Some omissions are likely or possible. It is not clear that Jesus and his followers applied blood to the doorposts and lintel, since the evidence for this practice after the first celebration is nonexistent. The gradual centralization of the feast in the temple renders this element obsolete. *Pesah* thus moved from family deliverance through the father's obedience to national deliverance through priestly ritual. It is only possible that Jesus' followers ate the meal in haste;[31] as *Pesah* evolved the haste gradually gave way to joy and memory (cf. Exod 12:14; 13:3; Deut 7:18; 16:3). Hence, loins were only possibly girded, sandals were possibly worn, and perhaps a staff may have been in place.[32] That basting and dipping the victim was permitted reveals this same lack of interest in haste.[33]

These are my judgments, more or less. *If* Jesus celebrated a *Pesah* meal during his last week in Jerusalem, then these are the elements he ritualized along with his followers. I have left to this point the reminder that Jesus subverted the *Pesah* story when he claimed that he was the bread and he was the wine. This rite, even if we don't know the details, embodies a story and defines a people— massive changes cannot enter into the rite without massive implications for group identity formation. I am suggesting that, if this is *Pesah*, then Jesus has redefined *Pesah*; and that means he has told a new story.

This previous discussion implies that the meal Jesus ate was *Pesah*. But the evidence for this final supper being *Pesah* is far from clear, and the balance of scholarship today is shifting away from that conclusion. That shift leads to the search for another kind of meal for understanding the last supper. And that shift

---

[31] But cf. D.C. Allison, Jr., *The Intertextual Jesus* (Harrisburg: Trinity Press International, 2000), 59–62. Isaiah 52:11-12 reverses the "haste" theme of Exodus 12:11 because the "Lord will go before you, and the God of Israel will be your rear guard."

[32] There is evidence of weapons later that night (Luke 22:35–38).

[33] See Bloch, *Biblical and Historical Background of the Jewish Holy Days*, 109–10.

also raises the issues of a new rite, a new liturgy, a new story, and thus a new identity for a new people—for that is the Christian understanding of the last supper. Each of these issues is shaped by the various accounts of the last supper, and each must be examined before we can determine what Jesus was doing; and furthermore, how what he was doing provides clues for how he understood his own death.

Chapter 13

Pesah and the Last Supper

To understand how Jesus divined his own death we have come to the conclusion that a variety of texts indicated he expected to die prematurely and that he sought for meaning in that death by exploring figures and texts in the Tanakh. But those gospel texts, including Mark 10:45 (at least as far as we have studied it), are not firm enough historically or not expressive enough of a theory of atonement for us to know *how* he interpreted that premature death.

A final tradition to consider is the last supper tradition, but to mine that text for clarity in our study involves several procedures. One of those has been done: what *Pesah* was like in Judaism. This study was undertaken in order to determine if the last supper was itself the *Pesah*. It is the purpose of this chapter now to turn to that question: is the last supper *Pesah*? To anticipate: if Jesus saw in *Pesah* a prefigurement of his own death, we would know that Jesus saw his death as analogous to the victim of the *Pesah*. If the last supper is not *Pesah*, however, then an interpretation of his death would have to be altered. It is the purpose of this chapter to lay the foundation to answer such a question.

There are four accounts of the last supper, including its redactional interpretations,[1] in the early Christian records: Mark 14:12-25; Matthew 26:17-29; Luke 22:7-23; 1 Corinthians 11:17-34.[2] In each, the focus is on the meal, which

---

[1] Since the Johannine texts (John 6; 13) do not concern the death of Jesus as expressed at the last supper but are, instead, later reflections on that event, I do not investigate them here. G. Theissen and A. Merz, trace three types of texts alongside the Synoptic witness: social presence (John 13), causal presence (*Did.* 9), and real presence (John 6); see their *The Historical Jesus* (trans. J. Bowden; Minneapolis: Fortress, 1998), 417–20.

[2] For a nice survey of the texts, see X. Léon-Dufour, *Sharing the Eucharistic Bread* (trans. M.J. O'Connell; New York: Paulist, 1986), 46–76. He exegetes the synchronic reading along three axes: vertical (Jesus with creation and God), horizontal (with the disciples), and temporal (imminent death, active community, and final banquet are each tied into Jesus' past and present). For a brief,

needed preparation. During the meal the possibility of betrayal is raised. Such dark actions stand in contrast to Jesus' own actions. Behind John 13 is a meal during which Jesus washed the feet of his disciples as a prophetic action to display to them the kind of character and service he desired of them. In each of the Synoptic accounts Jesus and the disciples are the *actors* and there are several primary *actions*: Jesus offers a blessing, breaks bread, distributes the bread; after the bread, he offers thanksgiving for the wine in the cup, gives the cup to the disciples, and tells them to drink. Finally, during the meal Jesus utters solemn words of interpretation to explain the bread and the wine, and then promises resumption of fellowship when the kingdom arrives. The Pauline form of this event can be dated to the mid-30s or mid-40s: Paul knows it as tradition when he writes 1 Corinthians in the spring of 55 CE; we can surmise that Paul got this tradition when he was a persecutor, or more likely, when he was in Damascus (Gal 1:17) or Jerusalem (Gal 1:18-24; 2:1-3, 6-10). These visits occurred between the mid-30s or mid-40s.[3] So much for the basics.

These four texts can be divided into the Markan-Matthean tradition, the Pauline, and only possibly a separate Lukan tradition in which he shears away any atonement theology. The shorter reading (SR) of Luke (22:15-19a) was most likely Luke's original text, to which scribes later added a conglomerate textual tradition, taken from Mark and Paul, to create a longer reading (LR). That account (LR) has two cups, and twice Jesus tells the table guests that he won't partake of a meal like this one again until the kingdom (22:16, 18). The broad family resemblance of these four traditions is, however, clearly evident in their faces and body types.[4]

---

traditional view, see D. Wenham, "How Jesus Understood the Last Supper," *Them* 20 (1995): 11–16. Other important studies include J. Jeremias, *The Eucharistic Words of Jesus* (trans. N. Perrin; Philadelphia: Fortress, 1977); J. Koenig, *The Feast of the World's Redemption* (Harrisburg: Trinity Press International, 2000). For a brief history of interpretation, see Theissen and Merz, *Historical Jesus*, 407–14; an older study is R.J. Daly, "The Eucharist and Redemption," *BTB* 11 (1981): 21–27.

[3] Cf. M. Hengel, *The Atonement* (trans. J. Bowden; Philadelphia: Fortress, 1981), 47–55; *Paul between Damascus and Antioch* (trans. J. Bowden; Louisville: Westminster John Knox, 1997), 288–90; Koenig, *Feast of the World's Redemption*, 11–14. See also J.D.G. Dunn, *Jesus, Paul and the Law* (Louisville: Westminster/John Knox, 1990), 110–13.

[4] Famously, Luke has a two-fold witness to the last supper: a shorter reading that ends at 22:19a and a longer reading. The latter has *two* cups, one dispersed and over which Jesus speaks a word of resumption of fellowship in the kingdom of God (22:17-18); and one which he interprets as the cup of the new covenant (22:20). Scholarship prefers today the longer reading. The most complete study remains Jeremias, *Eucharistic Words of Jesus*, 139–59; see also B.M. Metzger, *A Textual Commentary on the Greek New Testament* (London: United Bible Societies, 1971), 173–77; J.B. Green, *The Death of Jesus* (WUNT 2/33; Tübingen: JCB Mohr [Paul Siebeck], 1988), 35–42; but cf. B.D. Ehrman, *The Orthodox Corruption of Scripture* (New York: Oxford University Press, 1993), 197–209.

The longer text in Luke, however, adds elements from the Pauline tradition and these elements are, on other grounds, secondary. The shorter reading contains almost no soteriological interpretation of the elements of the last supper (wine, bread), and many scholars point out the shorter read-

For example, only the Pauline-Lukan (LR) traditions record the words "do this in remembrance of me" (1 Cor 11:24; Luke 22:19) and that "after supper" (1 Cor 11:25; Luke 22:20) Jesus took the cup. Positing three independent traditions oversimplifies the evidence. Xavier Léon-Dufour assigns Mark 14:25 (the eschatological saying) in the Markan-Matthean tradition (from Jerusalem or Caesarea) to the Pauline-Lukan tradition (from Antioch) to form two separate tendencies: a cultic (e.g., Mark 14:22-24 and 1 Cor 11:23-26) and a testamentary tendency (Mark 14:17-21, 23-24a [24b], 25). But, these two traditions are from "one and the same episode."[5]

The more original form is debatable because early Christians have introduced Jesus to some later liturgical/eucharistic theology and customs, as the Israelites had done to the earliest edition of *Pesah*.[6] Some scholars think little

---

ing's consistency with Lukan soteriology elsewhere (but cf. Acts 20:28). The most decisive evidence against the shorter reading is: (1) its witnesses are few; (2) its witnesses are geographically restricted; (3) this [so-called] Western reading lacks uniformity; (4) it is, liturgically speaking, the *lectio difficilior* [if, however, the meal is *Pesah* it would not be the more difficult]. J.B. Green, to his credit, argues for the longer reading but also that Luke transmitted such words because of their traditional value (see *Luke*, 761–64). The most significant weaknesses of the longer reading: (1) it is difficult to explain how and why scribes would have omitted 22:19b-20 and (2) the theology of atonement presented here is by most accounts non-Lukan, and Luke consistently avoids such a soteriology [observe the omission at Luke 22:27 of the ransom saying in Mark 10:45, a logion Luke presents as part of the last supper].

The issues are not simple. I am impressed by the erudition and argument of Bart Ehrman, and I see matters as follows: (1) I think if one preferred the shorter reading it would be best explained as Lukan *omission* of an earlier tradition rather than as *original tradition*. That is, it is most likely that Luke omitted the soteriological explanations because of his theology. If he did omit them, then they were previous to him and the Markan tradition would be confirmed; thus: original inclusion, Lukan omission, scribal restoration. (2) If the longer reading is preferred, the wording would be Lukan redactional working of the Markan tradition in light of the Pauline tradition. (3) In neither case are the Lukan textual traditions an independent tradition about the last supper words of Jesus. Ehrman's presentation has not received an adequate answer, and so I shall prefer the shorter reading for Luke's text. In what follows, however, I shall try to balance the evidence. Nothing in my argument ultimately depends on assuming the shorter reading, because I believe Mark had that soteriology in his reading, and I believe Paul did as well.

[5] The quotation is from p. 97. A chart can be seen in Léon-Dufour, *Sharing the Eucharistic Bread*, 78–79; discussion on pp. 96–101. Léon-Dufour prefers the Antiochene tradition because of its less hieratic character. However, this theory fails if one thinks the testamentary dimension just as integral to the original event as a cultic dimension. A *last* supper, implying per force some kind of *farewell* (thus, testamentary), in which Jesus identified himself with the bread and wine and which became a liturgized memory, would of a necessity have combined both the *testamentary* and the *cultic* from the beginning. A more precise division of the tradition revolves around the entrance of covenant atonement into what is on other grounds connected to Passover. Exodus 12 and Exodus 24 do not follow one another immediately, and the events there related are connected only by a narrative. See ch. 15 below.

[6] Cf. esp. B. Kollmann, *Ursprung und Gestalten der frühchristlichen Mahlfeier* (Göttinger Theologische Arbeiten 43; Göttingen: Vandenhoeck & Ruprecht, 1990). On the context of early Christian worship, see now esp. the excellent study of L.W. Hurtado, *At the Origins of Christian Worship* (Grand Rapids: Eerdmans, 1999); on Jewish worship, see L.A. Hoffman, *Beyond the Text* (Bloomington: Indiana University Press, 1987).

would be found after a salvage operation. In the words of Xavier Léon-Dufour, "The Eucharistic practice of the first Christians did not owe its origin simply to the action of Jesus at the Supper, but supposed the intervention of other factors." Further, "the purpose of the account is not directly to relate an episode in the life of Jesus but rather to proclaim a foundational one."[7] Before we can interpret Jesus' sense of his death as seen in the last supper, we must go through the texts with a fine-tooth comb to discover what we can of what occurred at the last supper.

THE MOST PRIMITIVE ACCOUNT OF THE LAST SUPPER

The previous generation of form critics argued that both the Synoptic traditions and the Pauline text reflect not history, but a mythic assignation to Jesus of their eucharistic customs (e.g., a *cult etiology*).[8] But now the exhaustive analysis of Rudolf Pesch, set up by the thorough response to Bultmann by Vincent Taylor,[9] has demonstrated that the case of that generation should at least be open to review.[10] Others see the primitive tradition to reflect a *farewell/testamentary meal*.[11] This view of the last supper finds its best support in appreciation of solid, historical tradition in the Johannine material (e.g., John 13) as well as in the

---

[7] Léon-Dufour, *Sharing the Eucharistic Bread*, 39, 84.

[8] Cf. R. Bultmann, *The History of the Synoptic Tradition* (trans. J. Marsh; New York: Harper & Row, 1963), 265–66, 278. The purpose of an "etiological cultic story" is to ground a current liturgical practice in a foundational, historical (even if legendary or mythical) event. For more recent denials of the historical value of the last supper traditions, beside the Jesus Seminar, cf. M. Borg, *Jesus: A New Vision* (San Francisco: Harper & Row, 1987), 177, 187–88, n. 27.

[9] For Taylor's responses to the form critics, see esp. *Jesus and His Sacrifice* (London: Macmillan, 1955), 11–42; *Mark*, 542–47. His conclusion: "In general, I believe it is true to say that, while liturgical interests may have determined what is told or emphasized in the gospel narratives, unhistorical elements have not been imposed upon the primitive tradition in any important degree" (*Jesus and His Sacrifice*, 117). Thus, Mark is the most ancient, but these primitive accounts "reveal the singularly original manner in which Jesus conceived the nature of His redemptive death and related the Eucharist thereto" (*Mark*, 543). Pesch's arguments build on these two foundations: the antiquity of Mark and its value for assessing Jesus' perception of his own death (see following note).

[10] R. Pesch, *Das Abendmahl und Jesu Todesverständnis* (QD 80; Freiburg: Herder, 1978), esp. 21–69; see also the summary in his *Markusevangelium*, 2:364–77. Pesch's argument is a tour de force, and I would disagree at points. However, as my argument unfolds below, it will be seen that I agree that the oldest textual tradition is Markan, though there are potentially independent features in the Lukan-Pauline tradition. My points of disagreement with Pesch are that he sees the Markan form as nearly identical to the words of Jesus; I think there are secondary features already in the Markan form as well. And, he (like many) thinks the last supper is the *Pesah*. See a response in J. Gnilka, "Wie urteilte Jesus über seinen Tod?" in *Der Tod Jesu* (ed. K. Kertelge; QD 74; Freiburg: Herder, 1976), 13–50, here esp. pp. 31–41; Léon-Dufour, *Sharing the Eucharistic Bread*, 157–79. For other important surveys of the issues and scholarship, cf. G.R. Beasley-Murray, *Jesus and the Kingdom of God* (Grand Rapids: Eerdmans, 1986), 258–73; Theissen and Merz, *Historical Jesus*, 420–23; Daly, "The Eucharist and Redemption," 21–27, provides a nice survey of the German debate.

[11] See Léon-Dufour, *Sharing the Eucharistic Bread*, 85–95.

famous eschatological word of the last supper (Mark 14:25; cf. Luke 22:16, 18).
Pesch, however, mounts a serious argument for Paul's text betraying all the signs
of a founding story that embodies the origins and liturgical directions for
Christian eucharistic practice,[12] but he also contends that the Markan-Matthean
texts are to be dissociated from this cult etiology. Instead, these traditions are a
window on a genuine historical account, a narrative of the last supper of Jesus
with his followers. He also concludes that the most primitive form of the four
accounts is that of Mark.[13] Its attention to *genre* makes Pesch's study a singular
contribution.

His argument has proven compelling.[14] I cannot here rehearse all the necessary details,[15] but a few illustrate his approach. First, the Matthean minor textual variations, when compared to Mark, reveal Matthean redaction instead of a
more original form. As an example, Matthew's use of "for the forgiveness of sins"
(26:28; cf. Mark 14:24) is a Matthean clarification as also is his rephrasing of
"and all drank from it" (14:23). Mark observes that they had drunk it; but this
statement is no longer significant for a eucharistic setting. So, Matthew gives
directions to his community for eucharistic celebration: "all of you, drink from
it" (26:27). This eucharistic setting is important to Matthew—observe the parallelism of the preparatory words over the bread and the cup in 26:26 and 26:27.
A case is clear: Matthean ecclesiology and his church's practices have shaped
Matthew's text.

A second example is from Luke. The Lukan textual differences are explained
as follows: Luke 22:15-18, a section largely unparalleled in the Markan-
Matthean tradition, is a Lukan redactional reworking of Mark's famous "vow of
abstinence" (Mark 14:25), while Luke 22:19-20, if part of Luke's earliest text
(and I doubt it is), is a Lukan redactional "conflation" of 1 Corinthians 11:23-

---

[12] E.g., many have seen such in "do this in remembrance of me" (Luke 22:19; 1 Cor 11:24).
However, Passover is noted by this expression: Exod 12:14 (*l' zikkaron*); LXX: μνημόσυνον.

[13] The account in *Didache* 9:1-5 reflects later Christian eucharistic practices and is interesting for
what it tells us about that period. See also Justin, *1 Apol.* 66 (where the words are "this is my body"
and "this is my blood").

[14] E.g., see Davies and Allison, *Matthew*, 3:465; P. Stuhlmacher, *Grundlegung Von Jesus zu Paulus*,
vol. 1 of *Biblische Theologie des Neuen Testaments* (2d ed.; Göttingen: Vandenhoeck & Ruprecht,
1997), 130–33, 136–37. In effect, Pesch overturns the technical scholarship of the young Heinz
Schürmann, *Der Pashamahlbericht Lk 22, (7-14) 15-18* (NTAbh 19/5; Münster: Aschendorff,
1955); *Der Einsetzungsbericht Lk 22, 19-20* (NTAbh 20/4; Münster: Aschendorff, 1955).

[15] An alternative view, favored especially by Roman Catholic scholarship of Europe, is that of
Heinz Schürmann: that the most primitive account is to be found through Luke, not Mark, and
that there are two separate traditions present (Luke 22:15-18 and 22:19-20, the first historical and
the second an etiological cultic account). Schürmann has since modified his view (as reported in
Jeremias, *Eucharistic Words of Jesus*, 190). Schürmann was followed in general by Léon-Dufour,
Sharing the Eucharistic Bread, though Léon-Dufour judges the developmentary model of K.G.
Kuhn more successful. Here we find two early traditions, one cultic and the other testamentary,
combined (cf. 87–94). Cf. K.G. Kuhn, "Die Abendmahlsworte," *TLZ* 75 (1950): 399–408 (a
review of J. Jeremias).

25 and Mark 14:22-25. Luke's overall redactional direction is that of an *Abschiedsmahltradition* ("farewell meal tradition"), with atonement theology skimmed off. Luke's text clearly omits historical particularities that are also found in the Pauline text. In so doing, Luke's text becomes an example of later eucharistic worship settings as well as conflationary redaction.

As examples: (1) Luke's longer reading has the Pauline *eucharisteo* rather than the Markan *eulogeo* (Mark 14:22; Luke 22:19); (2) Luke (LR) has the Pauline "do this in memory of me" which neither Mark nor Matthew show (Luke 22:19); (3) Luke (LR) has the Pauline "and likewise the cup, after dinner" which replaces Mark's "and taking the cup" (Mark 14:23; Luke 22:20); and (4) Luke (LR) has "this is the new covenant in my blood," as does Paul, where Mark has "this is my blood of the covenant" (Mark 14:24; Luke 22:20).

The majority conclusion is that Paul's text is secondary and Luke's original presentation is one that cuts out the atonement theology. Thus, it becomes a weighty judgment to conclude that Mark's text is the most primitive rendition of the last supper of Jesus. We are on solid ground here but, as is often the case with the Jesus traditions, they aren't that simple (as our discussion will show). But, in general, Pesch has proven the case for Markan priority of the last supper as well as its non-liturgical genre. We thus must begin with Mark to discern Jesus' intentions in the last supper, and one of the first questions present to any reader pertains to its relation to *Pesah*.

Is the Last Supper *Pesah*?

Four options present themselves.[16] First, it can be argued that the Synoptics are correct and that John has theologized the crucifixion of Jesus in such a way that Jesus becomes a *Pesah* victim. Thus, John (cf. 13:1; 18:28; 19:14, 36) depicts Jesus as a lamb dying on behalf of the community,[17] and John relocates some developed traditions about Jesus' body and blood back to John 6:53-58.[18] In the

---

[16] See most recently, R. Routledge, "Passover and Last Supper," *TynBul* 53 (2002): 203–21, here pp. 205–6. Unfortunately, Routledge seems unaware of the prevailing scholarship that the Passover *Haggadah* needs to be seriously questioned as a source for historical information about first century practice. On this, see now the popular statement by J. Klawans, "Was Jesus' Last Supper a Seder?" *BRev* 17 (2001): 30–33; see also B.D. Smith, *Jesus' Last Passover Meal* (Lewiston, N.Y.: Edwin Mellen, 1993), 99–108.

[17] For a complete study of all the possible allusions to Passover in John, see esp. S.E. Porter, "Can Traditional Exegesis Enlighten Literary Analysis of the Fourth Gospel?" in *The Gospels and the Scriptures of Israel* (ed. C.A. Evans and W.R. Stegner; JSNTSup 104/SSEJC 3; Sheffield: Sheffield Academic, 1994), 396–428. Porter's net is a bit wide. For example, *lamb* appears to necessarily be a "Passover lamb," but lambs were sacrificed other than at Passover. Nonetheless, it is to Porter's credit to show the potential significance of this theme in John's Gospel.

[18] G. Dalman, *Jesus-Jeshua* (trans. P.P. Levertoff; New York: Macmillan, 1929), 86–93 (John relocates the *Pesah* elements to John 6 and adjusts the chronology a day forward); Jeremias, *Eucharistic Words of Jesus*, 41–84 (with reservations); Stuhlmacher, *Grundlelung Von Jesus zu Paulus*, 1:132–33; Hagner, *Matthew*, 2:772–73; Keener, *Matthew*, 622–23. A recent study devoted to a similar view

words of Barnabas Lindars, the Johannine depiction of Jesus dying during the slaughter of the lambs is "a purely Johannine invention, dictated by his theological interests, regardless of the traditions which he was actually handling."[19]

Second option: John is correct and the Synoptics have "passoverized" the last supper into a *Pesah* celebration.[20] In this instance, Jesus actually died on the day before Passover—roughly when the victims were being slaughtered in the temple—but it was the Synoptics who converted the last meal of Jesus into a Synoptic Passover account. Mark 14:12-16 and Luke 22:8, 15 become secondary theology.

Third, John is correct but the Synoptics give off only an appearance of the last supper being *Pesah*—a more historically-nuanced reading of the Synoptics reveals that the Synoptic last supper is only a meal from the last week.[21]

Fourth, a view more popular immediately after the initial discoveries of the Dead Sea Scrolls than today, claims that both are correct: John was following the calendar of Qumran while the Synoptics were following the calendar of the Pharisees or, more generally, that customs of various Jews differed on when to slay the lamb for Passover (cf. *m. Zebaḥ* 1:3).[22]

Though this last view has some support in its favor, like the Syriac Didascalia, it needs to be noted that there is no evidence that priests slaughtered lambs on two successive days to satisfy the calendrical calculations of various Jewish groups. If there is no evidence for separate slaughters, then we are thrust

---

is B.D. Smith, "The Chronology of the Last Supper," *WTJ* 53 (1991): 29–45, but he argues that John and the Synoptics are harmonizable, pointing especially to Johannine elements evocative of *Pesah* (cf. John 12:1; 13:10, 29, 30; 18:1) as well as the imprecision attached to the terms designating the feast days. But his view topples if "to eat the Passover" in John 18:28 does not mean, as he requires, "to eat the festival offering," and if "preparation of the Passover" in 19:14 does not mean "preparation for the Sabbath of Passover week."

[19] Lindars, *John*, 446. Lindars thinks the homily the author was using did see the meal now in John 13 as *Pesah*; John, however, inconsistently at times altered it.

[20] Brown, *John*, 2:555–58; cf. also R.E. Brown, *The Death of the Messiah* (2 vols.; ABRL; New York: Doubleday, 1994), 2:1351–1373; J.P. Meier, *A Marginal Jew* (3 vols.; ABRL; New York: Doubleday, 1991–2001), 1:395–401; A.J. Saldarini, *Jesus and Passover* (New York: Paulist, 1984), 51–79; an older defense can be seen in M. Goguel, *The Life of Jesus* (trans. O. Wyon; New York: Macmillan, 1946), 429–37; cf. also the nuances in H. Gese, *Essays on Biblical Theology* (trans. K. Crim; Minneapolis: Augsburg, 1981), 123–27.

[21] This was argued by Mary Marshall (Murdoch University, Perth, Western Australia) "New Insights on Jesus' Actions at the Last Supper," (paper presented at the annual meeting of the SBL, Historial Jesus Section, Atlanta, Ga., 22–25 November 2002) where she argues for a farewell meal that had, as one of its concerns, equitable distribution of the gifts of the land. I am grateful to her for giving me a copy of her paper.

[22] This view was established by A. Jaubert, *The Date of the Last Supper* (trans. I. Rafferty; Staten Island: Alba House, 1965); it has been followed by one who sometimes offers an *outré* view, E. Ruckstuhl, *Chronology of the Last Days of Jesus* (trans. V.J. Drapela; New York: Desclee, 1965) and most recently by I.H. Marshall, *Last Supper and Lord's Supper* (Grand Rapids: Eerdmans, 1981), 57–75; D. Instone-Brewer, "Jesus's Last Passover," *ExpTim* 112 (2001): 122–23.

back upon the first three explanations, or a variant of the first two.[23] If there was only one official slaughter of lambs, there was only one official *Pesah*. Any other meal that week, whether intended by various groups to be a *Pesah* meal or not, was not *Pesah*. Accordingly, the argument comes down to this—on which day did Jesus die? Was it on Passover or the day before? or, more fundamentally, was the last supper a *Pesah* meal or a normal (Passover week) meal? At times, scholars have proposed other kinds of ancient meals as the background to the last supper, but none has commanded consent.[24] The options are either *Pesah* or another Passover week meal and, if the latter, various forms of ancient celebratory meals could be present.[25] The most precise method of sorting out this question is to assess the evidence for the last supper being *Pesah*. If the meal is *Pesah*, then Jesus died the next day; if not, he probably died on the afternoon of *Pesah*.

Various arguments are used to show the last supper as *Pesah*.[26] The Markan narrative three times seemingly states[27] that the meal was a passover meal (*to pascha*) connected to the first day of unleavened bread (Mark 14:12, 14, 16). It is hard to think of this meal being other than the *Pesah* meal since it occurs the evening after the slaughter of the lambs (Mark 14:12: *hote to pascha ethuon*). Some have tried to give "the first day of Unleavened Bread" a more expansive meaning, but "when the Passover lamb is sacrificed" is inflexible. At first blush, this verse seems to mean that Mark presents the last supper as *Pesah*.

[23] B.F. Westcott contended that the words of interpretation of the Synoptics can be fitted between the verses of John 13; cf. his *John*, 188 (the bread before 13:2 and the cup before 13:33). There are four significant similarities in a comparison of the two meals: warning of a betrayal, prediction of Peter's denial, fruit of the vine, and the theme of the covenant. Further, John has in common with the Markan-Matthean tradition the scattering of the disciples while Luke and John have in common the lesson on humility and the future of the disciples in the kingdom or house. On this, cf. Brown, *John*, 2:557.

[24] For a nice discussion, see Keener, *Matthew*, 627–29; see also Jeremias, *Eucharistic Words of Jesus*, 26–36; the fundamental study for Qumran is K.G. Kuhn, "The Lord's Supper and the Communal Meal at Qumran," in *The Scrolls and the New Testament* (ed. K. Stendahl; London: Harper, 1957), 65–93, 259–65; Gese, *Essays on Biblical Theology*, 117–40 (who finds the origins of the Lord's Supper [not last supper] in the *Todah*: "thank offering meal"); C. Burchard, "The Importance of Joseph and Aseneth for the Study of the New Testament," *NTS* 33 (1987): 102–34. The summary statement of G. Theissen and A. Merz may be taken to be a consensus: "The provisional conclusion at present is that in primitive Christianity a 'normal' fellowship meal was combined with a highly theological interpretation which we cannot derive satisfactorily from the religion of the world of the time. It is still a riddle how this combination came about. Paul did not create it; Jesus could have prompted it. But that is not certain" (*Historical Jesus*, 414).

[25] The suggestion of Léon-Dufour, *Sharing the Eucharistic Bread*, 41, that the meal is a covenant meal founders on a lack of evidence (his text, 2 QS 24,4, so far as I know is not a text; the best I can determine he means 1QS VI, 2-6). Nor is his suggestion of a *toda*-sacrifice plausible for Jesus, even if it might have significance for the early Christian rite's developments (see pp. 41–44).

[26] Undoubtedly, the most robust defense of the last supper traditions as *Pesah* is that of Jeremias, *Eucharistic Words of Jesus*, 15–88 (he discusses fourteen arguments); he has been summarized in Marshall, *Last Supper and Lord's Supper*, 57–75. I list only the most significant arguments.

[27] See France, *Mark*, 561; L.C. Boughton, "'Being Shed for You/Many,'" *TynBul* 48 (1997): 249–70.

The last supper took place intentionally in Jerusalem (14:13, 26), at a prearranged time and a prearranged location. The meal was for a fictive family which otherwise was apparently staying in Bethany (11:11-12; 14:3). When the meal was completed Jesus and his followers evidently did not leave Jerusalem, but instead went out to Mt. Olivet. This conforms to the *Pesah* requirement to remain in Jerusalem until the morning.

The last supper occurred at night, in the evening, rather than during the late afternoon, before evening. Ordinarily, Jews in the land of Israel ate two meals: at the fifth hour (e.g., 10:00 a.m. to 11:00 a.m.) and then late in the afternoon, before the evening (cf. Mark 6:35 [indicates an evening meal is a late meal]; Luke 24:29-30). Josephus, for example, tells us that the Essenes had their breakfast at 10:00 a.m. (the fifth hour) and then dinner "until evening" ("late afternoon"; *B.J.* 2:129-32). An assortment of evidence shows that *Pesah*, however, was celebrated at night: Exodus 12 set the agenda and it was always followed (*Jub.* 49:1, 12). *Mishnah Zebahim* 5:8 concurs: "The Passover is eaten only at night. And it is eaten only up to midnight." The custom was that at midnight the doors of the temple were opened, one may assume for entrance into the temple for the next day's festivities (Josephus, *A.J.* 18:29; *m. Yoma* 1:8). And the early Christian eucharistic practice memorializes a meal "on the *night* on which Jesus was betrayed" (1 Cor 11:23). At any event, that this meal took place at night conforms to the practice of *Pesah*.

Both Mark and Luke depict Jesus breaking bread in the *middle* of the meal (Mark 14:22 [cf. 14:18, 20]; Luke 22:19 [LR]), even though normal Jewish meals began with the breaking of bread. A much later Passover custom involved a child's question as to why on this evening the habit was to dip without bread; this tradition would, if first century (and it is not), simply confirm that bread was not eaten until the middle of the meal.[28] This is plausible but hardly compelling. We simply do not have all the details of the meal—perhaps they broke bread earlier as well. Perhaps ordinary meals could have a second or third breaking of breads.

During the last supper, Jesus dispatches Judas to do what he has to do "quickly," and the disciples are confused, thinking he has sent Judas out to purchase something or to give alms to the poor (John 13:27-29). That they are confused doesn't matter; it is what they were confused about that matters. They thought he was sent to give to the poor or to purchase something quickly because all purchasing would be prohibited when the day ended at 6:00 p.m. Such a confusion would be part and parcel of a Passover setting. Especially appropriate was their guess that Jesus had urged Judas to do something for the poor, for the poor were a special concern during *Pesah*. That the poor still are a concern in today's *Haggadah* is unquestionable.[29]

---

[28] See Jeremias, *Eucharistic Words of Jesus*, 49–50. The modern Passover *Haggadah* does not have the question Jeremias proposes.

[29] See N.N. Glatzer, *The Schocken Passover Haggadah* (New York: Schocken, 1981), 25. I find no

When the meal was over, according to Mark 14:26, they sang a hymn and departed for Mt. Olivet. The Passover *Haggadah* ends with singing the Passover *Hallel* (Pss 113–118; cf. *m. Pesaḥ* 10:6-7). Consequently, if the custom in the first century, in the land of Israel, was to finish off the *Pesaḥ* with the *Hallel*, then this evidence would fit into such a feast. There are, however, two problems: first, we are not sure that other Passover week meals did not end with hymns;[30] and second, we are not on firm ground when it comes to knowing if the *Pesaḥ* routine in the first century included such a *Hallel*. It is possible; what we are more sure of is that the Levites at the temple sang the *Hallel* during the slaughtering of victims.

During the last supper Jesus spoke words of interpretation over the bread and wine. This suggests a creative reuse of the custom of interpreting various elements of the meal during *Pesaḥ*. This act by Jesus is for Jeremias "the convincing argument."[31] Against such a view are two decisive considerations: words of interpretation could be proffered at any meal one chose to interpret—after all, the act is an innovation, and the argument assumes that the Passover *Haggadah* interpretations for children are pre-Jesus. Recent Jewish scholarship contends that the Passover *Haggadah* is a reaction to Christian practices, including Eucharist.[32] If so, is it perhaps only later that Jews began to (counter)interpret various elements to clarify their own identity?

What is necessary for an interpretive event is two-fold: an interpretation to be given and an element in a meal that can be interpreted analogously. A *Pesaḥ* meal is not required for Jesus to interpret elements of the meal as an imminent death. I don't, however, doubt that such an interpretation would be especially significant in a *Pesaḥ* setting. It is a mistake to think *Pesaḥ* is a requirement. If we grant the historicity of the fundamental sense of Jesus' words of interpretation (this is my body; this is my blood), even these do not require the *Pesaḥ* for meaning. Instead, they are appropriate during the entire week (after all, it was a redemptive week) or even at Yom Kippur.

---

evidence for Jeremias's assertion that somebody from the street could be invited into the *Pesaḥ*, implying that this somebody was poor and invited as such (*Eucharistic Words of Jesus*, 54). In fact, *m. Pesaḥ* 9:11 is about what happens when two parties are unsure about whether or not a victim was theirs. The text then states that they are to find a "third party" (so Neusner) or "stranger" (so Epstein-Slotki) and register with that party to avoid confusion and to maintain identity of the victim. I see no indication that the concern is one of compassion for the poor.

[30] Keener provides evidence for music at other festal meals; *Matthew*, 633.

[31] Jeremias, *Eucharistic Words of Jesus*, 55–61. Jeremias also offers five other arguments of dubious value: (1) that Jesus ate with the Twelve; (2) that they reclined at the table rather than sat; (3) that they ate in purity; (4) that they drank wine; and (5) that the wine was red. None of these is distinctive enough of the *Pesaḥ* meal and, by placing such arguments in equal place with the others, minimizes the case for the last supper being *Pesaḥ*.

[32] So J. Tabory ("Towards a History of the Paschal Meal," 62–80) and I.J. Yuval ("Easter and Passover as Early Jewish-Christian Dialogue," 98–124) in *Passover and Easter* (ed. P.F. Bradshaw and L.A. Hoffman; vol. 5 of *Two Liturgical Traditions*; Notre Dame: University of Notre Dame Press, 1999).

As can be seen by now, several of the arguments mounted for *Pesah* are problematic. That the meal took place in Jerusalem is not decisive. It is entirely plausible for Jesus to have arranged a meal for himself and his followers on any night of that week in Jerusalem; lenders would be more than willing to lease a room for the evening. Second, it is overly zealous to think that only a *Pesah* meal could be eaten at night, after the setting of the sun. In fact, we neither know enough about festal meals to assert such nor enough about the daily life of a Passover week celebrant to claim that a meal at night must be *Pesah*. It is not hard to imagine that Jesus, after a long day of arguing with Jewish leaders and warning pilgrims about God's imminent judgment on an unrepentant people, could have had meals later than most as a matter of course. I have stated already that breaking bread in the middle of the meal may be nothing exceptional at all. And, it is hard to imagine that Jesus would be concerned with the poor only at *Pesah*. At any rate, the extant data about concern for the poor at *Pesah* is late at best. The argument founders on a lack of clear evidence. Again, we don't know enough about first century custom to think that a hymn means *Pesah*; other meals, including a symposium, ended with hymns. In addition, the Synoptic order requires that a trial be held on Passover day itself (the night and then morning/afternoon of Nisan 14/15), a most unlikely scenario—though I would not rule it out as impossible since the restrictions of the Mishnah may not have been in force at this time.[33]

The view that the last supper was *Pesah* requires a seriously problematic set of events. J.P. Meier, in response to J. Jeremias, states it well:

> [H]e [Jeremias] cannot really establish the likelihood that, at the time of Jesus, the supreme Jewish authorities in Jerusalem would arrest a person suspected of a capital crime, immediately convene a meeting of the Sanhedrin to hear the case (a case involving the death penalty), hold a formal trial with witnesses, reach a decision that the criminal deserved to die, and hand over the criminal to the Gentile authorities with a request for execution on the same day—all within the night and early day hours of Passover Day, the fifteenth of Nisan![34]

Other considerations provide a fuller argument. The bread of the Synoptic accounts is nearly always called *artos* and not *azuma*, the more specific word for "unleavened bread." But there is evidence in the Bible to support the Synoptics' use of *artos* (cf. Exod 29:2 [LXX]; Lev 2:4; 8:26; and Num 6:19). One has to wonder why Eucharist became a *weekly* meal and not, like Passover, an annual meal. The disciples most naturally would have held a remembrance meal annually had it been seen as a new Passover. In addition, the last supper is restricted, apparently, to the twelve disciples, while *Pesah* was a family event.

---

[33] *M. Sanh.* 4:1 (the last line): "Therefore [since capital cases must be tried by day and completed by day], they do not judge [capital cases] either on the eve of the Sabbath or on the eve of a festival."

[34] Meier, *Marginal Jew*, 1:396.

Most decisively, there is the absence of the lamb in the Synoptic accounts. At no place does an Evangelist tell us that they ate lamb, the most significant element of the *Pesah* meal. And even more: had lamb been eaten, why did not Jesus suggest that "this *lamb* is my body"? Such is a virtual soteriological necessity for the one who is seeking to communicate to his followers that what is being consumed is analogous to the very offering of himself.[35] If the lamb was sacrificed and then consumed, it makes more sense for Jesus to have pointed to that. To be sure, this is an argument from silence. But sometimes silence is golden. The choice of Jesus to prefer the bread to the lamb for his sacrifice, if lamb was present, is nearly incomprehensible. To confirm this point, it is important that neither Jesus nor the disciples are described as going to the temple to offer their *Pesah* lamb. We have only a record that they entered Jerusalem and went to the home to eat a meal; we have no record they entered Jerusalem, then the temple, and then walked to the home for the meal. They didn't go to the temple, perhaps because it was one day too early to sacrifice the lamb. Jesus would be arrested that night (Nisan 13/14), tried, and then crucified at the time the victims were being prepared for slaughter (Nisan 14/15).

Finally: it is unlikely that Jesus could find a man who would loan out his own home during *Pesah*. It is a near certainty to think that the man would have used his own home for his own family. The only objection to this argument is that the man may have had a house big enough to enable two parties to celebrate *Pesah*. Or, perhaps he had two homes. It is not impossible.

We are left, then, with little substantial argument for the last supper being *Pesah*. John's record of Jesus dying during the slaughter of the *Pesah* victims is more plausible than Mark's (apparent) case that the last supper was *Pesah*.[36] Now let me retreat from this conclusion slightly: regardless of which position one takes, no one disputes that the last supper took place in a *Pesah* setting and that there are allusions to at least a *Pesah*-like meal in the texts.

Having concluded that John is most likely the more accurate account in matters of chronology, we need to observe that for some scholars, it is unconscionable to think John's record could get anything right. Historical Jesus scholars have, since the days of Strauss's study of Jesus in 1835, given John's Gospel a wide berth when it comes to the search for historical information about Jesus. However, scholarship since C.H. Dodd, C.K. Barrett, and J.A.T. Robinson has, if not overturned this view, given us the permission to grab Robinson's "long spoon," even if we do so with two hands.[37] The impact of this trend in assess-

[35] Gese, *Essays on Biblical Theology*, 124.

[36] See the abbreviated discussion in France, *Mark*, 559–63.

[37] C.H. Dodd, *Historical Tradition in the Fourth Gospel* (Cambridge: Cambridge University Press, 1963); C.K. Barrett, *John*; see also J.A.T. Robinson, *The Priority of John* (London: SCM, 1985), who, as a sometimes *renonçant*, finds the eccentric more suitable than the customary. For the "long spoon," cf. his "The Last Tabu?" in *Twelve More New Testament Studies* (ed. J.A.T. Robinson; London: SCM, 1984), 157. The most recent studies in favor of historical Jesus scholarship reconsidering the Fourth Gospel are by F.J. Moloney, "The Fourth Gospel and the Jesus of History,"

ing the question of history in John's Gospel is that the bits and pieces of this text are now up for grabs—and not just shoved into a bag in some dusty corner of historical unlikelihoods. In fact, John's Passion Narrative relates some facts significant for the historical Jesus and, in particular, for assessing whether the last supper was *Pesah*.

The critical texts are John 13:1; 18:28; 19:14 ("it was the time of preparation of the *Pesah*");[38] and 19:36. If these references are seen as historical, the following facts would emerge from these texts: (1) that John's last supper (cf. 13:38; also Luke 22:24-30) took place "before the feast of the Passover" (John 13:1), thus, at least Nisan 13/14 if not before.[39] (2) During Jesus' trials before Caiaphas and Pilate, the judges of Jesus did not want to enter the palace for fear that they might contract ceremonial uncleanness with respect to *Pesah*.[40] If they became unclean, they would be unable to eat the *Pesah* meal. Evidently, they had no thought of coming one month later for the second *Pesah* (Num 9:6-12). (3) When Jesus died, it was "the day of Preparation of the Passover," the sixth hour. This means the last supper could not have been *Pesah*. (4) Jesus' death, occurring as it did without breaking his bones, is understood by the author to be a fulfillment of the requirement for Israelites not to break the bones of the *Pesah* victim (Exod 12:46; Num 9:12; but cf. also Ps 34:20). Here we find a consistent interpretation. As well, there are present the kinds of details historians often see as incidental or accidental but nonetheless valuable for reconstructing history.

Valuable, also, for theology. It is true that John depicts Jesus, from the outset, as the "Lamb of God" (cf. John 1:29, 35), but this interpretive scheme need not have forced John to alter the facts of the death of Jesus. None of his details are inaccurate in this regard, and the evidence of the Synoptics is questionable at best. Further, if John is driving a theological agenda on the Lamb of God, he simply avoids direct comment over and over when he has opportunities in the passion account itself. The evidence is not as lopsided as one might think. John's lamb theology is hardly prominent.

What then are we to make of the problem left over from the discussion about the Synoptics—namely, what to do with Mark 14:12, 14, 16? These texts and John 19:14, if the term *pascha* has the same meaning, seem to be historically irreconcilable. Either Jesus instructed his disciples to prepare *Pesah* during the time of the slaughter (Mark) or he died when the victims were being slaughtered (John). There are, in my view, only two options: (1) that the term *pascha* has two different meanings or (2) that Mark has "passoverized" a Passover week

---

NTS 46 (2000): 42–58; C.L. Blomberg, *The Historical Reliability of John's Gospel* (Downers Grove: InterVarsity, 2001).

[38] I do not consider it impossible, though unlikely, that "the *Pesah*" in John 19:14 means "the *Pesah* week." This is found in Köstenberger, *John*, 537–38.

[39] Some have argued that the prepositional phrase and two participial clauses ("before . . . when Jesus knew . . . having loved") refer instead to the time Jesus washed feet prior to *Pesah*.

[40] Probably by not entering into a house in which leaven or impure items could be contacted. See the discussion in Brown, *John*, 2:845–46.

meal into the *Pesah* meal itself.[41] I have argued above that Mark's account is best not explained as a non-*Pesah* meal, and I have further argued that John's text is best explained as indicating that Jesus died Nisan 14/15, when the lambs were being slaughtered in the temple. He was buried before the feast actually began.

Finally, other considerations favor the Johannine chronology. The Sanhedrin wanted to put Jesus away *before* the feast, that is, before *Pesah* (Mark 14:1-2). Maybe they were not able to; but the text suggests they wanted to, and they pulled it off. Simon's coming in from the fields (Mark 15:21) gives the impression that he had been working—something not possible for the Synoptic chronology if one followed *Pesah* regulations. Also, it is unlikely Jesus could have been buried on the day of preparation, if it is preparation for *Pesah* (15:42). I also mention that the Pauline tradition of the Eucharist shows no signs of a connection to *Pesah*, even though Paul understands Jesus as the *Pesah* victim (1 Cor 5:7).

In conclusion, I suggest that John's Gospel is the one to be preferred here, and that we conclude that Jesus was crucified on Nisan 14/15, near to the time of the slaughtering of the *Pesah* victims. It would then have been historical realities that led Christians to see Jesus as the *Pesah* victim. Further, I take it as likely that Mark seems to have turned the last supper into a *Pesah*-like meal by deft language that brings out the Passover hues without the substance of the lamb itself. I do not think the evidence is certain, in fact far from it. Either view of these accounts (Mark being a real *Pesah* meal and John being a theologized account, or Mark "passoverizing" and John having a real *Pesah* death) can lead to a meal at which Jesus clearly articulated that his own death was imminent and that they were to ingest the elements of the meal as if they were his own death. The balance of the arguments and evidence leans toward Markan redaction rather than Johannine, but it is a balance and not an avalanche.

Having said this, it is not inappropriate in my judgment for Mark to call the meal *Pesah* because, in fact, Jesus turned a Passover week meal into a kind of *Pesah*. He did so by interpreting the various elements of that meal as symbolic of his own death. In so doing, the decisive act of redemption was no longer the exodus but instead what God was about to do through the death of his agent of salvation. If youth is a matter of perspective, so also was *Pesah*—here is the perspective that a lambless meal can be *Pesah*. That view belongs to the youth of Christian eucharistic practice, to a Jesus who was bold enough to celebrate *Pesah* a day early, without a lamb and in a home more readily available, and see in the bread his sacrficial body and in the wine his blood.[42] A farewell meal, indeed,

[41] See Léon-Dufour, *Sharing the Eucharistic Bread*, 163, 192–93. B.D. Chilton argues that a connection to Passover occurred at the hands of James; among other restrictions, Chilton contends the meal was designed only for the circumcised; see *A Feast of Meanings* (NovTSup 72; Leiden: E.J. Brill, 1994), 98–108. The requirement of circumcision, never clear in and of itself (could females connected to circumcised males participate?) because Exodus 12 enjoins a meal for a family, was however given up well before the time of Jesus.

[42] As stated earlier, B.M. Bokser argued nearly the same for *m. Pesah*: the *Pesah* became a substitute for temple ritual (see *The Origins of the Seder* [Berkeley: University of California Press, 1984]);

and one anticipating what was to occur the next day—both for himself and for Jews all over Jerusalem—the slaying of lambs.

A final point: we can infer that Jesus turned an ordinary Passover week into a morose, farewell meal. The meals of Passover week, not excluding *Pesah* itself, would have been joyous occasions celebrating God's past liberation and anticipating God's future liberation. In the middle of such a meal Jesus suddenly shifted the mood from joyous celebration of God's liberation to morose contemplation of his own death. This shift in mood reminds the participants of the tone of Exodus 12, the founding *Pesah*. If Jesus saw beyond that death to a final banquet, he only got to that vision by revealing to his followers that a dark day loomed on the immediate horizon. The last supper became tasteless for his followers, while an abstinence emerging from either mourning or focused attention consumed Jesus.

It remains for us now to consider the significance of Jesus converting a *Pesah* week meal into a meal at which he announced his imminent death.

---

see also L. Hoffman, "A Symbol of Salvation in the Passover Haggadah," *Worship* 53 (1979): 519–37.

Chapter 14

This Bread and This Cup

We have concluded that the last supper was probably, or perhaps only possibly, not technically the *Pesah*. But the view concluded in chapter 13 does not imply that the meal was an ordinary Jewish meal, with a skin or two of vino tinto, vegetables, grains, herbs, a stew, and an assortment of dips. Even if Jesus does not celebrate *Pesah*, he does eat with followers during festal week, and every meal that week would be swallowed up in *Pesah* celebrations. How could they not be involved? They were away from home, and they were in Jerusalem for one purpose: to celebrate *Pesah*. The week was alive.[1]

In the meal Jesus eats with his followers, he reportedly assigns to the bread and wine an apparent redemptive meaning that expresses exodus theology.[2] *Pesah* week meals, even unintentionally, evoke the events behind the rites of *Pesah*. With everyone gathering to Jerusalem, eating in special places, seeing old friends and making new ones, and with Jerusalem decked out in memory of its greatest event of salvation, and with the Roman soldiers on guard for any act of rebellion—with all this in the eyes of every celebrant, every meal begins to take on the themes of *Pesah*. This would include at least two exceptions: the rest of the meals that week were less formal and were absent of lamb. It was this kind

---

[1] An excellent account, though I disagree in some details about Jesus' life and family, can be seen in P. Fredriksen, *Jesus of Nazareth, King of the Jews* (New York: Knopf, 1999), 42–50.

[2] On the theological themes that can be extracted from the last supper traditions, cf. F. Hahn, "Die alttestamentliche Motive in der urchristlichen Abendmahlsüberlieferung," *EvT* 27 (1967): 337–74; "Zum Stand der Erforschung des urchristlichen Abendmahles," *EvT* 35 (1975): 553–63; H. Merklein, "Erwägungen zur Überlieferungsgeschichte der neutestamentlichen Abendmahlstraditionen," *BZ* 21 (1977): 88–101, 235–44; L. Goppelt, *Theology of the New Testament* (ed. J. Roloff; trans. J.E. Alsup; 2 vols.; 1975; repr. Grand Rapids: Eerdmans, 1981), 1:213–22; P. Stuhlmacher, *Grundlegung Von Jesus zu Paulus* (vol. 1 of *Biblische Theologie des Neuen Testaments*; 2d ed.; Göttingen: Vandenhoeck & Ruprecht, 1997), 130–43. See also the study of M. Casey, *Aramaic Sources for Mark's Gospel* (SNTSMS 102; Cambridge: Cambridge University Press, 1998), 219–52.

of informal meal that Jesus most likely makes his last and to which he attributes significance.

Most scholars today, the Jesus Seminar included, attribute some historical core to the last supper. E.P. Sanders classed it, along with the temple incident, as "almost equally certain,"[3] and nearly two decades later James Dunn concluded that there is a "core memory of what Jesus said" in the last supper traditions.[4] Jesus somehow found the bread and the wine to be a symbol. There is much here that speaks of a core of reliability in these two elements. To begin with, Jesus is known for the table he keeps and creates. Further, the astounding claim that "I am the bread/wine" has no parallel in Judaism and is the sort of prophetic behavior we have seen from Jesus before. It would not be unlike Jesus to take a significant event (a meal during *Pesah* week) and attribute to it a new significance and, in particular, make himself the center of it all.[5] In addition, as we have demonstrated, *that* a premature death was on Jesus' mind from the time of John onwards anchors the scene in the realities of Jesus' life. Finally, these two elements (bread, wine) *distinguished* the early Christian communities from all other Jewish communities and did so from the very beginning. There is no time period of earliest Christianity that does not know of the Lord's Supper, and there is no better explanation for its origins than the one given by the church itself: Jesus' last supper.[6]

But, we need not just to concentrate on the *words* of Jesus. The *actions* of Jesus during that last supper are as significant here as his words, even if it is words, or a story, that *articulate* meaning and interpretation.[7] It is consistent for Jesus, *qua* prophet, to perform symbolic actions and to interpret them. It is also consistent with Jesus to assume personal authority in acting and speaking *qua* prophet. But no prophet ever approached the sacred center that Jesus here enters, for in this event Jesus offers himself to his followers. By drinking and eating they receive or ingest him and his entire ministry. We will now look to see

---

[3] E.P. Sanders, *Jesus and Judaism* (Philadelphia: Fortress, 1985), 307.

[4] J.D.G. Dunn, *Jesus Remembered* (vol. 1 of *Christianity in the Making*; Grand Rapids: Eerdmans, 2003), 804–5 (with 229–31). For general arguments for the historicity of the last supper, cf. J. Koenig, *The Feast of the World's Redemption* (Harrisburg: Trinity Press International, 2000), 14–20.

[5] Sanders made this statement: "We should, I think, accept the obvious: Jesus taught his disciples that he himself would play the principal role in the kingdom" (*Jesus and Judaism*, 307).

[6] In general, see M. Hengel, *The Atonement* (trans. J. Bowden; Philadelphia: Fortress, 1981).

[7] On the symbolic, prophetic actions of Jesus, see my "Jesus and Prophetic Actions," *BBR* 10 (2000): 197–32; H. Schürmann, "Die Symbolhandlungen Jesu als eschatologische Erfüllungszeichen," in *Jesus* (ed. K. Scholtissek; Paderborn: Bonifatius, 1994), 136–56; on the last supper as prophetic action, see J.W. Bowker, "Prophetic Action and Sacramental Form," in *The New Testament Message* (ed. F.L. Cross; TUGAL 88; part 2 of *Studia Evangelica* II–III; Berlin: Akademie, 1964), 129–37; N.A. Beck, "The Last Supper as an Efficacious Symbolic Act," *JBL* 89 (1970) 192–98; Gnilka, "Wie urteilte Jesus über seinen Tod?" in *Der Tod Jesu* (ed. K. Kertelge; Questiones Disputatae 74; Freiburg: Herder, 1976), 36–41; D. Wenham, "How Jesus Understood the Last Supper: A Parable in Action," *Them* 20 (1995): 11–16; M.D. Hooker, *The Signs of a Prophet* (Harrisburg: Trinity Press International, 1997), 48–54.

if Jesus interpreted his premature death as atoning, whether through action and word, during *Pesah* week, and we will sift through the various interpretive accretions of the early churches.[8]

AN INTENSE DESIRE

Because the last supper was most likely not, in fact, the central *Pesah* meal, and because this last supper was construed as a *Pesah* without lamb, the *desire* on Jesus' part comes into clearer focus (Luke 22:15). The logion is unparalleled. However, the words are plausibly Aramaic (cf. 1QapGen XX, 10–11), and express an emotion of Jesus not typical in the Jesus traditions. Expressions of emotion are frequently taken to be an index to antiquity, even if such a criterion does fall short of complete persuasion. When the emotions are unfulfilled, as this was, then they are even more reliable. The passion story about Jesus anchors itself in history by revealing the trouble of Jesus' emotions (Mark 14:33, 35-36; John 12:27; see Ps 42:6, 12; 55:5; Jonah 4:9; 1QH VIII, 32).[9] The sense of the "intense desire" logion, when set in the above conclusion that the meal is not *Pesah*, evinces the eschatology of Jesus.

As he does at Mark 14:25, Jesus here expresses his belief that the kingdom is imminent. Jesus thinks he will die shortly as part of the Final Ordeal,[10] that the

---

[8] A very complicated, and speculative, tradition history of the last supper tradition has been offered by B.D. Chilton, *A Feast of Meanings* (NovTSup 72; Leiden: E.J. Brill, 1994); see his more popular presentation in *Jesus' Prayer and Jesus' Eucharist* (Valley Forge, Penn.: Trinity Press International, 1997), 52–97 (this latter book shows some slight adjustments). Chilton contends Jesus' last meals were alternative sacrifices to the impure temple sacrifices. It was only later that Peter turned the meals into a last supper tradition, and various alterations and liturgies developed. If, however, one anchors the last supper traditions in Jesus' unique, final supper in the last week, it will be seen that certain features of Chilton's theory and the one presented below show some similarities at critical points. See also Merklein, "Erwägungen zur Überlieferungsgeschichte der neutestamentlichen Abendmahlstraditionen," 235–44.

The older, history-of-religions school approach to this tradition history was that meals became analogous to "theophagy" (ingestion of the god) at the hands of early Christians and, in some measure, to Paul under the influence of Hellenistic religion. An example can be seen in R. Bultmann, *Theology of the New Testament* (trans. K. Grobel; 2 vols.; New York: Scribner, 1951, 1955), 1:133–52. Hans Lietzmann, *Mass and the Lord's Supper* (trans. D.H.G. Reeve; Leiden: E.J. Brill, 1976), thought the Pauline church Eucharist was combined with an eschatological agape meal of primitive Christianity to form a sacramental meal. Oscar Cullmann modified Lietzmann: the earlier meal joyously celebrated table fellowship in the presence of Christ and then Paul reintroduced into that meal the theme of the death of Jesus; see his *Early Christian Worship* (trans. A.S. Todd and J.B. Torrance; Philadelphia: Westminster, 1978), 7–36, esp. 14–20; "The Meaning of the Lord's Supper in Primitive Christianity," in *Essays on the Lord's Supper* (trans. J.G. Davies; Atlanta: John Knox, 1975), 5–23. For a brief tradition history, see Stuhlmacher, *Grundlegung von Jesus zu Paulus*, 1:130–33.

[9] Both Matthew and Luke soften the emotions of Jesus. See Taylor, *Mark*, 551.

[10] The addition of πρὸ τοῦ με παθεῖν is plausibly later redaction, though assigning such an expression is not clearly Lukan. But cf. Nolland, *Luke*, 3:1049.

kingdom will emerge, and he will only then renew his table fellowship with his followers—at *Pesah*? Thus, the logion most likely expresses an unfulfilled wish.[11] Jesus wanted to eat *Pesah* with them but would not be able to; he would suffer, as he has previously explained to his followers, before that year's *Pesah* would be eaten. This means that *this Pesah* (*touto to pascha*) evokes a story: "the *Pesah* proper I will not eat; *this Pesah* I want to eat," but "the *Pesah* that I am about to share with you as I unfold the meal's significance, I will eat with you."

THIS BREAD: "THIS IS MY BODY"

Scholars are divided over the authenticity of the words of institution. However, a significant shift is underway that is beginning to regard at least a reduced version of the separate logia over the bread and cup as genuine.[12] In particular, the logion over the bread in which Jesus, after giving thanks (cf. Ps 104:10-23, esp. 13-14, 27; *m. Ber.* 6:1),[13] affirms that the bread is his body has been given a wide hearing as probably said by Jesus during the course of the last supper. Perhaps most decisive is the formidable argument brought forward by Heinz Schürmann, and then followed particularly in Germany by Peter Stuhlmacher and Martin Hengel, that, apart from an origin in the life of Jesus, there is no foundation whatsoever for the early Jewish Christian practice of the Eucharist or an interpretation of the death of Jesus in redemptive categories. Such a view does not mean, however, that some or much of that interpretation is performed with words not used by Jesus himself.[14] In liturgical texts like this, especially, we often find ourselves looking over the shoulder of an early Christian exegete.

This saying over the bread, in nearly identical form, has survived in several independent traditions (Mark 14:22; 1 Cor 11:24; cf. also Luke 22:19). Its baldness has attracted an interpretive accretion or two, in the same way that unleavened bread seeks sauce (cf. "which is given/broken for you" at Luke 22:19, in several significant MSS). However, the absence of the "given for you" in the Markan-Matthean tradition, and the greater liturgical (in a soteriological) direc-

[11] So also F.C. Burkitt and A.E. Brooke, "St Luke xxii 15, 16," *JTS* 9 (1907–1908): 569–72; J. Jeremias, *The Eucharistic Words of Jesus* (trans. N. Perrin; Philadelphia: Fortress, 1977), 207–8. *Contra* Fitzmyer, *Luke*, 2:1395–1396.

[12] The order of Mark (bread then cup) may be a departure from normal festal occasions, though evidence is not consistent; cf. 1QS VI, 4-5.

[13] See the tradition-historical analysis of O. Betz, "Jesu Tischsegen," in his *Jesus* (WUNT 42; Tübingen: J.C.B. Mohr, 1987), 202–31. Betz bases his study on Psalm 104 and *m. Ber.* 6:1 and finds traces of Jesus' blessing in Mark 4:26-29; Luke 12:16-21; Jas 5:7-9, 17-18; Matt 6:11 par. Luke 11:3 (cf. Exod 16); Mark 6:30-44; John 6:26-59.

[14] See H. Schürmann, *Jesus—Gestalt und Geheimnis* (ed. K. Scholtissek; Paderborn: Bonifatius, 1994), 136–56, 186–92, 202–40; P. Stuhlmacher, *Reconciliation, Law, and Righteousness* (Philadelphia: Fortress, 1986), 16–29; Hengel, *Atonement*, 65–75; see also J.B. Green, "The Death of Jesus and the Ways of God," *Int* 52 (1998): 24–37, who contends that the death of Jesus "proved to be a historical event of extraordinary fecundity in the making of meaning" (25).

tion of the Pauline-Lukan tradition, means the Markan stubborn lemma, "this is my body," is more primitive. It is very probably the *ipsissima verba Jesu*. After the customary prayer for the bread, Jesus alters the direction of this meal by declaring the bread his own body. He then gives the bread to his followers to eat. The statement is stunning.

The *actions* of Jesus also speak here: they become performative utterances. Therefore, we should probably grant to Xavier Léon-Dufour his claim to have found in the Pauline-Lukan formula ("given for you") a shrapnel of authenticity: he argues that *for* (Greek: *huper*) need not carry the sense of expiation but (in my words) can signify: "I give myself to you to enable you to live, for you and your sustenance."[15] If this is the sense of *for you*, then there are plausible grounds for anchoring such an expression into the last supper of Jesus. This is, after all, what did happen. The *for you* thus at least brings out what is implicit in the action.[16] The fundamental problem for these words is that Mark excludes them, and it is hard to find a reason for Mark to omit what fits with the soteriological statement at Mark 10:45.

For Christians it is hard to appreciate the stunning nature of these words: far from the norm, Jesus, as *paterfamilias*, suddenly announces that the bread he has broken for them is *his own body*.[17] Moses instructed the children of Israel to eat *massot* in haste, but he did not suggest that the bread was either himself or representative of their dangers. He also provided manna for the children of Israel, but he never suggested that the manna was his own body. Jewish prophets and martyrs—and one is inclined in the context of Jesus' mission to think of Daniel 7, Isaiah 40–55 and 61, as well as Psalm 118—put themselves on the line for their vision and mission to Israel, but none ever suggests that they are offering themselves for the people.[18] But Jesus does just that. In the course of a meal, presumably on Nisan 13/14, in the middle of a *Pesah* week when Jews of all sorts memorialized God's redemption of the children of Israel from the onerous hand of Pharaoh, Jesus states that the bread they are eating is in fact his own body. It is no longer just *massot*, and it no longer memorializes the haste of the exodus; the bread of this meal is his body. He offers his body to sustain them after his death, or even perhaps to enable them to participate in his death.

---

[15] X. Léon-Defour, *Sharing the Eucharistic Bread* (trans. M.J. O'Connell; New York: Paulist, 1986), 120–23.

[16] So also Taylor, *Mark*, 544.

[17] The later Christian debate over the meaning of "is" (ἐστίν) emerges from unhistorical concerns; the Aramaic or Hebrew would have needed no is. Grammatically speaking, then, the issue is insoluble. Other factors, such as tradition and theology, dictate one's decision. See Léon-Dufour, *Sharing the Eucharistic Bread*, 123–29, 133–36 (who speaks of three dimensions: prophetic action, performative sign, and symbol); Hagner, *Matthew*, 2:772; Keener, *Matthew*, 631–32. In the act and word of Jesus we find his aesthetic as well as his sense of the need of theology to be concretely embodied.

[18] So I would also read *Mek. de R. Ishm.* (on Exod 12:1): "And so you also find, that the patriarchs and the prophets offered their lives in behalf of Israel." The author then appeals to Moses (Exod 32:32; Num 11:15) and David (2 Sam 24:17).

If a death is clearly in mind, it is nearly impossible to find the same clarity with respect to the Aramaic (or Hebrew) behind "body" (Greek, *soma*). Joachim Jeremias contended that it was *basar*; Heinz Schürmann argued for *gup*; Maurice Casey, not one to forget to think for himself, supported *geshem*.[19] The arguments are neatly divided. Though the majority follow Jeremias even when it would be more natural to translate *basar* with *sarx*, the evidence of Daniel 3:27, 28 suggests *geshem*. But the difference is minimal for understanding what Jesus intended. After all, the term *body* probably means "self"—"this bread is myself" (cf. Num 16:22; 27:16; Isa 40:5-6; Ps 145:21).[20] This would suggest that Jesus is sharing his life as a form of sustenance for his followers,[21] or perhaps that he is giving himself personally to his followers in the sense that he is to die bodily.[22]

The bread here so identified with Jesus needs to be understood in the context of *Pesah* week and as *unleavened* bread. It does not correspond to the divinely provided manna of the wilderness, though John's mind eventually drifted into the wilderness experience to interpret "bread" (John 6). If the *manna* concerns the provision of God in the wilderness wanderings, the *massot* (regardless of the day of the week) speaks of God's hasty redemption of Israel through a ritual of smearing blood on the entrance of the house and eating this *massot* with bitter herbs and roasted lamb. By identifying himself with the unleavened bread, Jesus speaks of himself as both *sharing his life* with his followers and as being the *means of sustenance* just prior to an act of God for redemption. And these two elements of meaning are inevitably present if Jesus uttered these words in the context of a *Pesah* meal.

We are entitled to say more about this bread because an important connection between bread and the death Jesus anticipates is forged in Judaism between the bread of *Pesah* and the "bread of affliction" (Deut 16:3). This theme is retained in the Passover *Haggadah* until today. The unleavened bread of *Pesah* was given various meanings in Judaism: it referred not only to the suffering of Egypt under Pharaoh, but also to self-denial and labor (Philo, *Congr.* 16–67), as well as to grief, to bread not kneaded with wine, oil, or honey, and to poverty (*b. Pesah* 36a). Into this whoil of interpretations Jesus, obviously captured by the meaning of suffering in Egypt as an analogy of his impending death, states that his body is this bread of affliction. That is, he will himself endure suffering not unlike that of the children of Israel. His suffering will lead to an exodus, a redemption not unlike that of the children of Israel. In light of what we have

---

[19] Jeremias, *Eucharistic Words of Jesus*, 198–201, 220–25; H. Schürmann, *Der Einsetzungsbericht Lk 22, 19-20* (NTAbh 20/4; Münster: Aschendorff, 1955), 107–10; for a nice summary discussion, cf. G.R. Beasley-Murray, *Jesus and the Kingdom of God* (Grand Rapids: Eerdmans, 1986), 263–64. Casey, *Aramaic Sources of Mark's Gospel*, 239.

[20] So Fitzmyer, *Luke* 2:1399. An ecclesial interpretation developed from the idea that Jesus offered himself (thus, the bread is the "body of Jesus/Christ"); cf. 1 Cor 5:7; 10:17; *Did.* 9:4. See also Léon-Dufour, *Sharing the Eucharistic Bread*, 119–20.

[21] See Pesch, *Markusevangelium*, 2:357.

[22] So Léon-Dufour, *Sharing the Eucharistic Bread*, 119–20.

already argued, it would not be surprising if Jesus saw the exodus affliction as a prototype of the Final Ordeal into which he was about to enter.

The redemption of Exodus took place at the expense of the death of the Egyptian firstborn. The actions of Jesus tie together the bread and the cup. If the bread is connected to the cup, and the cup to sacrificial death, then the bread of affliction Jesus shares is participation in his death.[23] This can only mean that the bread, now identified with Jesus, is given to the followers in order that they may share in the death of Jesus in order to accrue its benefits.

To be sure, unleavened bread did not connote redemption in the sense that bread in the Eucharist acquires, even if the *massot* was connected with blood and redemption in a looser sense at the exodus meal. But, by connecting bread with cup and the cup with sacrificial death, we must think Jesus' offering of himself to his followers was an act of offering them the protection of a sacrificial death or participation in that death. By this death they will be redeemed from the affliction and God will pass over them when he judges. That sacrifice can be implicit is confirmed by the consumption of the sacrificial victim in Jewish sacred meals, especially *Pesah* (e.g., Gen 14:18; Exod 12; 24:11; Lev 7:11-18). What should be noted is that the death of *Pesah* week is not an atoning death nor is it a forgiving death; instead, the operative term is *protecting*. Jesus' death protects from God's judgment, and that judgment surely finds its clearest expression in Jesus' warnings about Jerusalem's destruction.

A less certain observation can be offered.[24] If we assume that the last supper was not *Pesah* and that no lamb was present (had lamb been present Jesus would have identified it with himself), then we might put forward the suggestion that Jesus saw the bread as a replacement for the lamb[25] in this Spartan meal of bread, sauce, and wine. If our interpretation of Luke 22:15 is sound (that Jesus looked forward to eating *Pesah* but couldn't), then this suggestion gains some merit: he would like to eat a proper *Pesah* but can't. He knows he will die,

---

[23] See Nolland, *Luke*, 3:1052–1054.

[24] I consider the *aphikoman* tradition even less probable in light of the interpretation offered concerning bread (and blood). If Jesus' concern was primarily to predict his death and to invite his followers to participate in that death, then it is quite unlikely that he would have simply said "I am the Messiah" when he distributed the previously broken bread (*aphikoman*). For David Daube, and those who follow him, the primary purpose of "this is my body" would be to disclose privately to his followers that he was, in fact, the Messiah who was signified in the *aphikoman*. Why wait until then for such a disclosure? and, what significance would that identification have for his imminent death and their life without him? Because Daube's exclusive concern is with messianic identity, and because no such *Pesah* ritual explanation pertains to the cups of wine, the wine of Jesus' last supper is minimized and eventually absorbs the bread itself. See his *Wine in the Bible* (St. Paul's Lecture 13; London: London Diocesan Council for Christian-Jewish Understanding, 1974), 12–20. An alternative lopsidedness is found in C.H. Dodd: here he focuses exclusively on ecclesiology in the last supper accounts at the expense of Christology (*The Founder of Christianity* [London: Collins, 1971], 92–97).

[25] According to D. Daube, the replacement of lamb by the *aphikoman* survives in Sephardic Judaism; see *He That Cometh* (St. Paul's Lecture 5; London: London Diocesan Council for Christian-Jewish Understanding, 1966), 9–10.

so this meal must substitute for *Pesah*, the bread replacing lamb. This is not a new conclusion, so I appeal to one who has stated it with greater clarity, C.H. Dodd: "Although the day was perhaps not the official date for the celebration of Passover . . ., yet for them it was (or else took the place of) the solemn Passover supper; and the historic memories which the festival recalled were present to their minds, arousing the deep emotions with which these memories were laden."[26] Such a view survives in Paul's letter to the Corinthians (1 Cor 5:7): "Clean out the old yeast so that you may be a new batch, as you really are unleavened. For our paschal lamb, Christ, has been sacrificed."[27]

THIS CUP: "THIS IS MY BLOOD"

The general consideration that, apart from some statement to that effect by Jesus, the early churches would never have understood the crucifixion of Jesus in redemptive categories remains a foundational argument for the originality of the words over the cup.[28] And, as more study has shown, the sayings are plausibly Aramaic.[29] More particularly, the express notion that Jesus urged his followers to drink "my blood" cinches the argument for most. At first blush (and even further blushes!), drinking blood is intolerable to Jewish sensitivities (e.g., Gen 9:4; Lev 3:17; 7:26-27; 17:10-16; *Jub* 21:17-20). The words may have shocked his followers. Consumption of blood was also unacceptable to early Jewish Christianity, and thus they demanded Gentile converts to desist in their eating meats that had been strangled (cf. Acts 15:29 with John 6:52-59).[30] Morton Smith, neither confessional friend to Christianity nor bashful of expression, said: "To try to derive them [the eucharistic practices of early Christianity] from the passover ritual or any other Jewish rite is ludicrous. Strange as some rituals of Judaism may be, they do not include eating people." And, a paragraph later, he judges the Christian interpretation of Exodus 24:8 "an atrocity that can have

---

[26] Dodd, *Founder of Christianity*, 153–54.

[27] This raises the question about whether or not the slaying of the *Pesah* lamb was crucifixion-like. See J. Tabory, "The Crucifixion of the Paschal Lamb," *JQR* 86 (1996): 395–406, with bibliography and discussion of the Samaritan practice of slaying the *Pesah* lamb. The text most specific in this regard is Justin, *Dialogue with Trypho* 40.

[28] The Pauline-Lukan tradition speaks figuratively of the "the cup" rather than "the blood/wine," but nothing significant is to be inferred from the difference, though one might contend (see next note) that the Pauline-Lukan form softens the shock of Jesus' identifying the wine with his blood.

[29] See esp. now M. Casey, "The Original Aramaic Form of Jesus' Interpretation of the Cup," *JTS* 41 (1990): 1–12; *Aramaic Sources of Mark's Gospel*, 241–42.

[30] See W.D. Davies, *Paul and Rabbinic Judaism* (3d ed.; Philadelphia: Fortress, 1980), 244–50, who sees the Pauline expressions as Paul's attempt to come to terms with Mark's starkness and to do so in a "form palatable to his own delicate sensitivities" (247), a veritable "Rabbinization of the tradition" (250). See also the texts at Keener, *Matthew*, 632. On early Christian context, cf. R. Bauckham, "James and the Jerusalem Church," in his *The Book of Acts in Its Palestinian Setting* (vol. 4 of *The Book of Acts in Its First Century Setting*; Grand Rapids: Eerdmans, 1995), 415–80, esp. 452–67.

been conceived only by a circle bent on demonstrating its freedom from the Law."[31]

However, as Jonathan Klawans has pointed out, *if* these words were said within the context of the *Pesah* week and *if* there is sufficient context to explain them as metaphorical (for which there certainly is evidence), then the argument tends to weaken. It is highly unlikely, indeed virtually impossible, for anyone sitting with Jesus at the last supper to think that Jesus' words were anything but metaphors for himself. Therefore, if the meaning of drinking blood is not cannibalistic but instead metaphorical, then the dissimilarity argument founded on a cannibalistic reading of *blood* is eliminated. What makes this logion dissimilar is that Jesus sees the *Pesah* blood *as his own*, and the drinking of it to be the drinking of *his own blood* (metaphorically speaking, of course).[32] This would dissociate Jesus clearly from any form of Judaism prior to him without needing to appeal to the rather unimaginative cannibalistic interpretation.

The irregularity of Jesus' words then suggests originality, even though the cannibalistic interpretation of blood by Smith was not intended by Jesus and was almost certainly not even understood as so by his followers. The entire context is one of prophetic, symbolic action. Even so, it is like Jesus to utter jarring words and aphorisms (e.g., Mark 7:15, 18-20; Q 9:60; 14:26-27).

Further, the multiple attestation of the logion, even with variations, is a strong index of reliability.[33] The use in the Pauline-Lukan tradition of "this cup" (Luke's second cup) is later than the Markan-Matthean form; it is the early church's harmless and wise attempt to avoid the suggestion of cannibalism. The Markan words translated as "this is my blood" adequately reveal the *ipsissima verba Jesu*.[34] Thus, after giving thanks[35] and contrary to custom, Jesus declared the wine of the cup his very blood.

---

[31] M. Smith, *Jesus the Magician* (San Francisco: Harper & Row, 1978), 123.

[32] J. Klawans, "Was Jesus' Last Supper a Seder?" *BRev* 17 (2001): 24–33, 47; "Interpreting the Last Supper," *NTS* 48 (2002): 1–17; see also P.M. Casey, "No Cannibals at Passover!" *Theology* 96 (1993): 199–205.

[33] See Davies, *Paul and Rabbinic Judaism*, 246; E.P. Sanders, *The Historical Figure of Jesus* (London: Penguin, 1993), 263. The suggestion of Léon-Dufour, *Sharing the Eucharistic Bread*, 96–101, that we have here two independent traditions (Antiochene, Markan) amplifies widespread attestation, but the suggestion is unlikely. The Pauline-Lukan tradition has "after dinner"; this kind of information may belong to an attempt to "passoverize" the tradition or, more likely, is simply an incidental, genuine memory of what Jesus did. It gains meaning only if it was the *Pesah*.

[34] If one prefers the shorter reading (Luke 22:17) as the most historical, one finds no atonement soteriology. Instead, as with the bread, Jesus simply offers the bread and the wine to his followers for sustenance. The addition of *my* to *body* in Luke 22:19a, however, christologizes the bread. The wine is probably also to be understood as "my blood." Thus, Jesus offers himself to his followers— and this probably as an understanding of his death as "for them." Even in the case of the shorter reading, however, it is most likely that Luke has erased atonement theology from his traditions; in such a case, the atonement theology was more primitive.

[35] Again, cf. Betz, "Jesu Tischsegen," in his *Jesus*.

Cup: One or More?

That a cup or cups were used is not disputed, but we are in doubt about whether the disciples shared a drink from one cup or drank from individual cups.[36] The only contextual evidence available to sort out this issue is late and, as we have noted before, using rabbinic evidence requires an assumption of a high correlation between the later Passover *Haggadah* and a first-century seder and its attendant practices. To cut to the heart of the issue: if the meal was not *Pesah*, sharing a common cup is possible. But, if Jesus asked them in sharing a common cup to drink in a manner contrary to custom and so enact a new vision for Israel . . . *that* we do not know. The synoptic evidence is ambiguous enough to permit either interpretation: "Then he took a cup . . . he gave it [the cup] to them [so they could drink from the one cup? so they could pour into their own cups?]" (Mark 14:23) and "Then he took a cup . . . 'Take this and divide it [drink from the one cup? pour from this cup into your cups?] among yourselves'" (Luke 22:17).[37]

Background to Cup

In addition, the words in Mark 14:24, "poured out for *many*" (*to engchunnomenon hyper pollon*), reveal a soteriology that appears more particularistic than we find in the earliest Gentile churches, and evidently in most of the branches of Jewish Christianity.[38] This anchors the logion in the earliest Jerusalem-based dimension of the Jesus traditions before the struggle over including Gentiles began. The words allude to Isaiah 53, but that reference is surprising at *Pesah*, though not impossible since we have already offered evidence that Jesus did see in the Servant some scripts for his own life (ch. 10). Doubt further concerns "of the covenant" (*tes diathekes*) because it sounds like the language of Paul or the theology of Hebrews, even if covenant can be used to express Jesus' theology (cf. 1 Cor 11:25). However, the wording of Mark 14:24 shows significant independence from the Pauline-Lukan, where it says "this cup that is poured out for you is the new covenant in my blood" (Luke 22:20 [LR]; cf. 1 Cor 11:25), and

[36] Jeremias, *Eucharistic Words of Jesus*, 69–70 (common to drink from one cup); Daube, *Wine in the Bible*, 18 (perhaps messianic); Schürmann, *Jesus—Gestalt und Geheimnis*, 250–52 (symbolic to use a common cup); Stuhlmacher, *Grundlegung von Jesus zu Paulus*, 1:135, 137 (the "one cup" is the cup of Ps 116:13, the cup of messianic salvation).

[37] Some have argued that in early Christian celebrations the wine was optional, while the bread necessary. This goes back at least to Lietzmann, *Mass and the Lord's Supper*, but assumes two questionable hypotheses: (1) that the early Christians celebrated originally only a fellowship meal, to which later was added under foreign influence the notion of covenant blood in wine; and (2) that "breaking bread" in the early churches (e.g., Acts 2:42; *Gosp. Heb.* 8) means both the memorial meal we now call the Eucharist as well as the absence of wine.

[38] Recently, Lynne C. Boughton has mounted an argument for seeing "poured out" as futuristic ("will be poured out") and that it refers, not to the cup, but to the death of Jesus itself. See "'Being Shed for You/Many,'" *TynBul* 48 (1997): 251–70.

should therefore be given its day in court. Our exegesis will sort out the questions.[39]

To discern which of the three clarifying terms in Mark 14:24 is genuine, we are led to four scriptural texts from which Jesus could have drawn these words, texts that will be given consideration in our next chapter when we will ask more specifically if Jesus saw the last supper as a new covenant.[40] These scriptures would explain the meaning of "this is my blood,"[41] that is, his imminent death: Jeremiah 31:31;[42] Exodus 24:8;[43] Zechariah 9:11;[44] and Isaiah 53:12.[45] A full listing of the words in Mark 14:24 demonstrates a pastiche of scriptural texts: prima facie, it appears to be a combination of Exodus 24:8, Jeremiah 31:31-34, and Isaiah 53:12, perhaps with some of Zechariah 9:11 included. The history of scholarship favors the first three, but the history of scholarship does not always check results about scriptural allusions at the door of authenticity.

But before we can discern the background to Jesus' words, we need to sound an important alarm about blood: sacrificial blood may speak of the establishment of the covenant in Exodus 24:3-8, or of the blood on the door frame in Exodus 12 that enabled YHWH to pass over that house with his angel's avenging knife, or of the atonement rituals of Leviticus 4 and 16 that secured forgiveness. The inherent power of blood is its "life" (*nephesh*; Lev 17:11), and the idea of substitution is not always, or even often, present. Consider the blood of *Pesah*: smearing the blood of the *Pesah* victim was not seen as vicarious or substitutionary punishment but as an act of obedience; it was a "sign" (Exod 12:13). Christian theology tends to blur the distinct functions of blood in the Old Testament. Not every use of blood was atoning and forgiving. Jews did not connect *Pesah* either with Leviticus 4 or 16 (except perhaps at Ezek 45:21-25). *Pesah* blood, covenant blood, and atoning blood are three different kinds of blood (e.g., *Mek. de R. Ishm.* 1:56, 87–88 [on Exod 12:6, 13, 23]). As Hans Kosmala once observed, "Until the destruction of the second temple, the passover sacri-

---

[39] It is inherently likely that Jesus "gave thanks" for the wine (Greek: εὐχαριστήσας) as it is likely that he also "blessed" (Greek: εὐλογήσας) the bread. In each case the Hebrew/Aramaic narrator would have used *berak/barek*. On *covenant*, see the next chapter.

[40] As noted in a previous chapter, the methodological factors of D.C. Allison, Jr., *The Intertextual Jesus* (Harrisburg: Trinity Press International, 2000), 9–13, provide a useful orientation for detecting citations and allusions.

[41] Cf. R.J. Daly, *The Origins of the Christian Doctrine of Sacrifice* (Philadelphia: Fortress, 1978), 25–35.

[42] Beasley-Murray, *Jesus and the Kingdom of God*, 264–65, argues the eschatological notions of "new covenant" are more characteristic of Jesus.

[43] E.g., V. Taylor, *Jesus and His Sacrifice* (1937; repr. London: Macmillan, 1955), 136–39; see also the important sifting of texts in Davies and Allison, *Matthew*, 3:473–75 (for Matthew); M. Smith, *Jesus the Magician*, 123 (a connection he finds "amazing" since the Christians drank the blood; Moses merely sprinkled the blood).

[44] See Jeremias, *Eucharistic Words of Jesus*, 225–26, n. 5.

[45] Those who think "for many" is genuine inevitably connect the logion to Isa 53:12; e.g., Stuhlmacher, *Grundlegung von Jesus zu Paulus*, 1:136–42.

fice remained as a sacrificial offering to be eaten and, therefore, could not assume the role of an atoning sacrifice."[46]

What kind of blood did Jesus have in mind when he claimed the wine they were drinking was his blood? We need to look at the crucial texts behind the words over the cup, with the most important words italicized, to provide an answer to this most important question:

> Jeremiah 31:31: The days are surely coming, says the LORD, when I will make a *new covenant* with the house of Israel and the house of Judah.

> Exodus 24:8: Moses took the blood and dashed it on the people, and said, "See the *blood of the covenant* that the LORD has made with you in accordance with all these words."

> Zechariah 9:11: As for you also, because of *the blood of my covenant* with you, I will set your prisoners free from the waterless pit.

> Isaiah 53:12: Therefore I will allot him a portion with the great, and he shall divide the spoil with the strong; because he *poured out* himself to death, and was numbered with the transgressors; yet he bore the sin of many, and made intercession for the transgressors.

Since Jesus is a "Scripture prophet,"[47] it is as likely that he could put together a pastiche of texts as one of the Evangelists. It is not impossible to think Jesus could have loaded his interpretation with allusions; at least one text is like this at Qumran (4Q174). Most people don't speak in pluriform metaphors and images; but most people don't approach their death as did Jesus, and very few in history have even possibly looked at their death as having redemptive significance. Since these claims are possible for Jesus, we can't rule out a pastiche for Jesus.

But it is simpler, when examining oral communication, to see an allusion to one text than to many texts. Allusions at once to a variety of texts and contexts, not to mention language games, may be fraught with incommunicability. We prefer the text with the most direct connections to the last supper words of institution, though we cannot rule out multiple allusions a priori. Four critical expressions are used: *blood*,[48] *covenant*, *poured out*, and for *many*.[49] To which did Jesus refer? And to which did early Christians refer to interpret the words of

---

[46] H. Kosmala, *Hebräer–Essener–Christen* (StPB; Leiden: E.J. Brill, 1959), 174 (my translation).

[47] Chapters 8–10 in this study.

[48] On blood, see J. Bergman and B. Kedar-Kopfstein, "*dam*," in *TDOT* (ed. G.J. Botterweck and H. Ringgren; trans. J.T. Willis, et al.; 8 vols.; Grand Rapids: Eerdmans, 1974–), 3:234–50; also L.L. Morris, *The Apostolic Preaching of the Cross* (Grand Rapids: Eerdmans, 1965), 112–28.

[49] On which, see Kosmala, *Hebräer–Essener–Christen*, 174–91.

their Lord? Or, will we find here "an opening into the intellectual workshop of the early church"?[50]

JEREMIAH 31?

A text upon which early Christians meditated is Jeremiah 31:31-34. The author of Hebrews twice quotes these verse (Heb 8:8-12; 10:16-17; cf. 9:15), and we find at least traces of connecting the salvation of Christ with the new covenant in Paul (Rom 2:15; 11:27; 1 Cor 11:25; 2 Cor 3:2, 6, 14; 6:17-18), John (6:45), Luke (22:20 [LR]), and Matthew (26:28; cf. 23:8).[51] But Jeremiah 31:31, in spite of its general attractiveness to Christian thinking about how the Bible is to be put together, presents itself as the weakest option because it contains only one significant word, *covenant*, and Jeremiah is not as popular with Jesus' overall mission.[52] Further, Jeremiah's context is one of covenant renewal and the reestablishment of the Law, neither of which emerges as a prominent theme in Jesus' ministry or in the last supper (Jer 31:33-34).[53] Nor is the concept of a future covenant/new covenant in Judaism connected to sacrifice and blood (cf. Bar 2:27-35; CD VI, 19-21; VIII, 21; XX, 12-13; *Jub.* 1:15-25). Some MSS of Mark have *new* modifying *covenant*, forming what would be an even tighter relationship to Jeremiah 31:31, but those MSS are certainly later.[54] Those texts assimilate Mark to both the Lukan-Pauline tradition as well as the theology that emerged from belief that Jesus' last supper was in fact the fulfillment of Jeremiah's prediction.[55] This text can only with difficulty be brought to the last supper table.

EXODUS 24?

An allusion to Exodus 24:8, favored in the history of interpretation, is more likely: not only does it contain two prominent terms as parallel expressions, *blood* and *of the covenant* (Mark has *my* with *blood*), but that context is one of covenant renewal with the twelve tribal leaders after which a meal takes place in

---

[50] C.H. Dodd, *According to the Scriptures* (London: James Nisbet, 1952), 28.

[51] Dodd, *According to the Scriptures*, 85, noticed other echoes to Jeremiah 31 in the NT: cf. Matt 2:18; 13:27; Luke 6:21, 25; John 6:12, 35; 10:9; 11:52; Rev 7:16.

[52] Possible citations or allusions are found, without listing Synoptic parallels, at Mark 8:18 (Jer 5:21); Mark 11:17 (Jer 7:11); Mark 14:24 (Jer 31:31); Matt 7:7-8 (Jer 29:13-14); Matt 10:6 (Jer 50:6); Matt 11:29 (Jer 6:16); Matt 23:38 (cf. Jer 12:7; 22:5). This last text is the weightiest, appearing as it does in the last week and tied as it is into the temple system.

[53] Matthew's redaction, "for the forgiveness of sins," may draw its juice from Jeremiah 31:34, where forgiveness is also present.

[54] E.g., A *f*[1.13] 𝕸, etc.

[55] So also Davies, *Paul and Rabbinic Judaism*, 251: for Jesus "the concept of the New Covenant is only implicit," while Paul brings this theme into fuller display. For new being later, see Koenig, *Feasts*, 35. See ch. 15 for further discussion.

God's presence (Exod 24:11). The last supper of Jesus can, after some stretching, assume a covenant-ceremony reenactment.[56] At least one early Christian, the author of Hebrews, explained the covenant with Jesus as a renewal of Exodus 24:8 (cf. Heb 9:15-22, but with considerable difference in detail, some of which stems from Num 19; see also possibly at 1 Pet 1:2). Some have drawn lines from Exodus 24 to Isaiah 25, to see the latter's description of the eschatological banquet as a new covenant banquet.[57] But we should be careful about drawing such lines; lines are easier to draw than realities connected.

The context of Exodus 24 is Moses' establishment of the covenant, while the context of Exodus 12 is *Pesah*—and the two should not be confused since Judaism did not celebrate the *Pesah* as the reestablishment of the covenant (cf., e.g., *Tg. Onq.*; Exod 12). *Pesah* was a memorial to God's liberation of Israel from Egypt, an act of both deliverance and judgment. The connection between Exodus 12 and 24 seems no more than the presence of blood—and even here the blood of a lamb in contrast to the blood of oxen. In saying this we need to take in the bigger picture: the story of Israel is that the *Pesah* led to the exodus, and the exodus to the wilderness, and the wilderness to the mountain, and on that mountain the covenant ceremony occurred. Covenant takes its meaning from *Pesah*, though the two events are quite distinct. In Joshua we find this storied connection of covenant and *Pesah*, if in reverse order (Josh 3:7-5:12).

The evidence for a natural connection of *Pesah* and the covenant ceremony is not as clear as some assume. Indeed, it may be thought presumptuous to split the two apart. An example of the problem is seen when the presence of blood in both rites leads some to make such a connection. Perhaps a looser definition of covenant as the entire process of redemption might make such a connection plausible. Loose definitions often lead to sloppy thinking, and in this instance we land on only a general connection of ideas on the basis of one term.[58]

---

[56] The promises to Abraham were sealed in a covenant of blood (Gen 12:1-3; 15:9-11), and then renewed under Moses through blood (Exod 24:5-8) and memorialized in ritual blood (Exod 29:38-46).

[57] E.g., Stuhlmacher, *Grundlung von Jesus zu Paulus*, 1:140.

[58] A fellow member of the Jesus Project of the Institute for Biblical Research, Craig Evans, suggested that I consider 2 Kgs 23:21-23 ("Keep the passover . . . as prescribed in this book of the covenant") and 4Q265 3, lines 2-3 ("Why then are we faithless to one another, profaning the covenant of our ancestors? [Mal 2:10] Let not a young boy or woman eat the Passover feast"). In the former text, "covenant" refers to the Josianic reform's discovery of Deuteronomy and probably is not sufficiently specific to suit our needs. However, the Qumran text clearly connects *Pesah* with the covenant, though the term *covenant* might be broader in the sense of "what God expected us to do, with Passover being but one instance."

One could also argue that the tossing of blood in Exodus 24:6 and the later *Pesah* practice (e.g., *m. Pesah* 5:5-10) shows a similar rite of dealing with the blood, drawing the covenant ceremony into the fabric of the *Pesah* slaughter. This may be so; it appears that this rite replaces the older rite of smearing blood on the entrance to the home. Later, a connection between *Pesah* and Covenant ceremony is found in *Pirqe de Rabbi Eliezer* 28-29, and between the red heifer ordinance (Num 19:1-10) and *Pesah* (*Exod. Rab.* 19:2 (on Exod 12:43), but here the primary concern is an old one: purity.

Accordingly, I contend that the distinction between *Pesah* (deliverance from bondage) and covenant-ceremony (relationship and commitment) needs to maintained.[59] Another line of reasoning supports this claim: covenant establishment is not central to Jesus' message and vision, and neither does the book of Exodus feature in his mission.[60] One could even contend, as I will in the next chapter, that the category of covenant is peripheral to his vision and mission.[61] Consequently, covenant appears to be a developmental feature of the last supper traditions as we peer through the window of some early Christian's hermeneutical workshop. While blood naturally connects to both wine (Gen 49:11; Deut 32:14; Isa 63:3, 6; *Sir* 39:26) and *Pesah*, covenant does not naturally connect with *Pesah* as a festival. The term's presence in the last supper tradition of Mark is questionable enough that we should look to a more basal idea to determine the meaning of Jesus' words over the wine.

ISAIAH 53?

Isaiah 53:12 is our next candidate. It holds out hope, not only for its verbal connections but also because Isaiah is clearly one of Jesus' favorite prophets and the Servant image was at times used by Jesus (see ch. 10).[62] Isaiah 53's focus is on a figure of redemptive significance, the Suffering Servant (cf. 52:13–53:12), whom the Targum identifies as Messiah (*Tg. Isa.* 52:13) and to whom the term *covenant* was attached (cf. Isa 42:6; 49:8). This Servant is disfigured and marred (52:14); he is to sprinkle many nations (52:15); he suffers and is rejected (53:3); he assumes infirmities and sorrows (53:4) but is rejected by God (53:4) while God is behind his sufferings (53:10); his sufferings are redemptive, sacrificial, vicarious, and intercessory (53:5, 11, 12); he is a guilt offering (53:10); he is lamb-like in his innocence and vulnerability (53:7); he is oppressed (53:8) because of the transgressions of his people (53:8); but he pours out his life unto death (53:12); yet, he will be vindicated (53:10-11) and justify many (53:11).

---

[59] So also Gnilka, *Markus*, 2:245.

[60] Most references to Exodus in the Jesus traditions are from Exodus 20 (e.g., Mark 7:10 [Exod 20:12; 21:17]). Apart from the Decalogue, cf. the following: Mark 12:26 (Exod 3:6); Mark 14:24 (Exod 24:8); Matt 5:38 (Exod 21:24); Matt 11:10 (Exod 23:20 with Mal 3:1); Matt 23:17, 29 (Exod 29:37; 30:29); Luke 11:20 (Exod 8:15). Apart from moral requirements, the most influential exodus texts are Exodus 23:20 and 8:15, both eschatological, and neither covenant, in orientation.

[61] But see Sanders, *Jesus and Judaism*, 141–42, who concedes that "covenant" can be seen as a dimension of "kingdom" in the sayings tradition that deals with entering the kingdom (Matt 7:21; 18:3; 19:23). See chapter 15 below.

[62] Cf. B.D. Chilton, *A Galilean Rabbi and His Bible* (GNS 8; Wilmington: Michael Glazier, 1984); Allison, *Intertextual Jesus*, 101–22; see the listing of texts in R.T. France, *Jesus and the Old Testament* (London: Tyndale, 1971), 259–63; D.J. Moo, *The Old Testament in the Gospel Passion Narratives* (Sheffield: Almond, 1983), 79–172.

Two verbal connections are present, but two are absent: we find *poured out* and *for many* but we find neither *blood* nor *covenant*. Arguably, even if the theme is fundamentally similar (suffering as part of God's plan), as the themes of Psalm 118:22 are present in the passion predictions, the more important specific terms are absent. Nonetheless, what makes this passage attractive for setting the context for the last supper is that in both *a figure and his identity* are central: in Isaiah we have the Servant; in the Jesus traditions Jesus identifies *himself* as the bread and the cup/wine. (And, it ought to be observed that many is as characteristic of Daniel as it is of Isaiah 53; cf. Dan 9:27; 11:33, 34, 39; 12:1-3).

On the other hand, Isaiah's context does not concern *Pesah*, even if redemption of the people from bondage is always in view in Isaiah. Further, apart from the appeal to broad allusions and theological overinterpretation, the passage in Isaiah does not concern either *Pesah* or the covenant (cf. Isa 42:6; 49:8; 54:10; 55:3). The same absences concern other Isaian passages sought for as analogies to the last supper (25:6-8; 42:6; 49:8-13; 55:3).

In spite of this lack of persuasive power, another consideration may be brought in. Fundamental to the decision about "poured out for many" (Mark 14:24) is our previous decision regarding a similar phrase at 10:45. If the view taken there—that these words are possibly from Jesus because he thought of himself in terms of the Servant of Isaiah—is applied here, then we are led to think that "this is my blood, poured out for many" could have been said by Jesus at the last supper. There are reasons to think of Isaiah as the background: the history of interpretation has always pointed to Isaiah 52:13–53:12; there are notable terms, themes, and imagery in common, the terms used are peculiar enough to lead one to these passages in Isaiah; and the book is clearly one about which Jesus had thoughts. Further, that portion of the book was fundamental to Jesus' mission. We should not count our shares, however, until the bell rings.

ZECHARIAH?

Zechariah's prophecies as the context for Jesus' vision for Israel have made a recent furious comeback, and so this text deserves careful consideration.[63] Zechariah's context is one of pronouncing dire judgment on the nations oppressing the people of God (9:1-8a); to them God promises that oppression will end permanently (9:8b). To announce the coming end of oppression, God introduces the arrival of a king, "righteous and having salvation, gentle and riding on a donkey, on a colt, the foal of a donkey" (9:9), who will bring peace (9:10; cf.

---

[63] I think here especially of B.D. Chilton, *Rabbi Jesus* (New York: Doubleday, 2000), though Chilton does not see this text influencing the last supper tradition of Jesus. See also N.T. Wright, *Jesus and the Victory of God* (vol. 2 of *Christian Origins and the Question of God*; Minneapolis: Fortress, 1996); France, *Jesus and the Old Testament*, 103–10; Moo, *Old Testament in the Gospel Passion Narratives*, 173–224. There are no demonstrable allusions or citations of Zechariah in Q: cf. Allison, *Intertextual Jesus*.

Luke 19:38, 41-44).[64] The king delivers the people from oppression because "of the blood of my [God's] covenant" (9:11). It is possible that *Pesah* as well as the exodus, with its wilderness aftermath, is reactualized in this text in 9:14-15: "Then the LORD will appear over them [wilderness presence in a pillar of cloud: cf. Exod 13:21, 22], and his arrow go forth like lightning; the Lord GOD will sound the trumpet and march forth in the whirlwinds of the south. The LORD of hosts will protect them, and they shall devour and tread down the slingers; they shall drink their blood like wine, and be full like a bowl, drenched like the corners of the altar." Then they will "shine on his land" (9:16). It appears then that Zechariah's prophetic word re-actualizes for Judah the Exodus deliverance and wilderness protection under Moses.

More importantly, there are clear interpretations in the Targum to Zechariah 9 that suggest the translator saw this language as reminiscent of *Pesah*. Thus, at 9:11: "You also, for whom a *covenant* was made *by blood*, I have delivered you from bondage to the Egyptians, I have supplied your needs in a wilderness desolate as an empty pit in which there is no water."[65] The problem, of course, is that we have no firm date for this Targum and cannot know that Jesus would have been aware of it, or that its interpretive scheme was current at the time of Jesus, or even that the *blood* is about *Pesah*. The allusions to Egypt in the text of Zechariah 9 are, moreover, hardly lucid. Nonetheless, there is evidence here that fits our text, not the least of which is the fundamental phrase *the blood of my covenant*.

If Jesus appeals to this text, then he intends to tell his followers that he embodies, in this bread and wine, the *Pesah* blood that will deliver them from Rome and oppression as YHWH had delivered Israel from Egypt. Other support may be found for this text. Zechariah 8:7-8, 18-23 (cf. also Isa 25:6-8) can be seen to correspond to the prediction of the eschatological banquet at Mark 14:25 (cf. Q 13:28-30), suggesting Zechariah may have been in Jesus' mind at the last supper.[66] And, one should not forget Zechariah 9:9-10 as an antitype to Jesus' acted, symbolic event in his entry to Jerusalem. Zechariah's visions feature as a significant part of Jesus' mission.[67]

CONCLUSION: WHICH TEXT?

The evidence is a bit of stalemate: if we consider *blood* and *covenant*, we lean toward Zechariah and Exodus; if we consider *pour out* and *for many*, we lean

---

[64] See S. McKnight, *A New Vision for Israel* (Grand Rapids: Eerdmans, 1999), 229–33.

[65] K.J. Cathcart and R.P. Gordon, trans., *The Targum of the Minor Prophets* (ArBib 14; Wilmington: Michael Glazier, 1989). The italics are from the translators and indicate variation from the Hebrew text.

[66] Cf. Koenig, *Feast of the World's Redemption*, 22–23, 42.

[67] Cf. Mark 8:38 (Zech 14:5); Mark 11:1-11 (Zech 9:9); 11:15 (Zech 14:21); Mark 13:27 (Zech 2:10); Mark 14:27 (Zech 13:7); Mark 14:28 (Zech 13:8-9); Mark 14:58 (Zech 6:12-13); Matt 24:30 (Zech. 12:12); Matt 25:31 (Zech 14:5); Matt 26:15; 27:9-10 (Zech 11:12-13).

toward Isaiah. A way forward can be found by examining Paul's words. A more careful examination of Paul's tradition about the last supper reveals an important and decisive omission: "which is poured out for many" (Mark 14:24) is not present in Paul. The most dignified explanation of Paul's non-inclusion of these words is that they are later theological interpretation and not a part of the Pauline church Eucharist. It is not impossible that Jesus connected his death to the Servant of Isaiah, and brought it all together in this one expression. But, the Pauline evidence is noteworthy, and the absence of the crucial words there may well indicate a secondary, however profoundly hermeneutical, feature in an emerging liturgical text. Our methods run out at this fork in the road. We can only speculate that Jesus may have seen his blood as poured out for the many.

If, however, these crucial words are omitted from consideration as part of the last supper of Jesus with his followers (and here our confidence depends on the precise terms we choose), then the critical text forming the backbone of Jesus' explanation of his imminent death seems to be Zechariah 9:11, though Zechariah's words stream from the Exodus texts.[68] Furthermore, Zechariah's words appear to be the more appropriate because they contain not only important verbal parallels but also a concern closer to Jesus': God's redemptive and delivering work at and following the exodus.

This being said, however, the prominence of Exodus 24 in the history of Israel is undeniable. And that leads to the question of whether or not Jesus was thinking in terms of a new covenant or of a covenant reestablishment. It is the task of the next chapter to investigate whether or not Jesus thought of his own mission to be connected to the great covenant theme of the Tanakh. It is there, perhaps, that we will find an opening into the mind of Jesus on *how* he understood his death. Was it atoning?

---

[68] Cf. B. Lindars, *New Testament Apologetic* (London: SCM Press, 1961), 132–33.

Chapter 15

Jesus and the Covenant

Nearly every theological interpretation of the Lord's Supper concerns itself with the last supper as somehow expressing the "covenant theology" of Jesus. The question we ask in this chapter is whether or not, and if so in what way, Jesus thought of the last supper and his death as covenant-establishing. Which means that we are also concerned here with the origins of the "new covenant hermeneutic" of the earliest Christians or, better yet, the origins of various new covenant hermeneutics among various followers of Jesus who were Israelites of a special sort.[1] Because the unique concern of this chapter is what it is, we have ranged more deeply into other portions of the New Testament and, consequently, will proceed from these later portions back to Jesus.

The question of concern in this chapter is not whether or not *covenant* is useful as a hermeneutic, or whether it is a category sufficiently large and flexible

---

A much shorter version of this chapter was as a Festschrift contribution for my doctoral supervisor, Professor James D.G. Dunn. See "Covenant and Spirit," in *The Holy Spirit and Christian Origins* (ed. G.N. Stanton, B.W. Longenecker, and S.C. Barton; Grand Rapids: Eerdmans, 2004), 41–54. The original impetus of this piece, the origins of a new covenant hermeneutics, permitted a greater opportunity to explore the significance Professor Dunn has had in the scholarly debate over the development of covenant thinking in earliest Christianity. The present chapter focuses on Jesus and the covenant.

[1] Apart from Paul (2 Cor 3:14), an early Christian use of "New Testament" for the collection of books is Tertullian, *Marc.* 4.1 ("one for each Instrument, or Testament as it is more usual to call it"); see also Origen, *Princ.* 4.1.1. Melito of Sardis, however, refers to the Jewish Bible as the "Old Testament" (cf. Eusebius, *Hist. eccl.* 4.26.14; also Melito's *Peri Pascha*). Perhaps the earliest non-canonical uses of the category for understanding salvation-history are found in Clement of Alexandria, *Strom.* 6.5 (cf. also *Protr.* 11), and in Irenaeus, *Haer.* 9.1; 33.14; see also *Barn.* 4.6–8, 14; 6.19; 7.5; 9.4; 10.9; 13.1; 14.5; Justin, *Dial.* 11.2; 118.3; 123.4. See esp. W. Kinzig, "Καινὴ διαθήκη," *JTS* 45 (1994): 510–44; K. Backhaus, *Der neue Bund und das Werden der Kirche* (NTAbh NF 29; Münster: Aschendorffische, 1996), 306–24; "Gottes nicht bereuter Bund," in *Ekklesiologie*

293

enough to encompass the biblical witness—for this is manifestly true.[2] As a hermeneutic, covenant theology has proven useful to many scholars for centuries. Nor is the issue whether or not *covenant* is the central term for the Apostle Paul—some have made a plausible case for Paul as a covenant theologian. Again, the issue is not as concerned with whether covenant is a category that can be used to unite the entire biblical witness, but rather this: when do we see the origins of a covenant hermeneutic in the Jesus movement and earliest Christianity?

---

des Neuen Testaments (ed. R. Kampling and T. Söding; Freiburg: Herder, 1996): 33–55; "Das Bundesmotiv in der frühkirchlichen Schwellenzeit," in *Der ungekündigte Bund?* (ed. H. Frankemölle; QD 172; Freiburg: Herder, 1998), 211–31; "Hat Jesus vom Gottesbund gesprochen?" *TGl* 86 (1996): 343–56.

The key to our study is that we are looking at when and how the term *covenant* was used to *distinguish discrete periods of salvation history*, whether or not such persons envisaged a breaking up of the people of God into Judaism and Christianity, and whether or not this began with Jesus. Another similar schematic, and more redolent of New Testament authors, is *promise* or *expectation* and *fulfillment* or *realization*. One should not suppose, however, when one sees "covenant theology" that the early Christians automatically thought in terms of two covenants or even in terms of climactic salvation-history; scholars today are quick to point out an incipient Christian bias in such interpretive programs. For a nice survey of the transformation of the term from Jesus to Justin, cf. Backhaus, *Der neue Bund und das Werden der Kirche*, 324–44.

It is characteristic of Christian hermeneutics to synthesize such schemes within the larger scheme of covenant theology, which is a broader, soteriological scheme for understanding the biblical revelation. In my judgment, however, this focus in hermeneutics tends to beg two questions: (1) when did this hermeneutical scheme begin? and (2) how central is it to early Christian thinking? One can, of course, acquire a hermeneutical reading of the biblical revelation in terms of covenant; the issue is how accurate it is to do that reading. We need to be reminded once again that exegesis permits the authors to speak in their own terms and categories. Perhaps we also need to be reminded that the *varieties of rhetoric* enable a variety of language and hermeneutical games that can throw fresh light on biblical theology and modern life. It is critical here to recognize that when early Christians shifted the center of faith from Torah to Jesus Christ/Holy Spirit, some hermeneutical scheme or rhetoric was absolutely needed; covenant is one of the rhetorics chosen. The issue here is when this occurred.

This hermeneutical approach holds together the valuable study of E.J. Christiansen, *The Covenant in Judaism and Paul* (AGJU 27; Leiden: E.J. Brill, 1995). Her use of *covenant* is defended on p. 2. Our question is more specific: when and why did early followers of Jesus begin to understand their experience as the "new covenant" spoken of in Jeremiah, or when did they begin to sort out God's unfolding history in terms of covenant as a hermeneutical tool? A central feature of Christiansen's study is the emphasis given to rituals expressing identity in that covenantal theology.

[2] One thinks of W. Eichrodt, *Theology of the Old Testament* (trans. J.A. Baker; 2 vols.; London: SCM, 1961), who examines OT theology through the lens of covenant; Jon D. Levenson, *Sinai and Zion* (Minneapolis: Winston, 1985); E.P. Sanders, *Paul and Palestinian Judaism* (Philadelphia: Fortress, 1977), 618 (s.v., covenant); "The Covenant as a Soteriological Category and the Nature of Salvation in Palestinian and Hellenistic Judaism," in *Jews, Greeks, and Christians* (ed. R. Hamerton-Kelly and R. Scroggs; Leiden: E.J. Brill, 1976), 11–44; I.H. Marshall, "Some Observations on the Covenant in the New Testament," in his *Jesus the Saviour* (Downers Grove: InterVarsity, 1990), 275–89; M.D. Hooker, "Paul and 'Covenantal Nomism,'" in her *From Adam to Christ* (Cambridge: Cambridge University Press, 1990), 155–64; N.T. Wright, *The Climax of the Covenant* (Minneapolis: Fortress, 1992); M. Vogel, *Das Heil des Bundes* (Texte und Arbeiten zum neutestamentlichen Zeitalter 18; Tübingen: Francke, 1996); N. Lohfink, "Der Begriff 'Bund' in der biblischen Theologie," *TP* 66 (1991): 161–76.

More particularly, did this new covenant hermeneutic begin with Jesus? Did it have a generative point at the last supper? And, if Jesus did use this category, does it reveal an understanding of the value of his death? The issue here is complex. Consequently, this chapter will have to explore not only the question of the historical Jesus and the covenant, but also how the early church used this category. The task here is to untangle the thread of covenant theology as it became more and more a covenant hermeneutic in the development of earliest Christianity. To do this most efficiently, we will begin with the Apostle Paul, move on to Hebrews, and only then return to Jesus and the last supper—in our quest to understand how Jesus comprehended his own death.

The development of a covenant hermeneutic had both positive and negative edges and questions. On a positive front, where and when did some followers of Jesus begin to understand the relationship of Israel's heritage (Scriptures, salvation-history, and tradition) to their Christian experience of the Spirit in terms of an "old" and "new" covenant? When did some begin to recognize that what they had found in Christ and in the Spirit was the anticipated expectations of Jeremiah and Ezekiel, as can probably be seen already in Baruch 2:27-35?

On a more negative front, when did some begin to exercise a cutting covenant hermeneutic that relativized the Mosaic covenant through the realization of its completeness in the new age inaugurated by Jesus and the gift of the Spirit? More particularly, we ask: how "new" was the new covenant? And in what sense was the new covenant "new"? And, to deepen the same question, how much of this "new" covenant hermeneutic owes its impetus to Jesus himself?

Thus, the early followers of Jesus examined over and over the crater left by the impact of Jesus Christ but, we ask, when did some (clearly not all) describe that impact by use of the category of covenant? Did they follow a precedent established by Jesus in the last supper, or were they the creative energies behind such a hermeneutic? When did some perceive that what had been wrought in Jesus Christ fulfilled in one sense, but in another sense eclipsed or even superseded, what was inherited from Israel's traditions? And, it might be asked, how central was that category of covenant to the various early Christian siftings of salvation-history? In short, we are face to face again with one of those early partings of the way. A covenant parting, to be sure, but one that can be profitably explored today to bandage and heal time-worn Jewish-Christian relations.[3] This

---

[3] On which, cf. J.D.G. Dunn, "Two Covenants or One?" in *Frühes Christentum* (ed. H. Lichtenberger; vol. 3 of *Geschichte–Tradition–Reflexion*; Tübingen: J.C.B. Mohr [Paul Siebeck], 1996), 97–122. One of Dunn's strong points here is the suggestion that scholarship should learn to use *Israel*, which often is not ethnically marked, for both *Christianity* and *Judaism* to avoid the polemical contrast inherent to these terms. Accordingly, I have tried to appropriate this suggestion in what follows. Lest the posing of our question be seen in simplistic terms (e.g., "when did the covenant category bifurcate Christianity from Judaism?"), we should remind ourselves here of the importance of the centuries-long overlap of the sibling rivalry between messianic faith and the non-messianic faith, which Dunn's article so richly documents and explores. It is not that covenant bifurcated the two; it set into bold terms what some Christians perceived about the relation of the

chapter will begin with faith expressions in the early church (notably Paul and the author of Hebrews), as it attempts to probe deeper into the origins of this hermeneutic to see if it can be connected to Jesus' last supper.

(New) Covenant Hermeneutics in Paul

Outside the last supper tradition found now in Mark 14//Luke 22 and 1 Corinthians 11 (see below), the earliest record we have of early Israelite followers of Jesus sorting out their theology and experience of Christ and the Spirit in covenant[4] terms is most likely Galatians 4:24 (building on 3:15, 17 and the tem-

---

new age to the former age. See also M. Theobald, "Zwei Bünde und ein Gottesvolk," *TQ* 176 (1996): 309–25.

[4] On *covenant*, from a plethora of studies, the following are important: G.E. Mendenhall, *Law and Covenant in Israel and the Ancient Near East* (Pittsburgh: The Presbyterian Board of Colportage of Western Pennsylvania, 1955); Eichrodt, *Theology of the Old Testament*, esp. 1:36–69; D.J. McCarthy, *Old Testament Covenant* (Richmond: John Knox, 1972); *Treaty and Covenant* (2d ed.; AnBib21A; Rome: Biblical Institute, 1978); Sanders, *Paul and Palestinian Judaism* (Philadelphia: Trinity Press International, 1992), 241–78, esp. 262–75; C. Levin, *Die Verheißung des neuen Bundes in ihrem theologiegeschichtlichen Zusammenhang ausgelegt* (FRLANT 137; Göttingen: Vandenhoeck & Ruprecht, 1985); P. Kalluveettil, *Declaration and Covenant* (AnBib 88; Rome: Biblical Institute, 1982); E.W. Nicholson, *God and His People* (Oxford: Clarendon, 1986); S. Lehne, *The New Covenant in Hebrews* (JSNTSup 44; Sheffield: JSOT, 1990), 35–59 with nn.; N.T. Wright, *The New Testament and the People of God* (vol. 2 of *Christian Origins and the Question of God*; Minneapolis: Fortress, 1992), 244–79, esp. 260–62; Christiansen, *Covenant in Judaism and Paul*; H. Lichtenberger, "Alter Bund und Neuer Bund," *NTS* 41 (1995): 400–14; F. Avemarie and H. Lichtenberger, *Bund und Tora* (WUNT 92; Tübingen: J.C.B. Mohr, 1996); Backhaus, *Der neue Bund und das Werden der Kirche*; R. Rendtorff, *The Covenant Formula* (Edinburgh: T&T Clark, 1998).

The Greek term διαθήκη normally means "testament"; but, in light of the NT's frequent use of the Tanakh or LXX for its vocabulary, the term normally takes on the covenantal tones of passages like Gen 12; 15; 17; 22; Exod 19-24; Deut. Critical here are "בְּרִית," in *DCH* (ed. Clines), 2:264–67; M. Weinfeld, "בְּרִית, *berith*," in *TDOT* (ed. Botterweck) 2:253–79; E. Kutsch, "בְּרִית, *berit*," in *TLOT* (ed. Jenni) 1:256–66; G. Quell, J. Behm, "διαθήκη," *TDNT* 2:106–34; J. Guhrt and O. Becker, "Covenant, Guarantee, Mediator," *NIDNTT* (ed. C. Brown) 1:365–76; for a sketch of the tradition-historical development, cf. H.-D. Neef, "Aspekte alttestamentlicher Bundestheologie," in *Bund und Tora* (ed. Avemarie and Lichtenberger), 1–23. Neef emphasizes the need to distinguish the historical development and context of any use of the term *covenant*, though one must question whether Second Temple Israelites thought in such defined categories. The general impression one gets from this period is that the term functions, with varying degrees of emphasis, on three fronts: (1) the elective and establishing covenant with Abraham, (2) the law-revealing instructions of the Mosaic covenant [e.g., Exod 19–24], and (3) the inviolability of a Davidic presence as specified in 2 Samuel 7. In this wider sense, one is quite justified in speaking of an Old Testament concept of the covenant.

On a covenant hermeneutic in a canonical framework, with thorough interaction with a wide variety of scholarship, cf. the excellent study of Scott W. Hahn, "Kinship by Covenant," (Ph.D. diss.; Marquette University, 1996).

porality of the Mosaic Torah in 3:19-26), a line embedded in Paul's infamous allegory on Hagar and Sarah:[5]

> Tell me, you who desire to be subject to the law, will you not listen to the law? For it is written that Abraham had two sons, one by a slave woman and the other by a free woman. One, the child of the slave, was born according to the flesh; the other, the child of the free woman, was born through the promise. Now this is an allegory: *these women are two covenants.* One woman, in fact, is Hagar, from Mount Sinai, bearing children for slavery. Now Hagar is Mount Sinai in Arabia and corresponds to the present Jerusalem, for she is in slavery with her children. But the other woman corresponds to the Jerusalem above; she is free, and she is our mother. For it is written,
> > "Rejoice, you childless one, you who bear no children,
> > > burst into song and shout, you who endure no birthpangs;
> > for the children of the desolate woman are more numerous
> > > than the children of the one who is married."
> Now you, my friends, are children of the promise, like Isaac. But just as at that time the child who was born according to the flesh persecuted the child who was born according to the Spirit, so it is now also. But what does the scripture say? "Drive out the slave and her child; for the child of the slave will not share the inheritance with the child of the free woman." So then, friends, we are children, not of the slave but of the free woman. (Gal 4:21-31)

Paul's attractions to the rhetorical power of binary oppositions, or antinomies, is obvious here: slave vs. free; flesh vs. Spirit; flesh vs. promise; Hagar vs. Sarah; Ishmael vs. Isaac; Jerusalem "now" (=here? below?) vs. Jerusalem "above"; slavery vs. freedom; Pauline believers vs. Judaizing believers; persecutors vs. suffering righteous ones; children of the slave woman vs. children of the free woman. Paul's concern is with whom the Galatians will align themselves, and most today think Paul is responding to a new alignment proposed by the Judaizing opponents.[6]

But for Paul, who herewith is considered either apostle or apostate, the foundation is clear: there are, in some sense, *two* covenants (cf. Rom 9:4-5). One covenant, that originating in the promise to Abraham with Sarah in their son Isaac (cf. Gal 3:15-25), leads to Christ and the Spirit, to justification by faith and forgiveness of sins (cf. Rom 11:27), and not to the "works of the law";[7] the

---

[5] See C.K. Barrett, "The Allegory of Abraham, Sarah, and Hagar in the Argument of Galatians," in his *Essays on Paul* (Philadelphia: Westminster, 1982), 154–70; Lehne, *New Covenant in Hebrews*, 65–68; Backhaus, *Der neue Bund*, 297–306.

[6] Martyn, *Galatians*, 431–66.

[7] On which, cf. J.D.G. Dunn, "Works of the Law and the Curse of the Law (Gal. 3.10-14)," in his *Jesus, Paul and the Law* (Louisville: Westminster John Knox, 1990), 215–41; but see also M. Abegg, "Paul, 'Works of the Law' and MMT," *BAR* 20 (1994): 52–55, 82; Hahn, "Kinship by Covenant," 411–12 n. 72, 482–87 (where a salvation-historical modification of Dunn is presented).

other covenant, originating in Abraham and Hagar and their son Ishmael, leads to Moses and the works of the law and to the Judaizers (but not therefore to Judaism), but not to "justification" or "life" (3:21).

Both of Abraham's boys were circumcised; circumcision then is not the critical factor in the blessing. For Paul, one must learn to read the Bible (i.e., develop a hermeneutic) in terms of *Abrahamic promise* and not in terms of *Mosaic law*: there is *covenant promise* with Abraham and *covenant law* with Moses.[8] If the alternatives are fierce, the foundation is forceful: the same revelatory events to Abraham and Moses are part of the picture, but Paul, in contrast to the focus on Abraham as a man of the Torah (found in Sir 44:19, CD III, 2-4 and *m. Qidd.* 4:14), draws Abraham front and center as a man of *faith*.[9] Paul's concern, it needs to be recalled, is with the "Israel of God" (6:16), which is a people of faith.

A clarification is in order: it is most likely that Paul sees *one* covenant of YHWH with Israel, and not *two* covenantal arrangements.[10] Rather, there is one fundamental covenant, that accomplished through Abraham, with its own predecessors (Adam, Noah) and its own successors (Moses, David, the new covenant). Most importantly, Paul, however, is not framing a picture into which the right covenant can be set, but instead framing an *approach* to God's covenantal relations with Israel—and that relation is shaped by faith and not by the boundary-erecting works of the law. Here is where Paul allows himself to speak of two covenants, but it ought to be observed that it is the one covenant approached, or used (and abused), in two ways. It should also be observed that, because Paul is so concerned with the Gentile question, he finds the Abrahamic framing of the covenant with YHWH in its purest and most permanent form because that framing is soteriological. (But this is not a study of Paul's theology.)

Even if undeveloped in Galatians, the use of covenant to categorize "faith in Christ" in contrast to "obedience to the Torah" is destined to become a powerful organizing principle and hermeneutic in the regular debates between messianic and non-messianic Jews (cf. e.g., Eusebius, *Hist. eccl.* 4.26.13–14 [about Melito]). Paul has now crossed a threshold, the threshold of comprehending salvation-history in covenant terms. These two covenants, at least as expressed here, forge a fundamental contrast between the Mosaic Torah, which brings a curse (cf. Deut 28; Dan 9:11; Gal 3:13[11]), and the Spirit-empowered age that

---

[8] Dunn, *Galatians*, 249. Dunn here helpfully uncovers what amounts to one covenant with two understandings of that one covenant, and he posits that the potential misunderstanding of that one inviolable covenant with Abraham prevented Paul from regularly using covenant as his hermeneutical category.

[9] On Abraham, cf. B. Ego, "Abraham als Urbild der Toratreue Israels," in *Bund und Tora* (ed. Avemarie and Lichtenberger), 25–40.

[10] On the importance of this discussion, see now Backhaus, *Der neue Bund*, e.g., 246, 251.

[11] Cf. M. Wilcox, " 'Upon the Tree'—Deut 21:22-23 in the New Testament," *JBL* 96 (1977): 85–99, where the Aqedah is given significant value for understanding Galatians 3:13.

brings life which follows the death and resurrection of Jesus Christ. It may be hard for Christians today to comprehend the momentous significance of this hermeneutical axiom: at least from this point on, whether exploited or not, there is a foundation for a new rhetoric to express what distinguishes messianic Israel from non-messianic Israel.[12] The rhetoric is that the era of Jesus Christ fulfills (and possibly supersedes) the era of Moses, and the rhetoric dresses itself up in the language of the Torah: covenant.[13] And it is this rhetoric that is in gold on the cover of New Testaments and that bifurcates the Christian Bible, even if this statement recognizes a fundamental unity that many Christians miss.[14] That covenant hermeneutic,[15] however, was but one option for early followers of Jesus. It is not possible here to engage every text intensively for, to swipe the golden words of E.P. Sanders, "this is an essay not a library,"[16] but a few more examples beg for attention.

Paul's next instance of a covenant hermeneutic can be found in his midrash of Exodus 34:29-35 in 2 Corinthians 3, which moves along the salvation-historical plane to create a past of promise and a present of fulfillment, with a special emphasis on ministries.[17] This salvation-historical plane of contrasts,

[12] The pressing issue today is to what extent Paul is responsible for the parting of the ways and to what degree Paul saw the church within Israel and not just as Israel. A radical statement of Paul's inclusion within Judaism can be found in M. Nanos, *The Mystery of Romans* (Minneapolis: Fortress, 1996); *The Irony of Galatians* (Minneapolis: Fortress, 2002). A more balanced view can be seen in Dunn, "Two Covenants or One?" 113–18.

[13] For a comprehensive study of Paul's covenant hermeneutic in Galatians 3–4, cf. Hahn, "Kinship by Covenant," 370–489; note esp. the intriguing suggestions on pp. 393–94 n. 46, where the Abrahamic rite of circumcision—as Abraham's fleshly action—is linked to the Deuteronomic covenant curses and both are swept away in the curse-absorbing and flesh-eliminating death of Christ (Gal 3:10-14). Furthermore, Genesis 22 supersedes Genesis 17 in substance; that is, in criticizing the Judaizers, so Paul argues, their decision to move from Genesis 12 and 15 to Genesis 17 was not a sufficiently scriptural move—they needed to move all the way to Genesis 22 to set the covenant demand in context (cf. Gal 3:8's appeal to Gen 12:3; 18:18; and 22:18) (pp. 398–404).

[14] Kinzig, "Καίνη διαθήκη, 519–44.

[15] One of the most noteworthy examples of sorting the Old Testament through the lens of covenant is the monumental study of Eichrodt, *Theology of the Old Testament*. In volume one he organizes as follows: the covenant relationship, the covenant statutes (law and cultus), the name and nature of the covenant God, the instruments of the covenant (charismatic and official leaders), covenant-breaking and judgment, and fulfilling the covenant. Eichrodt's covenant theology can be challenged at the level of the diversity of the scriptural witness itself. In other words, while covenant is one organizing category, is that category meant to be the sole organizing category? Are there not other principial categories at work? And, as is obvious from this sort of challenge, what would the unity of the scriptural witness entail? Would it entail one thematic category, or is it multivalent from the outset?

[16] Sanders, "The Covenant as a Soteriological Category," in *Jews, Greeks and Christians* (ed. Hamerton-Kelly and Scroggs), 11–44, here p. 15.

[17] See J.D.G. Dunn, "2 Corinthians 3:17—'The Lord is the Spirit,'" in *Christology* (vol. 1 of *The Christ and the Spirit*; Grand Rapids: Eerdmans, 1998), 115–25; C.F.D. Moule, "II Cor. iii. 18b, καθάπερ ἀπὸ κυρίου πνεύματος," in his *Essays in New Testament Interpretation* (Cambridge: Cambridge University Press, 1982), 227–34. See also N.T. Wright, "Reflected Glory," in *The Glory*

which transcends the terms *midrash* and *allegory*, cannot be emphasized enough in Paul's words of 2 Corinthians 3. Paul's churches are "a letter of Christ, prepared by us, written not with ink but with the Spirit of the living God, not on tablets of stone but on tablets of human hearts" (3:3; cf. here to Exod 34:1; Ezek 11:19; 36:26). Here Paul extrapolates to the New Covenant (an allusion to Jer 31:33) with further (rhetorical) binary opposites, contrasting *Spirit* and *heart* with *ink* and *stone*. It is the "new covenant" that is "of the Spirit" and "gives life," while the old was of "letter" (that is, the written law of concrete demands that could not give life) and therefore "kills" (3:6).[18] To deepen his rhetoric, Paul employs a *qal vahomer* argument: if those killing tablets of stone "came in glory" (Exod 34:29-35), the ministry of the Spirit will come with even greater glory because it undoes condemnation by accomplishing justification (2 Cor 3:8-9). Crucial for Paul, in an aside, is that the old glory only lost its glory when the new glory arrived (3:10), showing that it is the same continuous glory.

Another opposition: Moses' resorting to an accommodating veil is in powerful contrast to the evangelistic boldness of the Pauline mission (2 Cor 3:12-13), but that (multi-faceted) veil remains for the hard-hearted (3:14-15) and is lifted for the gospel believer when that person turns to the Lord (=YHWH) (3:16). The clinching covenantal claim is that YHWH is now experienced[19] for messianic Israelites in the Spirit (3:17),[20] and where that YHWH (present in Christ as Spirit)[21] is present there is a beholding of the "glory of the Lord"[22] that creates freedom—from the Law, from sin, and from flesh—and transformation (3:17-18). What the Law did not, indeed could not do (bring life and overcome sin), the Spirit now can do. We are led to two critical conclusions: for Paul, the new covenant is a *pneumatic experience* and an *eschatological existence*, and the new covenant is rooted in the Abrahamic promise of *justification by faith*. Paul has tipped his hat toward a salvation-historical bifurcation of epochs of salvation, but that is not his focus: instead, his concern is with the ministry of the gospel in the Spirit in comparison with the Mosaic law and its revelation.

Regardless of the cruciality of the insights found in Galatians 4:24 and 2 Corinthians 3:1-18,[23] a new covenant hermeneutic is not central to Pauline theology.[24] It could have become his hermeneutic, since we find in these two

---

of Christ in the New Testament (ed. L.D. Hurst and N.T. Wright; Oxford: Clarendon, 1987), 139–50; G.D. Fee, *God's Empowering Presence* (Peabody, Mass.: Hendrickson, 1994), 296–320; Lehne, *New Covenant in Hebrews*, 68–71; Backhaus, *Der neue Bund*, 298–99.

[18] Cf. S. Westerholm, "'Letter' and 'Spirit,'" *NTS* 30 (1984): 229–48.

[19] For one example of the emphasis given to experience in early Christian theological developments, cf. J.D.G. Dunn, "1 Corinthians 15:45—Last Adam, Life-Giving Spirit," in his *Pneumatology* (vol. 2 of *The Christ and the Spirit*; Grand Rapids: Eerdmans, 1998), 154–66.

[20] Dunn, "2 Corinthians 3:17," in his *Christology*, 122–24.

[21] So Moule, "II Cor. iii.18b," in his *Essays in New Testament Interpretation*, 227–34.

[22] So in the oft-neglected suggestion of Wright, "Reflected Glory."

[23] One might note also 2 Cor 1:20; 5:14-17; 6:2.

[24] See W.S. Campbell, "Covenant and New Covenant," in *Dictionary of Paul and His Letters* (ed.

passages the very core of Paul's concerns (Spirit, life, faith, Abraham, freedom, etc.), but it did not do so. Paul chose other terms to sift reality and the transition to a new day in Christ and the Spirit, a reality thoroughly charged with the relations of non-messianic and messianic Israelites with Gentile believers, some of whom were sitting on the fence between the Mosaic covenant and the new covenant as articulated in the Pauline gospel. Covenant could have been the cutting edge for the Pauline gospel, but it was not used to that purpose often enough to give it the centrality that it was later to assume. One of the strengths of Ellen Juhl Christiansen's dissertation is her exploration of covenant in terms of identity, and her study of Paul's theology in Romans leads her to the view that covenant was not the tool Paul used to sift the pneumatic reality because his hermeneutical lens was pointed elsewhere.[25]

NEW COVENANT HERMENEUTICS IN HEBREWS

One who did sift reality with covenant was the author of Hebrews, whose provocative work and singular perception of the relationship of Jesus Christ to Israel's heritage, especially its cult, contributed in no small measure to the gold letters on the spine of the Christian Bible. If Paul's theology moved in the realm of polemics against a Judaizing disrespect for the sufficiency of the salvation made available in Christ and through the Spirit, the author of Hebrews explores the covenant theme with his readers,[26] some of whom have entered a period of spiritual malaise,[27] through the lens of temple worship available because of the eschatological completion in Christ (cf. Heb 7:11-12).[28] Two brief examples will suffice here.[29]

G.F. Hawthorne, R.P. Martin, and D.G. Reid; Downers Grove: InterVarsity, 1993), 179–83; Backhaus, *Der neue Bund und das Werden der Kirche*, 301–3; B. Longenecker, "Defining the Faithful Character of the Covenant Community," in *Paul and the Mosaic Law* (ed. J.D.G. Dunn; Grand Rapids: Eerdmans, 2001), 75–97. I must point to my own teacher's massive *The Theology of Paul the Apostle* (Grand Rapids: Eerdmans, 1998), and observe that his index is nearly a bare cupboard when it comes to the term *covenant*.

[25] See Christiansen, *Covenant in Judaism and Paul*, 214–32, 270–71 (summary).

[26] On which see esp. L.D. Hurst, *The Epistle to the Hebrews: Its Background of Thought* (SNTSMS 65; Cambridge: Cambridge University Press, 1990); Backhaus, *Der neue Bund und das Werden der Kirche*, with a history of interpretation on pp. 1–30; J. Dunnill, *Covenant and Sacrifice in the Letter to the Hebrews* (SNTSMS 75; Cambridge: Cambridge University Press, 1992); S.W. Hahn, "A Broken Covenant and the Curse of Death," *CBQ* 66 (2004): 416–36.

[27] See Koester, *Hebrews*, 64–79; see also B. Lindars, *The Theology of the Letter to the Hebrews* (NTT; Cambridge: Cambridge University Press, 1991), 4–15 (for a variant of the traditional view).

[28] Cf. Lane, *Hebrews*, 1:208–10; Theobald, "Zwei Bünde und ein Gottesvolk," 313–19. For a concise comparison of Paul and Hebrews, cf. Backhaus, *Der neue Bund und das Werden der Kirche*, 303–6.

[29] For a good survey of the material, cf. now Koester, *Hebrews*, 112–14; Lehne, *New Covenant in Hebrews*, 93–117 with nn.; J. Frey, "Die alte und die neue διαθήκη nach dem Hebräerbrief," in *Bund und Tora* (ed. Avemarie and Lichtenberger), 263–310; see also Hahn, "Kinship by Covenant," 490–633, 593–630.

First, Jesus (not Moses;[30] cf. Exod 19:1-6, 9; 24:2, 12, 15-18; 32:9-14, 30-34; *As. Mos.* 1:14; 3:12; Gal. 3:19-20), as the "first born son" with a superior "name" (cf. 1:4, 6), is the mediator of a "better covenant" (8:6: κρείττονός ἐστιν διαθήκης μεσίτης; cf. 1 Tim 2:5), which is in fact the "new covenant" (8:8), because it has been "enacted through better promises" (8:6; cf. 9:15). One hears here an echo of Paul or an early Christian tradition (cf. Gal. 3:21), for the radical juxtaposition of law and promise is a distinctive thought of early messianic Israel,[31] and one should not fail to see the emphatic *theocentric* and *christocentric* foci of the author's perception of this covenant—it is what God is doing in the economy of salvation for his people in the death of Christ.[32] This new covenant is Jeremiah's (as understood by the author of Hebrews), and it makes the first covenant "antiquated" and, therefore, "obsolete" (8:13; cf. 9:15; 10:9) and ready for an imminent disappearance (8:13).[33] The author's concern here is not so much with the Torah as inscribed in the heart of Jeremiah (cf. 10:22; 13:9), as is often asserted, but with the *eschatological effectiveness* of the new covenant in forgiving sins, another theme found in exilic expectation (e.g., Jer 31:34; Ezek 16:63; cf. also Rom 11:27 [Isa 59:20-21; 27:9]; *Jub* 22:14-15; *Pss. Sol.* 18:5).

Thus, second, and here the author makes his singular contribution in turning the cult on its head, Christ entered into the holy place as a Melchizedekian priest (cf. Heb 2:17-18; 7:1-28) "through the eternal Spirit" (9:14)[34] with his own blood to obtain eternal redemption (9:12).[35] And this entry, in another *qal vahomer* argument, enables the hitherto unavailable purification of conscience from sinful acts that lead to death (9:14); in addition, it is able to make the followers of Jesus eternally perfect (10:1, 14) and to sanctify them (10:10) through his inaugural sacrifice.[36] Thus, God's work is brought to its climactic completion through the death of Christ as the believer finds a correlative completion in forgiveness and holiness.[37] The death he endured makes Jesus Christ the "medi-

---

[30] Cf. Lehne, *New Covenant in Hebrews*, 22–27.

[31] By contrasting Jesus with Moses and using the term *better* for Jesus, it appears that the author of Hebrews thinks the Mosaic covenant was itself established on the basis of promise, even if an inferior promise, and this view would differ sharply from the Pauline polemic of Galatians 3–4, where the Mosaic covenant is contrasted with Abraham because the latter is given the promise. On the relationship of Hebrews to Paul, which was set back on its tracks due to the research of Hurst, cf. his *Epistle to the Hebrews*, 107–24.

[32] So Backhaus, *Der neue Bund und das Werden der Kirche*, 124, 258–64.

[33] We are reminded here again (cf. Gal 3:15-26) of the shocking nature of asserting the temporality of the Mosaic Torah for a Jewish context (cf. Koester, *Hebrews*, 388). The use of "new covenant" at Qumran did not lead in any sense to the antiquation of the "old" covenant at Sinai; instead, it rendered the Sinai covenant now fully applicable (see below).

[34] So Koester, *Hebrews*, 410–11; but cf. Attridge, *Hebrews*, 250–51.

[35] See Lindars, *Theology*, 71–84; Backhaus, *Der neue Bund und das Werden der Kirche*, 86.

[36] See Hurst, *Epistle to the Hebrews*, 38–41.

[37] See Koester's summary in *Hebrews*, 122–25.

ator of the new covenant" (9:15), and, with a gentle twist of the pen the covenant (perhaps, and only perhaps) becomes a testament (9:16-22).[38] It becomes eternally effective because he entered heaven itself, once, at the end of time, to offer himself (9:23-28). "Not only is it [the death of Christ] an atoning sacrifice, it is also a covenant-inaugurating event."[39] Violating this covenant, as an intensified warning, results in an even more intense punishment, the return to the curse conditions of the Deuteronomic code (6:1-8; 10:29).[40]

Here we have covenant categories more centralized to the theology of an early messianic Israelite, but this time in the direction of the eschatological effectiveness of sacrifice in the complete forgiveness of sins to enable purified worship. In other words, covenant is deployed by the author in a *polemical* fashion: it sets the Mosaic codes—and Judaism—in the past in order to exalt the Christ-code and Christianity. (One is entitled, therefore, to use the polemical terms *Christianity* and *Judaism* for the innovations of the author.) One further thought: consistent with Deuteronomy 30:6; Jeremiah 31:31-34; and Ezekiel 37:14, the new covenant of the author of Hebrews is tied to interiority through the presence of the Holy Spirit (Heb 9:14). Clearly not as central as it was to Acts 2 or to Paul, but nonetheless present, is the idea that it is the Spirit that generates new covenant thinking.

In the exegetical workshop of earliest messianism, then, the tool of covenant became a way of sifting the relationship of believers in Jesus Christ to the scriptural revelation of the Torah and its people, Israel. For Paul, it was a tool that separated the Mosaic covenant from the new covenant, primarily by recognizing the significance of the Holy Spirit. For the writer of Hebrews, it was a tool that ontologically separated the old system from the new system, primarily by recognizing the effectiveness of the forgiveness of sins through the sacrifice of Jesus Christ and his intercessory powers. If Paul crossed the threshold by sorting out the relationship of the old to the new in terms of covenant, the author of Hebrews set up shop and made the category his home to an unprecedented degree.

This leads to a historically significant question: when and where did that tool come out of the box to be used by early messianic Israelites? Where do we find the origins of the use of covenant as a hermeneutic for sifting the realities of this faith? And, another question also is formed: was it always a tool of separation so that it was used for the parting of the ways? And these sorts of questions lead us directly to the traditions of the last supper, upon which it seems the

[38] But see J.J. Hughes, "Hebrews ix.15ff and Galatians iii.15ff," *NovT* 21 (1979): 27–96, here pp. 28–66; Hahn, "Kinship by Covenant," 612–20. Hahn, in "Broken Covenant and the Curse of Death," *CBQ* 66 (2004): 416–36, offers perhaps the most definitive defense of the term *covenant* vs. *testament*.

[39] Attridge, *Hebrews*, 253.

[40] Cf. S. McKnight, "The Warning Passages of Hebrews," *TJ* 13 (1992): 21–59; Lehne, *New Covenant in Hebrews*, 104–8.

author of Hebrews built his case.[41] Is it possible that Jesus used the term covenant? if so, what did it mean for him? did he use it to explain the significance of his death?

JESUS AND A (NEW) COVENANT HERMENEUTIC

If one were tempted to think covenant unimportant to earliest Christian reflection on the relation of followers of Jesus to their ancient heritage because the term occurs only in three writings—Galatians and 2 Corinthians (but not Romans), and Hebrews—that temptation can be resisted by reminding ourselves that the early Christian eucharistic celebration almost certainly contained the term: Mark 14:24 (par. Matt 26:28; Luke 22:20; 1 Cor 11:25). If this tradition was widespread—that is, as often as whenever and wherever the early Christians celebrated the Eucharist—they were drawn into a covenant hermeneutic. And every covenant implies a body politic—a new Israel.

We should observe that the lack of centrality of the covenant category in Paul almost certainly reflects that it is not Paul who was responsible for its innovation in earliest Christianity. It was available to him, and he did make use of it. But, covenant remained on the periphery of his theology at the same time that a sense of a covenanted community was probably central in worship (1 Cor 11:25).[42] Even if it was not central to Paul, it was central to those who developed the eucharistic traditions, and we should perhaps remind ourselves of the cruciality of liturgical ritual for both expressing and shaping the beliefs of a community.[43]

If we take the tradition of the new covenant hermeneutic as prior to Paul, how early might this tradition be? We can remind ourselves here of another white elephant in the middle of the room: "Noteworthy and puzzling is the so-called 'covenant avoidance' in Jesus' preaching, an avoidance only interrupted in the tradition of the last supper."[44] Why is it that Jesus, if not in the last supper, never uses the term covenant while some (not all) early Christians found in this term the hermeneutic that unlocked the mystery of Israel's Scriptures?[45]

The question is best answered by inquiring into the most reconstructible original form of the last supper words, even though Martin Kähler's students get

[41] So, among many, Backhaus, *Der neue Bund und das Werden der Kirche*, 228–32.

[42] A.R. Millard, in his article dedicated to F.F. Bruce, argued that Paul used the covenant concept of punishment for covenantal unfaithfulness (e.g., the reference to the sick and "sleeping" in 1 Cor 11:30). See his "Covenant and Communion in First Corinthians," in *Apostolic History and the Gospel* (ed. W.W. Gasque and R.P. Martin; Grand Rapids: Eerdmans, 1970), 24–48.

[43] On this, cf. A.F. Segal, "Covenant in Rabbinic Writings," *SR* 14 (1985): 53–62, here pp. 56–62.

[44] H. Lichtenberger, "'Bund' in der Abendmahlüberlieferung," in *Bund und Tora* (ed. Avemarie and Lichtenberger), 217–28, here p. 217 (translation mine).

[45] The recent study of T. Holmén, *Jesus and Jewish Covenant Thinking* (BibInt 55; Leiden: E.J. Brill, 2001), while setting forth some powerful theses and conclusions, is not a technical argument about whether or not Jesus used the term *covenant*.

their knickers in a twist when such questions are posed. In speaking of an original reconstructible form of the words, however, we should recognize, along with
Kurt Backhaus, that it is highly unlikely that the earliest Christians would have
fundamentally altered the intentional direction of what Jesus was all about, even
if the specific term covenant is in dispute.[46] Here are the four principal texts over
the wine, texts that are somewhat independent:[47]

Mark 14:24   This is my blood of the *covenant*, which is poured out for
             many.
Matt 26:28   This is my blood of the *covenant*, which is poured out for
             many for the forgiveness of sins.
Luke 22:20   This cup that is poured out for you is the **new** *covenant* in
             my blood.
1 Cor 11:25 This cup is the **new** *covenant* in my blood.

To summarize what was discussed in the previous chapter, there are four elements here: A. blood, B. covenant, C. pouring out, and D. forgiveness of sins.
What matters here are the literary allusions to ancient traditions, and Jesus may
be alluding to one or more of the following four texts: (1) Jeremiah 31:31, (2)
Exodus 24:8, (3) Zechariah 9:11, (4) Isaiah 53:12.[48] We concluded that the evidence is in a bit of a stalemate: if we consider *blood* and *covenant* as preeminent,
we lean toward Zechariah and Exodus; if we consider *pour out* and *for many* as
the fundamental concern, we lean toward Isaiah. We should omit for the forgiveness of sins as Matthean redaction of his Markan *Vorlage*.[49]

If, however, these crucial words are omitted from consideration as part of the
last supper of Jesus with his followers (and here our confidence depends on the
precise terms we choose), then the critical text forming the backbone of Jesus'
explanation of his imminent death seems to be Zechariah 9:11, though

[46] K. Backhaus, "Hat Jesus vom Gottesbund gesprochen?" *Theologie und Glaube* 86 (1996): 347.
He concludes: "Daher erscheint es sachgemäß, in der gemeinsamen Überlieferungssubstanz der
neuttestamentlichen Einsetzungsberichte den Grundzügen nach die historische Selbstdeutung Jesu
zu vermuten" (347). Backhaus is the most recent and complete defense of Jesus' use of *covenant* in
the last supper. He disagrees with numerous German scholars (cf. pp. 347–48 n. 21).
[47] So Backhaus, "Hat Jesus vom Gottesbund gesprochen?" 352–53.
[48] When Backhaus appeals to the connection of eschatology with covenant under the category of
the criterion of dissimilarity he fails to observe that "new" is hardly integral to the Jesus traditions;
instead, it appears in the Lukan-Pauline tradition alone. And one should not make an immediate
connection of eschatology with new. Furthermore, his strong contrast of John and Jesus (over the
image of God, hence Jesus' "newness") is suspect, and neither does this constellation make for as
easy a connection to covenant as he suggests (pp. 354–55). Nonetheless, Backhaus' contention that
the presence of a covenant motif in the last supper traditions witnesses to a theme that is not common in the early Christian tradition is important and insightful (pp. 35–54).
[49] In part, this discussion hinges on the conviction that Mark reflects the most primitive evidence
for the last supper. Furthermore, it hinges on the conviction that the Lukan form of the last supper is both independent and later, an adaptation of the last supper and the Pauline church Eucharist
tradition. On this, cf. Pesch, *Markusevangelium*, 2:364–77.

Zechariah's words stream from the Exodus texts.[50] Furthermore, Zechariah's words appear to be the more appropriate because they not only contain important verbal parallels but their concern is closer to Jesus': God's redemptive and delivering work at and following the exodus. But, it is hard to push Exodus 24 out of the early Christian exegetical workshop. Is there a way to clarify the options?

The critical expression for determining whether our text appeals to Zechariah or Exodus, or not, is the term covenant (cf. Gen 12:1-3; 15:1-6; 17:1-8; Exod 19–24; 2 Sam 7).[51] The question is simple: Did Jesus use this term in the last supper?[52] Is this term a *Lorelei* or is it the Q.E.D.? If the term is *not* present in the words of institution, we must erase an allusion to either Exodus 24:8 or Zechariah 9:11. In this case, the *only* context of significance is *Pesah* and the meals connected to that week.

The general argument that the early church may have never come to such an understanding of the death of Jesus apart from a word to that effect from him is often set down as a firm observation.[53] But, we propose an alternative explanation. We should place on the table the following important observation, even if often neglected: as we said in the previous chapter, the *Pesah* event (Exod 12) and the covenant-establishing ceremony (Exod 24) are not one and the same;[54] nor are they naturally connected in the *Pesah* week celebration. When recently reading through the Exodus commentaries by B.S. Childs and W.H.C. Propp, I was again struck by the *absence* of covenant connection made by these authors between Exodus 12 and 24.[55] In fact, Jewish history reveals that "covenant renewal" is connected with *Pentecost* (cf. 2 Chron 15:8-15; *Jub.* 6:15-31) and not with *Pesah*,[56] apart from later scattered evidence (e.g., *Mek. de R. Ishm.* on Exod 12:6, 14).

To be sure, in the grand story or myth dream of Israel, *Pesah* and the *Berith* ceremony,[57] with its *olah* and *selamim* offerings that have (almost) nothing in

[50] Cf. B. Lindars, *New Testament Apologetic* (London: SCM, 1961), 13–33.

[51] Cf. also X. Léon-Dufour, *Sharing the Eucharistic Bread* (trans. M.J. O'Connell; New York: Paulist, 1986), 149–54; Lehne, *New Covenant in Hebrews*, 80–88; Lichtenberger, "'Bund' in der Abendmahlsüberlieferung," in *Bund und Tora* (ed. Avemarie and Lichtenberger), 21–28; Backhaus, *Der neue Bund und das Werden der Kirche*, 291–97.

[52] See esp. Backhaus, "Hat Jesus vom Gottesbun gesprochen?"; see also D.C. Allison, Jr., "Jesus and the Covenant," *JSNT* 29 (1987): 57–78, esp. pp. 65–66, where Allison, in a flourishing insight, contends that John the Baptist denied the efficacy of the Abrahamic covenant, that the early Christians at a very early date thought in terms of covenant, and that Jesus had an eschatological outlook that implied the downfall of the Mosaic dispensation.

[53] For defense of covenant as original, cf. J. Koenig, *The Feast of the World's Redemption* (Harrisburg: Trinity Press International, 2000), 33–34.

[54] As any reading of *Mek. de R. Ishm.* evinces [on Exod 12; tractate *Pischa*].

[55] See Childs, *Exodus*; Propp, *Exodus 1–18*.

[56] But, cf. J.D.G. Dunn, *Jesus Remembered* (vol. 1 of *Christianity in the Making*; Grand Rapids: Eerdmans, 2003), 816.

[57] On which, see R.S. Hendel, "Sacrifice as a Cultural System," *ZAW* 101 (1989): 366–90, who

common with the last supper, are integral parts of the story of redemption from Egypt (e.g., Hos 2:15-18; Jer 31:31-40; possibly Isa 42:6); and Pentecost is the fitting completion of Pesah, but the two events are nonetheless distinguished, both liturgically and theologically. Further, the commonality of blood (smeared at *Pesah*; tossed in the ceremony—even if later tossed in the slaughtering of the *Pesah* victim in the temple) does not make the *functions* or the *effects* of the blood the same.[58] Nor is the major theme of the two founding events the same: deliverance and liberation as compared to relationship establishment, threat of punishment, and commitment (forgiveness is not on the surface either). This distinction needs to be observed because far too many scholars assume that a connection between *Pesah* and covenant ceremony is natural enough that the two founding events can be identified as one big event.[59] Being covered by blood at *Pesah* differs functionally and effectively from being splashed with blood at the covenant ceremony. In one the person is protected from God's wrath; in the other, a person becomes a covenant member and is warned of extirpation if the covenant terms are ignored. The first is not about forgiveness; the second seals the commitment to YHWH in terms of atonement and purity.[60]

If there is any place the later Passover *Haggadah*—which could be a good test case of how *Pesah* was understood—can aid these concerns with Jesus and first-century practice, it is at the level of *theologizing*. In the first century and in later Judaism both groups would be reflecting on the significance of *Pesah* and its importance for communal identity. And one thing is clear: the later Passover *Haggadah* is neither about covenant establishment nor about forgiveness.[61] I

---

sees in Exodus 24:3-8 a communal act fostering unity as part of a larger cultural system. Hendel cleanly distinguishes the Exodus 24 offerings (*olah*, *selamim*) from the Exodus 12 (contra Deut 16:7, which we observed in a previous chapter) offering in that the latter is roasted as an act of disconnection with Gentiles (*Pesah*) (pp. 384–86).

[58] One might suggest the presence of a covenant-forming blood in the requirement of circumcision for participation in *Pesah* (cf. Exod 12:48), but, as has been seen, even that requirement was modified to include women.

[59] E.g., P. Stuhlmacher, *Grundlegung von Jesus zu Paulus* (vol. 1 of *Biblische Theologie des Neuen Testaments*; 2d ed.; Göttingen: Vandenhoeck & Ruprecht, 1997), 133; Koenig, *Feast of the World's Redemption*, 34.

[60] This has been seen by many, but especially the German, exegetes: e.g., P. Stuhlmacher, "Das Lamm Gottes–eine Skizze," in *Frühes Christentum* (ed. H. Lichtenberger; vol. 3 of *Geschichte–Tradition–Reflexion*; ed. H. Cancik, H. Lichtenberger, and P. Schäfer; 3 vols.; Tübingen: Mohr Siebeck, 1996), 3:529–42, here pp. 529–31. J. Dunnill, in his wide-ranging study of Hebrews, however, finds a possible mixing of *Pesah* with covenant ceremony, at Hebrews 11:28 where the term πρόσχυσις may echo a liturgical connection of *Pesah* with *m. Pesah* 5:6 (cf. Exod 24:8); see *Covenant and Sacrifice in the Letter to the Hebrews*, 127–28. The evidence is suggestive, but one is tempted to argue that a new verb ("toss/dash" vs. "smear") would be used because the *Pesah* event has moved from door lintels to the temple altar.

[61] Later rabbinic reflection (*m. Pesah* 5:1-9:11) did connect the blood of the *Pesah* victim with the sin offering, but this is clearly not first century: see on this J. Neusner, *Performing Israel's Faith* (Waco, Texas: Baylor University Press, forthcoming), ch. 5, under "Inside the Walls of the Israelite Household."

find the term covenant only one time in the *Haggadah*: when the *barekh* (the grace) is recited, all participants remember the history of God's working with Israel and, in so doing, they express thanks "for thy covenant which thou hast sealed in our flesh" (*we'al beritheka shechathametha bibesarenu*). Liberation and redemption and circumcision, which is how covenant is understood here, are everywhere; political vision and national hopes are as well. But covenant establishment is simply not the way Jews reflect on the significance of *Pesah*.[62] We can only guess, and a guess it is, that first-century Jews would have seen *Pesah* in a similar manner. If so, covenant and *Pesah* are countries and ideas apart. The difference of the two for interpreting the words of Jesus is dramatic, and is evident in nearly every Christian interpretation of the last supper/Lord's Supper. Consequently, we need to think through this argument more completely.[63] The following steps lead me to conclude Jesus probably did not use the term covenant to explain his death at the last supper.[64]

First, this term is attributed to Jesus in the entire tradition (including John) only in the last supper text, a text crystallizing a tradition that itself became a fundamental liturgical expression in earliest Christianity. This text also shows several variations and developments to make it more expressive of early Christian theology.[65] Thus, the term covenant may be part of the unfolding

---

[62] Cf. the similar view of J. Jeremias, *The Eucharistic Words of Jesus* (trans. N. Perrin; Philadelphia: Fortress, 1977), 195. Contra J.M. Cohen, *Moments of Insight* (London: Vallentine, Mitchell, 1989), 57–61.

[63] See recently the study of Backhaus, *Der neue Bund und das Werden der Kirche*, 291–97.

[64] Long ago, R. Otto, *The Kingdom of God and the Son of Man* (trans. F.V. Filson and B. Lee-Wolf; London: Lutterworth, 1943), 268, 273–74, 289–95, proposed that "appoint" (διατίθεμαι) in Luke 22:29 meant "I make or found for you the covenant" (e.g., *karath berith*) and, originally, immediately followed Luke 22:19a as the original word of interpretation of the bread. This connection establishes a soteriological foundation for the covenant; furthermore, it specifies the covenant being established as a pan-Israel restoration of the twelve tribes with Davidic overtones. However, besides the uncertainty of Otto's retro-translation (cf. Fitzmyer, *Luke* 2:1419; Nolland, *Luke*, 3:1066), Luke 22:29 is a verse unparalleled in Matthew. One is given even more pause because some critical scholars of Q omit 22:29 from Q altogether, finding it of later derivation. See J.M. Robinson, et al., eds., *The Critical Edition of Q* (Hermeneia; Minneapolis: Fortress, 2000), 558–61; R.A. Horsley and J.A. Draper, *Whoever Hears You Hears Me* (Harrisburg: Trinity Press International, 1999), 262–63; D.C. Allison, Jr., *The Intertextual Jesus* (Harrisburg: Trinity Press International, 2000), 138.

[65] Some have argued that Mark 14:24 is nearly impossible in Jesus' language, Aramaic; however, this is dubious (e.g., a noun with a personal pronoun would not be followed by a genitive in Aramaic [Greek: τὸ αἷμά μου τῆς διαθήκης]). For discussion, with the balance shifting today toward the existence of a similar Aramaic expression, see Jeremias, *Eucharistic Words of Jesus*, 193–95; *adam geyami*; M. Casey, "The Original Aramaic Form of Jesus' Interpretation of the Cup," *JTS* 41 (1990): 1–12 (*dmy dnh, dqym' hv*). Casey, in particular, proposes methodological factors of significance; he also suggests how a translator moved from his proposed Aramaic saying to the present Greek saying. However, Casey uncritically assumes that the Greek logion is a translation of what Jesus said, and he then seeks an Aramaic *Vorlage* to that Greek logion; he never considers whether or not the Greek saying corresponds totally or partly to what Jesus said.

development of that tradition rather than a stable element in its bedrock expression.[66] It is not, however, circular to hold up a warning flag to authenticity because the term is not found elsewhere in the Jesus traditions; it is, in fact, an argument based on a consistent pattern of language for Jesus.[67]

Second, central to Jesus is the term and category *kingdom*, and it is that term around which Jesus oriented his mission and vision for Israel. And the more one finds that Jesus fits into the mold of "prophet," the less explicable it becomes why he avoided the term covenant, for that is a characteristic term of the prophetic vision[68]—unless we recognize that he chose other terms to express his vision. Kingdom is the term Jesus chose to build his dream on; one doesn't surrender one's dream terms easily. It is unlikely (but not impossible) that on the last night Jesus would have altered his fundamental term for understanding what God was doing in and through him. To use our earlier language, kingdom is Jesus' hermeneutic; it is through kingdom that Jesus understood God's unfolding plan of history.

Third, it follows that in no place in the teachings of Jesus is kingdom coupled with covenant. If it is plausible to connect the two terms/categories theologically,[69] with kingdom as one way of expressing covenant or expressing (the Davidic) dimension of the covenant, it can be affirmed unambiguously that Jesus' teachings do not make that connection. His mission was not one that brought to expression a focus on covenant-establishment or covenant-renewal.[70] If kingdom is central to Jesus and if, as later interpreters suggest, covenant reestablishment becomes the focus of Jesus' last week, it is not a little surprising that the term did not emerge in other parts of the Jesus tradition.

Fourth, very importantly, the last supper betrays, apart from the wine (=blood), few signs of a covenant ceremony reestablishment. Regardless of how one understands a covenant, the ceremony inevitably spells out the human obligations required to maintain that covenant and reveals the required commit-

---

[66] K. Backhaus' assumption that the saying over the cup inevitably speaks of covenant stretches the skin over the table: a cup, even when symbolizing blood, need not speak of a covenant ceremony. Cf. *Der neue Bund und das Werden der Kirche*, 294.

[67] Contra Backhaus, "Hat Jesus vom Gottesbund gesprochen?" 352.

[68] So ibid., 344–45.

[69] Cf. e.g., 1Q28b V, 20–23; 4Q252 V, 2–5. In fact, in these texts we find eschatology, even personified in the "messiah of justice," and end-time covenant. The connection of kingdom and covenant is palpably Jewish and belongs to the sort of movement Jesus inaugurates. However, the fact that it is Jewish does not make it a dimension of Jesus' thought-world. *That* kind of evidence is missing. On covenant at Qumran, cf. G. Vermès, *The Dead Sea Scrolls in English* (3d ed.; London: Penguin, 1987), 36–41. A connection of covenant and kingdom can be seen in the curious addition at Exodus 23:22 LXX (cf. 19:5-6), clearly evoking the covenant renewal ceremony with its formation of a "kingdom of priests" who receive divine protection. I am grateful to members of the IBR Jesus project for discussion of these texts.

[70] John Koenig: "Jesus proclaimed the covenant in many ways without actually using the word" (*Feast of the World's Redemption*, 33).

ment on the part of those who come under the protection of the Lord.[71] The following are absent in the schema of the last supper as a *kinship* covenant: an oath and mutually binding commitments.[72] In addition, if the last supper is to be seen as a *grant* covenant, the following would be missing: an oath,[73] a fundamental promise,[74] blessings for the followers and curses for the opponents, an unconditional bond for the suzerain, a promise of blessings for an indefinite future for the followers of Jesus. Neither is it likely that anything is seen here of the covenant being a reward for fidelity (but cf. Luke 22:28-29). If Jesus is setting forth a new covenant, he does so without specifying it as a covenant.[75] Such a practice would be abnormal in Judaism. Nor, in the Markan and Lukan traditions, is blood in the last supper "sprinkled" or "tossed" (and of all things, *on* the people),[76] the terms used in Exodus 24, but rather "poured out" and drunk (cf. Mark 14:24; Luke 22:20).

Fifth, this means that the entrance of covenant, especially in the sense of a new covenant, is foreign to the mission of Jesus and would be an unexpected innovation in the final week. Accordingly, Jesus probably said only "this is my blood"—a tidy parallel to "this is my body."[77] Some have argued that tidy parallels are a sign of increasing the liturgical elements, but this argument is contrary to the evidence we now possess.[78] Most scholars think the Pauline-Lukan form is secondary to the Markan-Matthean form. The Pauline-Lukan form is *less parallel* than the Markan-Matthean form. There are no laws in transmitting

---

[71] The commitment, or obligation, is the major emphasis of Kutsch, "בְּרִית, *berit*," *TLOT* (ed. Jenni), 1:258–64; see also Weinfeld, "בְּרִית, *berith*," *TDOT* (ed. Botterweck), 2:262–65.

[72] See esp. Kalluveettil, *Declaration and Covenant*; Rendtorff, *Covenant Formula*.

[73] The recent discussion of G.E. Mendenhall, *Ancient Israel's Faith and History* (Louisville: Westminster John Knox, 2001), 226–30, but the evidence he cites is from some later, rather than earlier, materials.

[74] One could posit such in Luke 22:29, though this promise of inclusion in the kingdom is hardly new for the followers of Jesus.

[75] The (probably) later "do this" is not covenant obligations but liturgical directions; obeying those words would hardly constitute covenant obligation fulfillment.

[76] The detail is omitted in *Tg. Exodus* 24:8, though Philo renders it as expressing the unity of mind (*QE* 2.35) while the author of Hebrews follows Exodus 24 (Heb 9:19-20). *Jub.* 6:11 has similar words for Noah's covenant.

[77] Justin, *1 Apol.* 66 [ANF 1.185]; Justin anchors his eucharistic practices in the "memoirs of the apostles" in the two claims of Jesus: "this is my body" and "this is my blood." These may have been the words he heard in his community before 155 CE, but it needs to be remembered that his origins are in Samaria.

[78] A serious start for this argument was given by Jeremias, *Eucharistic Words of Jesus*, 114. Further, the text-critical principle of the simpler reading favors Markan priority as well. The reading to be preferred is always the reading that best explains the origin of the others, and it is easier to move from Mark to Luke than from Luke to Mark; further, it is easiest to move from a simple "this is my blood" to the others. I am using text-critical criteria, as many have, to explain a tradition process as opposed to a text process; see G.D. Fee, "A Text-Critical Look at the Synoptic Problem," *NovT* 22 (1980): 12–28; see also M.C. Williams, "Is Matthew a Scribe?" (Ph.D. diss., Trinity International University, 1996).

traditions. Instead, an appeal to text-critical principles here supports the primitivity of the Markan tradition. *Sixth*, what we do have is a Jesus who identifies the wine of the meal with his blood. In fact, that statement of his pollulated in the earliest churches and produced a variety of saving metaphors for Jesus' death.

It must be granted that some big steps are needed from "my *blood*," in the context of a *Pesah* sacrificial offering, to "my blood of the *covenant*" and then to "the *new* covenant in my blood."[79] But, it appears that it was some early Christians, or Paul and his associates (or, what is more likely, someone in the pre-Pauline tradition[80]), as well as the writer of Hebrews, who took those steps. These steps led to the Christian concept of Jesus as the creator and arbiter of a new covenant that superseded the old covenant with Abraham and Moses and brought into reality the covenant expectations of Jeremiah and Ezekiel.[81]

We propose then that covenant and kingdom are alternative, hermeneutical categories—categories useful to Jews who are trying to get a handle on the diverse theological expressions of Jewish tradition as well as grasp Jewish history. Inasmuch as Jesus chose kingdom, covenant appears to be left to the side for others to use. (I am not arguing that the terms are mutually exclusive, but that Jesus had at least two options and chose kingdom and not covenant.)

It might be asked, and should be asked, why Jesus made this choice to prefer kingdom instead of covenant. (That this could have been, and indeed was, a choice for him is beyond question.) It is not possible here even to sketch a resolution to this question, but this much can be said: covenant by and large in Judaism was an allusion to Moses and the Sinaitic Covenant (as the Dead Sea Scrolls testify). Inasmuch as Jesus' foundation was not placed near Sinai but instead closer to Jerusalem as the City of David, it can be argued that covenant spoke too directly of the central concerns of the Deuteronomic movements like the Essenes and the Pharisees. Covenant, in addition, did not speak directly enough of the sort of prophetic and apocalyptic movements into which he placed himself. Accordingly, covenant spoke too directly of the statutes and ordinances of Exodus, Leviticus, and Deuteronomy, too directly of figures like Moses, Josiah, Ezra, and Nehemiah—it was for these reasons that Jesus opted

---

[79] A plausible anchor in the historical Jesus to "new covenant" would be through the theme of interiorization of the Torah, found in such texts as Mark 7:1-20 par.; Matt 5:21-48 pars.; 7:15-27. Cf. C.H. Dodd, *The Founder of Christianity* (London: Collins, 1971), 76–77. But it is precisely that connection—interiorization—that is absent in the last supper. But, this theme permits one to think that Jesus may have thought of the new covenant in terms of God's rewriting the Torah onto the hearts of people through his teachings. The term *new* has suggestive hints in *anew* (Mark 14:25—but here the new is in the future, not in the meal) and in "new commandment" at John 13:34.

[80] So M. Hengel, *The Atonement* (trans. J. Bowden; Philadelphia: Fortress, 1981), 53. For the Pauline contributions, emerging as they did from inclusive table fellowship, see pp. 109–30. H. Merklein, "Der Tod Jesu als stellvertretender Sühnetod," in *Studien zu Jesus und Paulus* (WUNT 43; Tübingen: J.C.B. Mohr [Paul Siebeck], 1987), 186, finds covenant typology in Jewish-Hellenistic reflection.

[81] Cf. E. Kutsch, "Von der Aktualität alttestamentlicher Aussagen für das Verständnis des Neuen Testaments," *ZTK* 74 (1977): 27–90; here pp. 286–89.

for kingdom. While those figures, those movements, and those books are within his orb of kingdom-thinking, they are not the central players. More central to Jesus were the *visions* of the classical prophets, like Isaiah and Zechariah. It was their images that shaped his thinking, and through which he viewed the other figures of holy writ and history. Jesus' Bible, then, was not a flat text, but a contoured text, with a little hill at Sinai but mountain peaks in the classical prophets. Because we have raised this issue of the origins of new covenant thinking, and because we have argued that it probably did not get its impetus from Jesus at the last supper, we should continue this very argument to inquire into its genesis in earliest Christianity.

New Covenant in the Early Christian Hermeneutic

If it is unlikely that Jesus used covenant or new covenant as hermeneutical tools to sort out the realities of God's saving work in his mission, then it remains for us to ask the further question of where it got its start, how it came the last supper traditions and whether or not its placement there was appropriate. In light of what has been sketched above, we can say that the category is used at least as early as the earliest Pauline churches, but sometime after the last supper and Easter.[82]

A critical tool allowing us to sort out the data can be found in examining the evidence from the great prophets of the exile, Jeremiah and Ezekiel (Ezek 11:14-21; 34:25-31; 36:16-28; 37:20-28; cf. also Hos 2:20, 25),[83] for it is in them that the new covenant gets its definitive shape; or, perhaps we should say, that they give it a definitive shape that was then reused in the faith of early followers of Jesus. When these messianic Israelites understood the Christ-event as the formation of the new covenant, they were appealing to the fulfillment of Jeremiah's early exilic predictions and Ezekiel's expectations as they understood them, with a hint of Isaiah's hope added.[84] And their concerns with this way of sorting out the future expectation, rooted as it is in the "covenant formula" (Jer 31:33), are not only a valued category for expressing Israelite hope, but are fundamentally central to Israel's perception of the future as well as its own exegesis.[85]

---

[82] Lehne, *New Covenant in Hebrews*, 85, concludes that the view came early in Christian thinking, and furthermore that the perception of the last supper tradition was more along the lines of a covenant renewal ceremony.

[83] See R.L. Kohn, *A New Heart and a New Soul* (JSOTSup 358; Sheffield: Sheffield Academic, 2002).

[84] See J. Swetnam, "Why Was Jeremiah's New Covenant New?" in *Studies on Prophecy* (VTSup 26; Leiden: E.J. Brill, 1974), 111–15; Levin, *Die Verheißung des neuen Bundes*.

[85] On which, cf. Levin, *Die Verheißung des neuen Bundes*, 11–13. On p. 12 he states: "Die Verheißung des neuen Bundes bildet, auf ihre Vorgeschichte gesehen, das Ziel, auf das die Entwicklung der alttestamentlichen Bundestheologie zustrebt. Mit ihr had die wichtigste theologische Systembildung, in der Israel sein Verhältnis zu Jahwe zu verstehen unternommen hat, die volle Ausprägung gefunden. Und auf ihre Nachgeschichte gesehen ist die Verheißung des neuen Bundes einder der Haupt-Ursprünge der alttestamentlichen Heilsprophetie."

Jeremiah's and Ezekiel's expectations are rooted, of course, in the covenant promises and covenant-making ceremonies with Abram/Abraham (Gen 12; 15; 17; 22), with Moses in the famous Book of the Covenant (Exod 19–24), with their contemporary Deuteronomic revision (Deut 12–26),[86] and with David (2 Sam 7; cf. Pss 89; 110; 132). The fundamental promises of YHWH with Israel, embodied as they are in these key figures, revolve around eternal protection and relationship with Israel as manifested in land and temple, nation, royal dynasty, and offspring. In each of these covenant formulations and reformulations, there are either implied or explicitly stated *conditions* on the part of Israel in order to sustain the relationship[87] and acquire its blessings (Gen 12:1; 17:1, 9, 10; Exod 19:6; Deut 5:26, 30; 7:12-16; cf. also, e.g., CD III, 2-4). So, when Jeremiah and Ezekiel rise up to address their pre-exilic and post-exilic audiences with the news of a coming new covenant (cf. Ezek 11:19; 18:31; 36:26; Isa 42:9), they do so as reconstructions and revitalizations of the older covenant formulas, as well as countermeasures against current priestly leadership. It is not the place here to explore the history of Israel's covenant formulations, but the following distinctive features of the *future* covenant with Israel can be utilized to understand the origins of the "new covenant" hermeneutic used by early followers of Jesus.

First, there is the expectation of a *restoration of the twelve tribes*, a pan-Israel reunification, which according to Ezekiel's vision, will result in a total realignment of the land of Israel (Jer 31:27-30; 32:44; 33:26; 50:4-7; Ezek 47–48). This restoration theme is connected, of course, to the inviolability of the covenant (cf. Isa 54:10; 55:3; 61:8). Second, the new covenant will prove to be *unbreakable* (Jer 31:32; 32:40), implying both that the former covenant (of Moses) was both breakable and had been broken so often that God had to send his people into exile as punishment and purgation (cf. Jer 7:21-26; 11:1-13; Deut 28). Third, when the new covenant is finally established, it will be *internal*, a knowledge embedded in the heart (cf. Jer 24:7; Deut 30:6), rather than an external relation or ritual enactment (cf. Jer 31:33; 32:39).[88] That is, it will be an inwrought work of the Spirit or, differently expressed, the result of God's gracious care in taking once again Israel's hand in his (Jer 31:32; cf. Isa 32:15; 34:16-17; 59:21; Joel 2:28-32; Ezek 11:17-21; 36:22-38; 37:4-14). This *interiority* is how most of scholarship perceives the blunt force of the expectation of exiled Judeans like Jeremiah,[89] but most fail to perceive its original context: whether that be an anti-priestly/scribal strain (cf. Jer 8:7-9),[90] or an antitradi-

---

[86] I consider a possiblity that Jeremiah himself, or perhaps Baruch, was the Deuteronomist, but I leave that to the *Alttestamentlers* to unravel.

[87] On this see Rendtorff, *Covenant Formula*.

[88] Cf. Levin, *Die Verheißung des neuen Bundes*, 257–64.

[89] E.g., Nicholson, *God and His People*, 21–12.

[90] So Mendenhall, *Ancient Israel's Faith and History*, 186: "The internalization of Yahweh's will makes unnecessary the entire machinery of external enforcement and religious indoctrination . . . it is an aspect of personal character; as such, it exists irrespective of social distinctions altogether." Mendenhall sees this new covenant in part as a return to the old (lionized) Yahwism of the exodus

tional theology (as narrated in Job), or the expectation of a new temple, or a connection with the proximity of God's (written) word (cf. Jer 30:2) in synagogal readings of Torah, the practice of phylacteries, and family instruction (cf. Deut 6:6-8; 11:18; 30:11-14; Isa 51:7; 59:21; Ps 119).[91] An important corollary is close to hand: Torah and covenant are nearly synonymous. Fourth, the final covenant will be *democratic* in contrast to the royal and hierocratic priestly system (Jer 31:34; cf. 36:20-31). For some of the exilic prophecies, the final people of God will be ruled by YHWH alone, which is to be seen as a return to the pre-monarchical days of Moses, Joshua, and Samuel (cf., e.g., Ezek 34:11-16). Furthermore, there was a gravity in some prophetic utterances about the centrality of Israel as a people—not Israel through its royal and priestly leaders—in a mission to the nations (Isa 40-55), a vision that was partly demolished in the post-exilic reforms of Ezra and Nehemiah.

Fifth, the new covenant will result in *forgiveness of sins*, which means the covenant will be restored, the people will inhabit their land, the temple will be functioning properly with YHWH present, and Israel will enjoy peace because YHWH will choose to forget Israel's history of covenant-breaking and consider its time of punishment, or exile, over (Jer 31:34; 33:8; 36:3; 50:20; cf. also Isa 40:1-2; 55:7; Ezek 16:63; Dan 9:16-19).[92] Sixth, the *former* covenants will find their consummation in the new covenant (Jer 14:21; 32:40; 33:15, 20-21; 33:23-26; Ezek 16:60; 34:23). Seventh, the covenant of the future will result in *peace* (Ezek 34:25, 27; 37:26, 28; Isa 11:6-9; cf. Mal 3:2b-4, 12). Finally, if the covenant's restoration looks forward to the restoration of the twelve tribes, there is also a more universal outlook in view (Ezek 16:61; Isa 42:1-6; 49:6; 55:3-5; 56:6). At any rate, there is an expectation of a pan-Israel restoration as the "new seed" of the "new covenant" days (Jer 31:27-30). Accordingly, this expectation is for a new start with a new people shaped by a new covenant—but it should be noted that this newness, because it is in fundamental continuity with the old, is a renewed covenant (cf. Lam 5:21).[93] It is development, not evolution; it is both continuity and discontinuity.

In short, it needs to be observed here that in the Jeremiah and Ezekiel versions of the expected new covenant there is something substantially new; this expectation is not just the revivification of the Mosaic covenant. To quote the fecund words of G.B. Caird, "But a theology which did nothing but look back to the city of destruction would share the monumental sterility of Lot's wife."[94]

---

covenant where there was no corporate body and a fundamental departure from the now destroyed, corrupt form of the Solomon-based Yahwism.

[91] See Swetnam, "Why Was Jeremiah's New Covenant New?" 113–15; see also the discussions of Holladay, *Jeremiah*, 2:163–65, 197–99.

[92] In general, see N.T. Wright, *Jesus and the Victory of God* (vol. 2 of *Christian Origins and the Question of God*; Minneapolis: Fortress, 1996), 268–74.

[93] Cf. Levin, *Die Verheißung des neuen Bundes*, 138–41; see also W. Gross, "Erneuerter oder Neuer Bund?" in *Bund und Tora* (ed. Avemarie and Lichtenberger), 41–66.

[94] G.B. Caird, *New Testament Theology* (ed. L.D. Hurst; Oxford: Clarendon, 1994), 160.

These two prophets think history will turn the corner and head toward the eschatological goal.

To set these few early Christian attempts to reconceptualize history and identity in covenant terms, we ought to take a brief glance at the central and differing conceptions of the covenant in the writings of the Dead Sea sect.[95] For them, God is sure to remember his covenant (CD I, 4; IV, 9; 4Q504 II, 9; 1Q34bis 3 ii.5-6; 1QM XIII, 8; cf. also *Jub.* 1:17-18) but will also mete out the covenant curses Israel has agreed to (cf. CD I, 17-18; VIII, 1; XIX, 13-14; 1QS II, 12; V, 12). So central is covenant that its members are known as the people of the covenant, here describing the new covenant made at Damascus with this new community (cf. CD II, 2; VI, 11, 18-19; VII, 5; VIII, 18, 20-21; IX, 2; XIII, 14; XIX, 31, 34; 2XX, 11-13, 17, 25, 29; 1QS II, 26; V, 11, 18), defined here and there as a "covenant of mercy" (1QS I, 8, 16), a "covenant of peace" (1QM XII, 3), and a "covenant of justice" (1QS VIII, 9, 10). This covenant is understood as God's eschatological favor shown to the community. Fundamentally, however, this covenant is understood as a revelation (1QH XII, 5; XIII, 9; XV, 10, 20) of a new set of regulations and commandments (cf. CD VI, 19; VIII, 21; X, 6; XII, 11; XV, 1-9; XVI, 1-2; XIX, 33-34; XX, 12-13; 1QSa I, 5, 7; 1QSb I, 2; III, 24; 1QpHab II, 3), to which the members were to commit themselves daily (1QS X, 10). Those who broke these commandments were cut off. Covenant, occasionally as a new covenant, is a theme found in, but not central to, other Second Temple texts that cannot be surveyed in this context (cf., e.g., 1 Macc 1:11-15; 2:19-22; 2:49-70; 4:6-11; Jdt 9:13; 2 Macc 1:2-6; 7:30-38; 8:12-18; Wis 18:22; Sir 17:12; 24:8-23; 41:19; 44–50; Pr Azar 11; 2 Esd 2:5, 7; 3:15; 5:29; 7:83; Jub. 1:16-25; 2:26-33; 6:12-14; 14:19-20; 15:1-34; 22:15-19; 30:7-12; 33:10-14; 36:8-11; 49:1–50:13).[96]

---

[95] Cf. Sanders, *Paul and Palestinian Judaism*, 240–57; Lehne, *New Covenant in Hebrews*, 43–54; J.A. Huntjens, "Contrasting Notions of Covenant and Law in the Texts from Qumran," *RevQ* 8 (1972–75): 361–80; Christiansen, *Covenant in Judaism and Paul*, 104–85.

[96] Cf. A. Jaubet, *La notion d'alliance dans le Judaisme aux abords de l'ère chrétienne* (Paris: Le Seuil, 1963); A.M. Schwemer, "Zum Verhältnis von Diatheke und Nomos in den Schriften der jüdischen Diaspora Ägyptens in hellenistisch-römischer Zeit," in *Bund und Tora* (ed. Avemarie and Lichtenberger), 67–109; Backhaus, *Der neue Bund und das Werden der Kirche*, 283–324.

See also Lehne, *New Covenant in Hebrews*, 35–59 with nn., who states: "It is curious, therefore, that in all of these writings—with the exception of the Dead Sea Scrolls . . . there seems to be a studious avoidance of Jeremiah's phrase. . . . In fact, even the word 'covenant' seems to appear less frequently than in the Hebrew Scriptures" (35). Her view on Bar 2:20-35 and *Jub.* 1:16-25 is a trifle overly constrained for detecting allusions to the new covenant of Jeremiah. The issue turns on how one defines new in new covenant; in fact, on how radically new the new covenant is. If one perceives the new covenant as somehow continuous with the old covenant, then the allusions are given a surer footing.

A comment is in order about why the rabbis used *covenant* so rarely. It has been argued that they avoided the term largely because it was assumed. In my judgment, this is a Christianization of the rabbinic traditions. If one is to allow that covenant can be a central religious category to all of Judaism, one must also ask why the term appears so infrequently *both* in Judaism and earliest Christianity (which is a form of Judaism at times). More importantly, one is entitled to ask why

It is not possible here to enter into a vigorous discussion of the forerunners of the covenant of Qumran. Instead, I shall simply state my conclusion that the covenant theme is understood as a Moses-like (Abraham is at times mentioned; cf. CD XII, 11) covenant, and this covenant for the Qumran community is somewhat of an extension of the Book of the Covenant (Exod 19-24) and Deuteronomy (12-26). More broadly, the covenant of the Second Temple period is by and large the Mosaic covenant of obligation to keep the Torah— especially its flash-point regulations in circumcision, Sabbath, and food laws— in order to secure the blessings of YHWH for the people of Israel (e.g., Sir 39:8).[97] It is, in the terms of E.P. Sanders, "covenantal nomism."[98] If new covenant is appealed to, it is less with a view to the distinguishing features of that covenant (as sketched above) than with a view to the sectarian belief in the fulfillment of that eschatological hope in their own community. Thus, it is new

---

Sanders needs to contend that we need a "most convenient term" (*Paul and Palestinian Judaism*, 237). The point might be made as follows: when we ask the term covenant to carry this sort of load, we are using a term that was not used that centrally by those who wrote in the NT and whose evidence we count as important. In other words, my contention is that Christians have learned to understand history, especially salvation-history, through this covenant hermeneutic, a hermeneutic that is more often than not an imposition on the material rather than integral to it. We would do better to let the specific textual categories shape the discussion rather than forcing their categories into our systemic categories. The issue is *not* whether covenant is a good term—for it surely is; the issue is *how often* and *to what degree* one uses covenant as a hermeneutical explanatory category. The critical term for most of Judaism prior to Jesus, in my judgment, was Torah. But this does not make for legalism in the classical sense; rather, this term defines Israel's relationship to YHWH as one of guidance and obedience, and hence "covenantal nomism" would be a fine synthetic category. To be sure, covenant can be seen as the foundation for Torah or as a part of Torah. However, it is the term Torah that was preferred by those whose texts we now study. See Segal, "Covenant in Rabbinic Writings," who (1) permits the evidence of earliest Christianity to be part of the material one uses for understanding Judaism, and (2) argues that the liturgical evidence fills out the picture of a broader use of covenant. Circumcision was called the "covenant of circumcision" throughout rabbinic writings (57–58). Beside the issue of dating liturgical traditions, my only demurral is his assumption of the centrality of covenant in Christianity, for it is this that forms his point of comparison. For a nuanced understanding of the role the term covenant plays in Diaspora literature, and with nods in the direction of the value and sometimes synonymity of other terms, cf. Schwemer, "Diatheke und Nomos." For a defense of a theology of the covenant among the rabbis, cf. F. Avemarie, "Bund als Gabe und Recht," in *Bund und Tora* (ed. Avemarie and Lichtenberger), 163–216.

[97] On this see J.D.G. Dunn, *The Partings of the Ways* (Philadelphia: Trinity Press International, 1991), 23–31.

[98] See Sanders, *Paul and Palestinian Judaism*. The recent multi-authored volume edited by D.A. Carson examines the central proposal of Sanders—that Judaism was a religion of "covenantal nomism"—by examining the central theological views of the broad spectrum of Judaism. Where Sanders sought a "pattern of religion," the authors here seek for special nuances with each author or corpus and, hence, disagreements with Sanders are discovered sometimes at the expense of not recognizing the intent of Sanders. See D.A. Carson, P.T. O'Brien, and M. Seifrid, eds. *Justification and Variegated Nomism* (vol. 1 of *The Complexities of Second Temple Judaism*; Tübingen: Mohr Siebeck; Grand Rapids: Baker Academic, 2001). For a balanced examination, cf. H.-M. Rieger, "Eine Religion der Gnade," in *Bund und Tora* (ed. Avemarie and Lichtenberger), 129–61.

in the sense of eschatology, but not in the sense of a specific fulfillment of Jeremiah's or Ezekiel's specific expectations.

To *that* fulfillment, to see at work messianic Israel's grand *pesher*, one must point to the early Jerusalem church's definitive communal visionary, missionary, and glossolalic (or xenological; cf. Acts 2:9-11) experience. More broadly, we must point to the messianic community that found in its *pneumatic* experiences[99] a lever that could be pulled down with such force that it erupted into a movement (Jerusalem: Acts 2; 8:14-17; 9:26-29; Damascus: Acts 9:17; Galilee: Mark 16:7; Pauline churches: Gal 3:1-5; Rom 8:4-27).[100] They were firmly convinced it was on the day of Pentecost[101] that the fullness of God's work in Jesus Christ was completed (cf. Acts 2:17-21's use of Joel 2:28-32); and, furthermore, this experience shaped the tellings of pneumatic experiences elsewhere (e.g., Acts 4:31; 10:44-48).[102] Put differently, the soteriological Spirit, who is also the Spirit of prophecy, was at work at the end of times in order to enable God's word to be heard with power.[103] The "Man of the Spirit" became the "Dispenser of the Spirit."[104] "It was only at Pentecost by the gift of the Spirit that the benefits and blessings won by Jesus in his death, resurrection, and ascension were applied to the disciples."[105] So Luke's story-line is to be understood.

The Pentecostal charismatics of the post-Easter church in Jerusalem could easily have appealed to each of the distinctive features of the new covenant expectations of Jeremiah (and in a secondary way also to Ezekiel) to produce a *Pentecostal* new covenant hermeneutic. This proposal is that the new covenant hermeneutic owes its origins to the pneumatic experiences of early Jerusalem-based followers of Jesus. Before outlining this suggestion, however, we need to

---

[99] In general, see J.D.G. Dunn, *Unity and Diversity in the New Testament* (2d ed.; Philadelphia: Trinity Press International, 1991), 174–202; see also M. Hengel, *Between Jesus and Paul* (trans. J. Bowden; Philadelphia: Fortress, 1983), 1–29; *Atonement*, 47–55.

[100] On this, cf. Dunn, *Unity and Diversity in the New Testament*, 38–54; *Jesus and the Spirit* (Philadelphia: Westminster, 1975), 135–56; "Pentecost," in his *Pneumatology*, 210–16; F.J. Foakes Jackson and K. Lake, eds. *Acts of the Apostles* (part 1 of *Beginnings of Christianity*; 5 vols.; Grand Rapids: Baker, 1979), 1:22–23. For a judgment of Acts 2 as having less historical value, cf. Fitzmyer, *Acts*, 232; Levin, *Die Verheißung des neuen Bundes*, 265–79, who observes that early Christian new covenant thinking was the result of an experience and was also an exegetical backward gaze. Further, he questions the exegesis of earliest Christianity in its use of new covenant language.

[101] Cf. C.F.D. Moule, "The Post-resurrection Appearances in the Light of Festival Pilgrimages," *NTS* 4 (1957–1958): 58–61; Dunn, *Jesus and the Spirit*, 139–42; "Pentecost," in his *Pneumatology*, 210–15.

[102] Dunn, *Jesus and the Spirit*, 136–39.

[103] Dunn, "Baptism in the Spirit," in his *Pneumatology*, 222–42.

[104] For further study, see Dunn, "2 Corinthians 3:17," "Jesus—Flesh and Spirit," and "1 Corinthians 15:45," in his *Christology*, 115–25, 126–53, 154–66; and "Rediscovering the Spirit," "Spirit and Kingdom," "The Spirit of Jesus," in his *Phenomenology*, 74–80, 133–41, 329–42. See also G.F. Hawthorne, *The Power and the Presence* (Dallas: Word, 1991).

[105] J.D.G. Dunn, *Baptism in the Holy Spirit* (Philadelphia: Westminster Press, 1970), 44.

observe that the earliest hermeneutical reflection on the Pentecostal experience derived from Joel 2 and not from Jeremiah 31[106] or Ezekiel. If the first impulse of the messianic community was to explain Pentecost as a fulfillment of Joel 2, a second reflection soon followed (now embedded in the Lord's Supper traditions, in Paul and in Hebrews) that led directly and even more profoundly to the new covenant expectations of Israel's later prophets. And that conviction would have led at least to eight separate ideas.

But, prior to those ideas, we add that when the early messianic Israelites appropriated a new covenant hermeneutic there is no reason to suggest they were implicitly arguing that the old was inferior. Rather, they were arguing that the *promises were being fulfilled.* In other words, it is a claim of eschatological continuity, not one of switching religions. They saw what occurred as the realization of Israelite faith, not the acquisition of another faith. It was the old faith now raised to its highest level. In the words of James Dunn: "Christianity cannot understand itself except as an expression of Judaism; that Judaism is not true to itself unless it recognizes Christianity as a legitimate expression of its own heritage; and that Christianity, equally, is not true to itself unless it recognizes Judaism as a legitimate expression of that same common heritage."[107] And, for some, this new found faith was to become a powerful perception of God's plan along covenant lines.

First, its concern with *twelve* continues the community focus of the historical Jesus (cf. Mark 3:13-19; 6:7-13, 30) as it reappoints a successor to Judas (Acts 1:12-26). This story is told in such fullness and detail that it gives one pause to think it is a later fiction. Indeed, what becomes of the one who replaces Judas? As Dunn has observed, the attempt to replace Judas is "a misguided striving after community at an artificial and superficial level."[108] One might hear also an echo of the promise to the Twelve (cf. Luke 22:28-30) to begin to exercise their "ruling" over Israel by confronting the nation with the good news about Jesus' resurrection (Acts 2:14).

Second, if the claim is that the new covenant will be unbreakable (Jer 31:32; 32:40), there is evidence in the Ananias and Sapphira story to see that *unbreakable* means "immediate punishment" (Acts 5:1-11), and one is then tempted to think in terms of the community rules at Qumran and the Essene quarter in Jerusalem (1QS VI, 20, 24-25).[109] An elaboration of this theme is carried out in

---

[106] This lack of reflection of Jeremiah 31 in Acts 2 confirms our proposal above on the absence of "new covenant" language in the original last supper event. Even more, it is somewhat astonishing that Luke omits reference to Jeremiah 31 in Acts 2 after his "new covenant" language of the last supper (Luke 22:20).

[107] Dunn, "Two Covenants or One?" in *Frühes Christentum* (ed. Lichtenberger), 119.

[108] Dunn, *Jesus and the Spirit*, 145.

[109] Ibid., 166; cf. B.J. Capper, "The Palestinian Cultural Context of Earliest Christian Community of Goods," in *The Book of Acts in its Palestinian Setting* (ed. R. Bauckham; vol. 4 of *The Book of Acts in its First Century Setting*; Grand Rapids: Eerdmans, 1995), 323–56.

the warning passage of Hebrews as an instance of the gravity of sin for those who voluntarily embrace the covenant.

Third, the *interiority* of the new covenant finds its solid basis in the early experience of endowment and indwelling of God's Spirit (Acts 2:1-41, esp. vv. 3, 4, 33, 38b), a theme carried out quite remarkably in Paul's theology of the indwelling Christ and Spirit (cf. Gal 5:13-26; 2 Cor 3:18). Paul's theology was heavily anchored in the new-age significance of the gift of the Spirit.[110] More importantly, one of the themes of the Peter speech is the democratization of the spirit of prophecy, and this democratization can be quite naturally connected to the knowledge of Jeremiah 31:33-34, a knowledge embedded in the heart. If critical scholarship finds the speech of Peter as less than a historical report, what is expressed in this Lukan speech would be precisely the point: democratization of the knowledge of God. The polemical impact of such a view being taken by messianic Israel is also embedded in the early chapters of Acts: strife with the priests, temple authorities, and the temple itself (cf. Acts 3:1–4:22; 5:17-42; 6:8–8:1, etc.).

Fourth, the expectation of Jeremiah that God's Torah would be kept by all, from the youngest to the oldest, and that teaching one another would not be needed, finds its fulfillment in the appeal to Joel 2:28-32 in Acts 2:17-21 and in Paul's theology of the democracy of charismatic gifts (1 Cor 12–14). In fact, the idealized account of the church in the early chapters of Acts evokes the expectation of Jeremiah that the law would be written in the heart and would be obeyed by all: even further, that Israel would become a people that loved its God completely. It was this Pentecostal experience that set the standard for pneumatic life (cf. Acts 11:15, 17). It is likely that this pneumatic, democratic experience was in part responsible for the community of goods in the early Jerusalem church and its developing ethic of reciprocity.[111] In other words, the democratic interiorization vision of Jeremiah took on realistic and concrete hues in the Jerusalem-based churches.

Fifth, the emphasis on "forgiveness" in early messianic theology (Acts 2:38; 5:31; 10:43; 13:38) could easily have led to the new covenant theology of the early Jerusalem community, even if forgiveness is understood in more than individualistic terms in the prophetic expectations. One might just as easily suggest that the early preaching of Peter on forgiveness is more than individualism—in fact, that Peter sees in this new body of pneumatic eschatological followers of Jesus the core of the restored people of Israel so longed for by Jeremiah and Ezekiel.

Sixth, what occurs at Pentecost is later considered to be the fulfillment of the promises—probably those given to Abraham, Moses in the Deuteronomic

---

[110] For an important clarification by Dunn, cf. his "Baptism in the Spirit," in his *Phenomenology*, 242.

[111] See Capper, "Palestinian Cultural Context," in *Book of Acts* (ed. Bauckham), 19:324–156; "Reciprocity and the Ethic of Acts," in *Witness to the Gospel* (ed. I.H. Marshall and D. Peterson; Grand Rapids: Eerdmans, 1998), 499–518.

tradition (cf. Deut 30:6), David, and through the prophets (Acts 1:4; 2:33, 38-39; Gal 3:6-14). The eschatological significance of Pentecost suggests it is the fulfillment of Israel's expectations. And, if Paul's theology clearly moves in the direction of replacing the Torah with the Spirit (Gal 3:6-14; 5:1-26), he is at least suggesting Pentecost as the date when the salvation-historical clock struck daybreak, since it was at Pentecost that Jews remembered the giving of the Torah (cf. Exod 19:1; 2 Chron 15:8-15; *Jub.* 1:1; 6:17-31; 14:20; 22:1-16; 1QS I, 8-II, 25; *b. Pesaḥ* 68b).[112]

Seventh, Ezekiel declared that the final covenant would bring peace. If this theme is not characteristic of Jeremiah's expectations (where it functions as the empty promises of the false prophet), neither is it the focus of the early messianic experience (but cf. Acts 10:36) or of its imminent transnational movement![113]

Finally, the restoration of the twelve tribes surely looked forward to a larger Israel; perhaps an Israel that would transcend its national limitations. If so, then the preaching of the gospel to all at Pentecost evokes the universal expectations of ancient Israel.[114] Fundamentally, under all these experiences that led to a new covenant hermeneutic is the belief that God's Spirit had empowered and indwelt the little community of Jesus' followers in Jerusalem (Acts 2) and elsewhere.[115]

CONCLUSION

A sketch of a solution to the origin of the new covenant hermeneutic has been provided, and the evidence suggests that it was the Pentecostal experience of the early Jerusalem followers of Jesus that provided the foundations for a complete reflection on the significance of that pneumatic experience. For it is here that one finds a constellation of factors that correlates substantially with Jeremiah's prediction of a new covenant. Sometime *after* Pentecost (note that Joel's text becomes the focus there) and probably by someone other than Peter, an early Christian came to the conviction that the pneumatic experience of Pentecost was in fact what was expected by Jeremiah and Ezekiel. Therefore, it was inferred, messianic Israel has entered into the new covenant. Whoever it was, that person bequeathed to early Christians a category of wide-ranging implications, for it quickly became attached to the last supper tradition and found its way into the Pauline circle as well as the hermeneutic of the author of Hebrews. One might say that kingdom expectation as expressed at table, when considered in light of the cross and Pentecost, became covenant theology.[116]

---

[112] Dunn, *Jesus and the Spirit*, 140–41.

[113] Dunn, *Baptism in the Holy Spirit*, 48–49.

[114] See D.A. Fiensy, "The Composition of the Jerusalem Church," in *Book of Acts* (ed. Bauckham), 213–36, for a nice study of the social nature of the Jerusalem church.

[115] Dunn, "Spirit and Holy Spirit in the New Testament," in his *Phenomenology*, 3–21.

[116] See the similar observation of H.-J. Klauck, *Herrenmahl und hellenistischer Kult* (NTAbh.NF 15; Münster: Aschendorff, 1982), 314.

A final observation is, however, in order, an observation that expresses the sort of history that is characteristic of the gospel traditions. If it might be argued that covenant is part of an anachronistic early messianic reflection on Jesus' last supper, there is ample reason for the early messianic Israelites to have anchored their new covenant hermeneutic in Jesus himself. Those very lines of connection begin to make their way back to Jeremiah during the life of the historical Jesus. It was during his time that Jesus was perceived, at a basic level, as a "pneumatic," and for whom the power of the eschatological and history-bending Spirit was pressed into action (Luke 7:18-23; 11:20).[117] Further, the Twelve were called and commissioned as the nucleus of the restored Israel (Matt 19:28), the sharp tones of a commitment that brooked no rival were heard (Luke 9:57-62), the importance of an interiority in ethics was sounded (Mark 7:1-20; Matt 12:33-37), the power and authority of miracles were clearly evident (Mark 6:5, 14; 11:28), an imaginative inclusion of all sorts at table with Jesus was embodied (Mark 2:18-22; Matt 11:19), and the offers of forgiveness and peace were found (Mark 2:1-12; Luke 10:5-6).[118] When Jesus sat at table over that last supper and spoke of his blood as a *Pesah*-like event, it would only be a few furious months before his followers would see in that blood, as a result of their pneumatic life, the very reconstitution of God's new covenant with Israel. That which is anachronistic is often the historic because it is hermeneutical.[119]

Having now examined covenant, it remains for us to examine several other courses of the last supper to see if they might shed light on how Jesus understood his imminent, premature death.

---

[117] On which see still two predominantly exegetically oriented studies of C.K. Barrett, *The Holy Spirit and the Gospel Tradition* (London: SPCK, 1966), and Hawthorne, *Presence and the Power*, for a more historical approach, cf. Dunn, *Jesus and the Spirit*, 11–92; see also M. Borg, *Jesus* (San Francisco: Harper & Row, 1987), 23–75.

[118] On which, cf. S. McKnight, *A New Vision for Israel* (Grand Rapids: Eerdmans, 1999).

[119] Dunn, "Pentecost," in his *Phenomenology*, 213: "The already established link between Pentecost, covenant renewal, and the giving of the Law probably prompted the first believers to interpret their experience of the Spirit as the fulfillment of the promise of a new covenant, as the Law writen in their hearts (Deut. 30:6; Jer. 31:31-34; Ezek. 3:26-27; 37:14; cf. Acts 2:38-39; 3:25; 1 Cor. 11:25; Heb. 10:5-16, 29). But the implications of this insight for continuing faith and conduct were not recognized and elaborated until Paul (Rom. 2:28-29; 7:6; 2 Corinthians 3; Gal. 3:1–4:7; Phil. 3:3; Col. 2:11; 1 Thess. 4:8)."

Chapter 16

"Poured Out" and Eschatology

We have now nearly come to the end of the meal, but there remain two other traditions in the Jesus material of the last supper that potentially shed light on how Jesus understood his death. We have argued that the last supper was not, technically speaking, the *Pesah*. It was a meal during the week of *Pesah*, a meal eaten in Jerusalem the night before the official *Pesah*. We have argued that Jesus converted that meal from a normal *Pesah* week meal into a *symbolic* meal, and his symbolism ran deep into the *Pesah* tradition. In essence, he claimed his death could be shared by his disciples if they ate the bread and drank the wine. We have also argued that it is unlikely (though possible) that Jesus expressed his death in terms of the establishment of a "new covenant." He has stated that his death was a representative death; it was his death that would inaugurate the death of others. In that his blood (the wine) was symbolic of that death, it is highly likely that he thought his death benefited his disciples. His blood, as a replacement or reenactment of the *Pesah* blood of the original event, would protect his followers from the coming judgment of God against Jerusalem and its corrupt leadership. Is there any more we might know about how he understood his death?

"POURED OUT"

Still left on the table is the expression poured out (Mark 14:24; Matt 26:28; Luke 22:20 [LR]).[1] The expression has a solid parallel in other Jesus traditions (cf. Mark 10:45), though most judge it inauthentic. The expression is not in the Pauline tradition but it is clearly consistent with Paul's soteriology. As a result,

[1] Specifically, Mark has "poured out for many," Matthew has "poured out for the forgiveness of sins," and Luke has "poured out for you."

we should consider "poured out for many" to be *possibly from Jesus*. To omit "poured out for many" from the discussion is to pretend to know too much and to know that too precisely. However, to use it is to pretend the same. There is nothing in the last supper that suggests that a cultic metaphor like this would have been used by Jesus, and there is nothing in our discussion so far of Jesus' understanding of his death that would suggest he thought like this.

A careful comparison of the Synoptics reveals only one term consistent in the traditions: *poured out*. The *for many* could be attributed to Mark (cf. 10:45), while Matthew and Luke each clarify the *benefit* of the pouring out: Matthew sees "forgiveness of sins" (26:28) while Luke sees a benefit "for you" (22:20 [LR]). That the Pauline tradition does not have any of this suggests that early Christian extrapolation has occurred.

The last supper is to be seen in the context of *Pesah* week. It is not *Pesah*, even though it is a *Pesah* week meal that approximates *Pesah* in meaning and intent. As an anticipatory *Pesah* meal, Jesus sees his death as a reenactment of the smearing of blood on the doors of the homes of Israelites so that God would deliver his people from oppressors. Such a national explanation for Jesus' understanding of his own death conforms to the general tenor of his vision and mission.[2] Jesus sees his death as a reenactment of *Pesah*, without lamb, and offers himself to his followers in order to partake in the deliverance God is about to perform for Israel as part of the arrival of the kingdom of God. Those who eat his body (the bread is a substitute for lamb) and drink his blood (to imbibe his life and partake in the benefits of his life and death) are analogous to those who ate unleavened bread, drank wine, and smeared blood on the doorpost and lintel: his followers, like the Israelites of old, will be "passed over" in God's imminent judgment. Jesus sees in his death the act whereby God will liberate Israel and, for those who partake of his offering of himself, offers a *Pesah*-like token of blood sufficient for the imminent judgment. John's supposedly late step to see Jesus as "lamb of God" (1:29) has, I think, a firm historical anchor. His death would benefit his followers: they would be protected from God's wrath and set free.[3]

In light of the lack of certainty pertaining to *poured out for many*, we are led back to our previous conclusion: Jesus would have seen his death as the lamb's blood smeared to cover his followers. However, it remains a possibility that he also regarded his death as poured out for many. Why? Because if he thought his death was a benefit for others—either as a representative leader of those who are

---

[2] See S. McKnight, *A New Vision for Israel* (Grand Rapids: Eerdmans, 1999), passim; N.T. Wright, *Jesus and the Victory of God* (vol. 2 of *Christian Origins and the Question of God*; Minneapolis: Fortress, 1996).

[3] Cf. *Jub.* 49:15 where a similar protective (apotropaic) sense is presented. H. Kosmala, *Hebräer–Essener–Christen* (StPB; Leiden: E.J. Brill, 1959), 174–91, offers a similar suggestion, and he ties it into the "cup of wrath" of the prophets and Psalm 79:6. Kosmala's piece, full though it is with suggestion, is far too preoccupied with Psalm 79:6 specifically and too concerned with the Gentiles to be finally convincing. See also, D. Wenham, "How Jesus Understood the Last Supper," *Them* 20 (1995): 11–16.

to die, or as a vicarious substitute, or none of these—if he thought his death was beneficial, then he thought it was beneficial *for someone*. And that someone could have been expressed in language like *for many*. While *the many* (cf. Isa 53:11) is not quite the same as *all*, the term itself in Hebrew (*rabbim*) would have meant "the whole community" (Israel or Jesus' followers as a new Israel) rather than "some."[4] It is more likely that Jesus spoke *for the many* than *for the world*, which is not used, and was clearly the more prevalent term in later developments (but cf. Rom 5:12).[5] Jesus, then, said that in imbibing his blood the disciples would benefit from his death, a death poured out for his people. It is possible that he said something like *for the many*.

LAST SUPPER AND TEMPLE

If Jesus sees his own death as a *Pesah* offering and securing a *Pesah* protection, we are led immediately to wonder whether his followers continued to participate in the temple sacrifices. What about the temple? Is Jesus here replacing the temple as offering corrupt sacrifices? That there is an important mission connection between Jesus' entry into Jerusalem and staged action in the temple and the last supper ought probably to be maintained, as several of late have emphasized.[6]

---

[4] J. Jeremias, *The Eucharistic Words of Jesus* (trans. N. Perrin; 1966; repr. Philadelphia: Fortress, 1977), 179–82; P. Stuhlmacher, *Grundlegung von Jesus zu Paulus* (vol. 1 of *Biblische Theologie des Neuen Testaments*; 2d ed.; Göttingen: Vandenhoeck & Ruprecht, 1997), 139–40; but more precisely because it sees the ecclesially restricted sense, Pesch, *Markusevangelium*, 2:360.

[5] A confirmation of this particularism may be found in *Tg. Isa.* 25 where the universalism of Isaiah is rendered in such a way that it is Israel who is saved, and the Gentiles as judged. Cf. esp. *Tg. Isa.* 25:6: "On this mountain the LORD of hosts will make for all peoples a feast and a festival; they think that it is of glory, but it will be to them for shame, strokes from which they will not be rescued, strokes by which they will come to an end." Cf. also 25:7, 10, 12.

[6] See esp. J. Ådna, *Jesu Stellung zum Tempel* (WUNT 2/119; Tübingen: Mohr Siebeck, 2000), whose conclusions are not entirely consistent with early Jewish Christian practice; G. Theissen and A. Merz, *The Historical Jesus* (trans. J. Bowden; Minneapolis: Fortress, 1998), 433–36. This view has been especially presented in the many writings of B.D. Chilton. See esp. *The Temple of Jesus* (University Park: Pennsylvania State University, 1992); *A Feast of Meanings* (NovTSup 72; Leiden: E.J. Brill, 1994); but see most recently his *Rabbi Jesus* (New York: Doubleday, 2000), 248–57, where he states Jesus' meal practice was not a personal cult nor was it autobiographical, but instead a vision of how sacrifice ought to be offered, in its purest form (Zech 9), in the real temple. Chilton's view ultimately signifies no one understood the last supper, or at least Jesus' meals and, even more, everyone misunderstood these occasions as they came to terms with his death. Further, he posits a creator of the entire last supper/Lord's Supper liturgy in Peter in whose letters (or those attributed to him) we find no clear trace of the last supper/Lord's supper words. As Chilton's theory unfolds, he has names, such as F.C. Baur, assigned to various factions with various adjustments and compromises in the evolution of Christian liturgy. Thus, changes occurred under the hands of Peter (covenant, Mosaic Christology), James (exclusive), Paul (inclusive), Barnabas as reflected in the Synoptic tradition (separate with integrity), and John (who replaces *Pesah* with Jesus as the Lamb of God).

But does such a connection imply the replacement of sacrifices? Is Jesus then anti-sacrificial and anti-temple?[7]

One of the most important arguments in this debate concerns a sacrificial interpretation of Jesus' words of institution. If those words are about *Pesah* victims, rather than covenant ceremony and new covenant, then his last meal can legitimately be construed as a statement about the temple at some level. In effect, Jesus would say that his body and his blood are either substitutes for the body and blood of the lamb slaughtered inside the temple or an extension of temple elements to the table. His body and blood will become the food of his followers, rather than or as an extension of the *Pesah* food. In this construal, a traditional temple is neutralized at some level.

So understood, however, Jesus' criticism concerns the efficacy of the victims being slain. What the priests do is incomplete. It is important to understand that only at a secondary and tertiary level is he against the priests and the temple edifice; only at this level is he against the entire operation of covenant formation through the temple and its sacrifices.

Let me express this in a slightly more nuanced form. I am not persuaded that Jesus is saying, "Do not participate in the temple ever again." This the disciples clearly did not follow, for we see them around the temple for decades. Instead, he is saying this: "What you see there is what you get when you drink my blood and eat my body." In other words, by saying *my* in front of *bread* and *blood*, Jesus is putting a boundary around his followers as special and making a comment on the temple procedures. In this sense, he cordons off his followers from the rest of the temple participants and, in effect, provides a foundation for what will later be a more complete abandonment of temple piety.

When, however, we take into consideration the prediction of the temple's destruction and his anti-establishment words (Mark 11–13), we can safely argue that Jesus' last supper is a fundamental reorientation of the temple order. The scholars, wide-ranging as they are,[8] who connect these three dots (entry, temple incident, and last supper) have offered a potent hypothesis that helps explain how Jesus understood his death. The temple, standing for the nation, is about to be destroyed; God has appointed Jesus' death as the means of escape; those who eat his body and drink his blood will be passed over.

The coming judgment is also a theme in *Targum Isaiah* 28, a chapter probably reflecting at least a Tannaitic period of thinking if not earlier.[9] Several resonances of this rendering of Isaiah 28 confirm Jesus' stance against the temple authorities (cf. also *Tg. Isa.* on Isa 5 at Mark 12:1-12). A corrupt leadership, here the "proud, the foolish master of Israel" as well as the "wicked one of the sanc-

---

[7] J. Klawans, "Interpreting the Last Supper," *NTS* 48 (2002): 1–17.

[8] E.g, Theissen and Merz, *Historical Jesus*, 433–36; Chilton, *Temple of Jesus*; Wright, *Jesus and the Victory of God*, 406–28, 490–93.

[9] See B.D. Chilton, *The Isaiah Targum* (ArBib 11; Collegeville, Minn.: Liturgical, 1987), xxiv. Translations are from Chilton; italics indicate variation from the Hebrew text.

tuary," will meet defeat at the hands of the Gentiles who will force them into exile (28:2). But suddenly, in the targumic rendering, the Messiah (*mashycha*) appears in his kingdom (cf. 24:23; 28:16 [now King]) as a replacement of YHWH; this Messiah is the true crown (a reversal of 28:1), and he will accomplish judgment and forge peace (28:5-6).

As for a critique of the temple, *Targum Isaiah* 28:1 says: "Woe to . . . him who gives the crown to the proud, the foolish master of Israel, and gives the turban to the wicked one of the sanctuary of his praise" (cf. also at 28:3, 4). The people have not followed the Torah (28:9), but it is the leadership that concerns the targumist: "My sanctuary was as little in their eyes, to serve there; my Shekinah was as little in their eyes there" (28:10; cf. 28:21). To these the prophets uttered warnings, saying "This is the sanctuary, serve in it; and this is the heritage of the house of rest" (28:12). Because of these temple pollutions, "they will be handed over to the Gentiles. . . . And because my sanctuary was little in their eyes, to serve there, therefore they will be left as little among the Gentiles where they will be exiled; that they may go, and stumble backward, and be broken, and caught and taken" (28:13; cf. 28:17). The question of inevitability arises in the Hebrew text of 28:24-26; the targumist considers the repentance of God if the people turn to the Law (28:25—an interpretation of "when they have leveled its surface"). Would not God then gather them from exile (seen in "scatter dill" in MT of 28:25)? Yes, indeed he would, and they would be lined up in the land. The changes are dramatic to the Hebrew text; the theology shaping them is Deuteronomic. For our purposes, these changes are consistent with Jesus' warnings to the Jewish leaders regarding temple pollutions, and it is to this book (Isaiah), and sometimes with its interpretations, that Jesus frequently turns.[10]

But, before moving to other words from the last supper, an important nuance needs to be placed on the table: this view of the temple's destruction, when combined with the last supper as interpreted above, did not exclusively lead to anti-temple Christian Judaism. Stephen's example is the exception. In fact, there is strong evidence that many early Christian Jews lingered around the temple and made Jerusalem central to their perception of God's work in Jesus (e.g., Acts 2:42-47; 15; Gal 1–2; Jas). Paul used language of the temple and of sacrifice metaphorically to describe various dimensions of the Christian faith, but in so doing, he was not suggesting that the temple had been obliterated by Jesus' Eucharist. In fact, when early Christians did criticize the temple (e.g., Acts 7; Heb), the notion of the last supper as eucharistic meal did not reveal itself as part of that polemic.[11] That the last supper had implications for temple ritual is

---

[10] See McKnight, *New Vision for Israel*, 139–49. I find myself in disagreement with those scholars who find a significant departure from John over the issue of judgment and threat (cf. Luke 3:7-10; Luke 4:16-30; Q 7:22-23). Cf. J. Jeremias, *Jesus' Promise to the Nations* (trans. S.H. Hooke; SBT 24; London: SCM, 1967), 44–45. For Jesus' use of Isaiah and his understanding of Isaiah that at times parallels the targumist, cf. B.D. Chilton, *A Galilean Rabbi and His Bible* (GNS 8; Wilmington: Michael Glazier, 1984).

[11] This important argument has been offered by Klawans, "Interpreting the Last Supper," 9–15.

within a typical mapping of Israel; that it replaces the temple system draws lines right off the map.

A final comment about the cup (and the bread): C.H. Dodd is one of the few scholars who suggest that ingestion of bread and imbibing of wine are not only soteriological actions (the acceptance of Jesus' death as salvation from judgment) but also *moral acts of commitment*.[12] If the bread and wine embody the death of Jesus, his life given for his followers, then the consumption of that bread and wine entails a similar commitment to give one's life for Jesus and his followers. There is substance to this observation by Dodd. It is solid memory that Jesus saw his fate in the terms of the prophets and John, his predecessor (cf. Q 6:23; 11:49-51), and that he warned his followers of a similar fate (Q 6:40; cf. Matt 10:24-25). It follows, rather briskly, that if he made these connections earlier, then his disciples would have seen their fate in the consumption of bread and wine. If John and Jesus died at the hands of oppressors, so might they (cf. Mark 8:34–9:1 pars.). More importantly, however overwritten John 13 might be, there is here a solid memory of Jesus acting *déclassé* in serving his followers, an indication that even the elements of the meal could carry similar moral freight. If the slave's role is usurped by Jesus in washing feet, so also the same might be said of his serving the food and wine. The connection between Jesus' fate and the disciples' fate is the hinge upon which Mark's Christology and discipleship turn together. In fact, for Mark the cross has become the *mandala* of moral existence. Mark's theology is firmly connected, prior to the cross, to the table of the last supper.

THE MEAL AND ESCHATOLOGY: MARK 14:25 PAR. LUKE 22:16, 18

A final logion of the last supper that sheds some light on how Jesus envisioned his own death is the so-called "vow of abstinence," a logion that some have anchored into the oldest of Jesus' sayings. The logion is a reexpression of the hope for the final banquet (e.g, Isa 25:1-10a).[13] The *absence* of this logion specifically, as well as its *transformation* in the Pauline tradition (1 Cor 11:26: "until he comes") is an index to its authenticity. The arrival of the kingdom mutates here into the return of Christ.

---

[12] C.H. Dodd, *Founder of Christianity* (London: Collins, 1971), 108–9.

[13] See esp. J.P. Meier, *A Marginal Jew* (ABRL; 3 vols; New York: Doubleday, 1991–2001), 2:302–9, for whom the logion evinces major dissimilarity with early Christian traditions (Christology, soteriology, and eschatology). Also, cf. G. Bornkamm, *Jesus of Nazareth* (trans. I. and F. McLuskey and J.M. Robinson; New York: Harper & Row, 1960), 160–62 (with no revisions in the 12th German edition). I do not find the transition from Mark 14:24 to 14:25 as abrupt as some do. If Jesus said, "this is my blood" and passed around a cup expecting his followers to drink of it, then a statement that he would not drink wine (again) until the kingdom is not insuperable. Contra X. Léon-Dufour, *Sharing the Eucharistic Bread* (trans. M.J. O'Connell; New York: Paulist, 1986), 85–87.

> Truly I tell you, I will never again drink of the fruit of the vine[14] until that day when I drink it new in the kingdom of God. (Mark 14:25)

This text yields two questions: first, did Jesus affirm such a vow twice that evening or once? Second, what was its meaning? Luke records two vows, at 22:16 and 22:18:

> Luke: For I tell you, I will not eat it until it is fulfilled in the kingdom of God.[15]

and

> for I tell you that from now on I will not drink of the fruit of the vine until the kingdom of God comes.

The absence of a parallel to Luke 22:16 in the Markan tradition, as well as the growing liturgical tendency to make parallels tight and obvious, not to say increase them, leads to the probable conclusion that Luke 22:16 is *Gemeindetheologie*.[16] It makes explicit what is otherwise implicit in the disruption of fellowship with Jesus: if he will not drink wine with them until the kingdom, neither will he eat bread with them. Historically, however, it makes sense: if Jesus is about to die, then he will not fellowship with his followers until the kingdom arrives. And that means he will neither drink wine nor eat bread with them.

Materially, of course, the Markan and Lukan logia on the wine are nearly identical, though the following slight alterations can be seen:

> Mark: *Truly* I tell you, I will never *again* drink of the fruit of the vine *until that day when I drink it new* in the kingdom of God.

---

[14] The term *vine* finds a later echo in *Didache* 9:1-2, where it is interpreted eschatologically and messianically (cf. Isa 25:6-8; Hos 14:7; Joel 2:22; Zech 3:10; 8:12; 9:17; Mal 3:11). Precedent for this can be seen in the exegesis of Genesis 49:9-12 at 1QSb V, 27. Some have traced an echo of the original last supper in *Didache*; therefore, it is also suggested, the last supper was non-soteriological but instead an eschatological sacrament. See A. Schweitzer, *The Lord's Supper in Relationship to the Life of Jesus and the History of the Early Church* (vol. 1 of *The Problem of the Lord's Supper according to the Scholarly Research of the Nineteenth Century and the Historical Accounts*; ed. J. Reumann; trans. A.J. Mattill, Jr.; Macon, Ga: Mercer University Press, 1982).

[15] Later, as found in the *Gos. Eb.* 30:22, some made of Jesus' denial of bread to himself a theological foundation for vegetarianism, but that author overcomes such views by historical exegesis.

[16] *Contra* those scholars who have followed H. Schürmann, *Der Einsetzungsbericht Lk. 22, 19-20* (NtAbh 20/4; Münster: Aschendorff, 1955), 133–50, who argues for a double eschatological saying by Jesus in a *Pesah* context. The specificity of cups requires more knowledge than we have about the *Pesah* liturgy of the first century. For the view taken here, see also Meier, *Marginal Jew*, 2:304. R. Otto, *The Kingdom of God and the Son of Man* (trans. F.V. Filson and B.L. Woolf; Lutterworth Library 9; London: Lutterworth, 1938), 277–78, argued that Jesus would not have said such things twice in such quick succession and that Jesus would be saying that there will be a future *Pesah*. What he fails to note is that such an expectation would be dissimilar enough to Christian eschatology to count in its favor.

Luke: For I tell you that from now on I will not drink of the fruit of the vine until the kingdom of God *comes.*

Mark: ἀμὴν λέγω ὑμῖν ὅτι οὐκέτι οὐ μὴ πίω ἐκ τοῦ γενήματος.

Luke: λέγω γὰρ ὑμῖν, [ὅτι] οὐ μὴ πίω ἀπὸ τοῦ νῦν ἀπὸ τοῦ γενήματος

Mark: τῆς ἀμπέλου ἕως τῆς ἡμέρας ἐκείνης ὅταν αὐτὸ πίνω καινὸν ἐν τῇ βασιλείᾳ τοῦ θεοῦ

Luke: τῆς ἀμπέλου ἕως οὗ ἡ βασιλεία τοῦ θεοῦ ἔλθῃ.

The original order, whether that of Mark (after the cup) or Luke (before the cup), can no longer be determined, nor does it matter for interpretation. He could have said it before dispensing the cup, while it was being consumed, or afterwards. The original wording favors the Markan words (if only slightly), but once again the substance is not changed. Jesus states that he will not drink the cup until the kingdom comes, at which time he will resume drinking the cup, presumably in fellowship with his followers.[17] That Jesus expected a resumption of fellowship is confirmed by Q 22:28-30 (cf. Matt 19:28), where Jesus speaks about kingdom table fellowship and vindication of himself and the Twelve. Luke connects this statement to the last supper tradition. Not all are convinced the connection is secondary. But is Jesus' word a statement of (1) the disruption of fellowship until the kingdom and a promise of resumption of that fellowship in the kingdom?[18] (2) a simple statement that he will die? or (3) a vow[19] of abstinence due to the urgency of the hour and the seriousness of the task?[20]

The logion about the wine and cup has two essential formal features: eschatology and a vow of the inviolability of the words so uttered. Similar patterns of

---

[17] Matthean redaction makes this explicit (Matt 26:29: "with you").

[18] See Meier, *Marginal Jew*, 2:306–7, with variation. John Koenig says the prospect here is "almost defiant" (*The Feast of the World's Redemption* [Harrisburg: Trinity Press International, 2000]), 24. If Q 22:28-30, esp. 22:30, is to be anchored in the last supper tradition, then resumption becomes even more prominent. But, Luke 22:24-30 appears to be a Lukan collection of disparate traditions, none of which emerge from the last supper. Instead, they elucidate the strife of 22:23. On the themes of the Lukan motives, cf. Green, *Luke*, 766–67.

[19] J. Jeremias, most famous for this view, however, argued in the later editions of his book that "vow" was incorrect; instead, it was an "avowal" since Jesus used *amen* (cf. *Eucharistic Words of Jesus*, 207, n. 6). J.P. Meier labeled such back-pedaling a "distinction without a difference" (*Marginal Jew*, 2:306.).

[20] It is unclear whether Jesus drank the cup with them and then began a period of not drinking, or refused to drink even that evening; cf. Davies and Allison, *Matthew*, 3:475. James, brother of Jesus, is said to have taken a vow himself that evening, to the effect that he would not eat bread until he saw his brother raised from those who sleep. When Jesus appeared to James, he also had a table prepared with bread and said, "my brother eat thy bread" (Jerome, *Vir. ill.* 2; NPNF² 2.3, 362).

thought can be found in Mark 9:1 and 13:30 as well as at Matthew 10:23 (with parallels). Fundamentally, Jesus states that a condition will *necessarily* occur when a certain time arrives. Thus, the disciples will live until they see the kingdom arrive in power (Mark 9:1); this generation will not die out before the predictions of Jesus are realized in history (Mark 13:30); and the missionaries will not finish fleeing through the cities of Israel before the Son of man comes (Matt 10:23).[21] To these can be added the logion about wine: Jesus will not drink wine until the kingdom arrives. The eschatological synthesis looks like this: the kingdom is imminent; his followers will live until it arrives; they will see his predictions about Jerusalem's destruction fulfilled; they will be persecuted, but the end is not imminent enough that they will run out of places to go; and, now, they will not find Jesus at their table until that time. But, when that time does come to pass, all these things will certainly happen. These various logia are of one cloth.

Thus, Jesus connects the last supper with the eschatological banquet (cf. Ps 107:1-9; Isa 25:1-10a; 49:10-13; Joel 2:24; 3:18; Amos 9:13; *1 En.* 10:19; 62:14; *2 Bar.* 29:5; 1QSa).[22] But what is the central sense of the logion? The logion clearly states that Jesus will disrupt fellowship for some reason, and it is certain that he predicts his own imminent death.[23] Further, inasmuch as it predicts at the same time resumption of fellowship, the saying also implies vindication (through resurrection?) for both Jesus and his followers.[24] This is confirmed by Q 22:30: "you will sit on thrones judging the twelve tribes of Israel." This text has as much claim to the last supper as any other place.[25] In other words, Jesus' death will not disturb the victory of God nor will it impede the establishment of the kingdom of God. Can more be said? Is this not an overcooked statement if it is nothing more than a prediction of death?

Because scholarship has been preoccupied with whether or not Jesus drank wine with his companions at the last supper, the positive resonances have been missed. Jesus here predicts not just that he will die and that he will resume

---

[21] On Matthew 10:23, see my "Jesus and the End-Time: Matthew 10:23," *SBL Seminar Papers* (1986): 501–20.

[22] On which, see McKnight, *New Vision for Israel,* 149–54.

[23] Pesch, *Markus,* 2:360–61; Davies and Allison, *Matthew,* 3:477. An interesting suggestion was offered by C.H. Dodd about Christology as shaped by Psalm 80 (*According to the Scriptures* [London: Nisbet, 1952], 101–2). In application to the last supper, Psalm 80 shows several connections: first, not noticed by Dodd, is "bread of tears" (cf. Ps 42:3) which corresponds notionally with Deuteronomy 16:3 and the bread of suffering of the last supper; second, "vine" is prominent and this vine escapes Egypt and suffers (Ps 80:8, 14-16); third, son of man is connected with rule (80:17 and 80:1-2). We have here then an interesting collocation of significant themes: Exodus, son of man, and a vine suffering. Jesus offers to his followers his blood, "the fruit of the vine" (Mark 14:25).

[24] Meier, *Marginal Jew,* 2:308–9, however, argues that vindication is not so much in mind as the continuation of the kingdom—in spite of Jesus' death. But, we must ask, how did Jesus envision that vindication taking place? Surely we must think of resurrection (cf. Mark 12:18-27 pars.) and sitting at table with others. See further McKnight, *New Vision for Israel,* 149–54.

[25] Note the term trials (Luke 22:28; cf. Mark 14:38).

fellowship; no, in fact, this saying speaks of the abundance of the final banquet. John Koenig suggests Mark 14:25 is related to Joseph's words to Judah in Genesis 49:8-12, in which a Davidic king may be seen.[26]

> [8]Judah, your brothers shall praise you; your hand shall be on the neck of your enemies; your father's sons shall bow down before you. [9]Judah is a lion's whelp; from the prey, my son, you have gone up. He crouches down, he stretches out like a lion, like a lioness—who dares rouse him up? [10]The scepter shall not depart from Judah, nor the ruler's staff from between his feet, until tribute comes to him; and the obedience of the peoples is his. [11]Binding his foal to the vine and his donkey's colt to the choice vine, he washes his garments in wine and his robe in the blood of grapes; [12]his eyes are darker than wine, and his teeth whiter than milk.

It is possible to draw a straight line from Genesis to Jesus' words about judging the twelve tribes (Q 22:28-30) in your father's sons shall bow down before you and the scepter and staff (Gen 49:8, 10). This royal figure commands allegiance: "his act of washing his garments in it [the wine] probably envisions a triumphant revelry that would include imbibing."[27] The joy of victory on that day, graphically depicted in wine and the blood of grapes, inebriates the king. If this passage is behind Jesus' words in Mark 14:25, the resumption of fellowship beyond death is a time of abundance, of both joy and victory.

This joy must not be overinterpreted, because the saying fundamentally announces the grim reality of Jesus' imminent death. Did this grim reality reach back into the meal so extensively that Jesus refused to eat and drink? The influential study of Joachim Jeremias concluded that Jesus here makes an avowal of abstinence—he wanted to eat the *Pesah* meal with them (Luke 22:15), but his death loomed so large he chose not to eat (22:16) or drink the wine (22:18). Thus, he fasted throughout the meal. This fasting of Jesus, in fact, finds confirmation in certain sects of earliest Christianity who fasted on *Pesah*.[28] I quote the passages from Jeremias:

> Epiphanius of Salamis (d. 403) quotes from the *Diataxeis of the Apostles* (to be dated shortly after AD 200): 'The same apostles say, "While they (the Jews) are feasting (in the passover night) you are to fast, mourning for them."' [Epiphanius, *Panarion* 70.11.3] The *Apostolic Constitutions* give the following regulations for the passover fast: 'fasting . . . all of you with fear and trembling, *praying for those that are perishing*'. [*Apostolic Constitutions* 5.13.3f] 'He (the risen Lord) therefore charged us himself to fast these six days (of the passover week) *on account of the impiety and transgression of the Jews. . . .*'[29]

---

[26] Koenig, *Feast of the World's Redemption,* 25–30.

[27] Ibid., 27.

[28] Jeremias, *Eucharistic Words of Jesus,* 207–18.

[29] Ibid., 216–17, as printed.

A connection from this early Christian practice of fasting to Jesus' practice can be drawn, but a weakness is evident: the foundation for the practice of fasting during *Pesah* week is, according to the text cited by Jeremias, the Lord's command. At no point do these texts suggest they are following the practice of Jesus during the last supper. Furthermore, the motive of the fasting is one of *evangelism* as a result of prayer. This evidence, supporting something besides the practice of following Jesus, totters under the weight of the conclusion and eventually collapses. A lurking issue in this discussion, one we previously concluded against Jeremias, is whether or not the last supper is *Pesah*. It is not. Thus, the appeal even to *Pesah* meal texts misleads the discussion.[30]

A further argument, also given by Jeremias[31] and even more substantial, is this: if Jesus thought the bread and the wine were his body and his blood—and a token of his death in a redemptive sense—then it is highly unlikely that he partook of his own body and his own blood. Would such a decision not to partake amount to an avowal of abstinence? The recent study of Bruce Chilton points a way forward.[32] After setting the logion in the general context of Jesus' meals (rather than as the last supper which Jesus knows is his last supper),[33] Chilton argues, on the basis of Semitic syntax,[34] that the logion affirms *resumption of fellowship* more than *denial of food in the meantime*. In fact, according to Chilton, "every act of fellowship in expectation of the divine rule was an assurance that the kingdom he prayed for would come."[35] Parts of Chilton's evidence and argument are compelling: Jesus, whether he ate bread and drank wine or not (and I doubt he did), affirmed that participation in the meal expressed the confidence that the kingdom would come and God would establish a final banquet. The focus of the saying is not on abstinence until the kingdom's arrival, but on the imminent certainty of that kingdom's arrival and the resumption of fellowship. Jesus, therefore, in the words of Mark 14:25 predicts his death and promises resumption of fellowship *in spite of* that death. Jesus has not changed his language from kingdom to sacrificial death; instead, he is certain of the kingdom's arrival in spite of his death. That death, so he says, can be shared by his followers when they ingest his body and imbibe his blood. They are, in other words, covered by his blood.

For a long time, scholars have claimed that Jews connected, in the *Pesah* meal's liturgy, the deliverance from Egypt with the eschatological deliverance.

---

[30] The same applies to the view of D. Daube that Jesus drank the third but not the fourth cup of the Passover *Haggadah*; the fourth cup, so he argues, would be messianic realization. See his *The New Testament and Rabbinic Judaism* (1956; repr. Peabody, Mass: Hendrickson, n.d.), 330–31.

[31] Jeremias, *Eucharistic Words of Jesus*, 212.

[32] B. Chilton, *Pure Kingdom* (Grand Rapids: Eerdmans, 1996), 85–90.

[33] Chilton's argument, however, may be probed a bit by asking if perhaps Jesus was not saying that he would not have table fellowship with his followers qua followers until the Kingdom's arrival.

[34] Chilton, *Pure Kingdom*, 88 (*lo'* – *'ad* construction).

[35] Ibid., 89.

Thus, *Pesah* was understood to be redemptive both retrospectively and prospectively.[36] The evidence for such cannot be anchored before the early rabbinic writings. The evidence is, therefore, inadmissible in our study (e.g., *Mek de R. Ishm.*, Pisha 14, on Exod 12:42[37]).[38] Whether Jews of Jesus' time made such a connection is unnecessary: Jesus did, and he may have done so in an innovative manner. We know that Jesus sees his own death as imminent and that he does not think his death will deter the kingdom's arrival. If Jesus thinks he will not celebrate *Pesah* again before the kingdom arrives, we have reason to think that Jesus thought the kingdom of God was imminent. In the last supper Jesus almost certainly gave rise to Paul's notion that the supper was to be memorialized "until Jesus comes" (1 Cor 11:26). Eschatology, understood as an irresistible arrival of the kingdom, was an integral dimension of Jesus' final supper.

"DO THIS IN REMEMBRANCE OF ME."

Did Jesus call his followers to remember him in this manner? Even if the wording as we now find it in the Pauline-Lukan tradition is clearly liturgical,[39] there is one reason to think Jesus may have urged his followers to remember him: the language is as foundational to *Pesah* as any words we have so far seen (Exod 12:14). And, even if the meal is not *Pesah*, the week itself gives rise to memory. The absence of the words in the Markan-Matthean tradition, however, is difficult to explain, especially with their tendency to attribute Passover meaning to the last supper. Their absence leads me to think the words are secondary as well. However historically accurate that explanation might be, the fact is that the earliest Christians did remember what Jesus did and what he said.[40] The insertion of such liturgical markers, then, has a firm historical basis: not only did his followers remember him, he did things easily remembered. If the words are not historical at least his actions that night led to such words. The tradition about Jesus' last supper had been told over and over, and it apparently gained in the retelling.

It remains for us now to put all the strands of this discussion back together and to suggest how the language of Jesus might have generated early Christian atonement theories.

---

[36] E.g., Léon-Dufour, *Sharing the Eucharistic Bread*, 53.

[37] This is the judgment of R. Joshua; R. Eliezer says it will occur in Tishri (on Rosh Hashanah).

[38] See also the later texts in Jeremias, *Eucharistic Words of Jesus*, 58–60, 205–7.

[39] Cf. Pesch, *Markusevangelium*, 2:375.

[40] On which see Léon-Dufour, *Sharing the Eucharistic Bread*, 102–16.

Chapter 17

Conclusions

It matters to some historians of the development of earliest Christianity and to the Christian faith both *if* Jesus thought about his own death and, even more importantly, *how* or *what* he thought of his death. Robert W. Funk, for instance, contends that Jesus is not "the proper object of faith," that moderns ought to "give Jesus a demotion," that moderns "need to cast Jesus in a new drama, assign him a role in a story with a different plot," and that moderns "will have to abandon the doctrine of the blood atonement."[1] J.D. Crossan's proposal that Jesus offered an unbrokered relationship with God and advocated a sort of social egalitarianism constructs a Jesus whose death had nothing to do with his mission and accomplishment.[2]

On the other hand, G.B. Caird suggests that the mission of Jesus was to save and to reconcile, in some measure through the very death he died.[3] And N.T. Wright presents a Jesus who entered the city in the last week as the return of YHWH to Zion and whose death accomplished salvation for all.[4] Hidden in this wide spectrum of views is Heinz Schürmann who, in a variety of writings, depicts Jesus as one whose very life is a *Proexistence* for the redemption of his people.[5] What matters is that for each of these scholars what Jesus himself thought and taught is truly significant. Some may dismiss such a significance, and contend that Christian faith is not based on the vicissitudes of historical conclusions, or contend that what really matters is the church's canon or tradition. But it boggles to think that Christians could anchor their hope of forgiveness in a Jesus who never thought of his death as atoning.

[1] See R.W. Funk, *Honest to Jesus* (San Francisco: HarperSanFrancisco [Polebridge], 1996), 304–12.

[2] J.D. Crossan, *The Historical Jesus* (San Francisco: HarperSanFrancisco, 1991).

[3] G.B. Caird, *New Testament Theology* (ed. L.D. Hurst; Oxford: Clarendon, 1994).

[4] N.T. Wright, *Jesus and the Victory of God* (vol. 2 of *Christian Origins and the Question of God*; Minneapolis: Fortress, 1996).

[5] P. Schürmann, *Jesus—Gestalt und Geheimnis* (ed. K. Scholtissek; Paderborn: Bonifatius, 1994).

Fortunately, scholarship of the twentieth century (and now with a lead into the twenty-first century) has addressed the question and has argued that Jesus thought about his death and thought about it as having saving benefits. In fact, there is an astonishing variety of perspectives on how Jesus thought of his death—from it being an accident to it being an atonement. Unfortunately, recent scholarship (apart from a scholar here and there) has failed to address this issue in its attempt to determine the mission of Jesus. Most scholars are persuaded now that Jesus' mission, his aim, was about the restoration of Israel (or something along these lines), but few have asked how Jesus thought of his death in that overall mission. It has been nearly fifty years since anyone dedicated an entire volume to analyzing how Jesus understood his death (Vincent Taylor, *Jesus and His Sacrifice*, 1955)—not that a plethora of books touching on the subject indirectly or in shorter compass have not followed Taylor's book. But it is time for the subject to reenter the conversation about the historical Jesus. This book makes an attempt to call our attention once more to the stubborn presence of numerous texts where Jesus anticipates his own death and, at times, he does so with suggestions of interpreting that death.

RECAPITULATION

FIVE CONCLUSIONS

To recapitulate our study, the following conclusions may be noted: first, the bookends of Q 11:4 and Mark 14:36-38 make it patently clear that Jesus' mission is more than a "mission to die." In these texts Jesus petitions his Father to be exempted from the last and final ordeal. Second, Jesus knew that he had a *temporary presence* on this earth—more temporary, that is, than most humans. Texts like Mark 2:19-20; 10:38; 14:3-9 and Luke 13:32-33 evince a Jesus who knew of a premature death. Third, because Jesus believed he was called by his Father to Israel, there is every reason to think he thought his premature death was part, somehow, of *God's providential plan in history*. Behind texts like Mark 14:36, Luke 13:32-33, and John 10:15-18 is a Jesus who saw in his death the outworking of divine providence. Fourth, but still short of a soteriological perception of his death, Jesus clearly thought his premature death was the *fate of a prophet*. Jesus stands behind texts like Luke 23:27-31, Q 9:58, Luke 12:49-50, Matthew 23:29-35, and Mark 12:1-12. Fifth, because Jesus believed his Father would eventually, somehow, vindicate him, Jesus challenged his followers also to run the gauntlet of death if it was their destined calling. The figure of Jesus is heard in texts like Mark 8:34.

THREE FOUNDATIONS

These five conclusions are well established, but do not add up to a Jesus who thought his death was either saving or atoning. What they do amount to, however, is a threefold foundation for constructing as best we can how Jesus perceived his premature death. First, the evidence clearly reveals an *indissoluble connection* between John the Baptist and Jesus. It was an a posteriori relationship: as with John, so with Jesus. It was also an a fortiori relationship: if with John, certainly with me. It was also a *comparative* relationship: each compared his role with Elijah. That connection is especially obvious at Mark 10:38, Luke 13:32-33, and the fate of the prophet theme so redolent in the Jesus traditions (e.g., Q 9:58; Luke 12:49-50; 23:27-31; Matt 23:29-35; cf. Q 7:18-19, 22-23). When John was put to death Jesus became instantly aware that he too might die a similar death. And it is unlikely that John's death was the first time it occurred to Jesus that his mission to Israel could, or would, end in martyrdom.

Second, Jesus evidently did not see his death in *exclusively individualistic terms.* From his penchant for the expression and imagery of the Son of man (from Dan 7) to the last supper when he urged his followers to eat his body and drink his blood in order to share in his death, Jesus saw his death as not only his: it was a *representative* death. It is indeed possible, as I judge the evidence, that Jesus saw his death as vicarious; if not, however, the evidence is clear that he believed he was the representative Israelite: his death paved the way for others. When he urged his followers to be prepared to run the gauntlet, it was a gauntlet he had seen John run and one he was ready himself to run. He represented others, namely his followers, when he entered the waters of Jordan at the hand of John to reenact the crossing of the Jordan and the reentering of the land. If that is his beginning, so also his ending: he goes to meet his death having asked his followers to share in his body and his blood.

Jesus was indissolubly connected to John; Jesus knew his death was representative. Thirdly, Jesus saw his death as the *beginning of the eschatological ordeal.*[6] We began our discussion with what we called the bookends: Q 11:4 and Mark 14:36-38. In these two passages representing both the centrality of Jesus' vision and the last night, Jesus envisions two shadowy figures on the immediate horizon: (1) the eschatological ordeal and (2) his desire not to endure that ordeal. Here we find an interpretation by Jesus of what his death is: the onslaught of the eschatological tribulation. He, as representative, is about to cross the threshold into the last hour. Other passages fasten Jesus firmly to this perception of his death: Q 9:58;16:16; Mark 3:27; 10:38; Luke 12:49-50; 13:32-33; 23:27-31; Matthew 23:29-35; and perhaps Mark 12:1-12. This point should not be missed. Not only did Jesus see his death as the onset of the eschatological tribulation, he knew (as a Jew) that the tribulation was to lead into the kingdom. Thus, Jesus must have seen his death as the onset of the kingdom of God.

Like others, Jesus knows his death is likely. Like other prophets, he knows his death is destined as the fate of the prophet. Like those same prophets, he knows his death will be vindicated by his Father. But, unlike others, he believes

---

[6] For an excellent exposition, cf. D.C. Allison, Jr., *The End of the Ages Has Come* (Philadelphia: Fortress, 1985), 115–41. A sketch of the great tribulation in Jewish literature is found on pp. 5–25.

his death will reveal the presence of the eschatological ordeal. And, apparently like others, he knows his death is a representative death. He takes upon himself that role of representation when, in spite of his desire to be excused from the ordeal, he remains behind while the lurking figures associated with the Roman government in Judea seek an opportunity to capture him, try him, and kill him. Does the evidence justify going beyond a representative death as part of the eschatological ordeal?

MARK 10:45

Two other Jesus traditions suggest we can probe even deeper: Mark 10:45 and Mark 14:24. Mark 10:45, however, is beset with an interpretive tradition that prevents historical scholarship from peering through that text to the time of Jesus. Besides the question of authenticity—and the "ransom for many" elements of that logion are particularly challenging when it comes to the issues of authenticity—there is the fundamental issue of *how Jesus perceived his own mission*. It was argued that there were plenty of Jewish precedents for seeing one's life inscripturated. Borrowing language from Michael Wise, we called these various figures "scripture prophets," and we argued further that there is clear evidence that Jesus too saw himself as a scripture prophet. He saw his own life, either as destiny or as pattern, in a variety of figures in the Tanakh—and we pointed to texts like Q 9:58; 9:61-62; 11:20 and 12:51-53. But that leaves the critical issue: granted that Jesus saw his life as a Scripture prophet, did he see his life in the Servant of Isaiah—for, according to most, that is the tradition behind the ransom words of Mark 10:45. Our conclusion is that there is negligible evidence to suggest he saw his life as the Servant of Isaiah (cf. Mark 9:9-13; Luke 22:35-38; Mark 1:11; Luke 4:16-21 [Q 7:22]; and Mark 3:27). More importantly, the central perception of Jesus and his statements pertaining to his suffering emerge most likely from the Son of man figure in Daniel 7. This is where the passion predictions belong—in the Son of man tradition rather than the Servant tradition. Hence, we argued, the perception Jesus seems to have had about his premature death—besides the factors mentioned above—is that his death was as a *representative* and as the *first in a group*. That is, his death was corporate. The Son of man then is his "job description" as he leads his followers through death and into vindication before the Ancient of Days.

LAST SUPPER

However, Mark 14:24 takes us a step further in the direction of an early Christian perception of Jesus' death as atoning. The Jewish history of the *Pesah* celebration was briefly surveyed in order to ask if the last supper was *Pesah*. The conclusion was that Jesus' last supper was a quasi-*Pesah* celebration. It was not the right day (one day early), but Jesus *anticipated Pesah* in the last supper. More importantly, Jesus interpreted the bread and the cup as his body and his blood.

And he asked his followers to share in that bread and cup, that is, in his death. Once again, he sees his death as representative, but it appears also that he sees his death as somehow *vicarious and protecting*. In stating that the bread was his body and the wine his blood, Jesus suggested that he was the Passover victim whose blood would protect his followers from the imminent judgment of God against Jerusalem and its corrupt leadership (embodied in the temple especially). We have here the first genuine glimpse of a death that somehow atones. Jesus' theory of the atonement then is that his own death, and his followers' participation in that death by ingestion, protects his followers from the Day of YHWH, which in the prophets especially is often described as the wrath of YHWH. As the avenging angel of the Passover in Egypt "passed over" the first-born children whose fathers had smeared blood on the door, so the Father of Jesus would "pass over" those followers who ingested Jesus' body and blood. We concluded also that *covenant* probably was not language used by Jesus at that last supper, but was instead language used soon after Pentecost. Also, we argued that Jesus firmly believed that his death would not destroy the imminent arrival of the kingdom—instead, when that kingdom arrived Jesus would once again resume table fellowship (bread and wine) with his followers. In other words, Jesus believed that the kingdom was yet in the future and that his own death was what would guarantee participation for his followers.

The Early Church Theologians of the Death of Jesus[7]

Christian theories of atonement are rooted in a variety of images that have grown into a mammoth banyan tree—images as diverse as sacrifice, justification, reconciliation, and high priestly intercession vie with one another logically but find little tension at the level of spiritual appropriation. This variety was at one time unknown, and it is the task of this section to chart how the individual the-

---

[7] Several general studies are worth noting, including E. Lohse, *Märtyrer und Gottesknecht* (2d ed.; FRLANT 46; Göttingen: Vandenhoeck & Ruprecht, 1963); K. Kertelge, ed., *Der Tod Jesu* (QD 74; Freiburg: Herder, 1976); M. Hengel, *The Atonement* (trans. J. Bowden; Philadelphia: Fortress, 1981); G. Friedrich, *Die Verkündigung des Todes Jesu im Neuen Testaments* (BTS 6; Neukirchen: Neukirchener, 1982); H. Merklein, "Der Tod Jesu als stellvertretender Sühnetod," in his *Studien zu Jesus und Paulus* (WUNT 43; Tübingen: Mohr Siebeck, 1987), 181–91; M. de Jonge, *Christology in Context* (Philadelphia: Westminster, 1988), 173–88; K. Grayston, *Dying, We Live* (New York: Oxford, 1990); M. de Jonge, *Jesus, The Servant-Messiah* (New Haven: Yale University Press, 1991); M.D. Hooker, *From Adam to Christ* (Cambridge: Cambridge University Press, 1990); *Not Ashamed of the Gospel* (Didsbury Lectures, 1988; Grand Rapids: Eerdmans, 1994); G. Barth, *Der Tod Jesu Christi im Verständnis des Neuen Testaments* (Neukirchen-Vluyn: Neukirchener Verlag, 1992); J.T. Carroll and J.B. Green, *The Death of Jesus in Early Christianity* (Peabody, Mass.: Hendrickson, 1995); R. Schwager, *Jesus in the Drama of Salvation* (trans. J.G. Williams and P. Haddon; New York: Crossroad, 1999); J.B. Green and M.D. Baker, *Rediscovering the Scandal of the Cross: Atonement in New Testament and Contemporary Contexts* (Downers Grove: InterVarsity, 2000); J. Jeremias, *Jesus and the Message of the New Testament* (ed. K.C. Hanson; 1965; repr. Minneapolis: Fortress, 2002), 75–96.

ologians of earliest Christianity understood the death of Jesus. It is not possible here to provide a complete or detailed map; instead, it is our purpose merely to sketch how each theologian understood the death of Jesus. Such a panorama of the landscape will enable us to assess more accurately the central theories of atonement that dominate Christian theology today.

It is impossible here to sort out the vagaries of theological interpretation of early Christian atonement theology, or the complexities of how Jesus' death has been taken up and used and reused in the history of Christian theology. But we shall offer a few words, hoping that our historical study of Jesus might shed light on the parameters of atonement theology in the New Testament and the history of theology.

PRE-PAULINE FORMULAIC EXPRESSIONS

Before anything else happened to the followers of Jesus, they had to come to terms with following someone who was crucified. Evidence of acrimony and conflict over worshiping a crucified Messiah is found throughout the New Testament, including texts like Deuteronomy 21:22-27 and Galatians 3:13, as well as Acts 2:36; 5:30; 10:39-40. Finding the earliest pieces about that debate is not an easy task, but it can be at least attempted in brief fashion.

Before we arrive in the embattled field of Paul's theology, a brief on the pre-Pauline traditions swallowed up by Paul's battle with various churches on the Mediterranean. While no consensus will ever be reached on details, the majority of Pauline scholars do assign a significant number of lines about Jesus' death to traditions taken up by Paul, sometimes without modification and other times with modifications.[8] Among these are profound interpretive claims, the most notable of which is Romans 3:25-26a, wherein Jesus' death is understood as the "mercy seat"[9] and also a demonstration of God's faithfulness to his purposes. Others point to 2 Corinthians 5:14-15 where we learn that Jesus' death, in this pre-Pauline period, was understood as an act of Jesus' obedient love of God. As such, this act of love was a death for others as well as the corporate death of all humans.

---

[8] A good start can be made with A.M. Hunter, *Paul and His Predecessors* (Philadelphia: Westminster, 1961); V.H. Neufeld, *The Earliest Christian Confessions* (NTTS 5; Grand Rapids: Eerdmans, 1963); H.N. Ridderbos, "The Earliest Confession of the Atonement in Paul," in *Reconciliation and Hope* (ed. R. Banks; Grand Rapids: Eerdmans, 1974), 76–89; a recent summary can be found in J.D.G. Dunn, *The Theology of Paul the Apostle* (Grand Rapids: Eerdmans, 1998), 174–77; E.E. Ellis, "Preformed Traditions and Their Implications for Pauline Christology," in *Christology, Controversy and Community* (ed. D.G. Horrell and C.M. Tuckett; NovTSup 99; Leiden: E.J. Brill, 2000), 303–20; P. Stuhlmacher, *Biblische Theologie des Neuen Testaments* (2d ed.; 2 vols.; Göttingen: Vandenhoeck & Ruprecht, 1997), 1:191–95.

[9] On this hardly recent interpretation, see now D.P. Bailey, "Jesus as the Mercy Seat," (Ph.D. diss., University of Cambridge, 1999), as summarized in "Jesus as the Mercy Seat," *TynBul* 51 (2000): 155–58.

As Jesus' death led to a resurrection, so that resurrection enables those who die with Jesus to live for him and with him.[10] What has been presented here enables us to see that *prior to Paul* the death of Jesus was perceived in temple imagery and sacrificial terms, in terms of God's faithfulness to his own purposes, and in terms of a corporate death and resurrection. That the pre-Pauline churches knew of Jesus' entire life as one of redemptive action can be gleaned quite easily by reading the tradition at 1 Corinthians 15:3-4: his death, burial and resurrection were "for our sins" and "according to the Scriptures." Whatever one may say of the pre-Pauline formulaic expressions, they center on the death and resurrection of Jesus as "for us"[11] (e.g., 1 Cor 15:3-5; Rom 1:3-4; 3:25-26; 4:24-25; 10:8-9; 2 Cor 5:21; Phil 2:6-11), and they may derive from reflection on Isaiah 43:3-4 or 52:13–53:12. What I think important is that such formulations of the significance of the death of Jesus imply at least a mild critique of the efficacy of the temple. No one who claims that Jesus' death is a fulfillment of the Tanakh and the mercy seat itself will continue to think of Yom Kippur in the traditional manner. Some scholars, notably M. Hengel, find the eye of the storm in the Stephen circle, but wherever we locate it, this sort of interpretive storm was making its presence felt.[12]

The gravity of *creation*, then, precedes Paul, and it is unprofitable to look to Paul for innovation in this regard. In fact, Paul is more of a *Tradent* than an innovator when it comes to the locus of salvation in God's redemptive activity in the death and resurrection of Jesus Christ.

PAUL AND THE DEATH OF JESUS[13]

We could perhaps begin with no stronger reminder than that set down in true Teutonic rhetoric by Ernst Käsemann: "The history of Pauline interpretation is

---

[10] On the significance of the resurrection, see N.T. Wright, "Jesus' Resurrection and Christian Origins," *Greg* 83 (2002): 615–35.

[11] On which, see S.B. Marrow, "Principles for Interpreting the New Testament Soteriological Terms," *NTS* 36 (1990): 26–80.

[12] M. Hengel, *Between Jesus and Paul* (trans. J. Bowden; Philadelphia: Fortress, 1983), esp. 1–29; *Atonement*.

[13] The literature on Paul is immense. I have chosen to avoid getting caught in the middle of the battle between Peter Stuhlmacher and Martin Hengel (on the German side) and J.D.G. Dunn, N.T. Wright, and E.P. Sanders. Though I've purchased some share in the "New Perspective," the following sources are sufficiently descriptive to satisfy more than one side of the debate. The following ought to be noted: A. Schweitzer, *The Mysticism of Paul the Apostle* (trans. W. Montgomery; 1953; repr. Baltimore: The Johns Hopkins University Press, 1998); R. Bultmann, *Theology of the New Testament* (trans. K. Grobel; 2 vols.; New York: Scribner, 1951, 1955), 1:293–306; W.D. Davies, *Paul and Rabbinic Judaism* (3d ed.; Philadelphia: Fortress, 1980), 227–84; D.E.H. Whiteley, *The Theology of St. Paul* (2d ed.; Oxford: Blackwell, 1980); H. Ridderbos, *Paul* (trans. J.R. DeWitt; Grand Rapids: Eerdmans, 1975), 182–204; E.P. Sanders, *Paul and Palestinian Judaism* Philadelphia: Fortress, 1977), 434–515; M.D. Hooker, "Interchange and Atonement," *BJRL* 60 (1978): 462-481; J. Christiaan Beker, *Paul the Apostle* (Philadelphia: Fortress, 1980),

the history of the apostle's ecclesiastical domestication."[14] As with many of Käsemann's assertions, I am not completely sure what he means, but this seems to be his point: Paul's theology has a history of mismanagement. Pauline specialists debate where to begin, what is the center of Paul's theology, what are his historical influences,[15] and the precise meaning of many of his crucial expressions concerning the death of Jesus: which is to say that I would not only like to be excused from blunders caused by ignorance of current trends and also for proposing a few features of Paul's view of death that I take to be acceptable to a wide range of that scholarship.[16]

For Paul,[17] a fundamental notion is that Jesus' death and resurrection are indissoluble, complementary acts of God, and that together (cf. 1 Cor 15:14, 17) they effect the accomplishment of salvation, the dawn of the eschaton as the redemption of the cosmos (Gal 2:20; 5:24; 6:14; 1 Cor 15:12-20; 1 Tim 3:16; 2 Tim 2:11).[18] This is "according to Scripture" (1 Cor 15:3). The cross and resurrection accomplish the great reversal, the apocalyptic act of God; and, standing on top of that act, Paul thought all history was now to be read from that coign of vantage. Furthermore, the resurrection hope of Judaism was not about

---

135–234; A.J.M. Wedderburn, *Baptism and Resurrection* (WUNT 44; Tübingen: J.C.B. Mohr, 1987); J. Becker, *Paul* (trans. O.C. Dean, Jr.; Louisville: Westminster/John Knox, 1993), 386–420; C. Breytenbach, "Versöhnung, Stellvertretung and Sühne: Semantische and traditionsgeschichtliche Bemerkungen am Beispiel der paulinischen Briefe," *NTS* 39 (1993): 59–79; S. Travis, "Christ as Bearer of Divine Judgment in Paul's Thought about the Atonement," in *Jesus of Nazareth* (ed. J.B. Green and M. Turner; Grand Rapids: Eerdmans, 1994), 332–45, who attempts to remove retribution from Paul's theology; Stuhlmacher, *Biblische Theologie des Neuen Testaments*, 1:234–52, 289–305, 311–48; N.T. Wright, *What Saint Paul Really Said* (Grand Rapids: Eerdmans, 1997); G. Strecker, *Theology of the New Testament* (ed. F.W. Horn; trans. M.E. Boring; New York: Walter de Gruyter, 2000), 105–10, 116–78; Dunn, *Theology of Paul the Apostle*, 207–33, 23–65, 334–412, 482–87; P. Stuhlmacher and D.A. Hagner, *Revisiting Paul's Doctrine of Justification* (Downers Grove: InterVarsity, 2001).

[14] E. Käsemann, "The Saving Significance of the Death of Jesus in Paul," in his *Perspectives on Paul* (trans. M. Kohl; Philadelphia: Fortress, 1971), 46–47

[15] See here the older study of S.K. Williams, *Jesus' Death as Saving Event* (HDR 2; Missoula, Mont.: Scholars Press, 1975), whose ideas are taken up anew in D. Seeley, *The Noble Death* (JSNTSup 28; Sheffield: JSOT, 1990), who contends that the construct "Noble Death," derived mostly from 4 Maccabees and both Hellenistic and Roman philosophical traditions, best explains Paul's understanding of Jesus' death. The theme has been explored more broadly by A.J. Droge and J.D. Tabor, *A Noble Death* (San Francisco: HarperSanFrancisco, 1992).

[16] See the excursus at the end of this chapter.

[17] No attempt here will be made to dissect the genuine letters of Paul from the pseudepigraphic, nor does it matter in a sketch of early Christian thinking on the significance of the death of Christ. We have analyzed the letters in three groups: (A) Galatians, the Thessalonian correspondence, the Corinthian correspondence, and Romans; (B) the prison letters; and (C) the pastoral letters. For a recent overview of the continuities and discontinuities, cf. Stuhlmacher, *Biblische Theologie des Neuen Testaments*, 2:4–27.

[18] So, Wright, "Jesus' Resurrection and Christian Origins"; Beker, *Paul the Apostle*, 197, however finds this distinction within their unity: "The cross accentuates the judgment and death of the old age, whereas the resurrection and the Spirit announce the newness of the coming age."

the individual (though surely the individual righteous person hopes for the resurrection) but about national restoration and the general resurrection (e.g., Isa 26; Ezek 37; Dan 12:1-2; Wis 3:7-8).[19] Paul was of the mind that the time of the resurrection had already begun, and no one has stated this more profoundly than Albert Schweitzer:

> While other believers held that the finger of the world-clock was touching on the beginning of the coming hour and were waiting for the stroke which should announce this, Paul told them that it had already passed beyond the point, and that they had failed to hear the striking of the hour, which in fact struck at the Resurrection of Jesus.
>
> Behind the apparently immobile outward show of the natural world, its transformation into the supernatural was in progress, as the transformation of a stage goes on behind the curtain.[20]

Paul's message is the gospel[21] of the victory of the cross of Jesus Christ (Gal 3:1; Rom 3:21-31; 1 Cor 2:2; 11:26; Phil 3:18),[22] the transformation of the Old into the New (2 Cor 3:4-18); and opposition is often to the scandal of that cross (Gal 3:13; 5:11; 1 Cor 1:17-25).[23] The Second Adam, who in some sense is the recapitulation of Israel's entire history,[24] died for each person individually (cf. Rom 14:15), but the plan of God is for the reconciliation of the entire cosmos.[25] At the foundational level, Jesus "gave himself" unto death as a (representative) sacrifice[26] (cf. Gal 1:4; 2:20; Eph 5:2, 25; Phil 2:8; 1 Tim 2:6; Titus 2:14; draw-

[19] That Judaism, however, did not have one view of the afterlife has now been demonstrated by A. Segal, *Life after Death* (New York: Doubleday, 2004), 120–70, 248–396, 596–638.

[20] Schweitzer, *Mysticism of Paul the Apostle,* 99.

[21] On gospel, see Stuhlmacher, *Biblische Theologie des Neuen Testaments,* 1:313–26; Wright, *What Saint Paul Really Said,* 39–62.

[22] Emphasized by many, including Schweitzer, *Mysticism of Paul the Apostle;* Beker, *Paul the Apostle;* Ridderbos, *Paul.* The recent study of the function of cross in the rhetorical strategy of Paul has been elucidated by D.K. Williams, *Enemies of the Cross of Christ* (JSNTSup 223; Sheffield: Sheffield Academic, 2002).

[23] See esp. M. Hengel, *Crucifixion in the Ancient World and the Folly of the Message of the Cross* (trans. J. Bowden; Philadelphia: Fortress, 1977); D.W. Chapman, "Perceptions of Crucifixion among Jews and Christians in the Ancient World," Ph.D. diss., Cambridge University, 1999. He places Christian perceptions of crucifixion in a wider context than has previously been done, and redresses the imbalance created by a simplistic reading of 1 Corinthians 1:23. "The cross then is the abode not just of the bandit or the rebel, but also of the innocent and the martyr" (87).

[24] See here now the exceptional study of H. Boersma, *Violence, Hospitality, and the Cross* (Grand Rapids: Baker, 2004), 121–26.

[25] Recently emphasized in Stuhlmacher, *Revisiting Paul's Doctrine of Justification,* 33–53. See also R.P. Martin, *Reconciliation* (Atlanta: John Knox, 1981).

[26] The term *sacrifice* has been debated intensely, both in scholarship concerned with the Tanakh and the New Testament. The singular development is that sacrifices atone in the sense of purging the sanctuary of defilement, and the emphasis has shifted from what it does for the individual to what it does for the sanctuary. A comprehensive examination of theory and evidence can be found

ing surely at times on Lev 4; 16) as a completely obedient[27] Son[28] and, consequently, as the "mediator" between God and the human (1 Tim 2:5). At the level
of the Christian life, suffering is a (metaphorical? literal? mystical?) participation
in the suffering and death of Jesus Christ (Gal 6:17; 1 Cor 15:31; 2 Cor 1:5-7;
4:10-11; 11:23; 12:9-10; 13:4; Rom 6:11; 8:17-18; Col 1:24; Phil 3:10).[29] But,
how did Paul perceive the saving and atoning significance of the death of Jesus
Christ? How was it effective?

Five themes summarize how Paul saw the death of Jesus Christ, and each
(in my judgment) is to be given equal value in Paul's perception of atonement.
First, Paul saw Jesus' death as an eschatological *rescue of victorious power* from the
Adamic condition or, as N.T. Wright has put it, the Exilic condition.[30] Paul
expressed this in a variety of metaphors, notably that they were rescued from:

- death (1 Thess 5:10; 1 Cor 15:20),
- sins and this evil age (Gal 1:4),
- the curse of the law (Gal 3:13-14; 1 Cor 5:7; Rom 10:4),
- bondage and slavery (Gal 5:1),
- the Passover-night wrath of God (1 Thess 1:10; 2:15-16; 5:9; 2 Thess
  1:5-10; 2:8; Rom 2:16 [cf. 1:18-32]; 5:9),

---

in R.E. Averbeck, "Sacrifices and Offerings," in *Dictionary of the Old Testament: Pentateuch* (ed.
T.D. Alexander & D. Baker; Downers Grove: InterVarsity, 2003), 706–33; see also M. Douglas,
"Atonement in Leviticus," *JQR* 1 (1993–1994): 109–30, and her *Leviticus as Literature* (Oxford:
Oxford University Press, 1999); pride of place belongs to the massive three-volume commentary
on Leviticus by J. Milgrom, *Leviticus* (AB 3A-3B; New York: Doubleday, 1991–2000).

For the New Testament discussion, cf. B.H. McLean, "The Absence of an Atoning Sacrifice in
Paul's Soteriology," *NTS* 38 (1992): 531–53; J.D.G. Dunn, "Paul's Understanding of the Death of
Jesus as Sacrifice," in *Sacrifice and Redemption* (ed. S.W. Sykes; Cambridge: Cambridge University
Press, 1991), 35–56; C.F.D. Moule, "The Sacrifice of Christ," in his *Forgiveness and Reconciliation,
and Other New Testament Themes* (London: SPCK, 1998), 135–76.

[27] On obedience, cf. R.N. Longenecker, "The Foundational Conviction of New Testament
Christology," in *Jesus of Nazareth, Lord and Christ* (ed. J.B. Green and M. Turner; Grand Rapids:
Eerdmans, 1994), 473–88; see also his earlier "The Obedience of Christ in the Theology of the
Early Church," in *Reconciliation and Hope* (ed. R. Banks; Grand Rapids: Eerdmans, 1974),
142–52.

[28] A decisive contribution was made by Davies, *Paul and Rabbinic Judaism*, 259–84; but see also
now R.B. Hays, *The Faith of Jesus Christ* (2d ed.; Grand Rapids: Eerdmans, 2002); D.B.
Garlington, *"The Obedience of Faith"* (WUNT 2/38; Tübingen: J.C.B. Mohr, 1991); also his *Faith,
Obedience and Perseverance* (WUNT 79; Tübingen: J.C.B. Mohr, 1994).

[29] To begin with, Schweitzer, *Mysticism of Paul the Apostle*, 141–59.

[30] Many have overreacted to Wright's proposal. The exilic condition (even if one does not prefer to
label it as that) still existed to the same degree that the promises of the prophets were not yet completely fulfilled. See N.T. Wright, *The New Testament and the People of God* (vol. 1 of *Christian
Origins and the Question of God*; Minneapolis: Fortress, 1992), 145–338. See the various responses
in J.M. Scott, *Exile* (JSJ Suppl. 56; Leiden: E.J. Brill, 1997); C.C. Newman, ed., *Jesus and the
Restoration of Israel* (Downers Grove: InterVarsity, 1999); S. Bryan, *Jesus and Israel's Traditions of
Judgement and Restoration* (SNTSMS 117; Cambridge: Cambridge University Press, 2002), 12–20.

- the powers of this age (Rom 8:31-39),
- the unjust conditions existing prior to the death of Christ (Rom 3:24).

From the prison letters, we see a similar pattern of thought: Jesus' followers are rescued from darkness (Col 1:12-14), the principalities and powers of this age (Col 2:14-15; Eph 1:20-22; cf. 1 Cor 2:6-8), and the law (Eph 2:14-18). Rescue is still found in the pastoral letters, as we find Christ as a "ransom" (1 Tim 2:6) and one who rescues the believer from wickedness (Titus 2:14). This rescue operation was costly (cf. 1 Cor 6:20; 7:23).

Second, Jesus' singular righteous act of death provides the eschatological bounty of benefits for those who turn to Christ in faith (Rom 5:18-19).[31] What Jesus Christ provides, specifically through his obedient death, includes:[32]

- the eschatological gifts of grace (Gal 2:21),
- blessing (Gal 3:14),
- sonship (Gal 4:5),[33]
- freedom from the law and sin (Gal 5:1; Rom 6:13; 7:4-6, 24-25),
- salvation (1 Cor 1:18),
- power (1 Cor 1:18, 24; 2:4-5),
- cleansing (1 Cor 1:2; 6:9-11),
- forgiveness (1 Cor 15:3),
- resurrection (1 Cor 15:20),
- righteousness/justification[34] (Rom 3:21-25;[35] 5:9, 16; 2 Cor 5:21[36]),
- riches (2 Cor 8:9),
- mercy (Rom 3:25),
- new covenant (2 Cor 3:4-18),
- life (1 Thess 5:10; Rom 4:25; 5:1-2, 12-21),
- reconciliation (Rom 5:10).

---

[31] See Moo, *Romans*, 341.

[32] The various terms are metaphors for release from the Adamic condition; cf. esp. Dunn, *Theology of Paul the Apostle*, 493–98. It is simply not possible in this sketch to delve into the scholarly debates over Paul's terms of salvation, terms like redemption, reconciliation, and justification. The breakdown of Becker, *Paul*, 407–20, is profitable: he breaks down terms into *Christ* and *Spirit*. See also Breytenbach, "Versöhnung, Stellvertretung and Sühne," where he carefully distinguishes *reconcile* from *atone* (esp. pp. 60–65).

[33] See J.M. Scott, *Adoption as Sons of God* (WUNT 2/48; Tübingen: J.C.B. Mohr [Paul Siebeck], 1992).

[34] The literature is vast: see Dunn, *Theology of Paul the Apostle*, 334–89; Stuhlmacher, *Revisiting Paul's Doctrine of Justification*; also M.A. Seifrid, *Justification by Faith* (NovTSup 68; Leiden: E.J. Brill, 1992).

[35] See the short summary in S. Westerholm, *Preface to the Study of Paul* (Grand Rapids: Eerdmans, 1997), 41–49; also N.T. Wright, "Romans," in *New Interpreter's Bible* 10:464–78.

[36] But cf. the innovation on this text by N.T. Wright, "'That We Might Become the Righteousness of God,'" in *First and Second Corinthians* (ed. D.M. Hay; vol. 2 of *Pauline Theology*; Minneapolis: Fortress, 1993), 200–208.

Regardless of the listing of benefits, the *fundamental gift* for Paul is the Spirit, and all others are but manifestations of that Spirit.[37] In the prison letters, Jesus' cosmic death provides forgiveness of sins as a redemption (Col 1:12-14; Eph 1:7; 4:32), victory (Col 2:14-15), ethnic (Jew/Gentile) and corporate reconciliation (1:20-22; Eph 2:13, 17; cf. Zech 9:10-11), and sanctification/purity (Eph 5:25-27)—and these at times with their virtues extended into universal scope (Col 1:20; Eph 1:10). And, from the pastoral letters, what the death of Jesus the mediator (1 Tim 2:5) provides is salvation from sin (1 Tim 1:15 [which is connected to the law; cf. 1:9]; Titus 3:5 [though here the Holy Spirit seems the agent]) and deliverance from wickedness so that one can live in purity (Titus 2:14).

These eschatological bounties are not so much individual benefits (though that they surely are as well) but *instances* of (1) the fulfillment of expectations from the Old Testament, (2) the dawn of the eschaton and (3) what Jews were led to expect in the eschaton from the Tanakh. That is, the death and resurrection of Jesus usher in the final age, not the least indicators of which are such things as grace, forgiveness, redemption, justification, and reconciliation. These bounties indicate then the death to the old era of sin, flesh, the devil, and especially the death that inheres in the Adamic condition.[38]

Paul does not explain the *mechanics* of atonement or his theory of the atonement for a variety of reasons, not the least of which are his foci on eschatological transition, the bounties one finds in Christ, and the mission to the Gentiles. But, what he does claim is that Jesus Christ rescued believers from death, sin, and the flesh because (1) he died (2) for others (3) as an atonement for sins (4) at the end of the age.[39] Two comments are in order: first, while Paul's theory of atonement is not spelled out, he clearly believes Jesus effected atonement in his death (which becomes powerfully operative through the resurrection); second, his language constantly brushes up against sacrifice, and therefore his language implies the legitimacy of the sacrificial system as an analogy for the atonement of Jesus' death. Even if Paul's prepositions derive from traditional Christian language (*for us, for others*, etc.), his ubiquitous use of that language reveals his acceptance of that tradition. Thus, the apostle to the Gentiles may see Christ through the sacrifices associated with Passover (1 Cor 5:7), the sin offering (Rom 8:3), the burnt offering (Eph 5:2), and Yom Kippur (Rom 3:25).

Such language[40] emerges fundamentally from the temple sacrificial system, and to the degree that Paul's language derives from Leviticus 4 and 16, that sys-

---

[37] See here Becker, *Paul*, 414–20.

[38] For the importance of this type of salvation-historical reading of Paul's soteriology, cf. singular remarks by Bultmann, *Theology*, 1:279, 303; Ridderbos, *Paul*; Beker, *Paul the Apostle*, 191, 211; Wright, *What Saint Paul Really Said*, 141.

[39] On which, cf. a half-century of continuity from Davies, *Paul and Rabbinic Judaism*, 227–59, to Dunn, *Theology of Paul the Apostle*, 212–23.

[40] See esp. Breytenbach, "Versöhnung, Stellvertretung and Sühne," 66–79.

tem of sacrifice explains his theory of atonement. It won't do to sweep Paul's sacrificial terms under the rug of tradition, nor will it do to claim that other ideas (like reconciliation, or "in Christ" or participation) predominate. These latter terms just might be more frequent, and more instinctual for Pauline thought, but the other terms are found frequently enough for us to contend that Paul was thoroughly conservative on how the death of Jesus was grasped in earliest Christianity.[41] Inherent to that language are ideas like identification, imputation, interchange, exchange, incorporation, vicariousness, representation, and substitution.[42] It is not possible here to expand the latter two terms any more than to say that I see *representation* as "inclusive/participatory substitution" and *substitution* as "exclusive substitution." Substitution, then, is a "one for many" and an "instead of" place-taking, and it at times *might* carry along with it the notions of penal[43] substitution and satisfaction—though it need not.[44]

---

[41] One can begin with Hengel, *Atonement*, 33–75.

[42] On the prepositions, cf. the study of M.J. Harris, "Prepositions and Theology in the Greek New Testament," in *New International Dictionary of New Testament Theology* (ed. C. Brown; 3 vols.; Grand Rapids: Zondervan, 1975–1985), 3:1171–1215, here esp. 1179–80, 1190–93, 1196–97.

[43] Critical here is Romans 3:26: εἰς τὸ εἶναι αὐτὸν δίκαιον καὶ δικαιοῦντα τὸν ἐκ πίστεως Ἰησοῦ. That is, the cross resolved a fundamental theodicy: how can God retain his justice (either as personal attribute [just] or as relationship [fidelity to promise]) and, at the same time, justify the sinner. The death of Christ resolves both for Pauline theology—even if this is the only time Paul works out his theology in terms of a theodicy. In some senses, this approach anticipates Anselm's theory of atonement. How so? For Paul, God's *nature* is at stake—he cannot justify willy-nilly; he must act in accordance with his nature and covenant promises. Jesus' death is thus (and all need to admit this in this instance) both satisfaction of God's nature (which is about as close as we can get to Anselm) *and* covenant promise *and* the means of declaring in favor of the sinner (cf. Rom 1:18–3:20).

It needs also to be noted that *dikaion* can be understood as God's attribute of righteousness or, in accordance with that, an attribution of his covenant justice/fidelity. The notion of covenant justice/fidelity is worthy of careful reflection and can be found in Wright, "Romans," 473–74.

[44] The key, if often disputed, texts for representation vs. substitution in our sense are Gal 3:13, 16; 1 Thess 5:10; 1 Cor 1:13; 8:11; 15:22; 2 Cor 5:14-15, 21; Rom 5:8, 18-19; 8:3. On satisfaction theory, one still needs to read Anselm, *Cur Deus Homo* [*Why God Became Man*] in his *Major Works* (ed. B. Davies and G.R. Evans; Oxford: Oxford University Press, 1998), 260–356. The evangelical adaptation of Anselm into a penal substitution theory is best represented in L.L. Morris, *The Apostolic Preaching of the Cross* (Grand Rapids: Eerdmans, 1965); J.I. Packer, "What Did the Cross Achieve?" *TynBul* 25 (1974): 3–45; J.R.W. Stott, *The Cross of Christ* (Downers Grove: InterVarsity, 1986). See the study of F.W. Camfield, "The Idea of Substitution in the Doctrine of the Atonement," *SJT* 1 (1948): 282–93. Steven Travis ("Christ as Bearer" in *Jesus of Nazereth* [ed. Green and Turner]) offers an alternative evangelical reading of the issues. I am less concerned with the validity of the terms *penal substitution* and *satisfaction* than I am with the imbalance of these terms when they come to dominate the rhetoric. The fact is that this is not how Paul very often speaks of the death of Jesus. His concern is, to repeat, not with the *mechanics* but the *effects* of the death and resurrection of Jesus Christ. The imbalance comes when one focuses on the former instead of the latter. On the terms in the German discussion, see esp. D.P. Bailey, "Concepts of *Stellvertretung* in the Interpretation of Isaiah 53," in *Jesus and the Suffering Servant* (ed. W.H. Bellinger, Jr. and W.R. Farmer; Harrisburg: Trinity Press International, 1998), 223–50.

James Dunn offers this thumbnail explanation: "for Paul the earthly Jesus represents *fallen* man, man who though he lives again is first subject to death. Adam represents what man might have been and by his sin what man is. Jesus represents what man now is and by his obedience what man might become."[45] But, I.H. Marshall defines the terms as follows:

> The difference between them is that substitution means that Christ did that which sinners would otherwise have had to do for themselves, and traditionally the idea is that the has borne the penalty which otherwise they would have had to bear themselves. Representation, however, is usually taken to mean Christ did something not necessarily identical with what sinners would have had to do themselves but rather something which has the effect of releasing them from this obligation. On this kind of understanding Jesus did not suffer the judgment which sinners ought to bear but, for example, offered some kind of compensation to God as a result of which their debt is cancelled.[46]

Marshall, an advocate of substitutionary atonement, finds the weakness of representation in that it does not explain the mechanics of a *pro nobis* atonement. I think Marshall's definitions fall short of the mark. *Substitution* tends to turn the believer into a passive "benefactor" while *representation* permits the believer to be an active "participant" and "benefactor." No one seriously disputes (in this debate) that Christ does something for the believer that frees the believer from having to undergo death or being cursed. The issue is finding a language game that adequately summarizes what the early Christians actually say. I propose the following model to help us understand the two language games, a model that will be assumed in what follows.

The substitution model, which focuses rather pointedly as well on penal substitution and satisfaction, may be compared to the heat and fire deflector at NASA. When I was a child our family visited Cape Kennedy (this was not long after President Kennedy's death led the leaders to alter the name from Cape Canaveral) and I saw one of the earliest deflectors. It was not large compared to today's deflector. In this analogy, the flame of God's wrath is directed at sinners. Christ in his death deflects the wrath from humans, absorbing it himself; but, because of his indestructible nature, he survives the wrath to provide for believers a life of righteousness.

In the representational model, Jesus may be compared to an experience I had with my young daughter. In 1979 Chicago experienced a blizzard, and the snow fell furiously from Friday night through Sunday morning. Drifting made driving nearly impossible. On Sunday afternoon my daughter was determined to play in a clearing on the far side of our small yard. So, we bundled her up and let her go—she went about two steps and found herself dangling on a snow bank

---

[45] Dunn, "Paul's Understanding of the Death of Jesus as Sacrifice," 37.

[46] I.H. Marshall, "The Death of Jesus in Recent New Testament Study," *WW* 3 (1983): 12–21, here pp. 19–21.

and unable to move or even extricate herself. So, and here the analogy to the work of Christ becomes clear, I bundled myself up, grabbed the shovel, picked her up and put her on the steps, and then I shoveled a path through the drift and snow so she could follow me into the clearing to play. In this sense, I represented her by shoveling for her, cutting a path for her, and giving her a passage way to the clearing. Had I "substituted" for her I would have played "for her." Instead, I made it possible by carving a path for her, a path she couldn't have carved but which she needed so that she could travel at my expense.

In both models, it is important to observe, the power and the glory belong to Jesus Christ—he deflects the wrath and he cuts the path. (Every model is destroyed on the spot when anyone suggests otherwise.) But, in the former the believer stands behind the shield passively while in the latter the believer participates. This is not, it needs to be emphasized once again, synergism or anything like it. (The believer doesn't deflect any flame or shovel any snow.) It is instead a model designed to incorporate the ever-present language of participation (e.g. Rom 6) as a dimension of the soteriological work of Christ.

I would add here that it seems to me that many avoid the language of substitution because they simply do not like to think of God exhibiting wrath, and they do not like to think of the atonement in terms of penal substitution and satisfaction (names omitted to avoid acrimony). Representation, they might think, softens the sense of substitution. But, as we teach our students, it is exegetically immaterial what we would like Paul (or any biblical author) to say or think. Our task is to describe (so far as we are able) what Paul (or another biblical author) says, and to allow him to be who he was—whether we like the person's ideas or not. So, to prefer representation to substitution because we don't like the latter idea is not a personal option.

Having relieved myself of these definitions, it must be stated that Paul's theory of atonement is more than just a resolution of sin, guilt, and wrath problems. Instead, it is an *actual recreation and empowerment* (cf. 2 Cor 5:14-15). Paul's system is other than Anselm's, whose theory has dominated Christian thinking on the atonement. His system has a different logic: the problem is not how (in an academic, rational, philosophical system) one might cohere belief in an absolutely righteous and holy God who expresses wrath against human sinfulness with a simultaneous belief in forgiveness and reconciliation of human subjects. (I do not mean to suggest this isn't a real and fundamental issue for soteriology.) Instead, Paul's logic is the logic of death and life, Adam and Christ, flesh and Spirit, old and new covenant, sin and righteousness, and disobedience and obedience—to name but a few of Paul's possible tension points. His theory is not about the *how* but about the *what* and the poles at each end of the what.[47] It is Paul's indissoluble connection of death and resurrection that shatters the

[47] See Marrow, "Principles for Interpreting the New Testament," 276–77, 27–80.

cultic and quantitative reductionism in Anselm's theory of the atonement.[48] In the words of Morna Hooker,

> What has often been overlooked, however, is the close link between the resurrection and redemption which we have been exploring: if Christ's *death* deals with *sin*, it is his *resurrection* which is the basis of our *righteousness*.[49]

Jesus' death is more than a sacrifice that satisfies God's just requirements (though it was that, too); instead, it is a death plus resurrection that both *resolves* and *re-creates*, which (now to our third theme in Paul) can be described as a transfer. In this sense, substitution might be seen as an aspect of a larger theory of atonement which animated Paul, and that theory might be more comprehensive than substitution and seen better in the term representation.[50] In the words of E.P. Sanders,

> The heart of Paul's thought is not that one ratifies and agrees to a covenant offered by God, becoming a member of a group with a covenantal relation with God and remaining in it on the condition of proper behaviour; but that one dies with Christ, obtaining new life and the initial transformation which leads to the resurrection and ultimate transformation, that one is a member of the body of Christ and one Spirit with him, and that one remains so unless one breaks the participatory union by forming another.[51]

Jesus' death for Paul is fundamentally about the eschatological transfer from one sphere to another, or an interchange of what Christ (the Second Adam) provides for what sinners (First Adamites) had as their destiny.[52] This theme expresses the salvation-historical and national significance of Jesus' death and resurrection, or the eschatological shift in eras (and spheres) that his death and resurrection effect for Israel. It is a series of one-act performances by Adam and Christ, imputing their status to others. Thus, Jesus is considered by Paul to be the new Passover victim, whose death switches time from the "old leaven time" to the "new no-leaven time," or the time of "moral purity" (1 Cor 5:7).[53]

---

[48] This is where the atonement theologies of J. McLeod Campbell, *The Nature of the Atonement* (1856; repr. Grand Rapids: Eerdmans, 1996) and R.C. Moberly, *Atonement and Personality* (London: John Murray, 1901), made such an important contribution: atonement is more than satisfaction but is instead both retrospective and prospective.

[49] Hooker, "Interchange and Atonement," 477.

[50] Let me carp a little longer on this. Most studies I have seen that prefer *representation* over *substitution* tend, in one way or another, to incorporate substitution somehow in the explanation.

[51] Sanders, *Paul and Palestinian Judaism*, 514.

[52] See the very important studies of Hooker, "Interchange in Christ," *JTS* 22 (1971): 349–61; "Interchange and Atonement"; Davies, *Paul and Rabbinic Judaism*, 36–57; S. Hultgren, "The Origin of Paul's Doctrine of the Two Adams in 1 Corinthians 15.45-49," *JSNT* 25 (2003): 343–70.

[53] *Pace* Dunn, *Theology of Paul the Apostle*, 216–17.

Alternatively, it is an interchange of old-age sinfulness for new-age life and righteousness and vocation (Rom 10:4; 12:1-2; 13:14; 2 Cor 5:21[cf. Lev 16:21]) or of poverty for riches (8:9). Most central to Paul's concept of the transfer is that it is one from a sin-deserving death to the grace of life (1 Thess 5:10; Rom 4:25; 5:10, 12-21; 6:3-10; 8:2, 34; 14:9). Here Jesus is the Second Adamic head of the resurrected ones (1 Cor 15:20), who enables life in the Spirit (Gal 5–6; Rom 6–8) and the new covenant (2 Cor 3:4-18). In effect, the transfer is ontic transformation (Gal 6:15; Rom 8:29; 12:1-2; 2 Cor 3:18; 4:16; 5:1-5, 17). In the prison letters, the believer is transferred from darkness to light (Col 1:12-14), from bondage to liberation (2:14-15), from sinfulness to the graces of virtue (2:20–3:17), and from ethnic boundary-making to unity (Eph 2:11-22). This person has God's image transformed (3:10). What remains in the pastorals is the transfer from death to life (2 Tim 1:10).

Fourth, the believer acquires this transformed existence by inclusion in the eschatological Second Adam, in Christ, and by participation in the death and resurrection of the Representative One, that is, by *co-crucifixion and co-resurrection*.[54] Or as Paul also puts it, by making sure that his death is ours and ours his. That is, the believer participates in the finality of Jesus' death and resurrection. That participation is a mimetic dying and rising with Christ, and places that person in a new era and in a new sphere of life.[55] Co-crucifixion is both an utter confession of the sin that leads to death and a resolution to turn from the death that derives from sin.[56] Thus, in Paul's early letters we find the notion of "dying with Christ" to the law, to death, and to sinfulness in order to live before God appropriately in the fruits of the Spirit (Gal 2:20; 5:24; 6:14; cf. Rom 7:4-6, 24-25), as we also find his similar reflections on the sacraments: ingesting (at the Lord's Supper) the elements as an act of participation in the death of Christ (1 Cor 10:16-34), and baptism as co-crucifixion and co-resurrection (Gal 3:27-28; Rom 6:3-11; 1 Cor 15:20, 29). That act of dying with Christ generates the eschatological (new covenant) life (2 Cor 3:4-18; 4:7-12; 5:14-15; 12:1-10) because Christ is the "first fruits" (1 Cor 15:20) or, as Paul clarified, Christ's becoming sin allows those "in him" to become the "righteousness of God" (5:21; or, to be an instance of God's covenant—saving action or faithfulness?). They now worship the living and true God (1 Thess 1:9; 1 Cor 8:1-6; Rom 1:18-32).

---

[54] Scholars have debated the historical context of Paul's perception of union with Christ, but the study of Wedderburn, *Baptism and Resurrection*, has now laid to rest that the notion that Paul's views had anything serious to do with the mysteries. See also Strecker, *Theology of the New Testament*, 117–23.

[55] On which, cf. R.C. Tannehill, *Dying and Rising with Christ* (BZNW 32; Berlin: Töpelmann, 1967); Seeley, *Noble Death*; and M.J. Gorman, *Cruciformity* (Grand Rapids: Eerdmans, 2001), is perhaps the finest study on how Paul worked out the theme of the cross for spirituality in matters of faith, love, power, and hope.

[56] One of the better discussions of this remains the old work of James Denney, *The Death of Christ* (3d ed.; New York: A.C. Armstrong, 1903); *The Christian Doctrine of Reconciliation* (The Cunningham Lectures 1917; London: Hodder & Stoughton, 1917).

These are specific instances of Paul's profound grasp of the human response of faith.

The prison letters evince a similar notion, this time the death in him/with Christ is spread beyond baptism and the Lord's Supper to include suffering itself (Col 1:24) and (spiritual) circumcision (Col 2:11-15), but once again this participation in Jesus' death leads to a new life of loving conduct (2:20–3:17; Phil 3:10-11). We are face to face here with Paul's themes of Adam/Christ[57] and being in Christ[58] (cf. 1 Cor 15:20-22; Rom 5:12-21; Phil 2:5-11; Eph 1:13; 2:11-22): the sinner participates in the path of death in Adam, and the believer in the entirety of Christ as the dawn of the eschaton. Thus, for Paul, ecclesiology is a dimension of Christology.[59] The pastorals reflect this notion of co-crucifixion but once (2 Tim 2:11), where once again co-crucifixion accomplishes co-resurrection. What these texts demonstrate is that for Paul one finds the benefits of salvation by participating in the dawn of the eschaton in the death of Jesus Christ, the one who represents the Christ-lineage and delivers from the Adamic lineage. Co-crucifixion occurs through faith and, less often, through ingestion of the body and blood, through undergoing water baptism, and through spiritual circumcision. Thus, Paul calls his churches to *die with Christ* in order to find the new life of the Spirit through *rising with Christ.*

Finally, the Pauline letters speak of Jesus' death several times as an *exemplar of living*. Jesus is an example that Paul thinks he is imitating and that others ought to imitate when it comes to suffering (Gal 6:17; 1 Thess 1:6; Rom 8:17; 2 Cor 4:7-12), to being insulted (Rom 15:3), to humble living (Phil 2:5-11), and to the courage needed to maintain one's (spirit-inspired) confession in the teeth of death (1 Tim 6:13).[60] One thinks here of Galatians 3:1; 4:14 and especially of 2 Corinthians 2:14-16; 4:1-18 (cf. Col 1:24–2:5).[61]

One might best sum up this Pauline theology of the atonement by comparing principal gospel summaries in texts that are traditional, Pauline, and per-

---

[57] See, besides the studies of Hooker mentioned above, also C.F.D. Moule, *The Phenomenon of the New Testament* (London: SCM, 1967), 21–42; Dunn, *Theology of Paul the Apostle*, 199–204, 241–42.

[58] So Schweitzer, *Mysticism of Paul the Apostle*; Sanders, *Paul and Palestinian Judaism*, 431–523; Dunn, *Theology of Paul the Apostle*, 390–412.

[59] See Becker, *Paul*, 403–4. See also Sanders, *Paul and Palestinian Judaism*, 453–63.

[60] On this, cf. P. Stuhlmacher, "Eighteen Theses on Paul's Theology of the Cross," in his *Reconciliation, Law, and Righteousness* (Philadelphia: Fortress, 1986), 159–60 (theses #5–6); G.W.H. Lampe, "Martyrdom and Inspiration," in *Suffering and Martyrdom in the New Testament* (ed. W. Horbury and B. McNeil; Cambridge: Cambridge University Press, 1981), 118–35; S. Hafemann, *Suffering and Ministry of the Spirit* (Grand Rapids: Eerdmans, 1990); "The Role of Suffering in the Mission of Paul," in *The Mission of the Early Church to Jews and Gentiles* (ed. J. Ådna and H. Kvalbein; WUNT 127; Tübingen: J.C.B. Mohr [Paul Siebeck], 2000), 16–84 (who suggestively explores the significance of Gal 4:14).

[61] On Colossians 1:24, see now Hanna Stettler, "An Interpretation of Colossians 1:24 in the Framework of Paul's Mission Theology," in *Mission of the Early Church to Jews and Gentiles* (ed. Ådna and Kvalbein), 185–208.

haps even post-Pauline (Gal 2:20; 1 Cor 15:3-8; 2 Cor 5:14-15; Rom 1:3-4, 16-17; 8:2; Col 2:14-15; Eph 4:20-24 and Titus 2:11-14).[62] It is always dangerous to select a few texts from the Pauline corpus, pronounce them central, and then build a case, but these verses adequately depict the Pauline gospel as it relates to the death of Christ. What strikes the reader is that the death of Christ rescues by a co-crucifixion and co-resurrection that lead to behavioral change and to life in the Spirit. Paul's theology of the death of Christ is that persons benefit from his death by participating in that death and resurrection and thereby being transferred from Adam to Christ. The benefit, however, is fundamentally an *altered kind of existence*. Christ's death brings in the eschatological time for the new Israel, forgives sin, rescues God's people from death and the devil, and transfers the person from a life of sin leading to death to a life of righteousness leading to life. His focus is clearly not on a *substitutionary* death or even a *vicarious* death for individuals but on a death in which the new Israel *participates* by faith and, less often, by the Lord's Supper, baptism, and spiritual circumcision. That is, his theory is more along the lines of a representative death (Second Adam) and an eschatological shift, an interchange, even if at times Paul may well express the idea of exclusive substitution. It is important to let the focus of Pauline theology be the focus of Pauline theologians. For Paul, Jesus Christ leads the way, opens the door to life, and beckons others to find the benefits of that death and resurrection by participating in his death and resurrection.[63] It is not off the mark to say that for Paul the death of Jesus is the first step in the direction of God's accomplishment of the re-creation of humanity and the cosmos, and there simply aren't any more important steps—there are only in essence four steps: creation of Adam; the life, death, and resurrection of Christ; the advent of the Spirit; and the Parousia (cf. 1 Cor 15:20-28). Paul is not alone among the early Christian theologians in this comprehension of the death of Jesus.

Q AND THE DEATH OF JESUS

The most telling observation of how Q depicts the benefits of the death of Jesus is that it does not. While some have extrapolated from this that (the) Q (community? author?) did not believe in the atoning death of Jesus, others have countered simply that we should use what we do know and not guess at what we don't know. Thus, John Kloppenborg Verbin, who has spent a life studying Q, says, "All that we have to go on is what the text of Q itself offers."[64] What we do know is that Q depicts history on a crash course headed for God's judgment (e.g., Q 3:7-9, 16b-17; 17:23-24, 26-30, 37; 22:28, 30). In such an eschatological

[62] See Strecker, *Theology of the New Testament*, 64–78; Stuhlmacher, *Biblische Theologie des Neuen Testaments*, 1:317–26.

[63] See Dunn, *Theology of Paul the Apostle*, 223.

[64] J.S. Kloppenborg Verbin, *Excavating Q* (Minneapolis: Fortress, 2000), 371. For his view of Jesus' death in Q, cf. the discussion on pp. 369–74.

condition, the Q tradition has a Jesus who prays that he and his followers will not endure that ordeal (11:4). If the Q tradition does not speak of Jesus' death *per se*, it clearly believes that persecution is present. In particular, a Deutero-nomistic, prophet-like destiny awaits Jesus and his followers (6:22-23; 7:23, 31-35; 9:58; 10:3; 11:29-32, 47-51; 12:49, 51, 53; 13:34-35; 14:26-27;[65] 16:16). The readers/auditors are expected to run the gauntlet, as Jesus himself did. In so doing, his story becomes their story. While we will never know if the Q community thought of the death of Jesus in terms of an atoning death, it clearly thought of his death as the death of a martyred prophet, a death scripted in the pages of the Tanakh.[66]

M AND THE DEATH OF JESUS

While Q scholarship flourishes, M scholarship wanes. What remains is a set of traditions, composed mostly of the birth narratives, debates with Pharisees, traditions of specific ecclesial concerns—like forgiveness—and parables.[67] It is almost certain they were not from a single source but, for heuristic reasons, we have gathered them all into one bundle to see if this set of unparalleled traditions might say anything about the death of Jesus. What they say is less than what we found in Q. Jesus is one who saves from sins (Matt 1:21), though it is unclear how this salvation is effected or what precisely this salvation includes. We can presume that such salvation takes place because of his death (cf. also 8:16-17); there is no evidence that M understood the death of Jesus as saving. If one thinks in general terms of Judaism at this time, then salvation for this M tradition would most likely involve Jesus' healing, exorcisms, and presence as aspects of salvation.[68] In fact, we need to recall the socio-political connotations of both *forgiveness* and *sins*.[69] We are standing on big boulders if we think M's perception of salvation is an eschatological, messianic deliverance in all its many manifestations, rather than just a personal deliverance from the consciousness of guilt before God.

These M traditions depict Jesus as rejected by the Herods (2:1-12, 13-15, 19-23) and Pharisees (9:32-34; 23). The themes of persecution (5:10, M?), judgment (13:24-30, 36-43; 13:47-50), and the humble obedience of Jesus (12:15-21, M?) could be drawn together to present a Jesus who willingly goes to

---

[65] It could be argued (and has) that Q 14:26-27 is *post eventu* reflection on the realities of Jesus' presupposed crucifixion, in which case the Q tradition knows (perhaps) of the passion narrative.

[66] On Q and the Tanakh, see D.C. Allison, Jr., *The Intertextual Jesus* (Harrisburg: Trinity Press International, 2000).

[67] See S.H. Brooks, *Matthew's Community* (JSNTSup 16; Sheffield: Sheffield Academic, 1987).

[68] See S. McKnight, *Turning to Jesus* (Louisville: Westminster John Knox, 2002), 39–47, 133–38, where on sociological grounds conversion is expounded as an experience that may involve more than just the personal and spiritual.

[69] See my *New Vision for Israel*, 224–27.

death but who awaits vindication (27:62-66; 28:11-15). That Jesus was innocent of the charges is clear (cf. 27:19, 24-25; also 27:3-10). Once again, we must
refrain from speculating whether the so-called M tradition knew of but rejected
an atoning death, or did not know of an atoning death, or did know of it and
just did not provide evidence of that knowledge. One must deal not only with
our lack of a clear profile, but also with the unavoidable reality that no early
believer in Jesus could have affirmed salvation in Jesus without somehow fash-
ioning that faith around his ignominious end.

L AND THE DEATH OF JESUS

Jesus, according to L—which symbol, again, is merely a convenience for the special traditions in Luke—means Son of God and Davidic king, whereas the M
traditions translate the term literally (cf. Matt 1:21 [saves from sins] and Luke
1:31-33). At the bottom of Luke's theology is "salvation" and the L material is
similar (cf. 1:69-75, 77-79; 2:11, 14, 29-32). Is that salvation accomplished
through the death of Jesus? To begin with, Jesus is the rejected prophet (cf. 2:34-
35; 4:25-30), and he brings forgiveness through faith in his word (7:47-50).
Jesus is to suffer in Jerusalem the death of the rejected prophet (13:31-33), and
he predicts such a death (17:25) even if he strenuously and emotionally predicts
a coming judgment (13:1-9; 19:39-44; 21:34-36; 23:27-31). He summons his
disciples to muster their courage to run the gauntlet (22:31-34). The night
before his death he experiences profound anguish (22:43-45), in part because he
is completely innocent (23:4-5, 6-16, 39-43). The only solid indicator of an
atoning death is the recognition others make of Jesus in his *dispensing of the meal*
(24:13-32)—a meal that is surrounded by his statements that his death was fore-
told in Scripture (24:27, 44-49), and the claim of Jesus that his partner in crucifixion would join him in paradise (23:43).[70] There is no evidence that the L
tradition thinks of Jesus' death as atoning, unless it be in the meal tradition at
Emmaus. Even here, the scriptural testimony to Jesus' suffering is not a "suffering for sins" so much as a prophetic expectation that shows who Jesus is; and
only in light of the total "Christ event" are "repentance and forgiveness of sins
. . . preached in his name to all nations, beginning from Jerusalem" (24:47). But,
once again, we should not extrapolate from the *absence* of data from the *non-
existence* of that same data in those behind the L traditions. Maybe they had a
fully developed atonement theology; maybe they didn't. We don't know. What
we do know is that in the evidence plausibly connected to the L material there
is little theology of salvation on the basis of the death of Jesus.

---

[70] On which, see J.A. Fitzmyer, *Luke the Theologian* (New York: Paulist, 1989), 203–33.

MARK AND THE DEATH OF JESUS[71]

Jesus cannot be understood in Mark's Gospel until he is understood as the Son of God who was crucified, and so we need to begin by noting the *centrality of the cross* in Mark's Gospel. Confessions along the way as the Gospel unfolds are limp until the confession of the centurion immediately following Jesus' death (Mark 15:39). Only then is the veil of the messianic secret lifted. Mark's Gospel is noted by two structural features: (1) chapters 10–16 are all about the passion week, while 1–9 are his public ministry, revealing an imbalanced focus on the last week of Jesus; (2) the flow of the Gospel turns at 8:27–9:1: Jesus reveals to his disciples that he must suffer, explains that his suffering will become their suffering, and then indicates a vindication. But these two structural features of the gospel illustrate the emphasis Mark gives to the cross.

But, the reader of Mark has been in touch with Jesus' profound awareness of his premature death (2:19-20; 8:31; 9:9, 12, 19, 31; 10:33-34, 38-40; 12:6-8; 14:6-9, 20-21, 32-42, 49) and the depth of his sufferings (cf. 14:33) and horror (15:39). In fact, Mark reveals that Jesus is determined to die (8:33; 12:1-12; 14:3-9, 32-42), and, as the complement to that determination, he urges the disciples to run the gauntlet if that is their calling (8:34-9:1). The courage to look death in the face derives from the hope of vindication, another theme found throughout Mark (8:34-9:1; 10:29-31; 12:9-11; 14:62; 16:1-8). This is the scriptural witness (14:49). Thus, for Mark, the cross (with vindication) becomes the decisive *moment of revelation*—here we find Jesus (at 15:33-39) on the cross and publicly proclaimed as the Son of God by a Gentile, a claim previously permitted only of the Father (cf. 1:11; 9:7). Even more, this revelatory moment at the cross casts its shadow over the entirety of Mark's Gospel when it comes to *discipleship*: Christology shapes ecclesiology (or discipleship), and since the Son of God suffers, so must the disciples of Jesus (8:27-9:1; 9:30-37; 10:32-45).[72] We might observe that if Paul has a 50/50 relationship of death to vindication and Luke a 25/75, Mark has a 75/25 relationship. For Mark, the cross gains a heavy emphasis.

Most importantly, Mark is probably responsible for the famous gloss in Mark 10:45 to the servant passage: "to give his life as a ransom for many." In this text, Mark tips his hand toward an atoning significance for Jesus' death.[73] Jesus voluntarily surrenders his own life—that is, he willingly embraces the will

---

[71] See D. Senior, *The Passion of Jesus in the Gospel of Mark* (Wilmington: Michael Glazier, 1984); E. Best, *The Temptation and the Passion* (SNTSMS 2; Cambridge: Cambridge University Press, 1965); R.P. Martin, *Mark: Evangelist and Theologian* (Grand Rapids: Zondervan, 1972), 140–205; J. Marcus, *The Way of the Lord* (Louisville: Westminster/John Knox, 1992), chs. 5, 6, 8; Hooker, *Not Ashamed of the Gospel*, 47–67; Grayston, *Dying, We Live*, 164–237; Carroll and Green, *Death of Jesus*, 23–38.

[72] So Martin, *Mark: Evangelist and Theologian*, 117–20.

[73] See Hooker, *Mark*, 247–51; C.A. Evans, *Mark*, 2:119–25; Evans' views are similar to Morris, *Apostolic Preaching of the Cross*, 29–38.

of God, the witness of Scripture (perhaps Isa 43:3-4; 53: 12; Dan 7:13-14 [note: Son of man, not Servant]), and permits himself to be trapped and put to death. The term *ransom* (λύτρον) probably means that Jesus' own life was a kind of payment to a hostage power (LXX Exod 21:30; Sir 29:15; 1 Macc 2:50), a power undefined by Mark but clarified with dazzling confidence and imagination by the early fathers.[74] Any reading of Mark's Gospel leans in the direction that the hostile powers are sin (1:5, 15), Satan and his destructive cohorts (e.g., 3:27), and the fearful self (8:34-9:1). Jesus is the "ransom price" paid to free "the many" (cf. Isa.53:11, 12) from these powers.

The use of the term *for* (ἀντί) indicates either exclusive substitutionary death (his death instead of theirs; cf. Lev 27:11) or benefit for the many (his death brings freedom for the many; cf. Matt 17:27).[75] While I am sympathetic to the grammatical evidence for *anti* suggesting substitution, the logic of the language game of *ransom* breaks down my sympathy. The notion of ransom is a price paid in order to rescue someone from some hostile power. One thinks, naturally enough, of the children of Israel being ransomed by the Passover victim from the hostile powers of Pharaoh. What is unobserved by the substitutionary theory advocates is that the ransom cannot be a substitute, as we might find in theologically sophisticated language: where death is for death, and penal judgment for penal judgment. Here we have a mixing of descriptions: a ransom for slaves. Jesus, in Mark's language, doesn't become a slave for other slaves. He is a ransom for those who are enslaved. The difference ought to be given careful attention. To be a substitute the ransom price would have to take the place of another ransom price or a slave for another slave, but that is not what is involved here. What we have is a ransom price and slaves, and the price is paid so the slaves can be liberated. The ransom is the price paid to the hostile power in order for the captives to be liberated. The ransom does not thereby become a substitute so much as the *liberating price*. As the Passover victim did not become the substitute slave of Pharaoh, so Jesus did not become the slave to sin, self, and Satan. Instead, he paid the price, and his followers were set free. The ransom, in this case, is not that Jesus "substitutes for his followers *as a ransom*" but that he ransoms by being the price paid in order to rescue his followers from that hostile power. The notion is one of being Savior, not substitution. The best translation would be that Jesus is a "ransom *for the benefit* of the many."

We can conclude that the most probable theory of atonement here is that Mark thinks Jesus' death benefited the many because he died to ransom them from hostile powers. Yet another meaning can be suggested: Mark's theology might be along the lines of a representative death. Jesus died (as an *inclusive* substitute) for the many who will participate in his death in their own lives and

---

[74] The term *ransom*, however, could bear a softer meaning, something like "redemption." In which case, the notion is that Jesus' death redeems "the many." This is the meaning preferred by Hooker, *Mark*, 248–49.

[75] On this, see also B. Janowski, "Er trug unsere Sünden," in *Der leidende Gottesknecht* (ed. B. Janowski and P. Stuhlmacher; BAT 14; Tübingen: Mohr Siebeck, 1996), 27–48.

hearts, through faith and perhaps even through their own martyrdom. The language can be construed (even if not easily) in this manner, and such a view would be consistent with other early Christian reflections on Jesus' death. It needs to be recalled that the pericope in Mark is concerned with Jesus' exemplary role in paving the way for his followers: he serves, and so they should serve. He serves to the point of death for the many.

A third theme in Mark's presentation of the death of Jesus pertains to scriptural figures who color Mark's language: the righteous sufferer and (perhaps) the Servant of Isaiah. It is likely, as Joel Marcus has so ably pointed out, that Mark paints the suffering of Jesus in the passion narrative as the life of a righteous sufferer. Two examples suffice here: (1) in the last supper Jesus is eating with someone who betrays him, and in Psalm 41:9 [41:10] the righteous one suffers in trusting someone who proves to be false; and (2) the false witnesses of Mark 14:57 correspond to Psalms 27:12 and 35:11. Marcus points to others instances, but the point is sufficient for us to contend that Mark depicts Jesus' sufferings as a *reenactment* of the righteous sufferer of Psalms.[76] And, as Marcus points out as well, there is language from the Servant of Isaiah that is picked up by Mark in such a way that one might think Mark intended to depict Jesus as the Servant. Thus:

Servant	Jesus in Mark
Isa 50:6	Mark 14:65
Isa 52:15	Mark 15:5, 39
Isa 53:6, 12	Mark 14:10-11, 18, 21, 41-42, 44; 15:1, 10, 15
Isa 53:7	Mark 14:61; 15:5
Isa 53:6, 12	Mark 15:6-15
Isa 53:12	Mark 14:24

The implication is clear: if Mark thinks of Jesus in terms of the righteous sufferer and the Servant, it is in his *role of suffering* that redemption is achieved. The cross is far from being a simple stage in the journey to glory; instead, the cross is a place where all must stop to see the revelation of the Son of God and the nature of discipleship, as well as being the trigger of redemption. Many inferences can be drawn from this use of scriptural figures, not the least of which would be that Mark thinks Jesus' death was providential as well as part of God's design for salvation-history.

Fourth, we turn to the last supper tradition. Mark has "passoverized" the meal by turning an anticipatory *Pesah* into the *Pesah* itself (Mark 14:12, 14, 16). In this meal, Jesus identifies the bread with his body (14:22) and the wine with his blood (14:24). This meal forms "the blood of the covenant, which is poured out for many" (14:24). Here we are led to think of Exodus 24:8 (cf. 29:12),[77]

---

76 J. Marcus, *The Way of the Lord* (Louisville: Westminster/John Knox, 1992), 172–86.

77 So Martin, *Mark: Evangelist and Theologian*, 199.

though many want to move the term to an association with Jeremiah 31:31-33 or with Zechariah 9:11. That Mark also has the phrase which is poured out for many removes the text specifically from any of these three texts and thereby forms a pastiche of allusions (some point to Isa 53:12). Such a pastiche is perhaps mostly Markan, or the Markan recording of a developing and rich early Christian interpretation of Jesus' original declaration that the bread and wine were his body and blood. For Mark, then, the death of Jesus is the establishment of God's covenant with his followers. It is inappropriate here to insert "new covenant," and appeal to Jeremiah 31:31-33, because Mark does not make that connection—but others had already done so (cf. 1 Cor 11:25; Luke 22:20[LR]).[78]

A fifth theme: Mark is perhaps responsible for connecting the death of Jesus with profound apocalyptic imagery, indicating that he saw in the death of Jesus the *turn of the ages*. The death of Jesus is the great tribulation and leads to the general resurrection. All in one quick sweep of the brush, Mark has darkness cover the earth (cf. Amos 5:18, 20; 8:9-10; also Exod 10:22; Isa 13:9-16; Jer 4:27-28; 15:9; Joel 2:10; As. Mos. 10:5; Sib. Or. 3:801–2; 5:344–50), as a sign of apocalyptic judgment; he has the Son of God abandoned by the Father (Mark 15:34), he has the temple veil split in two as a fulfillment of Jesus' predictions (15:38; cf. 9:1; 11:12-25; 13:1-37; also see Josephus, *B.J.* 6.292–93; b. Yoma 39b); and he has the centurion confess this crucified one as the very Son of God (15:39)—a confession previously chased off Mark's stage every time someone tried to confess Jesus. Jesus' death for Mark reveals not so much the innocence of Jesus as the profound work he has accomplished in inaugurating the kingdom of God. Jesus has just experienced the Day of YHWH, the eschatological tribulation, the wrath of God. Once again, we are probably led to Jesus' death as an era-changing and representative death—he leads the way into the final ordeal and absorbs its brunt forces of assault. Jesus' death breaks the assault, paving a way for his followers to identify with him and enter into the era of vindication.

With this apocalyptic imagery we confront another dimension of Mark's understanding of Jesus' death: ultimately, it is tied to his vindication through the resurrection (Mark 12:10-11; 16:1-8). The recent commentary of R.H. Gundry sets out to demonstrate that Mark's Gospel is an apology of the cross.[79] Thus, Mark does not pit the suffering and death of Jesus against his successes [as is seen in some "corrective christology" approaches to Mark], but . . . Mark pits the successes against the suffering and death, and then uses the passion predictions, writes up the passion narrative, and caps his Gospel with a discovery of the empty tomb in ways that cohere with success stories, in ways that make the passion itself a success story.[80]

From the beginning of Jesus' anticipations of his own premature death, there were always comments following as to his resurrection and vindication

---

[78] See our discussion of covenant in ch. 15.

[79] *Mark*, 3. See also Martin, *Mark: Evangelist and Theologian*, 192–97.

[80] Gundry, *Mark*.

(e.g., Mark 8:31; 9:31; 10:33-34). Thus, the Son of man's vindication before the Ancient of Days (13:24-27) is the other (and bright) side of the death of Jesus. Death is a prelude to victory, the presupposition of vindication. Mark's Gospel may be a theology of the cross, but it is also a theology of ultimate glory. Here we find a foundation for the dialectic of Paul: death and resurrection for Jesus imply death to sin and resurrection to Spirit-filled life for the believer.

Which leads to our final point: for Mark, the death of Jesus (which leads to vindication for Jesus) is an exemplar of the life God has written into the fabric of human history. If Jesus is to die, so also must the follower of Jesus (Mark 8:34–9:1; 10:33-34 with 10:35-45). If Jesus is to serve unto death, so also will his followers:[81] "His death is not seen as a substitute for theirs, but rather as a pattern."[82] Once again, we are confronted by a depiction of the death of Jesus in which Jesus is the *representative*, and in which the Christology of Mark shapes the ecclesiology. As the disciples will ingest the body and blood, and so participate in the saving benefits of the death of Jesus, so in following Jesus they participate in his death. This is not quite 2 Corinthians 4:7-12 or Colossians 1:24, but the idea in Mark is groping directly toward such participatory suffering and death. If we appeal to Son of man or to Servant of Isaiah, the collective interpretation of Jesus' death remains fecund: Jesus' death is the paradigmatic, representative death that others will find true in their own lives.[83]

MATTHEW AND THE DEATH OF JESUS[84]

It is not necessary here to redescribe what is common to the Matthean traditions (Q, M, Mark) unless it is important to the overall Matthean presentation of the death of Jesus. Thus, like the other traditions, Jesus is rejected (e.g., Matt 2:1-23; 9:1-17; 11:17-19; 13:54–17:27; cf. 27:25), he warns of judgment (27:24-25), he anticipates his own divinely destined death (9:15; 16:21; 17:22-23; 20:18-19; 26:2, 52-54), and he calls his followers to run the gauntlet of obedience after him (4:1-11; 10:15-16, 17-25, 26-33, 34-39; 16:24-28; 18:1-5; 20:20-28) as did John before him (11:2-19; 14:1-12).[85] Thus, for Matthew also

---

[81] This is nicely drawn out in Hooker, *Not Ashamed of the Gospel*, 47–67.

[82] Ibid., 53.

[83] Again, see Martin, *Mark: Evangelist and Theologian*, 156–62, 163–205, where this theme is used to provide the *Sitz im Leben* for Mark's purpose.

[84] On the death of Jesus in Matthew, see R. Hummel, *Die Auseinandersetzung zwischen Kirche und Judentum im Mattäusevangelium* (BEvT 33; Munich: Chr. Kaiser, 1966), 76–108, where the interplay of temple, destruction, and deeds of mercy leads to a Matthean perspective on atonement; B. Gerhardsson, "Sacrificial Service and Atonement in the Gospel of Matthew," in *Reconciliation and Hope* (ed. Banks), 25–35; J.P. Meier, *The Vision of Matthew* (New York: Paulist, 1978), 26–39; J.B. Green, "The Death of Jesus," in *The Dictionary of Jesus and the Gospels* (ed. J.B. Green, S. McKnight, and I.H. Marshall; Downers Grove: InterVarsity, 1992), 154–57; Carroll and Green, *Death of Jesus*, 39–59.

[85] On this, cf. esp. Gerhardsson, "Sacrificial Service and Atonement," where ecclesiology is tied tightly into the death of Jesus as the expression of sacrificial service to God.

the death of Jesus is *exemplary* and his followers become so by *participation* in his representative death.

Matthew's particular contributions include, besides straightforward copying of the ransom logion (20:28), a focus on the *forgiveness of sins*.[86] The last supper has the additional clause: "for this is my blood of the covenant, which is poured out for many for the forgiveness of sins" (26:28). That addition appears to be a Matthean rendering of Isaiah 53:12. Forgiveness of sins figures in the Matthean landscape, if not prominently then at least quite obviously. The name *Yeshua* (1:21) is given to Jesus because he will save his people from sins and because he is *Immanuel* (1:22-23). Whether *Yeshua* is rooted in *Immanuel* or *Immanuel* is defined by the saving from sins is unclear and matters little here. But, Jesus' ministry of forgiveness is connected to his being the shepherd of Israel (2:6) and to his healing ministries (8:14-17; 9:1-8; 12:15-21). One can theologize that Matthew envisions forgiveness and healing in the cross, but one might just as easily argue that he sees *Yeshua* as the forgiving agent in all his ministries. Thus, the cross forgives because it is an instance of the ministry of *Yeshua*, or the cross forgives because it is there that sacrifice is offered. For Matthew, the forgiveness of *Yeshua* is ingested in the reenactment of Jesus' last supper as his followers participate in his death (26:28). The words of Birger Gerhardsson are worthy of careful attention, when commenting on salvation in Matthew: "There is no suggestion that this [saving] is to happen exclusively through his sacrificial death."[87]

Matthew extends the eschatological transition of the crucifixion of Jesus by highlighting not only the Markan texts that evoke the onset of the great tribulation, but also by adding apocalyptic signs. In particular, Matthew has Jesus' death trigger the general resurrection (27:51-53), which is a fulfillment of Zechariah 14:4-5 (LXX). Second, it is a Gentile who first confesses Jesus as Son of God (27:54), and this universalism is for Matthew a sign of the last days (8:5-13; 21:43; 22:1-14; 28:16-20). That confession by the centurion, in Matthew's rendering, is generated by the earthquake, an event of the great tribulation (27:54). Jesus' resurrection (28:2-4) is another event easily connected to the great tribulation and the turn of the ages.

LUKE-ACTS AND THE DEATH OF JESUS[88]

From beginning to end, and not unlike the other Christians traditions, Luke-Acts emphasizes the *divine necessity* of Jesus' suffering[89] as part of the scriptural

---

[86] See the nice study of C. Ham, "The Last Supper in Matthew," *BBR* 10 (2000): 53–69.

[87] Gerhardsson, "Sacrificial Service and Atonement," 26.

[88] See Carroll and Green, *Death of Jesus*, 60–81; Fitzmyer, *Luke the Theologian*, 203–33; L.L. Morris, *The Cross in the New Testament* (Grand Rapids: Eerdmans, 1965), 63–143; Hooker, *Not Ashamed of the Gospel*, 78–93; Grayston, *Dying, We Live*, 229–32.

[89] J.T. Squires, "The Plan of God," in *Witness to the Gospel* (ed. I.H. Marshall and D. Peterson; Grand Rapids: Eerdmans, 1998), 19–39.

plot in God's plan (Luke 1:1; 22:22, 37; 24:26-27, 44-49; Acts 2:25-28, 34-35; 3:17-18; 4:28; 8:35; 13:27). Jesus must die in Jerusalem, and his death there is the second exodus (9:31; 13:31-33). Another emphasis of Luke-Acts is the offer of forgiveness in Jesus, though once again this forgiveness is apparently not granted exclusively through the cross. Instead, as we saw with Matthew, a comprehensive salvation and forgiveness are brought by Jesus as Messiah in the totality of his mission and work (cf. Luke 1:77-89; 3:3; 5:20, 30, 32; 7:36-50; 11:4; 15:1-32; 18:9-14; 19:1-10; 23:3 Acts 2:38-39; 3:16; 4:12, 30; 15:11; 16:31; 20:21; 26:18).[90]

What strikes the reader, especially the one trained to think of atonement in the terms of Anselm, is that for Luke-Acts the grace of the Lord Jesus Messiah is effected by both *death* and *resurrection* as a single, comprehensive event that may also be seen as his exaltation. This is noticeable in the passion predictions, where death and vindication are tied together (cf. Luke 9:22, 43-45; 18:31-34; 20:17; 22:25-30), but it becomes a profound feature of the gospel message of Acts, and I list here an abundance of references where this is indicated: 1:3, 22; 2:23-24, 31-33, 36; 3:13, 16; 4:2, 10; 5:30-32; 7:54-56; 10:39-43; 13:27-31, 36-41; 17:3, 18, 31; 26:23. The divinely-ordained suffering of Jesus is a prelude to his resurrection, and the two combined make for the glorified, vindicated Lord Jesus as Messiah who dispenses the Holy Spirit. Luke's emphasis on Christ's glory has led some (especially those in the wake of E. Käsemann) to posit that Luke has replaced a *theologia crucis* with a *theologia gloriae*.[91] The lack of emphasis on the cross is most notable in Acts (where one expects it might appear more often in early Christian preaching summaries), but its absence in the Gospels is no more noticeable than in Mark and Matthew.

As in the other Gospels, in Luke's Gospel Jesus is rejected (e.g., 2:34-35; 4:22-30; 7:30-35) and anticipates his own death (e.g., 9:22, 43-45; 12:49-51; 18:31-34), warns of coming judgment (19:41-44; 21:5-38; 23:26-31), and calls his followers to run the gauntlet as he has done (14:27; cf. Acts 9:5). As the one who calls others to muster courage, he is the *exemplar* of the crucified life (9:23-27, 46-48; 22:24-27). At the last supper, Luke knows of Jesus' meal as a Passover meal (22:8), and if one prefers the longer text, a *new covenant* where Jesus' blood is poured out (22:19b-20). Jesus' death will not prevent the coming of the kingdom (22:16, 17). For Luke, the death of Jesus is the *hour of darkness* (22:53cd; 23:44-45) when the innocent man (23:4-5, 6-16, 39-43, 47) is put to death. But, that death is the onset of the eschatological turning of the tide when the darkness comes (23:44-45),[92] the curtain splits in two (23:45), and they recog-

---

[90] See C. Stenschke, "The Need for Salvation," 125–44, and B. Witherington III, "Salvation and Health in Christian Antiquity," 45–66, in *Witness to the Gospel* (ed. Marshall and Peterson).

[91] See E. Käsemann, "Ministry and Community in the New Testament," in his *Essays on New Testament Themes* (SBT 41; London: SCM, 1964), 63–94.

[92] Much is made of this for Lukan soteriology in F.J. Matera, "The Death of Jesus according to Luke," *CBQ* 47 (1985): 469–85.

nize the innocence of Jesus. But, as is seen in the Luke-Acts depiction, this innocent crucified man is raised from the dead and becomes recognized for who he
is at the meal at Emmaus (24:30-32). Clearly, then, the death of Jesus plays a
heavy role in the Lukan plan of redemptive history.[93]

Perhaps the most notable feature of Luke-Acts pertaining to the death of
Jesus is the textually contaminated statement of Acts 20:28. It is not possible here
to engage the textual evidence, but it is likely that the original text had *church of
God* (rather than *Lord*) and that was modified with *that he obtained with his blood*
(rather than *with his own Son*). In which case, Acts presents a Paul who sees the
church as having been ransomed/purchased at the price of the death of Jesus
Christ.[94] The theology is quite similar to Mark 10:45, much like Paul (e.g., Rom.
3:21-25), and quite unlike anything else in Luke-Acts, unless one appeals to the
soteriology of the last supper as part of a redemption theology.

Like the other Jesus tradition material, Luke-Acts does not focus salvation
on the cross but on the kingdom-bringing mission of Jesus as Messiah that
involved a life, a death, a resurrection, a glorified exaltation, and a sending of the
Holy Spirit to his followers to accomplish mission. Luke's theology ought to be
compared favorably with the primitive tradition behind Philippians 2:5-11.
Furthermore, without exploring the theme, Acts shows Jesus as the Servant of
Isaiah (Acts 3:13, 26; 4:27, 30; 8:32-33; cf. Isa 53:7-8, 11; 61:1). Thus, the cross
is an *integral part* of Jesus' kingdom mission, but is neither the entirety nor all-
consuming goal of that mission. Also like the other Gospels, the cross is an
instrument of shame, but more importantly, the divinely destined entry to the
completion of Jesus' kingdom mission in his resurrection and exaltation. As
such, it is fundamental to embrace the cross in order to embrace Jesus. Thus, the
depiction of Jesus' death in Luke-Acts is more along the lines of a representative
death for others to follow and embrace, an eschatological death that turns history's time clock to a new era, and the necessary prelude to glorification that
paves the way for others to experience the Spirit's transformation and power on
the path to final glory. Luke's theology focuses on this last feature, without min-
imizing the other two.

HEBREWS AND THE DEATH OF JESUS[95]

No theologian of earliest Christianity has transformed the message of Jesus
about the kingdom more thoroughly than *Auctor Hebraeos*, and he does so by

---

[93] So Fitzmyer, *Luke the Theologian*, 212; I.H. Marshall, *Luke: Historian and Theologian* (Grand
Rapids: Zondervan, 1989), 170–75.

[94] On this, cf. Barrett, *Acts*, 2:976–77.

[95] See O. Kuss, "Der theologische Grundgedanke des Hebräerbriefes," in his *Aufsätze zur Exegese
des neuen Testaments* (vol. 1 of *Auslegung und Verkündigung*; Regensburg: F. Pustet, 1963), 281–328;
B. Lindars, *The Theology of the Letter to the Hebrews* (NTT; Cambridge: Cambridge University
Press, 1991), 84–101; A.N. Chester, "Hebrews: The Final Sacrifice," in *Sacrifice and Redemption*
(ed. S.W. Sykes; Cambridge: Cambridge University Press, 1991), 57–72; Carroll and Green, *Death*

taking the cultus of ancient Israel and standing it on its head by exploring the fulfillment of that cultus in the death of Jesus. As Otto Kuss has so ably demonstrated, what was scandalous became salvific (the cross) and what was soteriological became typological (the cult).[96] And no early theologian has more profoundly *interpreted* the significance of Jesus (his death and resurrection especially) in light of the Tanakh—leaving behind a quasi-letter with insights—into the eschatological significance of Jesus and glimpses into a sort of Christianity that is about as knowable as *Auctor's* mysterious Melchizedek. What for moderns is rather mundane, old school stuff (the theology of Hebrews), is but one more example of the hermeneutical creativity and theological narration of the earliest Christians.

Where to begin? I suggest Hebrews 10:10, 12-14, and 12:18-24, quoted here in full to put on our table and as complete a disclosure of his perspective as we can find:

> [10]And it is by God's will that we have been sanctified through the offering of the body of Jesus Christ once for all. . . . [12]But when Christ had offered for all time a single sacrifice for sins, "he sat down at the right hand of God," [13]and since then has been waiting "until his enemies would be made a footstool for his feet." [14]For by a single offering he has perfected for all time those who are sanctified.

And in the author's final appeal:

> [18]You have not come to something that can be touched, a blazing fire, and darkness, and gloom, and a tempest, [19]and the sound of a trumpet, and a voice whose words made the hearers beg that not another word be spoken to them. [20](For they could not endure the order that was given, "If even an animal touches the mountain, it shall be stoned to death." [21]Indeed, so terrifying was the sight that Moses said, "I tremble with fear.") [22]But you have come to Mount Zion and to the city of the living God, the heavenly Jerusalem, and to innumerable angels in festal gathering, [23]and to the assembly of the firstborn who are enrolled in heaven, and to God the judge of all, and to the spirits of the righteous made perfect, [24]and to Jesus, the mediator of a new covenant, and to the sprinkled blood that speaks a better word than the blood of Abel.

These two sections illustrate the transformation of language at the hand of *Auctor Hebraeos*. We have "sanctified," "offering of the body of Jesus Christ," "once for all," "perfected," the "heavenly Jerusalem," "mediator of a new covenant," and "better." Most of *Auctor's* theology is here—as long as one recalls that it is God's grace (not his wrath) that sets it all in motion (2:9). It might be gathered into the following bundles of thoughts.

of Jesus, 133–39; Hooker, *Not Ashamed of the Gospel*, 112–24; Grayston, *Dying, We Live*, 254–75; Stuhlmacher, *Biblische Theologie des Neuen Testaments*, 2:92–97; Koester, *Hebrews*, 118–22; S.W. Hahn, "A Broken Covenant and the Curse of Death," *CBQ* 66 (2004): 416–36.
[96] Kuss, "Der theologische Grundgedanke," in *Aufsätze zur Exegese des neuen Testaments*, 1:312–13.

First, Jesus is the incarnation of God as a complete and total human being (2:11-18; 7:26-28) who descends into an earthly existence in order to be perfected (2:10; 5:9; 7:29), to live a faithfully obedient life (3:2), to be tempted (2:18; 4:15), to be sinless (4:15), to offer prayers and supplication with profound earnestness (5:7), and to suffer (2:10, 18; 5:7-8). The Christology could hardly be higher (cf. 1:2, 3, 6, 8, 10-12).

Second, this earthly life of Jesus is one that leads to an ascension into the heavenly Temple and, as with Paul and Luke-Acts, the issue of the earthly humiliation and heavenly exaltation provides the gifts of forgiveness and purification of sins (1:3b; 2:9; 9:14, 22; 10:10-14; 12:24; 13:12, 20), salvation (2:10; 5:9; 7:25), sanctification (2:11—a near equivalent of Paul's "justification"), destruction of the devil and death (2:14-15; 5:7), redemption (9:12, 15), "expiation" (2:17), an eternal inheritance (9:15), the removal of sin (9:26), the bearing away of sins (9:28), grace (12:24), and direct access to the "sanctuary" (10:19). For *Auctor*, however, the tilt is in the direction of the death of Jesus as a self-sacrifice, often spoken of as the blood (2:9, 17; 7:22, 27; 9:12, 14, 22, 26; 12:24; 13:20). If Luke-Acts leans toward the exaltation, *Auctor* speaks more often of the first member of the two-stage act of redemption. And, his focus on this first member is to depict what Jesus' death *provides* for the followers of Jesus, that is those who have faith (11) and are partakers of both Christ (3:14) and the Spirit (6:4).

As the one who provides all these dimensions of salvation, *Auctor* describes Jesus as "apostle" (3:1), "pioneer" (2:10; 12:2), the "source" (5:9), the "forerunner" (6:20), the "surety" (7:22), the "mediator" (9:15; 12:24), "perfecter" (12:1-2), and especially the "great high priest" who mediates the "new covenant" (e.g., 5:5, 10; 7:20-22; 8:6-13; 10:1-18 et al.). It is neither possible nor necessary to develop the concept of the new covenant for this author, but the concept is profound because for *Auctor* the days of the Torah and the old covenant are now obsolete (cf. 7:11, 18-19; 10:9, 18). In the new covenant Jesus is the Son (3:1-5), a sinless sacrifice (4:15; 7:26-28; 9:14), in the line of Melchizedek (6:13-7:28), perfect (8:7-13), eternal (7:3, 16-17, 24), made such by an "oath" (7:20-23) for the heavenly sanctuary (8:1-2, 6; 9:11-15, 23-28), and these from the Spirit (8:8-12; 10:16-18). As the great high priest, developing a thought in Psalm 110:4, Jesus perfects salvation for his followers because of his "once-for-all" mission (7:27; 9:12, 26, 28; 10:10, 12). *Auctor* sees in the accomplishment of Jesus the completion of Yom Kippur and the covenant ceremony of Exodus 24 on Good Friday (cf. Heb 9:1-10, 12, 14; Lev 16; Heb 9:15-28; Exod 24:4-8). Thus, one might say that Jesus' sacrificial act is *representative*—for he paves the way as apostle, pioneer, forerunner, source, and perfecter—and *vicarious*—for he does for others (2:9; 9:14, 28) what no priest could do before "the time of reformation" (9:10; RSV). There is, in my judgment, no indication that *Auctor* thought in terms of either penal substitution or of wrath being vented on Jesus in his death. In the theology of this book, Jesus offers himself as the sacrifice for others; his sinless sacrifice is not an endurance of punishment so much as the provision of redemption in the new era (7:27; 9:12, 26).

Where that wrath does appear is on the heads of those who do not follow Jesus as exemplar of one faithful to the covenant in obedience and moral perseverance. Thus, the warning passages of Hebrews evoke constancy (2:1-4; 3:7–4:13; 5:11–6:12; 10:19-39; 12:1-29),[97] and the readers are called to run the gauntlet with Jesus as the pioneer and perfecter of faith (11:1–12:11, esp. 12:1-2). It intrigues that *Auctor* so centralizes the example of Jesus that he can depict Moses thinking that "abuse suffered for the Christ" (11:26) is of more significance than wealth. And, as Jesus was cast from the city so also the followers of Jesus are to join him in the place of suffering because, for both, the eternal city is what matters (13:12-14).

THE PETRINE TRADITION AND THE DEATH OF JESUS[98]

We can dismiss 2 Peter as saying little about the death of Jesus. That author tells us that his readers have been cleansed from sin (2 Pet 1:9), have been bought by him (2:1), and have escaped corruption by their knowledge of Jesus Christ (2:20-22), but not once does he connect either of these provisions to the death of Jesus. We can assume, but it is an inference only, that the author saw these benefits in the death of Jesus Christ. And this in sharp contrast to 1 Peter, where the death of Jesus figures prominently, even paradigmatically.

1 Peter—whose author I shall call Peter, the single author who embodies a solid expression of the Petrine tradition—carries on the indissoluble connection of Jesus' death and resurrection. Thus, the "new birth" derives from the creative power of the resurrection (1 Pet 1:3, 23); the prophets were investigating the sufferings and subsequent glory of the Messiah (1:11); the living stone is the vindicated one who was previously rejected (2:4, 6-8); and Jesus' own death led to the vindication and glory of the resurrection (1:20-21; 3:18-22 [where Peter reuses the Enochic mythology]; cf. 4:6). Not that Peter does not find the gravity of salvation in the death of the sinless Jesus (2:22-23), for he apparently does (cf. 2:21-25), but the overall thrust of Peter's theology is that the death and resurrection accomplished salvation. In fact, Peter has Jesus explore the realm of the spirits and death to accomplish salvation.

Peter sees the death and resurrection, or the death by itself, as providing *salvation*—a massive term for Peter that refers to the past (3:20), the present (1:2,[99] 10; 3:21), and especially the future redemption at the coming of Jesus Christ

---

[97] See S. McKnight, "The Warning Passages of Hebrews," *TrinJ* 13 (1992): 21–59.

[98] See Carroll and Green, *Death of Jesus*, 139–42; Hooker, *Not Ashamed of the Gospel*, 125–30; Grayston, *Dying, We Live*, 238–53; Stuhlmacher, *Biblische Theologie des Neuen Testaments*, 2:75–78; Elliott, *1 Peter*, 103–9, 110–11.

[99] The twofold object of *eis* in 1:2, its connection to "elect sojourners" (1:1), and the formal way Peter divides believers from unbelievers by using "obedience" and "disobedience" (1:22; 2:8; 4:17), suggests that "sprinkled with his blood" refers to the establishment of the new covenant in the death of Jesus Christ (Exod 24:8), rather than the consecration or sanctification of the believer (cf. Exod 29:21; Lev 8:30).

(1:5, 9; 2:2; 4:18). In addition, Jesus' death provides forgiveness of sins (1:18-21; 2:24; 3:18a) and grace (1:10), and is the act of God that transfers the sinful person into a life of obedience (1:18; 2:24-25; 3:18, 21) where their wandering ends under the watchful care of the shepherd (2:25). For Peter, there is a special connection between the life of faith and baptism (3:21).

Of particular importance to the life of the baptized for Peter is the call to suffer with Christ (e.g., 1:6-9; 2:18-25; 3:13-22; 4:1-6, 12-18; 5:1, 10) because he has been the paradigmatic exemplar of the life of obedience, suffering, and final vindication (2:18-25; 3:13-22; 4:13; 5:1). The focus Peter gives to this running of the gauntlet after Jesus, contrasting as it does with what we know of his life in the Gospels (cf. Mark 8:27–9:1; 14:26-31, 66-72), evinces a radical transformation on the part of Peter. He now embraces the cross as the paradigm of life (yea, death and life). In a saying of considerable distress to interpreters, but evidently less to the readers of Peter, suffering with Jesus disciplines the life away from sinful behaviors (4:1).

Peter's lines at times suggest that he has thought more deeply on the *mechanics* of the atoning death of Jesus. Jesus is clearly a once-for-all (3:18) sacrifice (1:2) and a Passover victim (1:19), and he has suffered for others (2:21b) as a sinless sacrifice (2:22-23) and as one who has healed by his physical wounds (2:24). As such, Jesus carried away on his shoulders the sins of others (2:24) and suffered for sins, the just one for the unjust (3:18a). This atoning death of Jesus is not just an example: it transfers the faithful to a life of righteousness (2:24; 3:18c). There can be little question that Peter thinks Jesus' death is *vicarious*—he suffers for the benefit of others—and *representative*—as his suffering becomes theirs at times. It is entirely possible that "the righteous for (*hyper*) the unrighteous" is substitutionary, though Peter refrains from explaining how the death works to the benefit of the unrighteous. Was it a death instead of theirs or simply for their benefit? Peter does not tell us.

The Johannine Tradition and the Death of Jesus[100]

The tradition history of the Johannine tradition (John, 1–3 John, Revelation) is so intricate and complex that no attempt will be made here to layer the tradition and so to open up the discussion of the death of Jesus along tradition-historical lines. Themes will be traced from the Fourth Gospel to the letters to the Apocalypse, but no historical judgment about chronology is thereby offered.

Unlike the Synoptics, where the emphasis is kingdom, the Johannine context of the death of Jesus moves along several lines: Jesus is the incarnate word of God (John 1:1-14; 1 John 2:3; 2 John 7) who is also in his incarnational work the presence of the glory of God (e.g., 1:14; 21:19). In this work it is he who

---

[100] Carroll and Green, *Death of Jesus*, 82–109, 142–47 (where they omit 1 John); Hooker, *Not Ashamed of the Gospel*, 94–111, 130–37; Grayston, *Dying, We Live*, 276–335; Stuhlmacher, *Biblische Theologie des Neuen Testaments*, 2:238–47.

has been sent by the Father and who brings life (e.g., John 5:24-30) and love (3:16; 13:1, 15, 34-35), and in so doing separates light from darkness (8:12; 9:5; 12:46; 1 John 1:5-7). In this context, the death of Jesus takes on several distinctive as well as (by now clearly) traditional features.

First, Jesus knows his death is coming and knows this is the reason he has been sent to earth by his Father. Thus, he knows of and predicts his death pervasively in the Johannine Gospel (2:19; 3:14; 6:51; 7:33; 12:7-8, 23-26, 32-33; 13:1, 33; 14:19, 30; 16:16-24, 28; 17:11; cf. 18:32) as he is rejected—also just as pervasively (e.g., 1:10-11; 3:11-21; 15:18-25). Most especially, however, he knows he has come to die. Thus, in a new interpretation laid over the Gethsemane tradition, Jesus says in John 12:27-28:

> 27"Now my soul is troubled. And what should I say—'Father, save me from this hour'? No, it is for this reason that I have come to this hour. 28Father, glorify your name." Then a voice came from heaven, "I have glorified it, and I will glorify it again."

And, at 18:11, John writes,

> Jesus said to Peter, "Put your sword back into its sheath. Am I not to drink the cup that the Father has given me?"

It is not just that Jesus knows and faces his death more squarely in the Fourth Gospel, but that this is the mission the Father has given to him.

That is, secondly, the Father has sent the Son to die, and in so doing to save and give life and bring light. Thus, the Father sent the Son "to save the world through him" (John 3:17; cf. 4:42; 10:9; 12:47; 1 John 4:11); he sent the Son to the world in order that the Son, who has life in himself, might give life to those who believe in him (John 5:21, 24-30; 6:33; 10:10, 28; 14:19; 20:31; cf. also 1 John 2:25; 3:9); and he sent the Son to give light (John 8:12; 9:5; 12:46). A particular crystallization of this theme is that Jesus is the bread of life, and those who eat his flesh and drink his blood will find life (John 6:25-59). The Father's sending is surely indicated in the scriptural precedent for the Son's rejection and death (e.g., John 18:9; 19:23-24, 36-37; 20:9). This is why, when Jesus has finally died, his work is pronounced "finished" (John 19:30).

Without tracing a moment of tension, however, the Fourth Evangelist can also say the Son sacrificed himself, and that it is he who lays down his own life (6:51; 10:11-18; cf. 1 John 3:16). He knows he is to die, and he faces that death courageously; that death is part of the Father's plan, but the Son is also fully involved in the act of dying by making his death a self-sacrifice. This self-sacrifice is a death for others, for the world (*hyper*; John 6:51; 10:11-18; 1 John 3:16; cf. also John 11:51-52; 18:14). How that death is *for* the world/others is not spelled out. At the minimum, it benefits the world by removing sins and providing life.

Fourth, as with the rest of the early Christian theologians, the Fourth Evangelist makes the death and resurrection/exaltation indissoluble. Jesus is rejected and crucified according to the plan of the Father, but that death must be seen as part of a single act of glorification and exaltation, that is, a vindication through resurrection and ascension (2:19; 8:14, 28; 10:17; 13:1, 31-32; 17:5; 20–21). It is obvious that for the Fourth Evangelist the life Jesus brings through his ministry is a life granted because of the merits of a life-producing resurrection and exaltation. The entirety of his work is written into the fabric of his earthly ministry. But it is in this way that the author works into the life of Jesus an inclusive incorporation of believers into his life-giving work. Thus, the believer is "in him" as a branch is in a tree, and as the Son is in the Father (15:1-17) and Jesus prays that his followers may be "one" in him, as he is one with the Father (17:20-23). Their inclusion in him permits their death to be transformed into life.

It is this inclusion, fifth, that turns Jesus' very life into an exemplar of abundant living before the Father, the Son, and the Paraclete. The followers are to run the gauntlet after Jesus (12:23-26), they are to love as he has loved them (15:12-13), and in general they are to be like the master (15:20). This theme explodes with force in the Apocalypse, where the seer will urge the followers of Jesus to live faithfully through the great tribulation (see below). The same theme is found in the letters as well (1 John 3:16; 4:11, 19): as Jesus laid down his life, so they are to lay down their life.

It is difficult to know, sixth, what to make of the "water and blood" of the crucifixion of Jesus (John 19:34; cf. 1 John 5:6-9), but it is safe to think that the language functions as either an antic-docetic notation or a symbol for purification. Along similar lines, it is clear that John finds it important that Jesus dies at the same time as do the *Pesah* victims at the temple (18:28, 39; 19:14), but it is not altogether clear what kind of atonement theology he finds in such a connection. If Jesus is the Passover victim, ingested at some personal level for his followers, it would mean he is the center of the celebration and that in which they participate in order to memorialize the redemption. It would also mean he would be the protector from the wrath of the slaying angel of YHWH.

Seventh, it is this theology of the eschatological lamb of wrath that permits a tight connection of the death of Jesus with the witness of John the Baptist: John declares that Jesus is the "Lamb of God who takes away [*airo*] the sin of the world" (1:29, 36).[101] Scholars have debated vigorously the connotation of Lamb of God—connecting it to a variety of potential sources in the Tanakh and Jewish traditions—but none is as compelling as the eschatological Lamb (*1 En.* 90:9-12; *T. Jos.* 19:8; *T. Benj.* 3:8) who will occupy center stage in Revelation (e.g., Rev 5:6-14; 13:18).[102] As the eschatological Lamb, Jesus "removes sin"—

[101] On Lamb of God, see P. Stuhlmacher, "Das Lamm Gottes–eine Skizze," in *Frühes Christentum* (ed. H. Lichtenberger; vol. 3 of *Geschichte—Tradition—Reflexion*; ed. H. Cancik, H. Lichtenberger, P. Schäfer; 3 vols.; Tübingen: Mohr Siebeck, 1996), 3:529–42.
[102] Stuhlmacher, "Das Lamm Gottes–eine Skizze," in *Frühes Christentum* (ed. Lichtenberger), connects John 1:29, 36 (along with Rev 1:5; 5:9; 7:14; 12:11) to the *Tamid* offering of Exod 29:38-42; Num 28:3-8; Ezek 46:13-15 as well as to the Servant of Isaiah in Isaiah 53. From a priestly

that is, he is the one through whom the eschatological forgiveness of sins (e.g., Jer 31:31-34) will be accomplished (cf. John 1:29; 8:21, 24; 1 John 3:5). John's language then evokes the notion of Jesus as eschatological purger of Israel rather than sacrifice for individual forgiveness. Put differently, this is the Fourth Evangelist's equivalent of the Q tradition in which John sees Jesus as the one who will baptize with the Holy Spirit and fire (Q 3:16b-17).

Not that the Johannine tradition is unaware of individual forgiveness being found in the death of Jesus. So, for an eighth observation of the Johannine tradition, 1 John 2:2 and 4:20 describe Jesus' death as an atoning sacrifice. And that "not for ours only but also for the sins of the whole world" (2:2)—that is, Jesus' death provides for universal atonement. His death "cleanses" from all sin (1:7; 3:5) those who walk in the light and believe in Jesus (1:7, 9). Not only is Jesus an atoning sacrifice, but he is also an advocate with the Father (2:1-2). What might John have meant by atoning sacrifice (*hilasmos*)? The issue is simple: is Jesus that which propitiates the wrath of God or that which expiates the sins of humans? Is his work directed at the Father or at the people's sins or both?[103] The focus of both 2:2 and 4:10 is unambiguously the sins of the people, and leads to the conclusion that the language of the term, within the letter, is that of expiation, or atoning sacrifice rather than propitiation, especially if the Day of Atonement is in mind in 1 John 2:1-2 (Lev 16:30).[104] However, in light of the presence of wrath in the Johannine tradition, we would be remiss in omitting every sense of propitiation from the term (e.g., John 3:36; Rev 6:15-17; 19:15-21). Furthermore, 1 John 2:1-2 clearly depicts Jesus as mediating between the people and the Father, and this lends credence to the notion of propitiation, even if that sense is subordinate to the removal of sins.[105] What shouldn't be forgotten is that the author of this letter has an unmistakable setting for this sort of teaching: the issue is about the *transfer* from a life of sin to a life of righteousness. His context is moral: the one forgiven is the one who is walking in the light.

When we turn to the Apocalypse, we have an important tenth observation: the wrath of the Lamb occupies a central feature of the seer's vision of how history will unfold. Thus, the Lamb pours out his wrath as an expression of God's wrath (6:15-17; 11:18; 14:10, 19-20; 15:1; 16:4-6, 17-21; 19:15-21). Here we have an explosive force of wrath that emerges only rarely in the previous material examined (cf. John 1:29, 36). But it is this perspective on the death of Jesus

---

perspective, the *Tamid* offering is unquestionably the first connection made to the term *lamb*, and if John (who is putatively behind this term in John 1:29, 36) is developing an alternative to the temple cultus, then more weight can be given to this suggestion of Stuhlmacher. That the Lamb of God in John and the Apocalypse are to be connected directly to the Servant of Isaiah 53 is more difficult to demonstrate for Stuhlmacher's thesis.

[103] For an extensive, and balanced account, see esp. Brown, *Epistles*, 217–22.

[104] Ibid., 220–21.

[105] For two who see both propitiation and expiation, cf. Smalley, *1,2,3 John*, 38–40; Marshall, *Epistles*, 117–20.

that opens the window on how the Apocalypse sees the death of Jesus. The Lamb is the instrument of wrath because it is he who "was slain" (5:6-14; 13:18). It is his blood, as the slain Lamb of God, that purchases a people (5:9) and makes them fit to become a kingdom of priests (1:6; 5:10; 20:6; 22:5). In other words, the Lamb's death is all about securing a people who are fit for God's presence and heavenly worship. Thus, the blood of the Lamb makes people white in purity (7:14)—fit for worship—and enables them to overcome persecution so they can endure long enough to enter the new Jerusalem (12:11).

This Lamb of God paves the way for followers to worship in the final city of God, and the Lamb (through the seer) calls the "the followers of the Lamb" (14:4) to a life of steadfast endurance as they run the gauntlet after Jesus. In so running faithfully (e.g., 2–3), they will be invited to the wedding of the Lamb (19:6-9; 21:9-27). The Lamb's paving of the way is simply a variant of the early Christian refrain that Jesus' death and vindication cannot be separated: in Revelation, the death of Jesus is indissolubly connected to the resurrection and enthronement of the Lamb. The Lamb who was slain is the Lamb who now reigns from the center of the throne (1:5, 7, 18; 2:8; 5:5, 6, 12-13; 7:9-17; 11:15; 14:1; 22:1, 3). He is the firstfruits (14:4). Therefore, the followers are called to participate in and endure a similar type of suffering (1:9; 6:9-11; 7:13-17; 11:18; 12:1-17; 17:14; 18:24; 20:4): the who was slain and enthroned promises the suffering saints a share in his glory.

THE CHURCH'S THEOLOGIANS OF ATONEMENT

The beginning is the end. That is, the end of one's theology of the atonement is determined by where one begins. Aulén begins with the image of a rescue, Anselm (so they say) with a courtroom—though I think it better to see him in the academy working out a theory at the hands of his student Boso—and Abelard, well, who knows where he began? Each limits the horizon by the size of the window he looks from. Any self-respecting theory of the atonement must be broad enough to encompass the various biblical images, but we are getting ahead of ourselves.

I sketch here only the rudiments of what I call an *ecclesial atonement theory*. The issue, so far as I see it, is not the how of the atonement—there are various valid options for working out the how—but the whereunto. And the answer to the whereunto question is simple: the design of the atonement is to create a *community*, an *ecclesia*, a *koinonia*, a *zoe*, a *new creation*. The purpose is to take humans in one condition and put them in another condition, to take them from being enslaved—from being in Adam, from being sinful—and put them in freedom, in Christ, and in holiness.

The New Testament witness is that this transfer occurs through the death and resurrection of Jesus Christ—at Golgotha and on Easter morning (not to miss also Pentecost). It is an entire weekend, not just Good Friday or Easter morning; it is a weekend called Grace. In these events, Jesus is both representative and substitute, paving the way for those who are to follow by trusting in him, by obeying him, or in better terms, by loving him. The focus of the NT witness, again, is on the body and on the cosmos, not on the individual—though this does not rob individuals of significance. The death of Jesus protects the followers of Jesus from condemnation and ushers them into being right with God—so that, as an *ecclesial body*, they may worship God, love him, and serve him on earth while they await the final day when they will receive the total redemption of their bodies.[106]

This is what the New Testament tells us about the death of Jesus. What it tells us, very clearly, goes right back to Jesus, who told his followers that his death would protect them, liberate them, and usher them into the kingdom of God.

EXCURSUS: CHASING DOWN PAUL'S THEOLOGICAL SHIP

Debates surround the starting point of Paul's theology—should it begin with his experience of conversion? with his apostolic, missionary vocation? or with the systemic logic of his thought? Only of late has the first option been taken with utter seriousness, as can be seen in J. Becker, *Paul: Apostle to the Gentiles*, P. Stuhlmacher's *Biblische Theologie*, J.D.G. Dunn's *Theology of Paul the Apostle*, S. Hafemann's *Suffering and Ministry*, N.T. Wright's *What Saint Paul Really Said*, and (less completely) T.R. Schreiner, *Paul, Apostle of God's Glory in Christ: A Pauline Theology*.

(1) Older scholarship has focused on the centering of Paul's thought in the concept of justification, and this can be seen in Martin Luther as well as in E. Käsemann, *New Testament Questions of Today*, especially "'The Righteousness of God' in Paul," 168–82. (2) Rudolf Bultmann found the center of Paul's thought in the human crisis of the word of the cross, or in his anthropology; see his *Theology*; see also G. Strecker, *Theology of the New Testament*, 9–216. (3) A fundamental breakthrough occurred with the insight that Paul's theology was essentially grounded in *Heilsgeschichte* or salvation-history; see esp. J.C. Baker, *Paul the Apostle*; K. Stendahl, *Paul Among Jews and Gentiles*; one should also read in this context the great work of W.D. Davies, *Paul and Rabbinic Judaism*. (4) Albert Schweitzer, along with others, argued that "justification" was subsidiary to what he called "Christ-mysticism" in an apocalyptic setting (*The Mysticism of Paul the Apostle*) and he was followed in some important respects in the seminal study of E.P. Sanders, *Paul and Palestinian Judaism*. (5) The recent study of N.T. Wright, *What Saint Paul Really Said*, modifies several approaches to present a center in a politico-salvation-historical framework of fulfillment of Old Testament expectation. (6) Nearly all agree with J.D.G. Dunn, that the real center of Paul's theology is Christ (*Theology of Paul the Apostle*).

[106] See now the incisive study of R.R. Reno, *Redemptive Change* (Harrisburg: Trinity Press International, 2002).

It is my belief that the refocusing by Pauline scholars on the apostolic, missionary vocation and theology of Paul (e.g., Beker, Stuhlmacher, Hafemann) leads to a refocusing of Paul's theology of the death of Jesus so that it takes on an *ecclesial* rather than a *juridical* shape. However, one can begin presenting Paul's theology in a variety of locations and still be true to his theology: one might begin (as few have done) with the Torah, for it was there that Paul first experienced the gospel of Jesus Christ; or one might begin with the theological shaping of Romans (as did Dunn), or with theology proper (so T.R. Schreiner), or with a salvation-historical framework (Beker, Wright, Ridderbos), or with Paul's experience of the gospel (Becker). Thus, one might begin with what Paul discovered first in his experience, or what is most fundamental to Paul's theological thinking, or what is most often the issue at hand, or with what is the most complete statement (e.g., Romans). The issue is not so much where one begins; instead, it is the *decision* to integrates the multifaceted nature of Pauline thought. While some might disagree with Dunn's organizing of Paul's theology (which is a rather predictable set of Christian theological categories), what most impresses is the flexibility he maintains as he winds through each category, and the cross-references he enjoins upon his readers to other categories and sections of the book. If Dunn maintains that Pauline theology is a dialogue with Paul, he also demonstrates that the dialogue obtains as well for one category with another.

What is the meaning of *gospel* for Paul? Recent studies of gospel shed light on Paul's understanding of Jesus' death. In particular, the gospel needs to be understood as the declaration of eschatological redemption (the precise metaphor varies in Paul's preaching and teaching) in the life, death, burial, resurrection, and exaltation of Jesus the Messiah as Lord for all who believe, and this gospel is the climax of God's redemptive designs in and through the history of his people, beginning with Abraham and Israel and climaxing in the church. On this, cf. J.D.G. Dunn, *Theology of Paul the Apostle*, 163–81; N.T. Wright, *What Saint Paul Really Said*, 39–62; P. Stuhlmacher, *Biblische Theologie*, 1:311–26.

What is the meaning of *righteousness of God* in Pauline thought? This most troubled expression of Paul has received a nice taxonomy in Wright, *What Saint Paul Really Said*, 101, where the following breakdown occurs:

1.0 Subjective
    1.1   Moral
          1.1.1   Distributive justice
          1.1.2   Covenant faithfulness
    1.2   Salvation-creating power
          1.2.1   Acts of loving faithfulness
          1.2.2   Non-covenantal actions (cosmic, social)

2.0 Objective
    2.1   Standing from God
          2.1.1   Imputed
          2.1.2   Imparted (transformative)
    2.2   Standing with God
          2.2.1   Natural
          2.2.2   Divinely wrought

One might say that the old-fashioned impasse of righteousness being either imparted or imputed, or God's moral quality vs. forensic standing, is behind us. But, there are still those who think that E.P. Sanders' line is not to be followed, and these scholars tend to prefer the older objective interpretations of *righteousness of God.*

Paul's theology is not systematics; instead, he is grasped best when at least the following seven Pauline principles are kept on the table as we proceed through his letters. *First,* the gospel is the grace of God in revealing Jesus as Messiah and Lord for everyone who believes; *second,* everyone stands behind one of the twin heads of humanity, Adam and Christ; *third,* Jesus Christ is center stage, and it is participation in him that transfers a person from the Adam line to the Christ line; *fourth,* the church is the body of Christ on earth; *fifth,* (salvation-)history does not begins with Moses but with Abraham and the promise God gave to him, and finds its crucial turning point in Jesus Christ—but will run its course until the consummation in the glorious lordship of Christ over all; *sixth,* Christian behavior is determined by the Holy Spirit, not the Torah; *seventh,* Paul is an apostle and not a philosopher or systematic theologian. These principles springs into action when Paul meets his various threats (circumcision, wisdom, gifts, works of the Torah, ethnocentrism, flesh, rival leaders, and the eschatological fights about the Parousia or the general resurrection).

Works Cited

Abegg, M. "Paul. 'Works of the Law' and MMT." *Biblical Archaeology Review* 20 (1994): 52–55, 82.

Ådna, J., and H. Kvalbein, eds. *The Mission of the Early Church to Jews and Gentiles.* Wissenschaftliche Untersuchungen zum Neuen Testament 127. Tübingen: J.C.B. Mohr (Paul Siebeck), 2000.

Allison Jr., D.C. "'Elijah Must Come First.'" *Journal of Biblical Literature* 103 (1984): 256–58.

————. *The End of the Ages Has Come: An Early Interpretation of the Passion and Resurrection of Jesus.* Philadelphia: Fortress, 1985.

————. *The Intertextual Jesus: Scripture in Q.* Harrisburg: Trinity Press International, 2000.

————. "Jesus and the Covenant: A Response to E.P. Sanders." *Journal for the Study of the New Testament* 29 (1987): 57–78.

————. *Jesus of Nazareth: Millenarian Prophet.* Minneapolis: Fortress, 1998.

————. *The Jesus Tradition in Q.* Harrisburg: Trinity Press International, 1997.

————. *The New Moses: A Matthean Typology.* Minneapolis: Fortress, 1993.

————. *The Sermon on the Mount: Inspiring the Moral Imagination.* New York: Crossroad, 1999.

Andrews, M. "Peirasmos—A Study in Form Criticism." *Anglican Theological Review* 24 (1942): 229–44.

Ankersmit, F.R. *Historical Representation. Cultural Memory in the Present.* Stanford: Stanford University Press, 2002.

Anscombe, G.E.M. *Intention. Library of Philosophy and Logic.* Oxford: Basil Blackwell, 1979.

Anselm, *Cur Deus Homo* [*Why God Became Man*]. Pages 260–356 in his *Major Works.* Edited by B. Davies and G. R. Evans. Oxford: Oxford University Press, 1998.

Antwi, D.J. "Did Jesus Consider His Death to be an Atoning Sacrifice?" *Interpretation* 45 (1991): 17–28.

Appleby, Joyce, Lynn Hunt, and Margaret Jacob. *Telling the Truth about History.* New York: W.W. Norton, 1994. [=AHJ]

Arens, E. *The HAΘON-Sayings in the Synoptic Tradition: A Historico-Critical Investigation.* Orbis biblicus et orientalis 10. Göttingen: Vandenhoeck & Ruprecht, 1976.

Ashton, J. *Studying John: Approaches to the Fourth Gospel.* Oxford: Clarendon, 1994.

———. *Understanding the Fourth Gospel.* Oxford: Clarendon, 1991.

Aune, D.E. *Prophecy in Early Christianity and the Ancient Mediterranean World.* Grand Rapids: Eerdmans, 1983.

Aus, R.D. *The Wicked Tenants and Gethsemane: Isaiah in the Wicked Tenants' Vineyard, and Moses and the High Priest in Gethsemane: Judaic Traditions in Mark 12:1-9 and 14:32-42.* University of South Florida International Studies in Formative Christianity and Judaism 4. Atlanta: Scholars, 1996.

Avemarie, F., and H. Lichtenberger. *Bund und Tora: Zur theologischen Begriffsgeschichte in alttestamentlicher, frühjüdischer und urchrstlicher Tradition.* Wissenschaftliche Untersuchungen zum Neuen Testament 92. Tübingen: J.C.B. Mohr, 1996.

Backhaus, K. "Das Bundesmotiv in der frühkirchlichen Schwellenzeit: Hebräerbrief, Barnasbrief, Dialogus com Tryphone." Pages 211–31 in *Der ungekündigte Bund? Antworten des Neuen Testaments.* Edited by H. Frankemölle. Quaestiones disputatae 172. Freiburg: Herder, 1998.

———. "Gottes nicht bereuter Bund: Alter und neuer Bund in der Sicht des Früh-christentums." Pages 33–55 in *Ekklesiologie des Neuen Testaments: Für Karl Kertelge.* Edited by R. Kampling and T. Söding. Freiburg: Herder, 1996.

———. "Hat Jesus vom Gottesbund gesprochen?" *Theologie und Glaube* 86 (1996): 343–56.

———. *Der neue Bund und das Werden der Kirche: Die Diatheke-Deutung des Hebräerbriefs im Rahmen der frühchristlichen Theologiegeschichte.* Neutestamentliche Abhandlungen 29. Münster: Aschendorffische, 1996.

Bailey, D.P. "Jesus as the Mercy Seat: The Semantics and Theology of Paul's Use of Hilasterion in Romans 3:25." Ph.D. diss., University of Cambridge, 1999.

———. "Jesus as the Mercy Seat: The Semantics and Theology of Paul's Use of Hilasterion in Romans 3:25." *Tyndale Bulletin* 51 (2000): 155–58.

Bammel, E. ed. *The Trial of Jesus: Cambridge Studies in Honour of C.F.D. Moule.* Studies in Biblical Theology. Second Series 13. London: SCM Press, 1970.

———, and C.F.D. Moule, eds. *Jesus and the Politics of His Day.* Cambridge: Cambridge University Press, 1984.

Banks, R. *Reconciliation and Hope: New Testament Essays on Atonement and Eschatology Presented to L.L. Morris on his 60th Birthday.* Grand Rapids: Eerdmans, 1974.

Barbour, R.S. "Gethsemane in the Tradition of the Passion." *New Testament Studies* 16 (1969–1970): 231–51.

Barnett, P. *Jesus and the Logic of History.* Grand Rapids: Eerdmans, 1997.

Barnett, P.W. "The Jewish Sign Prophets—A.D. 40–70—Their Intentions and Origins." *New Testament Studies* 27 (1981): 679–97.

Barrett, C.K. "The Allegory of Abraham, Sarah, and Hagar in the Argument of Galatians." Pages 154–70 in his *Essays on Paul.* Philadelphia: Westminster, 1982.

———. "The Background of Mark 10:45." Pages 1–18 in *New Testament Essays: Studies in Memory of Thomas Walter Manson.* Edited by A. J. B. Higgins. Manchester: Manchester University Press, 1959.

———. *The Holy Spirit and the Gospel Tradition.* 2d ed. London: SPCK, 1966.

———. *Jesus and the Gospel Tradition.* London: SPCK, 1967.

———, ed. *New Testament Essays.* London: SPCK, 1972.

Barth, G. *Der Tod Jesu Christi im Verständnis des Neuen Testaments.* Neukirchen-Vluyn: Neukirchener Verlag, 1992.

Batey, R.A. *Jesus and the Forgotten City.* Grand Rapids: Baker, 1991.

Bauckham, R., ed. *The Book of Acts in Its Palestinian Setting*. Vol. 4 of *The Book of Acts in Its First Century Setting*. Grand Rapids: Eerdmans, 1995.

———. "The Son of Man: 'A Man in My Position' or 'Someone'?" *Journal for the Study of the New Testament* 23 (1985): 23–33.

Bayer, H.F. *Jesus' Predictions of Vindication and Resurrection*. Wissenschaftliche Untersuchungen zum Neuen Testament. Second Series 20. Tübingen: J.C.B. Mohr (Paul Siebeck), 1986.

Beasley-Murray, G.R. *Jesus and the Kingdom of God*. Grand Rapids: Eerdmans, 1986.

Beavis, M.A. "Women as Models of Faith in Mark." *Biblical Theology Bulletin* 18 (1988): 3–9.

Beck, N.A. "The Last Supper as an Efficacious Symbolic Act." *Journal of Biblical Literature* 89 (1970): 192–98.

Becker, Jürgen. *Jesus of Nazareth*. Translated by J.E. Couch. New York: Walter de Gruyter, 1998.

Becker, J. *Messianic Expectation in the Old Testament*. Translated by D.E. Green; Philadelphia: Fortress, 1980.

———. *Paul: Apostle to the Gentiles*. Translated by O.C. Dean, Jr. Louisville: Westminster/ John Knox, 1993.

Beker, J.C. *Paul the Apostle: The Triumph of God in Life and Thought*. Philadelphia: Fortress, 1980.

Bellinger, W.H., and W.R. Farmer, eds. *Jesus and the Suffering Servant: Isaiah 53 and Christian Origins*. Harrisburg: Trinity Press International, 1998.

Bennett, W.J. Jr. " 'The Son of Man Must . . . ' " *Novum Testamentum* 17 (1975): 113–29.

Berdyaev, N. *The Destiny of Man*. Translated by N. Duddington. London: Geoffrey Bles/Centenary, 1945.

———. *The Meaning of History*. Translated by G. Reavey. London: Geoffrey Bles/Centenary, 1945.

Berlin, I. "The Hedgehog and the Fox." Pages 436–98 in *The Proper Study of Mankind: An Anthology of Essays*. Edited by H. Hardy and R. Hausheer. Foreword by Noel Annan. New York: Farrar, Straus & Giroux, 1998.

———. *Historical Inevitability*. Auguste Comte Memorial Trust Lecture 1 (12 May 1953). London: Oxford University Press, 1954.

Best, E. *The Temptation and the Passion: The Markan Soteriology*. Society for New Testament Studies Monograph Series 2. Cambridge: Cambridge University Press, 1965.

Betz, O. "Jesu heiliger Krieg." *Novum Testamentum* 2 (1958): 116–37.

———. "Jesu Tischsegen: Psalm 104 in Lehre und Wirken Jesu." Pages 202–31 in his *Jesus: Der Messias Israels. Aufsätze zur biblischen Theologie*. Wissenschaftliche Untersuchungen zum Neuen Testament 42; Tübingen: J.C.B. Mohr, 1987.

———. *Sermon on the Mount*. Edited by A.Y. Collins; Minneapolis: Fortress, 1995.

Bickermann, E. *The God of the Maccabees: Studies on the Meaning and Origin of the Maccabean Revolt*. Translated by H.R. Moehring. Studies in Judaism in Late Antiquity 32. Leiden: E.J. Brill, 1979.

Bieringer, R. "Traditionsgeschichtlicher Ursprung und theologische Bedeutung der UPER-Aussagen im Neuen Testament." Pages 219–48 in *The Four Gospels*. Vol. 1. Edited by F. Van Segbroeck, et al. Bibliotheca ephemeridum theologicarum lovaniensium 100. Leuven: University Press, 1992.

Black, M. *An Aramaic Approach to the Gospels and Acts*. 3d ed. Oxford: Clarendon, 1967.

———. "The 'Son of Man' Passion Sayings in the Gospel Tradition." *Zeitschrift für die neutestamentliche Wissenschaft und die Kunde der älteren Kirche* 60 (1969): 1–8.

Blair, H.J. "Putting One's Hand to the Plough. Luke ix. 62 in the Light of 1 Kings xix. 19-21." *Expository Times* 79 (1967–1968): 342–43.

Blank, J. "Frauen in den Jesusüberlieferungen." Pages 22–28, 42–48 in *Die Frau im Urchristentum*. Edited by G. Dautzenberg et al. Quaestiones disputatae 95. Freiburg: Herder, 1983.

Bloch, A.B. *The Biblical and Historical Background of the Jewish Holy Days*. New York: Ktav, 1978.

Bloch, M. *The Historian's Craft*. Translated by P. Putnam. Introduction by J.R. Strayer. New York: Vintage, 1953.

Blomberg, C.L. *The Historical Reliability of John's Gospel: Issues and Commentary*. Downers Grove: InterVarsity, 2001.

———. "John and Jesus." Pages 209–26 in *The Face of New Testament Studies*. Edited by S. McKnight and G.R. Osborne. Grand Rapids: Baker, 2004.

Bock, D. *Blasphemy and Exaltation in Judaism: The Charge against Jesus in Mark 14:53-65*. Wissenschaftliche Untersuchungen zum Neuen Testament. Second Series 106. Tübingen: J.C.B. Mohr, 1998.

———. *Jesus according to Scripture: Restoring the Portrait from the Gospels*. Grand Rapids: Baker Academic, 2002.

———. *Studying the Historical Jesus: A Guide to Sources and Methods*. Grand Rapids: Baker Academic, 2002.

Bockmuehl, M., ed. *The Cambridge Companion to Jesus*. Cambridge Companions to Religion. Cambridge: Cambridge University Press, 2001.

Bode, E.L. *The First Easter Morning: The Gospel Accounts of the Women's Visit to the Tomb of Jesus*. Analecta biblica 45. Rome: Biblical Institute Press, 1970.

Boersma, H. *Violence, Hospitality, and the Cross*. Grand Rapids: Baker, 2004.

Boffetti, J. "How Richard Rorty Found Religion." *First Things* 143 (2004): 24–30.

Bokser, B.M. *The Origins of the Seder: The Passover Rite and Early Rabbinic Judaism*. Berkeley: University of California Press, 1984.

Bolyki, J. *Jesus Tischgemeinschaften*. Wissenschaftliche Untersuchungen zum Neuen Testament. Second Series 96. Tübingen: J.C.B. Mohr, 1998.

Borg, M. *The Heart of Christianity: Rediscovering a Life of Faith*. San Francisco: HarperSanFrancisco, 2003.

———. *Jesus, A New Vision: Spirit, Culture, and the Life of Discipleship*. San Francisco: Harper & Row, 1987.

Bornkamm, G. *Jesus von Nazareth*. 12th German ed. Stuttgart: W. Kohlhammer, 1980. [Translated as *Jesus of Nazareth* by I. McLuskey, F. McLuskey, and J.M. Robinson. New York: Harper & Row, 1960].

Botterweck, G.J., and H. Ringgren, eds. *Theological Dictionary of the Old Testament*. Translated by J.T. Willis, G.W. Bromiley, and D.E. Green. 8 vols. Grand Rapids, Eerdmans, 1974–. [= *TDOT*]

Boughton, L.C. "'Being Shed for You/Many': Time-Sense and Consequences in the Synoptic Cup Quotations." *Tyndale Bulletin* 48 (1997): 249–70.

Bowker, J.W. "Prophetic Action and Sacramental Form." Pages 129–37 in *The New Testament Message*. Edited by F.L. Cross. Part 2 of *Studia Evangelica* II–III. Texte und Untersuchungenzur Geschichte der Altchristlichen 88. Berlin: Akadamie, 1964.

Boyarin, D. *Dying for God*. Stanford: Stanford University Press, 1999.

Brabazon, J. *Albert Schweitzer: A Biography*. New York: Putnam, 1975.

Bradshaw, P.F., and L.A. Hoffman, eds. *Passover and Easter: Origin and History to Modern Times*. Vol. 5 of *Two Liturgical Traditions*. Notre Dame: University of Notre Dame Press, 1999.

Brandon, S.G.F. *Jesus and the Zealots: A Study of the Political Factor in Primitive Christianity*. Manchester: Manchester University Press, 1967.

Braumann, G. "Leidenskelch und Todestaufe (Mc 10 38f.)." *Zeitschrift für die neutestamentliche Wissenschaft und die Kunde der älteren Kirche* 56 (1965): 178–83.

Breisach, E. *Historiography: Ancient, Medieval, and Modern*. 2d ed. Chicago: University of Chicago Press, 1994.

Breytenbach, C. "Versöhnung, Stellvertretung and Sühne: Semantische und traditionsgeschichtliche Bemerkungen am Beispiel der paulinischen Briefe." *New Testament Studies* 39 (1993): 59–79.

Broadhead, E.K. "Mark 14:1-9: A Gospel within a Gospel." *Paradigms* 1 (1985): 32–41.

Brodie, T.L. "The Departure for Jerusalem (Luke 9:51-56) as a Rhetorical Imitatio of Elijah's Departure for the Jordan (2 Kgs 1:1-2:6)." *Biblica* 70 (1989): 96–109.

———. "Luke 9:57-62: A Systematic Adaptation of the Divine Challenge to Elijah (1 Kings 19)." *Society of Biblical Literature Seminar Papers* 28 (1989): 237–45.

Brondos, D. "Why Was Jesus Crucified? Theology, History and the Story of Redemption." *Scottish Journal of Theology* 54 (2001): 484–503.

Brooke, G.J. "4Q500 1 and the Use of Scripture in the Parable of the Vineyard." *Dead Sea Discoveries* 2 (1995): 268–94.

Brooks, S.H. "Matthew's Community: The Evidence of His Special Sayings." Journal for the Study of the New Testament: Supplement Series 16. Sheffield: Sheffield Academic, 1987.

Brown, C. *New International Dictionary of New Testament Theology*. 4 vols. Grand Rapids, 1975–1985. [= *NIDNTT*]

Brown, P. *The Rise of Western Christendom: Triumph and Diversity, A.D. 200–1000*. Malden, Mass.: Blackwell, 2003.

Brown, R.E. *The Birth of the Messiah: A Commentary on the Infancy Narratives in the Gospels of Matthew and Luke*. 2d ed. Anchor Bible Reference Library. New York: Doubleday, 1993.

———. *The Death of the Messiah: From Gethsemane to the Grave. A Commentary on the Passion Narratives in the Four Gospels*. 2 vols. Anchor Bible Reference Library. New York: Doubleday, 1994.

———. "The Pater Noster as an Eschatological Prayer." Pages 275–320 in his *New Testament Essays*. Garden City: Doubleday, 1968.

Brown, R.E., et al. *Mary in the New Testament*. Philadelphia: Fortress, 1978.

Brown, R.E., K.P. Donfried, and J. Reumann, eds. *Peter in the New Testament. From discussions by Paul J. Achtemeier, et al.* Minneapolis: Augsburg, 1973.

Brown, S. *Apostasy and Perseverance in the Theology of Luke*. Analecta biblica 36. Rome: Pontifical Biblical Institute, 1969.

Bruce, F.F. *The New Testament Development of Old Testament Themes*. Grand Rapids: Eerdmans, 1969.

Bryan, S. *Jesus and Israel's Traditions of Judgement and Restoration*. Society for New Testament Studies Monograph Series 117. Cambridge: Cambridge University Press, 2002.

Buchanan, G.W. *Jesus: The King and His Kingdom*. Macon, Ga.: Mercer University Press, 1984.

Bultmann, R. *The History of the Synoptic Tradition.* Translated by J. Marsh. Rev. ed. New York: Harper & Row, 1963. Repr. 1976.

———. *Jesus Christ and Mythology.* New York: Scribner, 1958.

———. *The Presence of Eternity: History and Eschatology.* The Gifford Lectures, 1955. New York: Harper, 1957.

———. "The Primitive Christian Kerygma and the Historical Jesus." Pages 15–42 in *The Historical Jesus and the Kerygmatic Christ: Essays on the New Quest of the Historical Jesus.* Edited by C.E. Braaten and R.A. Harrisville. New York: Abingdon, 1964.

———. *Theology of the New Testament.* Translated by K. Grobel. 2 vols. New York: Scribner, 1951, 1955.

Burchard, C. "The Importance of Joseph and Aseneth for the Study of the New Testament: A General Survey and a Fresh Look at the Lord's Supper." *New Testament Studies* 33 (1987): 102–34.

Burkett, D. "The Nontitular Son of Man: A History and Critique." *New Testament Studies* 40 (1994): 504–21.

———. *The Son of Man Debate: A History and Evaluation.* Society for New Testament Studies Monograph Series 107. Cambridge: Cambridge University Press, 1999.

Burkitt, F.C., and A.E. Brooke. "St Luke xxii 15, 16: What Is the General Meaning?" *Journal of Theological Studies* 9 (1907–1908): 569–72.

Burns, Robert. "My Native Land Sae Far Awa'." Page 462 in *The Poems and Songs of Robert Burns (1759–1796).* Collins: Glasgow, n.d.

Burridge, R.A. *What Are the Gospels? A Comparison with Graeco-Roman Biography.* Society for New Testament Studies Monograph Series 70. Cambridge: Cambridge University Press, 1992.

Byrskog, S. "A New Perspective on the Jesus Tradition: Reflections on James D.G. Dunn's Jesus Remembered." *Journal for the Study of the New Testament* 26 (2004): 45–71.

———. *Story as History—History as Story.* Tübingen: J.C.B. Mohr, 2000.

Cadoux, C.J. *The Historic Mission of Jesus: A Constructive Re-examination of the Eschatological Teaching in the Synoptic Gospels.* London: Lutterworth, 1941.

Caird, G.B. *New Testament Theology.* Edited by L.D. Hurst. Oxford: Clarendon, 1994.

Cameron, P.S. "Lead Us Not into Temptation." *Expository Times* 101 (1989–1990): 299–301.

Camfield, F.W. "The Idea of Substitution in the Doctrine of the Atonement," *Scottish Journal of Theology* 1 (1948): 282–93.

Campbell, A.F., and M.A. O'Brien. *Unfolding the Deuteronomistic History: Origins, Upgrades, Present Text.* Minneapolis: Fortress, 2000.

Campbell, W.S. "Covenant and New Covenant." Pages 179–83 in *Dictionary of Paul and His Letters.* Edited by G.F. Hawthorne, R.P. Martin, and D.G. Reid. Downers Grove: InterVarsity, 1993.

Cancik, H., H. Lichtenberger, and P. Schäfer, eds. *Geschichter–Tradition– Reflexion: Festschrift für Martin Hengel zum 70: Geburtstag.* 3 vols. Tübingen: J.C.B. Mohr (Paul Siebeck), 1996.

Carmichael, D. "David Daube on the Eucharist and the Passover Seder." *Journal for the Study of the New Testament* 42 (1991): 45–67.

Carmignac, J. "Hebrew Translations of the Lord's Prayer: An Historical Survey." Pages 18–79 in *Biblical and Near Eastern Studies: Essays in Honor of William Sanford LaSor.* Edited by G. Tuttle. Grand Rapids: Eerdmans, 1978.

Carr, E.H. *What Is History?* George Macaulay Trevelyan Lectures, January–March 1961. 1962. Repr. New York: Knopf, 1987.

Carroll, J.T., and J.B. Green. *The Death of Jesus in Early Christianity.* Peabody, Mass.: Hendrickson, 1995.

Carson, D.A., P.T. O'Brien, and M.A. Siefrid, eds. *Justification and Variegated Nomism.* Vol. 1 of *The Complexities of Second Temple Judaism.* Tübingen: Mohr Siebeck; Grand Rapids: Baker Academic, 2001.

Case, S.J. *The Christian Philosophy of History.* Chicago: University of Chicago Press, 1943.

Casey, M. "Aramaic Idiom and the Son of Man Problem: A Response to Owen and Shepherd." *Journal for the Study of the New Testament* 25 (2002): 3–32.

———. *Aramaic Sources of Mark's Gospel.* Society for New Testament Studies Monograph Series 102. Cambridge: Cambridge University Press, 1998.

———. *From Jewish Prophet to Gentile God: The Origins and Development of New Testament Christology.* Edward Cadbury Lectures at the University of Birmingham, 1985–1986. Louisville: Westminster/John Knox, 1991.

———. "General, Generic, and Indefinite: The Use of the Term 'Son of Man' in Aramaic Sources and in the Teaching of Jesus." *Journal for the Study of the New Testament* 29 (1987): 21–56.

———. "Idiom and Translation: Some Aspects of the Son of Man Problem." *New Testament Studies* 41 (1995): 164–82.

———. "The Jackals and the Son of Man (Matt. 8:20//Luke 9:58)." *Journal for the Study of the New Testament* 23 (1985): 3–22.

———. "No Cannibals at Passover!" *Theology* 96 (1993): 199–205.

———. "The Original Aramaic Form of Jesus' Interpretation of the Cup." *Journal of Theological Studies* 41 (1990): 1–12.

———. *Son of Man: The Interpretation and Influence of Daniel 7.* London: SPCK, 1979.

Cathcart, K.J., and R.P. Gordon, trans. *The Targum of the Minor Prophets.* The Aramaic Bible 14. Wilmington: Michael Glazier, 1989.

Ceresko, A.R. "The Rhetorical Strategy of the Fourth Servant Song (Isaiah 52:13-53:12): Poetry and the Exodus-New Exodus." *Catholic Bible Quarterly* 56 (1994): 42–55.

Chapman, D.W. "Perceptions of Crucifixion among Jews and Christians in the Ancient World." Ph.D. diss., Cambridge, 1999.

Charlesworth, J.H. "The Historical Jesus and Exegetical Theology." *Princeton Seminary Bulletin* 22 (2001): 45–63.

———. "Jesus and Jehohanan: An Archaeological Note on Crucifixion." *Expository Times* 84 (1972–1973): 147–50.

Charlesworth, J.H., et al., eds. *The Messiah: Developments in Earliest Judaism and Christianity.* Princeton Symposium on Judaism and Christian Origins. Minneapolis: Fortress, 1992.

Charlesworth, J.H., and J. Zias. "Crucifixion: Archaeology, Jesus, and the Dead Sea Scrolls." Pages 273–89 in *Jesus and the Dead Sea Scrolls.* Edited by J.H. Charlesworth. Anchor Bible Reference Library. New York: Doubleday, 1992.

Chavasse, C. "Jesus: Christ and Moses." *Theology* 54 (1951): 244–50, 289–96.

Childs, B.S. *The Book of Exodus: A Critical, Theological Commentary.* Old Testament Library; Philadelphia: Westminster, 1974.

———. *Isaiah.* Old Testament Library. Louisville: Westminster John Knox, 2001.

Chilton, B.D. *A Feast of Meanings: Eucharistic Theology from Jesus through Johannine Circles.* Supplements to Novum Testamentum 72. Leiden: E.J. Brill, 1994.

———. *A Galilean Rabbi and His Bible: Jesus' Use of the Interpreted Scripture of His Time.* Vol. 8 of *Good News Studies.* Wilmington: Michael Glazier, 1984.

————. *The Isaiah Targum: Introduction, Translation, Apparatus and Notes.* The Aramaic Bible 11. Collegeville, Minn.: Liturgical, 1987.

————. "Jésus, le *mamzer* (Mt 1.18)." *New Testament Studies* 46 (2001): 222–27.

————. *Jesus' Prayer and Jesus' Eucharist: His Personal Practice of Spirituality.* Valley Forge, Penn.: Trinity Press International, 1997.

————. *Pure Kingdom: Jesus' Vision of God.* Grand Rapids: Eerdmans, 1996.

————. *Rabbi Jesus: An Intimate Biography.* New York: Doubleday, 2000.

————, ed. *Targumic Approaches to the Gospels: Essays in the Mutual Definition of Judaism and Christianity.* Studies in Judaism. Lanham, Md.: University Press of America, 1986.

————. *The Temple of Jesus: His Sacrificial Program within a Cultural History of Sacrifice.* University Park: The Pennsylvania State University Press, 1992.

Chilton, B.D., and C.A. Evans, eds. *Authenticating the Words of Jesus.* New Testament Tools and Studies 28.1. Leiden: E.J. Brill, 1999.

————, eds. *Studying the Historical Jesus: Evaluations of the State of Current Research.* Leiden: E.J. Brill, 1994.

Christiansen, E.J. *The Covenant in Judaism and Paul: A Study of Ritual Boundaries as Identity Markers.* Arbeiten zur Geschichte des antiken Judentums und des Urchristentums 27. Leiden: E. J. Brill, 1995.

Clark, D.K. *Empirical Realism: Meaning and the Generative Foundation of Morality.* Lanham, Md.: Rowman & Littlefield, 2003.

Clines, D.J.A., ed. *Dictionary of Classical Hebrew.* 5 vols. Sheffield: Sheffield Academic, 1993–. [= *DCH*]

Coakley, J.F. "The Anointing at Bethany and the Priority of John." *Journal of Biblical Literature* 107 (1988): 241–56.

Cohen, J.M. *Moments of Insight: Biblical and Contemporary Jewish Themes.* London: Vallentine, Mitchell, 1989.

Cohn-Sherbok, D. *The Jewish Messiah.* Edinburgh: T&T Clark, 1997.

Collingwood, R.G. *The Idea of History.* Oxford: Clarendon, 1946.

Collins, A.Y. "The Charge of Blasphemy in Mark 14.64." *Journal for the Study of the New Testament* 26 (2004): 379–401.

————. "Finding Meaning in the Death of Jesus," *Journal of Religion* 78 (1998): 175–96.

————. "The Signification of Mark 10:45 among Gentile Christians," *Harvard Theological Review* 90 (1997): 371–82.

Collins, J.J. "The Root of Immortality: Death in the Context of Jewish Wisdom." *Harvard Theological Review* 71 (1978): 177–92.

————. *The Scepter and the Star: The Messiahs of the Dead Sea Scrolls and Other Ancient Literature.* Anchor Bible Reference Library. New York: Doubleday, 1995.

Corley, K. *Private Women, Public Meals: Social Conflict in the Synoptic Tradition.* Peabody, Mass.: Hendrickson, 1993.

————. *Women and the Historical Jesus: Feminist Myths of Christian Origins.* Santa Rosa, Calif.: Polebridge, 2002.

Cox, M, ed. *E.H. Carr: A Critical Appraisal.* New York: Palgrave, 2000.

Craig, W.L. *Reasonable Faith: Christian Truth and Apologetics.* Rev. ed. Wheaton: Crossway, 1994.

Croce, B. *History: Its Theory and Practice.* Translated by D. Ainslie. New York: Russell & Russell, 1960.

Crossan, J.D. *The Historical Jesus: The Life of a Mediterranean Jewish Peasant.* San Francisco: HarperSanFrancisco, 1991.

———. *In Fragments: The Aphorisms of Jesus.* San Francisco: Harper & Row, 1983.

———. *Jesus: A Revolutionary Biography.* San Francisco: HarperSanFrancisco, 1994.

———. "The Resurrection of Jesus in its Jewish Context." *Neotestamentica* 37 (2003): 29–57.

———. *Who Killed Jesus? Exposing the Roots of Anti-Semitism in the Gospel Story of the Death of Jesus.* San Francisco: HarperSanFrancisco, 1995.

Crüsemann, F. *The Torah: Theology and Social History of Old Testament Law.* Translated by A.W. Mahnke. Minneapolis: Fortress, 1996.

Cullmann, O. *The Christology of the New Testament.* Translated by S.C. Guthrie and C.A M. Hall. Rev. ed. Philadelphia: Westminster, 1963.

———. *Early Christian Worship.* Translated by A.S. Todd and J.B. Torrance. Philadelphia: Westminster, 1978.

———. *Prayer in the New Testament.* Translated by John Bowden. Overtures to Biblical Theology. Minneapolis: Fortress, 1995.

Cullmann, O., and F.J. Leenhardt. "The Meaning of the Lord's Supper in Primitive Christianity." Pages 5–23 in *Essays on the Lord's Supper.* Translated by J.G. Davies. Atlanta: John Knox, 1975.

Dahl, N.A. *Jesus the Christ.* Edited by D.H. Joel; Minneapolis: Fortress, 1991.

Dalman, G. *Jesus-Jeshua: Studies in the Gospels.* Translated by P.P. Levertoff. New York: Macmillan, 1929.

———. *The Words of Jesus Considered in the Light of Post-Biblical Jewish Writings and the Aramaic Language.* Translated by D.M. Kay. 1898; Repr. Edinburgh: T&T Clark, 1902.

Daly, R.J. "The Eucharist and Redemption: The Last Supper and Jesus' Understanding of His Death." *Biblical Theology Bulletin* 11 (1981): 21–27.

———. *The Origins of the Christian Doctrine of Sacrifice.* Philadelphia: Fortress, 1978.

Daube, D. "Death as Release in the Bible." *Novum Testamentum* 5 (1962): 82–104.

———. "The Anointing at Bethany and Jesus' Burial." Pages 312–24 in his *The New Testament and Rabbinic Judaism.* Peabody, Mass.: Hendrickson, n.d.

———. *He that Cometh.* St. Paul's Lecture 5. London: London Diocesan Council for Christian-Jewish Understanding, 1966.

———. *The New Testament and Rabbinic Judaism.* Peabody, Mass.: Hendrickson, n.d.

Daube, D. "The Significance of the Afikoman." *Pointer* 3.3 (1968): 4–5.

———. *Wine in the Bible.* St. Paul's Lecture 13. London: London Diocesan Council for Christian-Jewish Understanding, 1974.

Davies, P.E. "Did Jesus Die as a Martyr-Prophet?" *Biblical Research* 2 (1957): 19–30.

Davies, W.D. *Paul and Rabbinic Judaism: Some Rabbinic Elements in Pauline Theology.* 3d ed. Philadelphia: Fortress, 1980.

Dawson, C. *Religion and the Rise of Western Culture.* New York: Sheed & Ward, 1950.

Delling, G. "βαπτισμα βαπτισθηναι." *Novum Testamentum* 2 (1957–1958): 92–115.

Delobel, J., ed. *Logia: Les Paroles de Jésus—The Sayings of Jesus: Mémorial Joseph Coppens.* Bibliotheca ephemeridum theologicarum lovaniensium 59. Leuven: Leuven University Press, 1982.

Demel, S. "Jesu Umgang mit Frauen nach den Lukasevangelium." *Biblische Notizen* 57 (1991): 41–95.

Denaux, A. "L'hypocrisie des Pharisees et le dessein de Dieu: Analyse de Lc., XIII, 31–33." Pages 245–85 in *L'Evangile de Luc: Probleme littéraires et théologique.* Edited by F. Neirynck. Rev. ed. Bibliotheca ephemeridum theologicarum lovaniensium 32. Leuven: Leuven University Press, 1989.

Denney, J. *The Christian Doctrine of Reconciliation*. Cunningham Lectures, 1917. London: Hodder & Stoughton, 1917.

———. *The Death of Christ: Its Place and Interpretation in the New Testament*. 3d ed. New York: Armstrong, 1903.

Derrett, J.D.M. "Christ's Second Baptism (Lk 12:50; Mk 10:38-40)." *Expository Times* 100 (1988–1989): 294–95.

———. *Law in the New Testament*. London: Darton, Longman & Todd, 1970.

———. "The Lucan Christ and Jerusalem: τελειοῦμαι (Lk 13 32)." *Zeitschrift für die neutestamentliche Wissenschaft und die Kunde der älteren Kirche* 75 (1984): 36–43.

———. "Receptacles and Tombs (Mt 23 24-30)." *Zeitschrift für die neutestamentliche Wissenschaft* 77 (1986): 255–66.

Derrett, J.D.M. "'You Build the Tombs of the Prophets' (Lk. 11, 47-51, Mt. 23, 29– 31)." *Texte und Untersuchungen zur Geschichte der altchristlichen Literatur* 102 (1968): 187–93.

Dibelius, M. *Jesus*. Translated by C.B. Hedrick and F.C. Grant. Philadelphia: Westminster, 1949.

Didion, Joan. *Slouching Towards Bethlehem*. New York: Farrar, Straus & Giroux, 1968.

Dodd, C.H. *According to the Scriptures: The Sub-Structure of New Testament Theology*. London: Nisbet, 1952.

———. *The Founder of Christianity*. New York: Macmillan, 1970.

———. "The Historical Problem of the Death of Jesus." Pages 84–101 in his *More New Testament Studies*. Grand Rapids: Eerdmans, 1968.

———. *Historical Tradition in the Fourth Gospel*. London: Cambridge University Press, 1976.

———. *The Interpretation of the Fourth Gospel*. Cambridge: Cambridge University Press, 1953.

———. "Jesus as Teacher and Prophet." Pages 53–66 in *Mysterium Christi: Christological Studies by British and German Theologians*. Edited by G.K.A. Bell and A. Deissmann. London: Longmans, Green, 1930.

———. *The Parables of the Kingdom*. London: Nisbet, 1935.

Douglas, M. "Atonement in Leviticus." *Jewish Quarterly Review* 1 (1993–1994): 109–30.

———. *Leviticus as Literature*. Oxford: Oxford University Press, 1999.

Douglas, M. "Power and Praise in the Hodayot: A Literary Critical Study of 1QH 9:1– 18:14." Ph.D. diss., University of Chicago, 1998.

Douglas, R.C. "A Jesus Tradition Prayer (Q 11:2b-4; Matt 6:9b-13; Luke 11:2b-4; Didache 8.2)." Pages 211–15 in *Prayer from Alexander to Constantine: A Critical Anthology*. Edited by M. Kiley, et al. New York: Routledge, 1997.

Drescher, H.-G. *Ernst Troeltsch: His Life and Work*. Translated by J. Bowden. Minneapolis: Fortress, 1993.

Droge. A.J., and J.D. Tabor, *A Noble Death*. San Francisco: HarperSanFrancisco, 1992.

Dunn, J.D.G. *Baptism in the Holy Spirit*. Philadelphia: Westminster, 1970.

———. *Christology*. Vol. 1 of *The Christ and the Spirit: Collected Essays of James D.G. Dunn*. Grand Rapids: Eerdmans, 1998.

———. *Christology in the Making: A New Testament Inquiry into the Origins of the Doctrine of the Incarnation*. 2d ed. London: SCM Press, 1989.

———. *Jesus, Paul and the Law: Studies in Mark and Galatians*. Philadelphia: Westminster/ John Knox, 1990.

———. *Jesus Remembered*. Vol. 1 of *Christianity in the Making*. Grand Rapids: Eerdmans, 2003.

———. *Jesus and the Spirit: A Study of the Religious and Charismatic Experience of Jesus and the First Christians as Reflected in the New Testament*. Philadelphia: Westminster, 1975.

———. "Matthew 12:28/Luke 11:20–A Word of Jesus?" Pages 29–49 in *Eschatology and the New Testament: Essays in Honor of George Raymond Beasley-Murray*. Edited by W.H. Gloer. Peabody, Mass: Hendrickson, 1988.

———. "On History, Memory and Eyewitnesses: In Response to Bengt Holmberg and Samuel Byrskog." *Journal for the Study of the New Testament* 26 (2004): 473–87.

———. *The Partings of the Ways: Between Christianity and Judaism and Their Significance for the Character of Christianity*. Philadelphia: Trinity Press International, 1991.

———. *Pneumatology*. Vol. 2 of *The Christ and the Spirit: Collected Essays of James D.G. Dunn*. Grand Rapids: Eerdmans, 1998.

———. *The Theology of Paul the Apostle*. Grand Rapids: Eerdmans, 1998.

———. *Unity and Diversity in the New Testament: An Inquiry into the Character of Earliest Christianity*. 2d ed. Philadelphia: Trinity Press International, 1991.

Dunnill, J. *Covenant and Sacrifice in the Letter to the Hebrews*. Society for New Testament Studies Monograph Series 75. Cambridge: Cambridge University Press, 1992.

Eco, Umberto. *Serendipities: Language and Lunacy*. Translated by William Weaver. San Diego: Harcourt Brace, 1998.

Ehrman, B.D. *Lost Christianities*. New York: Oxford University Press, 2003.

———. *The Orthodox Corruption of Scripture: The Effect of Early Christological Controversies on the Text of the New Testament*. New York: Oxford University Press, 1993.

Eichrodt, W. *Theology of the Old Testament*. Translated by J.A. Baker. 2 vols. London: SCM Press, 1961.

Ellis, E.E. *The Old Testament in Early Christianity: Canon and Interpretation in the Light of Modern Research*. Grand Rapids: Baker, 1992.

Elton, G.R. *The Practice of History*. New York: Crowell, 1967.

———. *Return to Essentials: Some Reflections on the Present State of Historical Study*. Cambridge: Cambridge University Press, 1991.

Ernest, J.D., ed. and trans. *The Theological Lexicon of the New Testament*. 3 vols. Peabody, Mass., 1994.

Evans, C.A. "Messianic Claimants of the First and Second Centuries." Pages 239–52 in *Noncanonical Writings and New Testament Interpretation*. Peabody, Mass.: Hendrickson, 1992.

———, ed. *Jesus and His Contemporaries: Comparative Studies*. Arbeiten zur Geschichte des antiken Judentums und des Urchristentums 25. Leiden: E.J. Brill, 1995.

Evans, C.A., and P.W. Flint, eds. *Eschatology, Messianism, and the Dead Sea Scrolls*. Studies in the Dead Sea Scrolls and Related Literature. Grand Rapids: Eerdmans, 1997.

Evans, C.A., and W.R. Stegner, eds. *The Gospels and the Scriptures of Israel*. Journal for the Study of the New Testament: Supplement Series 104. Vol. 3 of *Studies in Scripture in Early Judaism and Christianity*. Sheffield: Sheffield Academic, 1004.

Evans, C.S. *The Historical Christ and the Jesus of Faith: The Incarnational Narrative as History*. New York: Oxford University Press, 1996.

Evans, R.J. *In Defence of History*. Rev. ed. London: Granta, 2000.

Faierstein, M.M. "Why Do the Scribes Say that Elijah Must Come First?" *Journal of Biblical Literature* 100 (1981): 75–86.

Farmer, W.R. "The Passion Prediction Passages and the Synoptic Problem: A Test Case." *New Testament Studies* 36 (1990): 558–70.

Fee, G.D. *God's Empowering Presence: The Holy Spirit in the Letters of Paul.* Peabody, Mass.: Hendrickson, 1994.

———. "A Text-Critical Look at the Synoptic Problem." *Novum Testamentum* 22 (1980): 12–28.

Feeley-Harnik, G. *The Lord's Table: The Meaning of Food in Early Judaism and Christianity.* Symbol and Culture Series. Philadelphia: University of Pennsylvania Press, 1981. Repr., Washington, D.C.: Smithsonian Institution, 1994.

Feuillet, A. "La coupe et le baptême de la passion (Mc., x, 35-40; cf. Mt. xx, 20-23; Lc., xxii, 50)." *Revue biblique* 74 (1967): 356–91.

Finkel, A. "The Prayer of Jesus in Matthew." Pages 131–69 in *Standing Before God.* Edited by A. Finkel and L. Frizzoli. New York: Ktav, 1981.

Fisk, B.N. "Offering Isaac Again and Again: Pseudo-Philo's Use of the Aqedah as Intertext." *Catholic Biblical Quarterly* 62 (2000): 481–507.

Fitzmyer, J.A. "More About Elijah Coming First." *Journal of Biblical Literature* 104 (1985): 292–94.

———. *Luke the Theologian: Aspects of His Teaching.* New York: Paulist, 1989.

Foakes Jackson, F.J. and K. Lake, eds. *The Beginnings of Christianity.* Vol. 1 of *The Acts of the Apostles.* 5 vols. Grand Rapids: Baker, 1979.

Fohrer, G. *Die symbolischen Handlungen der Propheten.* 2d ed. Zürich: Zwingli, 1968.

Fortna, R.T., and T. Thatcher, eds. *Jesus in Johannine Tradition.* Louisville: Westminster John Knox, 2001.

France, R.T. *Jesus and the Old Testament: His Application of Old Testament Passages to Himself and His Mission.* London: Tyndale, 1971.

Frankfurt, H.G. *The Reasons of Love.* Princeton: Princeton University Press, 2004.

Fredriksen, P. *Jesus of Nazareth, King of the Jews: A Jewish Life and the Emergence of Christianity.* New York: Knopf, 1999.

Friebel, K.G. *Jeremiah's and Ezekiel's Sign-Acts: Rhetorical Nonverbal Communication.* Journal for the Study of the Old Testament: Supplement Series 283. Sheffield: Sheffield Academic, 1999.

Friedman, R.E. *The Bible with Sources Revealed: A New View into the Five Books of Moses.* San Francisco: HarperSanFrancisco, 2003.

———. *Who Wrote the Bible?* New York: Summit, 1987.

Friedrich, G. *Die Verkündigung des Todes Jesu im Neuen Testament.* Bible et terre sainte 6. Neukirchen: Neukirchener Verlag, 1982.

Fuller, R.H. *The Foundations of New Testament Christology.* New York: Scribner, 1965.

———. *The Mission and Achievement of Jesus: An Examination of the Presuppositions of New Testament Theology.* Studies in Biblical Theology 12. London: SCM Press, 1954.

Fuller, R.H., and P. Perkins. *Who is This Christ? Gospel Christology and Contemporary Faith.* Philadelphia: Fortress, 1983.

Funk, R.W. *Honest to Jesus: Jesus for a New Millennium.* San Francisco: HarperSanFrancisco [Polebridge], 1996.

Funk, R.W., R. Hoover, and the Jesus Seminar. *The Five Gospels: The Search for the Authentic Words of Jesus.* New York: Macmillan [Polebridge], 1993.

Funk, R.W., and the Jesus Seminar, ed. and trans. *The Acts of Jesus: The Search for the Authentic Deeds of Jesus.* San Francisco: HarperSanFrancisco, 1998.

Gaddis, J.L. *The Landscape of History: How Historians Map the Past.* New York: Oxford University Press, 2002.

Galvin, J.P. "Jesus' Approach to Death: An Examination of Some Recent Studies." *Theological Studies* 41 (1980): 713–44.

Garlington, D.B. *Faith, Obedience and Perseverance: Aspects of Paul's Letter to the Romans.* Wissenschaftliche Untersuchungen zum Neuen Testament 79. Tübingen: J.C.B. Mohr, 1994.

———. *"The Obedience of Faith": A Pauline Phrase in Historical Context.* Wissenschaftliche Untersuchungen zum Neuen Testament 38. Second Series Tübingen: J.C.B. Mohr, 1991.

Gathercole, S.J. "The Critical and Dogmatic Agenda of Albert Schweitzer's *The Quest of the Historical Jesus.*" *Tyndale Bulletin* 51 (2000): 261–83.

George, A. "Comment Jésus a-t-il perçu sa propre mort?" *Lumière et vie* 101 (1971): 34–59.

———. " 'Par le doigt de Dieu' (Lc 11, 20)." Pages 127–32 in *Études sur L'Oeuvre de Luc. Sources bibliques.* Paris: Gabalda, 1978.

Gerhardsson, B. "The Matthaean Version of the Lord's Prayer (Matt 6:9b-13): Some Observations." Pages 207–20 in *The New Testament Age: Essays in Honor of Bo Reicke.* Edited by W.C. Weinrich. 2 vols. Macon, Ga.: Mercer University Press, 1984.

Gese, H. *Essays on Biblical Theology.* Translated by K. Crim. Minneapolis: Augsburg, 1981.

Gibson, J. *The Temptations of Jesus in Early Christianity.* Journal for the Study of the New Testament: Supplement Series 112. Sheffield: Sheffield Academic, 1995.

Girard, R. *Things Hidden Since the Foundation of the World.* Research in collaboration with Jean-Michel Oughourlian and Guy Lefort. Translated by S. Bann and M. Metteer. Stanford: Stanford University Press, 1987.

Glatzer, N.N. *The Schocken Passover Haggadah.* New York: Schocken, 1981.

Goguel, M. *The Life of Jesus.* Translated by O. Wyon. New York: Macmillan, 1946.

Goldingay, J. *Israel's Gospel.* Vol. 1 of *Old Testament Theology.* Downers Grove: InterVarsity, 2003.

———. *Models for Interpretation of Scripture.* Grand Rapids: Eerdmans, 1995.

———. *Models for Scripture.* Grand Rapids: Eerdmans, 1994.

Goppelt, L. *Theology of the New Testament.* Edited by Jürgen Roloff. Translated by J.E. Alsup. 2 vols. 1975. Repr. Grand Rapids: Eerdmans, 1981.

———. *Typos: The Typological Interpretation of the Old Testament in the New.* Translated by D.H. Madvig. Foreword by E.E. Ellis. 1939. Repr. Grand Rapids: Eerdmans, 1982.

Gorman, M.J. *Cruciformity.* Grand Rapids: Eerdmans, 2001.

Gorringe, T. *God's Just Vengeance: Crime, Violence, and the Rhetoric of Salvation.* Cambridge: Cambridge University Press, 1996.

Gray, J. *I & II Kings.* Old Testament Library. 2d ed. Philadelphia: Westminster, 1970.

Grayston, K. *Dying, We Live: A New Enquiry into the Death of Christ in the New Testament.* New York: Oxford University Press, 1990.

Green, J.B. "The Death of Jesus." Pages 154–57 in *The Dictionary of Jesus and the Gospels.* Edited J.B. Green, S. McKnight, and I.H. Marshall. Downers Grove: InterVarsity, 1992.

———. "The Death of Jesus and the Ways of God: Jesus and the Gospels on Messianic Status and Shameful Suffering." *Interpretation* 52 (1998): 24–37.

———. *The Death of Jesus: Tradition and Interpretation in the Passion Narrative.* Wissenschaftliche Untersuchungen zum Neuen Testament. Second Series 33. Tübingen: J. C. B. Mohr (Paul Siebeck), 1988.

Green, J.B., and M.D. Baker. *Rediscovering the Scandal of the Cross: Atonement in New Testament & Contemporary Contexts.* Downers Grove: InterVarsity, 2000.

Green, J.B., and M. Turner, eds. *Jesus of Nazareth: Lord and Christ. Essays on the Historical Jesus and New Testament Christology.* Grand Rapids: Eerdmans, 1994.

Grelot, P. "Michée 7,6 dans les évangiles et dans la littérature rabbinque." *Biblica* 67 (1986): 363–87.

Gubler, M-L. *Die frühesten Deutungen des Todes Jesu: Eine motivgeschichtliche Darstellung aufgrund der neueren exegetischen Forschung.* Orbis biblicus et orientalis 15. Freiburg: Universitätsverlag, 1977.

Guillaumont, A., et al. *The Gospel According to Thomas: Coptic Text Established and Translated.* San Francisco: Harper & Row, 1984.

Gunton, C.E. *The Actuality of Atonement: A Study of Metaphor, Rationality and the Christian Tradition.* Grand Rapids: Eerdmans, 1989.

Hafemann, S. *Suffering and Ministry of the Spirit: Paul's Defense of His Ministry in II Corinthians 2:14–3:3.* Grand Rapids: Eerdmans, 1990.

Hagner, D.A. *The Jewish Reclamation of Jesus: An Analysis and Critique of the Modern Jewish Study of Jesus.* Grand Rapids: Zondervan, 1984.

———. "Paul in Modern Jewish Thought." Pages 143–65 in *Pauline Studies: Essays Presented to Professor F.F. Bruce on his 70th Birthday.* Edited by D.A. Hagner and M.J. Harris. Grand Rapids: Eerdmans, 1980.

Hahn, F. "Die alttestamentliche Motive in der urchristlichen Abendmahlsüberlieferung." *Evangelische Theologie* 27 (1967): 33–374.

———. *The Titles of Jesus in Christology: Their History in Early Christianity.* Translated by H. Knight and G. Ogg. New York: World, 1969.

———. "Zum Stand der Erforschung des urchristlichen Abendmahles." *Evangelische Theologie* 35 (1975): 553–63.

Hahn, S.W. "A Broken Covenant and the Curse of Death." *CBQ* 66 (2004): 416–36.

———. "Kinship by Covenant: A Biblical Theological Study of Covenant Types and Texts in the Old and New Testaments." Ph.D. diss., Marquette University, 1996.

Ham, C. "The Last Supper in Matthew." *Bulletin for Biblical Research* 10 (2000): 53–69.

Hamerton-Kelly, R. "A Note on Matthew XII.28 par. Luke XI.20." *New Testament Studies* 11 (1965–1965): 167–69.

Han, K.S. *Jerusalem and the Early Jesus Movement: The Q Community's Attitude Toward the Temple.* Journal for the Study of the New Testament: Supplement Series 207. Sheffield: Sheffield Academic, 2002.

Hanson, A.T. *The Wrath of the Lamb.* London: SPCK, 1957.

Hare, D.R.A. *The Son of Man Tradition.* Minneapolis: Fortress, 1990.

Harris, M.J. *From Grave to Glory: Resurrection in the New Testament.* Grand Rapids: Zondervan, 1990.

———. *Raised Immortal: Resurrection and Immortality in the New Testament.* Grand Rapids: Eerdmans, 1983.

Harris, W.V. *Ancient Literacy.* Cambridge, Mass.: Harvard University Press, 1989.

Haslam, J. *The Vices of Integrity: E.H. Carr, 1892–1982.* New York: Verso, 1999.

Hawthorne, G.F. *The Presence and the Power: The Significance of the Holy Spirit in the Life and Ministry of Jesus.* Dallas: Word, 1991.

Hays, R.B. *The Faith of Jesus Christ: An Investigation of the Narrative Substructure of Galatians 3:1–4:11.* 2d ed. Grand Rapids: Eerdmans, 2002.

Hayward, C.T.R. *The Jewish Temple: A Non-Biblical Sourcebook.* London: Routledge, 1996.

Heinemann, J. "The Background of Jesus' Prayer in the Jewish Liturgical Tradition." Pages

81–89 in *The Lord's Prayer and Jewish Liturgy*. Edited by J.J. Petuchowski and M. Brocke. New York: Seabury, 1978.

Hendel, R.S. "Sacrifice as a Cultural System: The Ritual Symbolism of Exodus 24, 3-8." *Zeitschrift für die alttestamentliche Wissenschaft* 101 (1989): 366–90.

Hengel, M. *The Atonement: The Origins of the Doctrine in the New Testament*. Translated by J. Bowden. Philadelphia: Fortress, 1981.

———. *Between Jesus and Paul: Studies in the Earliest History of Christianity*. Translated by J. Bowden. Philadelphia: Fortress, 1983.

———. *The Charismatic Leader and His Followers*. Translated by J.C.G. Greig. Edinburgh: T&T Clark, 1981.

———. *Crucifixion in the Ancient World and the Folly of the Message of the Cross*. Translated by J. Bowden. Philadelphia: Fortress, 1977.

———. *Hellenism and Judaism: Studies in Their Encounter in Palestine during the Early Hellenistic Period*. Translated by J. Bowden. 2 vols. Minneapolis: Fortress, 1974.

———. *Jews, Greeks and Barbarians: Aspects of the Hellenization of Judaism in the Pre-Christian Period*. Translated by J. Bowden. Philadelphia: Fortress, 1980.

———. *The Johannine Question*. Philadelphia: Trinity Press International, 1989.

———. *Paul Between Damascus and Antioch: The Unknown Years*. With A.M. Schwemer. Translated by J. Bowden. Lousville: Westminster John Knox, 1997.

———. "Der stellvertretende Sühnetod Jesu. Ein Beitrag zur Entstehung des urchristlichen Kerygmas." *Internationale kirchliche Zeitschrift* 9 (1980): 1–25, 135–47.

———. *Studies in Early Christology*. Edinburgh: T&T Clark, 1995.

———. *The Zealots: Investigations into the Jewish Freedom Movement in the Period from Herod I until 70 A.D.* Translated by D. Smith. Edinburgh: T&T Clark, 1989.

Hengel, M., and C. Markschies. *The 'Hellenization' of Judaea in the First Century after Christ*. Translated by J. Bowden. Philadelphia: Trinity Press International, 1989.

Henry, M. *I Am the Truth: Toward a Philosophy of Christianity*. Translated by S. Emanuel. *Cultural Memory in the Present*. Stanford: Stanford University Press, 2003.

Heschel, A.J. *The Prophets*. 2 vols. New York: Harper & Row, 1962.

Heyer, C.J. den. *Jesus and the Doctrine of the Atonement: Biblical Notes on a Controversial Topic*. Translated by J. Bowden. Harrisburg: Trinity Press International, 1998.

Higgins, A.J.B. "'Lead Us Not into Temptation.'" *Expository Times* 58 (1946–1947): 250.

———. "Lead Us Not into Temptation: Some Latin Versions." *Journal of Theological Studies* 46 (1945): 179–83.

Hill, D. *Greek Words and Hebrew Meanings: Studies in the Semantics of Soteriological Terms*. Society for New Testament Studies Monograph Series 5. Cambridge: Cambridge University Press, 1967.

Himmelfarb, G. *The New History and the Old: Critical Essays and Reappraisals*. Rev. ed. Cambridge, Mass.: Belknap, 2004.

Hoffman, L.A. *Beyond the Text: A Holistic Approach to Liturgy*. Bloomington: Indiana University Press, 1987.

———. "A Symbol of Salvation in the Passover Haggadah." *Worship* 53 (1979): 519–37.

Hoffmann, P., N. Brox, and W. Pesch, eds. *Orientierung an Jesus: Zur Theologie der Synoptike: Für Josef Schmid*. Freiburg: Herder, 1973.

Hofius, O. "Ist Jesus der Messias? Thesen." *Jahrbuch für Biblische Theologie* 8 (1993): 103–29.

Holmberg, B. "Questions of Method in James Dunn's Jesus Remembered." *Journal for the Study of the New Testament* 26 (2004): 445–47.

Holmén, Tom. *Jesus and Jewish Covenant Thinking.* Biblical Interpretation Series 55. Boston: E. J. Brill, 2001.

Holt, J.C. *Robin Hood.* London: Thames & Hudson, 1982.

Hooker, M. *From Adam to Christ: Essays on Paul.* Cambridge: Cambridge University Press, 1990.

———. "Interchange and Atonement." *Bulletin of the John Rylands University Library of Manchester* 60 (1978): 462–81.

———. "Interchange in Christ." *Journal of Theological Studies* 22 (1971): 349–61.

———. "Is the Son of Man Problem Really Insoluble?" Pages 155–68 in *Text and Interpretation: Studies in the New Testament Presented to Matthew Black.* Edited by E. Best and R. McL. Wilson. Cambridge: Cambridge University Press, 1979.

———. *Jesus and the Servant: The Influence of the Servant Concept of Deutero-Isaiah in the New Testament.* London: SPCK, 1959.

———. *The Message of Mark.* London: Epworth, 1983.

———. *Not Ashamed of the Gospel: New Testament Interpretations of the Death of Christ.* Didsbury Lectures, 1988. Carlisle, UK: Paternoster, 1994.

———. *The Signs of a Prophet: The Prophetic Actions of Jesus.* Harrisburg: Trinity Press International, 1997.

———. "The Son of Man and the Synoptic Problem." Pages 1:189–201 in *The Four Gospels, 1992: Festschrift Frans Neirynck.* 3 vols. Bibliotheca ephemeridum theologicarum lovaniensium 100. Leuven: Leuven University Press, 1992.

———. *The Son of Man in Mark: A Study of the Background of the Term "Son of Man" and Its Use in St. Mark's Gospel.* London: SPCK, 1967.

Horbury, W. *Jewish Messianism and the Cult of Christ.* London: SCM Press, 1998.

Horbury, W., and B. McNeil, eds. *Suffering and Martyrdom in the New Testament: Studies Presented to G.M. Styler by the Cambridge New Testament Seminar.* Cambridge: Cambridge University Press, 1981.

Horrell, D.G., and C.M. Tuckett, eds. *Christology, Controversy and Community: New Testament Essays in Honour of David R. Catchpole.* Supplements to Novum Testamentum 99. Leiden: E.J. Brill, 2000.

Horsley, R.A. *Jesus and Empire: The Kingdom of God and the New World Disorder.* Minneapolis: Fortress, 2003.

———. *Jesus and the Spiral of Violence: Popular Jewish Resistance in Roman Palestine.* San Francisco: Harper & Row, 1987.

Horsley, R.A, and Jonathan A. Draper. *Whoever Hears You Hears Me: Prophets, Performance, and Tradition in Q.* Harrisburg: Trinity Press International, 1999.

Hoskyns, E., and N. Davey. *The Riddle of the New Testament.* London: Faber & Faber, 1931.

Howard, V. "Did Jesus Speak about His Own Death?" *Catholic Bible Quarterly* 39 (1977): 515–27.

Howell, M., and W. Prevenier. *From Reliable Sources: An Introduction to Historical Methods.* Ithaca: Cornell University Press, 2001.

Hughes, J.J. "Hebrews ix.15ff and Galatians iii.15ff: A Study in Covenant Practice and Procedure." *Novum Testamentum* 21 (1979): 27–96.

Hultgren, A.J. *Jesus and His Adversaries: The Form and Function of the Conflict Stories in the Synoptic Tradition.* Foreword by R.H. Fuller. Minneapolis: Augsburg, 1979.

———. *The Parables of Jesus: A Commentary.* Grand Rapids: Eerdmans, 2000.

Hultgren, S. "The Origin of Paul's Doctrine of the Two Adams in 1 Corinthians 15.45-49." *Journal for the Study of the New Testament* 25 (2003): 343–70.

Hummel, R. *Die Auseinandersetzung zwischen Kirche und Judentum im Mattäusevangelium.* Beiträge zur evangelischen Theologie 33. Munich: Chr. Kaiser, 1966.

Hunter, A. M. *Paul and His Predecessors.* Philadelphia: Westminster, 1961.

Huntjens, J.A. "Contrasting Notions of Covenant and Law in the Texts from Qumran." *Revue de Qumran* 8 (1972–1975): 361–80.

Hurst, L.D. *The Epistle to the Hebrews: Its Background of Thought.* Society for New Testament Studies Monograph Series 65. Cambridge: Cambridge University Press, 1990.

Hurst, L.D., and N.T. Wright, eds. *The Glory of Christ in the New Testament: Studies in Christology in Memory of George Bradford Caird.* Oxford: Clarendon, 1987.

———. *New Testament Theology.* Oxford: Clarendon, 1994.

Hurtado, L.W. *At the Origins of Christian Worship.* Grand Rapids: Eerdmans, 1999.

———. *Lord Jesus Christ: Devotion to Jesus in Earliest Christianity.* Grand Rapids: Eerdmans, 2003.

Ignatieff, M. *Isaiah Berlin: A Life.* New York: Metropolitan Books, 1998.

Ilan, T. *Integrating Women into Second Temple History.* Peabody, Mass.: Hendrickson, 2001.

———. *Jewish Women in Greco-Roman Palestine.* Peabody, Mass.: Hendrickson, 1996.

———. " 'Man Born of Woman . . .' (Job 14:1): The Phenomenon of Men Bearing Metronymes at the Time of Jesus." *Novum Testamentum* 34 (1992): 23–45.

Instone-Brewer, D. "Jesus's Last Passover: The Synoptics and John." *Expository Times* 112 (2001): 122–23.

Jacobs, Alan. *A Theology of Reading: The Hermeneutics of Love.* Boulder: Westview, 2001.

Janowski, B. "Auslösung des verwirkten Lebens: Zur Geschichte und Struktur der biblischen Lösegeldvorstellung." *Zeitschrift für Theologie und Kirch* 79 (1982): 25–59.

Janowski, B., and P. Stuhlmacher, eds. *Der leidende Gottesknecht: Jesaja 53 und seine Wirkungsgeschichte.* Forschungen zum Alten Testament 14. Tübingen: Mohr (Siebeck), 1996.

Jaubert, A. *The Date of the Last Supper.* Translated by I. Rafferty; Staten Island: Alba House, 1965.

———. *La notion d' alliance dans le Judaisme aux abords de l'ère chrétienne.* Paris: Le Seuil, 1963.

Jenkins, Keith. *On "What Is History?": From Carr and Elton to Rorty and White.* London: Routledge, 1995.

———. *The Postmodern History Reader.* London: Routledge, 1997.

———. *Refiguring History: New Thoughts on an Old Discipline.* London: Routledge, 2003.

———. *Re-thinking History.* London: Routledge, 1991, 2003.

———. *Why History?* London: Routledge, 1999.

Jenkins, Philip. *Hidden Gospels: How the Search for Jesus Lost Its Way.* New York: Oxford University Press, 2001.

Jenni, E., ed. *Theological Lexicon of the Old Testament.* With C. Westermann. Translated by M.E. Biddle. 3 vols. Peabody, Mass., 1997.

Jeremias, J. *Abba: Studien zur neutestamentlichen Theologie und Zeitgeschichte.* Göttingen: Vandenhoeck & Ruprecht, 1966.

———. "Die Drei-Tage-Worte der Evangelien." Pages 221–29 in *Tradition und Glaube: Das frühe Christentum in seiner Umwelt: FS K.G. Kuhn.* Edited by G. Jeremias, et al. Göttingen: Vandenhoeck & Ruprecht, 1971.

———. *Die Sprache des Lukasevangeliums: Redaktion und Tradition im Nicht-Markusstoff des dritten Evangeliums.* KEK Sonderband. Göttingen: Vandenhoeck & Ruprecht, 1980.

──────. *The Eucharistic Words of Jesus.* Translated by N. Perrin. Philadelphia: Fortress, 1966, 1977.

──────. *Heiligengräber in Jesu Umwelt (Mt. 23, 29; Lk. 11, 47): Eine Untersuchung zur Volksreligion der Zeit Jesu.* Göttingen: Vandenhoeck & Ruprecht, 1958.

──────. *Jerusalem in the Time of Jesus: An Investigation into Economic and Social Conditions during the New Testament Period.* Translated by F.H. and C.H. Cave. 1962. Repr. Philadelphia: Fortress, 1969.

──────. *Jesus and the Message of the New Testament.* Edited by K.C. Hanson. 1965. Repr. Minneapolis: Fortress, 2002.

──────. *Jesus' Promise to the Nations.* Translated by S.H. Hooke. Studies in Biblical Theology 24. London: SCM Press, 1967.

──────. *New Testament Theology: The Proclamation of Jesus.* Translated by J. Bowden. New York: Scribner, 1971.

──────. *The Prayers of Jesus.* London: SCM Press, 1967.

Johnson, L.T. *The Creed: What Christians Believe and Why It Matters.* New York: Doubleday, 2003.

──────. "The New Testament's Anti-Jewish Slander and Conventions of Ancient Rhetoric." *Journal of Biblical Literature* 108 (1989): 419–441.

──────. *The Real Jesus: The Misguided Quest for the Historical Jesus and the Truth of the Traditional Gospels.* San Francisco: HarperSanFrancisco, 1996.

Jonge, H.J. de. "The Sayings on Confessing and Denying Jesus in Q 12:8-9 and Mark 8:38." *Novum Testamentum* 89 (1997): 105–21.

Jonge, M. de. *Christology in Context: The Earliest Christian Response to Jesus.* Foreword by W.A. Meeks. Philadelphia: Westminster, 1988.

──────. *God's Final Envoy: Early Christology and Jesus' Own View of His Mission.* Grand Rapids: Eerdmans, 1998.

──────. "Jesus' Death for Others and the Death of the Maccabean Martyrs." Pages 142–51 in *Text and Testimony: Essays on New Testament and Apocryphal Literature in Honour of A. F. J. Klijn.* Edited by T. Baarda et al. Kampen: Kok, 1988.

──────. *Jesus, The Servant-Messiah.* New Haven: Yale University Press, 1991.

Juel, D.J. *Messianic Exegesis: Christological Interpretation of the Old Testament in Early Christianity.* Philadelphia: Fortress, 1988.

Kähler, Martin. *The So-Called Historical Jesus and the Historic, Biblical Christ.* Edited and translated by C.E. Braaten. Foreword by P. Tillich. 1896. Repr. Philadelphia: Fortress, 1964.

Kalluveettil, P. *Declaration and Covenant: A Comprehensive Review of Covenant Formulae from the Old Testament and the Ancient Near East.* Analecta biblica 88. Rome: Biblical Institute, 1982.

Kaminouchi, A. de M. *"But it is Not So Among You": Echoes of Power in Mark 10.32-45.* Journal for the Study of the New Testament: Supplement Series 249; New York: T&T Clark, 2003.

Käsemann, E. *Essays on New Testament Themes.* Studies in Biblical Theology 41. London: SCM Press, 1964.

──────. *New Testament Questions of Today.* Translated by W.J. Montague. Philadelphia: Fortress, 1969.

──────. "The Saving Significance of the Death of Jesus in Paul." Pages 46–47 in his *Perspectives on Paul.* Translated by M. Kohl. Philadelphia: Fortress, 1971.

Keck, Leander. *Who is Jesus? History in Perfect Tense*. Columbia: University of South Carolina Press, 2000.

Kertelge, K., ed. *Der Tod Jesu: Deutungen im Neuen Testament*. Quaestiones disputatae 74. Freiburg: Herder, 1976.

Kiley, M. "'Lord, Save My Life' (Ps 116:4) as Generative Text for Jesus' Gethsemane Prayer (Mark 14:36a)." *Catholic Bible Quarterly* 48 (1986): 655–59.

———. "The Lord's Prayer as Matthean Theology." Pages 19–21 in *The Lord's Prayer and Other Prayer Texts from the Graeco-Roman Era*. Edited by J. Charlesworth, et al. Valley Forge, Penn.: Trinity Press International, 1994.

Kiley, M., et al. *Prayer from Alexander to Constantine: A Critical Anthology*. New York: Routledge, 1997.

Kim, S. "Jesus—The Son of God, the Stone, the Son of Man, and the Servant: The Role of Zechariah in the Self-Identification of Jesus." Pages 134–48 in *Tradition and Interpretation in the New Testament: Essays in Honor of E. Earle Ellis for his 60th Birthday*. Edited by G. F. Hawthorne and O. Betz; Grand Rapids: Eerdmans, 1987.

———. *The "Son of Man" as the Son of God*. Wissenschaftliche Untersuchungen zum Neuen Testament 30. Tübingen: J.C.B. Mohr, 1983.

Kinzig, W. "Καινή διαθήκη: The Title of the New Testament in the Second and Third Centuries." *Journal of Theological Studies* 45 (1994): 510–44.

Kittel, G., and G. Friedrich, *Theologische Wörterbuch zum Neuen Testament*. Stuttgart: Kohlhammer, 1932–1979. [Translated as *Theological Dictionary of the New Testament* by G.W. Bromiley. 10 vols. Grand Rapids, 1964–1976.] [= *TDNT*]

Klauck, H.-J. *Herrenmahl und hellenistischer Kult. Eine religionsgeschichtliche Untersuchung zum ersten Korintherbrief*. Neutestamentliche Abhandlungen Neue Folge 15. Münster: Aschendorff, 1982.

Klawans, J. "Interpreting the Last Supper: Sacrifice, Spiritualization, and Anti-Sacrifice." *New Testament Studies* 48 (2002): 1–17.

———. "Was Jesus' Last Supper a Seder?" *Bible Review* 17 (2001): 24–33, 47.

Kleinknecht, K.T. *Der leidende Gerechtfertigte: Die alttestamentlich-jüdische Tradition vom "leidenden Gerechten" und ihre Rezeption bei Paulus*. Wissenschaftliche Untersuchungen zum Neuen Testament. Second Series 13. Tübingen: J.C.B. Mohr (Paul Siebeck), 1984.

Kloppenborg Verbin, J.S. *Excavating Q: The History and Setting of the Sayings Gospel*. Minneapolis: Fortress, 2000.

———. *Q Parallels: Synopsis, Critical Notes, and Concordance*. Foundation and Facets Reference Series. Sonoma, Calif.: Polebridge, 1988.

Knohl, I. *The Messiah Before Jesus: The Suffering Servant of the Dead Sea Scrolls*. Translated by D. Maisel. Berkeley: University of California, 2000.

———. *The Sanctuary of Silence: The Priestly Torah and the Holiness School*. Minneapolis: Fortress, 1995.

Koch, K. "Messias und Menschensohn: Die zweistufige Messianologie der jüngeren Apokalyptic." *Jahrbuch für Biblische Theologie* 8 (1993): 73–102.

Koenig, J. *The Feast of the World's Redemption: Eucharistic Origins and Christian Mission*. Harrisburg: Trinity Press International, 2000.

Kohn, R.L. *A New Heart and a New Soul: Ezekiel, the Exile and the Torah*. Journal for the Study of the Old Testament: Supplement Series 358. Sheffield: Sheffield Academic, 2002.

Kollmann, B. *Ursprung und Gestalten der frühchristlichen Mahlfeier*. Göttinger Theologische Arbeiten 43. Göttingen: Vandenhoeck & Ruprecht, 1990.

Kosmala, H. *Hebräer—Essener—Christen: Studien zur Vorgeschichte der frühchristlichen Verkündigung.* Studia Post-Biblica. Leiden: E.J. Brill, 1959.

Kraeling, C.H. *John the Baptist.* New York: Scribner, 1951.

Kuhn, H.-W. "Die Kreuzesstrafe während der frühen Kaiserzeit: Ihre Wirklichkeit and Wertung in der Umwelt des Urchristentums." *Aufstieg und Niedergang der Römischen Welt* 2.25.1 (1982): 648–793.

Kuhn, K.G. "Die Abendmahlsworte." *Theologische Literaturzeitung* 75 (1950): 399– 408.

———. "The Lord's Supper and the Communal Meal at Qumran." Pages 65–93, 259–65 in *The Scrolls and the New Testament.* Edited by K. Stendahl. London: New York: Harper, 1957.

Kuss, O. "Der theologische Grundgedanke des Hebräerbriefes: Zur Deutung des Todes Jesus im neuen Testament." Pages 281–328 in *Aufsätze zur Exegese des neuen Testaments.* Vol. 1 of *Auslegung und Verkündigung.* Regensburg: F. Pustet, 1963.

Kutsch, E. "Von der Aktualität alttestamentlicher Aussagen für das Verständnis des Neuen Testaments." *Zeitschrift für Theologie und Kuche* 74 (1977): 273–90.

Lachmann, J.M. *The Lord's Prayer.* Translated by G.W. Bromiley. Grand Rapids: Eerdmans, 1998.

Le Goff, J. *History and Memory.* Translated by S. Rendall and E. Claman. European Perspectives. New York: Columbia University Press, 1992.

Lee, D.A. "Presence or Absence? The Question of Women Disciples at the Last Supper." *Pacifica* 6 (1993): 1–20.

Lehne, S. *The New Covenant in Hebrews.* Journal for the Study of the New Testament. Supplement Series 44. Sheffield: JSOT, 1990.

Lemcio, E.E. *The Past of Jesus in the Gospels.* Society for New Testament Studies Monograph Series 68. Cambridge: Cambridge University Press, 1992.

Lenowitz, H. *The Jewish Messiahs: From the Galilee to Crown Heights.* New York: Oxford University Press, 1998.

Léon-Dufour, X. *Sharing the Eucharistic Bread: The Witness of the New Testament.* Translated by M. J. O'Connell. New York: Paulist, 1986.

Levenson, J.D. *The Death and Resurrection of the Beloved Son: The Transformation of Child Sacrifice in Judaism and Christianity.* New Haven: Yale University Press, 1993.

———. *Sinai and Zion: An Entry into the Jewish Bible.* Minneapolis: Winston, 1985.

Levin, C. *Die Verheißung des neuen Bundes in ihrem theologiegeschichtlichen Zusammenhang ausgelegt.* Forschungen zur Religion und Literatur des Alten und Neuen Testaments 137. Göttingen: Vandenhoeck & Ruprecht, 1985.

Levine, A.-J. "Lilies of the Field and Wandering Jews: Biblical Scholarship, Women's Roles, and Social Location." Pages 329–52 in *Transformative Encounters: Jesus and Women Reviewed.* Edited by I.R. Kitzberger. Biblical Interpretation Series 43. Leiden: E.J. Brill, 2000.

Lewis, J.J. "The Wilderness Controversy and Peirasmos." *Colloquium* 7 (1974): 42– 44.

Lichtenberger, H. "Alter Bund und Neuer Bund." *New Testament Studies* 41 (1995): 400–14.

———, ed. *Frühes Christentum.* Vol. 3 of *Geschichte—Tradition—Reflexion: Festschrift für Martin Hengel zum 70: Geburtstag.* Edited by H. Cancik, H. Lichtenberger, and P. Schäfer. 3 vols. Tübingen: J.C.B. Mohr (Paul Siebeck), 1996.

Lietzmann, H. *Mass and the Lord's Supper: A Study in the History of the Liturgy.* Translated by D.H.G. Reeve. Introduction by R.D. Richardson. Leiden: E.J. Brill, 1976.

Lindars, B. *Jesus, Son of Man: A Fresh Examination of the Son of Man Sayings in the Gospels in the Light of Recent Research.* Grand Rapids: Eerdmans, 1983.

———. *New Testament Apologetic: The Doctrinal Significance of the Old Testament Quotations.* London: SCM Press, 1961.

———. "Salvation Proclaimed. VII. Mark 10:45: A Ransom for Many." *Expository Times* 93 (1981–1982): 292–95.

———. *The Theology of the Letter to the Hebrews. New Testament Theology.* Cambridge: Cambridge University Press, 1991.

Lipton, P. *Inference to the Best Explanation.* 2d ed. International Library of Philosophy. London: Routledge, 2004.

Lissaggargue, F. *The Aesthetics of the Greek Banquet: Images of Wine and Ritual (Un Flot d'Images).* Translated by A. Szegedy-Maszak. Princeton: Princeton University Press, 1990.

Lohfink, N. "Der Begriff 'Bund' in der biblischen Theologie." *Theologie und Philosophie* 66 (1991): 161–76.

Lohmeyer, E. *The Lord's Prayer.* Translated by J. Bowden. London: Collins, 1965.

———. *Märtyrer und Gottesknecht: Untersuchungen zur urchristlichen Verkündigung vom Sühnetod Jesu Christi.* Forschungen zur Religion und Literatur des Alten und Neuen Testaments 64. Göttingen: Vandenhoeck & Ruprecht, 1964.

Lohse, E. *Märtyrer und Gottesknecht: Untersuchungen zur urchristlichen Verkündigung vom Sühntod Jesu Christi.* 2d ed. Forschungen zur Religion und Literatur des Alten und Neuen Testaments 46. Göttingen: Vandenhoeck & Ruprecht, 1963.

Long, V.P., et al. *Windows into Old Testament History: Evidence, Argument, and the Crisis of "Biblical Israel."* Grand Rapids: Eerdmans, 2002.

Longenecker, B. "Defining the Faithful Character of the Covenant Community: Galatians 2.15-21 and Beyond." Pages 75–97 in *Paul and the Mosaic Law.* Edited by J.D.G. Dunn. Grand Rapids: Eerdmans, 2001.

Longenecker, R.N. *Biblical Exegesis in the Apostolic Period.* Grand Rapids: Eerdmans, 1975.

Lowe, M. "From the Parable of the Vineyard to a Pre-Synoptic Source." *New Testament Studies* 28 (1982): 257–63.

Lüdemann, G. *Jesus after Two Thousand Years: What He Really Said and Did.* With F. Schleritt and M. Janssen. Amherst, N.Y.: Prometheus, 2001.

Lunde, J. "The Salvation-Historical Implications of Matthew 24–25 in Light of Jewish Apocalyptic Literature." Ph.D. diss., Trinity Evangelical Divinity School, 1996.

Mack, B.L. "The Anointing of Jesus: Elaboration within a Chreia." Pages 85–106 in *Patterns of Persuasion in the Gospels.* Edited by B.L. Mack and V.K. Robbins. Sonoma, Calif.: Polebridge, 1989.

Malina, B.J., and J.H. Neyrey. *Calling Jesus Names: The Social Value of Labels in Matthew.* Sonoma, Calif.: Polebridge, 1988.

Manson, T.W. "The Lord's Prayer." *Bulletin of the John Rylands University Library of Manchester* 38 (1955–1956): 99–113, 436–48.

———. *The Sayings of Jesus.* London: SCM Press, 1949.

———. *The Servant-Messiah: A Study of the Public Ministry of Jesus.* Cambridge: Cambridge University Press, 1953.

———. "The Son of Man in Daniel, Enoch and the Gospels." Pages 123–45 in *Studies in the Gospels and Epistles.* Edited by M. Black. Philadelphia: Westminster, 1962.

———. *The Teaching of Jesus: Studies of Its Form and Content.* Cambridge: Cambridge University Press, 1939.

Manson, W. *Christ's View of the Kingdom of God: A Study in Jewish Apocalyptic and in the Mind of Jesus Christ.* Introduction by H.R. Mackintosh. Bruce Lectures. London: James Clarke, 1918.

————. *Jesus the Messiah: The Synoptic Tradition of the Revelation of God in Christ, with Special Reference to Form-Criticism.* London: Hodder & Stoughton, 1943.

Marcus, J. "Jesus' Baptismal Vision." *New Testament Studies* 41 (1995): 512–21.

————. *Mark: A New Translation with Introduction and Commentary.* 2 vols. New York: Doubleday, 2000.

————. *The Way of the Lord: Christological Exegesis of the Old Testament in the Gospel of Mark.* Louisville: Westminster/John Knox, 1992.

Marrow, S.B. "Principles for Interpreting the New Testament Soteriological Terms." *New Testament Studies* 36 (1990): 268–280.

Marshall, I.H. "The Death of Jesus in Recent New Testament Study." *Word and World* 3 (1983): 12–21.

————. *Last Supper and Lord's Supper.* Grand Rapids: Eerdmans, 1981.

————. *Luke: Historian and Theologian.* Grand Rapids: Zondervan, 1989.

————. "Some Observations on the Covenant in the New Testament." Pages 275–89 in his *Jesus the Saviour: Studies in New Testament Theology.* Downers Grove: InterVarsity Press, 1990.

————. "Son of God or Servant of Yahweh?—A Reconsideration of Mark I.11." *New Testament Studies* 15 (1968–1969): 326–36.

————. "The Synoptic 'Son of Man' Sayings in the Light of Linguistic Study." Pages 72–94 in *To Tell the Mystery: Essays on New Testament Eschatology in Honor of Robert H. Gundry.* Edited by T.E. Schmidt and M.Silva. Journal for the Study of the New Testament: Supplement Series 100. Sheffield: Sheffield Academic, 1994.

Marshall, I.H., and D. Peterson, eds. *Witness to the Gospel: The Theology of Acts.* Grand Rapids: Eerdmans, 1998.

Marshall, M. "New Insights on Jesus' Actions at the Last Supper." Paper presented at the annual meeting of the SBL. Atlanta, Ga., November 22–25, 2003.

Martin, R. *The Elusive Messiah: A Philosophical Overview of the Quest for the Historical Jesus.* Boulder: Westview, 1999.

Martin, R.P. *Mark: Evangelist and Theologian.* Grand Rapids: Zondervan, 1972.

————. *Reconciliation.* Atlanta: John Knox, 1981.

Martola, N. "Passover Haggadah." Pages 3:1052–1062 in *The Encyclopedia of Judaism.* Edited by J. Neusner, A.J. Avery-Peck, and W.S. Green. 5 vols. New York: Continuum, 1999–2004.

März, C.-P. "Zur Traditionsgeschichte von Mk 14, 3-9 und Parallelen." *Studien zum Neuen Testament und seiner Umwelt* A 6/7 (1981–1982): 89–112.

Matera, F.J. "The Death of Jesus according to Luke: A Question of Sources," *Catholic Bible Quarterly* 47 (1985): 469–85.

McArthur, H.K. "'On the Third Day,'" *New Testament Studies* 18 (1971–1972): 81–86.

————. "Son of Mary," *Novum Testamentum* 15 (1973): 38–58.

McArthur H.K., and R.M. Johnston. *They Also Taught in Parables: Rabbinic Parables from the First Centuries of the Christian Era.* Grand Rapids: Zondervan, 1990.

McCarthy, D.J. *Old Testament Covenant: A Survey of Current Opinions.* Richmond: John Knox, 1972.

————. *Treaty and Covenant: A Study in Form in the Ancient Oriental Documents and in the Old Testament.* 2d ed. Analecta biblica 21A. Rome: Biblical Institute, 1978.

McCasland, S.V. "The Scripture Basis of 'On the Third Day,'" *Journal of Biblical Literature* 68 (1949): 124–37.

McKeating, H. "The Prophet Jesus," *Expository Times* 73 (1961–1962): 4–7, 50–53.

McKnight, S. Review of L.T. Johnson's *The Real Jesus*. *Catholic Bible Quarterly* 59 (1997): 159–61.

———. "Calling Jesus *Mamzer*." *Journal of the Study of the Historical Jesus* 1 (2003): 73–103.

———. "Covenant and Spirit: The Origins of the New Covenant Hermeneutic." Pages 41–54 in *The Holy Spirit and Christian Origins: Essays in Honor of James D.G. Dunn*. Edited by G.N. Stanton, B.W. Longenecker, S.C. Barton. Grand Rapids: Eerdmans, 2004.

———. "The Hermeneutics of Confessing Jesus as Lord," *Ex auditu* 14 (1998): 1–17.

———. *The Jesus Creed: Loving God, Loving Others*. Brewster, Mass.: Paraclete, 2004.

———. "Jesus and His Death: Some Recent Scholarship." *Currents in Research: Biblical Studies* 9 (2001): 185-228.

———. *A Light Among the Gentiles: Jewish Missionary Activity in the Second Temple Period*. Minneapolis: Fortress, 1991.

———. "Jesus and Prophetic Actions." *Bulletin for Biblical Research* 10 (2000): 197–232.

———. "Jesus and the End-Time: Matthew 10:23." *Society of Biblical Literature Seminar Papers* (1986): 501–20.

———. "Jesus and the Twelve." *Bulletin for Biblical Research* 11 (2001): 203– 31.

———. "Jesus' New Vision within Judaism." Pages 73–96 in *Who Was Jesus? A Jewish-Christian Dialogue*. Edited P. Copan and C.A. Evans. Louisville: Westminster John Knox, 2001.

———. "Jesus of Nazareth." Pages 149–76 in *The Face of New Testament Studies: A Survey of Recent Research*. Edited by S. McKnight and G.R. Osborne. Grand Rapids: Baker Academic, 2004.

———. *A New Vision for Israel: The Teachings of Jesus in National Context*. Grand Rapids: Eerdmans, 1999.

———. *Turning to Jesus: The Sociology of Conversion in the Gospels*. Louisville: Westminster John Knox, 2002.

———. "The Warning Passages of Hebrews: A Formal Analysis and Theological Conclusions." *Trinity Journal* 13 (1992): 21–59.

McKnight, S., and M.C. Williams. *The Synoptic Gospels: An Annotated Bibliography*. IBR Bibliographies. Grand Rapids: Baker, 2000.

McLaren, J.S. "Exploring the Execution of a Provincial: Adopting a Roman Perspective on the Death of Jesus." *Australian Biblical Review* 49 (2001): 5–18.

McLean, B.H. "The Absence of an Atoning Sacrifice in Paul's Soteriology." *New Testament Studies* 38 (1992): 531–53.

McLeod Campbell, J. *The Nature of the Atonement*. Introduction by J.B. Torrance. 1856. Repr. Grand Rapids: Eerdmans, 1996.

Meadors, E.P. *Jesus, the Messianic Herald of Salvation*. Peabody, Mass.: Hendrickson, 1995.

Meier, J.P. "The Circle of the Twelve: Did It Exist during Jesus' Public Ministry?" *Journal of Biblical Literature* 116 (1997): 635–72.

———. *A Marginal Jew: Rethinking the Historical Jesus*. 3 vols. Anchor Bible Reference Library. New York: Doubleday, 1991–2001.

———. *The Vision of Matthew: Christ, Church, and Morality in the First Gospel*. New York: Paulist, 1978.

Mendenhall, G.E. *Ancient Israel's Faith and History: An Introduction to the Bible in Context*. Louisville: Westminster John Knox, 2001.

———. *Law and Covenant in Israel and the Ancient Near East*. Pittsburgh: The Presbyterian Board of Colportage of Western Pennsylvania, 1955.

Menn, E. "No Ordinary Lament: Relecture and the Identity of the Distressed in Psalm 22." *Harvard Theological Review* 93 (2000): 301–41.

Merklein, H. "Der Tod Jesu als stellvertretender Sühnetod: Entwicklung und Gehalt einer zentralen neutestamentlichen Aussage." Pages 181–91 in *Studien zu Jesus und Paulus.* Wissenschaftliche Untersuchungen zum Neuen Testament 43. Tübingen: J.C.B. Mohr (Paul Siebeck).

———. "Erwägungen zur Überlieferingsgeschichte der neutestamentlichen Abendmahlstraditionen." *Biblische Zeitschrift* 21 (1977): 88–101, 235–44.

Metzger, B.M. "A Suggestion Concerning the Meaning of I Cor. xv. 4b." *Journal of Theological Studies* 8 (1957): 118–23.

———. *A Textual Commentary on the Greek New Testament.* London: United Bible Societies, 1971.

Meyer, B.F. "A Caricature of Joachim Jeremias and His Scholarly Work." *Journal of Biblical Literature* 110 (1991): 451–62.

———. *The Aims of Jesus.* London: SCM Press, 1979.

———. *Christus Faber: The Master Builder and the House of God.* Allison Park, Penn.: Pickwick, 1992.

———. *Critical Realism and the New Testament.* Princeton Theological Monograph Series 17; Allison Park, Penn.: Pickwick, 1989.

———. "The Expiation Motif in the Eucharistic Words: A Key to the History of Jesus?" Pages 11-33 in his *One Loaf, One Cup: Ecumenical Studies of 1 Cor 11 and Other Ecumenical Texts: The Cambridge Conference on the Eucharist, August 1988.* New Gospel Studies 6. Macon: Mercer, 1993.

———. *Reality and Illusion in New Testament Scholarship: A Primer in Critical Realist Hermeneutics.* Collegeville, Minn.: Liturgical [Glazier], 1994.

Meyers, C., T. Craven, and R.S. Kraemer, eds. *Women in Scripture.* Grand Rapids: Eerdmans, 2000.

Migliore, D.L. ed. *The Lord's Prayer: Perspectives for Reclaiming Christian Prayer.* Grand Rapids: Eerdmans, 1993.

Milgrom, J. *Leviticus.* AB 3A-3B. New York: Doubleday, 1991–2000.

Millard, A.R. "Covenant and Communion in First Corinthians." Pages 242–48 in *Apostolic History and the Gospel: Biblical and Historical Essays Presented to F. F. Bruce on His 60th Birthday.* Edited by W.W. Gasque and R.P. Martin. Grand Rapids: Eerdmans, 1970.

———. *Reading and Writing in the Time of Jesus.* The Biblical Seminar 69. Sheffield: Sheffield Academic, 2000.

Miller, P.D. *They Cried to the Lord: The Form and Theology of Biblical Prayer.* Minneapolis: Fortress, 1994.

Miller, R.J. "The Rejection of the Prophets in Q." *Journal of Biblical Literature* 107 (1988): 225–40.

Moberly, R. *Atonement and Personality.* London: John Murray, 1901.

Moloney, F.J. "The Fourth Gospel and the Jesus of History." *New Testament Studies* 46 (2000): 42–58.

———. "The Re-interpretation of Psalm VIII and the Son of Man Debate." *New Testament Studies* 27 (1981): 656–72.

Moo, D.J. *The Old Testament in the Gospel Passion Narratives.* Sheffield: Almond, 1983.

Moor, J.C. de. "The Reconstruction of the Aramaic Original of the Lord's Prayer." Pages 397–422 in *The Structural Analysis of Biblical and Canaanite Poetry.* Edited by P. Van der

Meer and J.C. de Moor. Journal for the Study of the Old Testament: Supplement Series 74. Sheffield: JSOT, 1988.

———. "The Targumic Background of Mark 12:1–12: The Parable of the Wicked Tenants." *Journal for the Study of Judaism in the Persian, Hellenistic, and Roman Periods* 29 (1998): 63–80.

Moore, G.F. *Judaism in the First Centuries of the Christian Era: The Age of the Tannaim.* 3 vols. New York: Schocken, 1971.

Morris, L.L. *The Apostolic Preaching of the Cross.* Grand Rapids: Eerdmans, 1965.

———. *The Cross in the New Testament.* Grand Rapids: Eerdmans, 1965.

Moulder, W.J. "The Old Testament Background and Interpretation of Mark x.45." *New Testament Studies* 24 (1977): 120–27.

Moule, C.F.D. *Forgiveness and Reconciliation, and Other New Testament Themes.* London: SPCK, 1998.

———. "II Cor. iii. 18b, καθάπερ ἀπὸ κυρίου πνεύματος." Pages 227–34 in his *Essays in New Testament Interpretation.* Cambridge: Cambridge University Press, 1982.

———. "Neglected Features in the Problem of the 'Son of Man.'" Pages 413–28 in *Neues Testament und Kirche: Für Rudolf Schnackenburg.* Edited by J. Gnilka Freiburg: Herder, 1974.

———. "The Post-resurrection Appearances in the Light of Festival Pilgrimages." *New Testament Studies* 4 (1957–1958): 58–61.

———. *The Origin of Christology.* Cambridge: Cambridge University Press, 1977.

———. *The Phenomenon of the New Testament.* London: SCM Press, 1967.

———. "'The Son of Man': Some of the Facts." *New Testament Studies* 41 (1995): 277–79.

Mournet, T.C. *Oral Tradition and Literary Dependency: Variability and Stability in the Synoptic Tradition and Q.* Wissenschaftliche Untersuchungen zum Neuen Testament. Second Series. Tübingen: J.C.B. Mohr (Paul Siebeck), forthcoming.

Moxnes, H. "The Historical Jesus: From Master Narrative to Cultural Context." *Biblical Theology Bulletin* 28 (1999): 135–49.

Nanos, M. *The Irony of Galatians: Paul's Letter in First-Century Context.* Minneapolis: Fortress, 2002.

———. *The Mystery of Romans: The Jewish Context of Paul's Letter.* Minneapolis: Fortress, 1996.

Neale, D. "Was Jesus a Mesith? Public Response to Jesus and His Ministry." *Tyndale Bulletin* 44 (1993): 89–101.

Neufeld, V.H. *The Earliest Christian Confessions.* New Testament Tools and Studies 5. Grand Rapids: Eerdmans, 1963.

Neusner, J. *Performing Israel's Faith: Narrative and Law in Rabbinic Theology.* Waco, Texas: Baylor University Press, 2005.

———. "Money-Changers in the Temple: The Mishnah's Explanation." *New Testament Studies* 35 (1989): 287–90.

———. *The Rabbinic Traditions about the Pharisees Before 70.* 3 vols. South Florida Studies in the History of Judaism 202–4. Atlanta: Scholars, 1999.

Neusner, J,. et al., eds. *Judaisms and Their Messiahs at the Turn of the Christian Era.* Cambridge: Cambridge University Press, 1987.

Newman, C.C., ed. *Jesus and the Restoration of Israel: A Critical Assessment of N.T. Wright's Jesus and the Victory of God.* Downers Grove: InterVarsity, 1999.

Neyrey, J.H. "Jesus' Address to the Women of Jerusalem (LK. 23.27-31)—A Prophetic Judgment Oracle." *New Testament Studies* 29 (1983): 74–86.

Nicholson, E.W. *God and His People: Covenant and Theology in the Old Testament.* Oxford: Clarendon, 1986.

Nielsen, H.K. *Heilung und Verkündigung: Das Verständnis der Heilung und ihres Verhältnisses zur Verkündigung be Jesus und in der ältesten Kirche.* Acta theologica danica 22. Leiden: E. J. Brill, 1987.

Noort, E., and E. Tigchelaar. *The Sacrifice of Isaac: The Aqedah (Genesis 22) and Its Interpretations.* Vol. 4 of *Themes in Biblical Narrative.* Leiden: E.J. Brill, 2002.

North, C.R. *The Suffering Servant in Deutero-Isaiah: An Historical and Critical Study.* 2d ed. Oxford: Oxford University Press, 1956.

Novick, P. *That Noble Dream: The "Objectivity Question" and the American Historical Profession.* New York: Cambridge University Press, 1988.

O'Connor, F. *An Only Child.* New York: Knopf, 1961.

O'Neill, J.C. *Who Did Jesus Think He Was?* Biblical Interpretation 11. Leiden: E.J. Brill, 1995.

Oberlinner, L. *Todeserwartung und Todesgewissheit Jesu.* Stuttgarter Biblische Beiträge 10. Stuttgart: KBW, 1980.

Otto, R. *The Kingdom of God and the Son of Man: A Study in the History of Religion.* Translated by F.V. Filson and B.L. Woolf. Lutterworth Library 9. London: Lutterworth, 1938.

Owen, P., and D. Shepherd, "Speaking Up for Qumran, Dalman and the Son of Man: Was Bar Enasha a Common Term for 'Man' in the Time of Jesus?" *Journal for the Study of the New Testament* 81 (2001): 81–122.

Packer, J.I. "What Did the Cross Achieve? The Logic of Penal Substitution." *Tyndale Bulletin* 25 (1974): 3–45.

Page, S.H.T. "The Authenticity of the Ransom Logion (Mark 10:45b)." Pages 137–61 in *Studies of History and Tradition in the Four Gospels.* Edited by R.T. France and D. Wenham. Vol. 1 of *Gospel Perspectives.* Sheffield: JSOT, 1980.

Pagels, E. *Beyond Belief: The Secret Gospel of Thomas.* New York: Random, 2003.

Palmer, D.W. "To Die is Gain." *Novum Testamentum* 17 (1975): 203–18.

Patterson, S.J. "Fire and Dissension: Ipsissima Vox Jesu in Q 12:49, 51-53?" *Forum* 5 (1989): 121–39.

Pelikan, J. *Credo: Historical and Theological Guide to Creeds and Confessions of Faith in the Christian Tradition.* Vol. 1 of *Creeds and Confessions of Faith in the Christian Tradition.* Edited by J. Pelikan and V.R. Hotchkiss. New Haven: Yale University Press, 2003.

Perrin, N. "The Use of (para)didounai in Connection with the Passion of Jesus in the New Testament." Pages 204–12 in *Der Ruf Jesu und die Antwort der Gemeinde: Exegetische Untersuchungen Joachim Jeremias zum 70: Geburtstag gewidmet von seinen Schülern.* Edited by E. Lohse, C. Burchard, and B. Schaller. Göttingen: Vandenhoeck & Ruprecht, 1970.

———. *Rediscovering the Teaching of Jesus.* New York: Harper & Row, 1967.

Perry, J.M. "The Three Days in the Synoptic Passion Predictions." *Catholic Bible Quarterly* 48 (1986): 637–54.

Pesch, R. *Das Abendmahl und Jesu Todesverständnis.* Quaestiones disputatae 80. Freiburg: Herder, 1978.

Pitre, B.J. "The Historical Jesus, the Great Tribulation and the End of the Exile," Ph.D. diss., Notre Dame, 2004.

Popkes, W. "Die letzte Bitte des Vater-Unser. Formgeschichtliche Beobachtungen zum Gebet Jesu." *Zeitschrift für die neutestamentliche Wissenschaft und die Kunde der älteren Kirche* 81 (1990): 1–20.

Porter, S.E. *The Criteria for Authenticity in Historical-Jesus Research: Previous Discussion and New Proposals.* Journal for the Study of the New Testament. Supplement Series 191. Sheffield: Sheffield Academic, 2000.

———. "Mt 6:13 and Lk 11:4: 'Lead Us Not into Temptation.'" *Expository Times* 101 (1989–1990): 359–62.

Porter, S.E., M.A. Hayes, and D. Tombs, eds. *Resurrection.* Journal for the Study of the New Testament. Supplement Series. Roehampton Institute London Papers 5. Sheffield: Sheffield Academic Press, 1999.

Propp, W.H.C. *Exodus 1–18: A New Translation with Introduction and Commentary.* Anchor Bible 2. New York: Doubleday, 1999.

Pryke, E.J. *Redactional Style in the Marcan Gospel: A Study of Syntax and Vocabulary as Guides to Redaction in Mark.* Society for New Testament Studies Monograph Series 33. London: Cambridge University Press, 1978.

Ranke, L. von. *Geschichten der romanischen und germanischen Völker von 1494 bis 1514.* Sämmtliche Werke 33/34. 2d ed. Leipzig: Duncker & Humbolt, 1874.

Rau, E. *Jesus: Freund von Zöllnern und Sündern: Eine methodenkritische Untersuchung.* Stuttgart: W. Kohlhammer, 2000.

Rebell, W. "'Sein Leben Verlieren' (Mark 8.35 parr.) als Strukturmoment vor- und nachösterlichen Glaubens." *New Testament Studies* 35 (1989): 202–18.

Reed, J.L. *Archaeology and the Galilean Jesus: A Re-examination of the Evidence.* Harrisburg: Trinity Press International, 2000.

Reiser, M. *Jesus and Judgment: The Eschatological Proclamation in Its Jewish Context.* Translated by L.M. Maloney. Minneapolis: Fortress, 1997.

Rendtorff, R. *The Covenant Formula: An Exegetical and Theological Investigation.* Edinburgh: T&T Clark, 1998.

Reno, R.R. *Redemptive Change.* Harrisburg: Trinity Press International, 2002.

Rese, M. "Einige Überlegungen zu Lukas XIII, 31-33." Pages 201–25 in *Jésus aux origines de la christologie.* Edited by J. Dupont. Bibliotheca ephemeridum theologicarum lovaniensium 40. Gembloux/Leuven: Duculot/Leuven University Press, 1975.

Ricoeur, P. *Time and Narrative.* Translated by K. McLaughlin and D. Pellauer. 3 vols. Chicago: University of Chicago Press, 1984–1988.

Ridderbos, H. *Paul: An Outline of His Theology.* Translated by J.R. DeWitt. Grand Rapids: Eerdmans, 1975.

Riesner, R. *Jesus als Lehrer: Eine Untersuchung zum Ursprung der Evangelien-Überlieferung.* Wissenschaftliche Untersuchungen zum Neuen Testament. Second Series 7. Tübingen: J.C.B. Mohr (Paul Siebeck), 1981.

Riniker, C. "Jesus als Gerichtsprediger? Auseinandersetzung mit einem wieder aktuell gewordenen Thema." *Zeitschrift für Neues Testament* 5 (2002): 2–14.

Rist, J.M. *Real Ethics: Reconsidering the Foundations of Morality.* Cambridge: Cambridge University Press, 2002.

Rivkin, E. *What Crucified Jesus?* Nashville: Abingdon, 1984.

Robinson, H.W. *The Cross in the Old Testament.* Philadelphia: Westminster, 1955.

———. *Redemption and Revelation in the Actuality of History.* New York: Harper, 1942.

Robinson, J.A.T. *The Priority of John.* Edited by J.F. Coakley. Oak Park, Ill.: Meyer-Stone, 1985.

———. *Twelve More New Testament Studies.* London: SCM Press, 1984.

Robinson, J.M., P. Hoffmann, J.S. Kloppenborg, and M.C. Moreland. *The Critical Edition of Q: Synopsis Including the Gospels of Matthew and Luke, Mark and Thomas with English,*

German, and French translations of Q and Thomas. Hermeneia. Minneapolis: Fortress, 2000.

Roloff, J. "Anfänge der soteriologischen Deutung des Todes Jesu (MK. X. 45 und LK. XII. 27)." *New Testament Studies* (1977–1973): 62–64.

———. *Das Kerygma und der irdische Jesus: Historische Motive in den Jesus- Erzählungen der Evangelien.* Göttingen: Vandenhoeck & Ruprecht, 1970.

Romano, R., ed. *Enciclopedia.* Turin: Einaudi, 1977–1982.

Rorty, R. *Achieving Our Country: Leftist Thought in Twentieth-Century America.* Cambridge, Mass.: Harvard University Press, 1997.

———. "Religion in the Public Square." *Journal of Religious Ethics* 31 (2003): 141–49.

Routledge, R. "Passover and Last Supper." *Tyndale Bulletin* 53 (2002): 203–21.

Rowley, H.H. *The Servant of the Lord and Other Essays on the Old Testament.* London: Lutterworth, 1952.

Ruckstuhl, E. *Chronology of the Last Days of Jesus: A Critical Study.* Translated by V.J. Drapela. New York: Desclee, 1965.

Ruppert, L. *Der leidende Gerechte und seine Feinde: Eine Wortfelduntersuchung.* Forschung zur Bibel 6. Würzburg: Echter, 1973.

———. *Der leidende Gerechte: Eine motivgeschichtliche Untersuchung zum Alten Testament und zwischentestamentlichen Judentum.* Forschung zur Bibel 5. Würzburg: Echter, 1972.

———. *Jesus als der leidende Gerechte? Der Weg Jesu im Lichte eines alt- und zwischentesta- mentlichen Motivs.* Stuttgarter Bibelstudien 59. Stuttgart: Katholisches Bibelwerk, 1972.

Saldarini, A.J. *Jesus and Passover.* New York: Paulist, 1984.

Sanders, E.P. "The Covenant as a Soteriological Category and the Nature of Salvation in Palestinian and Hellenistic Judaism." Pages 11–44 in *Jews, Greeks, and Christians: Religious Cultures in Late Antiquity: Essays in Honor of William David Davies.* Edited by R. Hamerton-Kelly and R. Scroggs. Leiden: E.J. Brill, 1976.

———. "Defending the Indefensible." *Journal of Biblical Literature* 110 (1991): 463–77.

———. *The Historical Figure of Jesus.* London: Penguin, 1993.

———. "Jesus and the Kingdom: The Restoration of Israel and the New People of God." Pages 225–39 in *Jesus, the Gospels and the Church.* Edited by E.P. Sanders. Macon, Ga.: Mercer University Press, 1987.

———. *Jesus and Judaism.* Philadelphia: Fortress, 1985.

———. *Judaism: Practice & Belief, 63 BCE–66 CE.* Philadelphia: Trinity Press International, 1992.

———. *Paul and Palestinian Judaism: A Comparison of Patterns of Religion.* Philadelphia: Fortress, 1977.

Satterthwaite, P.E., et al., eds. *The Lord's Anointed: Interpretation of Old Testament Messianic Texts.* Tyndale House Studies. Grand Rapids: Baker, 1995.

Schaberg, J. "Daniel 7,12 and the New Testament Passion-Resurrection Predictions." *New Testament Studies* 31 (1985): 208–22.

———. "A Feminist Experience of Historical-Jesus Scholarship." Pages 146–60 in *Whose Historical Jesus?* Edited by W. E. Arnal and M. Desjardins. Studies in Christianity and Judaism 7. Waterloo: Wilfrid Laurier University Press, 1997.

———. *The Illegitimacy of Jesus: A Feminist Theological Interpretation of the Infancy Narratives.* San Francisco: Harper & Row, 1987.

Schäter, P., ed. *Judentum.* Vol. 1 of *Geschichte—Tradition—Reflexion: Festschrift für Martin Hengel zum 70: Geburtstag.* Edited by H. Cancik, H. Lichtenberger, and P. Schäfer. 3 vols. Tübingen: J.C.B. Mohr (Paul Siebeck), 1996.

Schlosser, J. *Jésus de Nazareth.* 2d ed. Paris: Agnès Viénot, 2002.

Schmidt, D. "The LXX Gattung 'Prophetic Correlative.'" *Journal of Biblical Literature* 96 (1977): 517–22.

Schnackenburg, R. *All Things Are Possible to Believers: Reflections on the Lord's Prayer and the Sermon on the Mount.* Translated by J.S. Currie. Louisville: Westminster John Knox, 1995.

———. *Die sittliche Botschaft des Neuen Testaments.* 2 vols. Herders theologischer Kommentar zum Neuen Testament. Sonderband 1–2. Freiburg: Herder, 1986–1988.

Schnider, F. *Jesus der Prophet.* Orbis biblicus et orientalis 2. Göttingen: Vandenhoeck & Ruprecht, 1973.

Schottroff, W. "Das Gleichnis von den bösen Weingärtnern (Mk. 12:1-9 par.): Ein Beitrag zur Geschichte der Bodenpacht in Palästina." *Zeitschrift des deutschen Palästina-Vereins* 112 (1996): 18–48.

Schreiner, T.R. *Paul, Apostle of God's Glory in Christ: A Pauline Theology.* Downers Grove: InterVarsity, 2001.

Schröter, J. *Jesus und die Anfänge der Christologie: Methodische und exegetische Studien zu den Ursprüngen des christlichen Glaubens.* Biblisch-Theologische Studien 47. Neukirchen-Vluyn: Neukirchener Verlag, 2001.

Schröter, J., and R. Brucker, eds. *Der historische Jesus: Tendenzen und Perspektiven der gegenwärtigen Forschung.* Beihefte zur Zeitschrift für die neutestamentliche Wissenschaft 114. Berlin: Walter de Gruyter, 2002.

Schürmann, H. *Der Einsetzungsbericht Lk 22, 19-20.* Neutestamentliche Abhandlungen 20/4. Münster: Aschendorff, 1955.

———. *Der Pashamahlbericht Lk 22, (7-14) 15-18.* Neutestamentliche Abhandlungen 19/5; Münster: Aschendorff, 1955.

———. *Gottes Reich—Jesu Geschick: Jesu ureigener Tod im Licht seiner Basileia-Verkündigung.* Freiburg: Herder, 1983.

———. *Jesu ureigener Tod: Exegetische Besinnungen und Ausblick.* Freiburg: Herder, 1975.

———. *Jesus—Gestalt und Geheimnis: Gesammelte Beiträge.* Edited K. Scholtissek. Paderborn: Bonifatius, 1994.

———. *Praying with Christ: The "Our Father" for Today.* Translated by W.M. Ducey. New York: Herder & Herder, 1964.

Schüssler Fiorenza, E. *In Memory of Her: A Feminist Theological Reconstruction of Christian Origins.* New York: Crossroads, 1985.

Schwager, R. *Jesus in the Drama of Salvation: Toward a Biblical Doctrine of Redemption.* Translated by J.G. Williams and P. Haddon. New York: Crossroad, 1999.

Schweitzer, A. *The Kingdom of God and Primitive Christianity.* Edited and introduction by U. Neuenschwander. Translated by L.A. Garrard. New York: Seabury, 1968.

———. *The Mystery of the Kingdom of God: The Secret of Jesus' Messiahship and Passion.* Translated by W. Lowrie. New York: Dodd, Mead, 1914. Translation of *Das Messianitäts- und Leidensgeheimnis: Ein Skizze des Lebens Jesus.* Tübingen: J.C.B. Mohr, 1901.

———. *Geschichte der Leben-Jesu-Forschung. 9th ed. Uni-Taschenbücher 1302.* Tübingen: J.C.B. Mohr, 1984. Reprint of *Geschichte der Leben-Jesu- Forschung.* 2d ed. Tübingen: J.C.B. Mohr, 1913. Reprint of *Von Reimarus zu Wrede.* 1st ed. Tübingen: J.C.B. Mohr, 1906.

———. *The Mysticism of Paul the Apostle.* Translated by W. Montgomery. Foreword by J. Pelikan. Baltimore: Johns Hopkins University Press, 1998.

———. *The Psychiatric Study of Jesus*. Translated by C.R. Joy. Boston: Beacon, 1948. Translation of *Die psychiatrische Beurteilung Jesu*. Tübingen: J.C.B. Mohr, 1913.

———. *The Quest of the Historical Jesus*. Edited by John Bowden. Translated by W. Montgomery, J.R. Coates, S. Cupitt, and J. Bowden. Foreword by D. Nineham. Minneapolis: Fortress, 2001.

———. *The Quest of the Historical Jesus: A Critical Study of Its Progress from Reimarus to Wrede*. Translated by W. Montgomery. Forewords by F.C. Burkitt and D.R. Hillers. Baltimore: Johns Hopkins University Press, 1998.

———. *The Lord's Supper in Relationship to the Life of Jesus and the History of the Early Church*. Vol. 1 of *The Problem of the Lord's Supper according to the Scholarly Research of the Nineteenth Century and the Historical Accounts*. Edited by J. Reumann. Translated by A. J. Mattill, Jr. Macon, Ga: Mercer University Press, 1982.

Schweizer, E. *Jesus*. Translated by D.E. Green. London: SCM Press, 1971.

———. *Lordship and Discipleship*. Studies in Biblical Theology 28. Naperville, Ill.: Alec R. Allenson, London: SCM Press, 1960.

Scott, J.M. *Adoption as Sons of God: An Exegetical Investigation into the Background of huiothesia in the Pauline Corpus*. Wissenschaftliche Untersuchungen zum Neuen Testament. Second Series 48. Tübingen: J.C.B. Mohr (Paul Siebeck), 1992.

———. *Exile: Old Testament, Jewish, and Christian Conceptions. Journal for the Study of Judaism in the Persian, Hellenistic, and Roman Periods*: Supplement Series 56. Leiden: E. J. Brill, 1997.

Seeley, D. "Jesus' Temple Act." *Catholic Bible Quarterly* 55 (1993): 263–83.

Segal, A. "Covenant in Rabbinic Writings." *Studies in Religion* 14 (1985): 53–62.

———. *Life After Death: A History of the Afterlife in the Religions of the West*. New York: Doubleday, 2004.

Segal, J.B. *The Hebrew Passover from the Earliest Times to A.D. 70*. London Oriental Series 12. London: Oxford University Press, 1963.

Seifrid, M.A. *Justification by Faith: The Origin and Development of a Central Pauline Theme*. Supplements to Novum Testamentum 68. Leiden: E. J. Brill, 1992.

Senior, D. *The Passion of Jesus in the Gospel of Mark*. Wilmington: Michael Glazier, 1984.

Slater, T.B. "One Like a Son of Man in First Century CE Judaism." *New Testament Studies* 41 (1995): 183–98.

Slater, W.J., ed. *Dining in a Classical Context*. Ann Arbor: University of Michigan Press, 1991.

Sloyan, G. *The Crucifixion of Jesus: History, Myth, Faith*. Minneapolis: Fortress, 1995.

Smith, B.D. "The Chronology of the Last Supper." *Westminster Theological Journal* 53 (1991): 29–45.

———. *Jesus' Last Passover Meal*. Lewiston, N.Y.: Edwin Mellen, 1993.

Smith, C.W.F. "Fishers of Men." *Harvard Theological Review* 52 (1959): 187–203.

Smith, C. *Moral, Believing Animals: Human Personhood and Culture*. Oxford: Oxford University Press, 2003.

Smith, D.E. *From Symposium to Eucharist: The Banquet in the Early Christian World*. Minneapolis: Fortress, 2003.

Smith, D.M. "Historical Issues and the Problem of John and the Synoptics." Pages 252–67 in *From Jesus to John*. Edited by M.C. de Boer. Sheffield: JSOT, 1993.

Smith, M.H. "No Place for a Son of Man." *Forum* 4 (1988): 83–107.

Smith, Morton. *Jesus the Magician*. San Francisco: Harper & Row, 1978.

Snodgrass, K.R. *The Parable of the Wicked Tenants: An Inquiry into Parable Interpretation*.

Wissenschaftliche Untersuchungen zum Neuen Testament 27. Tübingen: J.C.B. Mohr, 1983.

Soards, M.L. "Tradition, Composition, and Theology in Jesus' Speech to the 'Daughters of Jerusalem' (Luke 23, 26-32)." *Biblica* 68 (1987): 221–44.

Stacey, W.D. "The Lord's Supper as Prophetic Drama: The A. S. Peake Lecture for 1993." *Epworth Review* 21 (1994): 65–74.

———. *Prophetic Drama in the Old Testament.* London: Epworth, 1990.

Stählin, G. "'On the Third Day': The Easter Traditions of the Primitive Church." *Interpretation* 10 (1956): 282–99.

Stanton, G.N. *Jesus of Nazareth in New Testament Preaching.* Society for New Testament Studies Monograph Series 27. Cambridge: Cambridge University Press, 1972.

———. "Presuppositions in New Testament Criticism." Pages 60–71 in *New Testament Interpretation: Essays on Principles and Methods.* Edited by I.H. Marshall. Grand Rapids: Eerdmans, 1977.

Stauffer, E. "Jeschu ben Mirjam (Mk 6:3)." Pages 119–28 in *Neotestamentica et Semitica: Studies in Honour of Matthew Black.* Edited by E.E. Ellis and M. Wilcox. Edinburgh: T&T Clark, 1969.

———. *New Testament Theology.* Translated by J. Marsh. London: SCM Press, 1955.

Steck, O.H. *Israel und das gewaltsame Geschick der Propheten: Untersuchungen zur Überlieferung des deuteronomistischen Geschichtsbildes im Alten Testament, Spätjudentum und Urchristentum.* Wissenschaftliche Monographien zum Alten und Neuen Testament 23. Neukirchen-Vluyn: Neukirchener Verlag, 1967.

Steinhauser, M.G. "Putting One's Hand to the Plow: The Authenticity of Q 9:61-62." *Forum* 5 (1989): 151–58.

Stendahl, K. *Paul Among Jews and Gentiles.* Philadelphia: Fortress, 1976.

Stern, D. "Jesus' Parables from the Perspective of Rabbinic Literature: The Example of the Wicked Husbandmen." Pages 42–80 in *Parable and Story in Judaism and Christianity.* Edited by C. Thoma and M. Wyschograd. New York: Paulist, 1989.

———. *Jewish New Testament Commentary.* Clarksville, Md.: Jewish New Testament Publications, 1992.

Stott, J.R.W. *The Cross of Christ.* Downers Grove: InterVarsity, 1986.

Strack, H.L., and P. Billerbeck. *Kommentar zum Neuen Testament aus Talmud und Midrasch.* 6 vols. Munich: C.H. Beck'sche, 1922–1961.

Strecker, G. *Theology of the New Testament.* Edited and completed by F.W. Horn. Translated by M.E. Boring. Louisville: Westminster John Knox, 2000.

Strobel, A. *Die Stunde der Wahrheit: Untersuchungen zum Strafverfahren gegen Jesus.* Tübingen: Mohr, 1980.

Stuhlmacher, P. *Biblische Theologie des Neuen Testaments.* 2 vols. Göttingen: Vandenhoeck & Ruprecht, 1992, 1997.

———. *Grundlegung Von Jesus zu Paulus.* Vol. 1 of *Biblische Theologie des Neuen Testaments.* 2d ed. Göttingen: Vandenhoeck & Ruprecht, 1997.

———. *Historical Criticism and Theological Interpretation of Scripture: Toward a Hermeneutics of Consent.* Translated by R.A. Harrisville. Philadelphia: Fortress, 1977.

———. "Der messianische Gottesknecht." *Jahrbuch für Biblische Theologie* 8 (1993): 131–54.

———, ed. *Reconciliation, Law, and Righteousness: Essays in Biblical Theology.* Translated by E. Kalin. Philadelphia: Fortress, 1986.

———. "Why Did Jesus Have to Die?" Pages 39–57 in *Jesus of Nazareth: Christ of Faith*. Translated by S.S. Schatzmann; Peabody, Mass.: Hendrickson, 1993.

Stuhlmacher, P., and D.A. Hagner. *Revisiting Paul's Doctrine of Justification: A Challenge to the New Perspective*. Downers Grove: InterVarsity, 2001.

Swetnam, J. "Why Was Jeremiah's New Covenant New?" Pages 111–15 in *Studies on Prophecy: A Collection of Twelve Papers*. Supplements to Vetus Testamentum 26. Leiden: E.J. Brill, 1974.

Sykes, M.H. "'And Do Not Bring Us to the Test.'" *Expository Times* 73 (1962): 189–90.

Sykes, S. *The Story of Atonement. Trinity and Truth.* London: Darton, Longman & Todd, 1997.

Sykes, S.W., ed. *Sacrifice and Redemption: Durham Essays in Theology.* Cambridge: Cambridge University Press, 1991.

Tabory, J. "The Crucifixion of the Paschal Lamb." *Jewish Quarterly Review* 86 (1996): 395–406.

Tan, K.H. *The Zion Traditions and the Aims of Jesus.* Society for New Testament Studies Monograph Series 91. Cambridge: Cambridge University Press, 1997.

Tannehill, R.C. *Dying and Rising with Christ: A Study in Pauline Theology.* Beihefte zur Zeitschrift für die neutestamentliche 32. Berlin: Töpelmann, 1967.

Taussig, H. *Jesus Before God: The Prayer Life of the Historical Jesus.* Santa Rosa, Calif.: Polebridge, 1999.

———. "The Lord's Prayer." *Forum* 4 (1988): 25–41

Taylor, J. "The Coming of Elijah, Mt 17, 10-13 and Mk 9, 11-13: The Development of the Texts." *Revue biblique* 98 (1991): 107–19.

Taylor, J.E. *The Immerser: John the Baptist within Second Temple Judaism.* Grand Rapids: Eerdmans, 1997.

Taylor, V. *Jesus and His Sacrifice: A Study of the Passion-Sayings in the Gospels.* 1937. Repr. London: Macmillan, 1955.

———, ed. *New Testament Essays.* Grand Rapids: Eerdmans, 1972.

———. "The Origin of the Markan Passion-Sayings." *New Testament Studies* 1 (1955): 159–67.

Theissen, G., and A. Merz. *The Historical Jesus: A Comprehensive Guide.* Translated by J. Bowden. Minneapolis: Fortress, 1998.

Theissen, G., and D. Winter. *The Quest for the Plausible Jesus: The Question of Criteria.* Translated by M.E. Boring. Louisville: Westminster John Knox, 2002.

Theobald, M. "Zwei Bünde und ein Gottesvolk: Die Bundestheologie des Hebräerbriefs im Horizont des christlich-jüdischen Gesprächs." *Theologische Quartalschrift* 176 (1996): 309–25.

Thiselton, A.C. *Interpreting God and the Postmodern Self: On Meaning, Manipulation, and Promise.* Grand Rapids: Eerdmans, 1995.

———. *New Horizons in Hermeneutics: The Theory and Practice of Transforming Biblical Reading.* New York: HarperCollins, 1992.

Tödt, H.E. *The Son of Man in the Synoptic Tradition.* Translated by D.M. Barton. London: SCM Press, 1965.

Tovey, D. *Narrative Art and Act in the Fourth Gospel.* Sheffield: Sheffield Academic, 1997.

Trembath, K.R. *Evangelical Theories of Biblical Inspiration: A Review and Proposal.* New York: Oxford University Press, 1987.

Troeltsch, E. "Historical and Dogmatic Method in Theology." Pages 11–32 in *Religion in*

History. Translated by J.L. Adams and W.F. Bense. Introduction by J.L. Adams. 1898. Repr. Minneapolis: Fortress, 1991.

Tuckett, C., ed. *The Messianic Secret.* Vol. 1 of *Issues in Religion and Theology.* Philadelphia: Fortress, 1983.

Twelftree, G.H. *Jesus the Exorcist: A Contribution to the Study of the Historical Jesus.* Peabody, Mass.: Hendrickson, 1993.

Vanhoozer, K. *Is There a Meaning in This Text? The Bible, the Reader, and the Morality of Literary Knowledge.* Grand Rapids: Zondervan, 1998.

Vansina, J. *Oral Tradition as History.* Madison: University of Wisconsin Press, 1985.

Vargas, LM. "Trench Town Rock." *American Scholar* 71 (2002): 56.

Vermès, G. *The Changing Faces of Jesus.* London: Penguin, 2000.

———. *The Dead Sea Scrolls in English.* 3d ed. London: Penguin, 1987.

———. *Jesus the Jew.* London: Fontana/Collins, 1973.

———. "New Light on the Aqedah from 4Q 225." *Journal of Jewish Studies* 47 (1996): 140–46.

———. *Scripture and Tradition in Judaism: Haggadic Studies.* Studia Post-Biblica 4. Leiden: E.J. Brill, 1961.

Vielhauer, P. "Gottesreich und Menschensohn in der Verkündigung Jesu." Pages 51–79 in *Festschrift für Günther Dehn.* Edited by W. Schneemelcher. Neukirchen: Erziehungsverein, 1957.

———. "Jesus und der Menschensohn: Zur Diskussion mit Heinz Eduard Tödt und Eduard Schweizer." *Zeitschrift für Theologie und Kirche* 60 (1963): 133–77.

Vogel, M. *Das Heil des Bundes: Bundestheologie im Frühjudentum und im frühen Christentum.* Texte und Arbeiten zum neutestamentlichen Zeitalter 18. Tübingen/Basel; Francke, 1996.

Vögtle, A. "Der 'eschatologische' Bezug der Wir-Bitten des Vaterunsers." Pages 344–62 in *Jesus und Paulus: FS. W.G. Kümmel.* Edited by E.E. Ellis and E. Gräßer. Göttingen: Vandenhoeck & Ruprecht, 1975.

Walker, N. "'After Three Days.'" *Novum Testamentum* 4 (1960): 216–62.

Wall, R.W. "The Finger of 'God': Deuteronomy 9.10 and Luke 11.20." *New Testament Studies* 33 (1987): 144–50.

Watson, F. *Text and Truth: Redefining Biblical Theology.* Grand Rapids: Eerdmans, 1997.

Watts, J.D.W. *Isaiah 34–66.* Word Biblical Commentary 25. Waco, Texas: Word, 1987.

Weaver, J.D. *The Nonviolent Atonement.* Grand Rapids: Eerdmans, 2001.

Weaver, W.P. *The Historical Jesus in the Twentieth Century, 1900–1950.* Harrisburg: Trinity Press International, 1999.

Webb, R.L. *John the Baptizer and Prophet: A Socio-Historical Study.* Journal for the Study of the New Testament: Supplement Series 62. Sheffield: JSOT, 1991.

Wedderburn, A.J.M. *Baptism and Resurrection: Studies in Pauline Theology against Its Graeco-Roman Background.* Wissenschaftliche Untersuchungen zum Neuen Testament 44. Tübingen: J.C.B. Mohr, 1987.

Weiss, J. *Die Predigt Jesu vom Reiche Gottes.* Edited by F. Hahn. Foreword by R. Bultmann. 3d ed. Göttingen: Vandenhoeck & Ruprecht, 1964.

Wellhausen, J. *Das Evangelium Matthaei.* Berlin: Reimer, 1904.

Wengst, K. *Christologische Formeln und Lieder des Urchristentums.* Studien zum Neuen Testament 7. Gütersloh: Gerd Mohn, 1972.

Wenham, D.W. "How Jesus Understood the Last Supper: A Parable in Action." *Themelios* 20 (1995): 11–16.

————. *The Rediscovery of Jesus' Eschatological Discourse*. Vol. 4 of *Gospel Perspectives*. Sheffield: JSOT, 1984.

Weren, W.J.C. "The Use of Isaiah 5, 1-7 in the Parable of the Tenants (Mark 12, 1-12; Matthew 21, 33-46)." *Biblica* 79 (1998): 1–26.

Westerholm, S. "'Letter' and 'Spirit': The Foundation of Pauline Ethics." *New Testament Studies* 30 (1984): 229–48.

————. *Preface to the Study of Paul*. Grand Rapids: Eerdmans, 1997.

Wheeler, R.H. *Corporate Personality in Ancient Israel*. Introduction by G.M. Tucker. Rev. ed. Philadelphia: Fortress, 1980.

————. *The Cross in the Old Testament*. Philadelphia: Westminster, 1955. [Reprint of *The Cross of the Servant: A Study in Deutero-Isaiah*. London: SCM Press, 1926.]

————. *Redemption and Revelation in the Actuality of History*. New York: Harper, 1942.

White, H. *Figural Realism: Studies in the Mimesis Effect*. Baltimore: Johns Hopkins University Press, 1999.

————. *Metahistory: The Historical Imagination in Nineteenth-Century Europe*. Baltimore: The Johns Hopkins University Press, 1973.

————. *The Content of the Form: Narrative Discourse and Historical Representation*. Baltimore: The Johns Hopkins University Press, 1987.

————. *Tropics of Discourse: Essays in Cultural Criticism*. Baltimore: The Johns Hopkins University Press, 1978.

Whiteley, D.E.H. "Christ's Foreknowledge of His Crucifixion." *Studia Evangelica* I (=TU 73 [1959]): 100–114.

————. *The Theology of St. Paul*. 2d ed. Oxford: Blackwell, 1980.

Wijngaards, J. "Death and Resurrection in Covenantal Context (Hos. vi. 2)." *Vetus Testamentum* 17 (1967): 226–38.

Wilcox, M. "'Upon the Tree'—Deut 21:22-23 in the New Testament." *Journal of Biblical Literature* 96 (1977): 85–99.

Williams, B. *Truth and Truthfulness: An Essay in Geneaology*. Princeton: Princeton University Press, 2002.

Williams, D.K. *Enemies of the Cross of Christ*. Journal for the Study of the Old Testament. Supplement Series 223. Sheffield: Sheffield Academic, 2002.

Williams, M.C. "Is Matthew a Scribe? An Examination of the Text-Critical Argument for the Synoptic Problem." Ph.D. diss., Trinity International University, 1996.

Williams, S.K. *Jesus' Death as Saving Event*. Harvard Dissertations in Religion 2. Missoula, Mont.: Scholars Press, 1975.

Williamson, H.G.M. *The Book Called Isaiah: Deutero-Isaiah's Role in Composition and Redaction*. Oxford: Clarendon, 1994.

————. *Variations on a Theme: King, Messiah and Servant in the Book of Isaiah*. The Didsbury Lectures, 1997. Carlisle: Paternoster, 1998.

Willis, G.G. "Lead Us Not into Temptation." *Downside Review* 93 (1975): 281–88.

Windschuttle, K. *The Killing of History: How Literary Critics and Social Theorists are Murdering Our Past*. San Francisco: Encounter, 2000.

Wink, W. *The Human Being: Jesus and the Enigma of the Son of Man*. Minneapolis: Fortress, 2002.

Wise, M.O. *The First Messiah: Investigating the Savior Before Jesus*. San Francisco: HarperSanFrancisco, 1999.

Wise, M., M. Abegg, Jr., and E. Cook, trans. *The Dead Sea Scrolls: A New Translation*. San Francisco: HarperSanFrancisco, 1996.

Wolff, H.W. *Jesaja 53 im Urchristentum.* 2d ed. Berlin: Evangelische Verlagsanstalt, 1950.

———. *Micah: A Commentary.* Translated by G. Stansell. Minneapolis: Fortress, 1990.

Work, T. *Living and Active: Scripture in the Economy of Salvation.* Sacra doctrina. Grand Rapids: Eerdmans, 2002.

Wrede, W. *The Messianic Secret.* Translated by J.C.G. Greig. Cambridge: James Clarke, 1971.

Wright, N.T. *The Climax of the Covenant: Christ and the Law in Pauline Theology.* Minneapolis: Fortress, 1992.

———. "Jesus' Resurrection and Christian Origins." *Gregorianum* 38 (2002): 615–35.

———. "Jesus' Self-Understanding." Pages 47–61 in *The Incarnation: An Interdisciplinary Symposium on the Incarnation of the Son of God.* Edited by S.T. Davis, D. Kendall, and G. O'Collins. Oxford: Oxford University Press, 2001.

———. *Jesus and the Victory of God.* Vol. 2 of *Christian Origins and the Question of God.* Minneapolis: Fortress, 1996.

———. *The New Testament and the People of God.* Vol. 1 of *Christian Origins and the Question of God.* Minneapolis: Fortress, 1992.

———. *The Resurrection of the Son of God.* Vol. 3 of *Christian Origins and the Question of God.* Minneapolis: Fortress, 2003.

———. " 'That We Might Become the Righteousness of God': Reflections on 2 Corinthians 5:21." Pages 200–208 in *First and Second Corinthians.* Edited by D.M. Hay. Vol. 2 of *Pauline Theology.* 4 vols. Minneapolis: Fortress, 1993.

———. *What Saint Paul Really Said.* Grand Rapids: Eerdmans, 1997.

Wuellner, W. *The Meaning of "Fishers of Men."* Philadelphia: Westminster, 1967.

Yoder, J.H. *The Politics of Jesus: Behold the Man! Our Victorious Lamb.* 2d ed. Grand Rapids: Eerdmans, 1994.

Young, B.H. *Jesus and His Jewish Parables.* New York: Paulist, 1989.

Zager, W. "Wie kam es im Urchristentum zur Deutung des Todes Jesu als Sühnegeschehen? Eine Auseinandersetzung mit Peter Stuhlmachers Entwurf einer 'Biblischen Theologie des Neuen Testaments.' " *Zeitschrift für die neutestamentliche Wissenschaft und die Kunde der älteren Kirche* 87 (1996): 165–86.

———. *Jesus und die frühchristliche Verkündigung: Historische Rückfragen nach den Anfängen.* Neukirchen-Vluyn: Neukirchener Verlag, 1999.

Zeller, D. "Zur Transformation des Χριστός bei Paulus." *Jahrbuch für Biblische Theologie* 8 (1993): 155–67.

Zias, J., and E. Sekeles. "The Crucified Man from Giv'at ha-Mivtar: A Reappraisal." *Israel Exploration Journal* 35 (1985): 22–27.

Zimmerli, W., and J. Jeremias, *The Servant of God.* Translated by H. Knight, et al. Studies in Biblical Theology 20. Naperville, Ill: Alec R. Allenson, 1957.

Zugibe, F. "Two Questions about Crucifixion: Does the Victim Die of Asphyxiation? Would Nails in the Hands Hold the Weight of the Body?" *Bible Review* 5 (1989): 35–43.

Scripture Index

I wish to express my deep appreciation to Sarah and Hauna Ondrey for their work in typing these indices and over the years with helping me acquire bibliographical materials.

OLD TESTAMENT

Genesis

1:26-28	143, 192
1:27	196
2:23-24	196
3	113
3:16	196
6-8	128
9:4	282
12	201, 313
12:1-3	306
12:1	313
12:3	186
14:18	281
15	201, 313
15:1-6	306
17	313
17:1-8	306
17:1	313
17:9	313
17:10	313
17:20	201
17:21	201
22	179, 236, 313
22:1	113
22:2	151
22:18	186
35:22-26	201

49:8-12	88, 332
49:8	332
49:10	332
49:11	289

Exodus

5:1–12:51	200
6:6-8	166
7:3	198
7:9	198
7:20-25	198
8:1-15	198
8:15	198
8:16-17	198
8:19	198, 204
8:20	198
8:23	198
10:1, 2	198
10:22	359
11:9	198
11:10	198
12–13	245
12	115, 244, 248, 254, 256, 267, 273, 280, 285, 288, 306
12:6	285
12:13	285
12:14	257, 334
12:23	285
12:24	271

13:3	257
13:21	291
13:22	291
14:1–15:12	200
15:23-26	200
15:25	113
16:1-36	200
16:4	113
16:25	114
17:1-7	200
17:7	112
17:8-13	200
19–24	306, 313, 316
19:1-6	302
19:6	313
19:9–20:26	200
19:9	302
20:12	94
20:20	113
21:30	357
23:14-17	246, 247
24	287, 288, 292, 306, 310, 365
24:1-8	200
24:2	302
24:3-8	285
24:4-8	365
24:4	201
24:8	282, 285, 286, 287–89, 305, 306, 358
24:11	281, 288
24:12	302
24:15-18	302
29:2 [LXX]	269
29:12	358
31:8	198
32:9-14	302
32:15-24	200
32:25-29	200
32:30-34	302
34:1	300
34:18	246, 247
34:23	246, 247
34:29-35	299, 300
Leviticus	
2:4	269
3:17	282
4	285, 344, 346
7:11-18	281

7:11	285
7:26-27	281
8:26	269
16	170, 285, 344, 346, 365
16:21	351
17:10-16	282
18:16	185
20:21	185
23	246, 247
27:11	357
Numbers	
1:5-16	201
1:44	201
6:19	269
9:1-14	246, 247
9:6-12	271
9:12	271
11:16-30	200
16:1-50	200
16:22	280
17:1-13	200
19	288
19:1	320
20:2-13	200
20:22-29	200
21:4-9	200
27:12-23	200
27:16	280
28:16-25	247
28:16-24	246
29:7-11	170
31:5	201
Deuteronomy	
1:22-23	201
1:23	201
3:26	217
4:27-34	115
5:26	313
5:30	313
6:1-8	303
6:6-8	314
6:16	112
7:12-16	313
7:18	257
7:19	115
8:2	113
8:16	113
9:10	198

10:29	303	Judges	
11:18	314	1:22-26	160
12–26	313, 316	2:22	113
13	53	1 Samuel	
13:2-6	96	10:1	131
13:4	113	15:27-29	199
15:11	131	16:13	131
16	246, 247, 248	17:44	143, 194
16:2	248	17:46	194
16:3	248, 257, 280	2 Samuel	
16:7	248	7	306, 313
17:1-7	53	7:23	166
18:15-22	96	1 Kings	
18:15	190	1:34-40	131
18:19	190	11:29-40	199
18:20	53	14:2	152
21:18-21	53, 94	14:11	143, 194
21:22-27	340	16:4	143, 194
21:22	93	17:42	214
21:23	82	18:4	149, 152
23:18-19	131	18:13	149, 152
26:5-8	250	18:20-40	185
28	235, 298, 313	19:10	149, 152, 179
28:6	143	19:13	185
28:26	194	19:14	149, 179
29:3	115	19:19-21	195, 196, 204
30:6	303, 313, 320	19:19	185
30:11-14	314	21:24	143, 194
32	179, 182	2 Kings	
32:14	289	1:8	185
32:43	179, 182	1:10	146
33:8	113	2:8	185
49:16-21	248	2:9-11	185
Joshua		2:12-18	199
3–4	182, 204	2:13-14	185
3:7–5:12	288	9:6	131
3:12	201	14:23-27	139
4	201	14:25	139
4:2	201	22:14	150
4:3	201	23:21-23	246, 248
4:5	150	1 Chronicles	
4:8-9	201	28:11-19	197
4:20	201	2 Chronicles	
5:10-12	246, 248	15:8-15	305, 320
18:24	201	24:20-22	134
19:15	201	24:20-21	149
21:7	201	24:21	152
21:40	201	24:22	150

25	246
30:15-16	250
32:31	113
35	248
36:14-16	152
36:51-21	149
Ezra	
6:17	
6:19-22	246, 248
Nehemiah	
9:25-26	152
9:26	140, 149
Job	
7:16-20	143, 192
25:6	192
Psalms	
2	190
8	175, 190, 212
8:3	197, 198
8:4-8	143, 192
8:4	192, 198, 204
11:6	127
22	54, 71, 190, 212, 215, 236
22:6	213
22:19-21	213
22:22	213
22:24	213
22:25-31	213
22:26	213, 215
26:2	113
27:12	358
31	190
33:6	197
34	190
34:20	271
35:11	358
37:32-33	180
38	190
41	190
41:9	358
42–43	190
42:6	277
42:12	277
49:7	159
55:5	277
69	54, 71, 190
75:8	127
78:42	166

79:1-3	169
80	190, 212
80:9-19	152
84:3	193
88	190
89	215, 313
89:38-51	213, 215
89:38-39	213
95:9	112
104:10-23	278
107:1-9	331
110	190, 313
110:4	365
113–18	250, 256, 268
118	190, 212, 213, 232, 236, 279
118:21-25	231
118:22-23	254
118:22	155, 213, 215, 231, 232, 235, 236, 290
118:25-26	256
119	314
132	313
139:23	109
143:2	113
144:3-4	143, 192
144:3	143, 192
145:21	280
146	220
Proverbs	
3:12	113
6:26	146
15:20	214
19:16	214
Ecclesiastes	
9:12	146
Isaiah	
5	152
5:1-7	152
6:1–9:7	190
10:16-19	142
11:1-10	90
11:6-9	314
12:17-21	198
12:31	198
13:9-16	359
16:18-19	220
20:1-6	199
24–27	230

24:21-23	223	42:9	313
24:21-22	198	42:18	220
24:23	327	43:1-2	127
25	288	43:1	166
25:1-10a	328, 331	43:3-4	87, 160, 169, 341, 357
25:6-8	291	44:1-2	219
26	343	43:10	219
26:16-19	212, 213	43:20	219
26:19	233	45:14-17	160
27:2-6	152	49	223
27:9	302	49:1-13	190
28:1	327	49:3	167, 222
28:2	327	49:4	221
28:3	327	49:5	167, 222
28:4	327	49:6	222, 314
28:5-6	327	49:7	214
28:9	327	49:8-13	289–90, 331
28:10	327	49:13	222
28:12	327	49:20	222
28:13	327	49:22-23	221
28:16	190, 327	49:24-26	222
28:17	327	49:24	199
28:21	327	50:4-11	190
28:24-26	327	50:6	358
28:25	327	51:7	314
29:8-9	186	51:17	126, 127
29:18-19	220	51:22	126, 127
30:27-28	146	52–53	62, 69, 167, 205, 224
32:15	197, 313	52:3	166
32:55-56	179, 182	52:13-53:12	64, 70, 87, 160, 168,
34:16-17	313		170, 190, 212, 214,
35:5-6	186, 220		215, 225, 226, 236,
40–66	209		289, 290, 341
40–55	209, 214, 219, 220, 222,	52:13-15	223
	224, 279, 314	52:14	168, 212, 289
40–50	202	52:15	168, 213, 289, 358
40:1-11	190	53	54, 67, 213, 223, 284, 289–90
40:1-2	314	53:2	181
40:3-5	199	53:3-4	181
40:5-6	280	53:3	212, 214, 215, 289
41:8-9	219	53:4	213, 289
41:18-19	181	53:5	213, 289
42	62	53:6	358
42:1–44:5	190	53:7	213, 289, 358
42:1-6	314	53:8	213, 289
42:1-4	198	53:9	213
42:1	217–18, 219, 220	53:10-12	213
42:6	290, 307	53:10-11	289

53:10	167, 213, 289
53:11-12	235
53:11	168, 213, 289, 325, 357
53:12	66, 167, 168, 213, 216, 217,
	222, 223, 285, 286, 289, 305,
	357, 358, 359, 361
54:1	142
54:10	290, 313
55:3-5	314
55:3	290, 313
55:7	314
56:6	314
59:20-21	302
59:21	313, 314
61	190, 279
61:1-9	209
61:1-3	220
61:1-2	197
61:1	186, 220
61:8	313
61:10	123
62:4-5	123
63:3	289
63:6	289
66:14-16	146

Jeremiah

2:21-22	152
2:30	149
4:27-28	359
7:21-26	313
7:25	149
7:33	143, 194
7:34	183
8:7-9	313
8:8-13	203
11:1-13	313
12:9-13	152
13:1-11	199
14:21	314
15:3	143, 194
15:9	359
16:4	143, 194
16:16	146
16:9	183
18:1-12	199
19:1-13	199
19:7	143, 194
24:7	313

25:10	183
25:15	127
25:17	127
25:28	127
26:20-24	149
26:20-23	134, 152
27:1–28:17	199
28:9	203
29:18-20	149
30:2	314
31	287, 318
31:10-34	190
31:11	166
31:27-30	313, 314
31:31-40	307
31:31-34	285, 287, 303, 370
31:31-33	359
31:31	285, 286, 305
31:32	313, 318
31:33-34	319
31:33	300, 312, 313
31:34	302, 314
32:39	313
32:40	313, 314, 318
32:44	313
33:8	314
33:11	183
33:15	315
33:20-21	315
33:23-26	315
33:26	313
34:20	143, 194
36:3	314
36:20-31	314
38:4-6	134
49:12	127
50:4-7	313
50:20	314
51:7	127
51:59-64	199

Lamentations

5:18	193
5:21	314

Ezekiel

2:8–3:3	199
3:14	197
4:1-3	199
4:7	199

5:1-4	199		214, 215, 230, 232, 236, 237,
8:1	197		238, 239, 279, 337, 338
8:3	197	7:9-14	87
11:14-21	312	7:9-10	161
11:17-21	313	7:13-14	192, 357
11:19	300, 313	7:14	161
16:60	314	7:21-22	129, 212
16:61	314	7:25	212, 233, 234, 235, 236
16:63	302, 314	7:26-27	161
18:31	313	8:14	235
19:10-14	152	9	167
21:3	142	9:11	298
23:31-33	127	9:16-19	314
29:4-5	146	9:24-27	178
29:5	143, 194	9:24	239
32:4	143, 194	9:26	220
34:11-16	314	9:27	235, 290
34:23	314	10:33	235
34:25-31	312	11-12	214
34:25	315	11	212, 215
34:27	315	11:29-35	54
36:16-28	312	11:30-35	212
36:22-38	313	11:30	212
36:26	300, 313	11:33–12:10	235
37	230, 343	11:33	212, 290
37:1	197	11:34	290
37:4-14	313	11:35	69, 212
37:14	197, 303	11:39	290
37:15-28	199	12:1-3	212, 215, 290
37:20-28	312	12:1-2	54, 212, 213, 230,
37:26	314		233, 236, 343
37:28	314	12:1	129, 203
38:14	233	12:2-3	69
38:22	146	12:2	233
39:4	143, 194	12:11-12	235
39:6	146	Hosea	190
45:21-25	285	2:14-25	123
45:21-24	246, 248	2:14-16	199
47–48	313	2:15-18	307
Daniel		2:20	312
2	232, 236	2:25	312
3:27	280	3:1-5	199
3:28	54, 280	3:4-5	234
6:16-18	122	6:1-2	233
6:25-27	54	6:3	233
7	69, 128, 155, 167, 168, 173,	10:1-2	152
	174, 175, 190, 193, 211, 212,	Joel	
		1:15	202

2–3	190	9:9	290
2	318	9:10-11	346
2:1-2	202	9:10	290
2:10	359	9:11	285, 286, 291, 292, 305,
2:24	331		306, 359
2:28-32	313, 317, 319	9:14-15	291
2:28-29	197	9:16	291
3:18	331	10:8	166
6:1-2	235	13:1	181
11	202	13:4	185
31	202	13:7	181
Amos		14:4-5 (LXX)	361
1:4	146	Malachi	
1:7	146	1:4	180
1:10	146	1:7	214
1:14	146	1:12	214
4:2	146	2:9	214
5:16	202	2:13-16	185
5:18	359	3-4	186, 211, 212, 221
5:20	359	3:1-5	184
6:1	214	3:1-3	184
6:4-7	249	3:1-2	184
7:10-17	134	3:1	185
8:9-14	124	3:2b-4	185, 314
8:9-10	359	3:2b-3	184
9:13	331	3:12	314
Jonah		3:19-24	184
4:9	277	3:19-20a	184
Micah		3:19	146, 184
4:10	166	3:23-24	184
7:1-7	202	3:24	203
7:2	203	4:1	184, 185
7:3-4	203	4:5-6	184, 185, 202, 210
7:5	203	4:6	202, 203, 204
7:6	202, 203, 204		
7:7	203	APOCRYPHA	
Habakkuk			
1:14-17	146	Jdt.	
2:16	127	8:12-14	113
Zechariah		8:22-23	113
3:8-9	232	8:25-27	113
6:9-15	199	9:13	315
8:7-8	291	1 Maccabees	
8:18-23	291	1:1-15	178
9–14	190	1:11-15	315
9:1-8a	290	1:41-43	178
9:8b	290	1:44-61	178
9:9-10	291	1:52	178

1:62-63	178	41:19	315
2:1	179	44-45	315
2:6-14	178	44:19-20	113
2:15-22	179	44:19	298
2:18	178	48:1-3	185
2:19-22	178, 315	48:10	210
2:23-26	178	50:14-21	170
2:27-28	178	51:10	109
2:28-38	179	Tobit	
2:29-38	178	14:4	140
2:39-41	178	Baruch	
2:42-48	178	2:27-35	287, 295
2:49-70	315	Wisdom	
2:50	88, 357	2:12-20	235
2:51	179	3:7-8	343
2:52	113	4:3-6	98
2:64	179	5:1-6	235
4:6-11	315	11:10	113
4:8-9	179	18:22	315
4:54	235	2 Esdras	
2 Maccabees		2:5	315
1:2-6	315	2:7	315
3:4	179	3:15	315
4:7	178	5:29	315
4:23-25	179	7:83	315
7	117, 182, 230		
7:30-38	315	NEW TESTAMENT	
7:37-38	88, 179		
8:3-5	179	Q	147–50
8:12-18	315	3:7-9	142, 184, 353
8:27-33	179	3:9	184, 185
15:6-11	179	3:16-17	142, 146, 184, 353, 370
Psalms of Solomon		3:16	125, 128, 184, 185
18:5	302	3:17	185
Sirach		6:22-23	140, 149, 354
2:1	113	6:23	196, 328
6:23	214	6:40	328
15:11-20	113	7:1-10	140, 161
17:4	143, 192	7:3-35	122
17:12	315	7:18-35	123
18:1-14	192	7:18-23	200
23:1	109	7:18-19	184, 337
23:4	109	7:19	184, 185
24:8-23	315	7:22-23	184, 337
29:15	88, 356	7:22	220–24, 338
33:1	113	7:23	354
36:27	193	7:24-28	144, 185
39:8	316	7:25	194

7:31-35	354	17:23-24	353
7:34	217	17:26-30	353
9:57-60	194	17:26-27	128
9:57-58	95	17:33	154
9:58	80, 143–44, 146, 147, 192,	17:37	353
	193, 194, 202, 336, 337, 354	22:28-30	330, 332
9:59-60	195	22:28	353
9:60	283	22:30	201, 331, 353
9:61-62	194, 202, 338	Matthew	
10:1-12	216	1:1-17	96
10:3	201, 354	1:16	97
10:5-9	201	1:18-25	97, 98
10:10-12	201	1:21	354, 355, 360
10:11-13	140	1:22-23	361
10:13-15	144	2:1-23	360
11:3	95	2:1-12	354
11:4	80, 101, 136, 145, 147,	2:6	361
	153, 336, 337, 354	2:13-15	354
11:7-19	186	2:18	150
11:16	198	2:19-23	354
11:20	94, 197, 199, 200, 223, 338	3:14-15	219
11:29-32	354	4:1-11	360
11:29-30	139	5:9	215
11:30	80, 234	5:10	354
11:31-32	144	5:17	162
11:34	53	5:22	146
11:44	250	5:39	215
11:47-51	354	5:43-48	215
11:47-48	237	6:10	136
11:47	149	6:13	101, 114, 127, 145
11:49-51	237, 328	7:19	146
12:2-31	95	8:5-13	361
12:4-9	154	8:14-17	361
12:9	154	8:16-17	354
12:49	354	8:20	143–44
12:51-53	94, 129, 201–4,	9:1-17	360
	211, 338	9:1-8	361
12:51	354	9:9-13	196
12:52-53	203	9:14-17	121
12:52	203	9:15	360
12:53	354	9:32-34	354
13:28-30	291	10:15-16	360
13:28-29	140, 144	10:17-25	360
13:34-35	142, 156, 237, 354	10:23	331
14:26-27	195, 283, 354	10:24-25	328
14:26	94, 196	10:26-33	360
14:27	154	10:33	154
16:16	123, 129, 203, 337, 354	10:34-39	360

10:34-36	163	23:29	148
10:34	145	23:30-32	149
10:38-39	154	23:30	149
10:38	146	23:31	149
10:40	163	23:34-36	80
11:2-19	360	23:37-39	80
11:12-13	82	24:8	114
11:17-19	360	25:1-13	123
11:19	94, 95, 163, 321	25:41	146
11:27	137	26:2	80, 228, 360
12:15-21	354, 361	26:17-29	259–73
12:18	218	26:26-29	246
12:33-37	321	26:26	263
13:24-30	354	26:27	263
13:36-43	354	26:28	263, 287, 304, 305, 323,
13:40	146		324, 361
13:47-50	146, 354	26:41	118
13:50	146	26:42	117
13:54–17:27	360	26:52-54	360
13:55	97	26:52	215, 216
14:1-12	360	27:3-10	355
15:24	163	27:19	355
16:17-19	200	27:24-25	355, 360
16:21	228, 360	27:25	360
16:24-28	360	27:51-53	361
16:24	153	27:54	361
17:12	213	27:62-66	355
17:22-23	228, 360	27:62-64	96
17:27	357	28:2-4	361
18:1-5	360	28:11-15	355
19:10-12	94	Mark	
19:28	321, 330	1:1-13	200
20:18-19	228, 360	1:4-5	184
20:19	229	1:4	219
20:20-28	161, 360	1:5	96, 357
20:28	361	1:6	185
21:28-32	184	1:7-8	184
21:33-46	150–53	1:11	185, 217–20, 222,
21:43	361		338, 356
22:1-14	361	1:15	357
22:1-4	123	1:16-20	195, 196
23	354	1:38	162
23:8	287	2:1-12	321
23:23-36	156	2:7	95
23:27-28	250	2:10	174
23:29-36	147–50	2:13-17	93, 196, 200, 249
23:29-35	336, 337	2:17	162
23:29-32	80, 143, 152	2:18-22	121, 122, 237, 321

2:18	123	9:13	79, 211
2:19-20	121–24, 132, 153, 336, 356	9:19	356
2:19	123, 124	9:30-37	356
2:20	79, 124	9:31-32	228
2:23-28	200	9:31	63, 66, 79, 134, 226–39,
2:24	94		235, 356, 360
2:28	174	9:32	17
3:13-19	318	9:34	94
3:16	200	9:37	163
3:22	94	9:43	146
3:27	221–23, 337, 338, 358	9:48	146
3:31-35	94, 195, 196	9:49	146
6:3	97	10:15	195
6:5	321	10:18	222
6:6-13	95	10:25	94
6:7-13	318	10:29-31	356
6:9-13	216	10:29-30	94
6:11	200	10:32-45	356
6:14	321	10:32-34	79
6:21-29	249	10:33-34	134, 226–39, 356, 360
6:30-44	200	10:34	229
6:30	95, 318	10:35-41	164
6:35	267	10:35-45	161, 166, 238, 360
7:1-23	200	10:35-37	161
7:1-20	321	10:38-40	356
7:1-4	94	10:38-39	125, 129, 161
7:15	283	10:38	79, 118, 124-29, 132,
7:18-20	283		143, 144, 153, 154, 155,
8:27-9:1	356, 367		336, 337
8:31-32	228	10:40	125, 161
8:31	79, 134, 226–39, 356, 360	10:41-44	161
8:32-33	232	10:43-44	164
8:32	171	10:44	167
8:33	356	10:45	64, 66, 69, 79, 137, 155,
8:34-9:1	328, 356, 357, 360		156, 159, 160, 177, 186, 205,
8:34-38	215		224, 239, 259, 279, 290, 323,
8:34	153–55, 336		324, 338, 356–58, 363
8:35	154	11–13	326
8:36-37	154	11–12	86
8:38	154	11:1-10	200
9:1	331, 359	11:9-10	256
9:7	217–20, 356	11:11-19	200
9:9-13	210–15, 223, 338	11:11-18	95
9:9-10	212	11:11-12	267
9:9	356	11:12-25	359
9:11-13	184, 185	11:15-17	185, 200
9:12	79, 210, 212, 213, 214,	11:20-25	200
	215, 356	11:27-33	186

11:28	321	14:23-24a [24b]		261
12:1-12	79, 149, 150–53, 156, 356	14:23		263, 264, 284
12:1-2	336, 337	14:24		64, 156, 166, 263, 264,
12:6-8	356			284, 285, 290, 292, 304,
12:8	152, 237			305, 310, 323, 338, 358
12:9-11	356	14:25		83, 89, 261, 263, 277, 291,
12:9	142, 152			328–34, 329, 331, 332
12:10-11	213, 231, 256, 359	14:26-31		367
12:13-17	215	14:26		256, 267, 268
12:18-27	94	14:27-28		80
12:29-31	109	14:27		138, 237
13	112, 129	14:32-42		116, 117, 356
13:1-37	359	14:32		256
13:8	114	14:33		116, 277, 356
13:12	94, 203	14:35		117
13:13	203	14:35-36		118, 277
13:24-27	360	14:36-38		106, 116, 336, 337
13:30	331	14:36		80, 109, 117, 119, 125,
13:31-35	79			127, 136–37, 145, 153,
14:1-9	79			237, 336
14:1-2	132	14:38		109, 116, 118, 119, 147
14:1	228	14:39		117
14:3-9	130–32, 143, 148, 153,	14:41-42		358
	336, 356	14:41		119
14:3	131, 267	14:43-52		216
14:4	131	14:44		358
14:6-9	356	14:49		80, 356
14:7	131, 132	14:50		80
14:8-9	130	14:51		217
14:8	131	14:57		358
14:9	131	14:58		63, 234
14:10-11	132, 358	14:60-61		80
14:12-25	259–73	14:61		358
14:12-16	255	14:62		356
14:12	266, 271, 358	14:64		95
14:13	267	14:65		80, 358
14:14	266, 271, 358	14:66-72		367
14:16	266, 271, 358	15:1		358
14:17-21	261	15:2		96
14:18	267, 358	15:3-4		80
14:20-21	356	15:6-15		358
14:20	267	15:5		358
14:21	80, 237, 358	15:9		96
14:22-25	64, 80, 125, 126,	15:10		358
	246, 264	15:12		96
14:22-24	261	15:16-20		96
14:22	256, 264, 267, 278, 358	15:21		272
14:23-25	256	15:26		96

15:28	216	7:30-35	362
15:29	63, 234	7:36-50	130, 362
15:32	96	7:39	96
15:33-39	356	7:47-50	355
15:34	80, 359	7:54-56	362
15:38	359	8:1-3	196
15:39	356, 358, 359	9:22	228, 233, 362
15:40	255	9:23-27	362
15:42	272	9:23	153
15:47	255	9:31	362
16:1-8	356, 359	9:35	218
16:1	255	9:43-45	362
16:7	317	9:44-45	228
Luke		9:44	66
1:1	362	9:46-48	362
1:3	362	9:54	146, 185
1:17	210	9:57-62	321
1:22	362	9:58	143–44
1:26-38	98	9:59-60	94
1:31-33	355	10:5-6	321
1:69-75	355	10:18	114, 223
1:77-89	362	10:39-43	362
1:77-79	355	11:1	109
2:11	355	11:4	106, 362
2:14	355	11:20	321
2:23-24	362	11:47-51	147–50
2:29-32	355	11:47	148
2:31-33	362	12:49-51	362
2:34-35	355	12:49-50	80, 125, 128, 144–47,
2:36	362		155, 237, 336, 337
3:3	362	12:49	145, 146, 163
3:10-14	184	12:50	145, 146
3:13	362	13:1-9	355
3:14-15	215	13:14	94
3:16	362	13:27-31	362
4:2	362	13:31-35	129
4:10	362	13:31-33	80, 91, 136, 143, 148,
4:15-21	220–24		153, 355, 362
4:16-21	221, 224, 338	13:32-33	132–35, 136–37, 144,
4:18-19	220		234, 336, 337
4:22-30	362	13:32	63, 143, 194
4:25-30	355	13:33	63, 237
5:20	362	13:34-35	91
5:30-32	362	13:36-41	362
5:30	362	14:1-6	94
5:32	362	14:16-24	144
5:33-39	121	14:27	362
7:18-23	321	15	138

15:1-32	152, 362	22:28-30	83, 318
15:1-2	249	22:28-29	310
16:1-7	151	22:31-34	355
17:3	362	22:35-38	66, 80, 215–17, 223,
17:18	362		237, 338
17:22	123	22:35-36	216, 217
17:25	80, 355	22:36	216
17:31	362	22:37	215, 216, 362
17:33	154	22:38	217
18:7-8	233	22:40	118
18:9-14	362	22:43-45	355
18:31-34	362	22:46	118
18:31-33	228	22:53	114, 362
19:1-10	362	23:2	96
19:10	163	23:3	362
19:38	291	23:4-5	355, 362
19:39-44	355	23:5	96
19:39	95	23:6-16	355, 362
19:41-44	142, 291, 362	23:14	96
20:9-19	150–53	23:26-31	362
20:17	362	23:27-31	140–43, 144, 148,
21:5-38	362		336, 337, 355
21:11	114	23:27-29	141
21:34-36	355	23:27-28	141
22	112, 164	23:29	141, 142
22:7-23	259–73	23:30-31	141
22:8	362	23:31	141, 142
22:15-19	260	23:35	217–20
22:15-18	263	23:39-43	355, 362
22:15	277, 281, 332	23:43	355
22:16	256, 260, 263, 328–34,	23:44-45	362
	329, 332, 362	23:45	362
22:17-18	256	23:47	362
22:17	284, 362	24:13-32	355
22:18	260, 263, 328–34, 329, 332	24:26-27	362
22:19-20	64, 246, 263, 362	24:27	355
22:19	261, 264, 267, 278	24:29-30	267
22:20	165, 261, 264, 284, 287,	24:30-32	363
	304, 305, 310, 323, 324, 359	24:44-49	355
22:22	362	26:23	362
22:24-30	161, 271	John	
22:24-27	165, 362	1:1-14	367
22:24	117, 164	1:10-11	368
22:25-30	362	1:14	367
22:25	164	1:19-28	185
22:26	164	1:21	185, 210
22:27-31	80	1:25	210
22:27	164	1:28	185

1:29	80, 156, 271, 324, 369, 370
1:34	218
1:35	271
1:36	369, 370
2:1-10	255
2:14-16	185
2:19	80, 233, 368, 369
3:11-21	368
3:13-14	237
3:14	80, 368
3:16	368
3:17	368
3:29	123
3:36	370
4:42	368
5:21	368
5:24-30	368
6	246, 280
6:33	368
6:42	98
6:45	287
6:51	368
6:52-59	282
6:53-58	264
7:33	368
8:12	368
8:14	369
8:21	370
8:24	370
8:28	80, 237, 369
8:41	97
8:42	98
9:5	368
9:16	98
9:39	163
10	137, 138
10:9	368
10:10	163, 368
10:11-18	368
10:14	137
10:15-18	137–38, 336
10:15	80, 137
10:17-18	80
10:17	137, 369
10:18	137
10:28	368
11:51-52	166, 368
12:1-8	130, 132
12:1-2	131
12:3	81
12:34	174
12:4-8	131
12:5	154
12:7-8	368
12:7	81
12:23-26	368, 369
12:25	154
12:27-28	368
12:27	277
12:31-34	237
12:32-33	368
12:33-34	81
12:46	368
12:47	163, 368
13	162, 246, 260, 262, 328
13:1	264, 271, 368, 369
13:15	368
13:27-29	267
13:31-32	369
13:33	368
13:34-35	368
13:37	137
13:38	271
14:19	368
14:30	368
15:1-17	369
15:12-13	369
15:13	137
15:18-25	368
15:20	369
16:16-24	368
16:16-19	234
16:16	63
16:28	368
17	63
17:5	368
17:11	368
17:20-23	369
17:20-21	368
18:8-14	166
18:9	368
18:11	116, 368
18:14	368
18:28	264, 271, 369
18:32	368
18:39	369

19	63	7:15-16	150
19:4	264	7:16	150
19:14	271, 369	7:35-40	199
19:23-24	368	7:52	140
19:25-27	255	7:56	174
19:30	368	8:14-17	317
19:34	369	8:32-33	363
19:36-37	368	8:35	362
19:36	264, 271	9:5	362
20:9	368	9:17	316
20:31	368	9:26-29	316
21:19	367	10:36	320
Acts		10:39-40	340
1:4	320	10:39	93
1:12-26	318	10:40	233
2	303, 317	10:43	319
2:1-41	319	10:44-48	317
2:9-11	317	11:15	319
2:14	318	11:17	319
2:17-21	317, 319	13:2-3	122
2:25-28	362	13:27	362
2:28	165	13:38	319
2:29	150	14:22	113
2:33	320	14:23	122
2:34-35	362	15	327
2:36	340	15:11	362
2:38-39	320, 362	15:29	282
2:38	319	16:31	362
2:42-47	327	20:21	362
3:1–4:22	319	20:28	363
3:12-26	199	26:18	362
3:13	363	Romans	
3:16	362	1:3-4	341, 353
3:17-18	362	1:18-32	344, 351
3:26	363	2:15	287
4:11	213, 231	2:16	344
4:12	362	3:21-31	343
4:27	363	3:21-25	51, 345, 363
4:28	362	3:21	298
4:30	362, 363	1:16-17	353
4:31	317	3:24	345
5:1-11	318	3:25-26	341
5:17-42	319	3:25-26a	340
5:30	95, 340	3:25	345, 346
5:31	319	4:24-25	232, 341
5:40	93	4:25	345, 351
6:8–8:1	319	5:1-2	345
7	327	5:9	344, 345

5:10	345, 351	10:16-34	351
5:12-21	345, 351, 352	11:13-26	246
5:12	325	11:17-34	259–73
5:16	345	11:23-26	261
5:18-19	345	11:23-25	64, 263–64
6–8	351	11:23	267
6	349	11:24	261, 278
6:3-11	351	11:25	83, 261, 284, 287, 304,
6:3-10	351		305, 359
6:3-4	125	11:26	328, 334, 343
6:8	154	12-14	319
6:11	344	15:3-8	353
6:13	345	15:3-7	28
7:4-6	345, 351	15:3-5	341
7:24-25	345, 351	15:3-4	341
8:2	351, 353	15:3	342, 345
8:3	346	15:4	232, 233, 342
8:4-27	317	15:7	342
8:17-18	344	15:12-20	342, 352
8:17	352	15:13-14	28
8:29	351	15:20-28	353
8:31-39	345	15:20	344, 345, 351
8:32	55	15:27	193
8:34	351	15:29	351
9:4-5	297	15:31	344
10:4	344, 351	2 Corinthians	
10:8-9	341	1:5-7	344
11:27	287, 297, 302	2:14-16	352
12:1-2	351	3	299, 300
13:14	351	3:1-18	300
14:9	351	3:2	287
14:15	343	3:3	300
15:3	352	3:4-18	343, 345, 351
1 Corinthians		3:6	287, 300
1:2	345	3:10	300
1:17-25	343	3:12-13	300
1:18	345	3:14-15	300
1:24	345	3:14	287
2:2	343	3:16	300
2:4-5	345	3:17-18	300
2:6-8	345	3:17	300
5:7	272, 282, 344, 346, 350	3:18	319, 351
5:21	351	4:1-18	352
6:9-11	345	4:7-12	351, 352, 360
6:20	345	4:10-11	344
7:23	345	4:16	351
8:1-6	351	5:1-5	351
10:13	113	5:14-15	100, 340, 349, 351, 353

5:15-16	154	1:13	352
5:17	351	1:20-22	345
5:21	100, 341, 345, 351	2:11-22	351, 352
6:17-18	287	2:13	346
8:9	345, 351	2:14-18	345
11:23	344	2:17	346
12:1-10	351	3:10	351
12:9-10	344	4:20-24	353
13:4	344	4:32	346
Galatians		5:2	343, 346
1–2	327	5:25-27	346
1:4	343, 344	5:25	343
1:17	260	Philippians	
1:18-24	260	2:5-11	352, 363
2:1-3	260	2:6-11	341
2:6-10	260	2:6	154
2:20	342, 343, 351, 353	2:8	343
2:21	345	3:10-11	352
3:1-5	317	3:10	344
3:1	343, 352	3:18	343
3:6-14	320	Colossians	
3:13-14	344	1:12-14	345, 346, 351
3:13	82, 93, 95, 298, 340, 343	1:20-22	346
3:14	345	1:20	346
3:15-25	297	1:24–2:5	352
3:15	296	1:24	344, 352, 360
3:17	296	2:11-15	352
3:19-26	297	2:14-15	345, 346, 351, 353
3:19-20	302	2:20–3:17	351, 352
3:21	302	1 Thessalonians	
3:27-28	351	1:6	352
4:5	345	1:9	351
4:14	352	1:10	344
4:21-31	297	2:15-16	344
4:24	296, 300	2:16	149
5–6	351	5:9	344
5:1-26	320	5:10	344, 345, 351
5:1	344, 345	2 Thessalonians	
5:11	343	1:5-10	344
5:13-26	319	2:8	344
5:24	342, 351	1 Timothy	
6:14	342, 351	1:9	346
6:15	351	1:15	346
6:16	298	2:5	302, 344, 346
6:17	344, 352	2:6	343, 345
Ephesians		3:16	342
1:7	346	6:13	352
1:10	346		

2 Timothy	
1:10	351
2:11	342, 352
Titus	
2:11-14	353
2:14	343, 345, 346
3:5	346
Hebrews	
1:2	365
1:3	365
1:4	302
1:6	302, 365
1:8	365
1:10-12	365
2:1-4	366
2:6-8	193
2:6	174
2:9	364, 365
2:10	365
2:11-18	365
2:11	365
2:14-15	365
2:17-18	302
2:17	365
2:18	365
3:1-5	365
3:1	365
3:2	365
3:7–4:13	366
3:14	365
4:15	365
5:5	365
5:7-8	365
5:7	117, 365
5:9	365
5:10	365
5:11–6:12	366
6:4	365
6:13—7:28	365
6:13	365
6:20	365
7:1-28	302
7:3	365
7:11-12	301
7:11	365
7:16-17	365
7:18-19	365
7:20-23	365

7:20-22	365
7:22	365
7:24	365
7:25	365
7:26-28	365
7:27	365
7:29	365
8:1-2	365
8:6-13	365
8:6	302, 365
8:7-13	365
8:8-12	287, 365
8:8	302
8:13	302
9:1-10	365
9:11-15	365
9:12	302, 365
9:14	302, 303, 365
9:15-28	365
9:15-22	51, 288
9:15	287, 302, 303, 365
9:16-22	303
9:22	365
9:23-28	303
9:26	365
9:28	365
10:1-18	365
10:1	302
10:9	302, 365
10:10-14	365
10:10	302, 364
10:12-14	364
10:12	365
10:14	302
10:16-18	365
10:16-17	287
10:18	365
10:19-39	366
10:19	365
10:22	302
11	365
11:1–12:11	366
11:26	366
11:37	150
12:1-29	366
12:1-2	365, 366
12:2	365
12:18-24	364

12:24	365	**2 Peter**	
13:9	302	1:9	366
13:12-14	366	2:1	366
13:12	365	2:20-22	366
13:20	365	**1 John**	
James	327	1:5-7	368
1:2	113	1:7	370
1:12	113	1:9	370
1:13-15	113	2:1-2	370
1 Peter		2:2	370
1:2	288, 366, 367	2:3	367
1:3	366	2:15-17	113
1:5	367	2:25	368
1:6-9	367	3:5	370
1:9	367	3:9	368
1:10	366, 367	3:16	137, 368, 369
1:11	366	4:10	370
1:18-21	367	4:11	368, 369
1:18	367	4:19	369
1:19	367	4:20	370
1:20-21	366	5:6-9	369
1:23	366	**2 John**	
2:2	367	7	367
2:4	231, 366	**Revelation**	
2:6-8	366	1:5	371
2:7	231	1:6	371
2:9	113	1:7	371
2:18-25	162, 367	1:9	371
2:21-25	366	1:13	174
2:21	367	1:18	371
2:22-23	366, 367	2–3	371
2:24-25	367	2:8	371
2:24	367	3:10	114
2:25	367	5:5	371
3:13-22	367	5:6-14	369, 371
3:18-22	366	5:6	371
3:18	367	5:10	371
3:20	366	5:12-13	371
3:21	366, 367	6:9-11	371
4:1-6	367	6:15-17	370
4:1	367	7:9-17	371
4:6	366	7:13-17	371
4:12-18	367	7:14	371
4:13	367	11:1-13	210, 235
4:18	367	11:15	371
5:1	367	11:18	370, 371
5:10	367	12:1-17	371
		12:11	371

13:18	369, 371	13	174
14:1	371	*Jubilees*	
14:4	371	1:1	320
14:10	370	1:12	149
14:14	174	1:15-25	287
14:19-20	370	1:16-25	315
15:1	370	1:17-18	315
16:4-6	370	2:26-33	315
16:17-21	370	6:12-14	315
17:14	371	6:15-31	306
18:24	371	6:17-31	320
19:6-9	371	14:19-20	315
19:7	123	14:20	320
19:15-21	370	15:1-34	315
20:2-3	198, 223	17:15–18:19	55
20:4	371	21:17-20	282
20:6	371	22:1-16	320
21:9-27	371	22:14-15	302
22:1	371	22:15-19	315
22:3	371	23:16	202
22:5	371	23:19	203
		23:29	198
OLD TESTAMENT PSEUDEPIGRAPHA		29:13	202
		30:7-12	315
Assumption of Moses		33:10-14	315
1:14	302	34:15-16	150
3:12	302	36:8-11	315
9:1-7	129	49:1–50:13	315
10:5	359	49	246, 248
1 Enoch		49:1	267
10:4-8	198	49:12	267
10:19	331	*Lives of the Prophets*	134, 150
37–71	174	10	139
62:14	331	10:11	140
90:9-12	369	*4 Maccabees*	
91–105	129	1:11	88
2 Baruch		6:27-29	88, 168, 179
25-29	129	6:28-29	55
29:5	331	9:23-24	88
32:1-7	114	17:21-22	55, 169
32:1	114	17:22	16, 179
40:1-4	114	18:3	169
71:1	129	18:4	88, 169, 179
4 Ezra	129	*Martyrdom and Ascension of Isaiah*	
5:9	203	5:1-14	134
6:24	202	5:4-16	113
6:26	210	*Prayer of Azar*	
9:1-13	114	11	315

Psalms of Solomon
  18:5 — 302
Sibylline Oracles
  2:187-88 — 210
  3:801-2 — 359
  5:344-50 — 359
  8:84 — 203
Testament of Abraham
  13:6 — 201
Testament of Benjamin
  3:8 — 88, 369
  10:7 — 201
Testament of Daniel
  2:4 — 146
Testament of Joseph
  19:8 — 369
Testament of Judah
  25:1-2 — 201
  25:3 — 198
Testament of Levi
  14:2–15:1 — 152
  18:12-13 — 223
  18:12 — 198
Testament of Moses — 129, 181
  1:14 — 182
  6:1-9 — 182
  9 — 179
  9:4-5 — 182
  9:6 — 182
  9:7 — 182
  10:1-10 — 182
  10:1 — 182, 198
  10:4 — 182
  10:5 — 182
  10:9 — 235

DEAD SEA SCROLLS

DAMASCUS DOCUMENT (=CD)
  I, 4 — 315
  I, 17-18 — 315
  II, 2 — 315
  III, 2-4 — 298, 313
  IV, 9 — 315
  IV, 15-16 — 146
  VI, 11 — 315
  VI, 18-19 — 315
  VI, 19-21 — 287

  VI, 19 — 315
  VII, 5 — 315
  VIII, 1 — 315
  VIII, 18 — 315
  VIII, 20-21 — 315
  VIII, 21 — 287, 315
  IX, 2 — 315
  X, 6 — 315
  XII, 11 — 315, 316
  XIII, 14 — 315
  XV, 1-9 — 315
  XVI, 1-2 — 315
  XIX, 13-14 — 315
  XIX, 31 — 315
  XIX, 34 — 315
  XIX, 33-34 — 315
  XX, 12-13 — 287, 315
  XX, 11-13 — 315
  XX, 17 — 315
  XX, 25 — 315
  XX, 29 — 315
1Q14 17-18 — 203
1Q28a 11-22 — 201
1Q34bis 3 ii.5-6 — 315
1QH
  II 29 — 146
  III 26 — 146
  V 8 — 146
  VIII, 32 — 277
  X 10:6-22 — 180, 181
  X 10:8 — 180
  X 13-14 — 114
  X 18 — 181
  X 33 — 180
  XI 29 — 142
  XII, 5 — 315
  XII 9 — 143
  XIII, 9 — 315
  XV, 10 — 315
  XV, 20 — 315
  XV 22-25 — 181
  XVI 4-10 — 181
  XVI 18 — 142
  XVI 20 — 142
  XVI 26-27 — 181
1QM
  II 1-3 — 201
  II 5 — 169

III 6	169	259	169
III 22-25	114	265	169
IV 16-19	114	266	54
V 6	169	491	235
VIII 6	169	504	170
IX 4-5	169	504	315
XI 20-21	143	508	160, 170
XII, 3	315	521	220
XIII, 8	315	521	210
1QapGen		541	169
XX, 10-11	277	558	210
1QpHab		558	210
II, 3	315	11Q19 [Temple]	
1QS		XVII 6-9	246
I, 8	315	XVII 11-14	201
I, 16	315	XIVI	131
II, 12	315	XXV10-16	170
II, 26	315	LIV	149
IV 18-19	198	LXI	149
V, 11	315		
V, 12	315	RABBINIC WRITINGS	
V, 18	315		
VI	249	MIDRASHIM	
VI, 20	318	*Genesis Rabbah*	
VI, 24-25	318	79:6	143, 192
VIII 1	201	98:11	139
VIII 2	201	*Mekilta de R. Ishm. 55*	
VIII 3	201	on Exod 12:6	285, 306
VIII, 9	315	on Exod. 12:11-14	55
VIII, 10	315	on Exod 12:14	306
X, 10	315	on Exod 12:42	116, 334
XI 20-21	192	*Pesiqta de Rab Kahana*	
1QSa	331	7.11.3	254
I, 5	315	*Sipre Deuteronomy*	
I, 7	315	333.5	169
1QSb		312	152
I, 2	315	333	160
III, 24	315		
4Q texts		MISHNAH	
159	169, 201	*m. Avot*	
171	180	2:1	136
174	286	2:4	136
175	199	*m. Berakhot*	
176	114	6.1	278
177	114, 143	*m. Eduyyot*	
225	54	1:7	249
257	169	*m. Qiddushin*	
		4:14	192, 298

m. Menahot
   7:6   248

m. Orlah
   2:5   249

m. Pesahim   248
   3:1   251
   5:9   255
   10   250
   10:6-7   268

m. Sanhedrin
   7:4-5   95

m. Sotah
   9:15   203, 210

m. Tohorot
   9:7   249

m. Yebamot
   4:13   98
                           170

m. Yoma
   1:8   267

TALMUND OF BABYLONIA
b. Berakhot
   28a   135
   60b   113

b. Horayot
   10   162

b. Mo'ed Qatan
   25b   141

b. Pesahim
   36a.   280
   68b   320

b. Qiddushin
   82b   192

b. Sanhedrin
   43a   96
   43b   48, 96
   67a   98
   89b   140
   93a   141
   97a   203
   107a   113

b. Temurah
   29   131

b. Ta'anit
   10   162

b. Yevamot
   109b   135

b. Yoma
   39b   359

TALMUD OF JERUSALEM
y. Avodah Zarah
   40d   98

y. Shabbat
   14d   98

TARGUMIM
Tg. Hosea
   6:1-2   233

Tg. Isaiah
   22:12-25   152
   28   326
   28:1-29   152
   28:1   327
   52:13   289
   On Isa 5 at Mk 12:1-12 326

Tg. Onqelos   248
   On Deut 16:2   250
   On Exod 12   288

Tg. Psalm
   8   143, 192

Tg. Pseudo-Jonathan   185

TOSEFTA
t. Bava Batra
   1:11   150

t. Hullin
   2:24   98

t. Shabbat
   1:4   135

t. Sukkah
   3:2   256

PHILO
De congressu eruditionis gratia
   16–67   280

De vita contemplativa
   70–72   162
   75–78   249

De specialibus legibus
   1.261   254
   2.145-75   246, 249

JOSEPHUS
Antiquitates judaicae
  2.286 — 182
  2.302 — 182
  2.332 — 182
  2.336 — 182
  4.206 — 131
  6.308-9 — 183
  9:208-14 — 140
  10.38 — 134, 149
  12.246-357 — 179
  17.149-67 — 254
  18.29 — 267
  18.63 — 95
  18.85-87 — 200
  18.116-19 — 184
  20.112 — 254
  20.97-99 — 182, 200
  20.167-68 — 200
  20.167 — 182
  20.169-72 — 200
  20.188 — 200
  20.6 — 183
Bellum judaicum
  2.129-32 — 267
  6.285-86 — 200
  6.290 — 254
  6.292-93 — 359
  6.301 — 183
  6.302 — 183
Contra Apionem
  2.205 — 150

GRECO-ROMAN LITERATURE

ARISTOTLE
Ethica nichomachea
  9.8 — 162

ATHENAEUS
Deipnosophistae
  15.702A-B — 256

PLATO
Symposium
  176E — 249

STRABO
Geographica
  16.4.26 — 162

TACITUS
Annales
  15.44 — 47, 93, 95-96

EARLY CHRISTIAN LITERATURE

Didache
  8:2 — 108
  10:6 — 83

EUSEBIUS
Historia ecclesiastica
  2.11: 1-3 — 182
  3.23 — 125
  4.26.13-14 — 298

GOSPEL OF PETER — 32

GOSPEL OF THOMAS — 32, 151
  10 — 145, 201
  16 — 145
  55 — 94
  65 — 150–53
  79 — 141
  82 — 146
  86 — 192
  101.1-2 — 94
  105 — 98

IRENAEUS
Adversus haereses
  2.22.5 — 125
  3.3.4 — 125

JUSTIN
Dialagous cum Tryphone
  69:7 — 96
  99 — 116
  120:14-15 — 134

ORIGEN
Contra Celsum
  1.28 — 98
  1.32-33 — 98

1.69   98
2.5   98
2.8-9   98
2:24   116
2.31   98

POLYCARP
Philippians
7:1-3   113

Protevangelium James
    7:1–16:2   98

PSEUDO-PHILO
Biblical Antiquities
    18:5   169

TERTULLIAN
De spectaculis
    30.6   98

Author Index

Abegg, M.   297
Abelard, P.   50, 73, 371
Adna, J.   325
Allison, D.C. 5, 19, 43, 57–58, 63, 79, 84,
             87, 88, 95, 112, 113, 127, 128
             129, 133, 142, 144, 148, 149,
             168, 173, 174, 175, 184, 189,
             190, 192, 195, 197, 199, 202,
             203, 210, 211, 220, 230, 257,
             285, 290, 306, 308, 337, 354
Andrews, M.   107
Ankersmit, F.R.   7-8, 33, 34–35, 45
Anscombe, G.E.M.   22
Anselm   50, 66, 347, 371
Antwi, D.J.   86
Appleby, J.   12
Arens, E.   144
Ashton, J.   97, 138
Attridge, H.   302, 303
Augustine   9, 33, 36, 50
Aulén, G.   50, 371
Aune, D.E.   15, 140, 199
Aus, R.D.   151
Avemarie, F.   316
Avemarie, F. and H. Lichtenberger   296
Averbeck, R.E.   344

Backhaus, K.   293, 294, 296, 297, 298,
                301, 302, 304, 305, 306,
                            308, 309, 315

Bailey, D.P.   51, 66, 340, 347
Baker, J.C.   372
Bammel, E. and C.F.D. Moule   215
Barbour, R.S.   105, 115, 117, 118
Barnett, P.W.   107, 140, 177
Barrett, C.K.   68, 69, 70, 78, 117, 118,
                   167, 168, 197, 208, 270,
                            297, 321, 363
Barth, G.   339
Barton, D.M.   193
Barton, S.   31
Batey, R.A.   134
Bayer, H.F.   226
Bauckham, R.   15, 29, 173, 282
Beasley-Murray, G.R.   107, 113, 139,
                   144, 146, 147, 197, 226,
                            239, 262, 280, 285
Beavis, M.A.   130
Beck, N.A.   276
Becker, J.   43, 73, 83, 92, 110, 191,
                   195, 342, 345, 346, 352,
                                     372, 373
Beker, J.C.   341, 342, 343, 346, 373
Bellinger, W.H. and W.R. Farmer   66, 190,
                                            208
Berdyaev, N.   33
Bergman, J.   286
Berlin, I.   18, 22, 33
Best, E.   172, 356

Betz, O.   66, 112, 113, 202, 208,
                   209, 278, 283
Bickermann, E.   154
Bieringer, R.   74
Black, M.   63, 130, 134, 172,
                   202, 209, 230
Blair, H.J.   196
Blank, J.   130, 131
Bloch, A.B.   245, 254, 257
Bloch, M.   16, 23, 28, 35
Blomberg, C.L.   97, 237, 271
Bock, D.   32, 95, 217
Bode, E.L.   233
Boersma, H.   343
Bokser, B.M.   85, 250, 251, 272
Bolyki, J.   200
Borg, M.   9, 11, 12, 36, 43, 91, 215, 262
Bornkamm, G.   328
Boughton, L.C.   266, 284
Bowker, J.W.   199, 276
Brabazon, J.   57
Brandon, S.G.F.   215
Braumann, G.   124
Breisach, E.   4
Breytenbach, C.   342, 345, 346
Broadhead, E.K.   130
Brodie, T.L.   195
Brondos, D.   49, 53, 73
Brooke, G.J.   152
Brooks, S.H.   354
Brown, C.   172
Brown, P.   25
Brown, R.E.   80, 91, 97, 109, 111,
                   114, 119, 137, 138,
                   141, 142, 232, 265, 266,
                   271, 370
Brown, S.   106
Bruce, F.F.   209
Bryan, S.   140, 193, 210, 211, 344
Byrskog, S.   5, 97
Buchanan, G.W.   215
Bultmann   33, 45, 52, 58, 60, 65, 73,
             74, 78, 130, 156, 160, 166,
             171, 195, 225, 226, 227,
             262, 277, 341, 346, 372
Burchard, C.   266
Burkett, D.   171, 173, 174, 193
Burkitt, F.C. and A.E. Brooke   278

Burns, R.   28
Burridge, R.A.   35

Cadbury, H.J.   208
Cadoux, C.J.   61, 101
Caird, G.B.   67, 68, 74, 113, 141,
                 175, 201, 209, 314, 335
Cameron, P.S.   111
Camfield, F.W.   347
Campbell, A.F. and M.A. O'Brien 247
Campbell, W.S.   300
Capper, B.J.   318, 319
Carmichael, D.   251
Carr, E.H.   13, 14–18, 19, 24, 36
Carroll, J.T. and J.B. Green   339, 356,
                 361, 363, 366, 367
Carson, D.A.   316
Case, S.J.   33
Casey, M.   192, 193, 210, 211, 227,
                 228, 229, 232, 234, 235,
                 275, 280, 282, 308
Casey, P.M.   36, 71, 124, 126, 162, 165,
                 172, 173, 230, 283
Cathcart, K.J. and R.P. Gordon   291
Ceresko, A.R.   208
Chapman, D.W.   48, 343
Charlesworth, J.H.   24, 29, 48, 63, 92,
                 109, 191
Chavasse, C.   197
Chester, A.N.   363
Childs, B.S.   208, 245, 306
Chilton, B.D.   11, 29, 30, 36, 43, 45,
                 54, 63, 74, 85, 88, 93, 96,
                 98, 110, 111, 160, 189, 190,
                 218, 277, 289, 290, 325,
                 326, 327, 332
Chilton, B.D. and C.A. Evans   189
Christiansen, E.J.   294, 296, 301, 315
Clark, D.K.   37
Coakley, J.F.   131, 132
Cohen, J.M.   247, 308
Cohn-Sherbok, D.   191
Collingwood, R.G.   23
Collins, A.Y.   54, 95, 166
Collins, J.J.   72, 191
Corley, K.E.   25, 36, 130, 255
Craig, W. L.   35
Cranfield, C.E.B.   122, 136

Croce, B. 23
Cross, M.D. 199
Crossan, J.D. 5, 11,19, 29, 30, 36, 43, 45
58, 63, 78, 162, 238, 335
Crüsemann, F. 245
Cullmann, O. 107, 112, 113, 116,
167, 172, 209

Dahl, N.A. 101
Dalman, G. 62, 63, 245, 264
D'Angelo, M.R. 130, 131
Daly, R.J. 260, 262, 285
Davies, P.E. 56, 62, 63, 72, 372
Davies, P.E. and D.C. Allison 114, 117,
124, 136, 140, 146,
149, 193, 197, 210,225,
226, 230, 234, 263, 330, 331
Davies, W.D. 282, 283, 287, 341,
344, 346, 350
Daube, D. 72, 117, 131, 251,
281, 284, 332
Dawson, C. 33
De Jonge, H.J. 154
De Jonge, M. 55, 70, 73, 168, 179,
194, 339
Delling, G. 125, 128, 146
Delobel, J. 172
Demel, S. 130, 141
De Moor, J.C. 110, 111, 152
Denaux, A. 133
Denney, J. 351
Denton, D.L. 4
Derrett, J.D.M. 127, 134, 148, 149, 152
Derrida, J. 7
Dibelius, M. 90
Didion, J. 101
Dodd, C.H. 51, 60, 68, 74, 78, 81, 82,
86, 87, 90, 95, 96, 105, 114,
123, 137, 148, 151, 153, 189,
190, 192, 199, 214, 226, 231,
232, 233, 270, 281, 282, 287,
311, 328, 331
Douglas, M. 180, 344
Drescher, H.G. 42
Droge, A.J. and J.D. Tabor 72, 342
Dunn, J.D.G. 5, 11, 12, 20–21, 25, 28,
29, 31, 32, 36, 39, 40, 51,
53, 69, 70, 83, 92, 107, 118,

125, 126, 145, 146, 164, 165,
175, 184, 197, 200, 208, 226,
228, 230, 236, 254, 260, 276,
293, 295, 297, 298, 299, 300,
301, 306, 316, 317, 318, 319,
320, 321, 340, 341, 342, 344, 345,
346, 348, 350, 352, 353, 372, 373
Dunnill, J. 301, 307

Eco, U. 48, 77, 78
Ego, B. 298
Ehrman, B.D. 31, 260, 261
Eichrodt, W. 294, 296, 299
Elliot, J.K. 366
Ellis, E. E. 189, 340
Elton, G.R. 3, 14–18, 19, 21, 24, 28
Elton, G. 8, 16, 36, 46
Evans, C.A. 68, 78, 83, 86, 88, 91,
115, 151, 152, 177, 190,
191, 226, 233, 288, 356
Evans, C.A. and P.W. Flint 191
Evans, C.S. 30, 107
Evans, R.J. 6, 8, 16, 21, 22, 24, 25,
27, 28, 36

Faierstein, M.M. 184, 210
Farmer, W.R. 66, 67, 228
Fee, G.D. 300, 310
Feeley-Harnik, G. 51
Feuillet, A. 124, 125
Fiensy, D.A. 320
Finkel, A. 108, 109, 118
Fisk, B.N. 55
Fitzmyer, J. A. 117, 118, 131, 133, 141,
184, 197, 210, 215, 217, 220,
278, 280, 308, 317, 355,
361, 363
Foakes Jackson, F.J. 172
Foakes Jackson, F.J. and K. Lake 317
Föhrer, G. 198
Fortna, R.T. and T. Thatcher 97
France, R.T. 60, 63, 69, 78, 118, 123,
128, 161, 167, 168, 189, 190,
208, 214, 216, 266, 270, 289
Franfurt, H. 37
Fredriksen, P. 59, 78, 85, 89, 90, 93, 275
Frey, J. 301
Friebel, K.G. 199

Friedman, R.E.   245
Friedrich, G.   339
Froelich, K.   112
Fuller, R.H.   61, 67, 75, 83, 84, 172
Funk, R.W.   43, 107, 110, 131, 148, 150,
                            154, 211, 335
Funk, R.W. and R.W. Hoover   122, 141

Gaddis, J.L.   8, 16, 21, 22, 25
Galvin, J.P.   92, 93
Garlington, D.B.   344
Gathercole, S.J.   57
George, A.   64, 19
Gerhardsson, B.   108, 360, 361
Gese, H.   88, 265, 266, 270
Gibson, J.   111, 115, 116
Girard, R.   50
Glatzer, N.N.   251, 267
Gnilka, J.   64, 71, 74, 75, 79, 90,
          122, 131,132, 174, 193, 197,
                  234, 262, 276, 289
Goguel, M.   265
Goldingay, J.   38, 40
Goppelt, L.   64, 74, 172, 189, 209, 275
Görg, M.   214
Gorman, M.J.   351
Gorringe, T.   49
Gray, J.   196
Grayston, K.   339, 356, 361, 364,
                            366, 367
Green, J.B.   56, 81, 161, 202, 217,
              260, 261, 278, 330, 360
Green, J.B. and M.D. Baker   49, 339
Grelot, P.   201
Gross, W.   314
Gubler, M.L.   54, 72, 140
Guelich, R.A.   122, 123, 218
Guhrt, J. and O. Becker   296
Guillaumont, A.   145
Gundry, R.H.   210, 223, 225, 227,
                       229, 236, 359
Gunton, C.E.   49

Hafemann, S.   352, 373
Hagner, D.A.   63, 264, 279, 342
Hahn, F.   71, 235, 275, 364
Hahn, S.W.   296, 297, 299, 301, 303
Ham, C.   361

Hamerton-Kelly, R.   197
Han, K.S.   148
Hanson, A.T.   119
Hare, D.R.A.   173
Harris, M.J.   347
Harris, W.V.   189
Haslam, J.   14
Hawthorne, G.F.   317, 321
Hays, R.   190
Hays, R.B.   344
Hayward, C.T.R.   246, 248
Hegel   9
Heinemann, J.   109, 118
Hendel, R.S.   306
Hengel, M.   15, 25, 48, 62, 63, 65, 74,
            75, 78, 84, 85, 86, 88, 97,
        154, 160, 170, 185, 196, 208,
        215, 260, 276, 278, 311, 317,
                  339, 341, 343, 347
Hengel, M. and C. Markschies   160
Henry, M.   20, 22
Hermisson, H.-J.   208, 209
Heschel, A.J.   95
Heyer, C.J. den   71
Higgins, A.J.B   113
Hill, D.   168
Himmelfarb, G.   6, 27
Hoffman, L.A.   245, 250, 253, 261, 273
Hoffmann, P.   229
Hofius, O.   92
Holmberg, B.   5
Holmén, T.   25, 304
Holt, J.C.   47
Hooker, M.D.   51, 67, 68, 69, 70, 78, 81,
            82, 97, 122, 151, 152, 167,
        172, 173, 174, 175, 193, 199
        208, 210, 211, 217, 218, 225,
        226, 229, 236, 237, 276, 294,
        339, 341, 350, 356, 357, 360,
                  361, 364, 366, 367
Hoover, R.   107
Horbury, W.   191
Horsley, R.A.   29, 30, 36, 43, 53, 74,
                95, 110, 140, 215
Horsley, R.A. and J.A. Draper   148, 308
Hoskyns, E. and N. Davey   34
Howard, V.   74, 124, 154
Howell, M. and W. Prevenier   34

Hugenberger, G.P. 207
Hughes, J.J. 303
Hultgren, A.J. 101, 151, 152, 350
Hummel, R. 360
Hunt, L. 12
Hunter, A.M. 340
Huntjens, J.A. 315
Hurst, L.D. 175, 301, 302
Hurtado, L.W. 41–42, 261

Ilan, T. 63, 97, 255
Instone-Brewer, D. 265
Isidore of Seville 33

Jacob, M. 12-14
Jacobs, A. 37, 38
Janowski, B. 165, 208, 357
Janowski, B. and P. Stuhlmacher 159
Jaubert, A. 265, 315
Jenkins, K 6–14, 15, 20–21, 34, 37
Jenkins, P. 107
Jeremias, J. 11, 12, 41, 62, 63, 64, 65, 70,
71, 74, 75, 85, 111, 115, 130,
131, 133, 134, 135, 139, 150,
167, 200, 216, 228, 229, 232,
233, 245, 255, 260, 264, 266,
267, 268, 269, 278, 280, 284,
285, 308, 310, 325, 327, 330,
331, 332, 339
Johnson, L.T. 9, 29, 52, 107, 148
Juel, D.J. 81, 190, 219

Kähler, M. 9, 36, 52, 304
Kalluveettil, P. 296, 310
Kant 45
Käsemann, E. 42, 44, 71, 341, 342,
362, 372
Keck, L. 85, 92, 93
Keener 113, 211, 218, 264, 266, 268,
279, 282
Kertelge, K. 64, 339
Kiley, M. 106, 108, 109, 117
Kim, S. 162, 163, 174, 191
Kinzig, W. 293, 299
Klauck, H.-J. 320
Klawans, J. 253, 264, 283, 326, 327
Kleinknecht, K.Th. 54
Kloppenborg Verbin, J.S. 70, 79, 194, 353

Knohl, I. 89, 180, 245
Koch, K. 92
Koester, C. 301, 302, 364
Koenig, J. 66, 74, 88, 260, 276, 287,
291, 306, 307, 309, 330, 331
Kohn, R.L. 312
Kollmann, B. 261
Kosmala, H. 165, 285, 286, 324
Köstenberger 271
Kraeling, C. H. 185
Kuhn, H.-W. 48, 141
Kuhn, K.G. 263, 266
Kuss, O. 363, 364
Kutsch, E. 310, 311

Lachmann, J.M. 113
Lake, K. 172
Lambrecht, J. 154
Lampe, G.W.H. 72, 216, 352
Le Goff, J. 16, 21, 31,
Lee, D.A. 255
Légasse, S. 148, 149
Lehne, S. 296, 297, 300, 301,
302, 303, 306, 312, 315
Lemcio, E.E. 35
Lenowitz, H. 140
León-Dufour, X. 64, 99, 245, 259, 261,
262, 263, 266, 272,
279, 280, 283, 306, 328,
332, 333
Levenson, J.D. 54, 294
Levin, A.-J. 130, 313, 317
Levin, C. 296, 312, 314
Lewis, J.J. 113
Leyerle, B. 245, 249, 250, 255
Lichtenberger, H. 296, 304, 306
Lietzmann, H. 277, 284
Limberis, V. 142
Lindars, B. 82, 159, 167, 172, 193, 214,
264, 292, 301, 302, 306, 363
Lipton, P. 7
Lissaggargue, F. 249
Llosa, M.V. 48, 49
Lohfink, N. 294
Lohmeyer, E. 88, 110, 111, 112
Lohse, E. 339
Long, V.P. 246
Longenecker, R.N. 189, 301, 344

Lowe, M. 151
Luedemann, G. 110, 136
Lunde, J. 129
Luther, M. 372
Luz, U. 57, 93, 141, 153, 154, 201

Mack, B.L. 130
Malina, B. and J. Neyrey 94, 98, 99
Mann, C.S. 151
Manson, T.W. 61, 68, 74, 87, 108, 113, 175, 198, 209, 217
Manson, W. 61, 74, 83
Marcus, J. 97, 122, 217, 218, 356, 358
Markschies, C. 208
Marrow, S.B. 47, 341, 349
Marshall, I.H. 48, 62, 65, 161, 164, 175, 217, 265, 294, 348, 363, 370
Marshall, M. 265
Martin, R. 107
Martin, R.P. 343, 356, 358, 359, 360
Martola, N. 251
März, C.-P. 130, 131, 132
McArthur, H.K. 233, 234
McArthur, H.K. and R.M. Johnston 152
McCarthy, D.J. 296
McCasland, S.V. 228
McConville, J.G. 191
McKeating, H. 199
McLaren, J.S. 48, 51, 56
McLean. B.H. 344
McLeod Campbell, J. 220, 350
Meadors, E.P. 148
Meier, J.P. 5, 11, 15, 36, 43, 45, 73, 97, 98, 110, 128, 145–46, 198, 200, 217, 218, 265, 269, 328, 329, 330, 331, 360
Mendenhall, G.E. 296, 310, 313
Menn, Esther M. 190
Merklein, H. 65, 83, 275, 277, 311, 339
Merz, A. 325
Metzger, B.M. 228, 260
Meyer, B.F. 5, 11, 20, 26, 29, 30, 34, 36, 37, 43, 50, 62, 65, 84, 92, 110, 112, 113, 114, 201
Michel, O. 172
Migliore, D.L. 106
Milgrom, J. 344

Millard, A.R. 186, 304
Miller, P.D. 116
Miller, R.J. 134, 148
Moberly, R. 220, 350
Moloney, F.J 192, 270
Moo, D.J 63, 69, 78, 168, 189, 190, 215, 216, 217, 225, 234, 236, 289, 290, 345
Moore, G.F. 63, 131
Morgan, R. 31, 32, 37, 41
Morris, L.L. 286, 347, 356, 361
Moulder, W.J. 167
Moule, C.F.D. 72, 90, 112, 113, 174, 175, 189, 299, 300, 317, 344, 352
Moxnes, H. 4
Moxter, M. 23
Mournet, T.C. 5

Nanos, M. 299
Nassif, B. 33
Neale, D. 53, 96
Neef, H.-D. 296
Neufeld, V.H. 340
Neusner, J. 84, 136, 191, 249, 251, 307
Newman, C.C. 344
Neyrey, J.H. 141
Nicholson, E.W. 296, 313
Nielsen, H.K. 197
Nolland, J. 118, 133, 141, 144, 193, 195, 197, 220, 225, 277, 281, 308
Noort E. and E. Tigchelaar 55
North, C.R. 61, 207, 209
Novick, P. 4, 17

Oakman, D. 107, 111
Oberlinner, L. 59, 60, 90
O'Connor, F. 59
O'Neill, J.C. 50, 90, 161
Otto, R. 60, 83, 308, 329
Owen, P. and D. Shepherd 173

Packer, J.I. 347
Page, S.H.T. 81, 162, 164
Pagels, E. 31, 32
Palmer, D.W. 72
Patterson, S.J. 144, 145

Pelikan, J. 7, 29
Perelman, S.J. 68
Perkins, P. 62
Perrin, N. 42, 44, 45, 73, 93, 122, 235
Perry, J.M. 233
Pesch, R. 64, 71, 74, 75, 122, 130, 162
214, 225, 245, 262, 263, 264,
280, 305, 325, 331, 333
Pitre, B.J. 57–58, 115, 128, 129,
162, 166, 210, 239
Pobee, J. 72
Popkes, W. 110, 115
Porter, S.E. 42, 45, 111, 113, 264
Propp, W.H.C. 245, 306
Pryke, E.J. 122, 130

Quell, G. 296

Rabe, S. 16
Ranke, L. 14, 15
Rau, E. 200
Rebell, W. 154
Reed, J.L. 139
Reiser, M. 82
Rendtorff, R. 310, 313
Reno, R.R. 372
Rese, M. 133
Ricoeur, P. 23, 25, 29
Ridderbos, H.N. 51, 340, 341, 343,
346, 373
Rieger, H.-M. 316
Riesner, R. 108
Riniker, C. 82
Rist, J. 37
Rivkin, E. 50, 51
Robinson, H.W. 61, 207
Robinson, J.A.T. 52, 95, 97, 123, 138,
185, 186, 189, 210, 270,
Robinson, J.M. 53, 145, 184, 194, 198,
202, 308
Roloff, J. 35, 92, 123, 172
Rorty, R. 6, 7
Routledge, R. 253, 264
Rowley, H.H. 61, 207
Ruckstuhl, E. 265
Ruppert, L. 54, 71

Saldarini, A.J. 245, 246, 254, 265

Sanders, E.P. 11, 12, 15, 25, 29, 30,
36, 42, 43, 62, 63, 73, 75,
83, 85, 89, 92, 95, 98,
124, 126, 153, 198, 248,
250, 254, 276, 283, 289, 294,
296, 299, 315, 316, 341, 350,
352, 372, 373
Satterthwaite, P.E. 191
Scott, J.M. 68, 344, 345
Schaberg, J. 97, 98, 234
Schlosser, J. 70, 82, 106
Schmeidel, P. and R. Bultmann 44
Schmidt, D. 139
Schnabel, E. 80
Schnackenburg, R. 109, 195
Schneemelcher, W. 171
Schottroff, W. 152
Schreiner, T.R. 372, 373
Schrötter, J. 23
Schürmann, H. 64, 67, 70, 71, 74, 75,
82, 83, 93, 109, 114,
263, 276, 278, 280, 329,
335
Schüssler Fiorenza, E. 5, 131
Schwager, R. 49, 66, 83, 339
Schweitzer, A. 56–58, 60, 71, 83, 84, 87,
90, 115, 128, 172, 175,
189, 236, 329, 341, 343,
344, 352, 372
Schweitzer, E. 71, 72, 230
Schwemer, A.M. 315, 316
Seely, D. 342, 351
Seesemann, H. 111
Segal, A.F. 55, 72, 229, 230, 238,
304, 343
Segal, J.B. 245, 246, 316
Seifrid, M.A. 345
Senior, D. 356
Shepherd, D. 174
Slater, T.B. 173
Slater, W.J. 249
Sloyan, G. 49
Smalley, S.S. 370
Smith, B.D. 264, 265
Smith, C.W.F. 37, 146
Smith, D.E. 249
Smith, D.M. 97
Smith, M.H. 192, 193, 282, 283, 285

Snodgrass, K.R. 151, 231, 232
Soards, M.L. 141
Spicq, C. 165
Squires, J.T. 361
Stacey, W.D. 199, 251
Ståhlin, G. 230
Stanton, G.N. 33, 35, 53, 96
Stauffer, E. 72, 97, 140
Steck, O.H. 54, 140, 149
Stecker, G. 372
Steinhauser, M.G. 195
Stendahl, K. 372
Stenschke, C. 362
Stern, D. 151, 152, 244
Stettler, H. 352
Stott, J.R.W. 347
Strecker, G. 41, 342, 351, 353
Strobel, A. 53
Stuhlmacher, P. 37, 41, 65, 66, 70, 71
74, 75, 78, 79, 84, 85, 87,
88, 92, 100, 133, 162, 205,
209, 263, 264, 277, 278, 284,
285, 288, 307, 325, 340, 341,
342, 343, 345, 352, 353, 364,
366, 367, 369, 372, 373
Swetnam, J. 312, 314
Sykes, S. 49

Tabory, J. 251, 268, 282
Tan, K.H. 91, 133, 135, 136
Tannehill, R.C. 351
Taussig, H. 107
Taylor, J.E. 184, 210, 217
Taylor, V. 60–61, 122, 123, 151, 168,
170, 210, 211, 213, 218, 234,
262, 277, 279, 285, 336
Theissen, G. 43, 44
Theissen, G. and A. Merz 110, 259, 260,
262, 266, 325, 326
Theissen, G. and Winter 42, 149, 160,
Theobald, M. 296, 301
Thiselton, A.C. 36, 37
Tödt, H.E. 171, 193
Tolstoy, L. 18
Tovey, D. 97
Travis, S. 342, 347
Trembath, K. 40
Troeltsch, E. 42

Trumbower, J.A. 182, 184
Tuckett, C. 117
Twelftree, G.H. 197, 198

Van Cangh, J.-M. 197
Vansina, J. 5
Vanhoozer, K. 37
Vermes, G. 11, 54, 92, 172, 309
Vielhauer, P. 171
Vogel, M. 294
Vögtle, A. 64, 71, 84, 90, 91,
109, 145, 172

Wall, R.W. 197
Walker, N. 233
Watson, F. 30, 36, 37, 38
Watts, J.D.W. 208
Watts, R. 69, 208, 209
Weaver, J.D. 49, 101
Webb, R. L. 184
Wedderburn, A.J.M. 342, 351
Weinfeld, M. 296, 310
Weiss, J. 56
Wellhausen, J. 109
Wengst, K. 88
Wenham, D.W. 142, 162, 260, 276, 324
Weren, W.J.C. 152
Westcott, B.F. 266
Westerholm, S. 300, 345
White, H. 6–7, 10, 11, 39
Whiteley, D.E.H. 116, 117, 226, 341
Wijngaards, J. 233
Wilcox, M. 165, 166, 168, 298
Williams, B. 11, 26
Williams, D.K. 343
Williams, M.C. 79, 310
Williams, S.K. 342
Williamson, H.G.M. 61, 207, 220
Willis, G.G. 113
Wilson, R. McL. 172
Windschuttle, K. 6
Wink, W. 173
Winter, D. 43, 44,
Wise, M.O. 88, 89, 179, 180
Witherington, B. 362
Wolff, H.W. 202, 203, 207, 208
Work, T. 40
Wrede, W. 62, 171

Wright, N.T.   5, 12, 21, 28–30, 36, 43, 49,
50, 63, 67, 68, 69, 71, 74, 75,
78, 79, 84, 85, 87, 88, 92, 95,
107, 110, 115, 128, 142, 190,
209, 215, 233, 238, 290, 294,
296, 299, 300, 314, 324, 326,
335, 341, 342, 343, 344, 345,
346, 347, 372, 373
Wuellner, W.   42, 146

Yoder, J.H.   215
Young, B.H.   151, 152
Yuval, I.J.   245, 268

Zager, W.   66
Zeller, D.   92
Zias, J. and E. Sekeles   48
Zimmerli, W. and J. Jeremias   167, 207,
                                    218

Subject Index

Abba	118
After Three Days	233–55
Alexandra	179
Amidah	136
Antiochus Epiphanes	178
Aqedah	48, 55
Apostle's Creed	29
Atonement	335–72
Baptism	125
Betrayal	235–36
Covenant Hermeneutic	293–321
Covenant, New	312–20
Creeds	101
Criteria of Authenticity	42–45
Critical Realism	26
Cult Etiology	262
Cup	119, 125, 126, 127, 128
Day of YHWH	142
Death of a Martyr	71
Death of a Prophet	71
Death of the Righteous One	71
Death as Example	71
Ecclesial Atonement Theory	371
Elijah	184–84, 194–96, 202

	203, 204, 205, 210, 211, 212, 213, 221, 336
Elisha	194–96, 204
Eucharist	243, 244, 261, 268, 269, 272, 278, 304, 327
Exemplar	352, 361
Facts	20–23
False Prophet	95
Farewell/Testamentary Meal	262
Fate of the Prophet	337
Final Ordeal	115–19, 121, 126, 127, 128, 138, 140, 142, 143 145, 146, 147, 154, 177, 205, 207, 210, 211, 216, 231, 238, 277, 281, 337
Finger of God	197–200
Fishers of Men	146
Forgiveness of Sins	314, 319, 361
Gath-Hepher	139
Glutton and Drunkard	94
Hasideans	178
Hebrews and Atonement	363–66
Hebrews and Covenant	301–4
Herod Antipas	134, 135, 137, 140, 143, 148, 194
Hermeneutics	36–42
Historical Jesus	28–42

Historical Jesus and Theology   32–42
Historiography   3–28
History   19–28
Holy Spirit   303
Hyrcanus II   179

Inclusive Substitute   357
Interiority   319

Jeroboam II   139
Jerusalem   133, 134, 140, 142,
            143, 144, 150, 156, 177,
            178, 250, 269, 362
Jesus and the Covenant   293–321
Jesus and the Servant   20–24
Jesus and Soteriology   47–50, 100
Jesus as "Scripture Prophet"   86–89
Jesus Ben Ananias   183–84
Jesus Seminar   38, 50, 107, 110, 122,
                        141, 151
Jesus and OT   189–205
Jesus' View of his Death,
    Scholarship on   56–74
John and Atonement   367–71
John the Baptist   48, 105, 123, 124, 125,
            129, 135, 140, 143, 146
            147, 150, 156, 171, 18–86,
            194–96, 202, 203, 204,
            221, 231, 337
John, the son of Zebedee   125
Jonah   139, 140
Joseph   98
Joshua   182, 200–201, 205
Judah Messiah   179–81

Kingdom   82–84, 309

Last Supper   26–73, 338
    Bread Saying   278–82
    Cup Saying   282–92
    "In remembrance ..."   334
    "Poured Out"   323
Lawbreaker   94
Lazarus   132
Love   37–38
Luke-Acts and Atonement   36–63
Luke and Atonement   355

M and Atonement   354–55
Maccabean Martyr Theology   117, 168
Mamzer   96, 98
Mark and Atonement   35–60
Mary   97, 98, 254
Mattathias   178–79
Matthew and Atonement   36–61
Meaning   23–24
Messiah   60–63
Method   99–100
Micah   201–4, 205
Moses   197–200, 204, 205, 302

Narrative   38–39
Narrative Representation   29–30
Nazareth   139
New Covenant   351
Ninevites   139

Oxford Hypothesis   79

Passion Predictions   225–39
Paul and Atonement   340–53
Paul and Covenant   296–301
Peace   320
Penal Substitution   347
Pentecost   317, 320
Pesah   229, 239, 24–73, 275–92,
                        338
Peter   126
Peter and Atonement   36–67
Pharisees   135, 148, 179
Phinehas   183
Prophetic Fate   140—56

Q and Atonement   353–54
Qaddish   109, 136

Rabbi Levi   139
Ransom   161, 165, 168, 170, 357
Rebellious Son   96
Representation   347, 348, 349, 360,
                        367, 372
Representative Death   337, 338, 343, 357,
                        359
Restoration of the Twelve Tribes 313

Sadducees   179

Samaritan   98
Second Adam   343, 350, 351
Servant   231, 238
Servant of Isaiah   60–68, 69, 78, 170,
                          171, 183, 208, 225
                                289–90, 360
Scripture Prophets   177–87, 189–205
Son of Man   68–70, 128, 143, 144,
                        154, 156, 168, 171–75,
                     191–94, 194–96, 205, 210,
                      212, 213, 215, 227, 230,
                      232, 234, 235, 236, 237,
                          238, 239, 337, 360
Shimeon ben Shetah   181
Soteriology   47–50, 100
Spirit   197–200
Stephan   327, 341
Stoning   96
Story   29, 30
Substitution   347, 348, 349, 353,
                                 367, 372

Table Fellowship   123
Taxo   181–82
Taxonomy of Views   100
Temple   131, 151, 152, 325–28
Temptation/Test   110–15
Theories of Atonement   339
Theudas   182–83
Tribulation   84
Truth   11–12, 25
Truthfulness   26
Twelve   200–201, 318, 330

Vicarious   339, 353, 367
Virginal Conception   98
Vow of Abstinence   330

Wrath   349, 370